Pen and Sail

LITERATURE AND HISTORY IN EARLY BANGKOK

Pen and Seil

LITERATURE AND HISTORY IN EARLY BANGKOK

Including

THE HISTORY OF BANGKOK IN THE CHRONICLES OF AYUTTHAYA

By

NIDHI EOSEEWONG

Edited By

CHRIS BAKER *and* BEN ANDERSON

With

CRAIG J. REYNOLDS

HONG LYSA

PASUK PHONGPAICHIT

PATRICK JORY

RUTH T. MCVEY

Silkworm Books

ISBN: 978-974-9575-92-5

This publication was made possible by a grant from
The James H. W. Thompson Foundation.

First published in 2005 by
Silkworm Books
430/58 M. 7, T. Mae Hia, Chiang Mai 50100, Thailand
info@silkwormbooks.com
www.silkwormbooks.com

Typeset in AGaramond 10 pt. by Silk Type

Printed and bound in the United States by Lightning Source

CONTENTS

EDITORIAL FOREWORD

It took Nidhi Eoseewong around four years to write *Pen and Sail.* It has taken ten people twenty years to translate it.

The chapters first appeared as seminar papers and journal articles between 1979 and 1982. They were collected and published as a book by Amarin in July 1984. Soon after, a project to translate the book was launched in Cornell University under the leadership of Ben Anderson, and involving Craig Reynolds, Ruth McVey, and Seksan Prasertkul with help from Thomas Hudak.

Somehow this project foundered. In 2000, I wondered aloud to Craig Reynolds why so little of Nidhi's work had ever been translated, especially this book. He told me about the Cornell project. On Songkran day in 2002, Ben Anderson handed me whatever remaining files could be found. It took one year and searches in Bangkok, Chiang Mai, and Ithaca to establish that the translation of the first and key chapter, comprising over half the book, had been lost. Seksan had translated it, Ben edited it, and Nidhi checked it, then all copies had disappeared from this world.

This first chapter, 'Bourgeois Culture and Early Bangkok Literature,' as it appears here has been translated by Chris Baker, Pasuk Phongpaichit, Patrick Jory, and Hong Lysa.

The second, 'Sunthon Phu: Bourgeois Poet Laureate,' was undertaken at the first round by Ben Anderson who has now completed the work.

The third, 'On the Phetchaburi Version of the *Mahachat,*' seems to have been omitted from the original Cornell project, and here has been translated by Patrick Jory.

The fourth, 'The World of Lady Nophamat,' was translated by Ruth McVey under the Cornell project; her translation has here been edited and completed by Chris Baker and Pasuk Phongpaichit.

The fifth, 'The Life of the Buddha and the Religious Movement of the Early Bangkok Period,' was translated by Craig Reynolds and was the only chapter in virtually final form after the first round.

The sixth, 'The History of Bangkok in the Chronicles of Ayutthaya,' was not part of the publication of *Pen and Sail,* but appeared as a separate book in 1980. However, it belongs to the same period of Nidhi's work, and the same set of research concerns; Nidhi cross-references it many times in the other essays. It is also a wonderful and classic piece. Hence it seemed to make sense to include it in this collection. The translation is by Chris Baker and Pasuk Phongpaichit.

During the original Cornell project, Nidhi compiled a glossary of authors, literary titles, and other matters referenced in the text. This glossary has been used to help compile explanatory inserts and footnotes. Notes added by the translators and editors are identified by [T]. Also during the Cornell project, Thomas Hudak was asked to translate the literary extracts scattered through the chapters. Some of his drafts were found in the files and were used to help finalize the translations. For some extracts, published English translations by Prem Chaya, Walter Vella, Montri Umavijani, and Thomas Hudak have been used and the sources indicated.

The bibliographies from each of the chapters have been amalgamated, and the style of referencing standardized. Quotations which Nidhi translated from English-language sources have been traced back to the original. Quotations from French-language sources are here rendered either using existing English translations (e.g., Pallegoix) or a direct translation from the original French (e.g., Malleret).

Wherever possible, Thai names are presented in the English spelling used by their owner. Otherwise they are transliterated using the Royal Institute (RI) method. Nidhi's own name presents a special problem. In his early English writings, he used the form, Nidhi Aeusrivongse, and that has been retained in the bibliography for works bearing this spelling. Under the RI system, his name would be transliterated as Nithi Iaosiwong, and this form is used in titles of works which contain his name. More recently, Nidhi has favored the spelling Nidhi Eoseewong, and we have followed that form elsewhere.

The essays are presented here in the order chosen for the original Thai publication of *Pen and Sail*, with 'The History of Bangkok in the Chronicles of Ayutthaya' tacked on the end. Readers interested in the development of Nidhi's thinking might prefer to read them in the order in which they appeared, namely: History of Bangkok (1978), Nang Nophamat (1979), Sunthon Phu (1981), Mahachat (1981), Bourgeois Culture (1982), Life of the Buddha (1982).

Each of these essays has a similar form. Nidhi introduces some texts which he proceeds to examine in detail in order to dispel false conceptions and determine their true historical importance. Then he uses this clarified view of the material as a springboard for some very original insights into the history of the early Bangkok period. 'Bourgeois Culture' is a little different in that the texts are replaced by economic data, and the essay is really two pieces wrapped as a sandwich, but otherwise follows the pattern. Readers who, in any essay, feel deterred by Nidhi's initial explication of the texts might try skimming ahead to find the point where the essay takes off.

Nidhi read the complete draft and offered pages of comments and suggestions which prevented several errors and drew attention to subtleties which sometimes defied our ability to render in translation. We are very grateful.

Many thanks to Attachak Sattayanurak, Chalong Soontravanich, Chatthip Nartsupha, Chetana Nagavajara, James Ockey, Porphant Ouyyanont, Saichon Sattayanurak, Somphong Witthayasakphan, Thanet Aphornsawan, Thongchai Winichakul, and Ukrist Pathamanand. Special thanks to Khun Arun for allowing us to reprint his caricature of Nidhi from 1981. Thanks to Trasvin Jittidecharak and everyone at Silkworm Books for their enthusiasm and professionalism.

This project has been very generously assisted by the James H. W. Thompson Foundation to which we are extremely grateful.

Chris Baker

PUBLICATION HISTORY

1. 'Watthanatham kadumphi kap wannakam ton rattanakosin' (Bourgeois Culture and Early Bangkok Literature). Number 20 in papers of the seminar 'Two Centuries of Rattanakosin: the Changes of Thai society,' organized by Thammasat University Thai Khadi Institute, Chulalongkorn University Social Research Institute, Social Science Association of Thailand, and Thammasat University Foundation for Textbooks in Social Science and Humanities, 3–5 February 1982.

2. 'Sunthon phu mahakawi kadumphi' (Sunthon Phu: Bourgeois Poet Laureate). Collected Papers of the Early Bangkok Social History Seminar, 17–19 January 1981.

3. 'An nueng ma chak mahachat mueang phet' (On the Phetchaburi Version of the *Mahachat*). *Warasan Thammasat* (Thammasat Journal), 10, 4, 1981.

4. 'Lok khong nang nophamat' (The World of Lady Nophamat). *Warasan Thammasat* (Thammasat Journal), 9, 1, 1979.

5. 'Phrapathomsomphotika kap khwam khluean wai thang satsana nai ton rattanakosin' (The Life of the Buddha and the Religious Movement of the Early Bangkok Period). Circulated in draft form in 1982, and appeared in print for the first time in *Pakkai lae bai ruea.*

6. 'Prawatisat rattanakosin nai phraratchaphongsawadan ayutthaya' (The History of Bangkok in the Chronicles of Ayutthaya). *Ruam pathakatha chak samakhom sangkhomsat haeng prathet thai* (Collected Lectures from the Social Science Association of Thailand), Bangkok: Social Science Association of Thailand, 1978; as a book, first published by Bannakit, 1980. Reprinted by Matichon, 2000.

Pakkai lae bai ruea: wa duai kan sueksa prawatisat–wannakam ton rattanakosin (Pen and Sail: Literature and History in Early Bangkok), published by Amarin Printing, 1984; reprinted by Phraeo in 1995 and 2000.

AUTHOR'S PREFACE

If this book were to be written today, it would not be longer than 50 pages, since many things I wanted to say two, almost three decades ago, are now well-known and understood in the Thai historical circle. But in those days I had to devote a great deal of space to presenting and explaining many things, interpreting the truth of certain matters, and even reiterating analysis and conclusions over and over again like someone giving a sermon. None of this would be necessary today.

Nowadays, the idea that there were major changes in many aspects of Thai society in early Bangkok; that understanding the changes which arise in Thai society (or any society) requires attention to the internal factors in that society more than seeing those changes as only responses to external forces; that literature can be used as one kind of historical source material; and that, conversely, historical change has more effect on literary creativity than was once understood in Thai society – all these ideas have become commonplace things which students of Thai history can accept. But whether they agree with them or not is another matter.

I cannot claim that this book alone created change in the discipline. There were many factors in Thai society, both related and unrelated to academic study, which had a part in bringing about this changing perspective on Thai history. But this would require more detailed analysis than should appear in a preface.

I think that anyone who is interested in Thai history and who reads Thai can derive the academic value of this book (if there is any) without reading it. The more important step for the study of Thai history is to escape beyond the various conclusions which the book presented, either by disagreeing with them, or by offering more detailed and more diverse perspectives on the changes which the book describes. That would certainly be progress in the subject.

I'm thus not certain whether the English version of this book will be of much use to students of Thai history, because these people should be able to read Thai already. But I hope it will be of some use for general readers who cannot read Thai, and for this reason I offer my profound thanks for the efforts of the translators who have done work of irreproachable quality.

Nidhi Eoseewong
February 2005

PREFACE TO THE THAI EDITION

At the end of 1979 I turned to the task of explaining the relations between literature and history in early Bangkok. My research from that time to now has resulted in the five essays collected in this *Pen and Sail.*

People have been saying for a long time that history has value for the study of literature, and literature has value for the study of history. But even though this idea commands general acceptance, no proper research has been done to realize these values. The work I present in this book is a first step in this direction, and like any pioneer work, its value will be proven if it rapidly becomes outdated.

These five essays have been presented earlier in various forms. Each occasion has given me an opportunity to receive comments from friends in academic circles. For this publication I have tried to incorporate those comments which I have found valuable, by correcting the text or adding footnotes. I have cited the names of those giving comments and indicated the value of their suggestions at various places through the essays, and here I would like again to offer my thanks.

Some comments and suggestions I have not incorporated, either because I did not agree with them, or because they were not directly related to the theme. But these comments and suggestions have still had a very profound value for my thinking, and I would like to offer my utmost thanks to Chatthip Nartsupha and Sombat Chantonwong.

Sujit Wongthet and Chukiat Utokaphan have given enormous encouragement for collecting these essays together in one volume, and I would like to offer them my gratitude also.

Finally, I cannot fail to mention that over the last three years while I have been laboring with great enjoyment over this work, I have stolen a lot of time that should have belonged to Daeng, Phrai, and Doi. Their continual understanding and forbearance has had a great part in the achievement of this book… for which, many thanks.

Nidhi Eoseewong
June 1982

I

BOURGEOIS CULTURE AND EARLY BANGKOK LITERATURE

TRANSLATORS' NOTE

Bangkok became a royal capital in 1782 with the establishment of the Chakri dynasty by King Rama I. The "early Bangkok period" conventionally extends from then until 1855, the year of the Bowring Treaty. (Nidhi actually uses, not "Bangkok," but "Rattanakosin," part of the city's ritual title.)

Sakdina was the system of ranking in the traditional social order. Nidhi (and others) use it as a more general term for the whole social order, rather as "feudal" is used in Europe.

Nidhi sometimes uses the terms phrai and *nai* or *munnai* to describe the broad division into two social groups. Phrai is usually translated as (common/ordinary) people, but left as phrai when referring to their legal requirement to perform several months of corvée labour each year. To organize this corvée, every phrai was legally attached to a *munnai*, and when used in this sense the word *munnai* is translated as overseer. But Nidhi also uses *munnai* in the general sense of all those with an official post and rank, and in these cases the word is translated as officials. The term *khun nang* is generally used to refer to the upper ranks of officialdom and here is translated as nobles or nobility.

I

BOURGEOIS CULTURE AND EARLY BANGKOK LITERATURE[1]

PREFACE

THE early Bangkok period (1767–1855) is usually placed in the era of "Old Siam." The meaning of this "Old Siam" is not very clear. Often it is a way to explain the changes that took place in Siam under royal leadership in the late nineteenth century. "Old Siam" is the opposite of the "New Siam" that resulted from the royal reforms. This approach may seem a useful way to study the history of the reform period, but deep down it has more pitfalls than benefits, in at least two ways. First, setting up the situation prior to the reforms as "Old Siam" blinds us to the many changes in Thai history over the centuries from the Lopburi era (seventh to thirteenth centuries) to the Fifth Reign (1868–1910). The long and eventful evolution of Thai society is not captured by a static phrase like "Old Siam." Second, emphasizing the contrast between "Old Siam" and "New Siam" does not help us to understand the real changes involved in the royal reforms. Such an approach can explain the changes in the late nineteenth century only by reference to external forces, especially from the west, that not only drive change but also shape it for the most part. Historians often measure change in Thai society by using the west as a yardstick, but have to face the problem that after the reform era Thai society was still very different from western society. This perplexity arises from overemphasizing external factors and picturing the momentum of the reform era solely as a response to the west. The "New Siam" era thus arises with no foundation inside the society. Ignoring the local foundations of change makes it impossible to explain how Thai society developed to its present state which is not like the west, and not like "Old Siam" either.

In truth, external drivers alone never truly determine the direction of change in any society. To understand the trajectory of a society, we need to give proper weight to the seeds of change inside that society. Without these internal factors, outside

1. The following people have helped in the thinking and writing of this essay: Professor Akhom Phattiya, Professor David Wyatt, and Achan Saichon Wannarat. Assistant Professor Em-on Chittasophon kindly gave explanations on Thai literature, including lending many of her own books and giving useful advice from the start of the research. In addition, she has given permission for the table of early Bangkok literary works which she compiled to be printed as an appendix to this work. All these people have earned my deep gratitude. However their expertise cannot totally overcome the writer's stubbornness. Any errors and inadequacies are my responsibility alone.

forces will not take root. To understand change in Thai society in the late nineteenth century, we need to analyze the seeds of change inside Thai society, the interest groups, and the struggles by various pressure groups to reap the greatest benefit. We need to examine "Old Siam" as a dynamic situation, not as something fixed and static as usually portrayed. We need to study the continuities between the eras of "Old Siam" and "New Siam" more than has been done in the past.

The early Bangkok era before the reforms is usually seen as a static age of continuities from Ayutthaya, not the starting point of any forces for social change. As a result, the actions of the kings in the late nineteenth century are seen as the impulse for changes in Thai society so drastic they can be termed a "total revolution." But studies of Bangkok's intellectual and economic history (Nidhi 1979, 1980; Wyatt 1979; Paitoon 1978) have revealed the emergence of ideas that would lead to deep changes, including adjusting the machinery of state to profit from a new economic environment. These new studies show there may be more continuities between the reform era of the late nineteenth century and the early Bangkok era, than between early Bangkok and Ayutthaya. However, the study of change in early Bangkok has not yet progressed very far. Many aspects of change are not yet clear. Understanding which groups were involved and how they were motivated are subjects that await further research. This essay focuses on changes in the thinking, values, artistic tastes, and some aspects of the worldview of the upper class of this era. It also hazards some explanations of the forces behind these changes, and the interest groups involved.

THE VALUE OF LITERATURE FOR THE STUDY OF EARLY BANGKOK INTELLECTUAL HISTORY

There are few written sources for Thai history prior to the mid nineteenth century. This is mainly because Thai society did not make much use of writing prior to this era. Most transmission of language and culture was oral. Even government affairs and major policy decisions relied more on the spoken than the written word. Yet in this drought of written sources, there are some literary works that have come down to us from various periods. In total, they are quite a significant amount—more than other kinds of historical sources. They are spread across all historical periods, though rather unevenly. For instance, there are fewer extant works from the Sukhothai period than from late Ayutthaya, and fewer from late Ayutthaya than from early Bangkok. Even so, there is a broader spread of literary sources than of official reports, orders, and records.[2] They can help develop the study of history because sources from two periods can be compared. For this reason, students of Thai literature have been more successful than Thai historians in narrating developments from the Sukhothai era to the early Bangkok era in a concrete form, rather than just lumping all this literature

2. *Bai bok*, reports from provincial governors to the central government; *san tra*, directives sent from the central government to provincial governors or tributary chiefs; *chotmaihet*, records of individual events, occasionally written in verse

under the heading "Old Siam" as historians do in their own discipline from time to time.[3] Hopefully, using literary works as historical sources will deliver similar benefits as in literary study, and help form a better view of historical development, especially for the Ayutthaya and Bangkok periods.

It is said that literature is a mirror of the society that creates it. This is true, but it is a mirror which reflects only certain things. Its major importance is that it gives us a view of the feelings and values of the people in a certain period. But such matters do not figure strongly in Thai written works. As is well known, works along these lines are not popular among the Thai. Writers of religious texts tend to be so dominated by religious ideas that it is not certain how much their writings actually reflect their time. Literature which reflects the values, feelings, and worldview of people in various periods—without the writers deliberate intention—are sources of great value for the study of intellectual history, especially as other sources are difficult to find.

Any work of literature has both a writer and a body of readers who, down through the years, have "consumed" the work in their lives. The work does not reflect the worldview, values, feelings, and thoughts of the writer alone; those of the readership are of no less significance. The work presents a particular view, and that view gains currency if the readership appreciates it. In brief, a literary work and the society that produces it are interrelated. From this perspective, the use of literary sources for studying intellectual history is not limited to study of the few intellectuals who produce such works. Rather it encompasses the trends of thought of both the intellectuals and their readers who interact with one another and with the social environment in which all of them live.

Although literature is valuable for the study of intellectual history, it also has some limitations. It is almost impossible to find Thai literary works in their pure original form. They have been embellished and added to by scribes making recensions, or by later scholars, and may have lost material along the way. In using these literary works as historical sources, the manuscripts have to be critiqued in detail, as literary specialists like Chantit Krasaesin and MC Chand Chirayu Rajani have done with certain works. The fact that the manuscripts are not original creates major problems in determining their age and identifying their authors.

Apart from problems concerning the manuscripts, written Thai literary works are products of the upper class which is a minority segment of the society. In many cases, these upper class literary works have not been consumed by the ordinary people. Examples include *Khamchan dutsadi sangwoei klomchang*, a Brahman chant for pacifying royal elephants,[4] and various *Khlong chaloemphrakiat*, epics eulogizing royalty. The literary mirror reflecting society is thus rather narrow. It reflects only the images, thoughts, and feelings of the upper class. At the same time the people's literature, which was transmitted orally, has almost completely disappeared. Only a

3. This can be seen from the studies by the old generation of literature specialists such as Plueang na Nakhon (1963), down to those of the new generation such as Saowalak (1977) or Nittaya (1972) and Somphan (1975).

4. A verse in the *chan* meter chanted by Brahmans in a royal ceremony of placating wild elephants captured for royal service.

small amount has survived in the memory of the poor and been written down, and even this cannot be dated. Using written literary works as historical sources implicitly forces us to study a history centered on the ruling class.

In contrast to the study of history, attempts to create a reasoned understanding of literary works should be done along with knowledge of the social and economic background to these works. The essay presented here is hoped to be some use to students of literature.

I: THE LITERATURE OF THE TWO CLASSES OF AYUTTHAYA

The widespread influence of foreign culture within the Thai ruling class meant that the cultures of the ruling class and of the people were very different. Relations between government and people were limited to corvée service, the collection of tribute in kind and rice taxes, and the formation of armies. The culture of the *munnai* or officials rested on education, and was thus bound up with written texts, the majority of which were in foreign languages such as Pali or Khmer. In contrast, the culture of the phrai or ordinary people was bound up with folk tales, stories, and legends that were transmitted orally and not recorded in written form. Religion for the ordinary people meant monks' sermons and beliefs that had been embedded for generations. The creative products of these two cultures were thus different. For the official class, the past was in the form of royal chronicles, while for the common populace the past was found in legends and folk tales. Officials begged for rain by performing dances based on Hindu mythology such as the dance of Orachun (Kukrit 1980, 7) while ordinary people conducted the *hae nang maeo* or cat procession,[5] mimicking nature's processes of birth, procreation, and so on.

The literatures produced by the two classes were equally different. Nowadays we tend to think that literature does not have much of a role in society aside from providing entertainment or promoting appreciation of the arts, hence the belief that when a country is not at peace, literary works will not be created (Nittaya 1972, 47–50). But in fact what we call literature, especially in olden times, had a larger social role than entertainment and artistic appreciation. The *Lilit ongkan chaeng nam* or water-oath verse[6] and *Kham su khwan* or spirit-soothing verse[7] are good examples of literature that had nothing to do with the two roles mentioned. The respective ways of life of the ordinary people and the official ruling class resulted in differences in the roles and functions of the literature they produced as well. These differences are significant and need to be examined comparatively in some detail.

5. A rain-generating rite featuring a procession with a female cat at the head, participants singing songs alluding to sexual activity, and spectators throwing water at the cat

6. An oath of allegiance in verse form chanted by Brahmans in the ceremony of taking the water oath.

7. A long verse chanted melodically to soothe one's spiritual essence in a marriage ceremony.

THE ENVIRONMENT IN WHICH LITERATURE WAS CREATED

The literature of the officials arose in the *mueang*, the town, or in other words, the communities that acted as the headquarters for government at one level or another. The majority of the extant works of literature from the Ayutthaya period would all have emerged from the capital city itself. However, there has recently been increasing research interest on literary manuscripts found in other towns (for example Nattawut 1979; Chuan et al. 1981). As "town" and especially "capital" are places where royal power is concentrated, Ayutthaya literature of the official class is permeated by kings, gods related to them in one way or another, and rituals associated with the glorious power of the monarch. At the same time, the town has a rather important role in the literature of this ruling class because the town is a device for reflecting royal power. Celebrating the town in a *kham pranamphot*[8] or invocation as in *Khlong kamsuan*,[9] is a defining characteristic of upper class literature. However, as the town is so closely associated with the king, the people of the town have a very minor role and scarcely appear in Ayutthaya literature at all.

In contrast, the literature of the ordinary people emerged from the countryside, and was intimately bound up with the ways of life of rural people. Even in instances where the king is mentioned, he is portrayed as an ordinary man, as found in many stories in *Phongsawadan nuea*,[10] the Northern Chronicle. In one story, the daughter of a king comes to savor gourds belonging to villagers; in another, a king's son sneaks through the fortress walls for an assignation with another king's daughter; and there is the tale about the village of *Ta monglai*.[11] On the whole, however, this literature had little to do with kings, but rather was about events in peoples' lives, courtship, and knockabout humor verging towards obscenity. Most was in the format of verbal exchanges between groups of males and females. These exchanges extended across the range from oral accounts of everyday life, to transmission of beliefs and values upheld since ancient times, to flirting and courtship, to cursing and abuse full of analogies to sexual behavior. It is highly likely that the use of ambiguous language with lots of sexual references originated from fertility rituals.

PROSODY[12]

The literature of the official class, or what might be called court literature, over time developed various different forms of verse of great complexity. One set of verse

8. A poem at the beginning of a literary work, calling on the power of the Three Gems and Hindu deities, and eulogizing the reigning king.

9. Title of a literary work probably composed in the sixteenth century.

10. A legendary history of kings who ruled kingdoms in the lower and central Chaophraya basin during the period before the foundation of Ayutthaya in the royal chronicles.

11. A tale about an elopement and severe punishment of the girl's father.

12. For fuller descriptions of Thai verse forms, consult: William Gedney, 'Siamese verse forms in historical perspective,' in Gedney, ed., *Selected Papers on Comparative Tai Studies*,

forms popular in early court literature may have originated in the Thai language, including various kinds of *khlong*[13] and *rai*.[14] However these forms apparently were not used in the literature of the ordinary people (except in provincial centers where the literature had strong ties to court literature and must be considered as literature of the official class). It can be surmised that these verse forms developed more complexity than anything that had existed earlier in the Thai language, rendering them unsuitable for the repartee and improvisation found in folk literature. True, there is a well-known story about Si Prat[15] at the court of King Narai (1656–1688), and the court's appreciation of his witty improvisation using the *khlong si suphap*[16] verse form. However, the sources for the Si Prat story are not reliable enough to count as history. In general terms, the trend of development in court literature was towards a style suitable for written composition. This reached its height in the *khlong kon*[17] that was probably very popular in the late seventeenth century judging from the number of examples in *Chindamani*, a manual of language and prosody from that era.

The official class was acquainted with classical texts in foreign languages, and thus adopted verse forms from foreign languages, especially Pali, for some literary works. The first of these foreign verse forms used in Ayutthaya court literature seems to have been *kap*.[18] Its earliest appearance in extant works was in *Mahachat khamluang*[19] (Great Jataka) which also used the *chan*[20] meter and which may be called the model for the adoption of Pali prosody into the upper class literature of Ayutthaya from the time of King Trailokanat (1448–88?). The *chan* meter enjoyed a revived popularity in the reign of King Narai in the late seventeenth century, to the point that a court

---

University of Michigan, 1989; Manas Chitkasem, 'Thai poetry: problems of translation,' in J. H. S. Davidson, *Lai Su Thai: Essays in Honour of E. H. S. Simmonds*, London: SOAS, 1987; James N. Mosel, *A Survey of Classical Thai Poetry*, Bangkok: Bangkok World, 1959; J. R. Cooke, 'The Thai *khlong* poem: description and examples,' *Journal of the American Oriental Society*, 100, 4, 1980. [T]

13. A special group of Tai and Siamese metrical forms. The commonest form uses lines of five syllables in stanzas of two, three, or four lines, with constraints on rhyme and tone for certain syllables.

14. A simple metrical form using lines of five syllables, with the fifth or last syllable rhyming in sound and tone with the first or third syllable of the next line.

15. An Ayutthaya poet whose story was told by another poet in the early Bangkok period and who was allegedly extremely well-versed in improvising the rigid type of *khlong* metrical form.

16. A metrical form of the *khlong* group with further requirements of tonal rigidity.

17. An esoteric type of *khlong* which demands knowledge of its secret arrangement to decipher its meaning.

18. A group of metrical forms with many variants, probably from an Indian model.

19. The Siamese version of the Vessantara Jataka; the extant text is supposed to have originated from one written in the fifteenth century (see chapter 3 of this book).

20. A metrical form imported from India with patterns of "heavy" (long vowel or final consonant) and "light" (short vowel or no final consonant) syllables.

poet decided to render Jataka tales in *chan* form for a *nang yai*[21] or shadow puppet play. This *Samutthakhot khamchan*[22] can be considered the first *khamchan* or book of *chan* verse in the Thai language (Dhanit in *Chindamani*, 151).

The Ayutthaya court liked to combine several verse forms together in a single work. The *Mahachat khamluang* blended several metrical forms including *rai*, *kap*, *khlong*, and *chan*. The combination of *khlong* and *rai* was popular as the poetic form known as *lilit*.[23] In late Ayutthaya, *kap* was often combined with *khlong* as the form known as *kap ho khlong*.[24] *Khamchan* came in many different variants. Among works understood to originate from the Ayutthaya period, only four used *rai* exclusively, namely *Kap mahachat*,[25] *Nanthopananthasut khamluang*,[26] *Phra malai khamluang*,[27] and *Pradon tham*[28] (Nittaya 1972, 51–9).

A significant change in court literature took place towards late Ayutthaya, probably from the early eighteenth century. This was the use of the *klon*[29] meter. This form does not appear in the *Chindamani* treatise on prosody, meaning that it was not popular in King Narai's time. There are reasons to believe that *klon* first became widespread in folk literature and only later was adopted by the court (as explained below). This was the first time that the upper class took one of the common people's verse forms into its own literature. Apart from this lone example, all other verse forms used by the upper class were either developed themselves from old versions in the Thai language, or borrowed from overseas. Conversely, there is no evidence that folk literature adopted any verse forms from the court.

There are no specific names for each metrical form used in folk literature; instead they are usually collectively termed *phleng*.[30] Each *phleng* meter must have been

21. Siamese-style shadow play using puppets made of hide (*nang*).

22. A romance composed in the *chan* metrical form by a seventeenth century poet as a script for the performance of shadow play.

23. A literary term, probably coined in the early Bangkok period at the earliest, designating poetic writings in which *rai* and *khlong* metrical forms are used alternately.

24. A genre of poetic writings in which a *khlong* verse briefly states a main idea followed by a number of *kap* verses elaborating the main idea.

25. Another version of the Siamese Vessantara Jataka composed in the *rai* metrical form, used for ceremonial recitation by monks in a religious festival.

26. A Buddhist teaching taken from the Sutta and composed in the *rai* metrical form, probably recited by monks on special occasions; the extant text was composed by a prince in the eighteenth century and probably granted by the king the status of a royal version, i.e., *khamluang*.

27. A Buddhist teaching in a Siamese version usually recited by monks in the cremation ceremony; the extant text was composed by a prince in the eighteenth century and has been regarded as the royal version.

28. A collection of religious fables written in the eighteenth century.

29. A metrical form related to a popular improvised verse form; usually with lines of two eight-syllable hemistiches, various patterns of rhyming link between the two hemistiches, and a rhyming link from the final syllable to the next stanza.

30. Popular verse of all metrical forms, invariably improvised and sung.

popular in a particular locality—for instance *phleng i-saeo* or teasing songs around Suphanburi, *phleng khorat* around Khorat, and *phleng ruea* or boat songs around Ayutthaya—though certain forms such as *phleng kiao khao* or rice harvesting songs may have been more widely popular. Generally, folk verse forms tended to be geographically limited while upper class forms spread much more widely through the urban areas. More study is needed to understand the *phleng* forms of folk literature, but as far as can be seen, the major forms can be grouped into three:

1. Those constructed with two hemistiches in each line; the last word of the first hemistich rhyming with the fourth or fifth word in the second; and the endings of each line rhyming with the same sound throughout the song. The *wai khru*, or section paying respects to the teacher, of one of the boat *phleng* provides an example:

sip niow pranom khuen nuea sian phrom thang thup lae thian lae kho bucha
cha wai khru son khru phak cha wai khru lak khru cham thang khru nae khru nam ram rian ma

Ten fingers pressed together above my head,
with incense and candles, I pay my respects
To teachers who teach, rest, skip, and recall
to good teachers all who served as my guide

This verse form appeared also in other forms of *phleng* such as *phleng kiao khao* or rice harvesting songs (Prathueang 1981, 6–8), and *phleng mahori*[31] which became so widely popular during the Ayutthaya era that they were almost like folk songs. *Phleng hong thong*, the song of the golden goose, is another in the same form:

phraya hong thong chao bin long loi khongkha
tin yiap sarai pak go sai ha pla
kin kung kin kang kin hoi kraphang maengda
kin laeo pho ma chap ton wa pho thong

Lord goose of gold glides down and alights on Ganga
His feet seize the weeds his bill feeds on fish
Eats shrimp and crabs eats dabs and shellfish
Having eaten, he flies, whish up to the bo tree of gold
(Panya 1974, 58)

The most notable thing about this verse form is that the rhyming of the second hemistiches in each line is exactly like a *klon*. This is true of all *phleng* in which the endings of each line rhyme throughout, including both the *phleng ruea* or boat songs, and *phleng kiao khao* or rice harvesting songs.

31. Songs for a kind of courtly musical ensemble.

2. Another form of *phleng*, popular for *phleng klom dek* or children's lullabies, has external rhyming very similar to that of *klon*, as in this example:

maeo miao	yaek khiao ying fan
suea pla na san	kat kan laeo wa

Kitty cat	baring teeth and fang
fishing tiger, flat face	bite one another like mad
	(Prathueang 1981, 5)

The same verse form is found in some Ayutthaya *phleng mahori* such as *Phleng thoi lang khao khlong* (Walking backwards into the canal) and *Phleng angkan si bot*. Even the *Manora*[32] play from Ayutthaya used a form of the *klon* that in some places is similar to children's lullabies (Panya 1974, 49–51).

3. Another verse form found in folk literature perhaps should not be called a *phleng* as it was used in the rituals of the ordinary people. Examples include the verses for *tham khwan chuk* or spirit-soothing during the tonsure ceremony, verses for *su khwan* or spirit-soothing in the marriage ceremony, and prayers to invite a spirit to take up residence in a spirit house. It is highly possible that the authors of these prayers were in some way connected to the official culture, for example by having entered the monkhood and learned to read, as these prayers make reference to Hindu gods and major spirits that figure in upper class literature. In addition, the meter used is similar or sometimes identical with forms used in Buddhist wat. This issue will be discussed further in the section on monks and the literature of the wat.

What is noticeable about the verse forms of folk literature is how suitable they were for improvisation. Folk literature was not a written form but oral and improvised on the spot. Village poets studied their craft by listening to teachers, learning their teachers' own verses, practicing by embellishing these, and eventually becoming adepts of the genre.

FUNCTIONS

The corpus of Ayutthaya court literature that still exists today by and large had functions which were religious (or didactic) and ritualistic. The *Ongkan chaeng nam* or water oath verse clearly had a ritual function as did *Chan dutsadi sangwoei klomchang* or verse for soothing elephants. As for *Mahachat khamluang*, *Kap mahachat*, and even *Mahachat klon thet*,[33] *Nanthopananthasut khamluang*, and *Phra malai khamluang*, all had religious cum ritual functions. *Khlong chaloemphrakiat* or verses in praise of the monarch such as *Yuan phai*[34] (Defeat of Lanna), should also be viewed as having a largely ritual function.

32. Title of a romance on which a script for a play from the eighteenth century was based.

33. Siamese version of the Vessantara Jataka, composed in a loose *rai* metrical form, for recitation by monks during a religious festival

34. A eulogistic poem of the fifteenth century commemorating the victory of an Ayutthaya king over a Chiang Mai king.

Court literature with no religious or ritual functions emerged from the mid Ayutthaya period onwards, and was mostly related to performance of the Ramakian, the Thai version of the Ramayana. The prime examples are the *khamphak* or scripts for Ramakian mask plays and shadow plays of which the extant versions seem to have been composed later than the reign of King Narai (Dhanit 1963, 149–50). Some extracts from scripts older than these extant versions were used to illustrate verse forms in *Chindamani*. Also the *Rachaphilap*[35] story may have existed in the Ayutthaya era as part of a Ramakian script or in some related way. These *khamphak* came in long and short forms for the shadow and mask plays respectively (Saowalak 1977, 125–36). *Samutthakhot khamchan* was composed as a script for a shadow play, and *Anirut khamchan*[36] probably had the same purpose. In late Ayutthaya, the court began to take up drama patterned on folk performances (the history and evaluation of drama appears below). This generated an increasing numbers of written literary works that were not connected to religion and ritual. These plays included *Anirut* (Dhanit 1960, 3–4), *Inao*,[37] various episodes from the Ramakian (Nittaya 1972, 116–7) and a number of other *lakhon nok* or "outer dramas" that cannot with certainty be attributed to the court.

If we ignore literature connected to performance, then we find that the literary works of the Ayutthaya upper class as a rule did not have a plot. Even those few that did have a plot were not designed to be read for the pleasure of enjoying a story. For example, the intention behind *Suea kho khamchan*[38] (Tale of a Tiger and a Cow) was didactic rather than entertaining. *Siriwibunkiti*[39] is a manual for the *klon konlabot*[40] meter rather than a story. The *Kap he ruea* or boating chants, *Kap ho klong*, *Kamsuan*, *Thawathotsamat* (Twelve Months),[41] and *Bunnowat khamchan*[42] all have no plot at all. This does not mean that the Ayutthaya upper class could not derive pleasure from reading literature (or listening to literary works being read). There is no doubt that the kings enjoyed listening to the *Khlong chaloemphrakiat* or poems of royal celebration composed by the master poets. *Kamsuan*, *Thawathotsamat*, and *Lilit yuan phai* probably gave great enjoyment to those in the court circle. But the enjoyment of works like *Kap ho klong* came from appreciation of the poet's eloquence, which is

35. A lyrical poem expressing Ram's sorrow after his wife has been abducted, written allegedly in the Ayutthaya period, after the form of the *khamphak* genre.

36. A romance written in the seventeenth century in the *chan* metrical form, and based upon a romance in the Sanskritic tradition.

37. A romance originating from the Panji cycles from Java.

38. A parable-romance written in the seventeenth century

39. A treatise on making various types of esoteric verse in the *klon* metrical form with expositions of those types by using them to narrate a romance; the work was composed in the eighteenth century before the fall of Ayutthaya.

40. An esoteric type of *klon*, with additional metricological regulations for each type of *konlabot*

41. Title of a work written around the sixteenth century about the poet's yearning for a lady all year round, hence the title meaning "twelve months."

42. Title of a work depicting the poet's journey from Ayutthaya to the Buddha's Footprint at Saraburi during its annual festival in the eighteenth century.

different from the enjoyment of reading a story. The crux is not the story or plot but the poet's ability to weave fine words and images to express his profound sentiments. One work seems to be an exception to this generalization, and that is *Lilit phra lo* (Lay of Phra Lo).[43] But careful study shows it is not a very important exception. Certainly the *Lilit phra lo* of the Ayutthaya period was written to be read rather than performed. Yet what marks *Lilit phra lo* off from other works is that it was based on Thai folk stories (Pho Na Pramuanmak 1971, unpaginated), and hence should be seen as the one Ayutthaya-era literary work heavily influenced by folk literature. At the same time, the plot of *Lilit phra lo* is clearly not very highly developed. The Thai technique for developing stories is to insert new plots into an existing work. This happened with the *Ramakian*, *Khun chang khun phaen*,[44] *Phra aphaimani*,[45] *Kraithong*,[46] and so on. But *Lilit phra lo* from the Ayutthaya era has only one storyline, and even later that characteristic was maintained. Apart from this, throughout the Ayutthaya period, *Lilit phra lo* did not inspire writers to adapt the same story into other forms. By contrast, in the Bangkok era, *Lilit phra lo* was developed quite differently: it was adapted into a drama, the plot of a *nirat*,[47] a *phleng yao*,[48] and much more besides. All this indicates that in the Ayutthaya time, upper class readers were not impressed by the story of *Lilit phra lo* so much as captivated by its supreme poetic eloquence that is even mentioned in many later works.

At the same time it should be understood that the Ayutthaya elite did know how to enjoy imaginative stories but they sought such entertainment from performances such as *nang* shadow plays, *khon* mask plays, and later *lakhon* theatrical dramas. The pleasure they derived from reading probably had nothing to do with a storyline.

From various sources, the corpus of Ayutthaya literary works which have a storyline and which are not about religion or ritual can be listed as follows.

Lilit phra lo, *Kap khap mai rueang phra rot*,[49] and four dramas which were later called *lakhon nai*[50] or "inner dramas," namely *Inao*, *Dalang*,[51] *Unarut* (the Ayutthaya version of which is called Anirut), and *Ramakian*.

43. Title of a fictional poem written around the sixteenth or seventeenth century in the *lilit* form.

44. A story of a love triangle widely known and extended by different poets, ultimately resulting in a story of manifold themes.

45. A poetic romance composed by Sunthon Phu so popular that the author was requested not to finish the work with the result it was developed into many cycles of adventurous stories.

46. A story of an adventure and romance in which different poets added more episodes to the main theme.

47. A literary genre whose main feature is lamentation of parting with the loved one, but descriptions of experiences, real or imagined, in the course of a journey also form an important element, especially in the later development of *nirat* writing.

48. A literary genre of a poetic love letter; the person addressed in the letter, as the missed one in the *nirat*, may be either real or imaginary.

49. Title of a romance written in the metrical form of *kap* for a specific melodic recitation.

50. In the early Bangkok period, plays were classified into "inner dramas" performed only in the court, and "outer dramas" performed elsewhere.

51. Title of a romance, another version of the Panji story.

Fourteen "outer dramas": *Karaket, Khawi, Chaiyathat, Phikunthong, Phimsawan, Phinsuriwong, Manora, Mongpa, Maniphichai, Sangthong, Sangsinchai, Suwannasin, Suwannahong, Sowat.*

Five other old dramas prior to the Second Reign which are understood to date from the Ayutthaya period: *Kraithong, Khobut, Chaiyachet, Phra rot meri*, and *Sinsuriwong* (Nittaya 1972, 92, 112–3).

Other works can be inferred from references found in Ayutthaya literary works themselves, although no texts are currently known. Two titles, *Prachit* and *Sutrathanu*,[52] are mentioned in *Thawathotsamat* (stanzas 25 and 26) but there is no documentation whether at that time they were in a form for reading or performance though *Thawathotsamat* refers to other literary works which are known to have been works for performance such as *Ramakian, Anirut, Samutthakhot,* and *Phra suthon manora*[53] (see chapters 21–4).

In *Chindamani*, there are references to *Phra nonthakasattrisangwat* and *Si umathikan*[54] (*Chindamani*, 49) but the nature of these works is unknown.

In the same period Phra Si Mahosot, the author of *Kap ho khlong*, referred to several works whose names do not seem to appear in the above list, including: *Burana* with a plot about a hero Thao Phithun who wins a beautiful lady at saka, Indian backgammon; another of unknown title with a plot about a king of Chulani[55] (China) whose queen is kidnapped and taken south without him giving chase; and *Kunalasan* whose plot is unknown (Si Mahosot 1959, 50–2).

The *Unarut* drama from the First Reign has references to other dramas which are believed to date from the Ayutthaya period on grounds that *Unarut* was written by the king at the beginning of the reign and to a great extent copied from an old version. Two of these works have leading characters who are probably different from those in works listed above, namely Phra Chunarat and Thao Worawong (Phutthayotfa 1972, 244).

Evidently, most of the works with a storyline were designed for performance. Almost all appeared in late Ayutthaya when the upper class became more interested in plot-based literature meant for reading. This was a critical turning point in court literature which resulted in many tales from overseas being transmitted into the Thai language. The *Nithan sipsong liam* or Duodecagon (literally, Tales of Twelve Corners) was adopted from a Persian tale (though its purpose was still primarily didactic rather than for reading pleasure). The Arabian Nights tale was adopted as *Nang tantrai* with a rather erotic flavour. In addition, many Sanskrit tales were adopted into the Thai language by various routes including the myths of *Paksi Pakoranam, Pisat Pakoranam, Wetan Pakoranam, Nonthuk Pakoranam*, and *Hitopathet Watthu Pakoranam*[56] (Dhani

52. Titles or more probably names of heroes of fictional romances.

53. Names of the hero and heroine of a romance.

54. Titles of two literary works of unknown nature.

55. Name of a state in the ancient Indian subcontinent, but when used in Thai *tamnan* (legends) usually meaning China or a power centre in southern China.

56. Titles of various stories from Sanskrit mythology.

1960, 17). Clearly these stories were not very widely disseminated as they were not adapted into the plots of dramas and were not known among the ordinary people (Kusuma 1978–9, 80–92).

Folk literature had a very clear function to generate entertainment. Different kinds of *phleng* were popular in different localities in different seasons. Some may originally have had a ritual function but later evolved towards entertainment. The *klon phleng* were not simply recited but were "sung" to a tune with instruments to give a rhythm, and dancing to add to the merriment. There was little of the sacred quality which permeated upper class literature such as the mask or shadow plays. In *phleng*, even the teacher-honoring *wai khru* section might include some knockabout comedy.

The entertainment value of folk literature was closely bound up with the central importance of the story. Some of the plots came from the Jataka stories, some from local tales, and others may have been created anew and passed on by memory. Domestic and temple festivals were occasions for disseminating story-based folk literature. For instance, it was customary to recite a tale at the tonsure cutting ceremony, while at religious festivals, stories were recited in *klon* form as prayers known as *oh-eh-wihanrai*,[57] either using Jataka stories which enabled the audience to gain merit, or other tales which were simply fun because rather obscene (Damrong 1950, 2, 10–11; and Damrong in *Kap mahachat*, 87–8). The custom of reciting these tales helped develop the *sepha*[58] form of ballad in late Ayutthaya.[59] There are records from the First Reign about a *sepha* master called Son who was a gatekeeper in the Ayutthaya period (Damrong 1950, 17–8). Because *sepha* was genuinely a folk genre in which the performers mostly improvised and the texts were passed on by memory, there are no written versions from the Ayutthaya era. The *sepha* poems which remain from Ayutthaya thus come from memorization, are few in number, and are only dubiously products of the Ayutthaya era (Damrong 1950, 12–3).[60] *Khun chang khun phaen*,

57. A melodic recitation of tales in verse by laypersons in pavilions surrounding the *ubosot* of a wat during a religious festival.

58. A kind of performance basically consisting of narrating a story in verse either with the help of a script or through improvisation.

59. It is commonly claimed that *sepha* originated in early Ayutthaya, on grounds that a section of the *Kot monthianban* (palace or royal household laws) on royal activities (clause 146) stated that the presentation of *sepha* music performances should take place at midnight. However, what we know nowadays as *sepha* is the *klon sepha* verse, which definitely had not yet come into existence in the reign of King Trailokanat. Furthermore, speaking of *sepha* together with music indicates this definitely cannot mean the *sepha* known today for there is evidence that *sepha* singing accompanied by a musical ensemble emerged only in the Second Reign. Therefore it can be concluded that either 1. the word *sepha* in the palace laws refers to a type of performance which is not the *sepha* we know today, or 2. the word *sepha* in the palace laws confirms that the laws were revised and amended in later periods. This is not surprising, for it should not be forgotten that the Three Seals Law was actually the code in force during the first Bangkok reign, not an ancient legal text. Old laws have to be constantly revised as long as they remain in force.

60. In his critique of this essay, Somphan Lekhaphan argued that *sepha* may have existed in written form since the Ayutthaya period, and offered 1–2 pages of *sepha* found at Amphoe

which was a very popular work in the form of *klon sepha*, is a different genre from the run of court literature because its story and verse form originated from the common people, and because its first use was for mass entertainment.

Many literary works written in the form of dramas contain hints that their plots came from somewhere not far removed from the lives of ordinary people. For example, some seem to have evolved from the Pannyasa Jataka[61] or even from village tales recited in some locality. Aside from this, drama itself probably evolved as a folk performance genre before it was adopted by the court. Hence most Ayutthaya literature which has a storyline is in the form of *lakhon* drama scripts. Although the court modeled such fixed written scripts on old forms of court performance such as shadow plays and mask plays, nonetheless *lakhon* plays overlapped with the folk culture of the ordinary people more than any other performance genre.

THE LINKAGE BETWEEN COURT LITERATURE AND FOLK LITERATURE

While we have been able to discern many differences between the cultures of the officials and the ordinary people, nevertheless the two cultures coexisted in the same social system, and there was interaction between them as a matter of course. Parts of the culture of the official class would have spread into that of the common people and conversely, parts of folk culture would have been adapted for use by the official ranks. However, in the Ayutthaya period up to the mid seventeenth century, the main direction of cultural interchange was from the officials down to the ordinary people. The court and officials organized performances of *khon* or mask plays, *mongkhrum*[62] and *duekdamban*[63] rituals, *nang* or shadow plays, and so on which offered good opportunities for the ordinary people to know and understand the stories and beliefs of the upper class, which were based on foreign sources. Ramakian, for instance, was so well known that some of the characters in the story were adopted as characters in local folk dramas. Many stories associated with local geography were linked to Ramakian characters. It is possible that the dance poses accompanying the *phleng* of the ordinary people were copied and adapted from those of upper class female dancers, which in turn had some admixture of foreign influence. The Hindu deities Siva, Rama, and Brahma became well known among the populace.

Aside from the normal interactions between them, officials and people were also the common inheritors of a number of cultural elements. They held some basic beliefs in

---

Saohai, Saraburi as evidence. However, Somphan cannot prove that these truly come from Ayutthaya, and though there may have been *sepha* written down in the Ayutthaya era, that does not mean that *sepha* evolved as a genre within the traditions of Ayutthayan written literature.

61. Title of an archaic Pali work written in Chiang Mai around the seventeenth century, being a collection of local folk-tales, told in the Jataka form, i.e., as stories of the previous lives of the Buddha.

62. A ritualistic performance usually part of a ceremonial procession.

63. A ritualistic performance believed to be a depiction of the scene of churning the primordial ocean in Hindu mythology.

common such as the belief in spirits, some of which were ceremonially invoked for their supernatural powers in the rituals of both the official class and of the ordinary people. Examples are the *phra song mueang*[64] and *phra suea mueang*,[65] protective spirits of towns. Members of the official class composed *nang yai* shadow plays using the *Samutthakhot* story from the Pannyasa Jataka—a story which originated from a common folk tale well known in some localities. Thus it is not surprising to find that in the culture of the ordinary people, tales such as Nang Manora, also from the Pannyasa Jataka, were very popular.

The channel which facilitated this interpenetration of the two cultures was the wat, which was the site of frequent interaction between the upper class and the ordinary people in activities ranging from ordination into the monkhood to participation in seasonal festivals. The standards, values, and beliefs of the official class were sculpted, engraved, and painted on wat buildings, and commoners would see them in the course of visiting these places. Equally important, the scholars in the wat had a large part in linking together the cultures of official and commoner by offering the same teachings and upholding the same standards of Buddhism for both parties. Thus, this study of literature should give special attention to the role of the wat as the producer of an intermediary literature known to both officials and ordinary people.

WAT LITERATURE

Scholars in the wat consisted of two groups: first, there were monks who had been ordained and studying for a long time, could read Pali, and were teachers both for the common people and the officials who ordained in their wat; second, there were lay persons with religious knowledge who were attached to the wat and belonged to it in some way. In the Sukhothai era, there are records about people who belonged completely to the wat because patrons had "bought" them and offered them to the wat just like a *kalpana* grant of land or other materials. These people were known as "pandits" (see the Wat Asokaram inscription, face 2). The duty of these people was to chant texts for the audience of Buddhist devotees.

These two types of scholar had a large part in the dissemination of Buddhist literature to the official and commoner classes because they translated religious texts into the Thai language for chanting to the audience of devotees in the wat. The Vessantara Jataka had been very popular and respected from long ago. It might have been the first text translated into Thai. The oldest extant version is the *Mahachat khamluang* which was translated by a council of scholars on royal command. However, there were probably earlier translations made in the wat (which is why it is called *khamluang*, the royal version, rather than *khamwat*, the wat version). Apart from this important Jataka, others were also translated for chanting or reciting to devotees, and many texts have survived to the present. Some legends and some Jataka tales were composed in the *klon suat* form for chanting in the wat during seasonal festivals (Damrong in *Kap*

64. The spirit whose turn it is to protect the town in a particular year.
65. The ancestral spirits of a town.

mahachat, 87–8, and Damrong 1950, 10). Listening to these translated works was considered a way of making merit.

In the translations made by wat scholars, it was conventional to retain Pali for the opening passage as a simple way to indicate that the work had been translated. It also made it easy for experts to keep track. In the Thai language part, it was conventional to use the metrical form known as *klon wat* (*klon* here means a meter) which was the same as *rai*. Sometimes it was interspersed with *kap* but only to a small extent. Even though the original Pali texts were not in any meter, the wat scholars would translate them into the form of *klon wat*. The reason for this lay in the status of *rai* in Thai literature, and is a good example of the way wat literature helped to link the respective literatures of the officials and ordinary people. Hence the *rai* verse form and its development needs to be considered in detail.

Dividing language into poetry and prose tempts us to overlook that both actually have a common descent. At one extreme is spoken language which is not very strict about grammatical rules and full of idiom. At the other extreme is poetry which has mandatory patterns of meter, sound, rhythm, rhyme, and so on. Between these two extremes there are many types of language ranging from coarse to refined. Within this view of language, the metrical form known as *rai* is a transitional form from prose, refined by the application of a small number of rules, especially that each hemistich (*wak*) or line (*prayok*) must be connected by rhyming vowels. On the ladder of refinement, *rai* is the first step above prose (which itself is one step above spoken language). Thus the rules applied in prose, which is already a refined and euphonious form of language, are also applied in *rai*. Although *rai* and prose are overlapping, they are clearly distinguishable by a listener (or reader). *Rai* is thus appropriate for use in situations which are more special than those in which prose or spoken language are used. One such special situation is addressing a god, spirit, or something sacred. It is highly possible that *rai* has been used for such purposes for a very long time. The choice of words and rhyme make *rai* into a sacred form of language. The documents which indicate that *rai* had such a status are prayers to the spirits and prayers for essence-soothing (*tham khwan*) in various ceremonies including marriage, pre-ordination, and the tonsure ceremony. All use the *rai* form, and these texts are considered sacred. They are the exclusive knowledge of spirit "doctors." They change very slowly and probably mostly retain the main characteristics of old "chants." One example is a current *bot tham khwan chuk* used in the tonsure-cutting ceremony among people from Amphoe Pa Mok, Ang Thong province:

khaphachao cha kho rian choen pho no nuea muni nat wa phra khwan chi
cha lum long nai duang don huai heow pha
nai thong than thara thale luang
pai long chom matchachat thang puang
an waek wai
pratsachak rangkai tae kao kon
phra khwan chao oei cha pai sop son non nai pa na anat
pen choeng pha silalat luan tae utakang

bang pen huai heow pleow plong pen plak plo trueng san nam so krasen s
pen raho olan
khwan pho chueng luem long
phra khwan chao oei chong khao ma yu nai rup song
cha re ruan lum long nai dong don raem thuret
pho cha yu loei nai thaeo thin prathet mai mi khon
pen thaeo thuen kluen klon duai raet chang. . .

I appeal to you, the offspring of a great benevolent religious sage [Buddha].
The life essence has fled far away, carried away by what it sees,
Into the hills, valleys, and crags, into the streams, lakes, and great oceans,
Captivated by all the fishes swimming,
Losing its former body.
Oh spirit, wandering and sleeping pitifully in the forests
Among the crags and mountains, full of lakes (*utakang*)
Where water splashes into deep gorges, forming pools, muddy and turbulent,
So remote and secret, far from sight.
Oh life essence, you have lost yourself, please return to your old form.
You have become scattered, losing yourself in the forest and hills,
Living in a pitiless and helpless state.
Are you going to stay in a place with no people,
So wild with many rhinoceros and elephants?
(Prathueang 1981, 11–2)

It can be seen that the rules about rhyme are not very strict. In some verses, the ends of each line rhyme, as in the common people's *phleng*, and in others the two hemistiches in each line rhyme, as in a *rai*. Yet the difference between this language and everyday language is quite apparent.

Both wat and court used the *rai* form in some of their literature. In wat literature, *rai* became the model for translating Pali into Thai. The wat scholars' choice of this form for translation can probably be explained by the fact that *rai* was already "sacred" and hence appropriate to convey the content of texts which were chanted so that listeners might gain merit. This was the reason why the wat translators deliberately converted the texts into *rai* even though the Pali original was not written in meter. It became almost universally customary to use *rai* for religious texts, and this form was called *phasa roi kaeo*[66] or stylized prose. It was almost the same as the metrical form known as *rai yao*,[67] only not so strict about having each hemistich rhyme with the next. This *rai yao* form eventually became the universal format for compositions written by court poets for chanting in the wat, as shown by the three Ayutthaya *khamluang*.

66. Prose-like language in which rhyme and poetic vocabulary are favored.
67. A metrical form which requires rhyming of the last syllable of a line with another syllable in the next line, with no fixed rules about either the number of syllables in each line nor the position of the rhymed syllables.

In court literature, the *rai* was modified by adding more rules to become the *rai suphap*[68] in which both the number of words per hemistich (*wak*) and the tones of words were governed by rules. In folk literature, *rai* was not used in works for entertainment, while in court literature *rai* retained a sacred quality and was mostly used to address the gods in the so-called invocation at the beginning of a work. This can be seen in *Khlong kamsuan* and *Lilit yuan phai* which used *khlong* throughout except for the invocation which was in *rai*, because *rai* had a sacred status for both officials and ordinary people. This custom was still practiced into early Bangkok when poets may not have known its true meaning. This can be seen in the royal version of the *Ramakian* in the First Reign and the *Nirat tam sadet lamnamnoi*[69] whose authors wanted to copy and compete with the poets of Ayutthaya.

The *rai* was a common property of the upper class and the ordinary people. But the wat helped to evolve this metrical form by adopting it for Buddhist purposes which confirmed its sacred qualities. It was also developed and used in court literature.[70] The *rai* thus illustrates the role of the wat in linking the literatures of the official class and ordinary people.

Another important characteristic of wat literature was that it was a written literature, both because it was produced by scholars with high levels of education, and because it was close to the upper class. Besides, court literature had foundations in the translation of sacred texts. The "use" of such literature was in chanting prayers in which the sacred words had to be pronounced exactly, and thus had to be written down. In this respect, wat literature was rather like that of the officials, but at the same time wat literature also evolved in the direction of folk literature, such as in *Lae saek chadok*, extensions of the Jataka tales which were probably created by monk-reciters through improvisation. There may be other wat literary works that date from the Ayutthaya era and originated from improvisation with no written form, such as *Suat lam*, sermons improvised in verse from Phetchaburi province (Sanit 1981).

Because wat scholars used the Jataka tales as a major source for teachings, many literary works from the wat have a storyline. Such works may be the model for the court's story-based literature in written form, as all early court works with a storyline were clearly based on the Jataka or religious texts. Examples include *Mahachat khamluang, Suea kho khamchan,* and two other *khamluang* works authored

68. A further development of the *rai*, adding requirements on tone and number of syllables in each stanza.

69. Title of a *nirat* composed in the *khlong* verse form by Phraya Trang (the governor of Trang) in the reign of Rama II, describing the king's expedition to the western frontier in a campaign against the Burmese.

70. In fact, the oldest use of *rai* in court literature which is not connected with Buddhism is in the *Ongkan chaeng nam* water-oath text. But some literature scholars have asserted that those *rai* were composed later by Prince Paramanuchit Chinorot (Pho Na Pramuanmak 1972, 236–86). The first widespread use of *rai* in court literature was in the *Mahachat khamluang* which clearly was influenced by the wat. Thus the wat probably had a part in promoting the use of *rai* by the court, even though the court was acquainted with the form already.

by Prince Thammathibet.[71] Even court performance literature which required a plot took several stories from the Jataka, as did *Samutthakhot khamchan*. Folk literature also made use of wat literature. The Jataka translated for chanting or reciting in the wat became stories for folk performance on a large scale. Almost all the *lakhon nok* outer dramas in the Ayutthaya period took their plots from the Jataka. Wat literature was evidently a major source for the stories found in Thai literature, both of the officials and the ordinary people. But the influence of the stories from the wat was different in each case. For the court, they provided a model for written literature. For folk literature, they provided plots.

Though wat literature in the Ayutthaya period acted as a crossover point between court and folk literature to some extent, it must be reiterated that in general these two literatures were separate. Right through to the end of the Ayutthaya era, court literature took very little from the folk tradition. For instance, the folk verse form known as *phleng* was not adopted by the court, and reading stories for pleasure was not a major element in Ayutthaya literature.

We have now made a broad survey of Ayutthaya literature to serve as a basis for understanding the trends of literary change in early Bangkok. In studying these changes, it will be necessary to limit the scope to the literature produced in the court circle because we have few—if any—good sources for folk literature in this period. A great deal more study is needed before we can reconstruct the folk literature of early Bangkok from the traditions passed down in the countryside in the form of memories and powerful *phleng* songs which the song masters and mistresses can still recall. Serious attempts to collect this information have just begun and not yet progressed very far.

II: CHANGES IN LITERATURE IN EARLY BANGKOK

Glimpses of the changes in literature in early Bangkok were visible since late Ayutthaya, that is, the early eighteenth century. But these changes did not blossom fully until early Bangkok when they grew into a new trend in court or upper class literature.

These trends may be described in broad-brush terms as two complementary and interrelated changes; first, adoption of folk literature into upper class literature, or in other words, closer connections between folk and court literature and in particular the court's adoption and adaptation of many properties of folk literature; second, reduction in the ritual element in court literature to the point the sacredness embedded in Ayutthaya court literature had greatly diminished. This latter aspect will be taken up first.

DECLINE OF THE RITUAL ELEMENT IN LITERATURE

Ritual was important in the written literature of the Ayutthaya court, not only in the works directly connected to ceremonies, such as *Ongkan chaeng nam* or *Khamchan dutsadi sangwoei klomchang*, but also in works designed to display poetic eloquence.

71. A famous poet of late Ayutthaya (d. 1755).

To a significant extent, ritual-style sacredness was embedded in performance literature such as the Ramakian which is saturated with sacredness because it is a story about the gods. Even shadow and mask plays were full of ritual. The importance of ritual in Ayutthaya literature is evident from the weight placed on the *kham pranamphot* or invocation, a tradition strictly upheld that a sacred ceremony must begin with a spoken offering to the gods. Offerings to the gods and to the king can be considered identical because the king is an avatar (incarnation) of a god. This is explicit in the *Lilit yuan phai*: "When the eight forms are assembled, along with everything that is pure, then the god is born as a king, doubling the glory of the royal line" (*Yuan phai*, 1). Such simultaneous eulogy of gods and king is found in another literary work of *Lilit yuan phai*'s era, *Thawathotsamat* (p. 1). From this dual eulogy, it is not a big departure to include the city in the invocation as well on grounds the city is the residence of the king and was created or established as a result of the king's accumulated merit. Ayutthaya is celebrated in the invocation of *Kamsuan*,[72] another old work of this vintage. Celebrating the glory of Ayutthaya meant celebrating the merit of the king himself[73] (*Kamsuan si prat*, 7–9), and celebrating the city could take the place of eulogizing the gods or the king, as in *Kamsuan*, because the association with the king and gods was clearly evident. All three could be eulogized together in the invocation, as in *Lilit phra lo*.

The convention of beginning literary works which were not directly for ritual or religion with such an invocation was strictly upheld through to the time of King Narai. *Anirut khamchan* begins with a passage about an avatar of Phra Narai (i.e., Vishnu) coming to rule Ayutthaya; this amounts to an invocation even though it is also somewhat connected to the plot (Si Prat 1960, 1; Dhanit in the same volume, ko–ngo). The same is true of *Samutthakhot khamchan* (pp. 1–2) which eulogizes the Buddha (who can be considered a god in a certain sense) and the king. Even the *Khlong chaloemphrakiat* of Phra Si Mahosot (1959, 1), which is entirely a eulogy of the king, begins with an invocation. Other works by this poet such as *Kap ho khlong* and the so-called *Nirat nakhon sawan*[74] invariably include an invocation (Si Mahosot 1959, 21, 40–52).

This strictness about beginning a literary work with an invocation declined steeply in early Bangkok. In four dramas composed in King Rama I's reign, only the *Ramakian* begins with an invocation. It seems that works which tended towards entertainment were excused from starting with an invocation. This practice may have begun from late Ayutthaya as Prince Thammathibet's *Kap ho khlong nirat thansok* had no invocation (in contrast to Phra Si Mahosot's *Kap ho khlong* which still had one). For this reason,

72. Title of a literary work probably from the early sixteenth century, variously called *Kamsuan*, or *Kamsuan samut* in some of the recensions.

73. MC Chand Chirayu Rachani states that the last verse of *Kamsuan* and the opening verse praising Ayutthaya were later additions, yet made during the Ayutthaya period (Pho Na Pramuanmak 1972, 414, 385), however the content of the verse was probably the same as before, namely praising the city.

74. A posthumous title of a literary work from the late seventeenth century.

works of the *nithan klon*[75] genre tended not to have an invocation from the very first example, *Sombat amarin*,[76] onwards (Chaophraya Phrakhlang (Hon) 1960, 15). The *nirat khamkhlong*[77] genre still upheld the tradition of starting with an invocation but with some exceptions such as *Nirat suphan*[78] (To Suphan) by Sunthon Phu and *Nirat talat kriap* (To Kriap Market),[79] attributed to Phra Thepmoli (Klin).[80] Only certain poets who can be considered lovers of old forms ("classic" poets), such as Prince Paramanuchit Chinorot,[81] adhered strictly to the practice of always beginning with an invocation.

Although in early Bangkok some poets continued to begin some works with an invocation, these invocations differed visibly from those of the Ayutthaya period. The celebration of the city expanded in importance, and especially in the form of eulogies of the king's accumulated merit and celebration of the city through the real actions of the king. *Lilit siwichai chadok*, Chaophraya Phrakhlang (Hon)'s rendering of the Sivijaya Jataka, written during the First Reign, is an early example of this change. Even though the invocation praises the king, it does not elevate him as a god, but emphasizes the skill and valour in battle through which he defeated the Burmese, Mon, Lao, Khmer, Lanna, and Vietnamese—claims which have at least some basis in the facts of King Taksin's achievements (Chaophraya Phrakhlang (Hon) 1972, 53–5). Similarly in the invocation to the *Lilit phayuhayatra phetphuang*, a work composed at royal command in the First Reign narrating a romance taken from a Jataka, the eulogy is not about the king as a god, but about the state under the king's rule (Chaophraya Phrakhlang (Hon) 1964, 1, 51). The invocations in the *Ramakian* dramas of the First Reign are also good examples of this change towards eulogizing the king by emphasizing reality based on experience rather than elevating him as a god or comparing him to a god. They refer to King Rama I's coronation, his defeat of enemies, his firm faith in Buddhism, his alms giving, his convoking of a Buddhist Council on the Tipitaka at Wat Mahathat, his renovation of Wat Phra Chetuphon, and so on. This change reduced the sacred element in the ritualism of the invocation and made the invocation more like a preface.

75. A literary genre created in the early Bangkok period for narrating romances in the *klon* verse form.

76. Title of a romance in *nithan klon*, written by Chaophraya Phrakhlang (Hon), a famous poet of early Bangkok.

77. A *nirat* written in the *khlong* verse form which was popular in the Ayutthaya period but outnumbered by *nirat* written in the *klon* verse form in the Bangkok period.

78. Title of a *nirat* by Sunthon Phu, written around 1841, describing his trip to Suphanburi; the work is unique because all his other *nirat* are in the *klon* verse form.

79. Title of a *nirat* in the *khlong* verse form written in the reign of Rama III.

80. But MC Chand Chirayu disputes this, suggesting it may be by a poet of the Third Reign who was ordered to inspect elephants on behalf of the king and so travelled to Phaniat (Pho Na Pramuanmak 1970, 166).

81. This renowned poet (1790–1853), a son of Rama I, entered monastic life in childhood and remained a monk throughout his life. His literary work was greatly admired by Rama III and Rama IV.

Another aspect of the change in the invocation occurred in the celebration of the city. In the invocations of the Ayutthaya period, this celebration was closely bound up with the accumulated merit of the king, and focused on the splendor of the temples and palaces or the strength of the fortifications. In these invocations of the Ayutthaya period, the people had no importance for the city. The invocation in *Anirut khamchan* does not mention people at all (Si Prat 1960, 1–7), nor do those in *Samutthakhot khamchan*, or *Nirat nakhon sawan* by Phra Si Mahosot. The latter work sacrifices many chapters to celebrating the Ayutthaya royal palace and the water procession without any reference to people (Si Mahosot 1959, 21). By contrast, the celebration of the city in the invocations of early Bangkok works always mentions the people as one part of the city, no less important than the temples, palaces, and fortifications. The well-being and contentment of the people are further evidence of the king's accumulated merit, as for example in the invocation of *Nirat phra phiphitsali*[82] (Pho Na Pramuanmak 1970, 124–7).

Another ritual element of Ayutthaya court literature lay in the content of the literature itself. Stringing words together to form a composition was seen as a form of recondite power which might bring good or evil to the author. The opening invocation is believed to have roots in rituals performed to gain protection against any evil that might arise from this recondite power, and to induce good effects from it. As Phra Si Mahosot states in the invocation of *Nirat nakhon sawan* (To Nakhon Sawan), may the "Three gods most fierce protect me and show me the path ahead. You who easily see all things, shield and protect me like an umbrella over the head. Burn up the countless spears so noble Ayutthaya may be a place of refuge, a land of contentment" (Si Mahosot 1959, 21). Here offerings are made to the gods through the literary work for the safety of Ayutthaya. Clearly the act of composing literature was a ritual in itself. People tried to achieve something they wanted by performing the ritual of literary composition. The poet who authored *Anirut khamchan* prayed that through the power of the merit from composing these verses,

> I beseech you for help, oh patron,
> In any task I desire to undertake.
> In the lines I compose about the *thamma*,
> Make the ideas manifest and clear.
> Remove the impurity of excess desire.
> Reveal man's maladies, man's misfortunes.
> Deliver eternal freedom from desire.
>
> (Si Prat 1960, 91–2)

Mahanak of Wat Thasai,[83] author of *Bunnowat khamchan* (p. 38), prayed in the

82. Title of a *nirat* in the *khlong* verse form written in the reign of Rama III, describing the author's trip to the south.

83. Name of a monk-poet in the late Ayutthaya period.

same way that he might have fame in the kingdom, suffer no hardship, disease, or danger, and finally go to heaven and achieve nirvana.

This view that composing a literary work is like performing a ritual scarcely appeared in early Bangkok. Rather the Bangkok poets valued a literary work for itself. Poems and prose were a way of embellishing the capital. Thus Prince Paramanuchit Chinorot explained his composition of *Samutthakhot* with the words, "Then with determination I started, ashamed it was unfinished. Poets have not disappeared from Siam" (*Samutthakhot khamchan*, 244; translation from Hudak 1993, 225, v. 2209). This has nothing to do with the merit-making of composing a literary work or some special form of sacredness.

The decline of ritual in early Bangkok literature is clearly visible in the final verse of the royal version of the *Ramakian* of the First Reign. The *Ramakian* is something rather sacred. The hero is called Ram(a), the name of the Thai king. The hero's capital has the same name as the royal capital (i.e., Ayutthaya). Ram himself and other characters in the *Ramakian* are referred to in the *Ongkan chaeng nam* or water oath text as if the gods summon them to witness the oath. Yet the early Bangkok *Ramakian* drama concludes the story like this:

> As for this royal composition of Ramakian,
> The king has faithfully followed the story full of the supernatural,
> But it has no core of substance at all.
> It is simply a ceremonial offering.
> Listeners should not get carried away by it,
> But rather, reflect on the transitoriness of life.
> (*Ramakian*, IV, 2975)

Viewing something sacred like the *Ramakian* as having "no core of substance" may have resulted from the desire to elevate Buddhism as the major ideology of the state, which was a key policy from the First Reign onwards (Nidhi 1980, 50–65; see chapter 6 in this book). For whatever reason, the sacred or ritual element in literature clearly declined in early Bangkok.

ADOPTING THE FOLK LITERARY TRADITION

From late Ayutthaya onwards, the folk literary traditions of the people became more widespread, and some of them were taken up by the court and adapted into its own literature. The decline in the ritual role of court literature opened up more opportunity for court poets to offer various forms of entertainment in their works. The relaxation in the tone and rhythm of court literature facilitated merging of folk literary traditions which emphasized the entertainment of listening to simple uncomplicated verse forms. This trend continued and intensified in the Bangkok era. These folk literary traditions refreshed and reinvigorated court literature, creating a lively revival, released from the stuffy atmosphere of ritual, sacredness, foreignness, and excessive classicism. But the traditions of folk literature alone were not enough to shake up court literature. Changes in the composition of the upper class in the court brought in groups who would adopt, adapt, and develop folk literary traditions into new aesthetic forms. We will concentrate on that part of the folk literary tradition which was adopted by the court, and developed into new forms, becoming the driving force of a major movement in the literature of the court circle.[84] This interplay between literary traditions, of which only key parts will be dealt with here, had a broad impact on court literature.

KLON: VERSE OF THE PEOPLE

The type of verse known as *klon* was the last to emerge among the categories of verse in court literature. The catalogue of verse forms in *Chindamani* does not mention *klon* at all. When the word *klon* was first used in the late seventeenth century it meant verse or poetry in general, as the *Chindamani* (p. 15) stated, "Anyone planning to compose *kap*, *khlong*, and *chan*, should look at the characters ri, rue, li, lue, and make sure they are suitable for using in *klon*."

It is often said that the *klon* was taken from a Chinese form, but this is difficult to believe. No other verse forms in Thai seem to have been adopted from Chinese and it seems impossible that *klon* could be the lone exception. Besides, there are good reasons to believe that *klon* originated from folk verse, and it would be impossible for a pre-literate culture to adopt a verse form from overseas.

The origins of *klon* must be sought among the verse forms used in folk literature. In many kinds of the verse form known as *phleng*, such as the rice-harvesting and boating *phleng*, the mandatory pattern for the last two lines (*bat*) is exactly the same as in the *klon*. In addition, the *phleng klom dek* or lullaby variant, and the variant used in late Ayutthaya drama and sometimes called *klon si* or *kan si*,[85] have exactly the same rules for rhyming. It is highly likely the *klon* is a verse form that originated in folk literature.

At the time *klon* was first used in court literature, *klon* and *phleng* were so clearly similar that this early use of *klon* must have been associated with *phleng* or some form of singing. The genre known as *phleng yao* used the *klon*. Prince Damrong explained that the reason why *phleng yao* was so named (rather than *klon yao*) was because it was a tradition adopted from courtship *phleng* (*kiao pharasi*) such as *phleng prop kai*[86] (Nittaya 1972, 126). *Klon* was used in dramas where the script was sung, similar to

84. A subject specially worth comparative study is the expansion of literary traditions from India or Lanka into the court literature of Ayutthaya, which probably peaked between the mid fifteenth and late seventeenth centuries. This had an impact on Ayutthayan literature of its time in the same way that ripples from folk literary traditions referred to here reinvigorated court literature between the mid eighteenth and nineteenth centuries.

85. A metrical form in which one stanza comprises four syllables; rarely used except in lyrics of old songs.

86. A kind of popular song-playing where male and female singers sing improvised dialogues in verse.

the usage in the lyrics of old mahori ensembles.[87] (Those texts in *klon suphap*[88] are believed to be no older then late Ayutthaya, if they date as far back as Ayutthaya at all.) The *klon* used in singing *doksoi*[89] and *sakkawa*[90] forms of improvised group singing was similarly intended for singing with a mahori ensemble. *Sepha* recitations used *klon*, and *sepha* certainly came from folk literature. As already noted, *phleng* and singing verses to a rhythm or tune for listening pleasure were among the distinctive characteristics of folk literature. In the early stages of the *klon*'s emergence from folk literature, it was always connected with *phleng* or singing.

From late Ayutthaya onwards, *klon* became a verse form which people in the court circle used more and more. Dramas were written in *phleng yao* and *klon* by people in the court circle. In the early stages, little emphasis was placed on internal rhyming (*samphat nai*) because the *klon* was mostly being used for singing. Only when the *klon* was used more for reading (or listening to reading) did the internal rhyming come to be considered necessary and indeed the very thing which made the *klon* so melodic. Strict conventions for external rhyme and the use of internal rhyme were distinctive and striking features of *phleng yao* which gradually evolved away from singing and became a literature for reading before other forms of *klon*. The *phleng yao* of Prince Thammathibet were very different from the *klon* dramas of Ayutthaya in this respect. Before the end of the Ayutthaya period, people in the court circle developed the *klon* into something much more complex than the *phleng* of the common people to the point the conventions of the *klon* were formalized in the treatise, *Siriwibunkiti*. Apart from having an external rhyme, *klon* also had to obey other rules. The number of words in each hemistich began to be fixed. It came to be known that words in certain positions should have a certain tone to achieve the melodic effect of the reading (note: not singing). The *klon* of court literature thus had its own character. Although it originated from folk verse, it became noticeably different from the original to the point that later this difference was recognized by calling it *klon suphap*, polished or respectable *klon*, to mark it off from the forms that ordinary people still used in their *phleng*.

In early Bangkok, *klon* thrived more than any other verse form and was used in many written works. Part of *klon*'s success stemmed from the popularity of drama both in the court and among the people. In early Bangkok, the verse form used in drama was fixed as *klon suphap*, the form which the court had developed from the *phleng* of Ayutthaya time. The composition of many dramas in early Bangkok thus

87. An ensemble which comprises wind, percussion, and string instruments.

88. The fully developed *klon* meter with loose constraints on the number of syllables in each line, tones of words in certain positions, etc., hence its name, meaning literally the polished *klon*.

89. A kind of popular song-playing in which participants are carried on boats and sing short poems in a dialogue-like manner.

90. A kind of song-playing in which poems are improvised as lyrics for the performance of an ensemble; usually musicians, poets, and participants are carried in boats and enjoy the "game" on the moon-lit water.

automatically expanded the use of *klon*. *Sepha* recitation was also taken up by the court to the extent that some tried their hand at composing their own *sepha*, and this again increased the usage of *klon* in court literature. *Nithan klon*, or romance in *klon* form, was a new genre which appeared at the start of this period and quickly developed with several major works written in the form. The writing of *phleng yao* and *chotmaihet*, which had begun to spread in later Ayutthaya (such as *Phleng yao mom phimsen banmueang di*[91]), continued with such compositions as *Phleng yao nirat tha din daeng* (To Red Earth Landing),[92] and *Phleng yao krommuen apsonsuda sinphrachon*.[93] The traditions of *phleng yao* and *chotmaihet* were merged with the genre of *nirat*, which in Ayutthaya times had been distinctly separate. As a result, *klon* become widely used for composing *nirat*, and in fact the most popular form. These new-style *nirat* differed from those like *Kamsuan* or *Thawathotsamat* not only in the use of a different verse form, but also in adopting the traditions of *phleng yao* and *chotmaihet* which described journeys, the realistic experiences in the course of these journeys, and the memory of a lady love left behind. New literary genres such as these expanded the use and popularity of the *klon* which became a verse form used both among the upper class and by the poets of the people.

One major reason for the widespread popularity of the *klon* verse form was that it is very versatile, and can be used for expressing many different moods. It can convey a very profound beauty like the *klon* of Chaophraya Phrakhlang (Hon). It can be sweetly pleasing to the ear like the *klon* of Sunthon Phu. Or it can be used for caustic humor such as that of Phra Mahamontri (Sap).[94] It is good for conveying a story and hence suitable for *sepha* recitations, *nithan* romances, and dramas. *Klon* is good for the lyrics of mahori songs because there is no mandatory pattern of stress, and the sound can be stretched to suit the rhythm of the music. The *klon* can even be used for texts and treatises with no difficulty because the conventions are not so difficult that authors need to use foreign words which would make such documents more difficult to understand. As a result, *klon* was used in medical treatises, records of royal sayings, and other texts. For these reasons the *klon* was widely and rapidly adopted.

At the same time, the *klon* which the court adapted from *phleng* had mandatory rhymes and other features which were not too complex and difficult. Importantly it retained the key feature of the folk *phleng*, namely that *klon* was something a skilled poet could improvise. Hence even though the *klon* became somewhat fancier in the hands of the upper class, it did not become a stranger to the people. The increasing

91. Title of a literary work by a Mom (a title of the nobility) Phimsen who lived in the "good old days" (*banmueang di*), written in the form of *phleng yao*; obviously the title was given in the Bangkok period when the reign of Borommakot was generally referred to as "the good old days."

92. Title of a *nirat* written by Rama I around 1786 when he led a campaign against the Burmese in Kanchanaburi.

93. Title of a work in the form of *phleng yao* recording the death of Princess Apson Sudathep, the favorite grand-daughter of Rama III.

94. A renowned poet in the reign of Rama III, whose masterpiece is a parody of *Inao*.

use and eventual domination of *klon* in drama performance came about effortlessly because the lead players of folk drama could improvise *klon* easily in the same way they had improvised since Ayutthaya times. The *lakhon nok* outer dramas adopted the *klon suphap* on a broad scale. The story of the origins and development of the *klon* illustrates the relations between folk literature and the court, showing how strong these relations were in early Bangkok.

EROTIC LITERATURE: THE FOLK TRADITION OF METAPHOR

The closer relations between the literatures of the upper class and of the people resulted in the use of metaphor and folk sayings becoming adopted by court literature. This had not happened in Ayutthaya times. It is interesting that the court inscribed the folklore collectively known as the "Sayings of Phra Ruang"[95] in Wat Phra Chetuphon, indicating the court's adoption of folk sayings and metaphor as its own property (*Prachum charuek wat phrachetuphon*, 665–9). Court poets such as Sunthon Phu, who were well acquainted with the sayings and metaphors used in folk literature, probably played a leading part in this adoption by court literature. One passage of *Inao* runs:

> Just as love goes through stages,
> So the water boiling vegetables turns from bitter to sweet.
> When love has gone, even sugar loses its flavor
> And an old favorite becomes totally sour and salty.
> (Phutthaloetla 1975, 1152)

This use of metaphor appears in the work of Sunthon Phu who may have been the author of this passage which well demonstrates the adoption of folk metaphor and sayings in upper class literature. However, no one has yet studied this matter in detail, and it will require some time to gain a proper understanding of many aspects of the literary traditions which appear in early Bangkok court literature. Although we do not yet have a sufficiently clear understanding of these matters, it is possible to analyze the increased use of folk sayings and metaphor in the depiction of erotic scenes which are popularly called *bot atsachan* or "wondrous scenes"—which itself is a form of metaphor.

Sexual activity is a rather major part of folk literature. Many forms of singing such as boat *phleng*, harvest *phleng*, courtship *phleng*, Khorat *phleng*, and *phleng thepthong*[96] are about flirting and courtship between men and women, and refer to sexual activity by using metaphor. Why sexual activity has such importance cannot be explained. It may be that these references to sex were once part of a fertility ritual (like the cat procession rite). At present there are no texts of the local people's songs

95. *Phasit phra rueang*, title of a literary work in the early Bangkok period, being a collection of old sayings in poetic form, attributed to Phra Ruang, a legendary king of Sukhothai.

96. A kind of popular verse-play.

which were popularly sung in the Ayutthaya period. But it is credible that the way metaphor was used in such songs was not very different from usage known from later periods. In folk literature, metaphors about sexual activity employed on the one hand comparisons with nature such as bees, flowers blooming, and rain, and on the other hand, comparisons with everyday life such as transplanting paddy, pounding rice, and weaving cloth.

References to sexual activity are also found in court literature. But in the old generation of court literature from Ayutthaya, there is little if any use of metaphor. The author of *Kamsuan* describes his memory of a girl he loves quite straightforwardly as "remembering your breast while sleeping, how inviting to look upon, dear lady" (*Kamsuan si prat,* 43). *Samutthakhot khamchan* uses up a lot of paper on "wondrous scenes" which have no trace of wonder but instead are absolutely explicit:

> His regal face against her fragrant face.
> His royal belly against her rounded belly.
> His chest pressed against hers.
> Gently from above, he presses her blooming lotus.
> Her heart overflows with joy,
> Her hands grasp the Lord of Men
> And lead, offering no resistance.
>
> (*Samutthakhot khamchan,* 70–1)

Metaphors of the type known as wondrous scenes first appeared in court literature in *Lilit phra lo*. But for the most part, *Lilit phra lo* describes sexual activity in a straightforward way. There is some metaphor using nature, but the metaphor is very close to sex in reality, for example "having fun in her pond, the fish come up to watch the rhythm, the flower blooms" (*Lilit phra lo,* 525). Yet the wondrous scenes of Phra Lo also become so truly wondrous that the hint at eroticism is almost buried, for instance:

> The sky trembles up to the heavens.
> The earth shakes in confusion.
> Massive waves crash and foam on the ocean.
> Trees swing and sway in all directions in wonderment.
>
> (*Lilit phra lo,* 537)

However, *Lilit phra lo* was significantly expanded later on, so there is a problem over knowing for certain in what period these extracts were composed. In addition, *Lilit phra lo* is a work adopted from folk literature, and seems to be an exception to Ayutthaya court literature. Other works retained the court literature's style of wondrous scenes using straightforward description. For example, *Rachaphilap* (which may have been composed in Bangkok from the text of the Ayutthaya *Ramakian*) has a reflective "wondrous scene" like this:

That time we were first together,
O supreme queen,
In utter happiness,
We tasted desire with joy.
I laid my hand on your youthful breasts.
Encircling, I embraced you
As a golden vine entwines a tree.
I gazed at your pure moon-shaped face.
We found ecstasy together.
Happiness lifted your heart.
Royal breast on royal breast,
Your legs spread far apart.
I kissed the fragrant edges of your lips.
Together in happiness and passion,
You swooned in my hands.

(*Rachaphilap khamchan*, 4)

Inserting wondrous scenes into such passages may have begun in late Ayutthaya but probably maintained the straightforward approach. However, the metaphors used in these wondrous scenes are very similar to those in folk literature in that they are about the natural environment of human life, and make no references to wonders on the scale of earthquakes or natural phenomena which are not regular occurrences. The merging of these two traditions can be seen in Chaophraya Phrakhlang (Hon)'s *Inao khamchan* which was composed at the turning point between these two literary eras, that is, at the start of the Bangkok era (it was completed in 1779).

With words and caresses
The king disturbs her sleep,
Kissing her alluring cheeks,
His chest against her firm breasts.
Two legs entwine two legs.
Two hands entwine two hands.
Two soft lips to savor perfection.
Eyes sparkle in her lustrous face,
Eclipsing the sun and moon.
Like an army, the storm roars.
Lightning streaks zigzag.
Rain sprinkles and splashes,
Brushing the flower
That smiles and opens.

(Chaophraya Phrakhlang (Hon) 1972, 210)

In early Bangkok, the writing of wondrous scenes increasingly adopted the folk tradition, that is, it rejected the straightforward description of Ayutthaya court literature completely, and totally used the form of metaphors with nature or with other familiar things in life such as a "Hainanese junk."[97] There was rivalry to compose scenes that were truly wondrous by describing natural phenomena in enormously exaggerated ways. Comparing the wondrous scene in the above extract by Chaophraya Phrakhlang (Hon) with contemporaneous passages in the royal *Inao* composed in the Second Reign, shows the direction of change very clearly: the approach is still the same but the parts which are straightforward description have been completely excised (Phutthaloetla 1955, 526).

Court literature adopted certain metaphors and used them repeatedly until they became a tradition which readers could understand instantly. The metaphors used most often were rainfall coupled with flowers blooming, and bees coupled with flowers. This repetitive usage had the benefit of creating symbols that readers readily understood, but had the drawback of lacking power and ultimately becoming bland. Even before the influx of Victorian morality from the west, wondrous scenes had already faded from Thai upper class literature. Although they still appeared in some works, they lacked life and color. This decline of the wondrous scenes in upper class literature happened while those composed by folk poets continued to have life and force and remained an important part of folk literature into the future.[98]

DRAMA: FROM THE PEOPLE TO THE COURT

If we discount the *rabeng* and *mongkhrum*, old semi-ritual forms of performance without storyline or script, the oldest form of court performance were shadow puppet plays and *rabam*, a combination of dance with music and perhaps singing depicting well-known episodes with no narration. It seems to have placed great emphasis on aesthetics. In *Thawathotsamat* there is a reference to *rabam* as a court performance which tended to be performed by women:

> Elegantly performing the *rabam*,
> Apsaras, heavenly nymphs,
> Dance in the sky.
>
> (*Thawathotsamat*, 34)

97. A metaphor used in *Khun chang khun phaen* (110): "Hearts thumped. Passions multiplied. Chaos approached. On the ocean, winds whipped up waves that crashed on the shoreline, recoiled, and crashed, over and over again. A Hainanese junk sailed into a small canal. The sky shivered with thunder, and rain sluiced down. The captain lost his way and turned the helm. The ship faltered, grounded on the shallows, and broke apart." [T]

98. Once western Victorian morality had come to totally dominate the upper class in the second half of the nineteenth century, wondrous scenes completely disappeared from upper class literature. The main reason why upper class literature deteriorated in the second half of the nineteenth century was because it moved away from folk literature and embraced western aesthetics which were totally foreign to the ordinary people. It seems that the evolution of "wondrous scenes" in upper class literature reflected the overall trend of development in upper class literature in the late nineteenth century.

There is no evidence that *rabam* performance was either a common property of both court and people, or something which spread from the court to the people. But there is a record from Narai's reign about a public performance of *rabam* which indicates it was a folk form (La Loubère 1969, 49). Yet this also indicates that it was significantly influenced by the court *rabam* as the performers wore costumes. In that era in Ayutthaya, there were professional *rabam* performers hired to perform at festivals for the general population. It was also popular for them to perform at marriage ceremonies (La Loubère 1969, 451).

The *rabam* emphasized the aesthetics of the dance postures, and maybe also the pleasantness of the music or singing, but it gave little importance to plot or story. Some *rabam* may have acted out scenes from religious stories or well-known tales, but there was no attempt to tell the whole tale in which the scenes performed were set. The form of court performance which gave importance to plot was shadow puppet plays (*nang*). There is no clear record of when shadow play performances began, but it is known they had been in existence for quite a long time by the Narai reign as there were already many scripts based on the Ramakian story which was the most popular source for shadow plays. The existence of these scripts is known because Phra Horathibodi (head court astrologer), author of *Chindamani*, referred to several examples of *kap* from Ramakian scripts of that era (*Chindamani*, 63–4, 66–7, 67–8). However, these old Ramakian scripts have completely disappeared. Those which have survived down to the present must be reckoned, on grounds of the language used, as dating from later than the Narai reign, possibly from King Borommakot's reign (1733–58) (Dhanit 1963, 148–50). In the shadow plays known as *nang yai*, only Ramakian stories were popular until the Narai period when other stories were composed, that is Samutthakhot and Anirut, for some performances. But they were not popularly received or perhaps were not performed very often as no puppets have been found from these two stories (Dhanit 1960, 11–2).

There are no sources to indicate whether shadow puppetry was originally a folk form of performance. But the court had always laid on shadow plays for a common audience as part of various celebrations. Shadow plays were one form of entertainment in the festival of the Buddha's footprint in late Ayutthaya as mentioned in *Bunnowat khamchan* (p. 25). They became widely popular in early Bangkok, and are mentioned in many literary works of this era as well. At least in early Bangkok (if not before), there were shadow play troupes that made a living by performing for hire by the ordinary people. This fact was used as a metaphor in *Inao* when Prasanta jokes with Sangkhamarata as follows:

> Going into combat this time,
> I'm sure to get so sweaty you could drink it,
> Because *this job is for pay.*
> I must play before the screen.
> This is not for free, so no grumbling,
> Not like the time in Melaka.
>
> (Phutthaloetla 1955, 986)

If shadow puppetry became more popular in late Ayutthaya and early Bangkok (which is not certain because the extent of its earlier popularity is not known), it was on the cusp of a rapid decline in the face of competition from other forms of performance, namely *khon* mask plays, and more importantly, *lakhon* dramas. Shadow puppetry was not a very flexible form of performance because it was limited to a single story, the Ramakian. Changing the story would have meant a high investment in manufacturing all the character puppets. Training drama actors to learn a new script was much cheaper. In addition, shadow play performances had a somewhat sacred character, with a lot of mysticism about the performance. For this reason they were out of step with the social atmosphere of early Bangkok, unlike the *lakhon* drama which was very much a matter of entertainment ('Tamra len nang nai ngan mahorasop').

From these shadow plays, the court developed another form which could equally be used to tell a story. But as this *khon* or mask play genre was developed from puppetry, it used only the story used in puppet plays, namely the Ramakian. This new genre was closely connected to the shadow plays. In fact, it was an attempt to enliven shadow plays by using actors in place of puppets. When it first began, the mask play was popularly performed in front of a screen. In addition, shadow play scripts were adapted and abbreviated for the mask play, and known as *khamphak san*, short scripts (Nittaya 1972, 96–7). The masked actors could show no feelings through facial expressions, and if they danced they usually turned sideways for people to see—a convention copied from puppetry (Phitthayalap 1974b). In the early stages when the mask play was performed among the upper class, it was still considered a royal property, and only the king could have a mask play troupe. Later permission was given for others (Dhanit 1965, 281). However, maintaining a whole mask play troupe was expensive and required a high investment. Whatever extract of the Ramakian was played, many people were needed. Training took a long time. As the mask play was a genuinely court genre, it probably involved costuming from the outset, and these costumes had to be paid for. Hence it was probably beyond the ability of ordinary people to have their own troupe. Even when the king ceased to maintain a troupe, the mask play remained a property of the aristocracy alone. The people could see it only during festivals or celebrations which the king organized and for which he enlisted the aristocrats' troupes to perform.

At first, mask plays had no singing, only continuous recitation like the shadow plays. However under influence from the *lakhon* dramas which emerged later, singing was interleaved with recitation and dialogues which the actors had to compose themselves on the spot (Phitthayalap 1974c, 253–5). Adopting singing under influence from the drama made the mask play become more like the drama. While the mask play had once been performed out in the middle of a field in front of the screen used for shadow plays, this became more difficult, forcing the mask play, like the inner drama, indoors where the sound could be better controlled. Mask play performance of this kind was called *khon rong nai* or indoor mask play. As a result of this closeness between mask play and drama, the Ramakian began to be used for some drama plays, and there are Ramakian drama scripts dating from Ayutthaya (Dhanit 1965, 65–7).

People could see mask play performances without much difficulty at major festivals or celebrations. Yet the mask play was developed from shadow plays which retained a lot of mysticism and sacredness in the performance. In addition, the plots of the mask play were limited because there was only one source, the Ramakian. Appreciating a mask play was not a simple matter of enjoying the story but required knowledge of dancing, acting, and recitation. This knowledge was something refined which aristocrats were taught from an early age so they could gain enjoyment from watching mask plays. But it was not something familiar among the people in general. The mask play was exciting and intriguing for the ordinary people because it was exotic and spectacular, but it did not have the same attraction of being enjoyable and entertaining that the people got from their own literature. Even later when the mask play was greatly influenced by the drama, it continued to be an aristocratic genre. There was no opportunity for folk literature to percolate into the mask play, as the Ramakian stories used in these performances always had a fixed script either in the form of a mask play (or puppet) recitation script or a drama script. Having a fixed script was a characteristic of upper class rather than folk performance.

Another plot-based performance genre for which there is a lot of source evidence from the Narai era onwards is *hun* puppetry. A puppet performance of Phra Chayathat figures in *Bunnowat khamchan* (p. 25). All plot-based performance genres seem to have been widely popular, including the *ngio* Chinese opera even though the audience might not understand them (La Loubère 1969, 47), while performance genres which had no plots, such as *rabam*, were not popular. Although in the Narai era there were professional dancers hired out for wedding ceremonies, by the end of the Ayutthaya period the composer of *Bunnowat khamchan* (p. 25) mentioned a *rabam* where "casually looking from outside, no one laughs joyfully." Plot-based performance genres developed considerably from late Ayutthaya onwards, especially in the form known as *lakhon* which originated in folk literature where stories were already popular as entertainment.

A useful and valuable study by Prince Damrong about the history of the Inao drama greatly aids understanding of the origins of *lakhon* drama. But it has a major shortcoming in that he relies too much on the tradition of drama in early Bangkok as the basis for explaining its development. This results in his explanation being confused and probably not accurate. In the early Bangkok era, the court developed the drama to a high degree, and this development was passed back as a model for the folk drama. This might make it seem as if drama was something which originated in the court, or that the cradle of the drama should be sought in court performance. Prince Damrong points to the *wai khru* (honoring teacher) sections of several *nora*[99] to show that Khun Sattha was trained to perform drama with the troupe of Phra Thepsinghon,[100] the son of Nang Si Khongkha in Ayutthaya. Khun Sattha then went

99. A kind of dance drama special to the south, playing only the story of Manora and hence its name.

100. A legendary figure who owned a drama company in Ayutthaya, according to one version of the legends about the origin of *nora*.

to give drama training in Nakhon Si Thammarat (Damrong 1965, 5–7). But at the same time, Damrong separates the mask play from the drama on grounds they had different origins—that is, the mask play was a performance for aristocrats of rank, while drama was a performance for people who had to work for a living (Damrong 1965, 14). In some places, he explains that the *nora chatri*[101] drama gave birth to the *lakhon nok* outer dramas, while in another place he mentions that *nora chatri* was played in the central region in the Thonburi period because the king brought it from Nakhon Si Thammarat when he went to attack that city (Damrong 1965, 64). All this makes Damrong's explanation about the origin and early development of drama confused and internally inconsistent.

In folk literature and performance, the key elements were singing, story, dance combined with singing, and improvisation of the script. These same key elements were present in the first generation of drama performances which appear in the sources. This seems to suggest that the drama was developed from folk literature and performance. Studying the early sources about drama shows that this assumption is probably right because it is well corroborated by the evidence.

The first source which refers to drama is by a foreigner, namely La Loubère who visited Siam at the end of the Narai reign. La Loubère wrote that drama used historical stories in verse form sung by a group of actors who also danced and postured. All the singing troupe was male. Although he does not state whether the actors were male or not, it can be inferred from the way he referred to the singing troupe that they were male also. In addition, La Loubère mentioned the performance was not costumed, and probably the actors were dressed like ordinary people (La Loubère 1969, 49). All this seems like a folk drama performance as known in the later period as outer drama. It is known for certain that in the Narai era, the drama was already in existence, at least the folk version.

Literary and historical sources produced by the court in the same period reveal no references to drama at all. The *Chindamani*, which took verses from various sources as examples of metrical forms, has no extract from a drama script. Phra Si Mahosot's *Kap ho khlong*, composed in the Narai era, similarly mentions many forms of entertainment but not the drama. When a girl catches the eye of a man at a festival, her heart cannot focus on the festival, and "bored of seeing shadow puppets, the widow averted her eyes" (Si Mahosot 1959, 41–2).

The fact that drama is not mentioned in court sources suggests that in the Narai era it had just begun to take shape among the people and was not yet widespread. Professional troupes had probably not yet appeared. La Loubère reports that while *rabam* and the *khon* mask play were performed at funerals and other ceremonies, *lakhon* drama was performed only at the dedication of a new temple or new Buddha image (La Loubère 1969, 49). This would be because at funerals and other ceremonies there was a host who laid on the entertainment, while the dedication of an image or

101. A kind of dance drama of the central plain, reportedly an adaptation of *nora* of the south.

temple involved people in general with no individual acting as a host. Drama was performed among the people themselves, in the same way as *phleng*.

The similarities between drama and the ordinary people's regular *phleng* performances went further than the way such performances were organized. *Phleng* performance had a distinctive style of interplay between males and females. In many kinds of *phleng* performance this interplay simulated a quarrel between a man and a woman. This quarrelling led to abuse and innuendo full of wit and obscenity. The first generation of drama such as Manora used verse forms similar to those used by the people in *phleng* such as *phleng klom dek* (lullaby) or *klon si*. According to La Loubère's report, the early drama was not costumed and thus resembled the *phleng* in which people did not dress up. In addition old dramas in late Ayutthaya and even those composed or updated in early Bangkok retained a trace of the quarrel scenes using *klon si* in some passages. In Ayutthaya dramas, this quarrelling probably employed a lot of coarse language, such as the passage when Nang Manora exchanges curses with an astrologer and with her own mother, and the passage at the end of *Sangthong* about the affair between Thao Yotsawimon and Nang Chantha (*Bot lakhon khrang krung kao*, 24–6, 31–6, 101–5). This quarrelling was a convention passed on to drama and maintained for a long time, although the use of *klon si* may not have been strictly maintained, and knockabout farce may have come to replace the quarrelling. This knockabout quarrelling was not limited to the type of *lakhon* known as outer dramas, as inner dramas also had such scenes. For example, the *Unarut* royal drama written in the First Reign has a knockabout quarrelling scene between Phra Unarut and Nang Sisuda, and Unarut chases the king's daughters of all 101 cities, slashing about with his sword (Phutthayotfa 1972, 217, 225). In the scene where Unarut rages at the spirit bomos and witches, the inner drama version of this story retained the old form of *klon si*, as follows:

> Hey you, old hag,
> You talk in riddles!
> You lie, you deceive!
> You talk in riddles!
> Hey you, low life,
> You have no shame
> Bragging on your good points.
> Why are you running away?
>
> (Phutthayotfa 1972, 232)

The scene at the end of the drama, when Nang Usa and Nang Sisuda quarrel with one another, is even closer to the quarrelling scenes in late Ayutthaya dramas though adjusted to be more genteel (Phutthayotfa 1972, 467–70). These quarrelling scenes were cut out of later inner dramas. For example, in the royal version of *Inao* from the Second Reign, the scene where Nang Chintara and Nang Butsaba meet has no knockabout quarrel scene like that between Nang Sisuda and Nang Usa in *Unarut*.

The royal version of *Ramakian* in the First Reign, which was a new composition, still had knockabout quarrelling written in the form of *klon si*, such as the scene where Thotsakan[102] loses his temper with his consorts over the death of his chief consort Nang Montho, as follows:

> 'Hey, hideous ones,
> I'll slice off your heads.
> Hey cursed women,
> Why do you all run away?'
> You came together to mock me.
> As he says this, the king
> Chases the women to and fro
> In confusion.
>
> (*Ramakian*, I, 151)

These quarrel scenes were probably retained in early Bangkok as an almost indispensable part of outer dramas. The royal version of *Kraithong* has a quarrel scene between Nang Wimala, Nang Lueamlaiwan,[103] the wives of Chalawan,[104] and Nang Taphaothong,[105] and another between Nang Wimala, Nang Taphaokaeo, and Nang Taphaothong[106] (Phutthaloetla 1958, 368, 392–401). The Front Palace prince who composed several outer dramas in the Third Reign also chose to include many quarrel scenes, for instance the passage in the *Ramakian* where Nang Benyakai and Nang Suwankanyuma[107] get jealous of one another, and the passage in *Khun chang khun phaen* where Nang Laothong[108] meets Nang Wanthong[109] (Damrong 1965, 158–9).

Another important feature of the drama which shows that it was developed from folk literature or performance is that the actors had to improvise everything, including *sepha* (which rather clearly originated in the cultural traditions of the common people). In *nora*, and dramas in the earlier period, the verses were all improvised. Those who trained for the drama but were not capable of improvising had to practice memorizing. Those with a clever tongue would compete to improvise improvements on their teachers' versions (Narisaranuwattiwong 1958, 6–7). Even in early Bangkok, when the influence of court literature had penetrated more into the folk drama, playing to a script was not yet common. As is well known, Sunthon Phu used to serve the very famous drama troupe of Nai Bunyang as versifier (*phu bok bot*), meaning that

102. "Ravana," the villain in the story of Ramakian, or the Siamese Ramayana.

103. Wives of the crocodile-villain of the story of Kraithong.

104. The crocodile-villain of the story of Kraithong.

105. A character in the story of Kraithong, who is captured by Chalawan and later rescued by Kraithong, the hero.

106. Nang Taphaothong's sister who was given as a wife to the hero as a reward for his success in rescuing Nang Taphaothong from the crocodile.

107. Two consorts of Hanuman in the story of Ramakian.

108. The second wife of Khun Phaen, the hero of *Khun chang khun phaen.*

109. The first wife of Khun Phaen, and also the heroine of *Khun chang khun phaen.*

he improvised verses for the singers during the performance (Sunthon Phu 1960, 269). John Crawfurd (1967, 337) mentioned drama (which is understood to mean the folk drama rather than the court version which Crawfurd does not seem to have witnessed) as follows: "The Siamese have no dramatic compositions,– that is to say, no performances containing a regular written dialogue.... the actors being left to their own wits for converting the subject into a suitable dialogue. A prompter stands by, and refreshes their memories from time to time." Written scripts appeared when the court, which was accustomed to composing literature through writing, adopted the drama from the people in late Ayutthaya.

After the Narai reign, the folk drama probably spread more widely. The growing preference for literature with a plot made the drama play a new channel for conveying plots in a new form of performance. The sources for these plots were stories from the oral tradition of recitation, or the well-known Jataka stories from wat literature. Even stories from upper class literature such as Ramakian and Unarut (or Anirut as it was called in the Ayutthaya period) could be used as the plot of folk drama. But stories from upper class literature which were specifically for reading, such as *Lilit phra lo*, were not well-known among the ordinary people and not used as plots for drama plays.

The court interest in literature with a plot in late Ayutthaya may also partly have helped to make the folk performance known as *lakhon* become popular in the court circle. It is not known when folk drama troupes first performed in the Ayutthaya court, but it was probably after the Narai era. Familiarity with this drama prompted the court to adapt the folk version by adding its own literary traditions, and changing the appearance by employing its own conventions for performance. The initial three major changes which the court made in the drama were, first, using females as actors, second, costuming the actors by adopting forms from the mask play (Damrong 1965, 20–8), and third, composing fixed written scripts.

Using female actors seems to have been necessary because there were not enough males to perform. But more important was probably the influence of *rabam*, a familiar form of performance at court in which all the performers were female because the aesthetics of the performance had priority. Costuming may also have been modeled on the *rabam*. In folk drama, female performers were probably excluded because of the obscene quarrel scenes. In *phleng* singing, it was traditional to have women performers as they had no need to feel shy or fear contempt; but the drama was new and did not have such a tradition, hence women were not considered suitable to be performers.

Writing fixed scripts was very much a literary tradition of the court which was already accustomed to composing literature in written form. When the drama started to become popular, it was inevitably composed in the same way as other performance genres such as shadow plays and mask plays which had scripts for the recitation. Having written scripts greatly changed the nature of the drama because the talent and ability for improvising verse lost its importance. Court drama players did not have to be good at improvising *phleng* songs or skilled at repartee, but had to become better at dancing. The lyrics were a matter for the poet. The brilliance of the composition depended on him and had nothing to do with the actors. Music and recitation must have become more important in the performance of court drama for the same reason. Apart from this, the fixed written script made the court drama diverge more and more from the folk version. The people could copy the use of female performers as long as there was no law forbidding it, and the folk drama did copy costuming from Ayutthaya times onwards. But the idea of having a fixed written script was in conflict with a key element of the folk drama. It downgraded the quick-witted skill of a drama performer which was the heart of the folk genre. The court drama required appreciation of dance and singing which were more refined and complex than what people were used to in their own culture. The royal scripts and outer drama scripts that today are considered excellent were not adopted by any folk drama troupe right through the Third Reign (Damrong 1963, 158). The old dramas, in which the important part of the performance was the skill in improvising the verse, must have retained their popularity.

Costuming contributed to the growth of the drama. It not only made it more magnificent to watch, but gave the performers a distinctive style of their own, with words and actions which matched that style. For these reasons, the drama began to diverge more from the *phleng* performances of the common people. The performers no longer had the ambiguity of being song masters in real life, and actors on the stage. Costuming made the actors more into drama characters rather than simply people on a stage. The adoption of costuming in the folk drama had this same effect, and made even the folk drama diverge from *phleng* singing.

Although the court drama initiated several innovations, within a short time these practices had spread down to the people as well. The earliest outer dramas were composed in late Ayutthaya. It is not certain whether all were composed in the court, but it is possible they were composed by people of rank who had their own drama troupes. They still used rather coarse language in certain passages of certain dramas, following the tradition of the folk drama. Although the Ramakian story was previously considered a sacred story, it was used to compose drama plays from the Ayutthaya period onwards. One text which has survived to the present takes the story from the point where Ram assembles his troops to the scene where Ongkhot[110] sends messages. It has been analyzed that in this text, "the language and words used seem very low; it must be an unofficial version written by one of the troupe leaders in the Ayutthaya period, or perhaps someone of that time had a poet compose it for a drama performance by his own troupe" (Dhanit 1963, 150–4). It appears that folk drama adopted some costuming in the Ayutthaya period. In sum, the interrelations between court drama and folk drama were so strong in the Ayutthaya period that we cannot easily separate them into inner dramas and outer dramas as in the later period.

Some analyze the drama of Ayutthaya using this division into two types found in early Bangkok, and are forced to seek the origins of inner dramas overseas. For example, in one version the model came from a Burmese teacher (Damrong 1965, 103–4). In truth, "inner dramas" and "outer dramas" were not very different in the Ayutthaya

110. A character in Ramakian, a monkey lord on the side of the hero.

period, at least, not so different that we can easily draw a dividing line between the stories dramatized by the outer drama on the one hand, and the Ramakian, Unarut, and Inao on the other (Damrong in Phutthaloetla 1958, k). There are surviving outer dramas from the Ayutthaya period based on Ramakian, and *Bunnowat khamchan* (p. 25) explicitly refers to Anirut as follows:

> In the *lakhon* they dance and sing
> Divine words streaming back and forth,
> Pleasing sounds from the Anirut legend.
> Groups of Kinnari dance the inner drama,
> Watched over by the Sovereign Discus Carrier.
> At the mountain's foot lies a theater
> Hidden from the eyes of men.
> The women chosen are shy, young, and beautiful.
> Anyone seeing them would rather die than watch their beauty fade.
> Their hearts yearn out for them in their dreams.
> They sing the story of Raden and Butsaba,
> Trysting together secretly in a cave,
> With caresses and loving embraces.

Apparently Anirut was played in outer drama which was clearly distinguished from those who "dance the inner drama." In the view of Mahanak of Wat Thasai, the author of this passage, the difference between the two types seems to have been one thing: the inner drama was performed by females, and males were barred from seeing it easily, probably because the performers were ladies of the court. As for Inao, there are no sources to prove whether or not it was performed as outer drama in the Ayutthaya period. Yet we can probably assume it was not, because Inao was a foreign story which had only recently been imported directly to the upper class of the court without passing through the general population (Phitthayalap 1974a, 203). The Inao story was thus unlikely to have been well-known among people outside the court circle at that time, and it is not surprising that it was not adopted for outer drama.

Even though there were already female drama performances in the court, through to the last Ayutthaya reign, folk drama troupes from outside were probably brought in to perform occasionally. There is a story that King Ekathat (1758–67) liked to bring in a troupe including the clowns, Nai Thaen and Nai Mi, who protested against the tax on *phak bung* vegetables[111] (Damrong 1965, 119–20). Undoubtedly this was an outer drama troupe. Prince Damrong explained that at the end of King Borommakot's reign, the court closed down its female drama troupe, hence King Ekathat had to bring in troupes from outside. But there is another story, as credible as the one about the protesting clowns, that after the Burmese had attacked and breached the city walls, the nobles went to inform King Ekathat but the king delayed until the Inao

111. Tax on a kind of water plant which was so easy to grow that it had little or no market value, and was generally consumed by the poor as a vegetable.

drama performance reached the point where Inao entered the cave. If Inao was a story played only in inner drama up to the end of the Ayutthaya period, then the court's inner drama troupe must still have been in existence. But the difference between the two types of drama was not such that the court considered it important. Besides, the Burmese are said to have taken away *lakhon* performers, resulting in four Thai dramas becoming popular in Burma, namely Inao, Sangthong, Ramakian, and Sangsinchai (or the story of Nang Kesonsumontha[112]). By the Bangkok period each of these four stories could be clearly distinguished as either outer drama or inner drama, but this was probably not the case in the Ayutthaya period, and the *lakhon* masters hauled away by the Burmese apparently played both types.

Before the fall of Ayutthaya, the popularity of the drama spread both among the ordinary people and the upper class. The developments which the court initiated in the drama did not completely destroy one major element of the folk version, namely the singing. In fact, the court's introduction of *rabam* to embellish the drama guaranteed the importance of singing in the drama in the future. One major difference between the mask play and the drama is said to lie in the fact that mask plays used mostly stylized recitation[113] while dramas almost always used singing (Dhani 1961, 64). Singing became very popular in the drama. The songs were probably existing *phleng* compositions with new lyrics taken from the play's plot and more captivating for this reason. Singing in the drama is mentioned in the *Kap ho khlong nirat tha thongdaeng* (To Thongdaeng Landing)[114] as follows: "Soft, gentle sounds in the lively *lakhon*" and "Melodious sounds of *doksoi* verse, pleasant songs in the lively *lakhon*" (Thammathibet 1962, 142). Later, themes from the drama came to dominate the lyrics of *phleng*. Because of its growing popularity, the drama became a model for other genres of performance. The mask play apparently copied singing from the drama as part of its evolution into *khon rong nai*, indoor mask play. As both the mask play and drama could use the Ramakian, subsequently the complete story was converted into the form of drama plays. The popularity of *rabam* declined, and ultimately became just a prologue for drama performances in the court (Damrong 1965, 15). And as mentioned in *Bunnowat khamchan*, the *rabam* performed in that role was "not enjoyable" at all.

Lakhon dramas were already composed in written form in the court. Possibly some parts of folk drama were also subsequently written, especially the song lyrics as this dispensed with the need to hire a skilled poet who could improvise as the narrator, and made training easier. The writing of scripts had great significance for literature because it gave rise to a new genre known as *bot lakhon*, drama scripts. Most were written in the *klon suphap* verse form, but using words of few syllables so as to be suitable for singing. This special form was later called *klon bot lakhon*, verse for drama plays. As *klon* was further developed into several separate styles, each was given a

112. The heroine of the story of Sangsinchai, sometimes used as the title of the story.

113. *Phak* is recitation with distinctive intonation.

114. Title of a *nirat* written in the late Ayutthaya period, on a trip to the Thongdaeng Stream near the Footprint Relic at Saraburi.

distinguishing name. Except for some outer drama scripts from Ayutthaya which used old-style *klon* very similar to the people's *phleng*, sometimes called *klon dan* or improvised verse, all drama plays were written with *klon bot lakhon*. Apart from developing their own distinctive style of *klon*, writers of drama plays also took over some traditions associated with performing. As a result, these traditions were carried over into other types of literature not composed for performance, including later generations of drama scripts which were written more for reading than performance.

These traditions would be interesting to study in detail, but here just two aspects will be mentioned to show the general trend. First, short words such as "then," "when," "oh, miss" were used to begin the first line of a *klon* verse. This tradition is believed to have been adopted from the common people's *phleng* as this was the origin of the drama as explained above. Possibly in some kinds of common *phleng* such as *phleng doksoi*, short words were used to facilitate the singing, and in others, such as in the *phleng* which was developed into *phleng yao*, the first line was deleted in its entirety. The *klon nirat* which was developed from *phleng yao chotmaihet*[115] also adopted the custom of cutting out the whole first line. The verse used in drama plays imitated *phleng yao* in using short words in the first line in this way, and later this practice became a convention for the *lakhon* plays of early Bangkok. The literature subsequently developed from drama plays but not intended for performance probably retained this style of opening because it had become conventional. This can be seen in Chaophraya Phrakhlang (Hon)'s *Inao khamchan* in which lines often begin with "then" or "when" but are then padded with extra words to conform to the mandatory syllable pattern of this type of verse.

The second of these traditions which began from drama plays and then spread to other types of literature were scenes in which characters bathe and dress themselves before embarking on a journey, short or long. The story is paused for these descriptions of bathing and dressing, after which the character can meet with others and the story can continue. The purpose of this tradition in drama performance is inexplicable. It was not popular in earlier forms of performing arts other than the drama. *Samutthakhot khamchan* has no such passages. In the *Khamphak ramakian* there is no bathing, and only some very brief mentions of dressing as in this passage of Mayarap[116] leading out an army:

> Mayarap of the Brahmaic sun dynasty,
> Moves elegantly and gracefully,
> Like Kuvera, the god of wealth.
> He polishes his weapons, his arms carrier, his arrow heads.
> His hands swing
> A jeweled club blazing.
>
> (*Prachum khamphak ramakian*, 87)

115. The later development of *phleng yao* in which the content changed from being a love letter to recording an event or series of related events.

116. A character in the Ramakian story, on the side of the ogre.

After the rise of the drama, this tradition became important in other story-based literature. *Inao khamchan*, for instance, includes such scenes describing the bathing and dressing of the characters. Even literature of the *lilit* form like *Taleng phai* (Defeat of the Mon)[117]—a genre very removed from drama plays—includes occasional such descriptions of bathing and dressing, for example in the passage where King Naresuan advances his army to engage with the Burmese Crown Prince,[118] as follows:

> So his majesty, the guardian of the earth,
> With his royal brother,
> Bathed in the fragrant water,
> Spreading and sprinkling the perfume around.
> He adorned himself in raiment radiant to the eyes,
> Two exotic side-sashes with shimmering red pattern;
> And an elegantly flowing front-sash,
> Over magnificent pantaloons.
> Incomparable royal finery:
> Brilliantly jewelled medallion on his chest;
> Belts decorated with lapis;
> Arm bracelets studded with the lustrous nine jewels;
> And royal rings sparkling and resplendent.
> (Paramanuchit 1960, 64–5)

Although drama plays in written form were invented by the court, the examples which have survived from the Ayutthaya period down to the present are a mixture of plays produced by people in the court circle and by folk drama troupes. The only exception is the Inao story which was not adopted into folk drama. There is definite evidence that princesses in the reign of King Borommakot of Ayutthaya wrote drama plays using this story, or at least certain passages from it, as there is a *klon* verse at the end of the First Reign's royal version of the Inao drama volume 38 as follows:

> As for Inao composed long ago
> With its melodious stanzas of verse,
> Whoever hears it, gains knowledge,
> Like celestial ambrosia for the ears.
> It ended with the episode of the nun disrobing.
> Over the years, the story surely would have disappeared.
> Now the King, follower of the Ten Royal Virtues,
> Who reigns over Dvaravati,
> Sitting on the heavenly imperial throne,
> Has composed beautiful verses

117. Title of a work written by the prince-poet Paramanuchit; a eulogic poem dedicated to King Naresuan (r. 1590–1605), using his victory in an elephant duel as the central theme.
118. Phra Maha Uparat, who was slain in the elephant duel with King Naresuan.

Continuing on from the nun's disrobing
Until the conclusion.
Whoever listens to this royal composition
Must return to the royal teachings
And not become carelessly captivated by something of little import.
(Damrong 1965, 133–4)

Also in the royal version of Inao from the Second Reign, there is a similar statement that "this Inao had been composed by a royal lady" which provides confirmation that Inao had existed as a drama play in the Ayutthaya period. Plays from this story were probably quite common among the upper class so that the story was well enough known for scenes from Inao to be painted as murals in buildings such as Tamnak Khiao or the green chamber, the residence of Princess Thepsudawadi[119] (Damrong 1965, 106). For Inao to be performed as a drama play, the audience would already have to know the story. Yet in fact only certain extracts of Inao were popular as drama performances. Moreover, there was not yet a custom in the drama of narrating an abbreviated version of the story before the performance. By comparison, in shadow plays for the mass audience, the Samutthakhot story, which would have been well known among the upper class, had to be narrated in summary form at the opening, and the characters introduced also (*Samutthakhot khamchan*, 2–8). This must have been a major reason why Inao did not spread into folk drama: the audience did not already know the whole story and hence it was difficult to perform a drama of certain extracts. Conversely, some in the upper class circle must have known the Inao story rather well. When Chaophraya Phrakhlang (Hon) composed *Inao khamchan* he must have used the Ayutthaya play script as his source. As a result his *Inao khamchan* and the royal version of the Inao drama from the Second Reign are alike in almost every detail because both were composed from the Ayutthaya version. Compare these two extracts:

Inao khamchan
Stolen beauty, whom my heart will not release,
Youthful beauty, if you split open my chest,
You will find a praiseworthy heart,
A heart truly truthful.
As for my faults long ago,
I beg you, my little one, not to pay heed.
Before, I devoted my life
To be together with you.
But now our merit has slipped away.
The old fate means I must depart.
Please stay here on the golden throne,
Oh beloved, and have no sorrow.

119. A chamber in green color in the Grand Palace arranged for the residence of Princess Thepsudawadi, an elder sister of Rama I.

Even if you return to the palace by this road,
I myself will enter the forest,
There to meet death.
Oh, beloved, do not mistrust me
That I will go to Manya.
If I have lost my honesty,
My life will end in the deep forest.

(Chaophraya Phrakhlang (Hon) 1972, 201)

Royal version of Inao from the Second Reign
Oh, love of my life,
It is not that I dislike you, my beauty.
I have forced myself on you because I love you, my angel.
It is difficult to express how much I love you.
If I could cut open my chest and take out my heart,
It would reveal everything clearly to you.
As for my former faults, I was truly in the wrong.
I have begged you, my beauty, for pardon,
But you have not granted it.
Do not doubt that I can survive.
Previously I said that if I did not get you, I would not live.
But now my merit is all gone,
Perhaps fate catches up with me.
We will see one another only today.
Stay well. I will say goodbye.
Do not believe that I want to return to Manya.
I will not break my promise.
I will fight to death in the forest.

(Phutthaloetla 1955, 516–7)

The fact that Inao became an exclusively court drama meant it had a major role in the development of the court version which had established a distinctive form by the time of the Second Reign. The king had a liking for choreographing dances in the drama performances along with Prince Phithakmontri,[120] and this was done in his composition of Inao. Inao can be said to have given birth to the inner drama that was clearly distinguished from outer drama.

Lakhon drama flourished in early Bangkok. This period may have seen the first composition of drama plays by the kings themselves. King Taksin adapted a Ramakian play from Ayutthaya (Phitthayalap 1974c, 228) with the result that it is not particularly different from the outer dramas surviving from the Ayutthaya period. For example the *kham na phat* melodies, which later were used to signal specific segments of the

120. (1770–1822) son of Rama I's eldest sister and brother to Rama II's chief consort, known to have contributed immensely to the standardization of the court drama.

inner drama, were still inserted anywhere in the verse without any rules. This reflected the lack of distinction between "outer" and "inner" drama in this era.

However, the fact that kings composed drama plays themselves was significant. It symbolized the greater readiness of the court in early Bangkok to adopt the traditions of folk literature into the court.

Descriptions of festivals in early Bangkok literature show that the drama became an indispensable part of royal ceremonies and various festivities. Professional drama troupes grew in number and popularity. To see something like the *nora chatri* drama, which originated in early Bangkok, it was not necessary to make a trip to a festival; if the drama players were at home and put their stage weapons in a box outside the house, it was a signal to let people know they could hire them to play (Damrong 1965, 77). In *Nirat phrabat* (To the Buddha's Footprint),[121] Sunthon Phu related the popularity of the drama among the general population in early Bangkok as follows:

> On the first day of the waning moon, the Phrakhlang
> Hires the troupe of Bunyang to celebrate the pavilion.
> When drama is performed, a big crowd gathers.
> Percussion instruments sound distinctly.
> Suwannahong goes out to play a kite one early morning,
> His followers set up a mechanical lance in the window;
> Upon return in the afternoon, he is struck with the lance.
> Country people are frightened and weep loudly.
> Some laugh heartily, standing in the crowd;
> Others talk or argue among themselves.
>
> (Sunthon Phu 1960, 96; translation from Montri 1990, 56)

The increasing popularity of the drama both in the court and among the general people made King Rama I shoulder the duty of composing versions of all the great stories that came from the Ayutthaya period—Unarut, Ramakian, Inao, and Dalang—in the form of drama plays. The first two stories were already well known among the ordinary people because they had long been used for other types of performance such as shadow plays and mask plays. The latter two stories were of foreign origin and had only recently come to Siam. They were not yet well-known by the ordinary people, although the upper class was reasonably familiar with them. The major intention of the king in composing these drama plays was not for them all to be performed. In the case of Ramakian, for example, the various divine legends connected to the Ram story were probably here collected together for the first time, and the main intention was probably simply to preserve them (Phitthayalap 1974c, 248–9). Given the importance of the Ramakian story in the *lakhon* drama, this act of preserving the story amounted to a form of patronage and facilitation which, at a time when communications were still limited, made the court the source of the stories used in drama performance. The drama was a device for disseminating the values, ideas, and prejudices of one group.

121. Title of a *nirat* describing a trip to the Footprint Relic in Saraburi.

By preserving a story usable for drama performance, the court was controlling the dissemination of a certain kind of information.[122]

The use of *klon bot lakhon* as a storage device for these stories was in tune with the way literature was consumed in early Bangkok. Any belief in the sacredness of these stories had already evaporated. Drama plays were the best possible way to present these stories in the form of entertainment. Comparison between the Ramakian as a drama play and as a *khamphak* script for shadow or mask plays reveals the differences. The drama play has more dialogue between the characters than the *khamphak*. For example, in the drama play the passage where Sukrip breaks the royal umbrella is preceded by a dialogue between Sukrip and Thotsakan. But in the *khamphak* this passage is missing and Sukrip is hence no more than a weapon despatched by Narai to destroy his enemies. The dialogue gives Sukrip sentiments and wit of his own, so that he becomes a "drama character" with more color. This approach emphasizes entertainment as the main point of the work, rather than extolling the power of Ram as the avatar of a god. In the same vein, drama plays often added battle scenes which did not appear in the *khamphak*. For example, in the *khamphak*, when Hanuman goes underground to meet Phanurat,[123] Hanuman immediately arrests Phanurat who confesses he was used by Thotsakan's magic against Ram's army, and Hanuman hence executes him (*Prachum khamphak ramakian*, 53). But in the Ramakian drama play, there is a dialogue between Hanuman and Phanurat and then a big fight before Hanuman is able to execute Phanurat (*Ramakian*, II, 1033–4). Comparing these two versions of the Ramakian shows that the drama play was composed from the *khamphak* but with minor adjustments throughout aimed principally at giving entertainment which had become the major purpose of literature in early Bangkok.

Drama plays were also a genre suitable for reading for pleasure because their verse forms are not complex and difficult to compose or to read. There are no fancy words. The story can be told clearly, unlike with *chan* and *kap* used for the scripts of shadow plays like *Samutthakhot khamchan* and *Anirut khamchan*, two works not meant to be read for entertainment, which show no interest in the story content or in establishing character, and aim to entertain through aesthetics rather than storyline. In early Bangkok there was a big growth in reading for pleasure (see below). Presenting these major stories in the form of drama plays responded to the needs of the upper class in that era.

The court of King Rama II contributed even more to the drama. At the behest of the king, the court drama developed into a format that was complex and detailed in every aspect. The king himself composed plays with the intention that they should actually be performed, for example the Ramakian plays composed in the Second Reign. The Inao play had a very different character from that of Unarut and Dalang in the First

122. Sombat Chantonwong asserted that these dramas may also contain political messages. Nobody has yet studied this matter seriously.

123. An ogre character in the Ramakian, ordered by Thotsakan to hide himself under the earth and to entice Ram's army to encamp over the area so that he could overturn Ram's whole army.

Reign. In particular, the similarities to outer drama completely disappeared. Dances were choreographed to correspond to the script. A large mirror was set up to enable the drama characters to see themselves dancing together with Prince Phithakmontri. All this gave the court drama a distinctive format of its own, decisively different from the folk drama. The true inner drama can be said to have appeared in this reign, in line with Prince Phitthayalap Phruethiyakon's statement that "the art of dance in the Bangkok era was shaped into its current character by King Rama II...and Prince Phithakmontri" (Phitthayalap 1974b, 212).

While King Rama II gave the inner drama its own special and distinctive character, he also adopted folk literary traditions into his court on a large scale. The ballad (*sepha*) of *Khun chang khun phaen*, which had its origins in genuinely folk literature, attracted the interest of the court to the extent that the king composed some of the verses himself, and commissioned court poets to compose many others. The king especially liked to listen to *sepha*, and also composed several scripts for outer drama. Such behavior stands in contrast to that of Ayutthaya monarchs, and was a result of the readiness to adopt the folk literary traditions on a large scale in early Bangkok.

Such adoption of folk literature was not limited to the court. In fact the upper class in general in early Bangkok fell under the same influence. Many other upper class nobles composed outer dramas including the Front Palace prince, Mahasakdi Ponlasep,[124] and Prince Phuwanetnarinrit[125] (who composed *Suwannahong*, *Nang kaeo na ma*,[126] *Nang kula*, etc.) (Damrong 1965, 158–60). Conversely, developments inside the court in this era were not reserved as "royal property" but spread to other people of rank as well. Even more in the Third Reign, when the king no longer wanted to maintain a royal drama troupe, the inner drama took root in other royal palaces and noble households such as those of Mahasakdi Ponlasep, Chaophraya Bodindecha,[127] and Chaophraya Nakhon (Noi)[128] who each trained a complete female drama troupe of their own (Damrong 1965, 155–6).

Outside the upper class circle, many other people composed drama scripts, both in written form such as the works of Sunthon Phu, and those relying on live improvisation. Countless drama scripts appeared in this time. The drama became the favorite form to tell popular stories. As a result, in the period following, people seemed to use this form to write stories even with no intention that they should be performed. The best example is the play *Raden landai*[129] by Phra Mahamontri (Sap).

124. (1785–1832) son of Rama I and the Front Palace prince of Rama III.

125. (1801–1856) son of Rama II, known as a poet.

126. Title of a romance in which the heroine leads an adventurous life by hiding her beauty underneath a mask with a horse's face.

127. (1772–?) Minister of the North in the Third Reign, best known for his long campaign in Cambodia warding off Vietnamese influence in that country.

128. Governor of Nakhon Si Thammarat, personal name Noi, who took office in the reign of Rama II and died in the reign of Rama III; remembered for his strong governorship, and close ties with the royal family.

129. Title of a parody of Inao by Phra Mahamontri.

The drama thus became a literature for reading as well. Even some of the plays which were composed at the start of this period may have been intended for reading as well as performance of some segments. Literature for reading became a prominent feature of early Bangkok, and should be given special consideration here because it greatly changed Thai literature, at least that produced by the upper class.

LITERATURE FOR READING

As stated above in the first chapter, Ayutthaya did not produce much literature for reading. One part of Ayutthaya literature was produced for use in ritual, for example the *Lilit ongkan chaeng nam* and *Khamchan dutsadi sangwoei klomchang.* Another part was literature for performance such as the scripts of *Ramakian*, *Samutthakhot*, and *Anirut khamchan.* Another part was religious literature for purposes of instruction or prayer such as the *Suea kho khamchan* and the three *khamluang* books. There was little literature for reading, and what there was tended to be upper class literature full of fancy words, and distinguished by a profound poetic elegance which the common people found difficult to appreciate. Examples are *Lilit yuan phai*, *Thawathotsamat*, and *Kamsuan.* Easier literature for reading began to appear from the time of King Narai onwards such as Phra Si Mahosot's *Nirat nakhon sawan* and *Bunnowat khamchan.* However even among the easier works of literature for reading in late Ayutthaya some were still not genuinely literature for reading. For example the main purpose of the *Kap he ruea* by Prince Thammathibet was to chant the rhythm in a boat procession. Drama plays were still more for performance than for reading. For this reason there is no complete work of this kind in the Ayutthaya period. Even Inao which had just been imported from overseas was unfinished. The form which was closest to literature for easy reading for pleasure in the Ayutthaya era was the *sepha.* But *sepha* in Ayutthaya was not yet in written form. It was still a genuinely folk literature which was always improvised.

In early Bangkok by contrast, a great deal of literature for reading was created. Apart from the small amount of reading literature produced by writers who were fond of copying ancient poets, early Bangkok literature was easy reading for the general population which had no great knowledge of books. These works were easy both in the words used and the stylistic form which was mostly dominated by the *klon.* As already noted, even performance literature such as drama plays were composed to be read for pleasure as well. A large number of *nirat* cum *phleng yao* composed in this era tell travel tales which are easy to understand. They include anecdotes and humorous passages for readers to enjoy. They are not in any way about ritual, performance, or instruction. They can be considered the most prominent form of literature of their time, and this reflected a change in the role of literature as there was nothing comparable in Ayutthaya times.

This change was recognized even in the works written in this era itself. Ayutthaya literature contains no references to reading for pleasure. Khlong Kamsuan tells his female lover to keep his verses in her pillow but also warns her: "Never, dear, never should you read them for fun" (*Kamsuan si prat*, 77). The verses were not something to be read, but rather a token of the writer's love which the recipient could feel without having to read them.[130] Conversely, Phraya Trang,[131] a classic early Bangkok poet, took *Kamsuan* as his guide but nevertheless departed from it by talking about reading, because in his era reading had become an integral part of the lives of the upper class, as follows:

> Recall another time like this,
> Sitting in a hall, ever so cool,
> Resting and reading *kap*,
> *khlong song*.[132]
>
> (Pho Na Pramuanmak 1970, 51)

In the same way, the *Kap he ruea* boating songs composed by King Rama II mentioned the pleasure of reading something with no ritualistic element:

> Some people boast how well they chant.
> But that is not like my love
> Who can recite *chan*, peerlessly and elegantly,
> Morning and evening,
> So sweet and gentle on the ear
> The verses flow seamlessly.
> My heart craves this beautiful sound.
> Every day I hope to hear her voice.
>
> (*Prachum kap he ruea*, 27)

Poets in the Bangkok era seemed to understand this change in the role of literature. Chaophraya Phrakhlang (Hon) was someone who always ventured experiment and innovation. This attitude shows in his work, *Lilit siwichai chadok*, which had an extremely interesting format. Even though the content was taken from the Jataka stories, the work was not intended for prayer chanting like the old Jataka stories because it was not composed in the form of *klon wat* or *klon thet*[133] but in the *lilit* form which was genuinely literature for reading. But at the same time he also preserved the tradition of *klon thet* by inserting Pali in places similar to other Jataka written in this form. Chaophraya Phrakhlang (Hon) was experimenting with presenting a religious work in a manner that was totally free from ritual. That is, the work was not written for monks to chant on special days because the verse form was not suitable for that

130. It is said that this verse was inserted into *Kamsuan* in the early Bangkok period, which further confirms that Ayutthaya literature does not mention "reading for pleasure."

131. A famous poet who lived through the reigns of Rama I and Rama II; his works are evidently inspired by Ayutthaya court poets of old times.

132. The variant of *khlong* with 2-line stanzas. [T]

133. A literary form in which the *rai yao* is mainly used, and occasionally interposed with Pali phrases and quotations.

purpose. Rather, it was written to be read, for both pleasure and for the intrinsic "merit." Chaophraya Phrakhlang (Hon)'s experimentation in this work did not succeed as no one else followed its example. The *Lilit siwichai chadok* is not among his famous works, but it reflects his understanding of the changing role of literature in early Bangkok. He found more success by initiating another type of literature for reading for pleasure, the *nithan klon* romance, which was a literary format which nobody had used before. His *Sombat amarin* and *Kaki*[134] started the practice of writing *nithan klon* that became very popular in early Bangkok. The first work of Sunthon Phu, *Khobut*, was a *nithan klon*, as was his greatest work, *Phra aphaimani*. The form became very popular for a long time after, along with *klon bot lakhon*. When printing appeared in Siam, the literary works printed in the very first era were mostly in one or other of these forms, *nithan klon* romances or *bot lakhon* play scripts.

Interest in reading for pleasure increased the importance of the plot in a literary work. A taste for fiction had begun in late Ayutthaya, but flourished fully in early Bangkok, prompting a search for new stories. Many drama plays were based on Jataka tales. In early Bangkok, stories were sought from other sources for the sake of novelty. This continued the tradition begun in late Ayutthaya with the court's discovery of the Inao story. Now, however, the search was not limited to the court but spread to the upper class in general. It followed the tradition of folk literature which was ready to adopt tales from the *wat* and from oral tradition. Chaophraya Phrakhlang (Hon) was one of the major writers who experimented with stories from new sources. In *Lilit phetmongkut*[135] he experimented with a plot unlike any other story in Thai literature. It is possible that he took it from mythology which had been translated into Thai in late Ayutthaya, as the Phetmongkut story is a Hindu story, and has a flavor totally different from the stories that the Thai were accustomed to. This experiment by Chaophraya Phrakhlang (Hon) was rather significant; if it gained good acceptance among readers, it would have opened up an enormous, accessible source of new stories. But unfortunately as it turned out, *Lilit phetmongkut* was another failure. It did not gain much favor among readers. Presumably the plot conflicted too much with Buddhist culture and with the trends of Thai literature. For example, the hero and his confidant play around and commit adultery with the wife of a merchant without suffering any consequences at all. The hero and his confidant cause the heroine's father to die tragically, overcome by the trickery of others. The hero also seems to lack patience because he could have asked for the girl's hand nicely without having to commit murder. Apart from this, the hero seems stupid, and has to rely on the intelligence of his confidant all the time.

Even though in the case of *Lilit phetmongkut*, Chaophraya Phrakhlang (Hon) failed to find a story from a new source to feed into Thai literature, he had greater success with other new stories. The works directly associated with his name are the *Three*

134. Title of a romance, originally a Jataka story.
135. Title of a romance, with a story probably taken from Hindu tales.

Kingdoms[136] and *Rachathirat.*[137] Both were novel stories for the general population. The Thai upper class may already have known the *Rachathirat* story, because King Rama I states in the preface that this *Rachathirat* story which had just been translated from the Mon chronicles was "totally different from the one heard before" (*Rachathirat*, 1), indicating that he already knew the story. The *Three Kingdoms* is understood to have become known for the first time in the Bangkok era. These two works along with *Sai Han*,[138] which was translated in the First Reign, and many other Chinese sources which were gradually translated into Thai, are especially interesting in that they were written in prose. This represented a new form of Thai literature that cannot be found in pre-Bangkok times. Owing to this novelty, these works had a very foreign quality compared even to others which originated from overseas. That is, they had little flavor of being Thai. The prose literature of early Bangkok is basically a "translated" literature. Those involved in translating or patronizing the translation of these foreign literary works seem mostly to have been associated with foreign trade. Chaophraya Phrakhlang (Hon) had an official post directly involved with trade and foreign countries. King Rama II also invested a great deal in overseas trade, beginning from before the time he ascended the throne. Another person who greatly patronized translation of Chinese literary works was Somdet Chaophraya Borommaha Sisuriyawong (Chuang Bunnag)[139] who had a large role in trading matters and marine shipping from the Third Reign onwards (see the list of translated Chinese romances in Damrong 1934, 1015). These plots from overseas were used in many other literary genres, including many drama plays based on the *Three Kingdoms* both in early Bangkok and in the subsequent period (Damrong 1934, 21–3).

The popularity of books like *Rachathirat* and the *Three Kingdoms* greatly expanded the use of prose in Thai literature. These translated works can be said to have opened up a new era of writing prose. In the Ayutthaya period, usage of prose was very limited, and was almost non-existent in works described as literature. The lines still had to have rhyme for euphony, and Pali or Sanskrit words to give a serious air and melodious ring. Such language was very distant from everyday speech. This was because prose in Ayutthaya was still closely bound up with religion. Mostly it was written by wat scholars who established the custom of translating Pali with this style of language. It was also, as already noted, bound up with the verse form known as *rai*. Ayutthaya prose was thus more like verse (Pricha 1972). The *Three Kingdoms* and *Rachathirat* (which was not a genuine chronicle) no longer used this stylized *roi kaeo* language of the Ayutthaya era but words and style very similar to common everyday speech. Such language was used in later translated works, and by the end of the early Bangkok era it was also used to compose original literature which had not been translated from

136. *Sam kok* or the 'Romance of the Three Kingdoms.'

137. The Siamese title of a Mon historical romance, "Rajadirit," meaning 'King of Kings.'

138. Title of a Chinese romance on the Eastern Han or the later Han Dynasty.

139. (1808–1883) born in the great Bunnag ministerial family as a son of the trade and foreign minister; heavily involved in foreign trade while gaining increasing political power; appointed the regent to King Chulalongkorn during his minority from 1868 to 1873.

another language, such as *Tamrap thao si chulalak*[140] or *Nang nophamat*[141] (Nidhi 1979; see chapter 4 of this book).

In the First Reign, most of the works in prose that differed from the stylized Ayutthaya version were translations such as *Mahawong phongsawadan langka* (Mahavamsa Chronicle of Sri Lanka), *Nithan iran ratchatham* (Persian Tales), *Chinnakanmalipakon*,[142] *Milinda panha* (The Questions of Milinda), and *Traiphum lokawinitchai* or *Trailokwinitchai* (Treatise on the Three Worlds).[143] Mostly these were translated or adapted from Pali originals. What is specially interesting about these works is that even though they were concerned with religion, the language in which they were written was not so poetic or formal. They still contained many fine words in Pali, but they no longer tried to make every line rhyme. This amounted to the emergence of true prose in Thai literature.

New sources for plots were sought in old texts as well as translations from foreign languages of works with which the Thai were not yet familiar. Attempts were made to compile collections of folk tales. There is a record from the very first years of the First Reign that King Rama I asked Vientiane for the *Nangsue chuang*[144] (Books on King Chuang), but it does not appear this "story" was used for any literature composed subsequently.[145] In the same way, at the end of the First Reign, a collection of historical legends was written up as the *Phongsawadan nuea* (Northern Chronicle). This showed the growing interest in the legends and stories of the common people.

Early Bangkok literature designed principally for entertainment had a large number of plots. The significance of the plot increased and rivaled that of a work's poetic elegance. Even religious literature developed in the direction of putting more emphasis on plot, as in the example of *Mahachat*. By describing the actions of the characters in more detail, and discussing more about their motivations, the characters became something more than just devices through which the Bodhisatta established his *barami*. The *Mahachat* chants composed from early Bangkok onwards explain the actions and motivations of the characters in detail (compare the *Mahachat mueang phet*[146] with

140. 'The Treatise of Lady Si Chulalak,' title of a tale about the Lady Nophamat who lived under a legendary king of Sukhothai (see chapter 4 of this book).

141. The personal name of the heroine of *Tamrap thao si chulalak*.

142. *Jinakalamalipakaranam*, "The sheaf of garlands of the epochs of the conqueror," a Pali work written in Chiang Mai in the sixteenth century about the history of Buddhism with emphasis on the introduction and expansion of Sinhalese Buddhism in the kingdom of Lanna.

143. Title of a work in Siamese on the Buddhist cosmology, written in the Bangkok First Reign.

144. Books on King Chuang, a semi-historical figure of the Lao and the Northern Thai. Many recensions of this literary work have been found.

145. Chalong Soontravanich kindly informed me about this request from sources in "Supha-akson wiangchan cs 1144" which is a record in the Manuscript Division, National Library. Let me here record my thanks to Achan Chalong.

146. A recension of the Siamese text of the Vessantara Jataka found in Phetchaburi, presumed to be the recension closest to the late Ayutthaya text (see chapter 3 of this book).

Mahawetsandon chadok chabap sipsam kan[147]). The emphasis on plot which the upper class initially adopted from folk literature also had an impact on the ordinary people. Characters from court literature such as Inao became well-known among the general population. Some folk literature such as *phleng* singing underwent change. Around the Third Reign at the latest, *phleng* players, both male and female, began to appear in some literary works as characters who sang dialogue, rather than singing about courtship or quarrelling and cursing one another as before. During his pilgrimage to Phra Thaen Dongrang,[148] Nai Mi[149] wrote that around midnight a performance of *phleng* was arranged among his entourage for fun: "Some sang the *phleng* together for enjoyment; those standing and listening were crowded together unbearably; they played the story of poor Khun Phaen when he traveled to fetch Nang Wanthong" (Sunthon Phu 1960, 787).

In sum, literature for reading expanded in volume along with the growing interest in literature with a plot. In parallel, more use was made of the *klon* meter because it was suitable for "reading" and "enjoying" a story. Sacredness and ritual, which had been the major functions of literature, greatly declined in significance as literature increasingly took on the role of generating enjoyment.

All of these developments noted above greatly changed the appearance of court literature in early Bangkok. Even calling it "court" literature seems a major misrepresentation because the production of written literature had proliferated among the aristocracy of rank far more than in the Ayutthaya period. In fact, although the ordinary people had not yet created written literature, many of the authors of early Bangkok literature were no more than minor officials such as Sunthon Phu or Muen Phrom Sampatson (the official title of Nai Mi), who was a collector of taxes on orchards. The poetess Khun Phum was daughter of an aristocrat but had no high official rank herself. Most of the people who composed the verses in the inscriptions of Wat Phra Chetuphon had junior positions in the bureaucracy. The poets who composed works in early Bangkok were different from their Ayutthaya counterparts who were genuinely people of the "court" such as Si Prat, who may have been an actual person though some argue it was the title of the court poet. Phra Maharatchakhru[150] and Phra Si Mahosot were Brahman posts close to the court. Others were high ranking members of the royal dynasty such as Prince Thammathibet, the composer of *Kamsuan*, who was probably a member of the royal family, as also the author of *Lilit phra lo*. Many other works such as the

147. A name for the Siamese recension of the Vessantara Jataka selected and edited by the Department of Education in 1902.

148. A pilgrimage spot in Kanchanaburi where there is an enshrined stone block believed to be the Buddha's bed.

149. A poet of the early Bangkok period, allegedly a student of Sunthon Phu, whose works resemble those of his teacher in many ways.

150. Title of the head of the council of legal experts, the *Lukkhun na san luang*, with sakdina equal to a minister; the poet of this title lived in the seventeenth century and wrote poetical romances, a eulogy for the king, and a *nirat*.

Mahachat khamluang and the *Kap mahachat* were commissioned by the king from the assembled "scholars of the royal academy."

Thus it seems correct to refer to the producers of Ayutthaya literature as "court poets." But in early Bangkok, although some producers of literature were tied to the court, such as Nai Narinthibet[151] and Sunthon Phu at one time, yet the biographies of these individuals, such as we know them, show that they were not really "court poets." Some such as Sunthon Phu were born in rather ordinary families, and so were different from people like Phra Horathibodi,[152] Phra Si Mahosot, or Si Prat (if the history of Si Prat has a real basis). Others had official duties which had nothing to do with being a poet, such as Phraya Trang or Chaophraya Phrakhlang. Their life experience seems to have been closer to the ordinary people than that of the true "court poets" of Ayutthaya, either as a result of their own family background or as a result of their official duties as administrators in the provinces. Even the works authored by royal family members were not always composed to supply the court. For example, the outer dramas authored by some royal family members were intended for performance by their own troupes. It is difficult to label such poets' works as court literature. Si Prat who composed *Anirut khamchan*, just like the author of *Lilit phra lo*, stated explicitly that his work was composed for presentation to the king. But many of the works composed in early Bangkok, even though composed by people in the court circle, were not recorded as works presented to the king. And because they were not presented in this way, the early Bangkok writers put their own names to the works more often than writers of the Ayutthaya era. We are not sure who were the authors of *Kamsuan*, *Lilit phra lo*, and so on, but Phraya Trang, Nai Narinthibet, Sunthon Phu, Prince Paramanuchit Chinorot, and so on put their names or titles to the works which they authored.

The changes in literature in early Bangkok were very evident because they were both broad and deep. For the study of literature, it makes more sense to treat early Bangkok literature as another era which can be studied for itself, and which has a focus of its own, not just as a continuation from the literature of the Ayutthaya era.

This flourishing new literary era which began in early Bangkok was sustained for a long time. The consumers of written literature increased in number, and were not limited to the court as had been the case in the Ayutthaya era. This literary change was thus something with real foundations, not something which happened because of the brilliance or special quality of a few writers. It depended on the tastes, values, and worldview of a readership which helped sustain continued growth over a century. Without such a secure base, this literary change would not have happened. Although "pathbreaking" writers might have appeared, their works would have faded from view in the absence of interest from the society which served as the market for this

151. Official title of a lowly page of the Front Palace; the poet of this title (personal name, In) lived in the Second Reign and wrote the famous *nirat* depicting his trip to the south in 1808 in the expeditionary force led by the Front Palace prince against the Burmese.

152. Title for a chief of the astrology department; the renowned writer of this title, who lived in the seventeenth century, wrote a royal chronicle and a treatise on the Siamese language.

literature. Describing the changes in literature does not explain them. We need first to look at the foundations which underpinned them. It is time for us to address these foundations in detail.

III: THE BOURGEOISIE IN THE EXPORT ECONOMY[153]

OVERSEAS TRADE AND THE EXPORT ECONOMY

Government in the early Bangkok period was clearly involved in overseas trade. In truth, overseas trade had been important for the governments established in the lower Chaophraya basin for several centuries. It was a major source of their revenue. Thus the early Bangkok government appears to represent no change in this respect. But in fact overseas trade was even more important to the survival of the early Bangkok government than to any of the Ayutthaya governments which relied on overseas trade. This was because the fall of Ayutthaya had also brought about a collapse in the Ayutthayan system of government. The control of phrai labor no longer worked as well as it had in the Ayutthaya period. It was a long time before the Bangkok government could do away with "informal" methods of controlling such labor. Only in the Third Reign, for example, did the king stop allowing the royal kin and senior nobles to gather bands of people in the forests to work for them. Such bands were outlawed in 1822 (Thiphakorawong 1961b, 10).[154] The decline of the bureaucratic system meant the government lost considerable revenue because the major base of

153. It is difficult to describe the economic and social changes that took place in the central region in the early Bangkok era because superficially the economy appears the same as or similar to that of the Ayutthaya period, suggesting there had been no fundamental change. But there was significant change if measured in terms of both geographical extent and social depth. In particular, the market economy expanded and dominated society incomparably more than in the Ayutthaya period. The difficulty is how to describe this change. Focusing on any single economic activity, whether overseas trade, government trade, or the reduction in the length of corvée, will not show the change since these were not innovations in early Bangkok. It is necessary to view the whole system, the connections between its components, and its internal logic in order to understand the changes—both how they developed, and what were their limitations. This is a big task. The author apologises if his efforts here have failed like many pioneer attempts have failed before.

154. The chronicles state "in King Borommakot's kingdom..." which leads us to believe that permission to establish these bands began in the Second Reign. But it is more likely that permission dates back to the First Reign (or even King Taksin's time). I will not deal with this issue here but simply mention that the words "King Borommakot" appear in three places in Chaophraya Thiphakorawong's chronicle of the Third Reign. In one other place (p. 69) it clearly means the First Reign when referring to the chedi at Phan Phrao "which King Borommakot built when he went to attack Vientiane." Although King Loetla (Rama II) took an army to attack Vientiane during Taksin's reign, he was too young at the time to establish this chedi, so there is no doubt this definitely means King Yotfa (Rama I).

government revenue was phrai labor. The government lacked any efficient means of generating revenue.

At the same time, the early Bangkok government made increasing use of wage labor, either because corvée was no longer efficient, or because hiring wage labor proved more efficient. Hence government needed more cash for hiring both unskilled Chinese labor and skilled Chinese or Thai labor. Government needed the knowledge and skill of Chinese, who were outside the phrai system, for activities such as woodworking for shipbuilding, crewing ships, trading, and sugar manufacture. As a result, the government needed more cash which it could not generate either from phrai or from *suai* taxes-in-kind. Also the early Bangkok government attempted to equip all its troops with guns which had to be obtained from overseas. Sometimes they could be acquired through bartering products, but in other cases they had to be purchased with cash.

These imperatives forced the early Bangkok government to pay great attention to overseas trade—even more than in the Ayutthaya period—because it was a major source of revenue and of cash (or silver which could also be used as a medium of exchange). Many early Bangkok records show the vigor of overseas trade, and also refer to its importance for government revenue. In the First and Second Reigns, the royal junk trade was the main source of revenue for paying *biawat*, allowances to members of the royal family and nobility. Any year when junk profits were insufficient to pay these allowances, chintz cloth was given instead, or sometimes gold from Bang Taphan or China (*Prachum prakat ratchakan thi 4*, II, 136). In the Second Reign, the royal junk trade still did not deliver enough profit in some years resulting in the *biawat* being paid in kind, or money being borrowed from the Front Palace prince whose junk trade had made a good profit (*Prachum prakat ratchakan thi 4*, II, 234). In the Second Reign, the royal junk trade suffered continual losses because of defalcation by officials; the royal trade was operated in a joint venture with Chaophraya Prakhlang (Dit Bunnag) who was able to push the losses onto the royal share (Burney 1910, 51). Hence the royal junk trade was unprofitable even though other royal kin and Chaophraya Phrakhlang made good profits. Some records claim that the royal junk trade in the Second Reign made up to 2 million baht a year for the treasury (Kiattisak 1990, ko), but these figures are questionable. Overseas trade generated revenue for government in many forms other than the royal junk trade. The total government revenue from overseas trade (including deck tax, customs, profits from monopolies, and so on) was significant even though the royal junk trade made occasional losses. John Crawfurd, who visited Bangkok late in the Second Reign, noted: "By far the most valuable branch of the revenue of the kingdom and the principal perquisites of the Officers of Government arise out of the foreign trade which is conducted in the river Me-nam" (Crawfurd 1915, 46). Ruschenberger, who visited Bangkok in 1835 during the Third Reign, gave a breakdown of government revenue in which gold tax-in-kind, fees, and internal taxes contributed over 400,000 baht a year, while the profits of the royal junk trade alone contributed over 1.9 million baht (Ruschenberger 1838, 282–4). These figures may be wrong, but the large difference between the two categories of revenue suggests the importance of overseas trade for the early Bangkok government (both the royal share and other revenues levied from private overseas trade).

TRADE AND TRADE POLICY

The most important trading partner throughout the Bangkok period was China (see details in Sarasin 1977). Captain Burney reported the trade between Bangkok and Chinese ports as far as he could discern it: each year, junks totaling 30,000 tons went from Bangkok to China, while twenty to forty-five big vessels from Hainan visited the Bangkok port, along with another thirty-six to fifty from Canton and other ports of western China. This China–Siam trade had a very high profit rate, estimated at a minimum of 300 per cent. Even if half of the ships sent to China were wrecked, the profit was still good (Burney 1911, 80). Apart from China, there was also considerable trade with other nearby countries, especially the British Straits Settlement. Among Siam's exports to the Settlement in 1820, the most valuable items were sugar worth over 300,000 rupees, rice of over 160,000 rupees, and tobacco another 130,000 rupees (Waraphon 1979, 137). Burney reported that thirty to forty junks went each year from Siam to Malay ports, and that in 1824 thirty ships went from Siam to Singapore carrying goods of 4,000 to 5,000 tons (Burney 1911, 81). By 1830, the volume of trade with British colonies had increased. To Singapore alone, Siam sent goods worth over 770,000 rupees, with sugar still the first-ranked product worth 350,000 rupees, while another 200,000 rupees of goods went to Penang and Melaka (Sarasin 1977, 206). Each year also some twenty to fifty small junks went from Siam to ports in southern Vietnam and Cambodia (Burney 1911, 82). This regional trade was an entrepot or re-export trade; Siamese junks exported products made in China and brought back local goods such as gamboge, wood, silk, hides, ivory, and eaglewood destined for the China market. Interestingly some products made in Siam such as iron, sappanwood, and rice were shipped to southern Vietnam and Cambodia (Waraphon 1979, 48–53; Burney 1911, 82).

As for the Indonesian archipelago, Siamese junks carried food products such as dried fish and rice to Batavia and other Javanese ports, and brought back European goods (Bowring 1969, II, 67).

There is another aspect of trade which is not mentioned much in foreign sources because it was not directly connected with Bangkok yet delivered a regular profit to the king in Bangkok. This is the trade between Trang and the Coromandel coast of India. Nakhon Si Thammarat probably oversaw this trade and arranged the supply of goods such as elephants and tin. The imports from India were white cloth of various kinds. The profit per trip, net of the investment and expenses, was almost 200 chang (see for example cho ro 2-16, cs 1175).

Besides Trang, junks from other non-Bangkok ports traded overseas in the same way. For example, small boats (called in Malay perahu, in Portuguese prau, and in English prow) owned by local people from ports in southern Siam such as Songkhla journeyed to Malay ports to trade and barter. Sometimes such boats came up to Bangkok carrying goods which had a good market in China such as birds' nests, gold dust, rattan, shark's fin, and Malay-style clothing. They returned with rice, oil, sugar, salt, iron, iron bars, sticklac, and benzoin (Burney 1911, 82). Also junks from Nakhon Si Thammarat and Chanthaburi went directly to trade in China (Waraphon 1979, 47). Records from Nakhon Si Thammarat and Songkhla show that junks from these two places went regularly to trade in Penang and Singapore.

The high volume of trade between Siam, China, and neighboring countries required a large number of junks. A significant portion of these junks belonged to people in Siam. Shipbuilding flourished in Bangkok because of the availability of raw materials and artisan skills. Bangkok was the base for a large number of merchants engaged in international trade, and ranked second to Canton in trade volume, excluding Asian colonial ports (Crawfurd 1967, 415). Various sources refer to the vitality of the Bangkok junk trade. The American trader, Morgan, who visited Bangkok in 1818, counted 700 ships of various types and sizes on the Chaophraya river, including two American sloops loading a large quantity of sugar (Frankfurter 1914, 6). In 1835 another foreigner recorded that he saw Chinese junks of 200–600 tons anchored for over two miles along the centre of the Chaophraya river (Ruschenberger 1838, 278).

The vitality and volume of Bangkok trade in this era can be gauged by comparison with foreigners' reports of trade at Ayutthaya in 1687. M. Veret of the French East India Company at Ayutthaya reported that in the trading season at Ayutthaya, "around ten or twelve junks arrived, some from China and some from Japan. Almost all belonged to the King of Siam. There were only two or three ships belonging to Portuguese from Macao. This year one special ship came belonging to the British.... In addition, there are two other small ships from Canton. These various ships are all loaded with blue-and-white ceramics for sale to people in Siam. Besides, the Portuguese load some raw silk, white and colored silk cloth,... metal rice-cooking pots, Chinese woods, gourd flasks, sugar, and gold" (*Prachum phongsawadan phak thi 43*, 518). However, Veret stated that government policy in the reign of Narai, especially the later part, had squeezed foreign merchants so much that Ayutthaya's trade had declined. After Narai's reign, trade between Ayutthaya and China increased greatly (Sarasin 1977), but Ayutthaya's trade could not compare to the vigor of Bangkok. A French merchant called Pierre Poivre visited Mergui in 1745 to investigate the prospects for trade at Ayutthaya and at this major Thai port on the west. He reported:

> Siam's trade is not substantial. Besides the fact that the country is poor and has little merchandise, the king, who is the sole merchant in his territories, creates so much difficulty and injustice for foreigners...that he has discouraged everybody except for the Moors, Chinese and Hollanders. The first come every year to Mergui...carrying two or three cargoes of coarse linen goods which they exchange with the king for tea caddies, ivory, and elephants.... The Chinese send to Siam each year four to five ships loaded with tea, porcelain, cowries, and various medicines worth less than what the king pays for them in tea caddies, sappanwood, eaglewood, and ivory; sometimes the Chinese take back rice from which they can make a sufficiently large profit in China as long as their junks are larger and can carry a big cargo. Among the Chinese who come to Siam, several settle in the country, establish themselves, and at present have a large

> quarter. It is these who carry out small-scale trade throughout the kingdom where they are spreading and establishing themselves as well as in the capital. There are over 6,000 of these foreigners in Siam, and their numbers increase each year. (Malleret 1968, 73)

The Hollanders were the only Europeans who still traded with Siam at this time. They carried poor quality linen from India along with pepper and two or three types of spice to exchange for tea caddies, sappanwood, and ivory. Their trade in Siam was small (Malleret 1968, 73–5).

Apart from the volume of trade with other countries in the Ayutthaya period, the important thing to notice is the roster of Ayutthaya's export products. In 1685, Veret reported that Siam's exports were tin, sappanwood, ivory, pepper, cowhide, and deerskins. By the end of the Ayutthaya period, pepper had to be imported, but rice which had not been a major export item in Narai's reign had increased in volume (Sarasin 1977), and tea caddies manufactured from metal alloys in Siam were also now exported. This listing excludes many other products which originated elsewhere and were re-exported from Ayutthaya, or which Ayutthaya merchants bought and stored for future sale as part of what is called entrepot trade. However, if rice and tea caddies are excluded, the articles that Ayutthaya sold overseas were mostly forest products such as sappanwood, elephants, ivory, and deerskins. Hence, however large the volume of the Ayutthaya government's overseas trade, its impact on society was not great because the *phrakhlang* imposed a monopoly on export products and collected most of them as taxes-in-kind. Because the volume of *phrakhlang* trade was not high, collection of these taxes provided the government with enough of these products.

Comparing early Bangkok and Ayutthaya shows that the type of export products changed greatly. The export volume increased beyond the capacity of the system of *suai* tax-in-kind. The range of products expanded to include some agricultural and industrial goods which required a more complex production process and higher labor input than simple forest collection. Many records confirm that the increase in the export of such products was the dominant economic trend throughout the early Bangkok era. It is worth making a rough survey of export products at various stages of this era.

In the Second Reign, the account book of a Chinese ship-owner trading to China on royal junks shows that the exports included sappanwood, snakehead fish, Phetchaburi beef, rattan (*calamus caesius*), cattle hide, balong bark (a medical plant), cardamom, arecanut, deerskins, myrobalan, rudders, wooden posts, tin, and ivory (cho ro 2–15, cs 1175 and 15/4, cs 1175). The only forest products were sappanwood, rattan, balong bark, deerskins, and ivory. Most of the other items required some form of processing. Besides, the goods carried on these royal junks probably tended to be either tax-in-kind products which required little investment, or products with high value-to-volume such as ivory and cardamom. Bulk exports of high-volume items like rice and sugar were probably left to private ships, especially those of the Chinese, based both in Siam and in China. The above list of export products in the Second Reign tallies with Crawfurd's record of goods subject to export taxes which included sappanwood, fragrant wood, ivory, sticklac, sugar, salt, dried meat, snakehead fish, dried shrimp, deer sinew, pepper, arecanut, balong bark, peacock feather, rayskins (probably dried), buffalo hide, birds' wing feathers, elephant bone, deerskins, deer horn, sharkfin, birds' nest, and seedless cotton (Crawfurd 1967, 382–3). Rice did not figure on this list.

Early in the Third Reign, Burney reported on exports in detail. The largest by volume was rice which came in two varieties: garden rice which cost 24–32 baht per *kwian*, and town rice at 15–20 baht. But the export tax on rice was rather high at 8 baht per *hap*.[155] (The government's policy was to guarantee sufficient rice for internal consumption and war stocks before allowing any remaining surplus to be exported. Government policy on rice in early Bangkok was rather ambiguous: government wanted to make money from rice but did not want to abandon the policy of guaranteeing sufficient internal supply. Exporting large quantities of rice would also have had an impact on the phrai system which the government was not prepared to undermine.) Teak and other timbers came from the Raheng region in large quantities but the government did not allow free export. The price was very cheap and the timber was used in shipbuilding, another export product. Some 50,000 *hap* of best-quality coconut oil was produced annually at a cost of only 7–8 baht per *hap*, and 20,000 *hap* were exported. At Penang the price of coconut oil was 18–20 Spanish dollars per *hap* which made the merchants a good profit.

Siam produced a type of benzoin even more purely white than that from Sumatra, and it formerly commanded a price of 120 baht per *hap*. But after a London chemist stated that Thai benzoin was not as pure as that from Sumatra, the price fell to only 50 baht per *hap*. Gamboge came in the form of both lumps and bars. Good-quality bars were priced at 50–60 baht per *hap*, but annual production was only 250–300 *hap*. Tin was plentiful in the south but only 10,000 *hap* was transported to Bangkok each year, and 5,000 *hap* exported. A lot more was exported directly from Thalang and Phangnga. Annual production of ivory was 800 *hap* at 150 baht per *hap*. Rhino horn sold well in the China market, with unusual pieces priced as high as 400 baht. Sticklac production was 15,000 *hap* per year, priced at 14–15 baht for good quality. Black pepper cost 11–12 baht per *hap* and annual production was 70,000 *hap*. White pepper was more expensive at 24–26 baht per *hap* but production was small at only 250 *hap*. The export tax on pepper was excessive making the final price so high that British merchants refused to buy. (Because pepper was exported to China on the royal junks in large quantities delivering high profits, supplies to foreign merchants were restricted.) Pepper had been a monopoly product in previous reigns. Salt was plentiful and annual exports were at least 2,000 *kwian*[156] at a price of only 3–6 baht per *kwian*. The best cotton was produced in the west of the country around Tavoy. Annual production of all three qualities was 50,000 *hap*. The best quality cotton was priced at 17–22 baht per *hap*, and the worst unseeded quality was only 5.50–7 baht per *hap*. Cattle and buffalo hides were plentiful and the annual volume could

155. A *hap* is equivalent to 60 kilogram. I suspect there is a mistake here in copying or printing, and it should be 8 baht per *kwian*, which would still be high in comparison to the cost.

156. A *kwian* is 25 *hap* or 1500 kilograms.

be 30,000 pieces at only 3.50–4 baht per piece. Cardamom came in three varieties, all sold to China. The combined annual production was 800 *hap* of which 100 *hap* was consumed inside the country. The price per *hap* was in the range of 150 to 280 baht according to quality. Beeswax was of good quality and low price. Each year some 250–300 *hap* reached Bangkok at a price of 50–100 baht per *hap* (Burney 1911, 103–7).

Burney's list of products tallies with other sources. The non-forest products which required some labor input in the production process included tin, lead, blackwood, musk, rice, arecanut, salted fish, sugar, pepper, cardamom, betel leaf, birds' nest, sticklac, redwood, myrobalan, tigers' tail, door planks, junks, salt, tobacco, oil, and pottery (Waraphon 1979, 76–80).

Late in the Third Reign, Malloch ranked Thai export products by export volume as follows: sugar, animal skins, raw cotton, sappanwood, sticklac, tin and tin products, fish, cotton cloth, iron, birds' nest, rice, pig oil and fat, cardamom, dried beef, bark, coconut oil, eaglewood, pepper, ivory, gamboge, and others (cited in Kiattisak 1980, 71).

To understand the change in the economy of the Siamese upper class in the early Bangkok era, it is not sufficient to study only the increasing trade volume and changing nature of export products. The policy on overseas trade, or the policy for generating government revenue from overseas trade, needs to be studied by comparing early Bangkok with Ayutthaya.

As noted above, foreign trade was an important source of government revenue since at least the Ayutthaya period. But the nature of government trade changed from period to period. In early Ayutthaya, China was the main destination for Siamese trade, not only as a market for goods, but also as the source of products which Ayutthaya could resell in the world market. Ayutthaya's main trade was of the entrepot type. The port was a centre for forest products coming from the Lanna kingdom, Cambodia, Vientiane, Burma, and elsewhere. It was also an important centre for products from China, Japan, and Ryukyu in the east. Products from places ranged around the Indian Ocean from the Middle East to the Malay peninsula were also brought to Ayutthaya. So too were spices from the Indonesian archipelago. Ayutthaya was a centre of international trade. Although it was not the only such centre in the region, and not as large as Melaka, yet it had some significance in trade between the west (the Indian ocean) and the east (the China sea). Ayutthaya maintained this status as a trading centre by two methods. First, it had its own junks (owned by both the king and private merchants) to collect and distribute products between Ayutthaya and China. Second, it attracted foreign merchants to bring their own ships to Ayutthaya or its tributary ports. What attracted foreign merchants most of all was the quantity and variety of goods available. They could get the type of goods they needed in the quantities they needed without traveling to the various sources of these products. Even though the prices might be higher, the expenses were less. The more ships that came, the greater the quantity and variety of products at Ayutthaya, and the more the needs of the merchants were satisfied.[157] The king benefited from this trading

157. I have described these characteristics of Ayutthaya's trade in detail in 'Kan kha tang

situation in two ways: through monopolies, and through the junk trade. Monopolies were imposed on domestically produced items in demand in the world market such as sappanwood which was acquired as tax-in-kind. The king took a profit from selling these goods, and also from imposing monopolies on export goods purchased at fixed prices (in the event the supplies from tax-in-kind were insufficient) and sold at an inflated margin. However, care was needed to ensure that such monopolies did not cause trade to decline because foreign ships came to prefer rival ports. Ayutthaya's foreign trade occasionally faltered because the rate of royal exploitation exceeded the optimum level. The king also made profits through imposing monopolies on some imports which sold well in the domestic market. Through the royal junk trade, the king made profits by exporting tax-in-kind products acquired without any investment, and importing goods sold to the local population or foreign merchants. The profits came directly from trade, not from production. In early Ayutthaya, the main source of the court's revenues was not domestically produced goods but the entrepot trade. The royal warehouse's monopolies delivered only a minor element of the royal revenues because the export products subject to these monopolies (which had to be domestically produced) were relatively few.

This form of trade and revenue-making had no broad impact on society. The ordinary people had absolutely no connection with such foreign trade, other than being forced to deliver tax-in-kind to their overseers. Only the overseers and foreigners, especially Chinese, got the full benefit of such commerce. At the same time, this kind of foreign trade had no tendency to transform the overseers into true merchants. This is an important conclusion because it remained true for a long time in Siamese history.[158]

> Although overseas trade involved the overseers a great deal, there was no tendency to transform them into true merchants. The reason lies in the fact that officials relied to some extent on their political power to create commercial benefits. For example, they acquired products through tax-in-kind and tribute, took commissions from government trade, asked bribes from foreign merchants, misappropriated government property they handled in the course of overseas trade, and so on. They also made use of phrai labor to acquire goods. These were not commercial methods since they did not depend on the price mechanism to realize a profit. The majority of officials did not accumulate wealth from overseas trade by profit-seeking, investment, or business risk.... They cultivated their political foundations, that is their political office, as this was the bedrock of their wealth and social status. Hence, whatever impact foreign trade had on the officials, that

---

prathet khong ayutthaya' (Ayutthaya's overseas trade) in *Sriramthepnakhon: ruam khwam riang kieo kap prawatisat ayutthaya ton ton* (Sriramthepnakhon: collected writings on early Ayutthaya history), which has been widely distributed in roneo form so here I have just summarized.

158. This conclusion is taken from the article 'Phon krathop khong kan kha to saphawa phai nai khong ayutthaya' (The effect of trade on the domestic situation in Ayutthaya) in the book cited in the previous note.

> impact had limitations. It did not change the structural foundations of the economy. It did not give rise to a free market, an independent business class, industrial production, large-scale investment in overseas trade, and so on (the factors which had a massive impact on political life, society, and culture in European societies of the same period).

From the mid Ayutthaya period, this trading situation changed as a result of western ships arriving to compete for a part of Asian trade. The Dutch East India Company carried a large volume of trade between Asian countries; more Chinese junks visited ports over a wide area; and Japanese became involved in migration and trading. As a result of these many factors, Ayutthaya's entrepot trade declined in importance, while goods produced inside the country, such as forest products and animal skins, increased in importance and were exported in larger quantities. Some of the main export goods required some input of human labor in the production process, particularly pepper which Ayutthaya exported in significant amounts. But most of Ayutthaya's export goods through to the end of the Ayutthaya period were still forest products collected under the tax-in-kind system. A new export opportunity arose when China's Qing dynasty government changed its policy to allow rice imports to supplement inadequate local supplies, rather than transporting rice by land from the interior which would have been more expensive. The nature of trade changed from low-volume luxury goods to increasing amounts of low-price high-volume goods. But with the exceptions of pepper in mid Ayutthaya and rice in late Ayutthaya, exports in general did not require an input of human labor, and hence had little impact on the society at large. From the reign of Trailokanat (1448–88?) onwards, the tax-in-kind system expanded as the power of the central government expanded, and this provided sufficient goods for Ayutthaya's overseas trade.

As the nature of trade changed in this way, so the nature of government's exploitation of trade changed in parallel. Monopolies were used in certain periods, such as the Narai reign when the king owned many ships, but this was not maintained for long. Later the royal fleet seems to have declined as sources mention private trade by both members of the official nobility and Chinese in Siam. Under the monopoly system, the king made profits like a sleeping partner: most of the export goods were articles available inside the country and in high demand in the world market; all the king had to do was to impose a monopoly. When the profitability of this trade dropped, the king allowed the junk trade to pass into the hands of foreigners and nobles. These groups had already accumulated experience in the junk trade, and were interrelated by both kin ties and common benefits.

In the early Bangkok era, Siam's overseas trade changed again. The volume increased, the range of goods widened, and more items incorporated some input of human labor in the production process. These changes had a great impact on the nature of trade and of government exploitation, which will be considered below. But another aspect of this change lay in the people who constituted the elite in early Bangkok.

In the period after the fall of Ayutthaya, the group gathered around King Taksin was just one of many groups of mid-level nobility. What really distinguished this group was that it was larger than others and got most of the benefits from reviving an Ayutthaya-style state. Other groups were composed of influential people in the provinces, including governors of provincial cities, who had little interest in the revival of an Ayutthaya-style state and hence little interest in expelling Burmese influence from the central region. Yet when King Taksin ascended the throne, he was not the central focus of the mid-level Ayutthaya nobles. The networks binding the Ayutthaya mid-level noble lineages through kinship and alliance over many generations found a new central focus in Chaophraya Chakri. Wyatt's study of late Ayutthaya noble lineages has interesting findings with a direct bearing on the changes in economic policy under the governments of the first three kings of the Chakri dynasty.

Wyatt found that the late Ayutthaya nobility had very varied origins. There were four big noble families whose members ascended to the rank of Chaophraya. All four were descended from people who were not ethnically Thai. The Bunnag family came from Persia; the related families of Singhaseni, Chantharotwong, Buranasiri, Thong-in, and Siriwatthanakun were Brahman; the family of Chaophraya Chakri (the Chakri dynasty) was of Mon descent; and the last, which had three of Chaophraya rank, was of Chinese descent. All four families had some connection with the office of *phrakhlang* and especially with the port department which had direct responsibility for overseas trade. All four families had been continuously in government service for a long time, and all were interconnected by marriage ties. They competed for power among themselves, but also retained power among themselves. The most striking thing in Wyatt's study is that all four families had marriage ties with the family of Chaophraya Chakri before 1782. This indicates that the Chakri dynasty had deep roots among the nobility of late Ayutthaya in a way that no previous dynasty had. So it is no surprise that the kings of the Chakri dynasty had closer relations with the nobility than the Ayutthaya kings had had, and it is no surprise that individuals from the leading Ayutthaya noble families should still have power in Bangkok under the Chakri dynasty (Wyatt 1980, 3–5).

The Chakri kings gave importance to overseas trade from the start. This reflects the prior experience of the Chakri and other leading nobles in early Bangkok. They had been involved in the royal junk trade since the Ayutthaya period. The Ban Phlu Luang dynasty (1688–1767) may have been involved in trade to some degree, but this was not the model for this new elite. They had already been making their private family incomes from the junk trade, and they now simply turned to the same source to find revenues for the treasury. Equally, allowing the nobles and Chinese to trade privately in parallel with the royal trade was something this upper class probably considered quite normal. The king and nobles had close relations. There was no reason for the king to obstruct the private junk trade, especially that of his relatives. Besides, having more junks exporting goods was another way to generate revenue for the king. In sum, the upper class in early Bangkok had roots in the circle of trade and official nobility. They were in a position to change the method of extracting profits from foreign trade because the trading environment was undergoing rapid change, and because they were not constrained by old traditions and practices.

The increased volume of trade in early Bangkok was the result of changes in political relations among countries in Southeast Asia, and changes in the policies of Qing dynasty China. These changes will not be covered here as they had no impact on Siam except for the greatly increased volume of shipping. When China opened the door to trade, many people (both inside and outside China) built junks in order to trade with China. At the same time more European colonies were founded and more of the European ships used in western oceans came to Asia. These ships were highly efficient. The cargo space was very large in comparison to the number of crew, and thus the cargo cost was many times cheaper than on Chinese junks. These changes in the quality and quantity of marine shipping were in line with Siam's need to export its own products to the world market now that the entrepot trade had declined. Most of the goods exported from Siam were bulk goods such as rice and sugar. The forest goods which Siam continued to export since the Ayutthaya period were mostly low-cost high-volume items such as sappanwood and sticklac. Some of these articles were exported in higher volumes in early Bangkok. Hence Siam's total trade volume increased greatly in this period.

The upper class in early Bangkok, which had a legacy of involvement in trade over several generations, actively participated in the opportunities for foreign trade. Kings, nobles, and Chinese invested in building ships in order to engage in foreign trade themselves, and helped to increase the range of exportable products. The immigration of many Chinese into Siam (which will be covered in detail below) supplied the entrepreneurship to produce many new goods, most of which were bulky cargoes.

The way that the government extracted profit from trade began to change in early Bangkok. Instead of exploiting trade directly, the new trend was to exploit production. The tax-in-kind system still operated and even expanded after people were transferred from the left bank of the Mekhong to the right bank and forced to remit taxes directly to Bangkok. Yet there was a clear trend for tax goods to diminish in importance even though the king was still directly involved in trade by owning junks and imposing monopolies on certain goods in demand in the world market. Sometimes the tax-in-kind supplies were insufficient for world market demand, and government had to buy additional supplies to fill its junks. Goods with more complex labor input than the collection of forest goods became more important. Both junks and western ships visited Bangkok port to buy such goods for export to various destinations. Sometimes the king imposed monopolies on such products, for instance pepper, but government monopolies in the early Bangkok era had a different purpose from that in Ayutthaya. Monopolies were used to ensure the royal junks acquired sufficient cargo to make a profit overseas, not to make a profit from the foreign and domestic merchants who wanted to buy these products for export. In other words, the purpose of the monopoly was to support the royal junk trade not to make a direct profit from the monopoly itself. When such products were available in quantities beyond whatever was needed for the royal junks, the surplus became free goods. As Crawfurd reported in 1823, the Chinese planted 60,000 *hap* of pepper a year, but the *phrakhlang* told him that the king took only 40,000 *hap* under his monopoly (that is, by forced purchase), leaving a surplus of 20,000 *hap* which was traded freely (Crawfurd 1967, 11–2). This change in monopoly policy is also evident on the import side. The early Bangkok government took little interest in making profits from import monopolies in the way that Ayutthaya governments had. In the Ayutthaya period, some imports were destined for re-export under the entrepot trade, and the government sought to make a profit from this trade before the goods changed hands in Ayutthaya. But imports in early Bangkok were mostly for domestic consumption (some were re-exported to Cambodia, Lanna, and Lao, but not in great quantity). Government took no interest in making a profit from this trade and various sources indicate there was a rather free environment for importing goods without passing through the *phrakhlang*. Chinese junks visiting the Chaophraya basin retailed goods directly to the people. The only way that government made some profit from imports was by buying foreign goods to fill the royal junks on their return journeys. The government was now more of a merchant than a sleeping partner.

These trends show that exploitation was increasingly focused on production. In the Second Reign government was able to collect over 2 million baht of revenue in cash from taxes, tax farms (*akon*), Chinese head tax, and so on. This amounted to two-fifths of total government revenue and did not include the taxes collected in kind such as those on tin and rice (Crawfurd 1967, 388). In the Third Reign government lifted most of the monopolies and concentrated instead on tax farms levied on production of goods for the market. Chaophraya Thiphakorawong reported in the chronicles of the Third Reign that dozens of new taxes were raised in this reign (Thiphakorawong 1961b, 182–3). In addition, foreign sources from the same period report that government revenue from tax farms on crops increased greatly after the abolition of monopolies, up to a level comparable with the profits from foreign trade in the Second Reign (estimated at over 2 million baht). This estimate did not include the rice tax which also changed from cash to kind during the Third Reign and had a value of 800,000 baht. In addition, reports on government tax revenues in the Third Reign show that some formerly important export goods dropped in volume and delivered the government little tax. The combined tax revenues from deer hides, deer horn, buffalo hides, buffalo horn, rhino hide, and tiger bone were only 4,400 baht (Ruschenberger 1838, 283–4).

Government was able to switch revenue policy from exploiting foreign trade to exploiting internal production because the country's economy was shifting more towards an export economy. That is, a significant volume of production was intended to supply the world market rather than home consumption. The more production there was for the world market, the more tax government was able to collect from the producers and export merchants. Siamese government documents indicate that Rama III "considered all people should seek livelihood through trade for everyone's benefit" (cho ro 3-1/1, cs 1191). He also had a policy to support production of export goods demanded in the world market such as sugar. In 1843, an order was sent to the governor of Nakhon Chaisi as follows:

> Nakhon Chaisi is a place where people and merchants make a living through gardens, sugar plantation, and sugar factories which generate revenue for the government. Sugar is a good example. These goods are sold to the western ships. Nowadays more ship captains come to trade in Bangkok than before. There is not enough sugar to fill their

> ships. The governor of Nakhon Chaisi must arrange for the Chinese, Lao, Khmer, and others to plant more sugarcane than before...and when sugar is planted to a full extent, encourage the Thai and Chinese to establish more sugar factories than before. (cho ro 3-20, cs 1205)

Because production of export goods was able to "generate revenue for the government," government focused more on taxes and tax farming, and the need for monopolies diminished.

This export economy flourished as long as Siam had access to markets which bought its products. The royal junk trade was thus one way to bridge the gap between internal production and external markets. Private trade by local or foreign merchants also had a role in distributing internal production into the world market, and so was important for the early Bangkok government. If there were no channels between domestic production and the world market, the export economy would collapse and return to subsistence, and government's revenue from export production would disappear. The early Bangkok government thus tried to promote trade by foreigners.

Foreign sources from some phases of the early Bangkok era suggest an exactly opposite trend. But using foreign sources in this case requires care because the authors of these documents were often writing under the influence of economic liberalism. They stressed the superiority of nineteenth century free trade, and portrayed eastern systems of quota and monopoly as evils which hindered the civilization of the world. This was a form of bias. Also foreigners, especially the British, had trading interests which conflicted with Siamese political interests. Every embassy sent to negotiate in Siam had a political agenda as well as a trade agenda.[159] The British demands over trade seemed to lack any attempt to understand the Thai trading system and the treasury's methods of raising revenue. Instead of taking up opportunities to make profits from the surplus which came into the free market after the monopolies, or to identify new products outside the monopolies, the British insisted on free trade in Siam which had not known free trade before. Under free trade the British would be in the best position to benefit. The British accounts of the monopolies and trade obstructions they found in Bangkok are thus rather exaggerated. They paint a picture of excessive controls on foreign merchants. For example Finlayson, an official in Crawfurd's mission, reported:

> Blind to their real interests, as well as ignorant of the practice of commerce, the king and his ministers still continue to be the sole merchants, retaining in their own hands the monopoly of all articles of consequence, and holding it contraband for any others to meddle. (Finlayson 1826, 166–7)

159. All British embassies which came to negotiate in Bangkok from Crawfurd to Sir James Brooke brought political issues for discussion. At first these political issues were about the problems of expanding Siamese power in the Malay states and on the western frontier between Siam and Burma. Later, when the problems of Siamese tributaries diminished, the British demanded extraterritorial judicial rights. See western embassies in the Bangkok period, *Prachum phongsawadan phak thi* 62.

These claims were patently false. In the Second Reign, government did not monopolize all the major products, only those which supplied the principal cargo on the royal junks. According to Burney, who knew Siam better and resided longer, monopolies were imposed only on sticklac, sappanwood, ivory, camphor, and pepper (Burney 1910, 180). In the same period, there were many other non-monopoly products which sold well in the external market such as tin, dried beef, dried snakehead fish, dried shrimp, arecanut, seedless cotton, animal hides, and wood for shipbuilding or house construction. These products were exported by China-based Chinese merchants in significant amounts. American traders also did good business during the Second Reign and had no complaints. The first American merchant came in 1818. Morgan, who arrived to trade at Bangkok in 1821, stated that the American sloop *Persia* had already visited Siam three times. American traders had presented 5,000 guns to the king and were given every facility for trade. By 1821 Morgan found that American ships had already made twelve visits to Bangkok to buy goods for export, and because of this flourishing trade and good profits the Americans intended to establish a warehouse in Bangkok before long (Frankfurter 1914, 6).

In the Third Reign, the monopoly policy was lifted by the independent decision of the Bangkok government, not under British pressure through the Burney treaty as some foreign scholars understand (Vella 1957, 117–28). Burney stated that King Rama III abolished the monopolies and allowed free trade from the first day he ascended the throne (Burney 1910, 50–1). This point tallies with the letter from a Portuguese to Crawfurd in Singapore in 1824:

> As soon as Prince Kroma Chiat [Rama III] ascended the throne, he gave orders to allow all nations that visited Siam to buy and sell, export and import, with any inhabitant they thought proper, without hindrance, they paying only the duties. This was done without any altercation with the Chiefs. (Burney 1911, II, 125)

This fact was well-known to the British in the colonies. Even Raffles, who edited Finlayson's volume in 1826, wrote a footnote stating that once Prince Chetsadabodin became king he permitted free trade by his subjects and foreigners except in arms, opium, and some other forbidden articles (Finlayson 1826, 200). Hence Burney's success in making a treaty with Siam in 1826 arose in part because of the imperatives of the political situation, but in part because the trade provisions in the treaty matched with existing government policy.

After the British acquired more colonies in the Far East and had more influence and interests in the China trade, they became dissatisfied with the Burney treaty and wanted to amend it, even though this treaty (and the treaty with the Americans) had been quite satisfactory for western merchants. The provisions which were later attacked had initially been welcomed by the western merchants. It was reported in 1835 that although the treaty provision on deck tax seemed on the surface to impose a very high rate of 4,275 American dollars on a ship with 25-foot beam, in fact this was equivalent to a tax of 10–12 per cent or less on high-value cargo (Ruschenberger 1838, 282).

The policy of free trade was fully supported by King Rama III even though it conflicted with the interests of senior nobles who had their own trading junks and used their roles in administering the monopolies for trading advantage; for example, Chaophraya Phrakhlang and his younger brother Phraya Siphiphat opposed free trade and created some obstructions for trade (Burney 1911, 223). However, the Burney treaty was respected by the Siamese government, and the trading environment was acceptable to foreign merchants, especially westerners. The treaty with the US in 1833, which reduced the deck tax from 1,700 to 1,500 baht, indicates the Siamese commitment to promote a flourishing trade by foreigners in the country, especially considering that this deck tax was once 2,200 baht (Thorneley 1923, 53). Trade among western and Siamese merchants increased rapidly. More western ships called at Bangkok to buy export goods, especially sugar. In 1842 it was reported that at least fifty-five ships, mostly under the British flag, called at the Bangkok port. Nine of these visited Bangkok port regularly each year. Apart from three or four ships which came direct from Britain, the majority came from Bombay, Singapore, or China. Most loaded sugar whose export volume in 1844 was 110,000 *hap* of first grade (Moore 1914, 27).

However, this atmosphere of free trade deteriorated late in the reign when government reimposed some monopolies, especially on the major export item of sugar. The true cause of this change in policy at the end of the Third Reign is not clearly known. Vella suggests that from the early 1830s onwards the government found a renewed interest in trading directly itself, and promoted production of high-selling goods such as sugar in order to make a high profit. But Siamese documents, such as the order to the governor of Nakhon Chaisi in 1843 cited above, show that the government was very interested in the western ships and wanted to increase domestic sugar production to supply them. St. John, secretary in the mission of Sir James Brooke, suggests that King Rama III truly appreciated the British but, after a dispute with Hunter over the purchase of a steamship, came to despise foreigners and caused the negotiations with Brooke to fail (St. John 1879, 221–2). This opinion seems to have originated from Hunter himself. In 1849, a British merchant who stated he had been in Siam for a long time wrote a petition to the British government in London relating the Siamese government's violations of the treaty over the sale of sugar, and claiming the government had begun to violate the Burney treaty since 1840. The British had not protested, even though in 1842 total monopolization raised the price of sugar in Bangkok by 40 per cent, with no differentiation according to the quality grade, and as a result, producers no longer produced the best quality sugar as they had before (cited in Thornely 1923, 57–8). It seems this petitioner was Hunter himself. The government began to totally monopolize sugar only in 1843. The foreign sources cited above show that in 1835 sugar was still traded in large quantities and western merchants bought a great volume for export. Credible sources to explain this change in government policy have not yet been found.

It may be that this change resulted from the complexities of internal politics. The power of the Bunnag family increased after the death of Chaophraya Bodindecha, at a time when the power of King Rama III had begun to wane. Perhaps the government's attempt to expand foreign trade using the phrai system had reached its limit, and increasing the production of sugar would require the release of phrai labor to plant sugarcane. Perhaps competition in export production from other colonial countries resulted in more efficient production. Perhaps western merchants had more political power and wanted to use that power to extract more benefit from Siamese trade for themselves. All these are just suppositions, and await more detailed study than previous attempts to explain the change in Siamese government policy towards foreign trade in the last five to six years of the Third Reign.

The rapid revival of overseas trade in the early Bangkok era reduced the importance of the profits of royal trade. Even though every king in this era kept junks and traded continuously, the aim was to generate royal income rather than government revenue. In some reigns, the royal trade made losses even though Chinese merchants, other royal family members, and nobles made large profits from their junk trading. The reason why the royal junk trade did not receive the care and attention it required was because many new economic opportunities had arisen which offered government higher potential revenues. These new economic opportunities lay in the rising production for the market and rising private trade. Taxes levied on export production and private foreign trade, rather than the royal junk trade or the monopolies, became the foundations of government revenue (Hong 1981, 87–92). The revenues which government collected from taxes levied on production for the market increased greatly in the Third Reign under the tax-farming system. The expansion of tax farming is testament to the expansion of production for the market. Increased production, possibly for export, enabled government to collect more internal taxes than before. Government stopped exploiting foreign trade and started exploiting production aimed at foreign markets.

Governments in the lower Chaophraya basin since at least the early Ayutthaya period had depended on trade. This trade went through changes induced by both internal and external factors. The entrepot trade in early Ayutthaya changed to export of bulky, natural forest products collected as tax-in-kind, and then changed again in early Bangkok to export of goods produced by agriculture or basic industry. In parallel with these changes, the upper class modified its methods of extracting profit from overseas trade. The trading environment and trade policies affected the people in the central region in different ways in different periods. In other words, the central region's economy was affected by the nature of foreign trade and by the way the upper class exploited foreign trade—both of which changed from period to period.[160]

160. This account of the changing nature of foreign trade and its effects on the Siamese economy and society from early Ayutthaya to early Bangkok should be considered as the writer's tentative ideas rather than a fixed and definite theory. The main point is that there are sources which indicate the evolution of foreign trade over this long period and its probable effects on economic and social systems. It is unlikely that foreign trade and the socioeconomic system remained unchanged from the fourteenth to nineteenth centuries, yet this view is found in most works of economic history. An important pioneer study in Thai economic history was the short article by van der Heide (1906) which used western sources to paint a static picture of the seventeenth to eighteenth centuries, and then expanded this picture to cover the total

MERCHANTS UNDER SAKDINA

The dynamism of overseas trade in the early Bangkok era and the government's increasingly free policy of allowing others to participate in trade, attracted many people to become merchants engaged in overseas trade. Even so, most of these were confined to two groups: the sakdina upper class of royalty and nobles, and the Chinese who were connected to the sakdina system by the grant of noble titles, by marriage links into upper class families, or by sharing profits with those in the sakdina system.

Royalty and nobles entered into foreign trade mainly by owning junks or owning cargo space on junks. From the start of the Bangkok era, the kings owned junks and made profits from the junk trade both for the government treasury and for themselves. The king's junks were also a means to provide for other royal kin. Cargo space was allotted to those who did not own junks, enabling them to send goods for sale in China. In the First Reign, Prince Issara Sunthon (the future Rama II) used cargo space in royal junks to export goods to China, and to import Chinese goods to sell at a profit in Siam (*Khattiyaratpatiphat,* 119). Each of the kings had junks or, in the later period, western trading ships. These ships mostly exported tax-in-kind goods, especially in the First and Second Reigns. Hence even if the royal junk trade did not deliver a business profit, it was a convenient way to distribute goods collected as tax-in-kind into the world market and bring cash into the royal treasury (*phrakhlang khang thi*). According to the trading accounts of a royal junk "Kim yok sun" trading in China in 1813, the goods carried were valued in total at 362 chang 12 tamlueng 1 baht and 1 salueng, but sales amounted to only 317 chang 7 tamlueng 1 baht and 1 salueng leaving a surplus of goods valued at 29 chang 17 tamlueng 1 baht and 1 salueng. The combined value of the sales and surplus was less than the original investment, without counting other expenses such as fees, lost goods, port permits, and wages for the junk crews (cho ro 2-15/4, cs 1175). Such losses were bearable because the king had acquired the goods such as tin, pepper, sappanwood, ivory, and rattan for nothing either as tax-in-kind or by using conscripted phrai labor to collect them. The royal junk trade in the Third Reign delivered higher profits because of the king's own trading expertise, yet he still loaded the junks with goods acquired without payment. For example, in 1838 several royal junks were loaded with rice acquired through the land tax for sale in China (cho ro 3-23, cs 1200).

---

evolution of the Thai economy, both before and after then until the late nineteenth century. Prince Damrong did not study economic history per se but commented on the government's foreign trade at many points in his works. His method was the reverse of van der Heide's. He used data on foreign trade in the early Bangkok era to explain foreign trade in all earlier periods, even back to Sukhothai. These errors are things which this writer is trying to avoid, yet he may not have succeeded in offering a credible theory of change in the nature of Thai foreign trade. The important point is that we must understand that there was change and evolution in the Thai economy. Another interesting work of economic history which gives a dynamic view of the pre-1855 period and this "evolution" rather than presenting a static picture is Paitoon Sayswang (1978).

Besides the king, other senior royal kin from the Front Palace prince downwards had their own trading junks. Except in the First Reign, all the Front Palace princes traded on a large scale. In the Second Reign he made enough profit from the junk trade to make loans to the king (*Prachum prakat ratchakan thi 4*, II, 234). The Front Palace prince of the Third Reign was involved in trade since the Second Reign when he held the rank of Prince Sakdiphonlasep. He was a relative of the governor of Nakhon Si Thammarat, and used his kin connections and the trading advantages of controlling the *kalahom* department (which oversaw the southern provinces). From the Second Reign, he built several junks for use in his own private trade. In the Scribes Department (*phanaek nangsue tua khian*), there are several letters dating from the Second and Third Reigns from Prince Sakdiphonlasep to the governor of Nakhon Si Thammarat on trading matters. In one of these letters he mentioned to the governor that "in the department nowadays a lot of money is being used to build junks" (cho ro 2-14, cs 1174).

Many other royal kin traded overseas. Prince Phithakmontri had his own junks trading with China from the First Reign (*Khattiyaratpatiphat*, 114). Prince Chetsadabodin made such large profits from the junk trade that his father called him "*chao sua*" (Waraphon 1979, 67). Prince Phrapinklao, while he held princely rank in the Third Reign, had a 200-ton sloop manned by three British sailors in his service for trading overseas (Ruschenberger 1838, 292). Prince Chakkrachetsada owned junks and had once allotted cargo space to King Rama III (Waraphon 1979, 70). These royal kin involved in foreign trade gained increased political power, probably because they had more wealth to support the king than their peers. The four princes who were entrusted with senior posts in the Second Reign were Prince Phithakmontri (regent but according to western sources in charge of the courts), Prince Issaranurak (in charge of *mahatthai*), Prince Sakdiphonlasep (*kalahom*), and Prince Chetsadabodin (port department) (Praphakonbowonwisutthiwong, 1938, 49–50). Sources clearly show that three of the four had previously been very active in foreign trade.

Some nobles, especially those in *phrakhlang*, also traded a great deal on their own account. Phraya Suriyawongkosa (Dit Bunnag), head of *phrakhlang* in the Second Reign, had a very large and profitable junk trade (Waraphon 1979, 67) which he maintained throughout his life. In the Fourth Reign, Bowring referred to him, then 68 years old, as follows: "He spoke of trade as the source of riches, and said he had five ships, trading with China, Singapore, and Java.... He grew coffee, and would send a sample" (Bowring 1969, II, 277–8). His son continued the private junk trade, and was also the first to think of building a western style ship. His younger brother, son, and grandson rose rapidly in government service. These nobles kept a tight grip on posts in *phrakhlang* because these posts conveyed direct benefits for their trading activity. Chaophraya Phrakhlang (Kun) in the First Reign was also rich from the junk trade (Waraphon 1979, 40). In the same way that the royal kin who traded overseas gradually increased their political power, so too did the nobles who grew rich from foreign trade. Although King Rama III put Prince Surinthararak in charge of the port department and *phrakhlang*, this prince was actually only a figurehead and the real power was in the hands of Chaophraya Phrakhlang (Burney 1910, 55).

Apart from these senior nobles, many lesser nobles also figure in records on the junk trade. Their names and titles suggest most were people of Chinese descent who had been appointed to posts in the port department. For example an 1844 list of those preparing a fleet of junks included Phraya Siphiphat, Phra Choduek, Phraya Kosa, Khun Thongsio, Phra In, Phra Sen, Luang Kaeo Ayat, Luang Aphai Phiphit, Phraya Thamma, Luang Surathon, Phra Sem, Phra Laoya, Phra Aphai Phiphit, and Prince Chakkrachetsada (Waraphon 1979, 69–70). Another record about a private junk in which cargo space was allotted free for the king to carry royal cargo had additional names including Chin Kao, Prince Thinnakon, Chamuen Waiworanat, Phra Sawatdiwari, Phra Sombatphanit, Luang Maitriwanit, Luang Phokhoratchasetthi, Luang Prasoetwanit, Khun Phakdi-akon, and Khun Watthanaphirom (Waraphon 1979, 72–3). Besides those of Chinese descent, there were also nobles of Vietnamese descent who traded with Vietnam, for example Luang Phakdiwanit who in the Second Reign sent two junks a year to Vietnam without fail (cho ro 2-4, cs 1183).

Many other Chinese who had some link with the bureaucracy but no official positions also played a large part in the junk trade, and may have been a majority of those engaged in trade. Crawfurd (1967, 415) stated that in Bangkok alone there were 9,000 to 11,000 boatmen engaged in overseas trade. Chinese who had settled in Siam owned junks and traded not only with China but also with other ports in Southeast Asia, and also not only from Bangkok but from other ports including Nakhon Si Thammarat and Songkhla in the south, and Chanthaburi in the east.

Those of Chinese descent along with the sakdina upper class reaped the main benefit from overseas trade.[161] However, the overseas trade of the Chinese differed from that of the sakdina upper class. Those Chinese who developed close relations with the sakdina system were able to take advantage of conscripted labor or political power to reduce the costs of trade investment. But there were many other Chinese junk traders who did not have the opportunity to trade in that fashion. Instead, they used trading methods brought from China. That is, several small merchants pooled their investments in a junk mission, and served as crew on the junk without payment in return for the right to a share of the cargo space in which they could transport goods or passengers. The junk owner had the largest share but had to leave some space for the crew in lieu of paying them wages. This system allowed small merchants with little capital to take part in the junk trade. Gutzlaff described such trade in detail, stating that each crew member "is a shareholder having the liberty of putting a certain quantity of goods on board, with which he trades wheresoever the vessel may touch, caring very little about how soon she may arrive at the port of destination" (Gutzlaff 1832, 55–8). This method of junk trading by small-scale Chinese merchants expanded the money economy to a wider circle of people since all the goods had to be purchased. To supply the large demand in the Chinese market, a large quantity of sappanwood beyond that required for tax-in-kind was felled and sold to these

161. In the original, this paragraph appeared in the section below on shipbuilding, beginning with a sentence, "More can be added on the Chinese migrants' participation in overseas trade." It has been moved here which seems more appropriate. [T]

small Chinese traders. Thus Siam was able to export 200,000 *hap* of sappanwood to China in 1832 (Sarasin 1977, 200). Apart from sappanwood, many other products were purchased (or acquired through barter) by small Chinese merchants for export. Thus production for the market also affected the Thai, whether or not they were yet drawn totally into this production system.

The Chinese were thus the main force in Siam's overseas trade in the early Bangkok era. They traded independently, traded in partnership with the sakdina upper class, and offered bribes or other benefits to this class.

Chaophraya Thiphakorawong, compiler of the chronicle of the Third Reign, referred to the wealthy people who built or renovated wat in the Third Reign, especially the major wat rather than the smaller ones, as "royalty, nobles, great merchants (*che sua*)—the people of property" (Thiphakorawong 1961b, 172). This description seems to encompass all the people involved in foreign trade. Their numbers probably increased greatly in the early Bangkok era after government opened up the junk trade. Although their trade to some extent competed with the royal junk trade, for reasons stated above government had begun to draw its revenues from taxes on domestic production of goods rather than from the junk trade. These groups thus had freedom to trade privately without government restriction. The nobles and Chinese relished this opportunity.

Talking of freedom to trade in this fashion may create the misunderstanding that a liberal economy had become fully established in early Bangkok. This is not true. Free trade was confined to those at the upper levels of the sakdina structure and their allies. In truth these "merchants" still leveraged their sakdina privileges for commercial benefit. The kings still acquired the goods for their private trade through tax-in-kind or conscripted phrai labor under sakdina. Similarly, while foreign merchants had freedom to import goods, the royal treasury had the first right to purchase them and used this right to control and exploit foreign merchants, or extract bribes from them. Many foreign records complain about this. Control over people was not the only source of wealth. Increasingly, commerce was becoming the main form of accumulation. But control over people—either directly or indirectly through influence over those who controlled many people as part of their official position—was a way to acquire goods cheaply in order to minimize the capital needed for trade. Hence these "merchants" were not true merchants independent of the sakdina system. On the contrary, they were born within the sakdina system, and tried to sustain the sakdina structure for their own commercial benefit. The Chinese, although not born within sakdina, tried to build connections with this sakdina upper class. Some were appointed as tax-farmers with official posts and titles. Some established connections through marriage. As the records constantly show, they had to give bribes or share their trading profits with the sakdina upper class, such as by allowing the king cargo space for nothing. Hence the private trade of the Chinese was not trade by independent merchants, but by merchants prepared to work with sakdina and be sucked into the system to gain its benefits. The rapidly increasing foreign trade in early Bangkok, instead of giving birth to a new class independent of sakdina, gave birth to nothing. Rather, it made the sakdina upper class more bourgeois, in the sense that the main foundations of their power came to rest on commerce. Their worldview, tastes, and preferences became like those of bourgeoisies in other places and eras (see below).

Because the bourgeoisie that arose in the early Bangkok era was closely connected to sakdina, the economic impact on sakdina was limited. For example, the release of phrai labor was in fact of considerable benefit to the government since labor was needed to produce export goods such as sugar, rice, pepper, and tin which provided government with increased revenue through taxes on both production and trade. But phrai labor was only freed to a very limited extent—by reducing the corvée period to only four months a year (and three months subsequently). It would take a long time before the profits of the bourgeoisie expanded to the point that the sakdina system no longer answered their needs. Only then could the administrative reforms of the Chulalongkorn reign abolish the old sakdina system.

THE CHINESE: THE MAIN FACTOR OF CHANGE

Labor was needed in many forms—for government work such as construction, for planting crops for the market, and for skilled tasks such as shipbuilding and mining. These activities developed the export economy from which the upper class harvested profit, and thus the early Bangkok government opened the country to the inflow of Chinese. In parallel, the internal situation in China drove people in the southwestern coastal region to emigrate (Skinner 1962, chapter 2). The number of Chinese in Siam increased rapidly. The Chinese had a philosophy of life different from that of the Thai. They viewed hard work, frugality, and diligence as the means to drag oneself and one's family up from the common ranks into the upper class. Seeking wealth through hard work was respectable and not at all shameful. In addition, the Chinese who migrated to Siam were naturally selected. Those who lacked aspirations would never dream of leaving home to seek their fortunes overseas. Only those with the drive to enrich and improve their families took the risks involved in migrating away from China. The migrants viewed those who did not dare leave their homes in China as weak and risible.[162] Because the migrants were looking for money to help their families in China, they had no interest in staking out plots of land for subsistence agriculture in Siam as this would not generate enough cash to send a surplus back to the family. They needed to find some way to make a profit so they could help their families in China. These were not cowards who left home just to save themselves (Skinner 1962, 93–7).

This natural selection ensured the Chinese in Thailand were people with certain qualities. They had the nerve to take commercial risks, were used to a cash economy, were diligent, and had the stamina for hard work. But at the same time, they were people who lacked certain other qualities. They had not succeeded in establishing

162. Skinner's data on this were not confirmed by later Chinese emigrants who gave a contrasting point of view in interview. They said those who left were looked down on because normally those with a job and future would not leave China. In other words, Chinese emigrants were those with no stake in Chinese society.

themselves in society or economy in China. They were not wealthy enough to transfer capital from China to start businesses in Siam. They brought with them only their labor. They had not gained any educational qualification in China and hence were not representatives of Chinese high culture. Rather, they lacked education and were ignorant of China's high art and culture. So their immigration did not result in any influence of Chinese high culture on Thai culture. More than that, because they lacked connections into Thai society, at least in the first generation, and were focused only on material profit, they were prepared to take on any activity without considering its social value, like people everywhere who have been uprooted from their own society.

The Chinese migrants in Siam fall into two identifiable groups, each with its own way of life. The first group found success in economy and society. They acquired a good economic standing and were able to penetrate into the sakdina system by gaining bureaucratic appointment, rank, or marriage connections with the sakdina upper class. They became closely involved with Thai sakdina society, and had opportunities to experience Thai high culture at first hand. They were prepared to be absorbed into the upper class of Thai society, and the faster it could be done, the sooner they gained both economic and social benefits. They were ready to cut off their pigtails and adopt Thai upper class customs. John Crawfurd (1915, 137) said of the Chinese in Siam that they "profess themselves Buddhists as soon as they come into the country, intermarry with the Siamese, give alms to the priests, frequent the temples, occasionally become priests themselves, and sacrifice the practice of burying their dead and erecting costly monuments over them." He was probably talking about the Chinese he had met in Bangkok who were among those who had successfully penetrated into the Thai sakdina upper class.

The second group of Chinese were those who found greater economic success than the run-of-the-mill Thai because at the least they entered into the cash economy while the Thai were half-way between the subsistence and market economies. These Chinese spread into the provincial centers where they entered mining, sugar planting, pepper planting, sugar making, or skilled work in shipbuilding, and so on. They had little opportunity to experience Thai high culture. Even though they lived in Thai communities and might marry a Thai, their relations with the Thai were confined to a single dimension, namely trade. There was no reason for such Chinese to merge themselves completely into Thai society because it gave them no profit, either economic or social. This group of Chinese was absorbed more slowly. They did not easily cut off their pigtails (which continued to be a symbol of being Chinese in Thailand for a long time), at least in the first two or three generations. Preserving their Chinese identity had more benefits for them than becoming Thai. They could retain the privileges which the king granted to the Chinese such as paying a head tax lower than the commutation fee paid by Thai phrai. In sum, the Chinese migrants had two choices: some were prepared to become absorbed into Thai sakdina, and chose to merge themselves into the Thai upper class; or else they retained their Chineseness, which gave them more benefits in every way, including the mental benefit of the sense of belonging together with those from the same motherland.

The different ways of life of these two groups had different effects on Thai society. The first group, which became absorbed into sakdina, had the opportunity to influence the upper class in both positive and negative ways. Their readiness to take commercial risk, acquaintance with the cash economy, commercial knowledge (of accounting for example), and so on, could serve as models and inspiration for the sakdina upper class. Equally, their excessive materialism, neglect of social values, and so on might be a "poison" which the Chinese migrants "injected" into the Thai upper class. Since the Chinese migrants did not bring along Chinese high culture, the most they could offer to the upper class were writing skills, plasterwork, Chinese style construction, and historical legends. Although these were things which high class Chinese looked down on as low culture, they were very exciting for the Thai upper class in the early Bangkok era. The acceptance of Chinese culture was evident among the upper class, but not among the Thai phrai. Only the wat of "royalty, nobles, great merchants—the people of property" in early Bangkok were built copying the Chinese *keng* or pavilion. The wat of the rural people were still built in the old Thai style.

The second group of Chinese had few connections with ordinary Thai, and also preserved their Chineseness for longer. The Thai and the Chinese were already differentiated by their respective cultures and ways of life. Economic factors tended to widen their difference and even introduce some bitterness between them. While the Chinese entered into the money economy, most of the Thai around them still lived mainly in the subsistence economy. Although market production had begun to affect the Thai, mostly they were still engaged in subsistence production and barter. The Chinese migrants became the people with cash wealth in a society where most of the people had none. They saw profit-seeking as the main purpose in life while ordinary Thai perceived other goals as of higher value such as face, merit, and social acceptance. When the money economy expanded in certain areas, it squeezed the Thai who were still based in a subsistence economy. Sometimes this gave rise to feelings of hatred against the Chinese. These feelings were a combination of jealousy, contempt, and dismay at the increasing hardship of their own lives. Such feelings surfaced in an incident involving Chinese gangs in Chachoengsao where the money economy had taken a firm hold because of the sugar industry. When government forces moved against these gangs, Thai who had fled from the disorder emerged from the forests and set to killing any Chinese they met in large numbers, whether or not they belonged to the gangs. As a result, "many thousands of Chinese died at that time and the Chachoengsao waterways were crammed with floating corpses" (Thiphakorawong 1961b, 130). The massacre reflected feelings against the Chinese in general, not just against the gangs. The account in the chronicles suggests why ordinary Thai were motivated to kill foreigners who kept cash firmly in their own grasp, as "after killing them, they took their clothing, cut the money belt, and sliced open the stomach to look for money. Some found money which was a bonus" (Thiphakorawong 1961b, 128–30).

Some argue that the Thai upper class took advantage of the migrant Chinese by using them as a front—the upper class could exploit the phrai yet divert the people's hatred away from the real source of their exploitation and onto the migrant Chinese. We cannot find sources which show such intentions on the part of the upper class in early Bangkok, yet it must be accepted this was the result, whether intentional or not. The privileges which the Chinese were granted by government gave them economic advantages over the general Thai population. But these privileges did not come free. The Chinese had to share much of their profits with the upper class who did not have to work hard, face hardship, or take business risks. Chinese immigration was most beneficial for the upper class, and that was why the country was opened up to the inflow. From the First Reign the royal junks which went to trade in China sometimes loaded people rather than goods for the return journey—up to 1,200 persons on a ship, delivering an immediate profit to the royal junk trade (Waraphon 1979, 41). The various benefits gained by the upper class will be considered further below. One particular benefit came from the special forms of expertise which the Chinese brought with them and which the upper class urban bourgeois made use of. For example, Chinese medicine, which was considerably advanced, was a very popular service in the towns where the bourgeoisie lived. Many pharmacists in Bangkok were Chinese or Vietnamese. Some doctors became famous and popular (Crawfurd 1967, 328). Sometimes government made use of Chinese technical expertise in mining to increase production from the phrai system. For example, there are records from 1836 that conscripts sent to pan for gold in the region of Sawankhalok, Sukhothai, Phichai, and Pak Hoeng were not skilled at the work so a Chinese called Sai Hu "who had expertise in making water systems for panning gold on marshland" was sought and sent to see whether his expertise could be put to use (cho ro 3-10, cs 1198).

The most important effect of Chinese immigration was economic. As Paitoon Sayswang concluded: "The economy of Siam up to 1855 was already expanding due to the growth in international trade especially of sugar, pepper, boat building, tobacco, but these activities were mainly accounted for by the continuous migration of Chinese" (Paitoon 1978, 37; see also Sarasin 1977, chapter 10, which summarizes the economic impact of Chinese immigration in the Third Reign). We will select some important aspects.

MARKET AGRICULTURE

The first type of market farming by the Chinese was probably vegetables and pig raising to feed the rapidly growing city in the early Bangkok era. Most agriculture in this period was close to the urban areas such as Bangkok (Skinner 1962, 113) and towns along the Maeklong River where most of the population was Chinese. In 1843 Chinese were planting gardens of long bean, sweet potato, cabbage, onion, aubergine, tobacco, and arecanut (Pallegoix 1963, 92; 2000, 48). The Thai also took up planting crops for sale. They did not produce solely for the market but simply added something on top of their subsistence production. During his travel to Suphanburi, Sunthon Phu (1960, 301, 308) mentioned cotton, beans, vegetable gardens, and bananas planted by Thai, Chinese, and Mon.

The most important of the crops which the Chinese planted for the market was sugarcane. It had been known in Siam for a long time, but the manufacture of sugar was certainly brought by the Chinese. Crawfurd states explicitly that production of sugar by the Chinese had started only twelve years before his visit to Bangkok (that is, in 1810), and that it was possible to produce "the whitest and best in India, to the extent of above 60,000 piculs" within that twelve years. According to Crawfurd's account in 1822, there was a lot of sugar growing and manufacture around Bangplasoi, Nakhon Chaisi, Bang Pakong, and Paetrio. Noticeably it had not yet spread to the western towns. In addition he reported that the sugarcane growers were all Thai while the sugar makers were all Chinese (Crawfurd 1967, 422–3). Chinese sugar production drew many Thai into production for the market and the money economy. Later reports mention many Chinese planting sugarcane also. When the world market demand for sugar increased, Chinese labor and Thai farmers were able to expand production. Chaophraya Phrakhlang told Finlayson that production could be expanded endlessly (Raffles 1826, 167–8). When Burney came to Siam he found that sugar was the European and American merchants' main export, that the Chinese were still the sole producers, and that government made considerable revenue from sugar by collecting internal tax of 2 salueng per *hap* and export tax of 6 salueng per *hap* (Burney 1911, 101–2). By the 1830s sugar had become the country's most important export. In 1832, 96,000 *hap* were exported to China alone (Sarasin 1977, 200). Sugar production expanded at this rapid rate with only modest initial investments. The sugarcane was crushed using both human and animal labor. The firewood used for boiling was freely available and cheap. In *Nirat phra pathom*, Sunthon Phu (1960, 369) described seeing small-scale sugar-crushing factories as follows: "the sugar mills crush the cane fed into them, people driving the buffaloes yell all the time.... they stoke the fires in the mills so the smoke billows." The mills could be expanded to any scale as long as the labor and raw material were available. In 1839 Pallegoix stated that in the Chachoengsao region there were at least twenty sugar mills mostly owned by Chinese. One mill where he stayed had two hundred workers. As a result of the scale of the sugar industry, the area around Chachoengsao town was flourishing with rice fields, fruit orchards, and sugar plantations (Pallegoix 1963, 74–5; 2000, 39–40). By the end of the Third Reign sugar production had spread to more places than those identified by Crawfurd. In 1858 in the Fourth Reign, the government divided the sugar tax farm into three parts corresponding to three regions. The first covered nineteen towns in the Chaophraya basin from Samut Prakan and Nakhon Khueankhan up to Phichai, Sawankhalok, and Kamphaengphet. The second covered a total of nine towns in the east including Chachoengsao, Nakhon Nayok, Prachinburi, Phanat Nikhom, Chonburi, Bang Lamung, Rayong, Trat, and Chanthaburi. The third region covered eight towns in the west including Sakhonburi, Nakhon Chaisi, Suphanburi, Samut Songkhram, Ratchaburi, Kanchanaburi, Phetchaburi, and Pranburi (*Prachum prakat ratchakan thi 4*, 236–7).

The expansion of the sugar industry also had an impact on the Thai who took up sugar planting to supply the Chinese-owned mills in competition with Chinese sugar planters. The government promoted sugar growing in order to increase the volume of sugar production. Chaophraya Chakri sent an order to the governor of Nakhon Chaisi to boost sugar planting by "arranging for Chinese, Lao, Khmer, and Thai (*ratsadon*) to plant sugar throughout the region more than before" (cho ro 3-20, cs 1205). Apart from drawing subsistence farmers into producing for sale, the government also itself ventured into planting cane and setting up its own mills in order to increase its revenue from sugar. Phraya Maha-amat sent an order to Phraya Wisetluechai, the governor of Chachoengsao, to buy sugarcane shoots for a plantation which King Rama III had directed Chaophraya Phrakhlang to create in Phanat Nikhom, and also to set up a sugar mill (cho ro 3-18/4, cs 1200). However, this government enterprise failed because of high expenses. Phraya Wisetluechai's accounts show that government's cash expenses in making the sugar plantation included buying land, digging canals, and paying Chinese to make equipment. In addition the labor used in the government sugar plantation was all Chinese wage labor (cho ro 3-9, cs 1201). The government's lack of business experience, and probably also corruption on the part of officials, caused this government enterprise to fail. Phraya Wisetluechai who had responsibility for government plantations in three Chachoengsao tambon, was called upon to settle the payments in 1841 (cho ro 3-19, cs 1201). The government had rarely considered undertaking business enterprise outside the phrai system in the past, and was certainly stimulated by the business initiative of the migrant Chinese.

Another agricultural export product of which the Chinese were major producers was pepper. There are records that Thai had planted pepper for export since the Ayutthaya period. But after the reign of King Narai, domestic pepper production had probably declined as there is no record of further pepper export until the early Bangkok era. The Taechiu Chinese who migrated into Siam in large numbers from the early Bangkok era onwards brought expertise in pepper planting from China. They probably started production in Siam with the original aim of exporting to the China market (Sarasin 1977, 177–8). The main area where the Chinese congregated to plant pepper was Chanthaburi (Raffles 1826, 256). Crawfurd (1915, 111–2) reported in 1823 that the Chinese exported 60,000 *hap* a year of pepper to China. In the early Bangkok era pepper production was probably completely in Chinese hands (Crawfurd 1967, 327) but the opening of the market for pepper in China greatly increased the production volume. Only a few years after Crawfurd, there are records that pepper production had expanded from Chanthaburi to many other areas, especially in the south. Pattani and Kelantan produced 16,000 *hap* a year and Trang 8,000 *hap* (Sarasin 1977, 201). Commercial pepper production entered into the way of life of many Thai.

Tobacco was grown commercially in China. In Siam it had probably been grown for a long time, but only within the subsistence economy. The ordinary Thai consumed a great deal of tobacco but the production in Siam was never adequate. La Loubère reported that both men and women consumed so much tobacco that imports came from Manila and China to supplement domestic supplies (La Loubère 1969, 50). The shortfall in tobacco production continued into early Bangkok when tobacco was imported from Java. But by the time of Crawfurd's observations, Siam produced enough for the high level of local consumption and even had a surplus for export to

Cambodia and southern Vietnam (Crawfurd 1915, 112; Crawfurd 1967, 314–5). The best and largest areas for tobacco growing were Chanthaburi and Bangplasoi (Crawfurd 1967, 424) which both had large Chinese communities, suggesting they had an important part in tobacco production for export.

Export agriculture generated considerable wealth for the Chinese and was a major base of the export economy which Siam had begun to develop. In fact the Thai had grown rice for export for a long time, but not in sufficient quantity to undermine the subsistence economy. By estimating the probable production capacity and subtracting the domestic consumption volume, Paitoon Sayswang (1978, 19) concluded that rice production was not large enough to allow much export. In the Third Reign, Siam exported only 1,500 metric ton of rice to China even though this was the largest market (Pallegoix 1963, 13; 2000, 7). However, the increase in the urban population and in the number of people engaged in specialized production expanded rice production for the domestic market. Even though rice was not produced much for export, supplies were needed to feed those who did not grow rice themselves, or those who had left the subsistence economy. Thai farmers' production of rice began to be affected by the market economy. Some Thai with investment capacity (either in cash or phrai labor) were inspired to replicate the success of export agriculture. In the Third Reign, there were orders to increase coffee planting in Chanthaburi where the coffee was found to have a good taste. Pallegoix (1963, 68; 2000, 36) sampled coffee at the governor's residence in Chanthaburi in 1848. Both the king and some senior nobles started large coffee plantations (Pallegoix 1963, 199; 2000, 110). When Bowring arrived to make a treaty in the Fourth Reign, Somdet Chaophraya Borommaha Prayurawong proposed to sell coffee to Bowring, as noted above. The Chinese did not invest in coffee planting because it required a lot of labor which they would need to hire. For this reason coffee plantations were limited to senior nobles who could use the phrai labor under their control.

MINING

The major mining ore was tin. It is not known for certain when Chinese first came to mine tin but probably in the Second Reign as in 1823 Crawfurd (1915, 109) reported that tin mining in the south was still in Thai hands. Production was small despite large numbers of people involved, and only 500 tons were sent to Bangkok. However not long after, Burney reported that most of those involved in tin mining at Phangnga and Thalang were Chinese, and those smelting the ore were totally Chinese. The Chinese entry into the tin mining industry increased production by applying more efficient techniques than those formerly used. Also, government allowed tin to be a free product in the market. Thus some tin was produced as tax-in-kind by Thai phrai labor, and some was produced directly for the market by the Chinese, as in Phangnga and Thalang. In the Third Reign, a tin tax farmer with a rank of *khun phra* was appointed from Bangkok to oversee tin production at Phangnga and Thalang. His responsibility was to deliver government 140 *phara* of tin (a *phara* is 240 kilograms) and forty flintlock guns a year. The king sent this tin to Penang to sell or barter against goods wanted from there. The tax farmer bought all the tin at 2 Singapore dollars for 3 *krabung* (a basket volume measure equivalent to 14–16 *chang*), and might cheat the miners by using *krabung* smaller than standard to increase his profit. The Chinese tin smelters bought the ore from the tax farmer, and had to smelt at least seven times to get 93 per cent purity (Burney 1911, 216–7). Tin of such purity could be exported to Penang and Singapore. Siamese ships also carried tin to sell on the Coromandel coast. Although the tax farming system exploited the miners, it was an advance over the tax-in-kind system which used forced labor and gave almost no benefit at all to the people involved.

In the Third Reign, Chinese tin mining for export expanded rapidly. At the end of the reign, Pallegoix (1963, 111; 2000, 60) reported that Chinese companies had tin mines in many places including Thalang, Chaiya, Chumphon, Ratchaburi, and Pak Phraek.

In parallel, skilled artisans among the urban Chinese developed use of tin within the country. Chinese established factories to cast tin for various utensils, and in Bangkok from the Second Reign polished them so they appeared like silver (Raffles 1826, 214).

The Chinese entry into the tin industry in the early Bangkok era paved the way for rapid expansion of tin mining once world market demand grew in the late nineteenth century.

Another mineral which the Chinese developed for export was iron. At the first stage of early Bangkok, the production of iron was insufficient for domestic consumption; King Taksin had wanted to buy iron pans from China to make weapons. The source of iron in this era was in the north, 200 to 300 miles away from Bangkok (probably around Nakhon Sawan, Phitsanulok, Rahaeng, and Tak). Iron ore was mined and smelted at those places but the resulting quality was poor. It was transported to Bangkok to make knives and other articles. Around the end of the First Reign or in the Second Reign, the Chinese entered into the industry of smelting iron and making iron articles. Probably because of better techniques for smelting and casting iron, the volume increased. Iron ore mining was probably still in Thai hands. Until the Third Reign, Chinese ironworks still purchased cheap iron carbonate in lumps brought by Thai boat traders. These ironworks produced thick ingots which were sent to Bangkok daily. As a result of their ability to produce more smelted iron, domestic supply was sufficient, and there was even some surplus for export to the Malay archipelago, Cambodia, and southern Vietnam (Crawfurd 1915, 108–9; Pallegoix 1963, 112; 2000, 60). Iron became a major export product. In Bangkok, Chinese established factories to cast and beat iron into tools and utensils. The iron price in Bangkok was very low, below 1.5 Malay dollars per *hap* of cast iron, and less than 3 dollars per *hap* for malleable iron which could be beaten without breaking (Crawfurd 1967, 323, 418). Export prices were similar. Ordinary iron bars cost under 4 rupee per *hap* (Crawfurd 1915, 108–9).[163]

163. Although iron was plentiful and cheap, it does not appear to have been used for tools by Thai farmers. In this period there are records of agricultural tools made with iron, but only

The export of iron probably began in the First Reign. In 1799 the Vietnamese ruler asked to purchase cast iron to manufacture guns, and the request was granted (Thiphakorawong 1960, 264–5). The iron-working industry developed considerably. In 1834, Pallegoix found the whole town of Tha Sung (near Chainat) was populated by true Chinese who had established twelve furnaces, some of which had 500–600 workers and operated both day and night. The iron industry had attracted Chinese to settle there and create a town (Pallegoix 1963, 83, 112; 2000, 44, 60).

SHIPBUILDING

The market for junks grew rapidly in the early Bangkok era. The raw material, hardwood, was available cheaply, and the building of junks both for use and sale developed quickly from early in the First Reign onwards. There was a large Chinese shipbuilding industry along the banks of the Chaophraya River. Both owners and skilled craftsmen were all Chinese (Sarasin 1977, 173; Crawfurd 1967, 50). Shipbuilding spread to several other towns outside Bangkok (*Phraratchaphongsawadan chabap phraratchahatalekha*, II, 610–1). It also stimulated growth in the timber industry. Rafts of timber were floated down from the north to sell in Bangkok. The government itself consumed more teak logs than it secured from tax-in-kind and had to spend money to buy extra supplies each year (cho ro 3-1/1, cs 1191). The cheap price of materials meant that junks built in Siam were cheaper than those from anywhere else. For example the price of a junk built in Siam was only 15 Spanish dollars per ton compared to 16.66 dollars in Vietnam, 20.83 dollars in Canton, and 30.58 dollars in Fukien. The junks made in Siam were also of better quality because they used hardwood throughout including the decks which in China were made of pine (Crawfurd 1967, 49). Before visiting Siam, Crawfurd (1820, 173) stated, "Almost all the junks employed in the commerce between the Indian islands and China are built at Bangkok, on the great river of Siam." In 1840, he reported to the lower house of parliament that at least eighty-one of eighty-nine large junks used in the eastern seas were built in Siam and owned by people in Siam. These figures excluded the Hainanese junks which were small, made in China, and owned by people in China (cited in Sarasin 1977, 201). The shipbuilding industry in early Bangkok evidently had a widespread effect on the economy because of its size. It increased the number of people in the towns who had moved out of the subsistence economy and were engaged in manufacture. It also had linkage effects on other industries.

---

for use by farmers growing cash or export crops such as sugarcane, while the majority still used ploughshares made with hardwood, especially in the northeast or outside the central region. The increase of domestic iron supply created profits for those involved in exports rather than stimulating an agrarian revolution. The increase in iron production and its limited domestic use illustrates well the nature of economic change in Siam of the early Bangkok era. That is, the impact was limited to the "royalty, nobility, great merchants—the people of property" or bourgeoisie rather than spreading to the general Thai population of phrai. This limitation is considered below.

One such industry already mentioned was the timber industry which had to increase in volume. Another hardwood besides teak, redwood, was exported to China in large quantities for furniture (Crawfurd 1915, 110). Other inputs for shipbuilding included plaited rattan, used extensively in junks in place of rope, bamboo strips used to make sails, nails, and caulking (Crawfurd 1820, 173–7). A large market arose for these items and drew more Thai into involvement with the market.

Although Chinese junks were of better quality than the Indian or Arab ships previously used in these waters, they had major disadvantages of being difficult to steer, clumsy, and requiring a high ratio of crew to tonnage. A 100-ton Chinese junk needed a crew of forty while a western sloop needed only four (Crawfurd 1820, 177). A major problem of the royal junk trade was the high expenses, especially the cost of paying wages to large crews. For this reason, at the end of the early Bangkok era the upper class was very interested in improving marine shipping. Hence western-style ships were built, and some attempts made to build steamships in order to reduce expenses and increase profits from the China trade (cho ro 3-55, cs 1205).

Although Chinese junks had several failings, the large increase in the number of junks used in trading opened up opportunities for more Thai products to be sold overseas. It both encouraged and reflected the increased production for export in Siam, especially in the central region.

INTERNAL TRADE

The expansion of the urban population outside the subsistence economy, along with the establishment of Chinese communities in market production areas such as the sugar tracts, iron mines, and tin mines, was enough to make internal trade grow. Merchants also traveled around to purchase or barter for products which could be sold overseas. Migrant Chinese had the right to travel throughout the kingdom, did not have to contribute corvée, and were motivated to make a trading profit to help their families in China. They thus had the major role in expanding and extending internal trade.

The internal trade by the Chinese can be divided into two parts. First, they supplied places outside the subsistence economy with necessities such as rice, cloth, and salt. These places included the towns which were growing rapidly, especially Bangkok and Ayutthaya which became large concentrations of people with specialized production. The traders also distributed imports to the same places. Imports of luxury goods increased because of higher demand resulting from increased domestic production for the market. The Chinese themselves consumed a large volume of imports from China such as tea, fans, umbrellas, paper, joss sticks, and silk. Both coarse pottery and porcelain were in growing demand along with Chinese silk, good quality cloth, carved ivory, birds' feather fans, and dried fruit (Sarasin 1977, 190–1). Gold jewelry was imported from China to meet the taste of the upper class, and began spreading to a wider circle. There was an expanding domestic market for such items among the "royalty, nobles, great merchants—the people of property" (Crawfurd 1967, 322). The second form of internal trade was collecting goods for export, especially to China. Products such as pepper, ivory, sappanwood, balong bark, and eaglewood were found scattered all over the country. Traders might undertake both types of trading by carrying imported goods to exchange for local products destined for export.

Water transport developed significantly in the early Bangkok era (see below), helping to extend Chinese internal trading. Sea routes were greatly used. From Bangkok junks traded southward down the coast to Chumphon, Chaiya, Ban Don, Nakhon Si Thammarat, Phatthalung, and Songkhla. To the east they went from Bangkok to Bangplasoi, Bang Pakong, Bangphra, Banglamung, Rayong, Chanthaburi, Thung Yai, and Kong Island all year round without needing to wait for the monsoon (Crawfurd 1967, 406, 413–4).

Other than the Chinese, there were Thai, Khmer, Lao, Mon, and others still in the phrai system who traded on the interior routes though not along the coasts which required junks and higher investment. Also several people of various ethnicities were involved in selling from shops and market stalls (other than peddling) as the market economy expanded and more people needed to trade or barter goods. The state of the market during the Third Reign is described in an order to Phraya Chainat to appoint Amdaeng Iam as a market overseer. This order specified the tax rates that the overseer should collect from buyers and sellers, and these indicate the range of products sold in the rural market and the nature of trading. According to the order, tax was to be collected from stalls, grocery shops, vendors, and peddlers. Specific rates were levied on shops selling specific products such as big mattresses, small mattresses, pillows, lotus-peel cloth (*pha bua pok*), cotton-silk cloth, pure silk, woven goods sold by peddlers, pork, rice, Chinese silk (*phrae mai*), white gold articles, Nanking cloth, crockery, benjarong ware, nails, pans, bronze goods, bowls, oil, rattan mats, garlic, onions, Chinese candy, lead articles, footwear, medicines, rice mills, pots for heating gold leaf, stoves for making gold jewelry, tinkers, metalworkers, dyeworks, oil presses, book makers, paper makers, liquor shops, stoves for sugar-boiling with pan and pot, stoves for *khanom chin*, iron stoves, hand towels, towels, rafts selling silk, rafts selling crockery, coarse mats, lacquered cane, rafts selling chairs, dolls, muslin shirts, gourd boats (*rue taeng*), brinjal boats from the north, mango boats, custard-apple boats, boats selling lime, boats selling *khanom chin*, boats selling coconut oil, boats selling arecanut and betel-leaf, sugar spindles, boats selling sundries, boats selling dried fish (*pla salit, pla chalat, pla krai*), boats selling foreign and Indian cloth, grocery boats, boats selling pancakes, boats selling haberdashery, boats selling durian, boats selling mangosteen, boats selling shells, boats selling water bugs, boats selling liquor, boats selling shrimp paste, shops selling bamboo, shops selling wooden planks and posts, boats selling firewood, boats selling thatch, boats selling fresh fish, boats selling charcoal, boats selling earthenware water jars and bowls, and so on (cho ro 3-3, cs 1191).

This list shows the extent of trading. It also suggests that some products were handled by Chinese and others by Thai, as the Chinese had no part in certain crops and products such as the sale of fruit, and the manufacture of earthenware jars and bowls. Equally we know that certain manufacturing and trading was mostly in the hands of the Chinese including sugar production, iron making, and sale of import goods (especially those from China such as Nanking cloth and crockery).

Apart from the major economic activities covered already, there are records of considerable Chinese involvement in fishing. For instance Bangplasoi, one of the large Chinese settlements, was a large fishing centre where fish were very cheap (Pallegoix 1963, 73–4; 2000, 39). Fish were also exported in this period. Dried fish appear on the lists of products exported to China. Another country which bought large quantities of fish from Siam was Java, where some twelve to fifteen ships went annually carrying sea fish (Pallegoix 1963, 14; 2000, 7).

Chinese economic activity focused on production for export. Even the junks built were often sold when they traveled to China if the price was good or if they were so damaged it would be difficult to make the return journey. One segment of internal trade was collecting goods for export. Major crops such as pepper, sugarcane, and tobacco were intended for sale overseas. Chinese migrants were the foundations of the export economy which arose in Siam before the Bowring Treaty. This export economy had a powerful and direct impact on the limited circle of the sakdina upper class and the Chinese, but also some effect on a broader range of people because it opened up opportunities for many more people to produce for the market, especially in the central and southern regions which had better communications with major ports such as Bangkok. These people did not totally exit from the subsistence economy, but produced for the market on top of their subsistence production, not as their principal economic activity. Yet this improved their economic situation a little, enough for them to consume more imports such as Chinese crockery.

Chinese enterprise spread along the routes running through the country. The Chinese established settlements for internal trade in almost every town in the central and southern regions. Industry and market farming drew the Chinese to manufacturing and commercial farming centers. Bangkok was the largest Chinese settlement in the country because of its external and internal trade and many kinds of production. Beyond the capital, Chinese spread into towns under *mahatthai* and the towns of the south, as shown by the records of the Chinese head tax. These records probably underestimate the true numbers because of government inefficiency and corruption. The main Chinese settlements with over a thousand Chinese were Ayutthaya, Nakhon Chaisi, Chachoengsao, and Phitsanulok. Towns with fewer Chinese included Suphanburi which sent poll tax for 432 Chinese. In the south, the largest Chinese settlement was the mining town of Phangnga. Other mining centers with several Chinese included Thalang, Phuket, and Takua Thung. This list omits large towns such as Chaiya, Nakhon Si Thammarat, and Songkhla for which there are no comparable data (cho ro 3-52, cs 1196; cho ro 3-185, cs 1202).

Chinese immigration affected not only the economy but also society and administration. This will be mentioned here only briefly as many others have dealt with the issue, and it is not the central concern of this work.

The Chinese success in accumulating wealth from their pioneer investments in trade and production made the sakdina upper class take interest in new forms of wealth different from old forms based on the control of people in the phrai system. This trend was evident from late Ayutthaya but became more marked in the early Bangkok era. Wealth (meaning also political power) could be gained by accumulating property. In some cases this method might be more important than controlling manpower. This was the first step towards a money economy.

One example of progress in this direction was the government's preference for using Chinese wage labor rather than conscripted phrai. Many public works in the early Bangkok era were carried out with wage labor. At the same time, government began to prefer that phrai pay commutation fees in cash rather than doing corvée. Some taxes formerly collected in kind, such as rice tax, were collected in cash from the Third Reign. Government was able to achieve this conversion because cash had spread widely enough in the country. In other words, people had the cash to pay instead of supplying labor or products (Sarasin 1977, chapter 10).

This change towards a market economy was the basis on which government was able to expand tax farming in the Third Reign. Taxes were collected only from articles which were "profitable," that is, were produced for the market not for consumption in the subsistence economy. Without such production for the market, the thirty-eight new taxes in the Third Reign would not have been possible. The tax farming system was introduced by the Chinese, and employed many Chinese as tax farmers. This was possible because of economic change. "By the mid 1820s, there was a sufficient level of production above subsistence—a situation arising from the expansion of trade and from peaceful internal conditions—for the king to think in terms of large-scale internal revenue collection.... The tax-farming system was complementary to the reduction of corvée labor and the encouragement to cultivate cash crops" (Hong 1981, 138, 140, see also 135–71). All this was the basis for the collapse of the phrai system in the later period. Without this economic and social foundation, the upper classes could not have responded to the Bowring Treaty with equanimity in the way they did.

INTERNAL TRANSPORT

The study of market production leads naturally to the study of internal transport since the two go together. Without good internal transport, market production and exports would remain limited in scope.

Transport routes were developed in the early Bangkok era. Water was still the main means of internal communication. Political control, trade flows, and tax flows all relied mainly on water-borne communications. From late Ayutthaya, foreign trade stimulated improvements in water-based communications, especially in the Chaophraya delta below Ayutthaya. Several canals were dug to shorten the distance along the Chaophraya River between Ayutthaya and the rivermouth. At least ten canals were dug in the delta in the Ayutthaya period (Paitoon 1978, 12). Also since the Ayutthaya period, canals were dug to connect the Chaophraya with nearby rivers in the lower central region, such as the Samrong Canal to the Bang Pakong River and Mahachai Canal to the Prachin River.

In the early Bangkok era, canals and dams were built to keep sea water out of agricultural areas, and also as highways to assist tax collection or military operations. The Saensaep Canal was built towards the east for sending reinforcements to support armies fighting in Cambodia (Paitoon 1978, 14). Other canals were dug or repaired to facilitate the flow of tax revenues to the capital, especially in the central region during the Third Reign (Vella 1957, 24). In fact there are records from the Second Reign about projects to repair canals but these projects failed through attempting to economize on labor. To overcome silting of the Bang Kaeo Canal and make it usable in the dry season, the king proposed to build a barrage to divert water from the river into the canal. This seemed more economical than re-digging the canal, but the barrage collapsed in the flood season (Thiphakorawong 1961a, 51–2, 63). In the Third Reign when the financial position of the government had improved, Chinese wage labor was hired for construction or repair of four large canal projects. In the biggest of these projects, the king commanded Chaophraya Siphiphat to oversee hiring Chinese wage labor to dig the Bang Khanak Canal to meet the Phrakhanong Canal, and to repair the long Phrakhanong Canal of over 1,337 *sen.*[164] In addition, the king had Chinese hired to dig the Sunak Hon (howling dog) Canal, along with a side canal to Ban Phohak designed to slow the silting in the main canal. All this was completed around 1837. Earlier in 1831, Phraya Choduek was commanded to hire Chinese for digging the Bangkhunthian Canal to join the Dan Wat Paknam Canal, and two Bang Bon side canals (Arunnipha 1938, 103; Thiphakorawong 1961b, 187). A ballad (*klon phleng yao*) composed by Nai Mi in praise of King Rama III refers to the digging of another canal, the old Samsen short-cut canal which had become so silted that boatmen had to hire buffaloes to drag boats along it (as mentioned in some of Sunthon Phu's *nirat*). Nai Mi's poem ran, "For digging the short-cut canal at Samsen to the rivermouth, the public works head conscripted skilled Chinese to complete the work. Now that is done the canal is well-known all over the world, its reputation has spread to other towns all over the place" (Sunthon Phu 1960, 680–1).

These canals extended not only between the capital and the rivermouth, but also outwards from the Chaophraya River across the lower central region. Although no direct commercial benefit may have been intended, merchants used these canal routes a lot. Similarly, building a fort at the mouth of the Chaophraya was ostensibly a purely military project, but merchants found a use for the fort as a refuge against natural dangers and robbers, as mentioned by Nai Mi: "At the rivermouth is a fort and armory where people coming and going from all over the world can take refuge along with their boats and rafts. For this peace of mind let us give thanks to the king" (Sunthon Phu 1960, 680). The *nirat* written by Sunthon Phu and other poets about journeys along these routes mention the rafts of various kinds of merchants using these canals. On his way to worship Phra Thaen Dongrang, Sunthon Phu passed through Bang Ma Hon (Howling Dog Village) and described the congestion of merchant boats on the Sunak Hon Canal:

164. A sen is equivalent to 40 meters, so this is 3.3 kilometers.

Approaching Howling Dog Village,
There are so many boats that the men wait holding their poles.
Rafts of Chinese, Mon, and Thai strung together
Move this way and that, bumping and crashing, in a merry tumult.
Some push this way, some that, some upstream, some down,
Seeking a way through but meeting obstruction.
They dodge the sappanwood boat, hit the salt boat, jam up against the firewood boat,
Vent their anger, raise their voices, and curse.
(Sunthon Phu 1960, 207)

Whatever the government's intentions in developing internal transport in the early Bangkok era, these routes expanded the boundaries of trading activity. They facilitated the task of collecting export products for despatch by boat to Bangkok. In other words, these canals serviced the export economy as well as achieving whatever else their builders intended. They made it possible for market production to be established over a wider area than Bangkok alone.

Apart from government, private interests also invested in repairing canals, such as the Bang Chueak Canal where boats and rafts had to be dragged by buffaloes: "Along the way through the middle of the settlement there are no houses, only open *sala* with no walls. The new *chek* Chinese and the Thai all want to build factories. They dig the earth out of the streams and waterways. The whole wide plain looks desolate under dark clouds" (Sunthon Phu 1960, 373). The interesting thing in this Sunthon Phu poem is that the canal being dug had nothing to do with irrigation since it passed through an empty area without houses, people, or ricefields. At the same time, even though it led to Phra Pathom Chedi, it was not another government project designed to facilitate travel to a religious site as Phra Pathom Chedi was not a popular place of worship in this period. Clearly people were improving this route specifically for trade. In fact, Bang Chueak Canal led to many densely settled communities such as Nakhon Chaisi.

Although there were such private projects to improve transport in this period, the records are very sparse. The key point, however, is that these projects themselves are evidence of development. Records show that wage labor was used in water transport. The accounts of their travels by Sunthon Phu and Nai Mi show interesting differences arising from their respective statuses and different periods. Sunthon Phu usually traveled in a small boat paddled by his disciples, children, or companions. But when Nai Mi traveled to Suphanburi as a tax collector he was able to hire "lots of *chek* as wage labor to paddle the boat." Tax collectors like Nai Mi were not the only ones hiring Chinese rowers. Nai Mi refers to a spot where many boats were passing: "the Chinese hired laborers shout 'yea yea', and 'you lady come eat with me' and 'where you go.' They raise their voices to show off to the women like playful monkeys" (Sunthon Phu 1960, 803–4). Chinese labor became engaged in transportation because of the increased demand for transport, and because of the Chinese laborers' need for cash wages. The fact that those owning or hiring the boats had money to pay the rowers is another indicator of the extent of the money economy.

Another development of waterway transport was the use of sail instead of human labor. The shortage of labor (because it was all captured in the phrai system) and increase of long-distance travel stimulated improvement in the technique of river transport. On Sunthon Phu's travels described in his *nirat* he tended always to use human labor. But on one of his later trips to Suphanburi, he sailed for certain sections: "the wind blows smoothly and softly so we can use sails" and "the winds billow the sails like dancing" (Sunthon Phu 1960, 289–90). This improvement was achieved totally by private enterprise as there are no records of government initiative, although government activities may unintentionally have provided the stimulus by extending the boundaries of travel. For example in the Second Reign, the court made some attempts to collect information for mapping the country (Crawfurd 1967, 332).

Sea travel also increased, facilitating relations between the central plain and the eastern or southern regions. Coastal shipping has been mentioned above in the account of trade. The main purpose was to collect products for export, and to distribute imports to local communities. But people moved as well as goods. In other words, better sea transport facilitated contact between people over a broader area. For example, there was a regular passenger boat running between Bangkok and Chaiya in the south, taking four to twenty-four days depending on the monsoon. Chaiya became the regular point of embarkation for southerners traveling to Bangkok (Burney 1911, 210). As a result, Chaiya became one of the major commercial centers of the south with a dense population. Nai Mi mentioned Chaiya during his journey to Thalang:

> To Chaiya town,
> A big town with huge houses
> Full of phrai and people,
> Looking prosperous, happy, and comfortable.
> Shops line both sides of the streets
> Full of people noisily buying and selling,
> Chit-chatting, both men and women,
> Shouting the sale of *luk phaniang* [*pithecolobium jiringa*], arguing noisily,
> Selling fresh plums, prunes and damsons (*mapring maprang masang*),
> Delicious durian for ten to a salueng.
>
> (Sunthon Phu 1960, 652)

Easier communications were a result of economic expansion, and also a cause of future expansion. They facilitated the quicker flow of goods, and also the transfer of people, ideas, standards, values, and preferences.

Records about the development of transport routes are sparse, but the expansion of transport itself indicates that the development was more extensive than the surviving records indicate. One major consequence was that people's horizons in life were broadened. This comes through in early Bangkok literature. When Khun Phaen from Suphanburi goes to fight in Chiang Mai, his baggage includes "Phetchabun tobacco, so pungent" (*Khun chang khun phaen*, 171). Khun Phaen's *Fa fuen* (Skystorm) sword is made with iron and other metals including "Fluid metal. Ore cast at the Phrasaeng mine. Iron ore and metal from Kamphaeng[phet] and Namphi. Gold. Bronze. Nak [an alloy] from Aceh." (*Khun chang khun phaen*, 327). The lives of people from Suphanburi and Kanchanaburi had become indirectly connected with far-off places whose names they associated with specific products including Phetchabun, Phrasaeng, Kamphaengphet, and even foreign locations such as Aceh in northern Sumatra. Trade and transport broadened people's horizons.

THE LIMITS OF THE MARKET ECONOMY IN EARLY BANGKOK

The above account show the rapid expansion of the export economy as a result of the early Bangkok governments' trade policies. The people directly involved in this export economy were the sakdina upper class of royalty and nobility, and the Chinese merchants and entrepreneurs in export production. We have seen that this export economy could not avoid affecting the lives of many others not directly involved in international trade. Some were drawn into market production on top of the usual subsistence production of the Thai. In other words, a market economy was becoming established in Siam, closely connected to the export economy. The next issue is to establish how extensive was the market economy, and how wide its social impact.

The terms market economy and money economy are closely connected and in some cases identical, hence the two terms are often used interchangeably. The expansion of the market economy requires money as a medium of exchange. Without sufficient money, a market economy cannot escape from sufficiency production. However, it is important to understand that while the market economy and money economy are closely related, they are not identical in this case. We are studying economic growth at an early stage of the market economy. The volume of money in circulation in the early Bangkok era was larger than in the prior period and affected many people, but it was still rather restricted. For the most part, money circulated within a limited circle of people. The expansion of the market economy was constrained by the small volume of money in circulation. Many goods were still bartered in the old way. Market production still made use of old systems of barter as long as they had a purpose. The expansion of the market economy often resulted in a shortage of money which deflated the prices of goods produced domestically and made them competitive in the world market.

The early Bangkok government seemed to realize the need to increase the supply of cash in the market, but whether it considered this need was critical is another matter. There are records from the Third Reign showing government was interested in establishing a mint in order to replace cowries with copper dollars like those used in Singapore. But after studying the machinery needed, King Rama III was not satisfied and canceled the order placed with Hunter (Moore 1914). Bullet money was probably still produced in a way that was slow, inefficient, and inadequate for market needs. There was no idea of producing paper money to replace specie at this stage.

This shortage of cash gave rise to a lot of "red money" (i.e., counterfeit) in the early Bangkok period. This is evident from King Mongkut's later remark during his own reign that the production and use of red money "nowadays is less than before"

(*Prachum prakat ratchakan thi 4*, I, 120). The problem of limited cash in circulation became more critical in the Fourth Reign after the Bowring Treaty accelerated the growth of the market economy. The government had to permit the use of foreign currency (*Prachum prakat ratchakan thi 4*, I, 178–82), and set up a mint for mechanized production of cash to meet market demand.

Because the money economy did not grow in pace with the market economy, capitalism did not develop fully in the early Bangkok era. Trader-nobles and merchants had rather limited amounts of cash. Burney stated that any noble with cash of 20,000 baht, or a shop owner with 10,000 baht, would be considered cash rich (Burney 1911, 229). At the same time, Malloch stated that Siamese government's cash revenues were no more than 2.5 million baht a year. Even though the government was the country's largest merchant, this money was not invested in trading but used to support the royal family, pay *biawat* allowances to the nobles, and finance the king's private spending, meaning mostly construction or repair of wat. In the treasury there was no more than 100,000 baht (Burney 1911, 229). Because growth of the money economy lagged behind the market economy, the upper class tried to sustain the sakdina system for the benefit of their own trading and export production. They continued to make use of forced labor at no cost, and leveraged the sakdina administrative system to support their trade. In the Second Reign, Phraya Ratchaburi was ordered to forward sappanwood "felled by conscripts" and purchase additional supplies up to the capacity of the junks leaving Bangkok for China. If he failed to meet the junks' sailing date, he "would be punished" (cho ro 2-3/3, cs 1183). This case shows how the sakdina system made it possible to trade even though capital was in short supply. Most of the sappanwood cargo was supplied through sakdina power over conscript labor, and only the balance purchased with money capital. Both old and new methods operated in tandem to make profits from export. The trend towards capitalism, and the survival of sakdina were muddled together. Other developments followed the same pattern. Labor was freed but only within limits. The corvée period was reduced, but the phrai system was certainly not abandoned because many people did not have the cash to pay commutation fees instead of corvée, and because the conscription system still delivered benefits to the upper class. The complete freeing of labor came only later, after the economy and system of administration had changed, the upper class no longer reaped much benefit from conscript labor which lacked knowledge and skills, and the government had no further use for phrai labor as government had withdrawn from foreign trade. Early Bangkok literature had the same dual character. It showed a tendency to become more bourgeois, but at the same time retained many traditions of sakdina literature from Ayutthaya, as will be explained below.

We have seen that the "royalty, nobility, great merchants—the people of property" were engaged in trade and the export economy, and became the centre of Siam's fledgling market economy. But to what extent did this market economy affect or incorporate other groups in society? There is no clear answer supported by reliable documents, but we can extrapolate from records about internal production and trade that the market economy was not limited within these three elite groups. Many others entered into the market economy, either fully or partially over their productive life.

Rice production, the main occupation of the people, was affected by the market economy. Before 1855, rice production for export was not a significant element in the economy, even in the central region. Comparing the size of the population to the volume of rice production suggests that the supply was needed to feed the growing population and any surplus for export must have been small. Records from the Second Reign show the Thai population was steadily increasing (Crawfurd 1915, 141). In addition, wars in areas around the kingdom required another large supply of rice. In 1839, Malloch reported that rice was ranked only fifth among exports behind sugar, cotton, sappanwood, and tin. The government probably still controlled rice exports closely in order to keep the price of rice down, and as a result, rice farmers had little incentive to increase production (Paitoon 1978, 19). Despite the small role of rice exports, rice production for the market began to expand to feed the large numbers of Chinese migrants who did not produce their own rice but bought their supplies in the urban markets, especially Bangkok. Industry and trade depended on supplies of rice to feed the people involved. Areas where export crops were grown also did not produce their own rice and had to buy supplies. Rising market demand for rice stimulated farmers in many locations to plant additional area in parallel with their own subsistence production. The area around Bangkok was not a zone of intensive rice growing. Most of the paddy land close to Bangkok was held only as temporary occupation (*tra chong*), and the main area of the country's rice production was in the north of the lower delta above Ayutthaya where most land was held as permanent occupation (*tra daeng*) (Paitoon 1978, 19–20). Bangkok got its rice supplies from this area (Paitoon 1978, 31), and government's interest in rice growing focused on this tract, and not on the lower delta. The paddy-season rainfall reports which governors and officials sent to Bangkok in the Third Reign all came from this tract (cho ro 3-6, cs 1193). The need for rice to feed the urban areas in the lower delta stimulated production of a surplus in this tract. But this production for the market was embedded within subsistence production. Studies in 1908 showed most land in the delta was held in small plots by commoners.

Apart from Bangkok, areas growing export crops also needed rice supplies from elsewhere. Pallegoix reported that in Chanthaburi in 1838 rice growing was neglected and the supply was barely sufficient for the province's inhabitants (Pallegoix 1963, 73; 2000, 38).

As rice production for the market was embedded inside subsistence production, collecting this rice to supply communities which did not grow their own was not a simple matter. Traders had to locate supplies left over from subsistence consumption, and often acquire them by bartering trade goods. The trading networks involved were widespread and complex. There is no detailed study of this trade, but records mention Chinese at the lowest levels of the trading network, who "spread out in the plains and even in forests and mountains.... to barter cloth, cutlery and Chinese hardware against rice, cotton and various products of the provinces which they travel through" (Pallegoix 1963, 305; 2000, 171). These peddlers sold the rice on to larger merchants with enough capital to transport it down to Bangkok. It probably passed through the hands of other merchants in Bangkok before reaching consumers in Bangkok or other communities. The price of rice in Bangkok was low because government had a policy to keep it that way, and hence the price which Chinese peddlers paid to the rice growers must have been very low indeed. Imports were best for such barter as the rice farmers did not know their true price, and also were tempted by their exotic origin.

This nature of the internal rice trade helps explain how the growth of the market economy could precede the growth of the money economy. There was no need for cash to circulate as far as the rice farmers. It could remain limited within the circle of the Chinese merchants and sakdina upper class. The peddlers acquired rice by bartering goods. Higher-level merchants sold it on, for ever increasing cash amounts. The higher up the economic system, the more one was in the money economy. People in the city were more in the money economy than those in the countryside, the Chinese junk traders more than the peddlers, the Bangkok nobles more than their counterparts in the provinces, and so on.

The network of rice trading which the Chinese established from the early Bangkok era greatly assisted the rice trade which accelerated after the Bowring Treaty when rice became Siam's leading export. In the second half of the nineteenth century, competition between Chinese and westerners to dominate the rice milling industry and rice export ended with a decisive victory for the Chinese. The networks for rice trading begun by the Chinese since early Bangkok lay behind the Chinese victory over the westerners.

Salt was a market product from the old days since salt is not found everywhere and cannot be manufactured in every region. Salt was traded in the old days, but in limited amount and extent. The salt trade extended more widely in the early Bangkok era as a result of improved transport, and expanded in volume because of demand from some export-oriented food industries such as salted fish and salted meat. Crawfurd (1915, 113–4) reported that Siamese sea salt of good quality was taken to Bangkok and other densely populated places along the maze of small canals and waterways. He thought the trade in salt was the largest segment of trade in the hands of local people.

The large volume of overseas trade greatly increased production for the market. Conscription and tax-in-kind failed to supply the full amount demanded in foreign trade, constantly forcing the government to resort to purchase. In the Third Reign, Phraya Nakhon was ordered to purchase pepper to fill up junks going to China (Waraphon 1979, 99–100). As Kiattisak Wongmukda (1980, 57–8) concludes, early Bangkok external trade increased the circulation of money because such purchases for export encouraged people to produce. Chinese peddlers penetrated into every nook and cranny to purchase goods for loading onto the junks. The combined volume of their purchases probably exceeded that of the government. These peddling networks survived into the later period. Records from the Fifth Reign show that Chinese who settled in Kanchanaburi and Ratchaburi to produce tobacco and sugar also purchased the sappanwood which was plentifully available in the forests of that area (Bock 1884, 95). Apart from the Chinese, "people of property" in the countryside, especially those in the lower ranks of the nobility with some ready capital, bought up local products to sell on for a profit. As a rich man of Suphanburi, Khun Chang purchased eaglewood from "Karen and Lawa in the big forest who came to weigh eaglewood" (*Khun chang khun phaen*, 377). Buying up goods to be sold on for export drew several people into the market economy.

In this way market production spread to the Thai. Writing about Chainat in 1834, Pallegoix stated that the small population of around 3,000 people was engaged in growing rice, tobacco, arecanut, and cotton, making torches, and constructing bamboo rafts which people floated down to sell in Bangkok because Chainat bamboo was of good quality (Pallegoix 1963, 73; 2000, 44). The crops which the Chainat people planted were "taxable," meaning that they were saleable. Cultivating tobacco, areca, and cotton and making torches using rubber oil could be done alongside paddy farming. All these items had a market both inside and outside the country. A significant part of the life of the people of Chainat was in the market economy. Similarly in the region of Sam Roi Yot (three hundred peaks) which Nai Mi traveled through on his way to Thalang, "the villagers of this area are not stupid, they plant their fields full of watermelon to sell" (Sunthon Phu 1960, 646). Muen Han, a character in *Khun chang khun phaen*, also farmed for the market, as his field is surrounded by a high fence and "teeming with workers"(*Khun chang khun phaen*, 305). Such market production brought buying and selling into more people's lives in place of subsistence production and exchange labor within the small community. In *Khun chang khun phaen* (p. 137), when Nang Thong Prasi considers marrying Phlai Kaeo off, she sends someone to "go to the saw mill and look into buying a newly made house. Take these three *chang* and buy it quickly." The life of urban people below the elite increasingly involved buying everyday goods because subsistence production was beginning to decline. When Bowring came to Siam he found that the lower cloths (*pha nung*) worn by ordinary people were all made from imported cotton (Bowring 1969, I, 238). The number of people involved in the market economy provided a basis for import of consumer goods. Although western consumer goods had a smaller market than those from China, an American merchant during the Third Reign spoke of the future for such goods with optimism:

> The chief merchants of Siam are the King, his ministers, the Chinese, and old women. They require from Europe and the United States arms and ammunition; perhaps a few military ornaments; coarse cutlery, glass ware, white cotton goods, which should be no less than two cubits in width [36–44 inches]; cotton twist, from No. 20 to 30; Siamese dresses, three yard long by forty inches broad, in star patterns, on red, green, and blue grounds, which colours should be bright; long ells, red and green; furniture chintz; ladies cloth, red, yellow, green, light purple, and light blue; steel in small bars, the size of nail iron, which for this market should be put up in tubs instead of cases, one hundred of which are enough at a time. American cottons are now sought for, though afforded at a higher price, because they have been found to be much more durable. There is an opening for the introduction of American cottons, through Bankok, to the countries lying north of Siam. (Ruschenberger 1838, 281–2, using information from Hunter)

The nature of the Chinese junk trade, as noted above, with several small merchants clubbing together and serving as the crew in return for cargo space for their export goods, helped to spread the export economy because these small merchants bought up export goods from people producing them outside the sakdina economy. They had to use fully commercial means to acquire the goods and make their profit. Those places which produced directly for export had the most intensive market economy of buying and selling. In describing the improved economic status of Thalang's people as a result of the development of tin mining, Nai Mi painted a favorable picture of the transition from subsistence to market economy:

> There are *laoka*[165] junks coming to trade,
> Moored at the end of the town with many sails flapping.
> The variety of goods available makes the townspeople merry and content.
> On the shore the market is full of people sitting close together.
> Tin exchanges for dollars, back and forth, bought and sold.
> Rows of Thai, Chinese, Indian, and Javanese sell patterned cloths
> And Chinese silk in myriad colors. Thalang people dress smartly.
> (Sunthon Phu 1960, 665)

Though mining attracted many Chinese, the Thai were not totally excluded. A record from Phangnga early in the Third Reign mentions 500 Chinese miners and 2,000 Thai and others, with another 500 Chinese and 600–700 Thai working in the mines further to the north (Burney 1911, 205–6). Such economic change, though more concentrated among the "royalty, nobility, great merchants—the people of property" had impact on the Thai population as well.

Although the money economy grew more slowly than the market economy, the use of cash as medium of exchange increased significantly, leading towards the full development of a money economy in the later period. Each year the government injected a large amount of cash into the market. In the Second Reign, Crawfurd estimated that the government's revenue in the form of cash or tax-in-kind which could be immediately converted to cash was 5 million baht. Each year government used up this money almost totally in various activities, leaving no more in the treasury than 240,000 baht, plus some Spanish dollars ready to be melted down into bullet money (Crawfurd 1967, 388–9). Chinese junks which traded between Bangkok and China brought some Chinese cash for melting down into bullet money (Gutzlaff 1832, 55–8). Most imported cash was converted into bullet money rather than accumulating in the royal treasury (Ingram 1955, 32–3). In the Third Reign, taxes collected in cash exceeded 2 million baht (Ruschenberger 1838, 283–4), and King Rama III used much of this revenue for building and repairing wat—an estimated 5 million baht between his ascent of the throne and 1839 (Kiattisak 1980, 29). The government's trading and expenditure in the Third Reign greatly increased the circulation of money (Vella 1957, 19–20).

165. Possibly meaning "big." [T]

One government expenditure in the early Bangkok era which injected cash into the market was the trend to use wage labor instead of conscripts for some public works, such as hiring Chinese for canal digging, as mentioned above. Skilled work was almost totally done by wage labor, especially in the Third Reign, because the results were perceived to be better than with conscripts. Nai Mi wrote about using wage labor to paint Jataka murals at Wat Krueawan: "By royal favor the artisans are paid one baht per panel as they demanded. With great merit and faith, there is no need to find painters as they keep coming, enticed by cash, and sit concentrating on their work, so happy they feel no back-ache. Those who came to find work are content, and all compete to show their skill" (Sunthon Phu 1960, 697–8). For the large amount of construction in the palace in this reign, the king hired Chinese and Thai artisans and rewarded them with *biawat* allowances or higher positions (Sunthon Phu 1960, 681).

As the volume of money in circulation increased, government preferred to receive cash in commutation of corvée. Commutation was introduced during the Ban Phlu Luang period, but not because the court needed cash at that time. Government still needed labor more than cash, and the proceeds from commutation were used to hire replacement laborers (Busakorn 1972, 296–7). But in early Bangkok, the government's need for cash increased as it preferred to use wage labor for skilled tasks and needed cash to hire them. In the Third Reign, the government stopped collecting rice tailings (*hang khao*), rice land tax, and all kinds of forced purchase of rice. It demanded cash instead at a flat rate of one salueng one fueang per rai for both categories of rice land (*na khukho* or *na fangloi*), but only on the cultivated portion of *na fangloi* (*Prachum prakat ratchakan thi 4*, II, 162–4). This change from kind to cash was very important since it increased the government's cash revenues. It also indicates that the village economy had changed far enough into a money economy for rice taxes to be paid in cash.

Apart from this change in rice taxes, many other new taxes were imposed on agricultural and industrial products during the Third Reign, especially on crops associated mostly with the Thai population. Taxes on gardens, orchards, and rubber oil indicate that these products were being produced commercially. Government was not interested in taxing products in the subsistence economy (except rice), but only items planted or manufactured "for selling at a profit." The proliferation of taxes reflects the expansion of the market economy and money economy in the Third Reign (see the new taxes in Thiphakorawong 1961b, 182–3).

The ability of the government to move from extracting labor and goods to levying taxes in cash suggests how much people had become engaged in the money economy. There was no major revolt by the people of the central region who were those most affected by this change in their obligations to government. This stands in contrast to areas outside the central region which rose in revolt against having to pay taxes in cash during the Fifth Reign. In early Bangkok the money economy was still geographically circumscribed, but within that circumscribed area it incorporated a wide circle of people. Records from the Third Reign show that increasing numbers were able to commute their corvée to cash. For example in 1845 people from a village in the Ayutthaya region who were conscripted to transport slabs of stone from Lopburi to Bangkok to repair Wat Phra Chetuphon preferred to pay money instead (Hong

1981, 97). Records about the appointment of market overseers, as well as passages from the literature of this era, attest to the amount of buying and selling which arose with the extension of the money economy.

Society was affected in many ways (see below). Increased sale and exchange in early Bangkok threw up new problems which old systems of administration and law could not deal with. Administrators resorted to religion for help in managing these problems—an age-old reaction in Siam. They hoped that religious teachings would be effective in combating commercial exploitation. In the inscriptions of Wat Phra Chetuphon, for example, the catalogue of sins and hells includes certain "sins" which come with the market economy and money economy:

> Anyone who dishonestly mixes paddy husk, shrunken grains, soil, and sand into paddy or milled rice, and fraudulently sells the result to make profit will go to hell number four, *Phutsanarok*, where there is a river of flaming husk and shrunken rice which they must eat until it burns their stomach and intestines, and shreds their liver and kidneys out through the anus....
>
> Anyone who dishonestly buys high-value goods at too low a price, in violation of the Five Aggregates (*benchakan*), will fall into hell number seven, *Tamphotnarok*. (*Prachum charuek wat phra chetuphon*,[166] 164–5)

BOURGEOISIE AND BOURGEOIS CULTURE

In the western world, economic growth was created by private capital. Sometimes this is pictured as the only route to economic growth, and factors which promote private capitalism are sought to explain economic growth. But in the east, economic growth may have evolved differently. In Siam of the early Bangkok era in particular, economic growth arose from the government's involvement in foreign trade, and the resulting inflow of Chinese who founded a domestic market economy. Thus the Thai bourgeoisie did not arise independently from sakdina. It was not a group which escaped the political power of sakdina by forming new trading communities which developed into politically independent towns. The Thai bourgeoisie emerged with the support of sakdina power. It was part and parcel of sakdina. In fact, members of the sakdina upper class, who were the major beneficiaries of economic growth, converted themselves gradually into a bourgeoisie. They built a power base in property and trading to supplement their control over phrai labor power. The early Bangkok bourgeoisie means the sakdina upper class combined with many Chinese or those of Chinese heritage, some of who had already been absorbed into sakdina and others who had not. This group had a stranglehold on political power under the sakdina system. They constituted the upper class of Thai society and played a role in developing the society's high culture. What these people created, consumed, and enjoyed was accepted both then and later as representative of Thai culture. This culture was grounded in

166. Panca skandha or the five aggregates are the elements of being or individuality, roughly: form, sensation, mentality, will, and consciousness. [T]

sakdina culture, but modified by new ways of life which began to distinguish the Bangkok upper class from its Ayutthayan predecessor.

The bourgeoisie's pattern of consumption was no different from that of the Ayutthaya upper class in that both favored products from overseas. But the number of people who could consume luxuries increased greatly in early Bangkok.

British cotton cloth was popular from the start of this period. Burney reported that imports were large and increasing, and that usage would expand further were the prices lower. Senior members of the nobility, especially women, liked to wear foreign patterned and pleated cotton cloth. Lengths of muslin were imported and dyed for offering to monks (Burney 1911, 100). As already noted, not many years after Burney's account, an American merchant found that imported cotton cloth was widely used among ordinary people. The Chinese introduced the popularity of drinking tea to the "royalty, nobility, great merchants—the people of property." Tea was imported from China for sale to the tea-drinking Chinese migrants, and the habit spread to the Thai, initially just those of high status but later a wider circle (Ruschenberger 1838, 413). Agencies were established in Bangkok to order luxury imports. After Hunter left the country in 1844, he wrote a report to the Governor-General of India stating there were five such permanent import agencies in Bangkok, all owned by British subjects. His was called Hunter and Hays, while another was owned by a Madrassi, and three were branches of Bombay stores (Moore 1914, 29). The popularity of foreign goods expanded because more people had the ability to purchase them. In *Khun chang khun phaen* (p. 359), when Nang Wanthong, who is an early Bangkok bourgeois character, is packing her belongings to chase after her wayward man, Khun Phaen, she "wrapped everything in a silk European handkerchief."

Being involved in trade or market production in order to acquire consumer goods was considered perfectly respectable among the bourgeoisie. Being successful enough to own a junk was something to flaunt, in the way that Somdet Chaophraya Borommaha Prayurawong boasted to Bowring. Local notables portrayed in *Khun chang khun phaen* exemplify the petty bourgeoisie. They have some relations with officialdom but their real occupation is business or producing for the market. Phan Sonyotha dies because "he went to trade with the Lawa and caught a fever" (*Khun chang khun phaen*, 39). Nang Thong Prasi flees from the king's punishment to settle in Kanchanaburi where she uses capital brought along with her to grow crops for the market: "Bit by bit, she began to earn a living and to acquire some money and property. She redeemed some slaves and phrai so they could farm. She bought land, elephants, horses, cattle, and buffaloes. She acquired property through trading. People looked up to her with respect." (*Khun chang khun phaen*, 32). Nang Kaeo Kiriya follows Khun Phaen to Ayutthaya when he is put in jail. She uses her little capital to "do good business selling low-priced goods like fruit, sweets, oranges, and lychees from a dry goods store with signs for 'good astringent betel,' 'Phetchabun tobacco,' and 'fresh banana leaves'" (*Khun chang khun phaen*, 430). The more Nang Thong Prasi's status improves, the more she invests in commercial agriculture, redeeming slaves, and retaining them to work on her many rice plots: "Lawa, Mon, and Lao servants came back from the fields. They lit smoky fires to ward off the mosquitoes and midges, as was the custom upcountry among the paddy fields." (*Khun chang khun phaen*, 482). Writers described all these activities without any shade of disapproval or disdain. The heroes in some literary works of this time were former merchants. Kraithong is an example.[167]

The early Bangkok upper class developed more detailed methods of accounting for use in their businesses. For example, accounts which junk captains reported to government about trade to China itemized the investment, expenses, and selling prices in cash broken down to salueng and fueang (e.g., cho ro 3-42 and 42/2, cs 1205). Such accounts reflected the nature of business enterprise. They showed what profit was made from what product and in what way, and they also showed the merchants' weaknesses. The early Bangkok bourgeois export merchants correctly understood that their own weakness was excessive expenses because Chinese junks were not efficient for carrying low-price, high-volume merchandise. Hence these bourgeois invested in constructing western-style sloops to make their business more "rational," and to reduce the element of speculation and politics in their business. In addition, business ventures such as planting sugarcane and manufacturing sugar using totally wage labor (see above) were long-term ventures, not one-off profit-seeking. This sort of enterprise increased the "rationality" of the bourgeoisie's activities, and was the basis of future development towards capitalism (Bendix 1962, 52–5).

This "rationality" orientated the bourgeois towards accepting western culture. Building western-style sloops was one example, and the idea of steamships was in their minds for a long time. Burney (1911, 219) related how the first visit of a steamship to Rangoon excited wide interest among the Thai nobles at Phangnga and Saiburi (Kedah). As noted above, late in the Third Reign there were attempts to build steamships. From early Bangkok, many bourgeois including King Mongkut, Somdet Chaophraya Borommaha Sisuriyawong, and Chaophraya Thiphakorawong sought western scientific knowledge through western missionaries. They were all involved in trading in some way, and, as is well known, were all interested in western science.

Literacy was not confined to the leading bourgeois, but spread among the bourgeois in general. Primers for reading and writing Thai appeared for the first time in this period, including *Prathom ko ka*, *Subinkuman*, *Prathom mala*, and *Prathom Chindamani lem 2*. Other literary works were used for practicing reading such as *Suea kho*, *Chanthakhorop*, *Anirut*, *Samutthakhot*, *Phetmongkut*, *Sangthong*, *Kaki*, *Phraya Chatthan*, *Sawatdiraksa*, and *Phra parammat* (Benchawan 1975, 11-–20). These books differed from the *Chindamani* of King Narai's time in that they were not meant for adults but were true primers (Chai 1974, 189). Literacy was prized. The inscriptions of Wat Phra Chetuphon state: "Because of this learned family's background, their noble bloodline and rank, they all studied to be literate, and knew how to compose poetry" (*Prachum charuek wat phra chetuphon*, 497). When children in the almshouse beside the Srisunthon gate showed their eagerness for study, the ruling class responded by teaching them the primary disciplines of reading, writing,

167. The idea that Khun Chang is the only bourgeois character in *Khun chang khun phaen* is baseless. In truth, all the main characters are bourgeois. *Khun chang khun phaen* (in the version currently known) is a truly bourgeois work of literature—about bourgeois characters who face bourgeois problems and solve them in bourgeois ways.

and arithmetic (Chai 1974, 46). Also in the Third Reign, missionaries established schools in Bangkok for Chinese children. A record dated 1838 shows that two or three such schools were already in existence, and another was opened. Establishing and developing these schools was not easy because Thai mothers saw little benefit in western culture, although Chinese fathers saw the value of education.

The interest in education, at least for literacy, increased the number of literate people. Some rough figures collected by missionaries in 1845 show that among 1,308 people (1,017 male and 273 female, adding error in the source) who attended the missionaries' clinic for fever, 414 could read, 513 could not, and 391 gave no information (*Chinese Repository*, 15, 2, February 1846, 82–3). According to these figures the literacy rate was 45.15 per cent which is not high, but those attending the missionaries' clinic were probably low class and mostly Chinese. Figures collected among the Thai population would probably have been higher, and much higher among the Thai bourgeoisie. Bowring stated that many Thai were literate (Bowring 1969, I, 143).

The attention to literacy was probably confined to the urban bourgeoisie. Their children had enough "free" time to devote to education, and they had a use for literacy in their lives. Trade required accounts, letters, petitions, and even the opportunity to enter government service for added business advantage. The general Thai farming population could not sacrifice their offspring's time to study enough to gain full literacy because the children's labor was needed from an early age. Besides, literacy was of no benefit at all to the life of a phrai. Literacy was a property of the bourgeoisie, and a property they sought for their descendants.

Bourgeois culture was thus a literate culture in the same way that the sakdina culture of the Ayutthaya era had been. Literacy added a cultural aspect to the close relationship and strong continuities between the early Bangkok bourgeoisie and Ayutthaya sakdina, despite considerable changes in cultural content across the two periods.

The literate culture of the early Bangkok bourgeoisie liked to claim its preferences, standards, and patterns of behavior were based on original written texts, especially those texts which were cultural products from the Ayutthaya sakdina era. Hence at a superficial level it is difficult to see the distinctiveness of early Bangkok culture.

Apart from being a literate culture, another main feature of the bourgeois culture of early Bangkok was that it originated and flourished in the town.

In Thai history, the town has two roles. First, it is the site of power (such as the king, governor, or ruler), and second it is the site of the "market." As the site of power, the town is also a community because the holders of power need people as servants and as soldiers. As the site of the "market," the town is usually located on trade routes so it may function as a centre of exchange for a wide circle of people. Because of this economic function, those who control the town also have power over the surrounding rural area. The power base of Thai sakdina was in the town, not in the countryside as in Europe.

Since the bourgeoisie emerged from within the sakdina upper class, and was closely bound up with the sakdina system, the Thai bourgeoisie was based in the town, just like sakdina. In truth, the bourgeoisie replaced the sakdina class in their old urban bases. Or in other words, the sakdina class transformed itself into a bourgeoisie in the old urban centers. Thus during this period of economic change and bourgeois social expansion, no new towns appeared outside the sakdina system. Industrial areas with tin mines, ironworks, and pepper plantations did not become new towns because old towns nearby, which were sited on trade routes and had been markets in the past, continued to serve as markets for these new communities.[168] This does not mean there were no communities which emerged in this period and became towns later, but such communities were under sakdina control from the start, and were elevated into towns by the sakdina government. Many towns were established in Isan for the purpose of sakdina exploitation. They were service centers for collecting tax-in-kind and controlling phrai. They appeared before the market economy reached Isan. Some mining communities had no old town nearby. Instead, local power-holders were co-opted into the administrative system to found and manage a new town—something which these power-holders relished. Ranong is an example of a mining community which developed later into a tributary town. As a rule, the Thai bourgeoisie had their power bases not just in towns, but in old towns which had been the power bases of sakdina. This further increased the continuity between sakdina and bourgeoisie. The old sakdina towns close to the areas of market production expanded rapidly, for example Nakhon Chaisi, Chachoengsao, Chanthaburi, Ayutthaya (the assembly centre for rice supplies to the towns in the lower delta), Chaiya (communication centre between the south and Bangkok), Chonburi, Songkhla, and Nakhon Si Thammarat.

The "market" in these places acquired new functions as a result of the expansion of external and internal trade. The market in many sakdina towns was a contact market, meaning a place of exchange where producers and consumers came into direct contact. But in early Bangkok these markets expanded into markets in the abstract sense of the word, that is where a wide range of goods were exchanged without the producers and consumers necessarily coming into direct contact.

Towns expanded in the early Bangkok era, especially in the central region. Bangkok grew at a particularly rapid pace. In 1839 (just half a century after Bangkok's foundation), Malloch estimated that Bangkok had a population of around 160,000, while other towns in the central plain had a combined population around 52,000. If the total population of Siam at the time was around 2 million (a generally accepted estimate), then 10 per cent of the total was in the urban area (Paitoon 1978, 31–2). These towns were the junctions of trade. In the view of the bourgeoisie, trade was a sign of urban prosperity and well-being. In *Inao*, when the town of Kalang celebrates the entry of Unakan, "the district officer calls on the people in the shops and houses along the street to have all the market women deck themselves out gaily and bring out their wares to sell" (Phutthaloetla 1955, 641). Foreign trade brought merchants and foreigners into the towns. It also brought strange new ideas and artistic forms. The towns of early Bangkok were lively, full of novelty and the dynamism of commerce.

168. On this point, it is worth making a comparison with Malaya, especially the mining area on the west coast. The major towns there were mostly outside the control of the sultans, and tended to undermine the sultans' power, creating an entry point for British imperialism to dominate the sultans.

Pallegoix left an excellent description of the atmosphere of part of Bangkok as an example of the bourgeois town of this era:

> Two rows of several thousands of shops float on rafts stretching out in front of us following the winding of a majestic river, crisscrossed in all directions by thousands of boats, mostly very elegant. The fortress, white as snow, the city with its towers and numerous gates, the aligned canals which cross the city, the gilded spire of the palace with its quadruple stacked up façade, the variety of edifices in Indian, Chinese and European styles, the singular dress of various nations, the sound of musical instruments the chants of comedies, the movement and life animating this great city, all this is for strangers a spectacle which elicits a pleasant surprise. (Pallegoix 1963, 55–6; 2000, 30)

The "hustle and bustle" of Bangkok portrayed here increased in parallel with the steady growth in population. In the Third Reign, taxes collected on wooden posts and thatch increased considerably because of the growth of urban areas like Bangkok (Ruschenberger 1838, 284).

As more people entered into the market economy and money economy, the commercial activity of the capital and major ports intensified. Descriptions of markets in late Ayutthaya indicate that trade was already lively in that era, and that most of the products in the markets were bought by urban people who did not produce for themselves (*Athibai phaenthi phranakhon si ayutthaya*, 72–7). But Ayutthaya's foreign trade was much less than that of Bangkok.

Urban life, here as everywhere, had comforts and conveniences but also vices. They were part of the money economy and thus spread in the towns where the money economy first dominated. Early Bangkok (as today) was full of prostitutes. These unfortunate women lacked the capital and the connections to survive in the new economy, and hence became victims of the change from subsistence to market economy. Most prostitutes in Bangkok were foreigners including Burmese, Mon, and Vietnamese who had either been seized as prisoners or had migrated of their own accord. There were also Thai women but in fewer numbers (Crawfurd 1967, 348). These prostitutes occupied a world below that of the bourgeois upper class. Even though they inhabited the same city, these two groups had no interrelations. The custom of flaunting status by having many wives meant the bourgeois upper class probably had little to do with these unfortunate women. The bourgeois literature of this period hardly mentions prostitutes in Bangkok.[169]

169. The absence of prostitutes in early Bangkok literature, and the lack of interest in this large urban group despite the fact that early Bangkok literature is a truly urban literature, stands in contrast to Vietnamese literature of the late eighteenth century.

Kim Vân Khiêu by Ngian Chu is about the fate of the daughter of an elite family. Even though she has a steady lover, she allows herself to be married in order to help her father who is being pressured by a nobleman. But the sale of her body turns out, in fact, to be sale into a brothel. After suffering the torment of this awful occupation for fifteen years, she escapes and meets her former lover. This is the most famous Vietnamese epic, and reflects changes in the Vietnamese economy and society in the late eighteenth century.

Drunkenness was another common vice in Bangkok and other major towns. The biggest consumers of liquor were probably the Chinese, and the production was also in their hands. In the Second Reign, the government made revenues of 102,000 baht a year from auctioning the liquor tax farm (Crawfurd 1915, 130). Around 1844 in the Third Reign, a foreign report states that government's revenue from the liquor tax was 96,000 dollars or 45 *hap* of silver (equivalent to over 200,000 baht), an increase of 100 per cent since the Second Reign. A foreigner who claimed to have been in Siam for a long time stated that formerly Thai did not drink themselves into drunkenness but, after the government auctioned tax farms to the Chinese with the aim of increasing revenue, liquor production expanded and drunkenness spread among the Thai to the point "even nobles and monks regularly get drunk" (Bruguière 1844, 202). This vice probably spread as much among the bourgeoisie as among the ordinary urban people.

The widening gap between the way of life of the urban bourgeoisie and that of the rural people who were less affected by the money economy gave rise to a feeling even among the Thai that urban and rural people were different. After detailing many bad aspects of the Thai in Bangkok, Crawfurd (1967, 349) stated: "I was assured, on what I considered good authority, that the character of the provincial inhabitants is much more favourable." The "good authority" was probably foreigners such as the Portuguese representatives in Siam. In the view of the Thai bourgeoisie, rural people or "country bumpkins" were stupid, dirty, lacking in manners, foolish, and excitable. The main point here is not whether rural or urban were the better people, but the consciousness among the Thai in general of the difference between town and country. As a result, bourgeois culture was self-consciously an urban culture.

In sum, the culture of the early Bangkok bourgeoisie was based in the culture of sakdina Ayutthaya, but was more diverse as a result of the bourgeoisie's greater readiness to accept strange, new, and exotic cultures, along with the liveliness of the common people's culture. Bourgeois culture was literate culture. It used written texts as legacies from the past, and as its own forms of expression, so that it could claim a basis in tradition (both real and false). At the same time, it tended to accept new knowledge with ease if that knowledge was known to have a textual basis even in strange new languages such as English. The town was the main environment of bourgeois culture, but it was not a town bathed in the recondite and majestic power of the king, like Ayutthaya. Rather it was a town of the "hustle and bustle" of merchants who were just as visible in the urban social landscape as the king and the king's men. They built wat just as big, and residences just as showy. Sakdina privileges about gold ornaments, sumptuary clothing, marriage, and so on were ignored. A new society emerged marked by greater equality, yet an equality which was based on property, urban residence, and urban business opportunities. Life and fortune were to some extent released from the influence of sakdina and the merit accumulated from past lives (*wasnabarami*). The bourgeoisie became more concerned with this world, and at the same time came to realize that fortunes in this world could to some extent be controlled.[170]

170. In truth, religious interpretation from the beginning of the Bangkok period began to focus on the spiritual improvement which could be achieved in this life. The ultimate purpose

THE LIMITS OF CHANGE

Although the survival of the sakdina system in bourgeois society has been mentioned several times already, yet the emphasis on economic change and its effect on the culture of the upper class might create a misunderstanding that this change was limitless. Hence the main limits on change need to be explained.

The first major limitation, as mentioned already, is that the volume of cash in circulation was much less than the volume of goods produced, resulting in export products being priced low and competitive with products from other countries. In addition, one drag on economic growth was the limited distribution of income. Vella estimated that government revenues in the Third Reign averaged only US$ 1.35 per head (around 2 baht at the exchange rate of that time). This came about because incomes were confined within the bourgeoisie and did not reach most of the population. The bourgeoisie could indulge in imported products while most people had no money. The internal market lacked purchasing power, and economic growth in the early Bangkok era focused on exports (hence it can be called an export-oriented economy) (Vella 1957, 24).

Because of their close connections with sakdina, and the benefits they gained from preserving the structure of sakdina, the bourgeois (especially those who came from the sakdina upper class) gave little thought to investing in production. Trading and exploiting the privileges of sakdina was less risky than investment, and thus there was little entrepreneurial capital. The limited money supply created opportunities for the bourgeois who had ready cash to invest in moneylending at high interest rates. According to custom, the interest rate was set at the already high rate of 33 per cent per year (Burney 1911, 229), yet in practice the lending rate was even higher at 50 to 80 per cent (Bruguière 1844, 213).

Although the market economy expanded greatly in the early Bangkok era, it was based on overseas trade which in turn relied a lot on the mechanisms of the sakdina system. The bourgeoisie had no interest in undermining sakdina because they themselves benefited from it. In the Third Reign, before the advent of free trade, government monopolies still supplied one segment of exports and made high profits for government. Because pepper enjoyed high demand in the markets of both

---

in life was increasingly found in this world (see the *Traiphum lokawinitchaikatha* which shows this tendency in many ways). The inscriptions of Wat Phra Chetuphon about hells include the statement that "wise men have just learnt there are many hells, which cannot be definitely determined. Any country which has only unavoidable suffering, that is called a hell" (*Prachum charuek wat phra chetuphon*, 165). This directly locates hell in this world. Prince Mongkut's religious reforms, known as the establishment of the Thammayut sect, emphasised the practises which Buddhists should adopt to gain benefit in this life. Prince Mongkut preached that one should make merit without knowing what merit is. He explained, "Whatever merit is called merit, where it is, is in the mind." He went on to describe how to purify the mind by avoiding greed, anger, and so on, so that actions in this life resulted in merit in this life (Chomklao, n.d; the original is a *samut khao* single volume in the William Gedney library, Michigan University.)

China and the west, the government acquired the whole supply from the producers by forced purchase. It purchased pepper in Chanthaburi during the Second Reign at 8 baht per *hap*, but sold it to foreign export merchants in Bangkok at 18 baht per *hap*. Cardamom at Chanthaburi was similar. Government bought at 120–140 baht per *hap*, but sold in Bangkok for as much as 270–280 baht and sometimes 300 baht (Raffles 1826, 256). Because demand for pepper in the world market was so high and the government's administrative machinery rather inefficient, there were opportunities to trade pepper outside the government monopoly. In the Second Reign, government had not yet found a method better than monopoly to profit from the growth of market production, and hence tried to prevent people producing pepper for free sale. For example, when pepper production expanded from the Chanthaburi area to Nakhon Si Thammarat where Thai-Chinese planted pepper for direct sale to merchants, government sent an order to the governor of Nakhon Si Thammarat stating: "Pepper is a government product which Thai and Chinese people...are not allowed to sell to their customers." The governor was ordered to use available cash to buy up pepper supplies at the Chanthaburi market prices (that is, forced purchase) and send everything to Bangkok (cho ro 2-10, cs 1181).

In the Third Reign, as noted already, the monopoly system based on the inefficient mechanisms of government became unsustainable. Government found it could increase its revenues by abandoning monopolies and instead levying taxes on domestic production through tax farming. Trade was liberalized from the start of the reign. But the tax farming system still depended on the structure of sakdina. Tax farmers were given official ranks and a certain degree of sakdina-style power. Government transferred the duty of collecting taxes to private bidders, and avoided taking responsibility for their exploitation of the people (Yada 1981). Besides, senior members of the nobility and royalty still benefited greatly from tax-farming by supporting the private individuals (usually Chinese) who bid for the tax farms and demanding a fee as reward. Some nobles and royalty were secretly tax farmers themselves, using Chinese to bid as a front. One example from the records is the case of the sugar tax in the Third Reign. The Chinese tax farmer, given the title of Khun Phithak, had to deliver only 30,000 baht a year even though the volume of sugar production at the time merited more than double this amount of tax. He undertook to supply sugar to the king, the Front Palace prince, and some other senior nobles at a price below that of the market. These people could export this sugar by junk and make abnormal profits. In effect, Khun Phithak was not the real tax farmer, only a front, whose role was to deliver the sugar at a low price. The real tax farmers were those who made piles of profit from this arrangement, namely Prince Surinthararak (in charge of the port department in the Third Reign), Phraya Siphiphat, and Chaophraya Phrakhlang (Burney 1911, 101–2).

Hence opening up a free market did not undermine the benefits of the sakdina upper class. In fact, the treasury was persistently short of funds because nobles and royalty behind the scenes took more and more of the profit from this taxation system, resulting in payments from tax farmers being held over to the following year. Yet in both the Third and Fourth Reigns, the kings did not seem very bothered by this, and gave no thought to a proper solution. This could happen principally because the king benefited more than under the monopoly system even though he was "cheated" a lot. The government in the Third Reign was able to collect a tax surplus without depriving the rest of the sakdina upper class of their benefits. This system survived in Siam for a long time, and did not alter sakdina, because it benefited this whole group, not just the king alone. As in the past, the nobles and royalty continued to share out the benefits—both the direct benefits and the benefits from corruption which the king accepted were the income on which the upper class lived. Only in the reforms of the Fifth Reign did the king try to gather all power to the throne, and deprive the upper class of all such traditional benefits.

This growing market economy did not create a class of Thai skilled laborers, even though there was a demand for skilled labor in the towns and in the zones of commercial agriculture. Wat, palaces, and houses for "great merchants—the people of property" were built based on new imported styles with more solidity and more complex structures than in the past. Crops grown in the new commercial areas were mostly new types which required different implements from those the Thai were accustomed to use. All this created a need for craftsmen, and a market for equipment, especially in the towns where incomes were growing and good quality products enjoyed increased demand. Thai craftsmen should have been stimulated to adopt new techniques, reap higher profits from their occupation, and elevate themselves into the ranks of the bourgeoisie. This in turn should have been stimulus for the bourgeoisie to start large-scale industries in the later period. Yet Thai craftsmen do not seem to have benefited much from this economic change, mainly because the sakdina system was still preserved relatively intact. Capable Thai craftsmen were not allowed to become free labor but were retained by the king or sakdina upper class as phrai for their private benefit. The ruling class had not developed methods for exploiting craftsmen's labor other than by conscripting them to work for nothing. There were no laws to collect taxes from craftsmen as money or tax-in-kind. Most other Thai were little affected by the money economy and had no cash to hire skilled laborers. People did their own craft jobs, just like they did other things for themselves in the subsistence economy. Ordinary Thai phrai were their own builders, woodworkers, and clothiers. The fact that people had such varied knowledge and ability meant there was no opening for developing higher skills (Bruguière 1844, 195). In the Third Reign, government began to have a policy of hiring skilled labor in place of conscripts, and felt this method delivered better results. But those hired by government were mostly artistic craftsmen. Most artisans with skills relevant for market production gained little or no benefit from this era of economic change.

The hiring of artisan labor existed alongside the surviving phrai system. Skilled labor was not truly released to become free labor. Only some kinds of artisan had opportunities to earn more income as cash. The survival of the phrai system was one of many reasons why the wage rate for labor in Bangkok was rather high. In the Second Reign ordinary wage laborers earned 1.5 salueng a day. Crawfurd (1915, 139) estimated this rate allowed a worker to buy enough rice to feed eighteen people for one month. Woodworkers earned half a baht a day. In the Third Reign wage rates remained high at around 4 fueang per day for ordinary labor (Pallegoix 1963, 15; 2000, 7). Hence it was impossible for ordinary people to hire laborers or skilled artisans.

The high wage rate for skilled labor was a result not only of high demand but also of low supply. The subsistence economy which supported most of the Thai population did not generate many artisans. In addition the phrai system was a barrier to the growth of skilled labor. The resulting gap attracted Chinese in large numbers. The Chinese were free laborers who brought from their homeland more knowledge and skills than those possessed by the general Thai population. The government seemed happy to allow the Chinese to be free labor, while at the same time happy to bind the Thai artisans into the phrai system under sakdina. Referring to repair work on the palace in the Third Reign, Nai Mi wrote: "Chinese artisans were hired for high wages rather than, as before, giving Thai plasterers, painters, and carvers *biawat* allowances and promotion to a higher title" (Sunthon Phu 1960, 168). Significantly, the Chinese received "wages" while the Thai received "*biawat*" and "promotion to a higher title." This continued attempt to bind Thai artisans under the phrai system severely reduced the number of Thai artisans. Pallegoix stated:

> They are witty and intelligent, and they imitate certain art objects which come from Europe very well. The majority desire to skill themselves in professions and industrial crafts, but because the King takes into his service everyone who is doing well in a profession, they dare not show their talent and work so to speak in secret. (Pallegoix 1963, 187; 2000, 103–4)

Some phrai with artisanal talent had to conceal themselves rather than having the opportunity to make a good income from the Bangkok labor market's high demand for skilled labor. Also, phrai had no opportunity to copy and reproduce western products, because those with the relevant artisanal skills were under the control of the upper class. The people who got the benefit from these skills were members of the sakdina upper class, such as Prince Phrapinklao or Chamuen Waiworanat who built western style ships for their own use. In other words, although the phrai possessed technical skills, the upper class monopolized the management of these skills, and hence could pioneer and guide change to accord with its own interests.

The expansion of the market economy also affected the phrai system (Anchali 1981, 160–71). The main trend of change in the phrai system was the gradual release into free labor. In fact laws reducing the annual length of corvée date back to late Ayutthaya. In 1748, departments which already had enough phrai were allowed to reduce corvée to four months a year (*Phraratchakamnot kao* (old laws), cs 1110, in Busakorn 1972, 294). But this law may never have been applied. It implies that labor was available in excess of government demand, yet another law from the Thaisa reign (1709–33) in the same era forbade overseers from using phrai for private purposes which would create a shortfall of labor for government (Busakorn 1972)—suggesting government was short of labor and thus any reduction in corvée was unlikely. However, in early Bangkok the corvée was truly reduced to four months a year, without any conditions about departments already having enough phrai. Crawfurd (1915, 27) states that this reduction began from the First Reign. The reason behind this reduction needs further study. The expansion of the market economy in early Bangkok was probably a factor, but there may be other reasons not known at present. At the same time, the early Bangkok government was happy to receive money in commutation of corvée. In the Ayutthaya era, the government allowed phrai to pay a commutation fee instead of corvée, but the purpose was to allow government to hire replacement labor at the same rate. The purpose in early Bangkok differed. It was the money which the government wanted because government activities now used more cash. There was no direct replacement with other labor. Also, the early Bangkok government preferred to hire Chinese labor for public works. Commutation fees were thus a change in line with the growth of the money economy. These two changes in the phrai system allowed people to become more productive in response to opportunities in the expanding market. At the same time, they gave phrai more options (in theory, in practice there were many other factors which prevented most phrai having the option to pay commutation fees instead of corvée).

These changes do not imply that government wanted to do away with the phrai system which was the basis of the privileges of the upper class in sakdina society. Power in the sakdina system came from large reserves of labor which could be used to generate profits through trading, or to generate political influence. The sakdina upper class still jealously harbored lots of phrai under its control and had no wish to see the system crumble. At a major bathing festival procession in 1829, an order limiting participating nobles to no more than 500 of their phrai and 50 sword-bearing attendants had no effect. In the actual procession, all the nobles showed off their rank and power to the full. Some had contingents of 1,000 phrai. Nobles of the rank *phraya phan thong* were all conscripted to join the procession. So many phrai were ordered by their overseers to take part in the procession that there was hardly a single male viewer, only women (Thiphakorawong 1961b, 97–8). The release of phrai in early Bangkok had a limited effect. It did not destroy the system.

The government tried to prevent the market economy disturbing the phrai system too much. As economic opportunities expanded, government departments found it more difficult to retain phrai who could leave their homes, disappear from the corvée registers without suffering any disadvantage, and take up waste land to plant crops for the market without any further contact with the bureaucracy. There are records from the Second Reign that newly arrived Mon "took their wives and children to make a living in all sub-districts...around Ratchaburi." Government worried they would run away and it would not be able to make use of them, so Phraya Ratchaburi was ordered to round them up and return them to the Bangkok area (cho ro 2-3/2, cs 1183). In sum, although the market economy was growing, most people still did not have liberty of movement. Only the Chinese and the official class had full liberty in this respect, and thus could monopolize the benefits from economic change.

The government's efforts to retain the phrai system are evident on the occasion in the Third Reign when government launched its own ventures to plant sugarcane and manufacture sugar. Most of the labor used in the plantations and factories was Chinese, even though Thai had long planted sugarcane to supply Chinese private sugar mills. Government avoided using corvée labor in the sugar plantations because corvée labor was reserved for traditional purposes such as transport, construction, warfare, and production of tax-in-kind. Sugar plantation and manufacture were new activities outside the scope of the government's use of phrai (cho ro 3-9, cs 1201).

The overseers could legitimately exploit phrai in the old system in ways other than in the course of export business, Pallegoix reported:

> princes and mandarins apply themselves continually to extorting money from their subordinates. High-ranking chiefs steal from lower-ranking chiefs and the latter steal from the poor. Moreover, in this country there is a host of vagabonds, fugitive slaves, gamblers, drunks and rascals who look for and use every opportunity to steal fruit from gardens, boats moored near houses, and goods of travelling merchants. (Pallegoix 1963, 189; 2000, 105)

Over-exploitation of the phrai ultimately had disadvantages for the bourgeoisie itself. Social disorder disrupted the bourgeoisie's own business. Hence in early Bangkok, the idea that phrai should be treated with some compassion became quite widespread. Officials became more sympathetic towards the suffering of phrai, as can be seen from passages in *Khun chang khun phaen* about the fortunes of the phrai. In truth, this work (at least, the version we have) is truly a literary work of the bourgeois court. It talks about the fortunes and million hardships of the phrai as something which should not happen because the upper class itself wanted to preserve a fair system. These passages are not an attack on the phrai system, but conform to the idea that overseers should treat phrai with some compassion, and not squeeze them too much as this might create other problems threatening to the bourgeoisie, as in the passage, "As a lay person, life will be tough. Do you want to disrobe and get yourself tattooed? Once your wrist is black, it's all hard times—carrying pack baskets on your shoulder until you collapse" (*Khun chang khun phaen*, 189).

The changes in the phrai system in the early Bangkok era were not intended to undermine the system, just adjust it for the benefit of the sakdina upper class or bourgeoisie whose interests were changing. As Anchali Susayan (1981, 219) interestingly concludes, "although the phrai system in early Bangkok was inefficient to the point some rules had to be changed, these changes were an attempt to maintain the system."

Thus even though the bourgeoisie was clearly dominant, it fitted into the pre-existing sakdina system. The bourgeois were few in number, including only some members of the sakdina upper class and some foreigners. They continued to use the sakdina structure of political authority, and the mechanisms of sakdina to retain old benefits and develop new benefits arising from commerce. They did not view the people as important except as tools to achieve some purpose (such as waging war, producing goods, delivering tax-in-kind, or serving as marks of status). There is a verse from the *Ramakian* which reflects attitudes towards the roles of various groups in society. This is a sakdina literary work influenced by bourgeois culture, and thus the attitudes exemplify the blending of bourgeois and sakdina:

> All cities are like bodies.
> The king is the soul which presides over the physical body.
> The left and right hands and feet are the four soldiers.
> The 32 parts-of-the-body are all in place, making this a bodily form.
> The various kinds of people are the weapons of different skills.
> Even the best of men will die if the soul leaves the body.
> Weapons with nobody to hold them cannot fight a war.
> (*Ramakian*, II, 777)

In government administration, the sakdina pattern was still maintained in full (although the content of government may have changed somewhat) (Nidhi 1980; chapter 6 in this book). Government was about control of people, not administration of people within a clearly defined area. Government mechanisms had to be adjusted in line with change but within the framework of the old pattern of administration. For example, there were problems over governing the increasing numbers of Chinese migrants. Such large immigration movements were not new. In the past government had seized people during wars against neighbors, and political refugees had moved in large numbers. The old method was to select an old leader of the foreign group and appoint him as an overseer within the sakdina system to continue governing these foreigners on behalf of the king. Mon, Khmer, Lao, and Cham were managed in this way. But the Chinese migrants in early Bangkok differed from previous immigrants. They arrived voluntarily in wave after wave with no old leaders who could easily be appointed to posts in the sakdina system from the time of their arrival. As a result they became free men who spread all over the country to make a living. The administration of these people was not clearly assigned to the provincial governors as that would have unduly increased the governors' political and economic influence (Mon and Khmer were not placed under provincial governors for the same reason). As the number of Chinese increased, some leaders had to be created. From the Third Reign, the government used the method of appointing Chinese district officers (*nai amphoe*), beginning in Bangkok and extending to towns where the Chinese had already settled. The Chinese district officers were "overseers" in the pattern of the old sakdina system, meaning they controlled people "of their own descent" in areas defined by the government. A Hainanese district officer had authority only over Hainanese in his area, and not over the non-Hainanese Chinese (cho ro 3-18, cs 1204). Thai governments in the past used this same method of appointing heads of various foreign communities so that they looked after themselves. Although changes in early Bangkok forced some adjustments, government clung to the old pattern of sakdina administration. These were the initial efforts to attach the Chinese to the Thai sakdina system.

For all the reasons explained, the early Bangkok economy should not be called a capitalist economy, even though some of its characteristics were similar. We should rather state that the foundations for a capitalist-style economy were laid in Siam in this era as the basis for fuller development after the Bowring Treaty. The bourgeois upper class was able to grab the benefits which arose from the Bowring Treaty because it had profited from the export economy for a long time. Thus the treaty had no bad effect on them at all, and was not the revolution which Sir John Bowring believed it to be. For this reason, although power based in sakdina now faced competition from power based on the accumulation of wealth and property, the sakdina system did not collapse. Those with wealth and those with power under sakdina were one and the same, or at least were closely related. The ambiguity of sakdina and bourgeois expansion in early Bangkok meant the economy had no trend of continuous profit accumulation (what Max Weber calls lacking rationality). A great volume of profits, especially among the sakdina upper class, was not circulated back as capital, but expended in activities not directly associated with business. Wealth was not accumulated to serve as "capital" on a large scale. Most of the labor used in production was not free labor. Even Chinese labor was not totally free because of Chinese secret societies (*angyi*) which probably had connections with the Thai nobles at the centre or in the localities. Especially in certain industries such as mining and sugar, Chinese labor was controlled by these organizations to the point it sometimes lost the character of free labor. The businesses of the Chinese and the Thai sakdina, and even the government administration, were family-based. Home and workplace were not separated, which is a feature of family business rather than true corporate enterprise (Weber 1958, 13–31).

Despite these limitations, the economy and society of early Bangkok cannot be analyzed on the pattern of the true sakdina system of Ayutthaya. The economic changes of this era transformed the character of the sakdina upper class. The Chinese who became integrated into the sakdina elite gave the upper class of Thai society a more bourgeois character. Understanding the bourgeois nature of the early Bangkok upper class is a prerequisite for understanding the changes which this upper class brought about after the Bowring Treaty. There was more continuity than formerly realized between the early Bangkok era and the "great reform" era which gave birth to "New Siam." Below we shall return to early Bangkok literature and show how understanding the influence of bourgeois culture illuminates this one activity of the upper class of the era, and the development towards the era of "New Siam." It is a route to understanding the evolution of Thai society from a viewpoint inside Thai society rather than a superficial survey of its outer husk.

IV: BOURGEOIS CULTURE IN EARLY BANGKOK LITERATURE

Wertheim (1964, 69) has stated that, "A society held together only by force is a rare phenomenon indeed. The secret of any domination is a partial imposition of one's own value system upon the members of the dominated groups."

This chapter, discusses the value system of the bourgeoisie, which, from the early Bangkok period onwards, was the ruling class in Thai society, as this value system appears in their literature. As a result of interaction between the ruling class and the general population, bourgeois values were disseminated to the lower classes through literary works. Indeed, as the mass media and print publishing began to spread throughout the country, these bourgeois values became even more widespread and entrenched in those works which later were elevated as the national literature.

The literary changes in the early Bangkok period discussed in section two above should be considered in conjunction with the socioeconomic changes that were simultaneously taking place. No literary work is produced within a vacuum; rather, it is created within a certain social environment. The social environment of Thai society of the central plains in the early Bangkok period explains not only the general character of "court" literature, but also the value system which is embedded in these literary works. Here the broad characteristics mentioned above will be analyzed in order to demonstrate certain values apparent in this literature.

URBAN LITERATURE

Court literature, or the literature of the Thai upper class, was always produced in the urban areas because it was in the towns that the producers and consumers of this literature resided. However in the literature of the Ayutthaya period the city was a symbol of the power of the king. It was described as similar to a heaven, the abode of the gods. Its power was apparent in the fortified city walls and the splendor of the royal palace. Merchants and the people have no place in the city of the Ayutthayan kings in this literature. However the city in the literature of the early Bangkok period is the city of the bourgeoisie, among them the king, who was one of those who had been transformed into a bourgeois. The city is therefore a place in which trade is given great importance. And since Siamese trade in the early Bangkok period was bound up with exports, the literature of this era gives great importance to ships and shipping, as though these were common things in the minds of the writers.

In literature of the Ayutthaya period, merchants and trade are accorded little importance. The king's wealth appears to arise from his superior store of merit rather than his control of commerce (at least as it appears in the literature, though not in reality). Thus in the *Khlong chaloemphrakiat* or verses in praise of the king by Phra Si Mahosot from the reign of King Narai there is just a single line referring to a trading vessel: "the junk was fully loaded with many goods" (Si Mahosot 1959; 7). Even this small reference gives no importance to trade, as the following line continues: "countless riches arose because of his great merit." Thus the wealth created by the junk trade was the result of the king's store of merit. Despite the fact that during the reign of King Narai there was considerable trade with western nations, in this writer's *Khlong chaloemphrakiat* there is not a single mention of westerners. There are, however, references to other nationalities who had either fled to seek the shelter of the king's benevolence or who had been captured as a result of warfare. This is because the labor of these migrants, which was managed through the phrai system, was part of the glory (*phrakiat*) of King Narai, while western merchants had no relevance to the king's glory. For this reason it can be concluded that trade was not a part of the king's glory during the Ayutthaya period, even though kings were interested in and benefited from trade.

In the early part of the Bangkok period this neglect of the importance of merchants and trade to the city is still apparent. The royal drama *Unarut*, which was based on a version from the Ayutthaya era and was one of the first literary works produced in the Bangkok era, describes the large size of the city but makes little reference to merchants and trade: "many merchants and their customers from all the twelve languages meet together" (Phutthayotfa 1972, 18). The lack of interest in foreign traders is demonstrated by the reference to the "twelve languages" which meant simply from all over the world. The author had no interest in mentioning where they might have come from. In a similar fashion the *Ramakian* by Rama I praises the city of Ayodaya under King Atchaban but says of the traders only that "many merchants also came to offer tribute" (*Ramakian,* I, 111). Later, however, the literature of the early Bangkok period reflects the thinking of the upper class by acknowledging the great importance of trade to their city. This literature describes trade and merchants in detail, for example, a verse in *Inao* by Rama II:

> Trading vessels row their way in
> Jamming up the rivers and canals.
> Barges are moored all along the harbor.
> It is very crowded on the water.
> So many goods are laid out for sale:
> Rolls of different silks in many colors;
> Cloth with gold thread, gold trim, and *chet takli* pattern;
> Precious gems, diamonds, onyx, and crystal;
> Such abundant treasures
> Including the nine precious gems and clothing.
> (Phutthaloetla 1955, 5)

In Rama I's *Ramakian*, trade is a means of enriching the king alone, as this work relates how the merchants who have come to trade offer tribute to the king. But in this excerpt from *Inao*, the wealth of the people in general symbolizes the prosperity of the city. *Inao* describes who the merchants of the "twelve languages" are:

> Merchants from many places come from foreign countries.
> Their trading vessels are moored in port:
> Muslim *(khaek)* sloops, Dutch merchant ships,
> Boats of the Chinese, Chams, and Acehnese who shout out loudly,
> The twelve languages all crowded together.
> (Phutthaloetla 1955, 5)

Merchants in these literary works are thus not simply part of the king's splendor (*barami*) but are important in their own right to the extent that they may be categorized according to each nation.

The power of the bourgeois king is thus expressed in the wealth that is spread among the ruling class generally. Moreover, such wealth has been generated by the efforts of people in this world, not as a consequence of the store of merit which the king has accumulated in previous lives. Thus the idea that the king's power as a *thammaracha* (ideal Buddhist king) will lead to the appearance of a Gem Treasurer,[171] who will indicate the existence of hidden riches in the kingdom, begins to wane, and is transformed into a belief that wealth is produced by trade, which is the action of human beings, or at least the upper class. A verse in praise of King Rama II at the end of *Kraithong* describes this idea well:

> Merchants from foreign countries
> Bring in special goods to offer the king,
> Many, many treasures
> To be distributed as part of the annual allowances.
> The soldiers who attend the king
> Become rich and set up as millionaires.
> Everyone is so happy and exuberant,
> Every day and night, every month, every year.
>
> (Phutthaloetla 1958, 429–30)

According to these literary works, wealth, riches, and prosperity are things that should be spread to the general population, rather than concentrated only in the person of the king. At the very least they should be available to the entire upper class. For this reason the city in early Bangkok literature is a place of abundance as a result of trade, because this demonstrates the real prosperity of the city. That is, people sell goods, and there are people with money to buy them. This situation is not limited to the capital. According to the ballad *Khun chang khun phaen* (p. 578), the market in Phichit is also bustling with trade:

> Shops selling cloth had barrels out front
> With bundles of patterned Surat cloths and uppercloths.
> Other shops were full of crockery,
> Pretty silk, and sundry goods
> Including rows of brassware and glassware.
> Lines of people crowded around to look.

The main characters in the literature of this era are themselves more involved in commerce. For example, all of the main characters in *Khun chang khun phaen* are

171. In the Three Worlds cosmology, the Gem Treasurer is one of the attributes of the ideal ruler. [T]

involved in trade (see above). Kraithong is a merchant from Nonthaburi who travels to Phichit to trade (Phutthaloetla 1958, 368).

Trade and the prosperity that results from trade among the bourgeois led to a greater literary interest in ocean shipping and navigation. A clear example that shows the difference between the earlier literature and that of the early Bangkok era on this point can be seen by comparing the *Kap mahachat* and the *Vessantara jataka* (*Mahawetsandon chadok,* Ministry of Education edition). There is a famous comparison in the Kuman chapter of the *Vessantara jataka* when Vessantara calls his son Chali out from the lotus pond where he is hiding in order to help him achieve the Perfection of Giving. In the Pali version the text uses the metaphor of the merchant's ocean-going ship, an ordinary boat which will capsize and sink if it runs into strong winds and waves. But his children Kanha and Chali are compared to a "*thamma* boat," because the children will help humankind cross the Sea of Becoming (*samsara*) if they let Vessantara give them away to Chuchok as an offering. There are two kinds of boat mentioned here. The first is the real boat of the merchant, which encounters real waves. The second is a metaphorical boat, which allows an important religious point to be made. A poet rendering the *Mahachat* could choose to expand the description of either boat. The *Kap mahachat* written in the Ayutthaya period only slightly develops the description of the first boat, such that the verse is almost a direct translation of the Pali:

> Also boats from different regions,
> All with masts, sails carefully done,
> Rudders, boat ribs, decks.
> The canoe-like *mat mun*
> Does not capsize,
> Running over the rolling waves.

By contrast, the poet chooses to expand the description of the second boat. He gives a detailed metaphor: the *thamma* is compared to the boat; meditation to the sail; and the rib, boat planks, and so on are all compared to some aspect of the *thamma* (*Kap mahachat,* 57). However Chaophraya Phrakhlang (Hon), the author of the Kuman chapter in the Ministry of Education version of the Vessantara Jataka, chooses to describe in considerable detail the first boat, the real boat of merchant traders, to the point of describing every aspect of the junks used at that particular time:

> A junk of some merchant
> Has its hull constructed
> Out of wooden planks nailed sturdily and tightly together,
> Sheets of metal fitted together, covered with a layer of caulking rubber to make watertight.
> The boards on the ship's deck are straight, there's a winch to haul up the anchor,
> The mast stands tall and steady, fastened by plates, attached to a pulley; it looks strong.

The rigging on the mast is secure.
The flag with a centipede insignia flaps in the breeze.
The craftsman has carved out reliefs of animals:
The royal lion proudly pushes out its chest decorated in the *kranok* style, holding a crystal ball in its mouth.
When the monsoon winds blow the shouts go up.
The cargo is lowered into the ship's hold and the stagnant water is bailed out.
The junk is heavily loaded, up to the washboards.
At the auspicious moment for departure three cheers go up.
A gun is fired from the ship, making a sharp bang.
The workers stand around all over the place,
Different accents and languages can be heard, "helo, lae, hela."
The anchor is hauled up and the gong is struck giving out a loud clash.
Flags flutter and wave atop the sail, blown by the wind god.
The book-keeper and the navigator look around intently.
They set the compass and look through the telescope to determine the direction in which the boat should sail.
The helmsman changes the boat's direction out towards the deep ocean; soon the coast can no longer be seen.

(*Mahawetsandon chadok chabap sipsam kan* 1957, 239–40)

The poet is clearly very familiar with ocean-going trading ships, but more important than that is the vividness of his description. The elaboration of this passage was not done just to demonstrate the poet's knowledge. It was the common interest of the poet and his readers in boats which was responsible for the vividness of the description. This early Bangkok poet's decision to describe real life trading ships well reflects a bourgeois awareness of boats and trade. Another interesting point about this description is Chaophraya Phrakhlang (Hon)'s interest in describing the equipment and means used to prevent the boat from sinking. The sturdiness and reliability of the boat are emphasized again and again. There are intricate methods of boat construction, including the use of planks, nails, metal sheets, and so on. The boat is covered all over with caulking rubber. The entire deck of the boat is made up of strong planks of wood. There are buckets to bail out the water. Ballast is loaded to make the boat steady. The measures taken to ensure the boat will withstand storms include the presence of plenty of crewmen such as the captain, second mate, and helmsman; the use of navigational instruments such as compass and telescope; and also magic rituals such as firing off guns, flying flags on the ship, and so on. All of this represents a human effort to combat nature using all the instruments and means that are available. Such a detailed description on this point reflects a confidence in human ability. It is possible for humans in this world to protect themselves from the forces of nature, up to a point. Such "humanistic" thinking will be discussed further below.

Boats have a role in other aspects of literature. One example which shows that ocean-going boats were embedded in the consciousness of poets is the use of a boat as a metaphor in the "wondrous scenes" between Khun Chang and Nang Phim, and again with Nang Saithong (*Khun chang khun phaen*, 123, 129). King Phanwasa compares Wanthong's love as

> ... having a reserve
> Deeper than the deep sea.
> Fill it with rafts, masts, weeds, and great junks.
> No amount will make any impression—
> Like a great ocean,
> So deep the floor is beyond fathoming.
>
> (*Khun chang khun phaen*, 790–1)

In this case the sea is something that the reader is so familiar with that the poet can use it as a realistic metaphor. Nothing like this can be found in the literature of the Ayutthaya period. In the early Bangkok period, a major literary work was composed using the sea as the main setting for the story—Sunthon Phu's *Phra aphaimani*. The sea of *Phra aphaimani* is the place where the lives of the characters are lived out. It is a real sea, in the sense that people have many different roles, the most important being the use of boats for transport and for war. There can even be sexual liaisons with creatures of the sea. This contrasts clearly with the sea of *Samutthakhot*, which is merely a place of death which the main character can escape only because of his great store of merit. The sea of *Samutthakhot* is a sea which neither the author nor the reader are very familiar with. It hardly exists outside of both their dark imaginations.

Like the sea, the city in the literature of the early Bangkok era is something "real," compared to the city in the literature of the Ayutthaya period. The descriptions of city life are more detailed, and include all kinds of different people. Apart from merchants and trade (which also existed in Ayutthaya, but which were not mentioned in its literature), these works also describe the lives of the petty bourgeois, for example:

> The women sellers from the raft people bring their children.
> The husbands, heads of the junks, are New Chinese,
> Who do not speak clearly, being unskilled in Thai.
> Wherever they sit the youth crowd together.
> The tax collector's minor wife isn't bad,
> But she flirts till her husband gets jealous.
> Loaded drunkards with tight faces
> Loudly and boastfully show off.
>
> (Phutthaloetla 1955, 51)

The interest of early Bangkok writers in realistically describing the city gives it a more international character in this literature, reflective of the real nature of cities at that time. These places, especially Bangkok, are full of foreigners who come from different countries and speak different languages. These foreigners have their own lives which give the cities a lively, diverse character. When literary works of the Ayutthaya period mention these people (if they mention them at all, which in fact is very rare), it is as an additional aspect of the phrai system with the king as the supreme lord. However the literature of the Bangkok era allows these characters to have their own roles, while not necessarily very prominent yet adding to the liveliness of the story. These figures are important in their own right, not as mere props to reflect the glory of the main character, the king. See, for example, the following verse from *Khun chang khun phaen* (p. 986):

> Crowds of people were watching and cheering.
> Khmer, Mon, Burmese, Vietnamese, Karen,
> Jek, and Farang had never seen such a sight.
> A Thai said, "Come and look if you dare!"
> Shy Tavoy ladies turned their faces and said in dialect,
> "We don't dare look or listen to the crocodile."
> A Mon said, "I'm leaving, sir," and left his pan and lime behind.
> A Lao said, "I don't know. I can't look. I'm really scared."
> On the riverbank, many people of many languages
> watched, sitting and standing.
> Jek and Khaek argued together in sing-song,
> "*Nung ning no na,*" sounding so cute.
> A Khaek said, "I am greatly fearful."
> The Jek argued back, "I disagree, you pudding face."

Besides illustrating the cosmopolitan character of the city, this verse also demonstrates a familiarity on the part of the author with foreigners and different languages, as if foreigners were a part of his life.

Growing foreign trade as well as the increasing income of the bourgeoisie led to the spread among the "nobility" of the use of luxury goods both produced locally and imported from overseas. This preference for luxury goods and living ostentatiously was a characteristic of the sakdina class since at least the Ayutthaya period because it was a means of expressing one's power (*barami*) over the common people. Since the bourgeois of the early Bangkok period were closely related to the sakdina class it was natural that they adopted the ostentatious lifestyle of sakdina as their own standard, even though this lifestyle was only allowed to "royalty, nobility, great merchants—the people of property." That is, the rule that the sakdina class could reserve the use of certain luxury items solely for their own use, which had helped distinguish classes in society, began to be relaxed. Gold jewelry could be worn by the children of the nobility even though sakdina laws forbade it. A regulation which once reserved performance of female drama for the king's pleasure alone was no longer strictly enforced by the Third Reign. Other royalty, nobility, and people of property now could own their own female drama troupes, and so on. Hence references to high quality goods from overseas are widespread in early Bangkok literary works, whether they were about the king or other people. Khun Chang, who is a classic minor noble except that he is wealthy, has many luxurious items in his house, for example:

A large frame held a picture of a seated Farang,
Looking out sideways in a pose that suited the face....
He walked past into a room full of glittering crystal,
Double screens, curtains, and blinds.
(*Khun chang khun phaen*, 345)

The best mirrors have to come from western countries: "I-Moei went into an inner room and picked up a big Batavia mirror, a genuine foreign one of good quality, fine clarity, and high price." (*Khun chang khun phaen*, 878). And because "expensive things" are common, even the harness of the king's horse has to be vaunted as being from overseas, for example the horse of King Phanwasa is decorated with "French filigree jewelry" (*Khun chang khun phaen*, 19).

The city, which was where literature originated and was consumed in the early Bangkok period, therefore appears in this literature as a place of sakdina-style splendor, but also of fun, liveliness, spectacle, and extravagant spending by the bourgeoisie. Economic problems have almost no place in the major literary works of this era. Khun Phaen might be less wealthy than Khun Chang, but he is not poor. This can be seen from the fact that even after the property of Khun Phaen's mother's is confiscated on the order of the king, she is quickly able to re-establish herself. Extravagant spending is something that did actually take place in the lives of the bourgeois who both produced and consumed these high literary works in this era. The standards mentioned in such literature are thus not imaginary or beyond the imagination of the reader. In an account of the annual *chong priang* lantern-lighting royal ceremony during the Third Reign, there is a description of the ostentatious displays of wealth by the upper class bourgeoisie when the nobility is requested to make *krathong* (decorative floats) to join in the royal ceremony procession.

> Some made them into barrels, some made them into boats fashioned out of banana tree stalk, 8 or 9 cubits (*sok*) wide and 10 or 11 cubits high. They competed among each other. Some made them into the shape of Mount Sumeru and the four continents; others as multi-tiered baskets. They were ornately decorated. Those who made them were counted in the hundreds. The investment in making the *krathong*, including the cost of meals for the people and the monks, was 20 chang or somewhat less. On the fourteenth day of the waxing moon they were done in green; on the fifteenth day in white; and on the first day of the waning moon in red. Fresh flowers were found according to the color of the *krathong*. Every *krathong* was different. In some a musical band was playing. The number of different styles of *krathong* is beyond description. Everyone competed with each other to win. The boats came to see the *krathong* at 4 in the afternoon. At 5 o'clock the boats towed the *krathong* into position. The boats were so crowded together it was hard to get out of their way. It was an amazing scene. (Thiphakorawong 1961b, 28)

What is especially interesting in these descriptions is the way they reflect both bourgeois and sakdina characteristics mixed together. Ostentation and contests of lavish displays of wealth are a new social "virtue." There is a liking for new, different things such as placing an engine inside the *krathong* so it can move about and so stand out from the others. But at the same time there are sakdina elements mixed in as well. For example, making such a large and beautiful *krathong* requires a lot of manpower, which is essentially a statement of one's power (*barami*) to conscript or control more labor than anyone else. In 1826 King Rama III ordered *krathong* to be made again, but even though he expressly forbade the nobles from spending large amounts of money he was unable to stop them, since in this year the *krathong* cost up to 23 chang (Thiphakorawong 1961b, 29–30).

This quality of displaying wealth by the use of "expensive" things, and demonstrating one's power (*barami*) through the display of phrai is a feature of the characters that the poets want to portray as upper class bourgeoisie. As Phra Wai is about to have an audience with the king,

> He called out to Simala to fetch a betel box,
> Cloth for wrapping, nak kettle, Japanese umbrella,
> Red pipe tipped with gold
> Which a servant filled with tobacco, and water pipe.
> Phra Wai bathed his body,
> Went into the house, took off his old clothes,
> And put on a *pha-muang* lowercloth of olive green imported silk,
> And uppercloth of plain chicken-skin silk, genuine Pakthao.
> (*Khun chang khun phaen*, 765)

In this lifestyle, enjoyment became important, but it was enjoyment of changes—not the simple, everyday things to which people were accustomed, but travel, watching entertainment, plays, fairs, or exciting spectacles. Of the five kings of this period, Rama II appears to have been the most bourgeois in this regard. He greatly enjoyed his private life. Chaophraya Thiphakorawong, who wrote the royal chronicle of this reign, summarized the king's achievements by stating that he did not carry out many royal duties. He composed the *Ramakian*, *Inao*, and other literary works. In the evenings he watched plays. He left the administration of the kingdom entirely in the care of the nobles, royal family members, and relatives (Thiphakorawong 1961a, 203–4).

Similarly, enjoyment, color, and excitement at new things are prominent features of most early Bangkok literature. As discussed in section 2, the popularity of fictional tales (*niyai*), a tradition of folk literature that had been adopted by the upper class, was due to the fact that "enjoyment" in literature was now regarded as important. Apart from the appearance of fictional tales another trend that distinguishes early Bangkok literature from that of the Ayutthaya era is the increase of colorful and lively details in the narration of the story—for example, the description of the city as discussed above. In fact this merely represents an increase in the lively details in the portrayal of the "city." Such details add to the enjoyment of reading the book and also make the "city," or whatever the poet is describing, appear more "real" based on one's own experience, compared to the style of description in the older literature (this interest in reality based on experience will be discussed in the next section). The use of these colorful details that increase the reader's enjoyment visibly developed through the literature of the early Bangkok period. That is, the literature written in the early part of the period places less importance on these things than that which appears in the later part. Those literary works that are adaptations of older versions dating from the Ayutthaya era attribute less importance to those details that aim to increase the reader's enjoyment. For example, the royal version of *Dalang* presents a very brief description of the cockfight scene with no attempt to describe the cocks actually fighting. This contrasts with Rama II's version of *Inao* in which the cockfighting scene is very lively and the fighting is described in considerable detail for the enjoyment of the readers of the tale (Phutthaloetla 1955, 678–81).

One passage in *Inao* describing the city seems to reflect very well this disposition of the bourgeoisie to love pleasure as it is about an ideal city full of happiness. The city's inhabitants seem to spend all their time in festivals. Life is about comfort, pleasure, and young men and women's enjoyment of courting. There is no work to be done, and no responsibilities.

> The crowd of city ladies take care of their looks, making themselves very pretty.
> They anoint their skin with turmeric and floral perfume to make it firm.
> They comb and trim their hair to look elegant.
> All the children of noble (*phu di*) families are beautiful, with good figures.
> They hide for fear they will be kept as women of the inner palace.
> So even if there is a big festival, they will not attend.
> Perhaps for those who are just coming of age,
> A groom will build a bridal house and ask for their hand.
> Some have secret trysts with their lovers, exchanging betel and flower garlands.
> All the young men keep coming by, intent on loving them and dreaming of them.
> They walk by playfully, eying them and engaging them with words of hidden meaning.
> Some flick their fingers, whistle tunes. All are skilled womanizers showing off.
> They go this way and that at leisure seeking pleasure. Women and men are happy night and day.
>
> (Phutthaloetla 1955, 6)

The city in early Bangkok gave opportunities for people of non-sakdina rank to relate with one another in a more equal way. Status deriving from birth, which was the main principle of sakdina, declined in favor of a new qualification—wealth and property. In the expanding networks of market relations, people had to deal with one another in a more equal way. Hence, at least amongst the bourgeois themselves, relations were less and less determined by sakdina principles. The city in early Bangkok literature tends to reflect this increasingly equal character of the city. When Dalang courts the heroine without revealing who he truly is, he refers to the Unarut story where a human and a *kinnara*, a mythical bird with a human head, can cohabit because "all this depends on love," and thus: "You live on the earth, so why are you perplexed? We are both human. Please allow love to change your heart" (Phutthayotfa 1956, 342–3). Dalang and the king's daughter may relate as man and wife because both are humans. This mentality is based on a view of mankind as fundamentally equal (though certainly not to the extent found in today's literature). Many activities in the city of early Bangkok literature made the division into social classes more difficult. Drama performances pitched the upper and lower classes together on a more equal footing. Popular culture was increasingly adopted into the performance literature of the upper class. Entertainments performed in the city were enjoyed by both the bourgeois upper class and the ordinary people. This is stated very clearly: "People's cheering echoed across the water. Gentlefolk mingled with riffraff without complaint." (*Khun chang khun phaen*, 985).

With growing bourgeois prosperity, bourgeois women took a larger role in society. Even though the bourgeoisie imitated many aspects of the lifestyle of sakdina, they had difficulty imitating the behavior of sakdina ladies, because their bourgeois counterparts had to play a greater part in the economy of the family. Crawfurd (1967, 115) refers to Thai women in Bangkok and the freedom of women in Thai society about sexual relations:

> Women mixed in the crowd, unveiled, as indeed they always are, and were neither shy nor timid; on the contrary, there was considerable familiarity between the sexes; and our conductors, Mohammedans, hinted to us, although I cannot pretend to say with how much truth, that the temples were frequent places of assignation. All this levity certainly formed a very striking contrast to the decent and reverential devotion of a Christian, or even of a Mohammedan people, and struck us with surprise.

In this social environment with more contact on equal footing between people of different sakdina status and with more freedom for upper class women, parents of girls faced new problems. Marriage still had a function of creating connections into the nobility and bringing political and economic benefits for the parents. But bourgeois girls tended to want to choose their own partner without listening to anyone. This free choice of partner was the practice of the ordinary people among whom there was less social class division than within the upper ranks. Bourgeois parents were concerned they might not be able to arrange a desirable match for their daughters. Pallegoix reported that women commonly eloped with male lovers because parents tended to demand too much as dowry (Pallegoix 1963, 209; 2000, 115–6). A new type of literature appeared of didactic manuals teaching unmarried girls how to care for and preserve their own body, rather than teaching married women how to minister to the wants of a husband. Yet women were not fully liberated because marriage was still viewed as the sole path for women to acquire standing in society. In *Ramakian*, Sida emphasizes just this point to Ram: "no matter how much status and respect she deserves, a woman without a husband will not be seen as such in the eyes of the world. She is like a jewel with no gold setting" (*Ramakian*, I, 482).

Because relations between young men and women within the bourgeoisie were more liberal, a new theme which had growing importance in literature was love. In truth, love was an important theme of Thai literature since the Ayutthaya period, but the love which becomes a theme in early Bangkok literature was rather different. The love between characters in Ayutthaya literature was something ordained by the power of the gods, or the power of their accumulated merit. In stories taken from the Jataka, the heroes are Bodhisatta and the heroines always turn out to be reincarnated as Nang Pimpha, the wife of Siddhattha. Because Ayutthaya literature made the heroes into Bodhisatta, the relations between hero and heroine were completely determined by the power of fate. Sida had to be the wife of Ram, not because of any mental attachment between the two individuals, but because Sida is an avatar of Lakshmi and Ram is an avatar of Vishnu. Phra Lo falls in love with Phoen and Phaeng because of the secret power of an old hermit. The well-known *nirat* poems from the Ayutthaya period dwell on the hero's longing for the absent wife rather than describing the feelings of two individuals towards each other.

In early Bangkok literature, love was a new emotion, namely a mental attachment between individuals not bound up with social ties of family, economic standing, and sakdina rank. Khun Phaen's love for Wanthong is clearly in conflict with social convention because Wanthong is already the wife of Khun Chang. Inao's love for Chintara is explicitly in conflict with the social and political order in the same way. His later love for Butsaba again does not conform to social convention. Sunthon Phu wrote *nirat* openly reflecting on his feelings for and attachments with a large number of women who were not his wives. Love in this meaning was something unknown in Ayutthaya literature, but became the totally dominant theme in early Bangkok literature. Because it was a new emotion, many early Bangkok literary works still could not deal with love as a motive in an explicit way. In *Inao*, love is the motive behind the plot throughout. It is a love which does not conform to various "proprieties," and hence amounts to a love based on an individualist consciousness. Significantly, throughout the Inao story, the affairs between Inao and Chintara, Inao and Butsaba, Choraka and Butsaba, and many other women who fall in love with Inao and Unakan, are all stirred by falling for appearances. The good looks of the characters are just a device to explain this new emotion which is not yet so familiar that its development can be described in the characters' hearts. Instead simple devices are used to explain this emotion, such as the beautiful appearance of Inao, or the magical love breath of the hero in *Khun chang khun phaen*. The characters meet and fall in love without reference to social standing, but because their feelings towards one another cannot be explained, devices such as magical love breath have to be used.

Although love became a major theme in early Bangkok literature, the society of this era was not yet familiar with this new emotion. There are virtually no references to love as something universal, as a kind of emotion which is not the property of any single person. One well-known verse from *Inao* runs: "And so, alas, love once revealed is like flowing water which rushes down in eddies, incapable of flowing back" (Phutthaloetla 1955, 304). This does not refer to love in the universal sense of the word but is specifically love for Chintara. The verse appears in a passage of longing.

It is not talking about love in a universal sense which probably appears for the first time in *Khun chang khun phaen* in the closing stages of the story (which may have been written in the Third or Fourth Reign) in a passage where Khun Phaen ponders on the love of Phra Wai for Nang Simala as follows:

> Khun Phaen pondered quietly to himself.
> "Phlai Ngam is lost in dreams about Simala
> Because he's just known love for the first time
> And sees everything from the good side.
> Oh Son, you don't yet know the bad taste
> When love changes and takes flight.
> The worst pain in the world
> Can't equal the pain and woe of love.
>
> (*Khun chang khun phaen*, 604)

Significantly, here love, rather than the characters, becomes the focus of the narrative. Moreover, it is a universal emotion rather than the love of one single person. The word love in this sense is not much used in early Bangkok literature, and apparently not at all in that of Ayutthaya. The reference to love in this passage shows Thai literature's growing maturity in handling this emotion which is a major theme of literature in general. This was another development that took place in early Bangkok.

LITERATURE FOR READING

As noted above, one striking characteristic of early Bangkok literature was that it was designed for reading. Literacy was more important for the bourgeois than for the ordinary people. Through their intimacy with the sakdina nobility, the bourgeois adopted this skill. The reading primers written in early Bangkok, which can be counted the first literacy primers in the Thai language, stressed the value of education, especially reading, writing, and arithmetic:

> A boss (*chao khun*) with enormous merit will have servants and clerks at his service.
> A person studious in learning must try hard to write.
> A troublemaker with a stupid character will become a vagrant walking the streets begging others for food, roaming for ever...
> If you are going to study arithmetic, do not shirk. Practice your multiplication and division. Do not play the troublemaker. You will get into difficulty and be put in the stocks for a long time.
>
> (*Prathom ko ka*, 31–2)

The same primer also states: "Books are the ultimate, the source of learning. Remember that" (*Prathom ko ka*, 53). The bourgeois associated literacy with economic and social progress. The illiterate are stupid people who have to walk destitute in the street, have constant difficulties, and end up flung in jail, while those with knowledge of literacy can become big nobles with a retinue of people. The bourgeois lived in the city where literacy was on the increase. The few ordinary people who became literate did not gain much advantage, and most probably remained illiterate. For this reason, King Mongkut stated: "Among the people of Siam, illiterates outnumber literates. The ordinary people in the provinces cannot read" (*Prachum prakat ratchakan thi 4*, 120). Bourgeois literature in early Bangkok thus placed a lot of emphasis on reading. It distinguished itself from the recitation tradition characteristic of popular literature, and from the prayer chanting and performance traditions of sakdina literature. In response to the taste for reading (or listening to reading), *niyai* folktales were assembled into complete stories in the form of drama scripts. Prose style which departed from the *roi kaeo* stylized version favored by monks for translating Pali became increasingly widespread in the Bangkok era, as shown by the style used in translating *Three Kingdoms*, *Sai Han*, and so on from the Chinese. This style of language was an innovation in Thai literature because, unlike *rai* or *roi kaeo*, it placed no emphasis on rhyme or using elegant vocabulary. This was clearly language specifically for reading while *rai yao* was language for chanting out loud. The inner rhyming of *klon* assumed greater importance because people read *klon* rather than listening to it with musical accompaniment. Several developments in verse forms and literary themes in early Bangkok can be understood when it is realized this was the first literature for reading (or listening to reading) in Siam.

Yet in this era, this literature was designed to be read by the ear—meaning that listening to reading was still an important way of consuming literary works, especially those in prose. This method of consumption affected the way authors worked. They had to compose for the ear. The meanings in works designed for listening could not be so profound. Verses in the *klon* form became more popular because *klon* could communicate without using fine words in an attempt to convey profound meaning. At the same time, listening to reading depended more on imagination than performance. Listeners had to create their own image without the help of music or acting. Thus there was a development in early Bangkok literature towards more detailed scenes, events, and characterization, sometimes to the point of excess.

Subsequently, there was another important change in consuming literature—from reading with the ear to reading with the eye. Not much prose was designed for reading with the eye, and not all authors attempted this form. Most still composed prose for the ear in this period. The writer who is often celebrated as the first to compose for the eye (or intended for reading by the eye) is Prince Paramanuchit Chinorot. His compositions are not very distinctive, except in the sense that he initiated a new way of consuming literature, and this lends his works some special interest. In reading with the eye, the meaning and emotions enter the mind without any role for sound. For this reason, Prince Paramanuchit Chinorot was the first author to pay attention to stress in his *chan* composition. Generally in the Ayutthaya period and early Bangkok, *chan* composition was not strict about stress. In literature which is consumed by listening, such as the recitation for a shadow play, or the chants of a Brahman in the Dutsadi Sangwoei Klomchang ceremony, the stress is a matter for the chanter or reciter, not totally the responsibility of the composer. In the same way, if verses are read with the ear, it is the duty of the reader to put the stress on the syllables. But when verses are read with the eye rather than the ear, the pattern of stress becomes more important because the words have no stress of themselves. The eye receives the form of the word and passes it directly on to the brain or heart. Prince Paramanuchit Chinorot composed for reading with the eye, and hence was more strict about stress in his verse than previous poets.

Prince Paramanuchit Chinorot composed other works intended for reading mainly by eye. Their distinctiveness can be seen through comparison with works of other authors. For example, in the *Lilit taleng phai* Prince Paramanuchit Chinorot (1960, 111) described the march of Naresuan's army prior to the single combat with the Burmese prince as follows:

> Reaching the great hour of victory,
> The Brahman soothsayers,
> Skilled in the mystic arts,
> Ring the bell of victory to celebrate that auspiciousness.
> Unfurled pennants sway.
> The drum of Indra echoes,
> Joining the horn and conch,
> Together with drums and musical instruments.
> Then His Excellency the King,
> The greatest among men,
> Mounts his elephant, the first in rank.
>
> (*Lilit taleng phai*, 111)

This scene is an opportunity for the poet to portray the magnificent power of King Naresuan by atmospheric description of the valor and might of his army. Prince Paramanuchit uses the *rai* meter here for this purpose. The atmosphere is created through the meaning and emotional content of the words which tend to be grand and awe-inspiring. There is no attempt to convey the clamor of a great army on the move. Even if the passage were read along with gongs and loud music, it would not convey the message of loud noise through the ear but through the meaning of the words (via the brain). There is no attempt to convey the sound and fury through words which imitate real sounds. Compare this to a *rai* verse in *Lilit phetmongkut* by Chaophraya Phrakhlang (Hon): "The water bubbles curiously, khruen, khreng, khran, khron, khrik; the booming wind swirls around the mountain and the grove of *salao* trees" (Chaophraya Phrakhlang (Hon) 1972, 80). The words imitate the natural sound of water, and convey the sound of booming wind. Conversely, attempting to grasp the meaning of this example from the words alone without taking their sound into account would not convey the impression of loud noise. Only if the verse is read aloud, letting the ear receive the meaning, does the noisy splashing of swiftly flowing water come across. Prince Paramanuchit Chinorot's compositions have an especially interesting character.

Understanding that most early Bangkok literature was literature for reading, and that each work aimed for the distinctive character this implied, is important for taking a correct approach to their study. Efforts to appreciate the poetic taste of many literary works of this time by going sentence by sentence would seem to be a waste of time. The authors were not trying to instill emotional atmosphere into each letter. The work of Sunthon Phu is a good example. The softly sweet rhythm of Sunthon Phu's verse can be felt through listening. There is no deep meaning which demands great thought or study. The same is true of the royal drama scripts composed in the First Reign, and the outer drama scripts in the Second Reign. Simple wording is used to tell stories full of colorful and detailed description. There is none of the solemnity of ritual or didacticism. It is just for listening for genuine "fun." The ballad of *Khun chang khun phaen* or *Raden landai* and many *phleng yao* and drama scripts are all literature for reading by the ear. *Phra malethethai* is the most highly developed work of literature for reading by the ear because without the sound, the wording has no meaning and makes no sense as reading. Whether insane or not, the author captured the main principle of the literature of this time, and experimented successfully with writing which had meaning without meaning.

There are some other early Bangkok works which differ from the literature for reading referred to above. These are works which imitate or are modeled on works from the Ayutthaya era. Examples are the *nirat* written in *khlong* meter by Phraya Trang and Nai Narinthibet, which are comparable with *Kamsuan*, *Thawathotsamat,* or the *nirat* sections of *Lilit phra lo*. The Ayutthaya originals were the property of the nobility. They are few in number, well studied, and display literary ability through fancy words and complex verse forms. The compositions which are modeled on Ayutthaya literature retained these key characteristics. Even though they might be for reading, it was contemplative reading, imbibing the meaning and emotion with each letter, not like reading the works of Sunthon Phu. This group of works, which might be called classic style poetry, is not extensive. They do not seem to have been as widely popular among readers of the time as the work of Sunthon Phu. In the late nineteenth century when upper class literature again began to diverge from the popular tradition, becoming a literature with no power or inspiration other than unthinking imitation of the west, these classic literary works were reintroduced to readers through printing, and celebrated by academics and authors, thereby gaining a larger readership.

As already noted, prose literature is especially interesting because it was clearly literature for reading. In the first stage of the early Bangkok era, prose works were mostly translations from foreign languages. In the Thai literature of the Ayutthaya period, there had been no prose fiction. Unlike the Chinese or western literary traditions, the Thai language had no tradition of writing prose for artistic effect. Chinese tales first began to be translated in early Bangkok and became increasingly popular among readers. Pali works were also translated into Thai, including many which were not true translations, but rather the contents of Pali works rewritten in Thai, such as the *Traiphum lokawinitchai* (Treatise on the Three Worlds). Works of this sort were religious. Probably there were works of this sort in a language close to prose during the Ayutthaya period. But the major difference of religious works in early Bangkok was the increased use of prose, and reduction in its "stylized" character (meaning rhyme and many elegant words), for example in the *Traiphum lokawinitchai*. Many religious passages in the inscriptions of Wat Phra Chetuphon are in prose (*Prachum charuek wat phrachetuphon*, 56–179), and also many documents in the Wachirayan Library in the category of *thammakhadi*, works on Buddhist theory. Using prose to expound Buddhist religious principles was probably part and parcel of changes in the conception of king and government which began in early Bangkok, stressing the duty of the king to lead people to escape from suffering, both physical and mental, both in this world and the next, and portraying the king as a Bodhisatta (Nidhi 1980, 50–65; see chapter 6 in this book). This made it necessary for the upper class or bourgeoisie to have better understanding of the principles of Buddhism. Teaching in stylized prose might create faith in religious teachings but may not have created good understanding of them. The development of prose continued through the Bangkok era. Around the Third Reign, an author composed a semi-fictional work in prose, namely the tale of Thao Si Chulalak or Nang Nophamat (Nidhi 1979, 11; see chapter 4 in this book). This was a milestone in Thai literature.

REALISM AND HUMANISM

The bourgeois were the major consumers of upper class literature in early Bangkok, and their worldview to a great extent dominated early Bangkok literature. The bourgeois wanted to enjoy exotic things far removed from themselves and from the monotonous life of the city. Yet at the same time, they did not enjoy descriptions of heavenly cities or tales of true sakdina characters whose power and might came from high birth. These two needs superficially seem in conflict with one another. Thai upper class literature from ancient times had been all about exotic matters. Samutthakhot's adventures happen in the Himmaphan forest. Ramakian is about Lanka, with giants and monkeys. These settings did not coincide with the real life of the upper class. For this reason, the bourgeoisie ought to have liked the upper class literature of Ayutthaya. But the exoticness in Ayutthaya literature was in conflict with the "reality" which the bourgeois could accept. Business and business success taught the bourgeoisie to give more importance to this world and rationality. This might be called the springs of realism.

As a result of this bourgeois preference, many *nirat* were produced because *nirat* tell a tale that is exotic but at the same time not beyond "realism." Among fictional literature, a work such as Inao became increasingly popular because it preserved an exotic atmosphere by using Malay words and describing strange customs such as worshipping a Buddha image in a cave, a suicide ritual, using a kris, and so on. Because of more extensive trading in the early Bangkok period, the bourgeoisie knew that such customs or something similar existed in reality in Java. This was the flavour of realism that they relished.

The fictional work which most clearly reflects such bourgeois taste is *Khun chang khun phaen*. Even though this ballad may have been recited since late Ayutthaya, there is no original Ayutthaya manuscript available for comparison. According to the version which appeared in early Bangkok, *Khun chang khun phaen* differed from earlier generations of Thai literature in the aspect of realism. Although the story is "exotic" with respect to time, yet it begins by stating the date, reign, and location (Suphanburi) very exactly (*Khun chang khun phaen*, 1–2). Furthermore, the time and place identified in this way were "real" for the reader, unlike the Jataka stories in which the time and place were identified yet obviously imaginary, conveying an idea of "the distant past" or "once upon a time." In addition, *Khun chang khun phaen* maintains this realism by describing customs of birth, death, house building, marriage, and so on. It thus belongs to the approach of modern fiction, namely a specific story, about specific people, in specific situations. Prince Damrong explained: "The key point is that it was composed to appear as a true story. For instance, the words used in dialogue are the words that a person of that type truly would use, and are spoken in the way such a person would speak.... The writing of this ballad seems to have required a lot of research about the geography" (Damrong 1950, 20). To give the impression of realism, care was taken to describe many situations as they were in the Ayutthaya period in which the story was set. For example, on his search for the horse Color-of-Mist, Khun Phaen goes to "Ratchaburi, Suphanburi, Phetchaburi" without success, but then by chance meets an official who has been commissioned to acquire foreign horses for the government:

> Now to tell of Luang Songphon and Phan Phan.
> They had been sent to Tenasserim on the king's orders.
> Along with thirty-four accompanying phrai,
> They stayed in Mergui for half a year,
> Because Luang Siworakhan had gone to the western lands
> To buy horses and had not yet returned.
> He had to wait for the season of the wind
> For the ship to sail back from the western lands.
>
> (*Khun chang khun phaen*, 329)

In early Bangkok when the tale of *Khun chang khun phaen* was composed, Siam had no power over Mergui and Tenasserim, and the two places were no longer important ports on Siam's western side. Any trade with India would most likely come onshore at Trang from where a route led to the major provincial headquarters of Nakhon Si Thammarat. All through the early Bangkok period, elephants were exported to India through Trang. The author of this passage in *Khun chang khun phaen* probably would have known about the contemporary trade with India, and yet described the pattern which was known to have prevailed in the Ayutthaya period.

The use of realistic settings was not limited to *sepha* ballads. Tales which retained the "exoticness" of foreign countries still inserted realistic elements to give a flavor of realism. For example in *Inao*, the royal horse which Inao rides "had been presented by the Khmer prince Chan" (Phutthaloetla 1955, 1057). Chintara gives presents to the six concubines of Inao:

> The ring with the big jewel, not an imitation,
> Was bought for a thousand baht from a wealthy king.
> The ring with a ruby set in gold enamel
> Was given by the noble governor to keep.
> One emerald of about eight chang
> Was bought by the royal treasurer from the new city.
>
> (Phutthaloetla 1955, 1158)

These were realistic situations and people with which early Bangkok readers were acquainted as a matter of course.

The interest in realism in these works had some impact on the consciousness about relationships among individuals in society. As already noted, Sunthon Phu's *Suphasit son ying* (Sayings for the Instruction of Ladies) differs from earlier Thai traditions of didactic literature for women in Thai by instructing young ladies about the search for an appropriate partner rather than about ministering to the needs of husbands with no other major role in the family. Compared to *Kritsana son nong* (Krishna Instructs a Younger Sister), *Suphasit son ying* is more in line with bourgeois expectations of a more prominent role for women in society, and more in line with the actual situation within bourgeois society. The inspiration must have come from realism. Sunthon Phu also wrote didactically about another aspect of social relations, namely the duties and everyday practice of people of different classes with respect to the king. Several such didactic works had been written since the Ayutthaya period such as *Pali son nong*. This genre focused heavily on ways in which royalty and nobility could pledge their constant loyalty to the king with body, word, and heart, acknowledging the difference of status between themselves and the king. Such actions were considered auspicious and would be rewarded with prosperity and happiness. Sunthon Phu's *Sawatdiraksa* (Protection of Well-being) is understood to have been composed in this tradition. Even the title is similar to *Ratchasawatdiwat*, an old didactic *klon* poem which was copied into the inscriptions of Wat Phra Chetuphon. But Sunthon Phu's version differs from the old style by focusing on the benefits which officials in government service will receive as a result of their actions, rather than as a result of pledging their utmost loyalty to the king as in *Ratchasawatdiwat*, as follows:

> When attending the king, do not be too close or too distant.
> Stay where you can hear his address clearly and understand the content.
> Be intent on loving and being close to
> The king with honesty and loyalty.
> Even though the remains of the water washing his feet are thrown on your head,
> Do not be angry, vengeful, or distressed.
> Do not try to approach closely a consort beloved of the king.
> Avoid words which are inconsistent with tradition.
>
> (*Prachum charuek wat phra chetuphon*, 488–91).

Such advice, which was the outstanding element in such literature in the past, does not figure in *Sawatdiraksa*, making Sunthon Phu's work more in line with the true situation of the nobility and bourgeoisie.

This interests in things which are exotic but realistic can be seen clearly in *nirat*. As trade broadened the horizons of the bourgeoisie, the *nirat* become more widely popular than at any previous time in Thai literary history.

The *nirat* is a genre which emerged rather late. In the sense of a certain literary form, the *nirat* is understood to have appeared and developed in early Bangkok. From the Ayutthaya period, there are certain works which are called *nirat*. With the sole exception of *Nirat hariphunchai*, all are from the central region. One work from late Ayutthaya is called *Nirat mom phimsen*, but in the original version it was not called a *nirat* but rather *Phleng yao mom phimsen banmueang di,* indicating that it was retitled as a *nirat* in early Bangkok.

Literary works which use the theme of separation from a female lover to display poetic eloquence were composed in the Ayutthaya period, such as *Kamsuan* and *Thawathotsamat*. The tradition was popular throughout the Ayutthaya period, such as Phra Si Mahosot's *Nirat nakhon sawan* (which was titled as a *nirat* only when first printed) and Prince Thammathibet's *Kap ho khlong sadet praphat*. The main aim of this literature of separation is to use poetic eloquence to describe the author's love and longing for a beloved women, by having the names of places, birds, or trees trigger comparisons with the heart's feelings of missing the lover. Travel and experiences during travel are not considered worthy of description. In some works of this kind, such as *Kamsuan*, it is not clear where the author is going. Even in *Nirat nakhon sawan*, the destination is known only by supposition. Hence the authors' true experiences are completely missing from this type of work.

In late Ayutthaya, the *phleng yao* form, which originally was used to express love in the same way as the *phleng* in popular literature, was developed to make a record of the author's traveling, or of some important events in the author's life. By relating real experience, this genre of *phleng yao* diverged from the literature of separation mentioned above. In late Ayutthaya, these two genres began to merge into *phleng yao chotmaihet* in which the author described his longing for a lover left behind. These works retained the tradition of *phleng yao* as an expression of love. *Nirat mom phimsen* was of this nature. The early passages, following the tradition of *phleng yao*, contain expressions of love and remembrance of past events between the author and his lover. Thereafter, the author reflects on his separation from her as a result of having to go to Phetchaburi, but there is very little description of real experiences on the journey as found in *phleng yao chotmaihet*. For example, throughout the story the reader does not know why Mom Phimsen has to go to Phetchaburi. Instead, it is all about his feelings triggered by the names of places, birds, fishes, trees, and so on. This is little different from Prince Thammathibet's *Kap ho khlong sadet praphat*, except in using a different metrical form.

However, such use of *klon phleng yao* for recording events and feelings of longing made way for the birth of a new genre. In early Bangkok, many more *phleng yao chotmaihet* were written. During Taksin's reign, Phraya Mahanuphap wrote *Nirat kwangtung* about being sent to China (the titling as *nirat* is understood to have been added later). Yet the work is more like a genuine *chotmaihet* than a *nirat*. In contrast to *Nirat mom phimsen*, there is no description of love or longing at all. The composition was intended for presentation to King Taksin (or King Rama I), as it states: "This is a record offered with loyalty" (Mahanuphap n.d., 382–404). *Nirat tha din daeng* (To Red Earth Landing) from the First Reign may be counted as the first true *nirat* as it includes both expressions of longing for the lover along with description in the form of a record. Yet the aspect of longing for the loved one is very limited, and the work used to be classified together with old *phleng yao*. But soon after this, more *nirat* were written which combined longing for the loved one along with narration of the journey, and the word *nirat* was used to name all literary works of separation.

The development of the *nirat* in early Bangkok can thus be classified into two directions. One type was developed from *phleng yao chotmaihet* by blending in the literature of separation. It was usually composed in *klon*, but this was not mandatory as the example of Sunthon Phu's *Nirat suphan* (To Suphan) was composed in *khlong si suphap*. The striking characteristic of this type of *nirat* was the description of real experience during the journey rather than the display of poetic eloquence to express longing. Some *nirat* of this type hardly mention the loved one at all, for example Sunthon Phu's *Nirat phukhaothong* (To Golden Mount). However, there are some exceptions to this. Sometimes authors used this form of *nirat* to display poetic eloquence about imaginary events involving the separation of the characters, for example *Nirat inao*, or about ancient times in the style of *Thawathotsamat*, for example *Nirat duean*. This indicates that old Ayutthayan literary models still influenced this new kind of *nirat* though not to a very great extent as no literary tradition exerts such tight control. The crux of this type of *nirat* is the author's interest in the real experience during the journey. This was probably not a convention imposed by anyone, but reflected the taste of both writers and readers whose interests diverged from those of people in Ayutthaya because of economic and social change. For this reason, there was a great deal of experimentation with this kind of *nirat*. For example, Sunthon Phu's *Nirat phukhaothong* can be considered an experiment because it does not mention the loved one or the separation at all. Another form of experiment was the adaptation of famous works like Ramakian or Inao into the *nirat* form. Prince Mahasakdi Phonlasep of the Front Palace composed *nirat* of this kind but used the *lilit* form rather than *klon*, which was an experiment in verse forms ('Lilit nirat' in Damrong 1920, 56–114).

Authors who closely adhered to Ayutthayan traditions continued to compose works of separation. But in early Bangkok these were called *nirat* in the same way as the new type of *nirat* mentioned above. This was the second type of *nirat* in which the author tried to retain the key characteristics of the literature of separation from Ayutthaya. Mostly these were composed in *khlong* meter since this rather than *klon* was the verse form used for *nirat* in Ayutthaya. But this was not always the case. For example, Prince Wichaichan of the Front Palace (at the time he had the title of Prince Yodyingyot Krommuen Bowon Wichaichan) composed *Nirat mueang nakhon* (To Nakhon Si Thammarat) in imitation of the Ayutthaya literature of separation but in *khamchan* meter. The striking characteristic of *nirat* of this type lay not in their verse form but in their focus on the feelings in the heart of the writer rather than description of the real experience of the journey. Yet the metrical form can be used as a broad principle for distinguishing these two types of *nirat*. For example, Prince Damrong explained that authors of *nirat* in the First and Second Reigns fall into two groups. The first "had the old idea that *khlong* was important and more difficult to compose than *klon*. This group composed *nirat* in *khlong* following the example of Si Prat. The other group liked *phleng yao* as it was used in the late Ayutthaya period. They composed *nirat* in *klon suphap*" (Damrong 1971, 84). This principle works but ignores an important aspect of Thai literary history. The distinctive characteristic of these two types of *nirat* is their interest in real experience, which was no less prominent than the display of poetic eloquence about love and longing. Old-style *nirat* had shown almost no interest in real experience of this sort. Even in late Ayutthaya, Prince Thammathibet continued to compose the old-style "*nirat*" of *Than sok* and *Than thongdaeng* with erotic musings about birds, trees, animals, and so on which obviously have little to do with any real experience of the author in journeying to the Sok and Thongdaeng streams.

The interest in real experience in the new *nirat* which gained wide popularity especially with the dissemination of the works of Sunthon Phu, was part of an interest in realism which increasingly dominated early Bangkok literature. It arose because of the widening horizons of the bourgeoisie and their acquaintance with many other real places which they had visited or heard of and wished to know more about or see in reality, not just as artistic similes as in old-style *nirat*.

The Ayutthayan traditionalists among early Bangkok authors did not emphasize real experience during the journey or describe the reality of locations, but they were still significantly influenced by the demands of their bourgeois readers. Hence even their style of *nirat* contained more real experience and realistic description of places than the "*nirat*" of Ayutthaya. *Nirat narin* has many more passages of this kind than its model, *Kamsuan*, for example stanza 19: "The raft people expand their trading plans, selling things like silk, clothes, gold-threaded linen, foreign dyes." Stanzas 60–9, when the army marches to Phetchaburi, are full of description of the army's actions and of Phetchaburi town market. When the army passes Bang Saphan, there is mention of the gold panning for which this place was already famous (stanza 94). In the same way, Prince Dechadison's *nirat* on the army expedition to Vientiane has many passages of real experience and realistic description of places. Passing Wat Dusit and Wat Daowadung, the author writes: "Look at the raft, examine the women's faces. Some are Chinese with rings hanging from their ears" (Pho Na Pramuanmak 1970, 194, stanza 24). In stanza 31, he writes: "Look at the young betel growing in rows. How fertile and productive it is." In stanza 35, he describes the history of Samsen in the same way that Sunthon Phu did: "Look past the village at Samsen. Some say an estimated 300,000 diggers were recruited, and hauled off with force. With heavy heart, admire it." Passing Mon people, he tells their history (stanza 63). Passing Ayutthaya, he describes the ruins and devastation, and the forest which has engulfed the monuments (stanzas 99–100).

Prince Wongsathiratsanit wrote *Nirat phra pathom* (To Phra Pathom Chedi) in 1834 (Pho Na Pramuanmak 1970, 253–297) with many such passages of realistic experience. He mentions the construction of Phaulcon's fort in the Ayutthaya period (stanza 22), the moving of the palace by "Khun Luang Tak" and King Rama I (stanzas 23–4), the incomparable beauty of Wat Pho (stanza 25), and the covered way to the water palace which is thronged by people in attendance when the king travels by water (stanza 33). On passing a Chinese village, he remarks there are so many "*chek*" (stanza 99). When he reaches a customs post, the people who inspect him find no goods but only gold and are greatly shocked to know a member of royalty has come (stanza 117). Passing a tax office, he sees a lamp and a Thai lady attending to the tax collector and is jealous of him. Such passages are found throughout this work, even though it attempts to uphold the traditions of old-style *nirat*.

Hence, the interest in realism and the narration of real experience were important characteristics of early Bangkok literature. Even in *nirat* which were composed on the traditional model paying no attention to real experience, several passages of this sort were inserted. As a result, the *nirat* literature of early Bangkok, even those modeled on old traditions, have their own character distinct from the "*nirat*" of Ayutthaya.

As a result of this realism, the upper class literature of early Bangkok deprecates supernaturalism (*saiyasat*). Ayutthaya literature showed no such tendency. *Lilit phra lo* describes very solemnly the supernatural power of a hermit which forces Phra Lo to travel to meet Nang Phuean and Nang Phaeng, and the spells which can change the forest into a place either of fear or shelter. The author's acceptance of such power is absolute. But writers in early Bangkok tended to view such covert, supernatural power, especially of rishi and hermits, as something comic and worthy of ridicule.

In *Ramakian*, the ruler of Rommaphat performs a sacrificial rain-making ceremony because the country has suffered a long drought on account of Thao Kalaikot's ascetic practice. In the rain-making ritual, someone goes into trance to find the reason for the drought. This give the author an opportunity to ridicule such behavior by recounting the behavior of the spirit-medium who enters the trance, and his wrong divination:

> He stands up, swings his body around, and blows on the cheroot.
> He pretends to speak repeatedly,
> Dancing this way and that, challenging his four friends and falling over them.
> He calls on the minions to help his faux pas.
> He then says, the sacred guardian who lives in the base of the big spirit-house
> States that, if he receives what he wants, the ruler will be helped with no worries.
>
> (*Ramakian*, I, 260)

Readers have been told from the beginning that the real reason for the drought in Rommaphat is because Lord Kalaikot had been practicing asceticism so severely. The divination by the spirit-doctor thus amounts to ridicule for the whole business of trances. Supernaturalism is built into the theme with asceticism being capable of provoking a drought. This royal version of Ramakian retains this story for the sake of the plot, but inserts passages such as these to ridicule and mock supernaturalism at the same time. At the end, the author advises the reader that the whole Ramakian story with its embedded supernaturalism "has no core of substance at all." Similar mockery of trances and supernaturalism is found in other works such as *Inao* (Phutthaloetla 1955, 256–8). At the same time, rishis and hermits increasingly became comic characters in literature. When Phra Phrot leads his army homewards following Phra Ram, the rishis see him and are scared into thinking that giants have come to molest them: "Some snatch canes, palm leaf fans, spitoons and stuff them into big bags. They run and crawl into the forest, falling down, unable to control themselves" (*Ramakian,* I, 556).

Supernaturalism such as treating illness with spirit doctors or trances in this way was popular among the ordinary people. Sunthon Phu was a major writer who ridiculed and castigated such practices. He took the view that this was deceit and trickery, including the instances in *Ramakian* and *Inao.* Like Nai Mi, he criticized the Chinese who went into a trance, cut their own tongues, and wrote characters to distribute to people: "Seeing that, I realize it's a trick, designed to relieve people of their money. They are prepared to lose blood by cutting themselves, with no fear of death. They play tricks on people to bamboozle them" (Sunthon Phu 1960, 209).

Because of realism, certain kinds of supernaturalism were looked down upon. At the same time, the Buddhism which flourished in early Bangkok placed greater importance on "this world." The interest in real experience made the upper class perceive the importance of humanity more than in earlier times. We might call this humanism in a broad sense, namely, placing humanity at the centre of events, and believing more in man's ability to control his own fate. This kind of humanism surfaced clearly in early Bangkok literature, marking another major difference from the literature of the Ayutthaya period.

Such humanism scarcely figured in the literature of Ayutthaya, as can be seen by studying the fictional literature. The leading characters in such works have special powers because they are gods or because they have received special protection from a god or deity. Phra Ram is a Bodhisatta and the avatar of a god who comes to overwhelm monsters (*yak*). Similarly, Orachun and Phra Samutthakhot are also Bodhisatta.

In Ayutthayan works, the leading characters' special powers are endowed by birth just as being royal is endowed by birth. Even works which are not about gods or Bodhisatta make a lot out of birth. For instance, Phra Lo describes Nang Bunluea as "completely from a *thao* lineage or *phaya* lineage" (*Lilit phra lo*, 5). This was because birth was an important factor for allocating power in the sakdina system. High birth, along with the special power and authority which come from such birth, equip the heroes of Ayutthaya literature to face dangers from the other characters. They are privileged by the protection acquired as birthright. The Samutthakhot story was taken from the Jataka and hence, as usual, the hero must be a Bodhisatta. Even so, *Samutthakhot khamchan* is very meticulous about the Bodhisatta-ness of the hero. Indra, the god who protects Buddhism, helps the hero throughout. He does not just come down to resolve everything in the finale, as in the Sangthong story.

When Samutthakhot competes in an art contest, Indra presents him with a vehicle (*Samutthakhot khamchan*, 92). When he is separated from Nang Phinthumadi, Indra helps by giving him a kris. Even when Samutthakhot leads an army to catch elephants, crowds of gods go along to "give their blessing with such loud shouting the air vibrates" (*Samutthakhot khamchan*, 34).

The heroes of early Bangkok literature are very different from those of Ayutthaya. The early Bangkok bourgeoisie did not feel that they could compare themselves to gods. Birth had less importance for them because birth was not the decisive factor in becoming powerful (though it still had some importance). The characters in early Bangkok literature thus tend to have power or authority in their own right as a result of education, which was something that every human had access to. Khun Phaen, Phlai Ngam, Phlai Chumphon, Phra Aphaimani, Sudsakhon, Sinsamut, and Sangthong (who acquired magic from his wet-nurse) all had power and authority as a result of education. Some works like *Khun chang khun phaen* even devote space to describing the education of these characters. Early Bangkok literature emphasized the humanity of its characters.

Because the characters were more human, more attention had to be paid to making the environment in which they were placed also appear more human in the same way. Take the example of scenes about the preparation of armies. An Ayutthayan hero could organize an army in the literature without mentioning soldiers at all (*Samutthakhot khamchan*, 105–10, 113–8). But equivalent scenes in early Bangkok works could not avoid describing the soldiers, as in Unakan's preparation of an army:

> He selects able soldiers who have killed enemies and never run away,
> All brave men who are invulnerable to harm. Each has his own saddle.
> Some have two swords crossed on their back,
> And a sacred headband from their mentor.
> The artillerymen look fearsome, in belts of lead charms carved with sacred formulae.
> The phalanx dress Malay-style, carrying double lances, looking as sturdy as Macassars.
> They will not flee the gunfire but run into the breach, stabbing with their lances.
> (Phutthaloetla 1955, 704)

Because of growing emphasis on humanity and this world, descriptions of cities and their inhabitants became more realistic in early Bangkok works. The hero is a human in a city of humans. Portraying the city as a place inhabited by real human beings is a way of reinforcing the humanity of the hero as well.

Sometimes this humanism affected the way even divine characters behave. Human ways of behavior are the norm and thus even gods behave like humans. When Phra Iswara (Siva) is about to kill Tripuram with the fire eye above his temple, he "spoke thus then grasped his jeweled lens, whirled it round flashing brilliantly, and skillfully directed its brilliant force at the giant" (*Ramakian*, I, 54). This fire eye or third eye of Siva represents his magical power as a god. Usually he does not use this eye. But in this *Ramakian*, he uses this "tool" to increase his special power in human fashion, just like using a gun in order to extend the range of weaponry.

This point is crucial to understanding early Bangkok literature. Works which failed to portray the hero in more human light were not so popular. For example the Unarut or Anirut story had been highly popular in late Ayutthaya, as can be seen from many references to the characters and staging of this drama script. It was also the first drama authored by King Rama I. But the popularity of the Unarut story seems to have declined sharply in early Bangkok because the drama largely maintained the Ayutthaya style and had no humanism at all. The hero is constantly associated with the gods. The opening passage has nothing to do with the Unarut story at all, but is included because it is about Phra Borom Chakkrit who is an avatar of King Narai and the grandfather of the hero, Unarut. Throughout the story the hero's divine descent is mentioned. Gods are repeatedly brought into the plot. The golden deer who comes to lure Unarut is a deity who has been transformed because Indra is concerned about his consort. When Unarut goes to fight his enemies, he claims the privilege of being the descendant of a god, as follows:

> By the good grace of merit and *barami*,
> I come from the lineage of the rider of Garuda.
> I will eliminate those who are jealous and evil.
> The irksome Asura will suffer the heaviest blow
> From the power and might of weapons that have been blessed
> In place of the discus of the god,
> Bringing peace and happiness to the world
> At every time of adversity.
>
> (Phutthayotfa 1972, 366–7)

Unarut's special powers do not come from study which humans could emulate, but from divine associations and divine weaponry. The villain of the story, Thao Panasun, also has special power. He has studied magic to become invulnerable, and each time he is killed he is born again—normally an attribute of the hero not the villain. Unarut thus has no way to defeat Panasun except by again deploying the privileges of birth—using a ring which his grandfather Phra Borom Chakkrit gave him and then praying for the power of the avatar to help him (Phutthayotfa 1972, 370). Both as a book for reading and as a drama, Unarut was not so attractive for the early Bangkok bourgeoisie and rapidly lost popularity.

By contrast, the Ramakian, which is also an Ayutthayan story about the avatar of a god, did not suffer a decline of popularity in early Bangkok because it was modified by Bangkok authors to give a more humanistic character to a story which is all about the gods.

In the early Bangkok version of the drama, the characters are still born as gods because the Ramakian story compels as such. Similarly, several tales not directly connected to the Ram story are included at the beginning because of an obligation to retain some "supernatural stories" from oral tradition. But whereas such extraneous material in the prologue to Unarut is designed to associate the hero with the gods, there is no equivalent imperative in the Ramakian. Moreover, in the early Bangkok Ramakian, Hanuman becomes the hero on a par with or even more so than Ram himself. Although Hanuman is born from the gods, the plot makes him more human than divine. For example, his own mischievousness is a weakness which results in Uma casting a spell to reduce his power by half (which seems to conflict with the gods' original intentions of sending Hanuman as their soldier to suppress the *yak* demons). Ram has to stroke Hanuman's back to revive his full power. Hanuman has to suffer while waiting for his special power to return. Similar to the way Khun Phaen or Kraithong have to undergo education. Hanuman learns from experience like an ordinary human being, rather than acquiring knowledge by birth. When he teases the rishi on Lanka island, he gets overwhelmed by the rishi and subjected to severe torture (*Ramakian*, II, 842–3). Hanuman is thus a very attractive lead character. In the performances of Ramakian as a *khon* masked play, *lakhon* drama, or *nang* shadow play (and *khon sot* later), Hanuman gained the love and affection of the early Bangkok audience more than any other Ramakian character.

Even Ram has more human qualities in the early Bangkok version. The revisions in some minor passages of the early Ramakian drama scripts composed during the First Reign show this trend. In the *Ramakian khamphak* of the Ayutthaya period, Ram sends Khonthan to find a resting place for the army; Phanurat uses magic to create a beautiful forest and trick Ram into halting where he can overturn the earth and bury Ram's army; Khonthan inspects cursorily and returns to tell Ram he has found a site for the army to spend the night; Hanuman goes to check and finds the place suspicious and unsuitable, so dives underground to fight and defeat Phanurat; he returns to tell Ram who is very angry and orders that Khonthan be publicly disgraced before the paraded army and then executed (*Prachum khamphak ramakian*, 54). The *Ramakian* of the First Reign follows this story on every point except the ending. Ram does not order Khonthan's execution but only has him expelled from his army (*Ramakian*, II, 1036). This revision highlights the mercy of a human king ruling over human subjects. Mercy and compassion are proper attributes of a human ruler, but unnecessary for a divine ruler who is outside human rules and displays his compassion towards humankind by coming as an avatar to suppress demons. He does not have to show mercy towards humans as a person. This revision makes Ram more human—a human king rather than a god king.

The contrast between Ramakian and Unarut is replicated in the contrast between Dalang and Inao. In the Ayutthaya period, Inao was already more popular than Dalang (if indeed Dalang existed at that time). In early Bangkok, Dalang fell even further in estimation. It was said this play was never performed at all. Both Inao and Dalang are heroes who come from the circle of the gods. But whereas Dalang retains the old Ayutthaya style with no sense of humanism, Inao seems to have more humanity. Dalang comes from a high lineage respected and worshipped by the ordinary people like something created by human imagination. Inao, however, has the divine qualities which bring success, but is also briefly described as undergoing study and education: "The king studies and understands completely. With superior celestial power, he is an expert in everything" (Phutthayotfa 1956, 10). In the Dalang story, the god Pratarakala constantly intervenes to help the principal characters. For instance, he comes down to help Raden Chawangkananglo who is ensnared by Raden Sirikan with a magic rope (Phutthayotfa 1956, 527). He carries Dalang's theatre house in his arms up into the sky at Manya to escape the chaos (Phutthayotfa 1956, 572). Butsaba Kalo also gets even more help from Pratarakala than she does in the Inao story. For example, when she ventures into the forest in the Inao story, the god just comforts her and gives her a kris for protection, but in Dalang the god even transforms the gender of Butsaba Kalo and her companion into male, and promises to give lots of other help. The characters in Dalang thus constantly impress on their bourgeois readers that they are gods in human bodily form. The hero likes to refer to his godly status, or his association with the gods. When the armies go to war, for example,

> Oh deity with magical power,
> Use the mystic cord to garner success
> Against the governor, dishonest and low.
> He is not afraid of the grandfather.
> Will you let him kill us, sacrifice us,
> We the honest line of Asanya?
>
> (Phutthayotfa 1956, 796)

In places it says directly that these heroes come from divine lineage "and certainly will not die" (Phutthayotfa 1956, 602). By comparison, the leading characters in Inao are much more human. Even though the troubles and tribulations they experience during their adventures in search of one another are created magically by the gods, they are not from a privileged class which can escape such hardships.

When man becomes the focus of the plot, the conception of humanity becomes more complex. In the past, the heroes in literature were gods or descendants of the gods, and the villains were enemies of the gods. Now the difference between heroes and villains is not so simple. Relations with the gods are no longer the main criterion. To date, there has been no systematic study of the characters in early Bangkok literature. But this rough survey shows that authors' more complex consciousness of humanity affected how they portrayed physical appearance. Heroes tend to have a slender physical form. This image was inherited from Ayutthaya and the sakdina upper class deprecation of physical work. In *Inao*, Choraka's ugliness is described as follows: "Look at his body like that of a laborer, large, tall, and strong, ugly, and totally base, an inappropriate match for a royal daughter" (Phutthaloetla 1955, 365). Choraka's robust and hard body is considered ugly because it resembles a phrai commoner who has to do hard work all the time. The sakdina or bourgeois upper class disliked physical work and allowed their bodies to atrophy, making slenderness a standard of physical beauty. Khun Phaen has a slender form "with a body as though it was molded." The upper class ideal was a tall, slender form. Choraka is thus described as having "a body like a laborer, not a prince" (Phutthaloetla 1955, 366). In early Bangkok literature, the heroes are not necessarily upper class—for example, Khun Phaen, Kraithong, Khongbeng, and Makatho—but their physical appearance tends to imitate the sakdina upper class ideal.

High birth is still appreciated but the power of money is now accepted as giving people no less merit than high birth or beautiful appearance. When Nang Thepthong, the mother of Khun Chang, instructs her son to stop thinking about loving and marrying Nang Phim on grounds Phim always looks down on Khun Chang, she says:

> You have heaps of money so why not use it
> To redeem somebody. Listen to your mother.
> Go to the city of Ayutthaya and choose a pretty thing who suits you,
> Someone with a slender figure like a kinnari.
> Stop being unnecessarily miserable.
> With all your money, you'll have no trouble.
> Why go begging after someone who doesn't want you?
>
> (*Khun chang khun phaen*, 95)

The power of money is something that people accept has a certain high influence. Yet the leading characters on the side of good in early Bangkok literature are not necessarily wealthy but, like Khun Phaen for example, are not hopelessly poor either. The primer *Prathom ko ka* (1963, 53) teaches that doing good is a route to acquiring riches and retinue. People with property and retinue are called *phu di*, gentlefolk or literally "good people." Khun Chang tells his men to make elaborate arrangements for a sermon because "they count me as among the *phu di*" (*Khun chang khun phaen*, 50). However, early Bangkok authors could distinguish between *phu di* and *khon di*, noble people and good people. Good people and people with rank were not the same thing. As Nai Mi wrote:

> Among humans who populate the world
> It is difficult to come across one who is good.
> But those who have merit and a little power
> Are not difficult to find.
>
> (Sunthon Phu 1960, 811)

This amounts to a rather complex idea about people.

Because of the changing values, tastes, and worldview of the bourgeoisie, literature entered a new era. Understanding these changes and their roots is a precondition for a more rational appreciation of early Bangkok literature.

SUMMARY AND CONCLUSION

The rapidly expanding export economy in early Bangkok changed the sakdina upper class towards becoming a bourgeoisie with its power founded as much on property as on the control of manpower. The migrant Chinese who flowed into Siam in great quantity made production for the market larger in scale and extent than ever before in Siam. Market production and exporting impacted greatly on the Siamese people through the bourgeoisie's purchase of goods for export in the junk trade. The growth of the city, and of people outside the subsistence economy, resulted in expanding internal trade alongside the collection of local goods for export. In response to these changes, the phrai system had to be modified to sustain the benefits of the noble class.

The social impact of these economic changes was that the upper class acquired a bourgeois character, and the interrelations between this upper class and the ordinary people became as dense as those among the upper class, bourgeoisie, and foreigners. The social bonds established under the sakdina order began to loosen. In some cases, the upper class was ready to accept such relaxation, for instance by reducing the period of corvée, and supporting the replacement of corvée by a commutation fee. People became more free though not to the point of creating a society of free labor. Most labor was still in subsistence production and tied by the surviving bonds of sakdina. Free labor was confined to foreigners who had the option to remain outside the phrai system—namely, the Chinese who flooded into occupations for which no Thai labor was available such as free labor in sugar plantations, mines, pepper gardens, and so on. The Chinese also became itinerant traders, junk traders, and import-export traders, who all shared their profits with the ruling class.

Early Bangkok literature was produced and consumed in this economic and social environment. The sakdina literary traditions of Ayutthaya were loosened. Popular literary traditions with power, liveliness, and adaptability were adopted into upper class literature. As a result, upper class literature acquired the same power as some popular literature. In this major period of Thai literary history, upper class literature achieved a power, liveliness, and ability to evolve new forms appropriate to its environment. The content of literature developed to serve the present. Most of the dark, stifling character of Ayutthaya sakdina literature was discarded. Openness to foreign literary traditions created new opportunities to sample different values in the Thai cultural context with no compunction to retain anything which could not justify its place. The number of literary experiments that failed in early Bangkok were at least as numerous as those that succeeded. Naturally it was the consumers of literature, namely the newly emerged bourgeoisie, who freely selected new literary traditions including those adopted from the popular tradition, those imported from overseas, and those invented anew. Bourgeois literature remained lively because there were no fixed models for literary creation, no dominant tradition that had to be followed. The form and content of literary creativity was decided only by risk, initiative, the communal approval of the literary community itself, and the decisive role of the expanding consumer market. Such force and liveliness has not arisen often in Thai literary history.

After the early Bangkok period, the Thai upper class began to know more about western literature. It began to believe that knowledge of western culture was a major condition of its social leadership. The ability to speak and read English qualified them to be kings, ministers, and so on. In parallel with this lapse of the Thai upper class into mental slavery to the west, the court circle from the Fourth Reign onwards became increasingly conscious of difference between themselves and the ordinary people. They tried to revive the "sacred" power of sakdina and reinforce their own sakdina-ness which had been neglected under the influence of bourgeois culture in the early Bangkok era (Nidhi 1980, 68–73; see chapter 6 in this book). But they could no longer reach back to the "sacredness" of Ayutthaya-style sakdina power because it conflicted with the rationalism adopted from the west. Hence they looked elsewhere for new philosophies, especially from the west itself. At first they focused on western knowledge but then found this threatened the "sacredness" of sakdina. Instead they turned to a safer source in the Sanskrit culture from the ancient era of the Vedas—especially its emphasis on the kshatriya caste as warriors and defenders of the kingdom. In many old poems translated from Pali, kshatriya is translated as lord of the paddyfields, not warrior. This translation seems to reflect the attitude of the court towards themselves, changing from an emphasis on their "right" towards an emphasis on their "duty." This duty was the reason they were rulers. Although ideas from Sanskrit about the relations between kings and gods were not used directly to justify kingship in this era, yet such beliefs underlay the general historical trend. One example is the emphasis on gentility (*sukhumalachat*) in qualification by birth (*chatwut*) (which King Mongkut made a condition for choosing entrants to the military cadet school; see the royal essay on the four-wheeled carriage). Through a monopoly on western knowledge, which was elevated as the highest form of knowledge, "birth" became a major condition for holding power. The administrative reforms which gave the royal institution absolute power reduced the age-old customary powers of the central nobility, provincial nobility, rulers of tributary states, and the Sangha. They also increased the importance and prominence of ideas about birth. In the late nineteenth century, Siam advanced into absolutism in the full meaning of the word for the first time in its history.

Driven by these political changes, upper class literature began to distance itself again from the popular literary tradition. The upper class—meaning the court or those under its patronage—turned to follow western literary traditions, while the majority of the people still knew nothing about foreigners except their strange appearance. The literature of the urban bourgeoisie and the rural people thus became totally distinct. The performances which the people developed in this era such as *lamtat*, *li-ke*, *phleng choi*, and so on, were looked down upon. The literature on which these performances were based was deprecated contemptuously as "all kings and courts," meaning nonsense. (Compare this to the First Reign when the King himself stated that the Ramakian was "all kings and courts," that is, nonsense, and himself wrote a *phleng yao chotmaihet*. Compare *Nirat tha din daeng* with King Chulalongkorn's *Klai ban* (Far from home). How many people read and enjoyed Klai ban? Without knowledge of the west, it probably made no sense at all. For example whatever is a "duke"?). At the same time, printing destroyed the opportunity for free literary experimentation. Only the propertied upper class could distribute printed books. The market for printed books was still narrow, and most upper class literary works in the late nineteenth century were printed for giving away as mementoes on various occasions such as cremations, and 60-year anniversaries. Alternatively, they were sold on behalf of government amongst officials themselves to raise funds for buying warships or funding the military exercises of the Wild Tiger Corps. (The writer of this essay once bought several old books of this era whose pages had not been cut open by the previous owner, making him wonder just how many readers these books had at that time.) Books printed commercially for profit were of another type such as those from "opposite Wat Ko"[172] or the works of Sunthon Phu, and such literature was looked down upon. In the late nineteenth century, the divergence between the literary traditions of the people (including a few bourgeois) and the literature of the court ensured that court literature became pretentious, with no relation at all to the social and economic situation of the country. There were dramas played for officials and courtiers to watch, and books distributed for officials and courtiers to read, but it was not important whether they inspired anyone. Amid the increasingly complex life of Bangkok society, awash with the sound of the people's laughter and tears, court poets continued to compose plays and poems using Sanskrit stories from two thousand years ago. The inspiration (if there were any) of such poets was the work of a group of academic Orientalists working in the English language. Both they and the consumers of their works constituted a tiny group in their own society, and an equally tiny group in Siam, but the latter group fortunately had a grasp on political power and thus could find more readers than usual by giving away books. The creators of this literature floated away from Thai society, borne by an insignificant breeze from the westerly direction.

Early Bangkok's upper class literature of such power, liveliness, and intellectual creativity met its final death. It turned into a pretentious, derivative literature for half a century and then disappeared from this world, leaving behind a lifeless corpse in textbooks which the Ministry of Education has to force students to study with great reluctance. Time had to pass until a new circle of writers emerged from a petty bourgeoisie closer to the people. Then again works were written with creative power, energy, and spirit, and Thai literature acquired a new lease of life.[173]

172. Early in the Fifth Reign, a printing house in front of Wat Samphanthawong (Wat Ko) produced many romances about royal deeds and court affairs, and this genre was later dubbed *na wat ko*. [T]

173. Most of this conclusion consists of observations from preliminary study. There may be some overstatement in emphasizing the key points. The aim of the writer is to explain the trends of change in upper class literature in the era following the early Bangkok period, not to present facts in detail, with the idea it might encourage a new, balanced study of this literature, not under the influence of the *Wannakhadi samoson* whose status differs little from that of books distributed at cremations. (The *Wannakhadi samoson* or Literary Society founded by Prince Damrong defined a canon of old Thai literature consisting almost wholly of court works. [T])

TABLE OF LITERARY WORKS

PROSE WORKS: FIRST REIGN

Period	*Title of work*	*English*	*Author-translator-editor*
1782	Kotmai tra sam duang	Three Seals Law	Recension of old work
	Iran ratchatham	Persian Tales	Somdet Chaofa Krommaluang Anurak Thewet
	Sai han	Eastern Han	
1802	Sam kok	Three Kingdoms	Chaophraya Phrakhlang (Hon)
1805	Rachathirat	King of Kings (Mon Chronicle)	Chaophraya Phrakhlang (Hon)
1802	Traiphum lokawinitchai	Treatise on the Three Worlds	Phraya Thammapricha (Kaeo)

PROSE WORKS: FOURTH REIGN

Period	*Title of work*	*English*	*Author-translator-editor*
	Phra Boromrachathibai, e.g., Tamnan Phrakaeo morakot, Prakat rueang tang tang	Royal works, e.g., History of the Emerald Buddha, Various Declarations	Phrabat Somdetphra Chomklao Chaoyuhua (Rama IV)
	Phraprawat trat lao thetsana phraratchaprawat phrabat somdet phra chomklao chaoyuhua	Autobiography of King Rama IV	Somdet Phramahasamana-chao Kromphraya Wachirayan Warorot
	Chotmaihet ratchathut thai pai mueang london	Journal of a Thai envoy to London	Mom Rachothai

POETIC WORKS: FIRST REIGN

Period	*Title of work*	*English*	*Author-translator-editor*
	Bot lakhon rueang ramakian	Ramayana drama	Phrabat Somdetphra Phuttayotfa Chulalok (Rama I)
	Unarut	Anirut	
	Dalang	Dalang	
	Inao	Inao	
1785	Nirat rop phama thi tha din daeng	Battle against the Burmese at Din Daeng	
1786	Nirat pai prap phama thi nakhon si thammarat	Defeat of the Burmese at Nakhon Si Thammarat	Kromphra Ratchawang Bowon Maha-surasinghanat
	Klon prarop rueang ti mueang phama	On the wars in Burma	
	Phleng yao thawai phayakon muea ploeng mai phra thi nang inthraphisek	Prophesy on the fire at the Inthraphisek palace	

POETIC WORKS: FIRST REIGN (CONT.)

Period	*Title of work*	*English*	*Author-translator-editor*
1791	Klon lae rai charuek rueang sang phukhao wat ratchakhrue	Inscription on building the mount at Wat Ratchakhrue	Chaophraya Phrakhlang (Hon)
1794	Khlong phayuha-yattra phet phuang	On royal processions	
	Rai yao mahawetsandon chadok kan kuman lae kan matsi	Maha Vessantara Jataka, Kuman and Matsi chapters	
	Kaki kham klon	Kaki	
	Lilit si wichai chadok	Sivijaya Jataka	
	Sombat amarin kham klon	Poems on Sombat Amarin	
	Khlong suphasit lae phleng yao tang tang	Various sayings and ballads	
	Rai yao mahawetsandon chadok kan mahaphon	Maha Vessantara Jataka, Mahaphon chapter	Phra Thep Moli (Klin)
	Nirat talat kriap	To Kriap market	
	Khlong kathu bettalet	Miscellaneous poems	

POETIC WORKS: SECOND REIGN

Period	*Title of work*	*English*	*Author-translator-editor*
	Khun chang khun phaen	Khun chang khun phaen	Phrabat Somdetphra Phutthaloetla Naphalai (Rama II)
	Inao	Inao	
	Bot lakhon nok 5 rueang: Sangthong, Kraithong, Khawi, Chaiyachet, Maniphichai	Five outer dramas: Sangthong, Kraithong, Khawi, Chaiyachet, Maniphichai	
	Kap he chom krueang khao wan	Poem in praise of food	
	Bot phak khon	Script of mask play	
1809	Khlong nirat narin	Narin's journey	Nai Narinthibet
	Khlong nirat tam sadet lamnam noi	Royal journey to Lamnam Noi	Phraya Trang Khaphumiban
	Khlong nirat thalang	To Thalang	
	Khlong dan chaloem phra-kiat ratchakan thi song	Euology of King Rama II	
	Phleng yao		
	Kan ruapruam khlong khong kawi boran	Collection of old poems	
Early 1807	Nirat mueang klaeng	To Klaeng	Sunthon Phu
Late 1807	Nirat phrabat	To the Buddha's footprint	
1828	Nirat phukhaothong	To Golden Mount	
c. 1832	Nirat wat chaofa	To Wat Chaofa	
1841	Nirat mueang suphan	To Suphan	
1842	Nirat phra prathom	To Phra Pathom Chedi	
1842	Ramphan philap	Lamentations	

POETIC WORKS: SECOND REIGN (CONT.)

Period	*Title of work*	*English*	*Author-translator-editor*
1845–9	Nirat inao	Inao	Sunthon Phu
c. Rama I	Kho but	Khobut	
c. Rama III	Phra aphaimani	Phra Aphaimani	
c. Rama III	Phra chaisuriya	Phra Chaisuriya	
	Laksana wong	Laksanawongse	
Early Second Reign	Singha trai phop	Singha Traiphop	
1821–4	Sawatdiraksa	Protection of well-being	
1830	Phleng yao thawai owat	Offering advice	
1837	Suphasit son ying	Sayings for the instruction of ladies	
	Aphainurat	Aphainurat	
Second Reign	Sepha khun chang khun phaen ton kamnoet phlai ngam	Khun Chang Khun Phaen: birth of Phlai Ngam	
Fourth Reign	Sepha phraratcha phongsawadan He rueang chap rabam He rueang kaki He rueang phra aphaimani He rueang khobut	Ballad on the Royal Chronicles Chants on dance Chants on Kaki Chants on Phra Aphaimani Chants on Khobut	

POETIC WORKS: THIRD REIGN

Period	*Title of work*	*English*	*Author-translator-editor*
	Charuek wat pho	Inscriptions of Wat Pho	Somdetphra Mahasamana Chao Kromphra Paramanuchit Chinorot et al.
1836	Khlong ruesi dat ton	On ascetics doing yoga	
	Rai lae khlong ban phanaek		
	Khlong phap khon tang phasa	On pictures of different peoples	
1845	Khlong dan rueang patisangkhon wat phrachetuphon	On the restoration of Wat Phra Chetuphon	Somdetphra Mahasamana Chao Kromphra Paramanuchit Chinorot
	Khlong charuek sala rai	On the Sala Rai inscription	Somdetphra Mahasamana Chao Kromphra Paramanuchit Chinorot et al.
	Khlong charuek sala na phra maha chedi	On the inscription in the sala before the great chedi	Somdetphra Mahasamana Chao Kromphra Paramanuchit Chinorot
	Khlong konlabot	Konlabot	Somdetphra Mahasamana Chao Kromphra Paramanuchit Chinorot et al.
	Lilit taleng phai	Defeat of the Mon	Somdetphra Mahasamana Chao Kromphra Paramanuchit Chinorot

POETIC WORKS: THIRD REIGN (CONT.)

Period	*Title of work*	*English*	*Author-translator-editor*
1844	Lilit krabuan phayuhayatra	On royal processions	Somdetphra Mahasamana Chao Kromphra Paramanuchit Chinorot et al.
	He phra kathin thang sathonlamak chonlamak	On the land and sea kathin processions	
1831	Suphasit khamchan	Proverbs	
1831–3	Kritsana son nong kham chan	Krishna teaches a younger sister	
1842	Tamra chan wannaphruet lae mattraphruet	Manual on the composition of chan	
	Chan dutsadi sangwoei klom chang phang	Poem for calming female elephants	
	Kap khap mai klom chang phang	Song for calming female elephants	
	Chan sangwoei klong winitchai pheri	Offering to the Winitchai Pheri drum	
	Chakkrathippani tamra horasat	Manual of astrology	
1849	Samutthakhot khamchan ton plai	Samutthakhot, final part	Somdetphra Mahasamana Chao Kromphra Paramanuchit Chinorot
	Phleng yao chao phra mahachat		
	Pathom somphothikatha	Life of the Buddha	
	Rai tham khwan nak luang	Spirit soothing for the royal ordinand	
	Prakat boromrachaphisek ratchakan thi si	Announcement of King Rama IV's coronation	
	Phra thamma thetsana	Sermons on Buddhism	
	Phraratchaphongsawadan sangkhep	Abridged Royal Chronicles	
	Phraratchapongsawadan krung sri ayutthaya	Royal Chronicles of Ayutthaya	
	Khlong lokkanit	Lokkanit Poem	Phrachao Borommawong-thoe Somdet Krom-phraya Dechadison
	Nirat sadet pai thap mueang wiangchan	The king leads an army to Vientiane	
	Chan klom phrasawet lae chan dutsadi sangwoei uen uen	Lullaby of the white elephant and other songs of calming	Krommaluang Phuwanetnalinlit
	Phleng yao lae bot sakkawa		
	Khlong nirat chachoengsao	To Chachoengsao	Krommamuen Kraison Wichit
	Klon konlabot		
	Nirat suphan kham khlong	To Suphanburi	Krommaluang Wongsathiratsanit
	Nirat phra prathom kham khlong	To Phra Pathom Chedi	
	Khlong chindamani	Chindamani	
	Phleng yao		

POETIC WORKS: THIRD REIGN (CONT.)

Period	*Title of work*	*English*	
	Itsarayan phasit	Itsarayan's proverbs	Phra-ong Chao Itsarayan
	Raden landai	Raden Landai	Phra Mahamontri (Sap)
	Phleng yao wa krathop phramahathep	Critique of Phra Maha Thep	
	Phleng yao chaloem phrakiat ratchakan thi sam lae si	Eulogies of King Rama III and Rama IV	Khun Phum
	Phleng yao chotmaihet rueang krommamuen apsonsudathep prachuan	On the illness of Princess Apson Sudathep	Khun Suwan
	Phleng yao rueang mom petsawan	On Mom Petsuwan	
	Phra ma-le-the-thai	Phra Male-the-thai	
	Unarut roi rueang	A hundred stories from Unarat	
	Nirat thalang	To Thalang	Muen Phrom Somphatson (Samian Mi)
	Phrasubin ko ka	Royal dream primer	
	Nirat duean		
	Phleng yao sansoen phrakiat phrabat somdet phranangklao	Euology of King Rama III	
	Nirat phra thaen dongrang	To Phra Thaen Dongrang	
	Nirat Suphan	To Suphanburi	
	Ramakian ton phra ram doendong	Ramakian segment: Ram travels in the forest	Phrabat Somdet Phrachomklao Chaoyuhua (Rama IV)
	Rai yao mahawetsandon chadok 5 kan (Sakkabap, Wanapawet, Mahaphon, Chulaphon, Chakasat)	Maha Vessantara Jataka, 5 chapters	
	Nirat london	To London	Mom Rachothai
	Nirat phra prathom	To Phra Pathom Chedi	Luang Chakkraprani
	Nirat thawarawadi	To Dvaravati	
	Nirat phra patthawi	In the stern of a royal boat	
	Nirat krungkao	To Ayutthaya	
	Khlong phap ramakian thi wat phra kaeo	On the Ramayan illustrations in the Temple of the Emerald Buddha	
	Sepha rueang abuhasan	Ballad of Abu Hasan	
Third Reign	Nirat phra phitthasali pai chumphon lae chaiya	Phra Phitthasali travels to Chumphon and Chaiya	Phraya Isaranuphap (On)
	Suthon khamchan	Suthon	
	Suthanu khamchan	Suthanu	
	Uthen khamchan	Uthen	

2

SUNTHON PHU: BOURGEOIS POET LAUREATE

TRANSLATORS' NOTE

The following summary of Sunthon Phu's life is based on Montri (1990), Prem Chaya's introduction to Sunthorn Phu (2001), and Sombat (1980).

Born in 1786 at Bangkok in a family hailing from Rayong; educated at Wat Si Sudaram, Thonburi; childhood in Rear Palace where his mother was wet-nurse to a princess; became government clerk; wrote *Khobut* when aged around 20; fell in love with a palace lady, Chan, for which they were both imprisoned.

1807: on release, traveled to visit father in Rayong, recorded in *Nirat mueang klaeng*; traveled to the Footprint Relic in Saraburi, recorded in *Nirat phrabat*; married Chan but they soon fell out.

1809: taken into the court of King Rama II; wrote the romances *Laksanawong* and *Singha traiphop*; legendarily offended future Rama III by improving one of his compositions.

c. 1821–4: started *Phra aphaimani* while jailed for drunkenness; commissioned to write part of *Khun chang khun phaen*; wrote *Nirat inao* as a parody.

1824: entered monkhood after the death of Rama II; wrote *Phleng yao thawai owat.*

1827: *Nirat phukhaothong*; 1831, *Nirat mueang phet*; 1834, *Nirat wat chaofa;* 1841, *Nirat suphan*; 1842, *Nirat phra pathom.*

1832: got renewed court patronage from a son of Rama II and others at court; went to stay in Wat Thepthidaram but fell out with the abbot; his patron died in 1835 and he traveled a lot.

c. 1841: renewed patronage from future Front Palace prince of King Rama IV, Prince Phrapinklao; probably wrote the etiquette manuals, *Ramphan philap*, and lullabies in this period.

1856: died famous.

All references to works by Nai Mi, and to Sunthon Phu's various *nirat*, *Kap phra chai suriya*, *Phleng yao thawai owat*, and *Aphainurat* are to the collection cited as Sunthon Phu 1960 in the bibliography.

2

SUNTHON PHU: BOURGEOIS POET LAUREATE[1]

THE ROLE OF THE BOURGEOISIE IN THE LITERATURE OF EARLY BANGKOK

IT is conventional to view the literature of early Bangkok as a continuation of that of Ayutthaya. But a comparative analysis of what survives of Ayutthayan court literature with the court and "semi-court" literature of early Bangkok shows clearly that this conventional view is quite superficial and of little value for serious study of the latter. The search for patterns in Ayutthayan literature to explain those of early Bangkok offers no illumination to the student

The truth is that in certain respects the upper class literature of early Bangkok abandoned so many of the patterns of Ayutthayan literature that it eventually developed a distinct character of its own. Its key feature was the massive adoption of patterns from the literature of the populace, whereas most Ayutthayan literature (till near the end) had a true sakdina character. The few Ayutthayan texts that were meant to be read made use of literary forms, vocabulary, and poetic locutions which could not be appreciated by the ordinary person (for example, *Thawathotsamat*, *Kamsuan*, and *Bunnowat khamchan*). The bulk of Ayutthayan literature was composed, not for the pleasure of readers, but rather for ceremonial and religious purposes (for example, *Lilit ongkan chaeng nam*, *Mahachat khamluang*, *Kap mahachat*, *Nanthopananthasut khamluang*, and *Khamchan dutsadi sangwoei klomchang*). Although some Ayutthayan literature was meant to entertain, the entertainment came not through reading but through performance (for example, *Samutthakhot khamchan*, *Anirut khamchan*, and *Khamphak ramakian*). It was not until the very end of the Ayutthayan period—when popular performances developed into the *lakhon* drama—that literature for performance began to flourish within the court in new forms. By contrast, it appears that the distinctive feature of early Bangkok literature was the habit of reading (or listening to others reading aloud) for pleasure. The production of *lakhon* texts of great length, and thus quite unsuitable for performance in their entirety, is strong evidence

1. The core theme of this section is analyzed in detail in my 'Bourgeois culture and early Bangkok literature' (chapter 1 of this book). Hence I cover it here quite briefly and without adducing any detailed evidence. My main aim in this essay is to examine Sunthon Phu as a "case study" using the critical methodology that I have proposed. I believe that I can thereby propose a view of Sunthon Phu which is closer to historical reality than the conventional one to which we are so accustomed.

for this contention. The ceremonial aspects of literature gradually disappeared, as demonstrated by the deliberate omission of the *kham pranamphot*, the traditional eulogistic invocation (of king or gods) at the start of literary texts. Of the four *lakhon* composed in the name of Rama I, only the *Ramakian* opens with such an invocation. In fact, the court taste for popular literature was then so avid that the monarch himself composed both *sepha* ballads and *lakhon nok* outer-dramas. Literature with a storyline grew steadily more popular. Efforts were made to expand its range and repertory by translating exotic narratives, by unearthing and rewriting ancient tales (e.g. from the Jatakas and books of antique fables), and by inventing wholly new stories. In addition, a number of the characteristic literary forms of early Bangkok were developed out of popular literature, such as the *klon phleng yao*, *sepha*, *nithan khamklon*, and so forth.

Although these changes had their origins in late Ayutthayan times, they only became conspicuous in the literature of early Bangkok, indicating that developments were occurring in the economic and social system which encouraged the florescence of these new literary forms.

In studying literature, we are accustomed to concentrate on its producers and to neglect its consumers. The truth of the matter, however, is that all literary work is social activity involving continuous interaction between producers and consumers. To be sure, a few writers or poets will have thoughts and feelings that diverge from the norms of their times: in such cases they are likely to be forgotten or ignored by their contemporaries. But the changes in early Bangkok literature were pervasive, affecting all writers and poets, not merely a few individuals. They were thus not changes that arose without a solid base, but rather were founded on a particular sensibility, a particular value system, and a particular way of life. It was this foundation that sustained the florescence of this new literature for almost a century. The new sensibility, value system, and way of life, far from being confined to the producers of literature, were so widely spread among the consumers that they had no difficulty enjoying the new literature. The combination of literary producers and consumers was the vital factor shaping the character of early Bangkok literature.

It was in early Bangkok times that commerce with China reached its apogee. The overseas junk trade with other regions was also by no means inconsiderable (for details, see Waraphon 1979, and Kiattisak 1980). The most active and direct participants in the junk trade consisted of three groups which were closely interlinked by family ties, business relations, and political interests. First was the monarch and the immediate royal family, who invested their money in shipbuilding and became the largest junk traders in the realm. To be sure the monarch's trading activities were still grounded firmly on a sakdina base, in that most of the goods he offered for sale came from compulsory tribute. Yet some genuinely commercial features also began to be evident—since at least some of the export commodities could not be obtained by tribute exactions but had to be acquired by purchase or barter. Official documents still preserved in the manuscript department of the National Library reveal the large-scale purchase, sale, and bartering of goods for collection and lading into junks engaged in long-distance trade. Such commercial activities also extended to speculative investment in the production of goods known to be in demand on the world market. For example, during the reign of Rama III, experiments were made in the construction of royal sugar mills.[2] These texts indicate very clearly that speculative commercial operations for profit were being carried on, and that the sakdina mode of production was being abandoned. In other words, the crown was now using Chinese laborers, both as workers in the sugar mills and as field hands on the sugar plantations; and this workforce was hired for wages, not mobilized by the sakdina corvée system.[3]

The second group now involved in commerce was a section of the nobility (*khun nang*), which, using bureaucratic office and private financial resources, also invested heavily in the junk trade. Even though these aristocrats' mode of participation in the junk trade remained tied to the sakdina system (insofar as that system continued to be the basis of their power), yet they were becoming even more heavily involved in speculation than the ruler. Since their rights to tribute were relatively limited, they mostly had to purchase the trade goods that they loaded onto their own junks, or into cargo space rented in those of other people. All the same, even if commerce made some noblemen extremely wealthy, opportunities for engaging in it derived primarily from tenure of bureaucratic offices or from bureaucratic connections. This is why the nobility never came into serious conflict with the sakdina system.

The third group to become involved in a big way with the junk trade were certain Chinese. Here again, those who succeeded in establishing themselves as men of wealth were probably only too happy to be absorbed into the sakdina system, not least because absorption greatly facilitated the conduct of their businesses, and opened up opportunities for commercial ventures in new fields (for example, various tax farms). Accordingly, relations between these Chinese, the nobility and the monarch were harmonious, since the activities of each group benefited the others. Another sizable group of Chinese consisted of traveling traders who formed a very profitable network for bringing junks into Siam, in spite of the fact that the ruler, the nobility, and the established Chinese were themselves owners of junks. This network also helped to expand the internal market, meaning higher prices for, and larger profits from, imported merchandise. Both those Chinese who were already fully absorbed into the sakdina system through acquisition of honorific titles, and those not yet so fully absorbed, were deeply involved in the economic transformation of the country, above all in the central region with its easy communications (Skinner 1957, chapter

2. See, for example, Document No. 5/1838 in the Third Reign archive of the National Library's Manuscript Section regarding the accounting of the money spent on a royal granular-sugar mill; Document No.18/4/1838, a letter from Phraya Maha Ammat to Phraya Wisetluechai, the governor of Chachoengsao, ordering a large purchase of cane shoots; Document No. 9/1839, the accounts of Phraya Wisetluechai's cash expenditures for sugarcane plantations.

3. It should be noted that in this period increasing numbers of Chinese were being brought into the country. The government had come to prefer hiring cheap "free" labor to various types of corvée forced on the *phrai luang*. This also helps us to see how the old sakdina order was beginning to decay. Not only the monarch himself, but those lesser royalty who had secured a growing role in running the country, participated in this lively junk trade.

2; Ingram 1955, 19–21). The descendants of these people, who had become Thai by education and upbringing, had a considerable role in determining the form and substance of early Bangkok culture.

The impact of the junk trade on the three above-mentioned groups—whom we may categorize as the ruling class, with vast political and cultural influence—was very extensive. Although they continued to rely on the sakdina system as the foundation of their political power, their interest in trade, capital investment, and profits drastically changed their values and worldview from the old sakdina norm. Since the bulk of their profits derived from investment of their own capital, they were in reality "capitalists" within a sakdina society—or at least a society in which capitalism was narrowly restricted to the upper class. Capital investment for the purpose of profit-making "at home" was still something inconceivable, since the mass of population lived outside the money economy. Hence, the system of extracting surpluses from this population, by compulsory labor (corvée) in the sakdina manner, remained in force. Yet it was ready for change the minute that the ruling class realized that hiring free labor would bring in greater "profits." For the time being, the one avenue open to these "capitalists" to make a profit on their investments was foreign trade, combined with exploitation of their sakdina status to exact domestic corvée labor. They were thus simultaneously sakdina lords and capitalists.

Although the economic activities of the ruling class did not immediately have an impact sufficient to undermine the sakdina framework of Thai society, they did exert a wide-ranging influence on a broader section of the population than simply the three groups described above. Quantitative increases in the junk trade involved a heightened demand for certain goods which the sakdina tribute system could not fully satisfy. The purchasing of goods from the common people for the junk trade meant in effect urging a part of the population to produce for export—particularly those producing commodities, such as pepper, which were in continuous demand on the world market (Waraphon 1979, 99–100). A scrutiny of the statistics on exports in the early Bangkok era (Kiattisak 1980, 68) reveals that the Thai were no longer merely middlemen, but were now actual producers of export commodities. Production of this type—by the massive use of labor for both the production of rice, coconut oil, shrimp paste, fermented fish, sugar, salt, and so on, and for the harvesting of natural resources such as forest products and lumber—surely affected a much wider milieu than just the three ruling groups. Even though an export economy in the true sense had not yet developed in the early Bangkok period, nonetheless a growing number of people were beginning to produce for markets far more distant than ever before. We should regard this change as an important basis for the very rapid development of rice exports in the wake of the Bowring Treaty.

In turn, these developments contributed to the undermining of the subsistence economy. More and more people began to be affected by the money economy, especially in those parts of the central region where communications were suitable. Early Bangkok literature makes frequent mention of market-oriented agriculture. References to markets and trade are a common feature of the contemporary *nirat*. More and more people—especially Chinese active in commerce—were getting rich without having any status in the sakdina society. Trade in commodities spread ever more widely because the flourishing of commerce also continued to broaden horizons—at least for some social groups.

Within this still limited milieu, economic change had a considerable impact on both the ruling class and that section of the common people which came to be indirectly involved with the change. Although the bulk of the population was still not involved, the numbers of those affected were becoming significant. Such people developed values, ideals, and worldviews that were different from those of the rest of the society; their ideas of truth and beauty came to diverge from what had long been traditional. But the new outlook bore strong similarities to the values, ideals, and worldviews of the bourgeoisies in other societies. It was thus these people who became both the producers and consumers of early Bangkok court literature, and who gave it its distinctive character—a character which cannot properly be regarded as continuous with the literature of Ayutthaya.

The poet Sunthon Phu provides an excellent "case study" in two respects common to poets everywhere. On the one hand, he was a product of his times. In this respect his works amply reflect the typical changes in the worldview of the bourgeoisie of that era. On the other hand, his greatness as a poet enabled him to establish standards of truth and beauty for his contemporaries (standards of a type that careful analysis shows to be characteristically bourgeois). Understanding his work requires placing it in its true historical context. It is useless to compare him with poets from other societies and other epochs, for the truth of the matter is that a poet is not a divinity immune to the flow of time, but a human being bound to his era just like the rest of us.

SOME ISSUES IN THE LIFE HISTORY OF SUNTHON PHU

One could well say that Sunthon Phu was very much a poet of the early Bangkok era—not simply because he was born in its opening years, but because most of his works were composed during those times. He was wholly molded by the age, and wrote specifically for his contemporaries (see the bibliography of his works in Chuea 1973, 36–7; Damrong and Dhanit 1956, 1–47; and Sombat 1980, 275–8). In addition, his long life afforded him the opportunity to observe and experience conditions right through the early Bangkok era.

A very interesting aspect of Sunthon Phu's life is that he cannot be regarded as a court poet in the full sense of the word, since the period in which he enjoyed the glories of life as a court official was very short. And what survives today from this part of his life are only minor sections of large works like royal compositions (*phraratchaniphon*) and *bot sepha*. Such texts allowed him only limited freedom, and tell us little about him. Even now we still do not know precisely which portions of the royal *Inao* are his handiwork, though we know for certain that he participated in its composition. Soon afterward Sunthon Phu fell from royal favor and lost his position at court. Although he subsequently found princely patrons, the works he created after the Second Reign (except for *sepha* versions of sections of the Royal Chronicles) were not produced under royal patronage. Consequently, he had ever increasing freedom in his writing. While it is true that some of his poems continued to be commissioned by princely patrons (for example, it is said that his *Phra aphaimani* so delighted Princess Apson Sudathep that she told him to keep adding to it), he still had much more freedom to write as he pleased than when he was composing dramas at the monarch's behest. Still more important, a large part of Sunthon Phu's oeuvre, particularly his *nirat*, was aimed at a far wider audience than a few aristocratic patrons. In fact, it is said that he even earned money from freelance composition. In this regard he differed from his major contemporaries, for he had to be sensitive to the tastes of a much wider circle of readers than was the case with the court poets. To put it another way, we can expect to find him responding, far more than the court poets, to the tastes of commoner readers. Hence his works reflect the conditions of life of a broader milieu than is true of the texts of such court poets as Narin-in and Prince Paramanuchit Chinorot. This is why Sunthon Phu became so widely popular in his own lifetime. His independence of the court and of the old system of artistic patronage marks the beginning of the disintegration of this system, a process that was greatly accelerated by the later appearance of print.

Another point to bear in mind is that the very fact such relative autonomy from the patronage system was possible for Sunthon Phu must mean that the pool of consumers of written literature outside the court was steadily widening. The literature which the Thai common people had consumed from ancient times was an oral literature, and thus unlikely to be written down. Written literature was the property of the very small minority with education. It was only religious literature that the common people and the ruling class "used" in common—for example, the *Kap mahachat* or the *Phramalai khamluang*. Since Sunthon Phu's works were written texts, we can be sure they could only be disseminated among the broad masses of the people via the medium of public performance. Hence those who stepped in to replace members of the upper class as his patrons were not ordinary commoners, but rather a group which, even if it did not make up the majority of the population, was still sufficiently numerous to spread his fame far and wide. It was first in the early Bangkok period that this stratum made its historical appearance. Its members were distinguished from the common people in that they were literate and thus could consume literature by means of reading (or listening to others reading aloud)—in the same manner as people in the court of Ayutthaya and in contrast to the common people who consumed their literature via public performances and songs.

The new popularity of literature-for-reading outside the milieux of court or wat intellectuals was the direct result of the spread of literacy, especially among the bourgeoisie. If one compares textbooks on the Thai language composed during the reign of King Narai with those of the early Bangkok period, one realizes that they were intended to serve very different purposes. The *Chindamani* is a text for the learned, in that it is fundamentally a treatise on the bases of the language from the perspective of grammar and versification. On the other hand, the *Prathom ko ka*, a Thai-language textbook of the early Bangkok era, is a primer for teaching children to read. It contains spelling exercises and other things needed by a child practicing to read. Emphasis on the importance of being able to read thus arose and spread, not during the reign of King Narai, but in the early Bangkok period. The *Prathom ko ka* praises highly the ability to read and write—what we could call literacy today: "For those born as men / Books are the main source of knowledge / If someone is unknowledgeable, shame and embarrassment befall him / Groups of friends ridicule and tease / Calling him stupid and dull" (*Prathom ko ka*, 53). In this way literacy spread among the "leisured class," which could afford to have its children spend considerable periods of time studying to read and write in the wat. The development of this "leisured class" determined that the characteristic feature of Sunthon Phu's work was that it was designed specifically for reading (or listening to reading aloud)—something of which the poet himself was keenly aware, as evidenced by these lines from his *Nirat phrabat* (97): "Whoever cannot go [to Phrabat] / May remember this description explaining the details to both the reader and the audience." This in itself confirms that he was in no way the lineal descendant of any Ayutthayan poet.

THE LITERARY GENRES OF SUNTHON PHU

A literary genre does not in itself have much significance. As a rule, poets everywhere take over genres inherited from their predecessors. But the intentions embedded in these genres may shift at any time. Genres are thus merely vessels for accommodating intentions as they change from epoch to epoch.

One segment of Sunthon Phu's work was composed in the genre *klon bot lakhon*, verse for drama scripts. This particular literary form had existed from late Ayutthayan times. Interestingly enough, it most probably originated in popular literature and only later was taken up by the court.[4] But in the Ayutthayan period it was used exclusively for theatrical performance, whereas in the early Bangkok era it came also to be employed for reading. In fact to preserve intact the entire story of the *Ramakian*, Rama I resorted to the *klon bot lakhon* as a storage vessel, without any intention of using the entire text for theatrical performance. Hence one can say that from the very beginning of the early Bangkok era, the *klon bot lakhon* was no longer composed solely for performance, but had become a genre of literature-for-reading. And even though at one point Sunthon Phu did serve as a versifier for Nai Bunyang's drama troupe (*Nirat suphan*, 269; see above p. 38–39), the *bot lakhon* he himself composed were by no means always meant for the stage. His *Laksanawong*, *Aphainurat*, and *Singha traiphop* are all drama scripts he never completed. These were literary works intended more for reading than for recitation. The custom of composing drama scripts for reading flourished further over the course of his lifetime. An outstanding example is Phra Mahamontri's *Raden landai*. And the "kings and queens" stories subsequently produced in considerable numbers were also written in the *klon bot lakhon* form.

4. I have already analyzed this matter in detail in the essay 'Bourgeois culture and early Bangkok literature' cited above (chapter 1 of this book).

But even aside from these texts, one can safely say that all Sunthon Phu's surviving works are literature-for-reading, befitting an age in which readership was expanding. There were ever more well-off people with sufficient leisure time to seek entertainment from reading. These people formed the market for Sunthon Phu's literary production. Their tastes were by no means the same as those of the Ayutthayan upper class, who were rather captivated by the *khlong* and *chan* verse forms with their elevated vocabulary, and meanings which by tight compression within a few lines of poetry were designed to arouse a deep emotional resonance. The education and lifestyle of Sunthon Phu's readers were quite different from those of the sakdina lords of Ayutthaya. They wanted simple entertainment, not something deep requiring much time for reflection. What they most enjoyed in literature were three things: first, entertaining, exciting tales of adventure and rivalry in love; second, travels to exotic places; and third, simple teachings on the theme that good deeds bring immediate rewards in this life.

Sunthon Phu exploited existing literary genres to respond to his readers' desires. In the genre of fiction he was an accomplished master, since he both knew a great many ancient tales (*nithan*) and could invent new ones of his own. *Khobut*, his very first composition, falls into the fiction genre. His masterpiece, *Phra aphaimani*, is a *nithan khamklon*, a tale told in the *klon* meter. This type of poetic composition had been invented earlier by Chaophraya Phrakhlang (Hon) in his *Sombat amarin*. In fact, the *Siriwibunkiti*, a *klon konlabot* text of Ayutthayan times, is also really a *nithan khamklon*—with the difference that the storyline is of less importance than the intricate rhyme patterns of the *konlabot* metrical form.

For those curious about new, exotic places, Sunthon Phu adapted the type of *phleng yao* traditionally used for recording events and travels, mixing in the *Kamsuan* genre of poetic lament. His *nirat* thus had a quite novel appearance. Composed mainly in *phleng yao* and describing things he himself had actually seen in the manner of the old *phleng yao* recording historical events (like the *Nirat tha dindaeng* or the *Nirat mom phimsen* of the Ayutthayan era which were originally categorized together with *phleng khongkao*), they included lovers' laments in the style of *nirat* like *Kamsuan*. The texts thus provided the reader with both flavors. In this way Sunthon Phu's *nirat* had a new spirit to them, quite unlike that of the *phleng yao* recording events in olden times, or of *Kamsuan*. This is why they were so enormously popular, and became models for this type of *nirat* for many years thereafter. The new genre spread because it responded to the hunger for information about new and different places whose names people had heard mentioned, as well as offering ideas and witticisms, and smoothly-phrased laments for real-life loves—not at all the type of idealized love and female beauty found in the *nirat* favored by the old sakdina lords.

Another segment of Sunthon Phu's work consists of didactic poems such as the *Suphasit son ying* (Sayings for the instruction of ladies), the *Sawatdiraksa* (Protection of well-being), and the *Phleng yao thawai owat* (Offering advice). But the teachings they contain are simple, not at all deep, and easily put into practice in everyday life, since for the most part they accept everyday reality and include no supramundane ideals. Their most important aspect was that their "morals" agreed perfectly with the values of Sunthon Phu's bourgeois readers. This is why quoting from them for the instruction of bourgeois children became so popular, and why they were so widely read, a point to be discussed further below.

As for the poetic genres which made Sunthon Phu so famous—the *klon phleng yao* and the *klon talat*—literary critics have attacked them as offering readers merely beautiful sounds without any profound meaning, and as maintaining a stereotypical metrical pattern regardless of the length of the work in question. But these critics miss the point, since they fail to understand the social environment of Sunthon Phu's literary production: i.e., that they belong historically to the first group of Thai texts composed for reading (or reading aloud for listeners), and that their author's aim was to respond to the demands of the three types of reader specified above. Light entertainment was a prominent element in these demands. Adults liked to read, or listen to children read aloud, poetry which gave pleasure by its euphonious phrasing, and was immediately accessible, with no need for intense, word-by-word concentration.[5] If the composition was of the type that had a narrative line, then the story should be recounted with rapidity. For example, in *Phra aphaimani*, the heroine manages to get pregnant and give birth in the course of a mere handful of stanzas. Listeners to Sunthon Phu's *nirat* were delighted by the descriptions of scenes he inserted, along with their sometimes real, sometimes fictitious histories, no less than by his easy-to-understand but witty epigrams. If they happened to lose concentration and miss a section here and there, they would be none the worse for it. His sweet, euphonious style of versification immediately engaged the ear, without requiring much attention to its meaning. Hence, once one understands correctly the purpose behind the reading of his works, and the milieu in which it occurred, one will readily see why it would be hard to find anyone to excel him in the composition of *phleng yao*. But his excellence is also limited by precisely these conditions; that is why it makes no sense to compare him with poets of our own time who write with other purposes in mind.

For the same reasons, it is useless to look for structural integrity or elegance in the works of Sunthon Phu. Critics have pointed out that his *Phra aphaimani* lacks a basic framework, and that it consists essentially of a series of interlinked episodes, without any controlling narrative, unlike the *Ramakian* or the *Wetsandon chadok* (Vessantara Jataka). Indeed, if one judges his works by this kind of western literary criterion, they are obviously seriously flawed. But in fact, we have to realize, for the reasons given above, that Sunthon Phu's poems were composed simply to entertain his readers—whether they really listened or not, or, if reading, merely skimmed the text. The virtues of his poetry lie in its parts, almost in every individual couplet. The amusement and pleasure one gets from each succeeding segment flows on and on, without necessarily leading up to anything grander, deeper, or more beautiful. One could thus compare his poems to a profusion of gems scattered randomly in heaps. But it was precisely this characteristic that made the poems answer so well to the

5. This cannot be done with the poetry of Angkarn Kalayanaphong, Chit Phumisak, or Naowarat Phongphaibun.

demands of readers in the early Bangkok period. These people did not have the leisure for any deep thought, and were perfectly content to consume everything strange and novel, glittering and colorful, and emotionally banal and superficial—exactly like the bourgeoisies of other societies and other epochs.

BOURGEOIS SOCIETY IN THE WORKS OF SUNTHON PHU

Like many other literary works of the early Bangkok period, the texts of Sunthon Phu are far more concerned with the condition of the country—as they saw it—than those of Ayutthaya. The very fact that written literature was spreading out beyond the royal court to the commoner bourgeoisie meant that writers were required to depict the lives of ordinary people—hence such new narrative backdrops as festivals, marketplaces, and highways. Such settings were almost totally absent from the written literature of Ayutthaya. In the case of Sunthon Phu, a determination to insert in his *nirat* naturalistic descriptions of things he himself had seen is particularly evident. Just for this reason, his *nirat* are of the greatest value for recapturing the ambience of that sector of society with which he was concerned. Indeed, it seems more than likely that he made a conscious decision to record what he saw as faithfully as possible, to judge from these words from his *Nirat phrabat* (stanza 97): "I record what was there in detail, without adding anything / Whoever has not been there / May remember the description." In this way he created the model for a type of *nirat* into which scenes from everyday life are inserted—a model that was imitated by Nai Mi, one of Sunthon Phu's pupils and also a contemporary. Let us now consider the *nirat* of both men from this angle.

The descriptions they both provide of life in the central region of Siam show a society in which commerce is actively pursued and an export economy is significantly expanding. The export commodity most frequently mentioned is sugarcane (produced mainly by Chinese capital and labor). It is clear that this sugar production was oriented almost wholly to the market, unlike rice which still remained embedded in the subsistence economy. As Nai Mi put it in his *Nirat suphan* (stanza 805): "See the crushing factory, squeezing sugarcane, delicious to the taste / Sugarcane juice trickles down drop by drop, of its own accord. / A large pan, a big stove with a fire / Make nothing else but granular sugar." The *nirat* of Sunthon Phu also mention sugar mills and sugar production in various localities. At the same time, neither poet described any other form of production for export—either because it was of a type they had never seen for themselves, such as teak logging, or because, concealed within the subsistence economy, it was simply too familiar (for example, rice).

As the result of the growth of this export sector, part of the population entered the money economy, and thereby in turn stimulated further the growth of commerce and the production of surpluses—beyond subsistence needs—in a significant number of peasant communities. Under these circumstances, markets or places for commercial exchange grew up in urban areas where both foreign imports and domestically produced export commodities were available. Here, for example, is a description of the market in Bangplasoi (Chonburi):

> We gaped our way through the market place.
> Two rows of buildings flanked a crowded street.
> Some stood, others sat in shops, chorusing noisily,
> Looking at the figures of the women vendors
> Who were stringy thin, and of moderate comeliness.
> On sale were clams, mussels, horse-crabs,
> Squids, beetles, and pickled shellfish in dishes,
> Brought here by Chinese traders.
> Eggplants, taro, pickled cabbage,
> Merchants sold cloth in the open air,
> Many women as well as men came to make purchases,
> About twenty of them packed up in bundles.
> I roamed and watched until evening.
>
> (*Nirat mueang klaeng*, 40; translation adapted from Sunthorn Phu 2001, 330)

In settlements close to the "forest people," local markets worked to bring those still living within the subsistence economy substantially under the influence of commerce or the money economy. The provincial dispersion of Chinese, whether for purposes of retail trade or for granular sugar production, was an additional important factor in the development of this money economy. Sunthon Phu described the market in the large settlement of Potharam as follows:

> On the slope of the river bank where things are sold
> Boats coming to and fro stop in large numbers.
> Many Chinese merchants sell goods like tea and chinaware.
> Dried sour tamarind in lumps and coconut oil
> Are some of the goods which forest dwellers bring to sell
> Along with kapok and cotton in tall white baskets.
> Thai, Yuan [Vietnamese], and Lao fishermen trap fish
> And grill them in a long stall on the river bank.
> The sugar factory at the end of the village
> Is a junction of many directions,
> A terminus for carts from the depths of the forest.
>
> (*Nirat phra thaen dongrang*, 213)

This kind of lively commerce was surely by then an everyday matter in the environs of Bangkok, which at that time was the largest urban settlement in the country. Just for that reason it would have seemed commonplace to Sunthon Phu's readers. Accordingly, he felt no need to go into great detail, contenting himself with such brief comments as "Go beyond the temple, and look at the landing at the levee / Permanent rafts are moored here to sell goods / Various kinds of silk, such as purple and light green / And many white and yellow wares from the junks;" (*Nirat phukhaothong*, 152) or "I could see only Indian rafts, strange kinds / Selling foreign goods and Thai, all to be used" (*Nirat mueang phet*, 167).

The expansion of the money economy to ever wider sectors of the population meant that growing numbers had cash in hand for consumption. The domestic market thus became an excellent place for the purchase of luxury wares. It offered profitable opportunities for the sale of various consumer goods to people who had stopped producing them themselves and had a taste for those foreign commodities which in Ayutthayan times had symbolized upper class wealth:

> Hainanese junks and other ships
> Drop anchor in rows. Chinese and farang
> Organize tribute to give to the king.
> When many goods come at the same time, prices fall.
> Patterned silk cloth and other things are sold cheaply.
> Men and women get whatever they like
> And walk around showing them off,
> Even wearing them when working in their villages.
>
> (*Klon phleng yao sansoen phrakiat khong nai mi*, 683).

This description reflects the characteristics of an export economy which in later years became predominant in Siam. As the commercial production of primary agricultural commodities flourished, so more and more people had more and more money to spend on imported consumer goods. Importing such goods for a hungry domestic market became increasingly competitive, and this competition drove prices down. It is fair to say, however, that it was above all the urban population whose standard of living was most strongly affected by the new market economy. Such people could now afford to wear nice clothes even when doing housework. To put it another way, the very bourgeoisie that derived the greatest profit from the export economy, now became slaves of the profusion of commodities they bought from overseas.

The *nirat* of Sunthon Phu and Nai Mi show us how substantially production for the market was spreading among the general population. One of the first occupations likely to have been so affected was fishing, in which a high level of specialized skill developed. It is possible that fishing as a specialized occupation originated in communities of foreign immigrants or their descendants, since they maintained greater fishing skills than the indigenous people. Sunthon Phu says of a certain Vietnamese lineage in the vicinity of Samsen that "I reached the Yuan village where there were lots of warehouses / There were fish-baskets, shrimp, and fish for sale / In front fish-traps were set up / Men and women all came and looked" (*Nirat phukhaothong*, 153). And his description of a Chinese community on the Maeklong River provides another example of references to fishing as an occupation, to fish-markets, and to the profits to be made from commerce in this type of foodstuff:

Reaching the Maeklong, where both banks are settled with houses
And many cheerful-looking houseboats.
Some are grilling fish with lots of slaves
Who rush to and fro, looking busy in differing degrees.
Some sell everything including duck and chicken, along with preserved eggs,
Sting-rays, mullet, mackerel, as well as crabs and shellfish.
Their customers number in thousands.
Small fish are heaped in baskets.
The women selling salty dried fish are all beautiful.
They make a good profit, collected until their moneybags are full,
Or put in their waistband, making their bellies bulge.
They all make themselves up to look very elegant.
(*Nirat mueang phet*, 176–7)

From this description we can clearly see that the Maeklong fishermen did not simply catch the small quantities of fish typical of a subsistence economy, but rather operated on such a large scale that slaves were needed to provide the necessary additional manpower. The fishermen themselves had to "rush to and fro" to cut open and prepare the fish for sale. Fish and shellfish are excellent food for ducks, so it is not at all surprising that the sale of duck eggs on a mass scale also developed in such fishing settlements. The sheer quantity of the eggs for sale again clearly demonstrates that it was not a matter of raising poultry merely for home consumption in the manner typical of a subsistence economy. On the contrary, people were raising ducks specifically for the market. Sunthon Phu's reference to preserved eggs also tells us that these fishermen were Chinese or at least the descendants of Chinese. He also shows, with great clarity, how the standard of living of the Maeklong fishing settlement was affected by the profits made from production for the market.

In the same way, the market economy made notable inroads on existing modes of agricultural production. Even though subsistence agriculture remained the foundation of people's everyday livelihood, the money economy spread out into the rural areas, stimulating small farmers to produce for sale. Sunthon Phu provides a picture of such a farming community in his *Nirat suphan* (stanza 301):

Groves of tall prathiw and bambax trees and sturdy-looking banyans.
This is a forest village with cotton fields.
The Chinese, living among groups of Mon and Thai, grow beans on their fences,
And plant vegetables and various bananas in profusion along the pathways.

Even though they do not say so explicitly, these lines describe a type of agriculture showing traces of a market orientation, insofar as the quantity of plants is said to extend "in profusion along the pathways." The same poem refers to banana orchards in another settlement, in a way that demonstrates still more clearly an intent to increase production for the market:

This is a village which Thai and Chinese call Ban Thawai.
Sweet banana orchards abound, attracting buyers.
Bunches are turning yellow, showing almost ripe, with flowers at the tip.
For one to four fueang the whole lot can be bought.
(*Nirat suphan*, 308)

The commercial economy expanded to include even the Karen, who produced raw cotton for sale in exchange for domestic utensils brought to them by riverboat traders. The scale of this traffic is indicated by Sunthon Phu's observation that the boats were "moored in line along the landing" (*Nirat suphan*, 317).

Even though the money economy in the early Bangkok period did not yet dominate the Thai economy as a whole, it did nonetheless expand extensively, especially in the central plain. As a consequence, people of very different social status, ethnic background, religion, and place of origin were forced into ever-increasing contact. To put it another way, the old closed society began to disintegrate in various localities. The ancient sakdina standards, while still maintained by law, began to totter on their foundations. Gold was becoming a commodity which wealthy people could use for commerce, even though the law forbade it. New standards were created by the bourgeoisie. Even if they continued to be based on the sakdina model, these rules were more liberal—they were no longer tied to birth-rank or social status. The only conditions required for the adoption of these standards were the necessary wealth and leisure time. Hence they spread rapidly in tandem with the changing economic situation. Sunthon Phu records the dissemination of the standards of the urban bourgeoisie into the countryside in the following lines:

At the row of rafts, there are many beautiful women
Radiant with a yellow sheen. Formerly, turmeric was used only in the town,
But now is spreading to the north, including those living on rafts.
The women fishers and vendors of fish and turtles
Are no longer sooty, no longer classifiable as fisherfolk.
(*Nirat wat chaofa*, 258).

Closer contact, whether direct or indirect, with foreigners and foreign languages, brought about a notable broadening of horizons. Like other literary texts of his time, the works of Sunthon Phu depict a society with an increasingly "cosmopolitan" perspective. We will recall that one of Phra Aphaimani's skills was his ability to speak several languages—the result of having lived for a time with *khaek*[6] and *farang* on Magic Jewel Island. That he studied these languages fitted perfectly with his roving life, insofar as he acquired his various skills by lived experience—in contrast to Phra Unarut or Anirut who had magical, supernatural power from birth. The composer of the *Nirat phra thaen dongrang* reflects an awareness of the internationalized character

6. Dark-skinned people, primarily Malays and Indians. [T]

of the society he knew in the picture he paints of the raft-dwelling settlement of Bang Ma Hon, Howling Dog Village (stanza 207):

> Approaching Howling Dog Village,
> There are so many boats that the men wait holding their poles.
> Rafts of Chinese, Mon, and Thai strung together
> Move this way and that, bumping and crashing, in a merry tumult.
> Some push this way, some that, some up, some down,
> Seeking a way through but facing resistance.
> Dodge the sappanwood boat, hit the salt boat, jam up against the firewood boat,
> They vent their anger, raise their voices, and curse.
> A Khmer swears, "ma jui ai tui na." A Lao says, "pa si mae bor fae su."
> A Chinese scolds, "mi nang ti kang fu."
> A Mon voice growls, "takork tork khami."
> With so many coming from one direction,
> Boats for oil, betelnut, prawn, crab, and fish paste,
> Push against one other, and some are smashed.
> Some have broken gunwales. Some have the roof holed and caved in.

The money economy stimulated rapid social mobility in a way that defied all the traditions of the old sakdina society. Hence, even in the absence of political change, men who did not hold bureaucratic offices closely attached to the monarch could still be upwardly mobile through control of wealth. It was becoming possible for wealth, on its own, to command a social prestige no less than that of rank in the old sakdina system. Indeed, in some cases, the prestige could even be greater, as suggested by Nai Mi's plaintive muttering that "The bracelets covering their hands are a sign of wealth / Nowadays people respect golden wrists" (*Nirat duean*, 726). Conversely, high birth alone might no longer ensure continuing high social status. It was essential now to have wealth. This might be acquired as a result of holding bureaucratic office which was deemed respectable. Prince Bowonsathanphimuk, for instance, had a great many children, who lost so much status that by the reign of Rama III they had all fallen on hard times in various ways:

> Several have fallen into utter poverty,
> While others work in government offices and are very cheerful
> To get praise, favor, and blessings from the king.
> They have lots of junks and feel content,
> With no worries and hosts of wives.
>
> (*Nirat suphan khong nai mi*, 797)

This increasingly rapid social mobility aroused great perplexity and anxiety in people like Sunthon Phu, who lamented,

> Oh, what is prestige and honor? Will it not disappear before our eyes?

> Being upper class and then falling into poverty,
> This is Impermanence.
>
> (*Nirat phukhaothong*, 161)

The most perplexing and alarming phenomenon of all was the rise of Chinese to the highest positions. Some Chinese had found ways to get rich extremely quickly—most of them foreigners who had special monopoly privileges from the government. Men who had once been mere coolies; men with conspicuously alien cultural values; men who won from the government various tax farms (for lotteries, gambling dens, liquor shops, and so on, which in the eyes of Thai Buddhists were sources of vice); men who used the wealth they accumulated to "buy" whatever they desired—intimacy with the monarch, the royal family, and the nobility, to the point of marrying into these circles, or offering their children as wives; special privileges; official offices and titles; even the "purchase" of beautiful Thai girls to serve as concubines—all this was a source of bitterness for Sunthon Phu. That wealth had become a new factor determining a man's public rights and social status was for him deeply perplexing. He expressed these feelings in the following lines:

> At Bang Luang on the small canal where so many Chinese sell pigs,
> Their wives are so young, fair, pretty, and rich it makes me feel shy and small.
> Thai men like me who asked for their hand would be blocked as if by iron bars
> But if you have money like these Chinese, the bars just melt.
>
> (*Nirat mueang phet*, 168)

Elsewhere, Sunthon Phu satirized the Chinese, for example:

> At the mouth of the canal amid the fields,
> Chinese are brewing liquor with lots of smoke
> And channels on two levels for the liquor flow.
> They tie a string to pull and control the filling.
> The wealth of Khun Phat deserves praise.
> He has so much money and gold, plus income from taxes,
> That all his minor wives are happy and nicely made up
> With better fate and fortune than the Thai.
>
> (*Nirat phra pathom*, 374-5)

It goes without saying that while the money economy brought wealth and prosperity to some, it imposed hardship on others who were caught unprepared, particularly those in urban areas. Having little or no cash in hand made it virtually impossible for them to live a normal life. Selling oneself as a slave (*that*) was one way out. Evidence has been found to show that during the early Bangkok period, there was a marked increase in the number of such slaves (Vella 1957, 25–6). Others had to live from hand to mouth, although we do not yet have concrete evidence to prove this conclusively. We can observe another "way out" in *Nirat suphan* where Nai Mi shows how young women sold themselves or were sold by others as prostitutes in sugar-producing areas where there were many Chinese laborers with cash in hand:

> He knows that the dripping sugarcane
> Brings hordes of ants from Bangkok for sale.
> But all are female ants. What a shame!
> They let themselves be sold, and face ruin.
>
> (*Nirat suphan*, 805)

The popular expression "dripping sugarcane" suggests that it was well known that cane was a lucrative business. The girls who became prostitutes were brought in from Bangkok—the opposite of contemporary trends, where upcountry girls come to the capital to work in the sex trade. In those days Bangkok, like the countryside today, was the first to feel the devastating impact of the money economy. Bangkokians then were ill-adapted to a monetized economy, like rural people these days who are forced to sell themselves to find the cash needed in order to survive. Indeed, over and over again, in a persistent pattern, we can see economic change forcing the "little people" to swallow this bitter pill.

Just as the monetized economy brought into contact people of quite diverse backgrounds, so the increasingly popular *nirat* reflected social traffic that was becoming busier than ever before. As commercial linkages expanded, more and more people came to seek out far-off production sites and markets, especially in places famous for local specialties, scuh as Phetchabun for its tobacco. Phetchabun was no longer at the far end of the Bangkokians' world. It had become a real place, even for those who had never set foot there. There were real people there, too, whom one could contact through the tobacco trade. As a result of market forces, the mental horizon of the Thai was vastly expanded to include not merely places within Siam itself, but other locations which produced commodities that urban Thai consumed, or from where various groups of traders migrated into the country. The outlook of the Thai bourgeoisie was thus increasingly based on concrete experience, in contrast to the imaginary world of the *Traiphum* (Nidhi 1979, 2–31; see chapter 4 of this book). Sunthon Phu's work perfectly reflected the widening consciousness of this bourgeoisie (see for example Khun Wichitmatra's *Phumisat sunthon phu*, The geography of Sunthon Phu). An extract from *Phra aphaimani* illustrates this consciousness:

> The Chinese sail on the route towards the east,
> Taking the outer course around the peninsula
> Then to Kuengtang, Kangchio, Chunchiochiang,
> Then a short-cut to avoid Ai Mui, sailing straight.
> The Indians take a different route to foreign lands
> Via Arumakhet, the bay of Surat, Pattani,
> Pahang, Pangaro, and then Java;
> To Melaka, Kailaiwang, then Trengganu.
> The Dutch come via Laem Lo, Ban Kham,

Entering the shark-infested bay of Laem Ngo, to Rahu Island.
The Chams of Aceh pass by Malaya.
The Yuan cross over from Vietnam.
The Brahmans cross to Sawathi town, Wesali, Ulong, Romwisai,
Kabinlaphat, and Romaphat, in sequence.
The town of Aphaisali is where they live.
The Thai, once they catch the wind, sail to Ayutthaya of Siam.
Burmese and Mon veer off to Phukam Bay.
Some *farang* cross over to Yiaraman Bay,
While others go to the Bay of Wilat,
The town of Ma-ngat, Ma-ngada, Ma-ngasawan,
Past Chaomali Island, full of shrimp paste,
Looking for their kin and relatives.

(*Phra aphaimani*, 383)

Phra aphaimani could actually be termed an Asian literary work, since it uses almost the entire Asian continent for its scenes. Such a vast setting for a literary work was not new for the Thai: indeed the *Ramakian* made use of the entire universe. The novelty was that the settings of *Phra aphaimani* were experienced realities (or at the least its creator tries to convince us of this). Most of the travel it described, whether for pleasure, for military purposes, or to visit kinfolk, was by sea—fitting exactly the trans-Asian maritime traffic with which Sunthon Phu and his bourgeois contemporaries were well acquainted. Once upon a time, the sea had evoked a feeling of terror; now it was where the main characters went to seek pleasure or to relax. The trading junks of the early Bangkok period had accustomed both author and readers to oceanic travel. When Suwanmali feels depressed, she asks to go to sea, rather than to the forest as in other (traditional) Thai literature. Her ladies-in-waiting accompany her, anticipating enjoyment rather than fear. One of them even contemplates "going to sea to find a hundred [kinds of] shellfish" (*Phra aphaimani*, 152–4).

Increasingly intensive travel in the early Bangkok period made Thai literature see the forest in a more friendly light. In Ayutthayan literature it was a terrifying place. As late as its final phase, Prince Thammathibet was still full of anxiety when his love was about to set out for the Footprint Relic in Saraburi.

For one who has never seen the forest, the first sight is so exciting.
Animal sounds are deafening. Such isolation makes one nervous,
The more one thinks, the more one becomes agitated.

(*Phleng yao chaofa kung*, 303)

Early Bangkok literature described the forest in a more relaxed manner. Admiration for a beautiful bird or tree would remind a character of his or her lover, or of a beautiful forest landscape—just like today. When Nang Laweng is left wandering alone in the forest, she gives a very cheerful description of what she observes (*Phra aphaimani*, 514). In *Inao*, when Butsaba and some of her ladies-in-waiting are carried off by the wind and set down in the midst of a forest, she is not in the least scared. Sunthon Phu described forests in a number of his *nirat*. As a rule, if he did not intend to describe a character's suffering, he would dwell on the beauty of the forest, as in this passage:

> The way was smooth with soft sand.
> Payom flowers of the forest were fragrant.
> Comforted by the gentle breeze,
> We glanced up and around us all the way.
> .....
> At Phadon Sakhon there was a spouting spring,
> The water poured down through a crevice
> In a clear, swift current, beautiful to behold.
> We dipped our delicate scarves and pressed them to our breasts.
> Then we walked up a slope into a grove of sweet-smelling wood,
> Full of floral delights,
> Where soft breezes blew, wafting
> The scent of flowers, cheering our spirits.
>
> (*Nirat mueang klaeng*, 47–48; translation adapted from Sunthorn Phu 2001, 539, 556)

SUNTHON PHU'S WORKS IN THEIR BOURGEOIS SETTING

Although Sunthon Phu was much loved by his contemporaries, the fabric of the evolving bourgeois society of his time was not yet strong enough to allow even a popular writer to make a living by his work, nor was the existing technology adequate for such a professional career. The printing press had only just begun to appear, and printing as a business was still over the horizon. It is therefore not surprising that all his life Sunthon Phu had to depend on various wealthy bourgeois patrons, in a manner reminiscent of the clientelism of the old sakdina social order. Yet it was under these conditions that he managed to create works which were read widely among the bourgeoisie and made him famous. Of all his contemporaries he has been far the most quoted. Up to the present, maxims and witty *bon mots* from his poetry continue to crop up in the oral and written language of the Thai. It is commonly held that his huge popularity is due to the quality of his writing. The plausibility of this argument is hard to deny, but somehow it is not quite satisfactory on its own. There were other poets of the early Bangkok period, many of whose works were very similar to those of Sunthon Phu—for example, Chaophraya Phrakhlang (Hon) and King Rama II—but they were not nearly so widely read. (The writings of King Rama II are today more put on a pedestal than actually "appreciated.") A more probable reason for Sunthon Phu's greater and more enduring popularity is that he shared the values and attitudes of the rising bourgeoisie and expressed them in his works. And this bourgeoisie has increasingly formed the bulk of the reading public—up to this day. It is not that the works of his contemporaries, royal and otherwise, do not reflect the values and outlook of the bourgeoisie of the time, but that they do so to a markedly lesser degree.

The values and outlook of the early Bangkok bourgeoisie cannot be likened to those of their counterparts today. The early Bangkok period was a time when the nascent bourgeoisie began to exert political power and hence to have, in certain respects, a decisive influence on Thai culture. Yet the bourgeois were also willing to sustain the sakdina system where it happened to further their own interests. After all, despite their considerable numbers, they were still only a small minority in the total population. Since their written literature was confined to what they themselves produced and consumed, they adhered to their values and outlook quite unselfconsciously. This is why their literature seems so remote from us these days. Only if we draw a comparison with what existed previously, say in Ayutthayan times (except its very last phase), will we become aware of affinities between the values and outlook of early Bangkok and our own. Thus, to appreciate the quality of Sunthon Phu's works, we have to compare them with Ayutthayan literature, rather than with contemporary literature. Then we will discover the vastly different attitudes and values latent in his poetry.

One distinctive feature of this bourgeois way of thinking was its emphasis on rationality. The mystical and the miraculous had little appeal to this class, no matter whether in the political, economic, or religious aspects of life. Sunthon Phu's works reflect this rationality, even though they still incorporated elements of sakdina Ayutthaya's fondness for the occult and the magical. Phra Aphaimani had supernatural powers, but they were not given to him at birth in the manner of Phra Samutthakhot or Phra Anirut. He had to "win" them by study and experience, like other human heroes of early Bangkok literature, such as Khun Phaen, Phra Wai, and Kraithong. This way of thinking about heroes could only arise in the freer atmosphere of early Bangkok by comparison with the Ayutthayan age. We have already observed how upward mobility was beginning to be achieved through education and commerce. It is therefore not surprising that Phra Aphaimani is more human than the heroes of Ayutthayan literature, even though supernatural events crop up in the narrative of his life. In this way, *Phra aphaimani* was more "progressive" than its contemporaries, *Inao*, *Ramakian*, or *Dalang*, but no more so than *Khun chang khun phaen*, the greatest bourgeois literary work of the period. Its characterization was more realistic, in that its protagonists were shown to have strengths and weaknesses, good points as well as bad, and they reaped what they had sown. The figures in *Phra aphaimani* were not simply puppets playing out parts ordained for them by the gods, like those in the *Ramakian,* or agents of occult forces beyond their own intentions, like Phra Lo, Lady Phuean, and Lady Phaeng in *Lilit phra lo.* The rationalism of the poem was pointed out long ago by the great bourgeois thinker Thianwan, who commented that "in *Phra aphaimani* nobody flies. When arrows miss their mark, they do not automatically return to their sheaf. People use their brains and make plans, just like in real history" (quoted in Plueang 1963, 552).

Sunthon Phu was critical of belief in magic, as his works demonstrate. But before investigating this topic, we need first to define our terms. I take supernaturalism or faith in magic to mean belief in something which cannot be logically proven, and which is not based on empirical evidence. Of course it is true that everyone has some magical beliefs in various degrees, such as "blind faith" in some things not accessible to proof. This means that what we call magic differs widely in different circumstances. Hence, certain supernatural beliefs are peculiar to certain classes, with each class confident in the truth of its own, while scorning those of other classes as either wicked or nonsensical. Naturally, Sunthon Phu was only critical of the supernaturalism of the ordinary people and of foreigners. Like any other bourgeois of his time, he did not question the magical beliefs associated with the precepts of Buddhism. In *Phra aphaimani* the monk Pipo is endowed with considerable supernatural power. For example, he can foresee future events. Nonetheless, he lives his life according to the Buddhist doctrine of the impermanence of bodily matter, and his power seems to be connected to the mastery of written treatises and to practical study. Sunthon Phu himself believed in alchemy, astrology, and magic charts that could lead one to buried treasure (see his *Nirat wat chaofa*). This kind of thing was quite beyond the horizon of the ordinary people. (Note that, for all his attempts at reforming Buddhism to make it more rational, King Rama IV remained a firm believer in astrology.) The magical beliefs of the ordinary people and foreigners of which Sunthon Phu so disapproved were mostly connected to the treatment of illness. Shamanism was a common and inexpensive form of "medicine" that ordinary people could afford.

When Sunthon Phu fell ill in the town of Klaeng, his relatives resorted to the traditional shamanistic treatment to help him. As he told it:

> A medium who was consulted when my hand was injured
> Said it was because I picked flowers[7] behind the hill.
> I had not asked permission respectfully and slighted
> The guardian spirit, who, angered, took revenge.
> After the doctor asked forgiveness it was granted.
> In my heart I knew it was a fraud
> But the villagers believed the doctor,
> So I kept my thoughts quietly in my breast.
>
> (*Nirat mueang klaeng*, 60; translation adapted from Sunthorn Phu 2001, 919)

The funny thing is that he was actually cured! But he had already chosen to insist that shamanism was "quackery." Such thinking is commonplace among the bourgeoisie everywhere, because they believe it is more respectable to be treated by doctors who

7. This passage probably has a double meaning. On the one hand, picking flowers would offend the forest spirit. On the other, "picking flowers" has the same meaning as "deflowering", and those "slighted" and "not asked leave respectfully" in the following line may be the girl(s) and their parents. [T]

are specially trained over many years and who read special books. This bourgeois outlook offers a sharp contrast to the view of the hermit Pu Chao in *Lilit phra lo*.

In other places, Sunthon Phu was quite explicit in his view of shamans as "quacks:"

> At the edge of the village is the villagers' spirit-house
> Where they are making offerings of propitious rice.
> Seeing spirit mediums, I feel how wretched they are.
> They lure people to swallow their tricks
> By dishonestly saying the gods will help them.
> I do not think that the people will get what they want.
> Even if the spirit consents to help, things may turn out different.
> It is better to depend on the patronage of nobles.
>
> (*Nirat phra pathom,* 376)

What is of special interest here is that the poet did not consider shamanistic spirit-possession itself as a sinful or heretical practice, but merely a racket; yet he strongly condemned the villagers' belief in the shaman as a serious sin for which they would go to hell. His unstated assumption was that it was a great sin to have more faith in spirits than in Buddhism's Triple Gems (the Tipitaka). The mentality of people who have become Buddhists through extensive reading and study is not at all peculiar to Buddhism, but can be found everywhere in other religious traditions. It is the mentality of the bourgeois whose faith is based on texts, and not on the lived practice of strictly observant religious leaders (for Buddhists, the abbots of temples). Yet instead of encouraging the common people to relinquish their spirit beliefs in favor of faith in the Triple Gems for their own good in the next life, the poet made a plea for them to turn to the nobility, rather than the spirits, on grounds the nobles could provide protection, and procure posts for their dependents as tax collectors or low-ranking state officials. Thus, the poet's attack on the supernatural beliefs of the ordinary people did not stem wholly from a religious standpoint, but rather from a combination of religious and worldly concerns and interests—the normal religious outlook of the bourgeois everywhere

Even though no European-style reformation movement against traditional religious authority ever took place in Siam, what the Thai bourgeoisie chose to emphasize in Buddhism gave the religion a new dimension. Religion plays a very important role in affirming values, yet the values held by believers should not contradict their material interests. For example, *ahimsa* (non-violence) cannot possibly be a value for hunters or warriors. In Buddhism, the fundamental doctrines of impermanence, of suffering as imprisonment in materiality, and the separation of the soul and the body, make the accumulation of material wealth the act of a fool. Such doctrines clearly conflict with the bourgeoisie's interest in capital accumulation, so it is no surprise that they preferred to push these doctrines into the background, and continued to consider the amassing of wealth as quite "legitimate." (Note that "legitimate" is a relative term, and changes according to time and mental outlook.) In other words, seeking worldly comfort (or in Buddhist parlance, "material comfort") was taken as quite normal. It might not be saintly, but it was no worse than how people acted as a matter of course. It was nothing to be ashamed of.

Sunthon Phu's poetry clearly reaffirms this bourgeois mentality. His male protagonists were unfaithful womanizers, exactly like most of their counterparts in the work of other poets of the early Bangkok period. This trait marks them off sharply from the heroes of Ayutthayan literature. Neither Phra Ram, Phra Anirut, Phra Lo nor Phra Wetsandon were depicted as womanizers, while Sunthon Phu's heroes abandon everything to do with religion in their pursuit of women. Phra Aphaimani enters the monkhood to attain nirvana, but once he sees Nang Suwanmali, he "gleefully forgot his meditation, for his heart was still young, and he fell for her" (*Phra aphaimani*, 173). Weakness of the flesh might cause the hero various problems in the course of his life, but in the end he always achieved his goals, undergoing no retribution for abandoning nirvana for worldly passions. "Low" things, like women and music, which kept human beings chained to the terrestrial world, were not that bad; in fact, they could turn out to be of real value (for instance, Nang Suwanmali proved to be a great help to Phra Aphaimani). Sunthon Phu had his hero describe the value of music this way:

> But in my heart I love the way of the *nak leng*.
> I think music is really wonderful.
> Even though the performance is indulgent
> Yet it dispels unhappiness for men and women.
>
> (*Phra aphaimani*, 4)

Being a *nak leng* (in the early Bangkok sense, equivalent to "playboy" today) was a typical trait of the heroes of that period, even though *nak leng* behavior clearly conflicts with Buddhist values. In various *nirat*, Sunthon Phu depicted himself as a *nak leng*—adventurous, an inveterate drunkard, and promiscuous. In the course of his *nirat* poems he claimed to have had sexual relations with no less than ten women. It is more than likely that he exaggerated his *nak leng* qualities in order to fit the picture that the bourgeoisie had of a *nirat* writer and to give more color to his poetry. Interestingly enough, he wrote of his sexual activities without apologies, and without mention of any sinfulness. That he dared to offer this self-portrait to his Buddhist readers shows that his behavior was quite in accord with the bourgeois-Buddhist morality of his time. By comparison, in *Kamsuan* or *Thawathotsamat, nirat* of the Ayutthayan age, the writers focus on a relationship with only one woman, with no skirt-chasing at all, while Sunthon Phu, especially in his *Nirat mueang phet*, vaunted his innumerable affairs with women.

This readiness to seek the pleasures of the flesh was easy to extend to a readiness to seek wealth. Sunthon Phu's readers were taught the value of riches from a very early age. In his primer, *Prathom ko ka hat an*, then a widely read text, he instructed children in this manner:

Young lads, seek out teachers and study subjects properly and thoroughly,
So when you are grown up, you can seek out wealth and riches, make a living, and yearn to have money, material goods, and attendants.
Wealth is near at hand. Anyone with intelligence can gain it in no time. Riches are to be found anywhere. Only the lazy cannot get them...
Do not be a playboy, singer, or musician. Do not even think of it. Do not be content to get hoarse with a sore throat. You are not meant for such.
You will waste your money on food and lodging, on booze, betelnut, and tobacco, on fancy clothes and people's wages, just to get aching ears and eyes.
Do not learn to play the Indian drum, get carried away, and beat it in the street so much that people are irritated by the noise and complain. It's pointless.
Do not be a drunkard. Do not take opium or alcohol...
Do not go to the big gambling den or cock fighting. Winning is rare.... Concentrate on your work.

(*Prathom ko ka hat an*, 74)

Notice that throughout the lesson, emphasis is put on wealth as the reward for good deeds, with no mention of heaven or nirvana. Learning led to wisdom, which in turn brought riches which were everywhere to be had. The logic of the lesson moves towards a conclusion which represented a core belief of the bourgeois class, to wit: cleverness or intelligence was the product of a child's serious devotion to study from an early age; and this devotion in turn came from avoiding bad behavior. Put in a nutshell, good behavior led to cleverness which led to wealth. The moral code was that proper behavior and riches were inseparable. A man's wealth was strong evidence of his fine moral character. By contrast, people who got involved in "improper" behavior were fools and would suffer "hardship." Hence poverty was inseparable from bad behavior, and wealth was man's highest value.

Sunthon Phu emphasized this bourgeois logic very often. For example, he wrote that "To be a man is to seek fulfillment and the achievement of perfect happiness" (*Ramphan philap,* 341; translation from Vella 1986, 52). The poet also pointed out that the value traditionally attributed to high birth was really secondary to that of wealth. Obviously this viewpoint won the approval of the bourgeoisie, who by definition were not of noble origins. Privileging birth-rank would necessarily thwart their interests and aspirations. Sunthon Phu put the point this way:

There is a saying someone coined
That a person with a beautiful face and of high birth,
Even if of the lineage of the Sun and the Chakra,
Without wealth is nobody.

(*Suphasit son ying*, 15)

The new value placed on worldliness, wealth, and man's control over his own destiny affected the traditional Thai belief in the importance of karma. On this matter, Sunthon Phu never made himself clear, even though he often used the term karma and occasionally borrowed from the theory of karma to explain certain difficulties (see Sombat 1980, 273–315). One has to remember Sunthon Phu was not a man capable of revolutionizing the old Thai philosophy of life. He was merely the product of a time of social and economic change. Hence, his thinking was a mixture of the old and the new. The interesting thing, however, is that, unlike the Ayutthayan poets, he tried to explain the workings of karma in a rational manner acceptable to his bourgeois audience, rather than simply accepting on blind faith the influence of the traditional conception. In several passages we can find him attempting to show that karma arises directly from the deliberate actions of individuals. This stance is best illustrated in his *Aphainurat*, a play in which the protagonist is put under a curse by a forest spirit. The man's misfortunes come from his own senseless burning of a spirit's house. Yet instead of the curse having an immediate, mysterious effect, it emerges gradually through the man's own decisions and actions. He falls in love with a court lady who is really an evil spirit, and so governs his country negligently and unjustly. In the end, he loses everything including his crown. (Sunthon Phu left the story unfinished, but the ending can be logically surmised.) Past good and bad deeds did affect one's destiny, but not by the impact of an inscrutable, inexplicable power. They led men to take actions which could lead to further actions, good or bad, with further logical consequences. This way of thinking was highly acceptable to the poet's bourgeois readers.

Sunthon Phu's attitude toward the institutions of Buddhism, especially the Sangha (monkhood), was rather relaxed and even a bit irreverent. When he himself became a monk, he continued to exchange poetic repartees with lay people, and to write *nirat* about women, for example *Ramphan philap*. It is true that irreverent attitudes of this kind, which gave rise to folk stories about "Grandpa Monk and Grandma Nun," were long known among the Thai common people. But they were not written down. The poet must have picked up this popular irreverence in oral literature and supplied it to his bourgeois readership. The most striking example is the sex scene in his *Kap phra chai suriya*. The poet tried to break with the conventional "wondrous scenes" of early Bangkok literature by exoticizing it whenever he could. Of his contemporaries he was far the most daring in this regard.

> The monk came down from his cell
> And ran amok, pulling a novice by the hand.
> The senior nun ran away from the senior monk
> Into the mud, and frolicked around.
> The temple-dwellers wandered off into houses,
> Bald head hitting bald head and lolling aside.
> Trees swayed to and fro
> As monkeys and gibbons swung around.
> The spirit who molds children
> Attached the nose and eyes
> But then collapsed in laughter.
> It could not mold as fast as it wished

And became frustrated.
Two people made love, shaking the ground,
And woke up feeling exhausted,
Unable to walk and out of sorts.

(*Kap phra chai suriya*, 123)

That Sunthon Phu dragged monks and temple-goers into sex acts was meant to be comic. His depiction of abbots and abbesses was tinged with the *nak leng* sarcasm at which the poet was particularly skilled. He did not show serious reverence for the monkhood, and this sat well with many bourgeois laymen who had long been critical of the activities of certain monks (for example with regard to the Sangha disciplinary code laid down in the *Kotmai tra sam duang* or Three Seals Law) and thought the monks generally "old-fashioned" (as King Rama IV described them in one of his royal decrees). Long-term monks of his time did not come from the bourgeoisie, but from the phrai or poor upcountry families. Furthermore, the early Bangkok bourgeois were rich enough to build temples of their own for monks to live in. Such monks were therefore their "dependents." The monks' religious education did not help them to upgrade their teaching so as to capture the hearts and minds of the bourgeois laity, who knew far more about the wide world. Consequently, they no longer commanded the old respect. This new attitude to the monkhood led to the religious reforms initiated by Prince Mongkut.

Thus the sakdina system, which ranked people according to birth, began to decline. Some noblemen had more power than members of the royalty. Some Chinese became extremely rich, and were respected for it. On the other hand, there were even some princes who suffered serious financial hardship. In other words, the social transformations then occurring, quite visible to contemporaries, meant that the birth-based status system was no longer firmly in place. The rising status of the bourgeoisie was not based on birth, and naturally its members began to look to other qualifications for respect. This new bourgeois pride is clearly reflected in Sunthon Phu's writings. Even though the poet never called for equality, he no longer accepted a social order based on rank at birth. In Ayutthayan literature there is nothing comparable to the lament for a loved one contained in *Ramphan philap*, which patently broke out of the sakdina framework. It is instructive that Sunthon Phu presented this lament in the form of a dream. The reader would have understood immediately that it was really no dream, but incorporated elements from the poet's own life. He knew very well, of course, that this "dream" could not happen in reality. That is why he called his love a "fairy" (*nang fa*)—also to be consistent with her name, Apson [Apsara] Sudathep. The important thing, however, was to commit his dream into writing, and Sunthon Phu did so with pride: "Because I was born a royal retainer, I aspired to join an angel in bed" (*Ramphan philap*, 340; translation from Vella 1986, 32).

Love was indeed an innovation of bourgeois literature, Under Ayutthayan sakdina, love as we understand it today was not very meaningful. Nowadays, love arises because we have the right to make our own choice of partners. By contrast, in an age when mates were selected for political reasons, or purely on the basis of birth-rank, love was neither necessary nor relevant. In Ayutthayan literature, love is an expression of appropriate social status, or of the invisible power of the gods who decide men's fates. Good examples are Phra Ram and Nang Sida, Wetsandon and Nang Matsi, Phra Samutthakhot and Nang Phinthummadi, Phra Anirut and Nang U-sa. But early Bangkok literature began to touch on loves which ran against the traditional social grain. Lovers chose each other of their own free will—something really unprecedented. Clear examples are Inao with Nang Chintara, and later with Butsaba, Khun Chang with Nang Phim, and Khun Phaen with Nang Phim, the wife of Khun Chang. *Ramphan philap* presented a new kind of love with real emotional involvement, something only possible in a society more open and egalitarian than that of Ayutthaya. Even before *Ramphan philap,* Sunthon Phu had described his love for Nang Chan, who became his first wife despite the wishes of the sakdina authorities:

> If in this life we gain not what we desire
> Because the Almighty One is severe
> Let my beloved be true to her vow
> And we shall meet again some day, as we desire.
>
> (*Nirat mueang klaeng,* 58; translation from Sunthorn Phu 2001, 876)

The reality was that his love for Nang Chan was blocked by Kromphra Ratchawanglang (prince of the Rear Palace) whom the lady served. Sunthon Phu was punished for his love on several occasions, but he persisted. We can take this as a love which rejected existing social rules. "Almighty One" (*ong itsararak*) is an elegant phrase for the lord who thwarted the writer's pure and constant love. For all this elegance, it is clear that the poet was not prepared to submit to the lord's power; he even asked his lady to be ready to meet him "some day" when the lord's power was no more. His love was a typically bourgeois love, a sentiment freed from social ties, having nothing to do with marriage, and refusing to bow to sakdina pressure. (See the two poems cited above, but also Sombat 1980, 266, where an analysis opposite to mine is offered.) This is why Sunthon Phu's kind of love charmed and captivated the bourgeoisie who were already experiencing similar feelings.

Aside from his treatment of love, the poet also ignored other traditional social constraints based on birth. He composed *phleng yao* for the instruction of young royalty and included elements taken from his own life. Sometimes, for example, he complained of the "Great One" acting strangely toward him. At other times there was a political nuance, for example, "May you live 10,000 years / And continue the line of the kings of Ayutthaya / Protecting the people and religion for 5,000 years," ending with, "Stay in your gold-ornamented room / Until you are grown up and strong / Then you will fly in the heavens for people to see / That you are of the royal lineage of the swan, mighty and brave" (*Phleng yao thawai owat,* 133, 147). It was most unusual for a commoner to instruct young royalty in this manner, and the poet had to keep reminding them of his loyalty, for example: "This advice is well-intended / If perchance you find it overbearing / Do not be angry and think it was offered in disrespect / It was given with love, and I beg your forgiveness" (*Phleng yao thawai owat,* 143–4). But however unusual these lines might be, the attitude behind them was typically bourgeois. The poet's status as an older man and teacher was more important than mere birth-rank. Thus, like an elderly relative, he was entitled to instruct the young on trivialities like deportment, but also on serious matters such as how to choose a partner in marriage, how to handle people, and how to govern them, no matter if he went so far as to touch on politics.

Bourgeois readers of Sunthon Phu's verses would empathize with the poet, and not feel at all awkward or embarrassed, since they shared his point of view. The young heroes of *Phra aphaimani*, Sinsamut and Sutsakhon, both born to lowly mothers, were popular with readers because their origins were like those of prominent bourgeois whom the readers themselves respected, and not far from those children of established aristocrats whose mothers were the daughters of Chinese towkays, packed off by their fathers to serve in upper class families or to marry into them. Conversely, the same readers would feel uncomfortable with the main characters in *Ramakian*, *Dalang*, or *Unarut* since they were either gods incarnate or the descendents of god—and therefore never "failed."

With their more rational way of thinking, their changed religious outlook, and their decreasing respect for high birth, the bourgeoisie came to expect more efficient government. Small in numbers, and benefiting financially from the existing sakdina structures, they had no wish for radical political change. They wanted to abolish only those sakdina practices that interfered with their interests. Stability and security were important to them, because of the support thereby provided for their import and export businesses. They did not think to engage in large industrial projects, but invested in agriculture to some extent. They had no interest in a system of free labor, since the sakdina structure guaranteed them the cheap labor of the phrai. What they most desired, therefore, was a status quo adequate for protecting their financial interests, and providing a plentiful supply of cheap labor. Specializing in the export trade, they were not concerned to increase domestic purchasing power. They did not worry about the exploitation and immiseration caused by the phrai system, since it ensured low labor costs for the business of export agriculture.

Sunthon Phu's works responded politically to the needs of the bourgeoisie by criticizing certain government activities, But, over all, he accepted the status quo, asking only that the government act rationally toward the bourgeoisie. He never called for equality for the phrai. The most he ever did was to ask the ruling class to show pity and kindness to the mass of the population, who were mainly phrai.[8]

8. This is probably one reason why the government of the early Bangkok period had no wish to use the phrai as hired labor, preferring to import Chinese for enterprises where hired labor produced higher profits. When the government experimented with the industrial production of granular sugar in the Third Reign, the workforce in the royal cane-fields was composed exclusively of Chinese coolies, whereas the labor power of the phrai was kept isolated inside the age-old corvée system.

Furthermore, Sunthon Phu seems never to have imagined any kind of king-less polity. Accepting fully the institution of monarchy, he still wanted its power to be exerted predictably: what needed to be done should really get done, while what did not need to be done should be left undone. He himself had suffered from monarchical unpredictability and arbitrariness, as we can see from Phra Pipo's advice to his disciples in *Phra aphaimani*:

> The priest says, do not slander the king.
> It is difficult to judge his disposition.
> When he is good, he can be as cool as the ocean.
> When he is angry, he is like fire burning the heart.
>
> (*Phra aphaimani*, 524)

It never entered Sunthon Phu's head to call for a basic law, such as a constitution, to limit the monarch's power. He simply wanted this power used rationally (in Max Weber's sense of the word), in the form of policies explainable in terms of generally acceptable objectives, such as the "happiness of the people" (meaning only the bourgeoisie). A monarch should not fly into a rage merely because someone upset his personal feelings. But he could rightfully get angry and order someone executed in the interest of the state. King Aphainurat's decision to order the execution of his senior adviser was a good example of the irrational exercise of kingly power. The poor fellow was killed, not because he was trying to incite rebellion or was engaged in corrupt practices, but merely because he warned the king, who was madly in love with a concubine (in reality an evil spirit), that he was governing unjustly. Before his execution, the elderly adviser

> Announced loudly to everyone:
> Because of my devotion, I am punished with death.
> Those present will soon see
> The city and the people facing ruin
> Because the evil spirit has taken possession of a wicked woman.
> I must die before my karma decrees.
>
> (*Aphainurat*, 404)

The fact that he died for his "devotion" showed the irrationality and unpredictability of the monarchical institution. Suffering spread far and wide among the people because the king no longer "governed the realm" (407):

> The people feel hot as if burned by fire
> Because their words are full of accusations and appeals.
> Drums are beaten. Countless petitions are made.
> So many cases are backed up in the old court.
> People do not know who is giving judgment.
> Old and new petitions pile up in the palace.

The judge delays advising the king,
But if the king objects, he is forced to speak,
As ministers great and small are waiting to hear.
(*Aphainurat*, 409)

Phra Aphaimani, on the other hand, was a highly rational ruler. Although he was not much of a warrior, and did not have a great deal of authority, he was very shrewd. He dispatched some of his followers, disguised as merchants, to various townships, so that he could rapidly be informed about changes going on in the world. Sunthon Phu extolled his ability to employ good and capable people in affairs of state. Nang Wali, for example, was promoted to the rank of First Concubine because of her keen intelligence. The consequence of Phra Aphaimani's action was

That afterwards all the retainers, officials,
And common people knew everything
That the king thought about developing the kingdom,
And that he loved people with knowledge.
The subjects of the realm were pleased.
Even though she [Nang Wali] was just a woman, they loved her dearly.
(*Phra aphaimani*, 332)

Nang Wali was not of noble birth, and she was plain and swarthy. Her asset was education, which the bourgeoisie valued highly. A good monarch should think highly of educated people, indeed, probably more highly than of the high-born. This kind of thinking on the part of Sunthon Phu and his class contemporaries is exactly that of T. W. S. Wannapho (Thianwan), another distinguished bourgeois from a later period (Chai-anan 1979).

At the same time, Sunthon Phu satirized and criticized crooked government officials. It is noteworthy that for the poet, this "crookedness" did not stem from any immorality in the officials' acts themselves, but rather from the degree to which they acted outside their authority. This judgment, too, reflected the changing mentality of the bourgeoisie. The officials most often attacked by Sunthon Phu were judges and customs officers, followed by "high government officials" in general. In the following passage, the poet belabors judges:

The craftiness of the judges is like a mangle.
They make threats all the time,
And collude to find fault without cause.
A mangle squeezes tighter and tighter.
Just thinking about this
Makes one sick at heart.
....
A heron stands motionless, poised to catch a fish,
To eat and be content.

If a judge has faith in honesty,
That is good.
If he desires to swallow money,
He is like the heron.

(*Nirat suphan*, 272, 276)

For customs officers he had these biting words:

At the Bang Sai customs post, a sign announces tax collection.
Many bad fellow sit in the customs house,
Smoking ganja in a hookah, and licking sugar from their fingers.
They scold people, and threaten to ransack their boats.
If they find no contraband, they still demand
Papaya, dried shrimp, cucumbers, aubergines,
Oranges, and condiments like chilies and salt.
The boatmen are fed up and curse them silently.

(*Nirat wat chaofa*, 241–2)

His general attitude towards the nobility was not very favorable. He gave the impression that the nobles abused their "big shot" power to cause suffering among the people.

While traveling alone in the forest, Nang Laweng runs into a brigand and tries to make him mend his ways. "[Why] are you robbing people for a living, as if you had no morals / Even if you make a fortune, it is still shameful / A reputation for good or evil remains with you beyond death, for ever." However,

The forest brigand, fierce and wicked,
Responded to this attack with his own words:
'Even officials exploit the people
Why scold us, mere forest-dwellers?'

(*Phra aphaimani*, 518)

The poet once compared the "rascally" nature of the nobility to crows which, hunting for fish, swarm high in the sky so that they can spot their prey from afar. The nobles took advantage of their high social and political position to seek out victims, while the common people were like fish—weak, defenseless, and unable to detect the peril looming over their heads.

A crow and an eagle hover in the sky,
Then swoop down to catch the fish.
Officials, like the crow and eagle, seize their prey, so shamefully.
They swoop down to collect fines
And abuse people like slaves, scolding and beating them.

(*Nirat suphan*, 276)

In all fairness, there is no firm evidence that the nobility and officialdom of early Bangkok were more "crooked" than those of other periods. Tax officials who were *phrai leo* (commoners) with no salaries or other source of profit had to make a living by seizing goods from boats they inspected as well as by taking bribes. For Thai society, this was something to be expected. Corrupt and unjust judges were also nothing new. Over the history of the judiciary way back to Ayutthayan times, prohibitions on the taking of bribes were issued repeatedly, yet bribery seems always to have been a normal part of the judicial process. Likewise, exploitation and oppression of the people was taken as the due "privilege" of a poorly paid nobility. The bureaucratic system itself offered every opportunity for such practices. The interesting thing about Sunthon Phu's criticism is not so much that it offered a true picture of the early Bangkok bureaucracy than that it reflected the view of the increasingly influential bourgeoisie that these practices were no longer tolerable. The peculations of the customs officers adversely affected the bourgeoisie's trading operations, while the long-standing judicial system, on which the bourgeoisie was heavily dependent for such matters as enforcing the repayment of debts, did not help the expansion of their enterprises.[9]

Bourgeois discontent did lead to some reform, but not of the bureaucratic system as a whole. The aim of the reformers was merely increasing the efficiency of specific elements in the state machinery and the administrative order—for the benefit of the bourgeoisie. For example, the exactions of petty officials, which were seen as obstructing commerce, were to be reduced. At the same time, bribes for high-level officials could be taken as necessary parts of the negotiations for business deals. It was the government's duty to "support the monks, Brahmans, and people of the realm" in a manner that promoted the economic activities of the bourgeoisie: for example, by reform of existing civil and commercial law, fixing standards and stable tariffs, expanding domestic transportation networks, and so on.[10] These demands were much in line with the serious "reform" of King Rama V's reign. Yet the desired changes were to be effected within the status quo sakdina framework inherited from Ayutthaya. It would be many years before changes in their interests convinced the bourgeoisie that the sakdina system was intolerable, and so they made a "revolution" to bring it down.

9. Among the files contained in the Manuscript Section of the National Archives there are a number of documents containing appeals in cases involving commercial debts. What is striking is that, in some of the cases connected to domestic trade, the debtor lived as far away as Sukhothai. In this particular instance, the debtor had purchased goods again and again from a creditor-plaintiff in Bangkok without sending any money as down-payment. This case shows that the geography of trade between individuals was continuously expanding, It also demonstrates that the traditional judicial method of forcing repayment of debts by arresting the debtor was no longer thought convenient. In effect, various old-style practices of the courts were proving an impediment to long-distance commerce.

10. It should be noted that early Bangkok was a period in which there was considerable private investment by individuals in the development of domestic communications, above all in the central region.

Thus there is a continuity between the criticism of the early Bangkok bourgeoisie and the reforms of the Fifth Reign, and the former should be considered as having laid the foundations for the latter.

The values evident in Sunthon Phu's works were of a kind that clearly supported the bourgeois way of life, and the tastes they expressed were absolutely bourgeois tastes. Writing about education for "young ladies," the poet stressed the values associated with the "rational" economy of the bourgeoisie, namely the importance of economic activities logically designed for material gain. For example, he pointed out to young ladies the financial costs and benefits of different types of behavior:

> When you see upper class people with wealth and jewelry,
> Do not compete with their heaven-sent fortune
> Or else what little you have will decline day by day,
> Like using up capital without any profit.
> (*Suphasit son ying*, 12)

Lack of modesty was thus not a bad thing in itself, nor was it something that society punished; but it did mean a "loss" or, as the poet put it, "using up capital without any profit." Sunthon Phu and the bourgeoisie detested female go-betweens because they represented "loss." We can see how the poet tried to explain to his young ladies the dangers of using go-betweens, and warned against trusting them:

> Pay no heed to go-betweens.
> They will exaggerate everything,
> Claiming all their men are good sons of high officials with merit.
> They invent things to make young girls fall for men.
> Whether the men are truly good or bad cannot be seen.
> You do not know where you are being led.
> It is as if these go-betweens are luring you to seek your fortune
> In far-off lands. Do not be enticed by sugared words.
> (*Suphasit son ying*, 3–4)

The significant thing about these lines is the portrayal of marriage as a risk, like searching for a windfall in a distant land. Not any ordinary risk, but one more like a business venture. If someone comes with a story about a "bit of luck" in a far-off city, the penalty for trusting this story is compared to a business venture where the capital invested turns out irrecoverable. This is a truly bourgeois outlook, wherein marriage is conceived as a business, with consequences which the bourgeoisie must calculate, as will be explained below.

In Sunthon Phu's view, a good wife was not merely someone as well-behaved and elegant as a folded cloth (as Nang Krishna taught her young sister in *Kritsana son nong khamchan*), but also a member of the family with an economic role equal (or almost equal) to that of her husband. Thus the good bourgeois wife was quite unlike the good sakdina wife, who had only to minister to her husband's desires and had no reason to be concerned about the financial status of her family, since it was secure from birth. This is why Sunthon Phu offered the following advice:

At home you should concentrate
On knowing everything about women's duties
In case your husband is an ordinary person like yourself
So that both can making a living all your lives.
(*Suphasit son ying*, 11)

As commoners—outside the circle of the nobility and others privileged by birth—the daughters of the bourgeoisie had to prepare themselves to take part in the economy of their future families. In some passages, Sunthon Phu even gave instruction on commerce:

If you are to learn to be a merchant,
Do not be foul-mouthed. Speak nicely,
Then customers will buy easily, sales and profits will be good,
Because buyers are not put off nor find you irritating.
(*Suphasit son ying*, 9)

Consistent with the quotations given earlier, speaking nicely was seen not as something good in itself or as a sign of "gentility," as described in the literature of sakdina Ayutthaya, but rather as a skill that could bring commercial benefits or turn a good profit, and thus something well worth practicing. In addition, neither Sunthon Phu nor the bourgeoisie in general found anything objectionable in the fact that commerce necessitated dealing with many different kinds of people. In fact, there was nothing wrong in a woman talking to a number of men. Keeping a wife at home, away from other people, just for the sake of one man, was a financial waste. A bourgeois husband would not dream of letting this happen, since his wife was an economic asset in her own right.

Suphasit son ying is clearly different from any previous poem of the same genre. It was a response to early Bangkok bourgeois life. To understand this point fully, one has only to compare it with *Kritsana son nong khamchan* (Krishna's instruction of her younger sister). Like other works of Prince Paramanuchit Chinorot, *Kritsana son nong khamchan* was an adaptation of an existing text. The oldest extant manuscript, copied by a scribe in the reign of King Borommakot, was composed by the monk In (Em-on 1970). Prince Paramanuchit Chinorot faithfully followed the storyline of the older version, which was a truly sakdina literary work, designed to instruct girls within the sakdina context. Nothing was expected of a woman except to be a good wife, obliged to serve and respect her husband.

A king is the head
Of a big realm with extensive territory.
A husband is the light and the protector

With supreme authority over [his] women.
(*Kritsana son nong khamchan*, 9)

Even a woman unlucky enough to have an ugly, stupid, and cruel husband had no right to despise him. This attitude is miles away from what we see in *Suphasit son ying*, where the husband was not to be regarded by his wife as the man above all others, the pennant and the crowning glory of her life. Instead, Sunthon Phu taught her to use her intellect in choosing her husband with care, and, by the same token, to be prepared to be critical of his behavior:

Think about yourself. Finding a husband is hard.
Many men are bad. Do not fall for them.
Those who smoke opium or drink liquor will bring ruin.
Women living with them will become poor.
They will take your money and beat you.
It's like keeping a monitor lizard as a pet—useless.
......
Having a bad husband makes everything difficult.
Life becomes so burdensome. Do not fall prey.
(*Suphasit son ying*, 4–5)

Although the poet did not go so far as to suggest that the wife should divorce a bad or stupid husband, he did make it clear that if she did not get away from him the consequences could be ruinous. Thus the woman in *Suphasit son ying* was much freer to exercise her personal judgment than her counterpart in *Kritsana son nong khamchan*. Since Sunthon Phu was instructing bourgeois girls, he had to respond to the specific problems of the bourgeois milieu. The poem was primarily aimed at unmarried young women because the problems facing the early Bangkok bourgeoisie arose from the contradiction between personal freedom and profit making. About sixty percent of the poem was devoted to teaching them the importance of preserving their virginity, and to making them fearful of elopement and premarital pregnancy. Only forty percent was left for the teaching of good manners.

The monetization of the economy gave rise to markets in towns and other large communities. The fact that the bourgeoisie was the group most deeply involved with these markets created among them a certain degree of egalitarianism. The nobility also, as buyers in these markets, got used to such equality in face-to-face encounters with the merchant-sellers, Over time, men of high sakdina rank and wealthy commoners more and more became accustomed to conversing on an equal basis. In turn, this made it easier for men and women of different social status to form relationships based on what we can call "love" outside the traditional restrictions imposed by lineage and rank. As noted earlier, love of this kind never appeared in Ayutthayan literature. It was something new, founded on a growing individualism (that is, family background and social and economic standing became less important than the personal feelings of the parties for each other) developed by "the market" and the general conditions of life of the bourgeoisie. Now and then, love could even lead to real-life marriage.

Nonetheless in the early Bangkok period marriage was generally speaking not a matter of personal choice, but rather a business transaction. For the bourgeoisie of the time the essential condition for a marriage was still equality of status between the man and the woman. Within the existing sakdina structure, the bourgeoisie still manipulated marriage ties for financial and political advantage. Marriage was not something on which a young man and a young woman could freely decide for themselves. Yet at the same time bourgeois parents disliked impediments to the market economy that was bringing them so much profit, and they were impressed by, and sympathetic to, "love." We shall see how these sentiments were used as key pivots of conflict in the thematics of various literary works of the period. In Sunthon Phu's *Suphasit son ying* the conflicts and contradictions are especially conspicuous. On the one hand he taught young women to become more independent and self-reliant, and to play economic and roles no less important than those of men. But on the other hand he forbade them to make their own marriage choices, and told them to leave this responsibility to their parents: "Take the advice of your family / If you love yourself above all / Marry like a royal swan" (*Suphasit son ying*, 5). Unsurprisingly, the contradictions between "reality" and the wishes of the bourgeoisie could always give rise to those "love problems" which parents were most eager to avoid. Occupations which encouraged or facilitated the new kind of "love" were detested; for the bourgeoisie, the worst offenders were professional female go-betweens or matchmakers. Of these women Sunthon Phu wrote:

> Go-betweens are aggressive devils.
> They work for whoever asks them.
> Do not believe them. Their livers are larger than their ribcages.
> They will do anything to convince, so they can collect their fee.
> (*Suphasit son ying*, 4)

In fact, in the culture of the common people, the matchmaker was a highly respected elderly woman who, because of her knowledge of local customs and traditions, was entrusted with the responsibility for approaching a potential bride on behalf of her suitor's parents The practice of employing these go-betweens had long existed among the common people because it allowed the girl's family to turn down an approach without the unpleasantness of a face-to-face rejection. But in the urban communities of the early Bangkok period, and especially in wards where the bourgeoisie mainly resided, the matchmaker had become a liaison between lovers, and did not necessarily concern herself with arranging marriages. Her activities were highly suspect, since they were carried on without the knowledge or consent of parents. She herself was greatly despised.

Subsequently bourgeois standards in this regard gradually seeped down and spread among the ordinary people, weakening the position of women who had traditionally had more freedom and rights than their counterparts among the aristocracy and the bourgeoisie. Their condition only improved again after western attitudes and values entered the country.

Even though the bourgeoisie did adopt and practice various elements from the culture of the common people, they did not do so "on purpose." Mostly they were quite unconscious of the origins of their borrowings. In their conscious minds they looked down on the culture of the common people and revered the old sakdina tastes and values—even if in a superficial manner. This is quite understandable if we remember that they still needed the support and protection of the sakdina social order, and so enjoyed making use of its symbols and ways of thinking. Contempt for, and mockery of, the common people are conspicuous features of the works of Sunthon Phu and his disciple Nai Mi. The following quotations show Sunthon Phu's contempt:

> I asked the price of knives and axes I wanted to buy.
> The conversation was loud and full of local dialect.
> Sweet words of endearment were hard to come by.
> I was bored to death with listening.
>
> (*Nirat mueang klaeng*, 56; translation adapted from Sunthorn Phu 2001, 795)

> I saw peasant girls busily ploughing,
> Some were chatting in country fashion, sounding ngur, ngur.
> There were rings of dried sweat around their necks,
> Their crossed breastcloths stained with dried areca spit
>
> (*Nirat mueang klaeng*, 52–3; translation adapted from Sunthorn Phu 2001, 696)

Generally speaking, the standards that the bourgeoisie upheld were a blend of those of the common people and of the sakdina upper class, adapted to be useful for their style of life. These people were not at all tolerant of ways of life different from their own, which in their eyes were ridiculous or repulsive. (It appears that while the sakdina also found standards other than their own unacceptable, they also regarded these standards as belonging to another world with which they themselves had nothing to do. They jealously guarded their "cultural" possessions, with no thought of sharing or circulating them outside their own circle. In the Ayutthayan period, for example, they hoarded the *khon* masked-dance, palaces, plays performed exclusively by women, regal tableware, and so on, as monopolies of and for their own class.) Since the bourgeoisie existed only in urban areas, they regarded urban standards as the best and the only ones to be followed, while those of rural folk were ludicrous or disgusting. Although Bourgeois Poet Laureate Sunthon Phu and his disciples often took trips upcountry, they made not the least effort to understand the standards and values of the rural folk. The countryside in Sunthon Phu's works offers the reader the beauties of nature and the ugliness of its human beings.

At Thap Nang, a sense of loneliness filled my heart,
There were only huts for peasants to dwell in.
The peasant women had no cause to rejoice,
Covered as they were with sweat as if stained with indigo.
City women, even if they are slaves,
Are twice or thrice as pretty as these.
O, away from the city all beauty is gone!
To think of it makes one lose heart and long for the city.

(*Nirat mueang klaeng*, 32; translation adapted from Sunthorn Phu 2001, 91)

Passing Bang Lao, there are some villagers
Busy harvesting and carrying thatching-grass.
Their skin looks very dark, as if painted with indigo.
All of them combined cannot match the beauty of one court lady.

(*Nirat phra thaen dongrang*, 213)

Rural values were completely unacceptable to Sunthon Phu, who found even the upcountry nobility laughable because they lacked the "grandeur" to which the Bangkok upper class and bourgeoisie were accustomed. On one occasion the poet made fun of the *yokkrabat* or state prosecutor of the township of Klaeng this way: "The *yokkrabat* polishes spoons morning and evening / His wife of lady rank sits grilling fish" (*Nirat mueang klaeng*, 57; translation adapted from Sunthorn Phu 2001, 821). At the same time, someone from upcountry who adopted bourgeois standards was also absurd, since he or she could not successfully imitate the bourgeoisie for lack of social training and financial resources.

The female country bumpkins gaze wide-eyed.
They hang on their husbands, never sitting or standing far away.
They cover themselves untidily with doubled pieces of colored silk.
All of them dress to the hilt.

(*Phra aphaimani*, 122)

On the other hand, the poet and his disciples appear to have regarded upcountry people in trade more as "petty bourgeois" than as peasants. Their descriptions of female hawkers were more ribald than scornful:

In the River Khwae region, rafts line up at the Khwan market
Of the town of Chantaprathet, a magnificent place.
On the east bank there is a *sala* and an open space
Where many boats are moored in rows. There is lots of noise.
The market-women, all good-looking,
Challenge and chivvy you in loud voices.

They squeeze themselves into tight blouses.
I'm looking for a plaything, but am disappointed.
(*Nirat phrabat*, 68)

The raft-owner with a long pigtail has a Thai daughter
Who shaves the hair back from her forehead.
The garden-workers look grimy, both adults and children.
But the wives of the Chinese comb their hair, and anoint their skin.
When a boat passes, they give it a sidelong glance,
Sitting in elegant poses, to show off their hands and figures.
(*Nirat phra thaen dongrang*, 208–9)

The economy of early Bangkok encouraged a growing division of labor. Certain specializations began to afford their practitioners the possibility of independent and stable livelihoods. It is true that the persistence of the sakdina structure and the bourgeoisie's lack of serious interest in industry forced most artisans to attach themselves to wealthy patrons in the old manner. But the money economy did offer unprecedented opportunities for certain types of specialized occupations. We have already spoken at length about merchants. But there were also oarsmen for hire on long journeys (in place of phrai on whose labor many of the bourgeoisie had no legal claim), and also people specializing in entertainment. On this latter group we have a great deal of information. Formerly, actors and dancers from commoner backgrounds had been unable to make full-time livelihoods from their skills. Some had been recruited into the retinues of the great sakdina lords or extremely wealthy bourgeois. But most used their professional skills as a seasonal sideline to their main source of livelihood, which was farming. Thus their performances remained part of the age-old subsistence economy. (A good comparison is provided by the *mo lam* players of Isan, who traditionally performed only after the harvest was brought in, to secure a little extra income, and who only quite recently have been able to make performing a full-time occupation.) But in thickly populated urban areas, acting had already become a full-time profession in the early Bangkok period. By then there were sufficient numbers of well-off bourgeois "patrons" to hire them to perform, so that a kind of "entertainment market" came into being. We know the names of several actor-dancers of the era who worked outside the sakdina patronage system. Some became successful and wealthy. A few, like Nai Bunyang and Chao Krap, could build their own wat. The bourgeoisie's respect for knowledge was changing its frame of reference. The knowledge that was valued was no longer confined to the fields of religion and traditional customs and etiquette, but extended now to anything that could produce a steady profit. A famous line of Sunthon Phu states, "knowledge is nothing compared to expertise." By "expertise" he probably meant technical, professional knowledge as compared to broad general knowledge because, as stated in the following line, specialized knowledge in bourgeois society made one "know how to survive successfully in life" (Nidhi 1979, 9–27; see chapter 4 of this book). This new respect for expertise as a route to success is plain from the scene in *Phra aphaimani* where the hero's father, learning that his son is studying music, upbraids him in words reflecting the old sakdina outlook:

As for the music of the *piphat* ensemble and two-headed drum,
You are as skilled as the crude players at mask and shadow play.
Any of my court women
Could learn to be just as expert.
As for knowledge of arms and armor,
You ought to like this as you come from a warrior line.
You are illustrious royalty, so why become a musician?
(*Phra aphaimani*, 8)

But Sunthon Phu went on to show that what the boy was studying allowed him "to survive successfully in life," even if it was hardly in the "grand imperial" manner. The poet also had Sisuwan console his elder brother in the same vein: "You have knowledge within you / Why are you afraid? / If life does not abandon you, you should succeed" (*Phra aphaimani*, 9). The knowledge to which Sisuwan referred was plainly specialized (and to be employed in a specialized occupation). Elsewhere Sunthon Phu taught that "a single branch of knowledge, if mastered, brings excellent results." This attitude could only be born and be diffused in an urban bourgeois society that opened up space for new professionalized career occupations.

The changing socioeconomic structure of early Bangkok brought about parallel changes in the mentality of the ruling class, which became more and more bourgeois, and more and more removed from the truly sakdina outlook of their predecessors in Ayutthayan times. The new values of the ruling circle also spread far more rapidly among the bourgeoisie than among the sakdina lords. In one section of his panegyric for King Rama III, where the beauty of the royal palace was extolled, Nai Mi wrote lines in which the full force of bourgeois tastes and values was only barely concealed:

Every place, outside and inside, is spick-and-span.
Wherever you look, there is nothing depressing.
Throughout the city everything is newly built
And looks cheerful and fun,
Truly magnificent.
The more you look, the more you are uplifted and impressed,
By the whole city, like a wonder wrought by Indra.
It is so delightful to stroll about sightseeing different things,
Everything so superbly fashioned.
Anyone who has the chance to examine carefully
Will want to see still more and admire more.
Other royalty came to copy, then built imitations of everything.
Almost every noble has built imitations
In the districts to the front and rear,

Including Chinese and *farang* structures, creating congestion
And hub-bub around the royal palace.
(*Klon phleng yao sansoen phrakiat phranangklao*, 682)

The poet emphasized the palace's "cheerful and fun" atmosphere. No matter where one went, one found nothing "depressing." in other words, everything was colorful, exciting, and, of course, superficial. The contrast with similar descriptions in the literature of Ayutthaya is striking; there what is stressed is regal elegance rather than the colorfulness and "fun." The reason for this was that the "city" of Ayutthaya was thought to display the meritoriousness of rulers who wielded real power, while the "city" of Bangkok was felt to display the merit of rulers who responded to the desire of the bourgeoisie to "stroll about sightseeing." Bourgeois members of the ruling class always enjoyed novelty. The excitement and admiration for the royal palace and for Bangkok found in Nai Mi's panegyric arose from their being so "superbly fashioned," or in other words, their novelty and strangeness. The monarch himself was the leader in spreading bourgeois tastes and values, first to the upper class as a whole, and later on down the social pyramid. These novelties might properly have been reserved for the royal household, but the Bangkok monarchs were not true sakdina people like the kings of Ayutthaya. Rather, they were leaders of the bourgeoisie. Thus the Chinese-style pavilion (*keng*) and western-style building (*tuek*) which the rulers glorified were widely copied by the bourgeois class.

Sunthon Phu's works suited his bourgeois readers with their love of excitement, novelty, and enjoyment, as well as their shallowness. We have noted that some critics have judged the poet's shallowness to be a serious weakness. But the truth is that it is exactly the facile and superficial qualities of his verse that made him such a popular favorite. And he did make innovations in the field of literature; even if he was not always himself their originator, he certainly popularized the new practices. One true novelty lay in the way he composed his poetry, as Chit Phumisak, a great literary critic of our own times, has written:

> His *klon paet* [8-syllable hemistiches] are most melodious, with internal and external rhymes, alliteration, and assonance. Each line is laced with carefully weighted words, some light, some heavy, very suitable for musical recitation. It is sweet to the ear, smooth-flowing, and catchy. It is this quality that makes Sunthon Phu's *klon paet* something unique and novel in the Thai poetry of the Bangkok period. (Chit 1975, 151–2)

Rhythmic melodiousness of this kind was perfect for bringing to readers (and those read aloud to) stories that were entertaining and easy to understand. It effectively conveyed superficial emotions, the writer's opinions, and explanations of various things either seriously (in the manner of the chronicles) or comically. This is why his works spread widely and rapidly in tandem with the expansion of the country's readership.

Another new literary genre that Sunthon Phu's work helped to spread in Thai society was the fable-in-verse (*nithan khamklon*). This was a genre aimed solely at readers, and was not intended for performance. There was nothing "magical" or sacred about works in this genre. They were simply "tales," quite unconnected to religion or to supernatural power.

Sunthon Phu also played a central role in the diffusion of a new way of writing *nirat* based on true events and the writer's personal experience. The Ayutthayan *nirat* stressed poetic eloquence rather than true accounts of real journeys. In Prince Kung's *Nirat than sok* and *Nirat than thongdaeng* the journeys themselves are barely mentioned. The verses express admiration for birds, trees, and animals with the nuanced eroticism of the Ayutthayan literary tradition. The reader understood immediately that he was not being given an account of a real journey made by the writer. In still older *nirat*, such as *Kamsuan* or *Thawathotsamat*, the reader was not even told clearly where the traveler was going. It was sheer poetic eloquence, and had nothing to do with the real world of experience. But the *nirat* of early Bangkok, even those composed by poets who tried to preserve the *nirat* in its classical form, showed a growing interest in exactly that world of experience (for example, *Nirat narin* stanzas 19, 60–2, 66, and 69). In a good many of Sunthon Phu's *nirat* the poet's interest is fully concentrated on real experiences in the course of real journeys that he had made. In *Nirat phukhaothong*, for example, the traditional love-lament for an idealized woman is completely absent; instead, the poem records episodes from "real life" (or what is skillfully made to seem like "real life") and the writer's own "real" feelings about them. Nothing remotely like this can be found in Ayutthayan literature. This new style of *nirat* spread and developed after Sunthon Phu's time, with innovations fitting the changes in the way of life of the Thai bourgeoisie. As commerce flourished and travel became easier, people's horizons widened, and they wanted to know more about places of whose real existence they were quite confident, such as Phetchaburi, Phukhaothong, Suphanburi, Klaeng, Phra Thaen Dongrang, and Phra Pathom Chedi. Travel was becoming an adventurous pleasure, involving little or no danger. And if one could not, or did not, make the journey, one could still taste the excitement by reading.

Sunthon Phu's tales in verse marked a "step forward" in the general trend of early Bangkok literature. For example, he picked out strange and new bits from existing tales, such as the *Khobut* and turned them into something fun to read. Eventually, he created tales of his own such as *Phra aphaimani* and *Aphainurat*. The importance assigned to the "story" is what is distinctive about early Bangkok literature. More and more tales appeared that were adapted from foreign sources and ancient legends. But Sunthon Phu was surely the first poet who created tales of his own in response to readers' desire to be entertained, and they became a treasure-house of bourgeois culture. At the same time, his tales were of things "strange and new" such as pirate boats, Nang Laweng's exotic musical instruments, the seal of Rahu functioning like a modern air-conditioner, characters different from those appearing in other literary works, and so on. He also described distant countries with weird practices, like Ceylon with its westerners. All these novelties aroused his bourgeois readers' admiration.

BOURGEOIS POET LAUREATE

The popularity of Sunthon Phu's works is clearly demonstrated by their wide circulation, even after the onset of the age of print in Siam when editions of his poems can be said to have opened the age of commercial publishing. Over the years—up till today—they have been constantly in print. Time has in no way diminished his popularity. Among our national poets, who were overwhelmingly of royal or aristocratic origins, he stands out by his common birth.

This enduring popularity requires some explanation. It has usually been justified purely on literary grounds. There is no doubt that he was a poet of exceptional gifts. But the durability of the admiration for his poems suggests that there must be additional factors at work. This essay has tried to show that Sunthon Phu lived in a changing society that was substantially different from that of Ayutthaya. Moreover he moved in the social milieu that was most affected by, and also contributed to, these changes. These people were leaders of the transformation of sakdina Ayutthaya into bourgeois Bangkok, since their new positions of power derived from their connections with the export economy. Such connections were not in themselves new, since the Ayutthayan ruling class had had quite comparable ties. But in early Bangkok their importance dramatically increased. The volume of trade was on a different scale, and so were the numbers of people drawn into its networks. Thus the upper stratum of Thai society became increasingly bourgeois in its tastes and preoccupations, even though the structure of sakdina still remained in place. All the poets of this period were attached in one way or another to this upper stratum. Hence to a greater or lesser degree their works reflected the outlook of the bourgeois within it. But it was Sunthon Phu who most completely mirrored the mentality, as well as the values and tastes, of this bourgeoisie as it moved away from the old sakdina system. This is why his poems were devoured by the consuming public, which was overwhelmingly bourgeois.

After his time, social and economic change continued, and in wider and wider spheres. The signing of the Bowring Treaty provided a powerful stimulus to the acceleration of this trend. More and more people became involved in the expanding market economy. Preserving the old structure of sakdina political power was becoming less and less feasible. Even the wide-ranging reform under King Rama V managed to extend the life of sakdina political power for only a further half-century. The bourgeois revolution of 1932 was aimed at the reallocation of political power among the bourgeois themselves. Essentially its lineage can be traced back to the early Bangkok period.

The bourgeoisie, who have managed to retain their leadership from that time until today, have no difficulty in feeling that Sunthon Phu is close to them. They understand his feelings extremely well. His kind of humor is just the kind that tickles their ribs. They find it very easy to accept for themselves what Sunthon Phu found to be good or beautiful. This is why this poet's popularity has never faded. The more bourgeois culture has become pervasive, the more Sunthon Phu, the most distinguished poet representing this culture, has been esteemed.

It is not enough to study carefully the poetry of Sunthon Phu (and his poet contemporaries of the early Bangkok period) simply in order to understand it and to admire it (what some students of literature like to call "literary criticism"), no matter whether this is done simply to tag along with tradition or as a polite pretence. Analysis has to be undertaken with a full cognizance of the economic and social environment which produced the works. Literary composition is a social activity, and never exists in a void. Hence any study of literature that focuses on its aesthetic aspects in disregard of the constraints of period is a waste of time and will not bring about any serious understanding. It is also an illusion, because in reality it cannot be done. The simple reason is that if one tries, one will unconsciously use present-day conditions for making judgments. It also has the effect of tyrannizing the minds of young students who are forced to bow to the authority of their teacher or of the texts themselves, and thus think and feel in the same vein. Sadly enough, this amounts to destroying the students' humanity. Hence an awareness of the social and economic environment of literary works is really important, for it will help students to use their brains and their imagination as true students should. Then they will not wander around in a maze without contact with the truth, but will gain the knowledge to understand that the flourishing of the mind and the imagination is always framed by economy and society. The core of literary studies lies in the ability to think and imagine within the framework of a systematic methodology, guided by serious knowledge—and not at all in infantile and narcissistic fantasizing.

I believe that this essay's consideration of Sunthon Phu as the Thai bourgeoisie's Poet Laureate will be useful in providing a frame for the ideas and the imagination of young people studying his works. I hope it will make it possible for them to feel as the poet felt, to like what he admired, to believe as he believed, to think as he thought, and to hope as he hoped. That is to say, to put one's own heart within his, to "empathize" with him. The whole aim of literary studies is to train a person to use the imagination in a systematic way, so that he can put himself or herself in the shoes of someone in a different social position, from another era, and in a changed environment.

3

ON THE PHETCHABURI VERSION OF THE *MAHACHAT*

TRANSLATOR'S NOTE

Mahachat means the "great birth" or "great Jataka." The Jataka or "birth stories" are accounts of the previous lives of the Buddha before his final incarnation as Siddhattha, the historical Buddha. In the popular religious tradition throughout Buddhist Southeast Asia, the Jataka stories were perhaps the main form of moral instruction, expounded in sermons, recited at festivals, dramatized in various forms of performance, and depicted in wat decoration.

The Buddha is said to have had 550 prior lives. In the Jataka, these are presented as recalled and recounted by the Buddha. The last ten Jataka are of special importance for they are the stories of how the Bodhisatta or Buddha-to-be achieved the Ten Perfections (*thotsabarami*)—giving, moral conduct, renunciation, wisdom, energy, patience, truthfulness, resolution, loving-kindness, and equanimity. Most important of all is the tale of Prince Vessantara (Phra Wetsandon), the very last life before incarnation as Siddhattha. This Jataka illustrates the Perfection of Giving. In the Thai tradition it is known as the *Mahachat.*

In the tale, Prince Vessantara first gives away the white elephant which had helped to protect his kingdom, and as a result he is banished by the people. He then successively gives away the stags hauling his carriage, his children, and his wife. The recipient of the wife is a disguised Indra who then helps to restore to Vessantara his wife, children, white elephant, and kingdom. It is by this feat of giving that Vessantara—the Bodhisatta—is able to achieve the state of Perfection (*barami*) that will enable him to be enlightened as the Buddha in his next life.

As Nidhi describes below, the tradition of reciting this tale has been the focus of a major festival for a long time. However, it became especially important in the early Bangkok era when the popular tradition was supplemented by royal patronage as part of the court's interest to promote Buddhist teaching. By the Second Reign, an annual recitation of the *Mahachat* was held at the major royal wat housing the Emerald Buddha. King Rama III mimicked Vessantara's giving away of his son as part of his coronation ritual. By the Fourth Reign, the annual *Mahachat* was the occasion for a massive display of alms giving by the king. Such patronage of the *Mahachat* was copied by nobles and local leaders.

With a shift towards a stricter, canonical interpretation of Buddhism in the court, royal patronage of the *Mahachat* ceased in the Fifth Reign, and the importance of the recitation festival declined steeply after the centralizing reform of the Sangha in 1902.

3

ON THE PHETCHABURI VERSION OF THE *MAHACHAT*[1]

THE Ministry of Education's Bureau of the National Cultural Committee has recently published *The Phetchaburi Version of the Mahachat* for free distribution to the public (*Mahachat mueang phet* 1980). The publication is based on original manuscripts from Wat Ko and Wat Phetphli, Mueang district, Phetchaburi province. The Wat Ko version is a palm leaf manuscript written in *khom*[2] script, and states that it was written or inscribed in 1873. The Wat Phetphli manuscript is believed to have been copied from the Wat Ko version. It is exactly the same except for the Chulaphon chapter[3] which is somewhat different. The Phetphli manuscript was completed in 1922. In the Bureau of the National Culture Committee publication, Achan Saman Sohem of Phetchaburi Teachers College has transcribed the Wat Ko version from *khom* into Thai script, as well as providing a commentary in the footnotes and an appendix.

Close study of the Phetchaburi version of the *Mahachat* reveals many interesting aspects of this work. The Phetchaburi *Mahachat* is an important key for the study of the literary history of central Thailand. This would require a more detailed study than the article presented here, but it would certainly not be a wasted effort for the literary scholar.

THE CHANTING OF THE *MAHACHAT*

The custom of chanting the Vessantara Jataka to laymen and women clearly dates from the Sukhothai era. For example, when King Lithai describes the Five Disappearances (*pancha antarathan*)[4] he mentions the disappearance of the Jatakas, "the dhamma sermons, firstly the Mahachat" (Nakhon Chum Inscription). The

1. The author would like to thank Achan Chanthima Buwanit from the Phetchaburi Teachers College for her kindness in giving me the gift of the Phetchaburi version of the *Mahachat*, which led to this study.

2. Old Khmer. [T]

3. The *Mahachat* is divided into thirteen "chapters" or *kan*. [T]

4. A prophecy referring to the gradual extinction of the Buddhist religion. The Five Disappearances were (in order): the Tipitaka (Buddhist scriptures); proper monastic conduct; the achievement of enlightenment and nibbana; the monkhood; and finally the Buddha's relics. [T]

Vessantara Jataka was a highly respected scripture. The purchase of an "embroidered text (*samut lai pak*) for the cost of one tamlueng...on which to place the Vessantara Jataka" was a form of merit making of such importance that it warranted mention in an inscription (Wat Khema Inscription). "Listening to the Mahachat" was an important form of making merit (Inscription No. 49, a record of the merit-making deeds of laywomen and nuns). However, it is not clear whether the version of the Vessantara Jataka that was chanted during the Sukhothai era had been translated from the Pali into Thai. Listening to chanting or to monks' sermons in Pali was believed to be a way of gaining merit for the laity, even if one did not understand the words.[5] Apart from this, during the Sukhothai era the chanting of the Tipitaka or Pali scriptures seems to have been quite popular. When Phra Ratchathepi Sichulalak restored Wat Asokaram she presented to the temple a scholar by the name of Sangkhason whose duty was to chant the Pali scriptures (Wat Asokaram Inscription, second face). If the laity went to the temple to gain merit the Vessantara Jataka may still have been in this form, that is, chanted in Pali from the *Nibat chadok* (*Nipata Jataka*) scripture.[6]

Although the Vessantara Jataka may once have been chanted in Pali, soon after the Sukhothai era and perhaps even during the Sukhothai era itself scholars began to translate the Pali version into Thai, interspersed with Pali text from the *Nibat chadok* or the Tipitaka. This made it possible for people to understand what was being chanted and hence enjoy the story. This assumption is based on evidence from the *Mahachat khamluang* which dates from the reign of King Trailokanat (1448–88?).

Scholars of the Royal Institute have long debated the meaning of the term *khamluang*. Some agree with Prince Damrong's explanation that *khamluang* is similar to the term *phraratchaniphon* used in the early Bangkok period to mean a literary work that the king ordered the royal pundits to compose under his direction. (However, from the reign of Rama IV, *phraratchaniphon* had come to mean a literary work written by the king himself.) While this explanation of the term *khamluang* is not wrong, it misses the more important meaning of the term.

Old literary works under the title *khamluang* are all religious works, such as *Mahachat*, *Nanthopananthasut*, or *Phra malai*. These works were originally produced by the wat. They were perhaps written by monks, or "pundits" as mentioned above in the Wat Asokaram Inscription. This included those who had left the monkhood or laymen who had studied religion at a high level. These people associated with the wat, along with members of the upper class, were the educated whose livelihood was

5. In the popular story of Phra Malai, the faithful are exhorted to listen to the "thousand verses" (in Pali) of the Vessantara Jataka as a form of making merit to ensure their rebirth in the era of the future Buddha, Mettreya. These verses were believed to have been actually uttered by the Buddha himself. Their recitation in Pali became an essential part of the ceremony of the recitation of the Vessantara Jataka. [T]

6. The *Nipata Jataka* is a book in the Khuddakanikaya collection of texts found in the Sutta Pitaka, the second book of the Tipitaka, the collection of teachings regarded as the canon of Theravada Buddhism. [T]

derived partly from writing books or other literary works. Religious scripture was translated and written into prose form for chanting to the laity at the wat. If the Vessantara Jataka had already been translated into Thai by this time there would have been numerous versions of the *Mahachat* in use by different wat, more or less similar to each other and written for chanting. Over time the versions that were superior in literary terms came to dominate the poorer ones, and new versions appeared to compete with the most popular versions. The chanting of the *Mahachat* in the late Sukhothai or early Ayutthaya era is likely to have led to the emergence of numerous versions of the *Mahachat* in Thai. King Trailokanat assembled the royal pundits to compose a version of the *Mahachat* to compete with these wat versions for chanting in the royal wat or those wat under special royal patronage. *Khamluang,* therefore, is distinguished from *khamrat* (the people's version), or *khamwat* (temple version). So *Mahachat khamluang* refers to this version *as opposed to* the popular versions. Similarly, there must have been popular versions of the *Nanthopananthasut.* However, when the king had the royal wat chant the version composed by his son, Prince Thammathibet, this version became known as the "royal version" (*khamluang*). This misunderstanding of the term *khamluang* led to the *Phra non khamluang,* which has made the term become even more confused.

If we follow this explanation of the term *khamluang* then there must have been versions of the *Mahachat* written in Thai in existence prior to the reign of King Trailokanat, and perhaps even as early as the Sukhothai era. In fact, Prince Damrong himself explained that in former times (he did not state in which period) the Jatakas, especially the *Mahachat,* were translated and recited at the wat. This developed into the extremely popular custom of composing Jatakas in verse form for readings during temple festivals (Damrong, 'Explanation of the *sakabap* verse poem,' in *Kap mahachat,* 87–8).

The *Mahachat khamluang,* then, was not a literary work used by monks for recitations (*thet*) but was chanted by the laity. The custom of having the "pundits" chant in Pali dates from the Sukhothai period. This later developed into chanting in both Thai and Pali, as appears to have been the case with the *Mahachat khamluang* before the reign of King Trailokanat. But the only evidence we have is this one literary work. The chanting of the *Mahachat khamluang* by monks, therefore, suggests that even though there were other Jatakas which had been translated for chanting, they were not used by the monks but rather were probably left to the laity. As to whether the monks were using recitation versions of the Vessantara Jataka by this time, there is no evidence to suggest that in the Sukhothai or early Ayutthaya periods there were recitations of the *Mahachat* in Thai by monks, or at least none survive from that period. Nevertheless, given the great respect in which this particular Jataka and the Jataka stories generally were held, as described above, it is likely that the Vessantara Jataka was already chanted by monks in this period. The question is, was it chanted in Pali or Thai?

RECITATIONS OF THE VESSANTARA JATAKA IN THAI BY MONKS

The oldest recitation version (*klon thet*) of the *Mahachat* is the *Kap mahachat.* Certain parts of this work are believed to have been composed during the reign of King Songtham (1610/11–28). This is based on an assumption by Prince Damrong, who concluded that the passage in the Royal Chronicle stating that King Songtham "composed the *Mahachat khamluang*" (*Phraratchaphongsawadan chabap phanchanthanumat*, 213; RCA, 210) actually referred to the *Kap mahachat* (Damrong, introduction to the *Mahachat khamluang*, cho). But the language of the *Kap mahachat* is not old enough to conclude that it was composed in the reign of King Songtham. One literary scholar states that: "I believe that the language used in the work is much later than that era. There are not many archaisms. It is easier to read and understand than the *Mahachat khamluang*. Even compared to the literary style of the literature of the reign of King Naresuan the style used in the *Kap mahachat* is more recent" (Plueang Na Nakhon 1963, 90).

The *Kap mahachat* is a text composed specifically for recitation. It does not mix other verse forms, as are found in the *Mahachat khamluang*. It is a true *klon wat*, the popular literary form used in the wat to translate Pali into Thai. It was only much later that the Royal Chronicle stated that the work that King Songtham had commissioned was the *Mahachat khamluang*. There is no apparent reason to think that the Royal Chronicle was referring to this recitation version of the *Mahachat.* It is very likely that certain chapters of the extant version of the *Mahachat khamluang* were composed in the reign of King Songtham or were adapted during the reign of King Songtham from an older version dating from the reign of King Trailokanat. The linguistic and historical evidence indicates that the extant version of the *Kap mahachat* is definitely *not* from the reign of King Songtham, and is most likely considerably later than this. The *Kap mahachat* has one very important feature: there are no accompanying Pali verses as in the *Mahachat khamluang* or in later recitation versions. Even the Pali words that are commonly used to introduce a section, known as *chunniyabot*, are rarely used. The work is mostly in Thai. Prince Damrong explains that the *Kap mahachat* was written for monks to recite to the faithful. It was written in a style copied from the *Mahachat khamluang* chanted by laymen, but without the Pali. Only a little Pali was retained at the start of each section. The recitation versions of the *Mahachat* which later became popular were intended to give the audience the chance to listen to both the Pali and the Thai. So in these versions there are much longer sections of Pali interspersed in the text than in the *Kap mahachat*; and in order for the recitation of the thirteen chapters to be completed within one day the Thai sections are shorter than in the *Kap mahachat* (Damrong, 'Explanation of the *sakabap* verse poem,' in *Kap mahachat*, 88–92). In fact, the Thai sections of the recitation versions of the *Mahachat* are much longer than in the *Kap mahachat,* so the explanation that the recitation versions of the *Mahachat* originated out of the need to complete the recitation within one day is unsatisfactory.

The literary style of the *Kap mahachat* is another interesting feature. The entire work is written in *klon thet* or recitation verse, which is in fact *rai yao*. The rules for writing in *rai yao* verse are easy. One needs only to find a rhyme linking each line or hemistich. There are no rules regarding sound, the number of words, or the position in each line for the words that need to rhyme. *Rai yao* or recitation verse is one of the oldest Thai literary forms, dating from the *Mahachat khamluang*, and was probably used even earlier than that in the popular (*khamrat*) translated versions of the Jatakas which existed before the *khamluang*. *Rai yao* is a style of composition which is common to the literature of both the people and the court, and was the most popular form of wat literature. It seems that in Thai tradition *rai* was the basic style of composition used for communication between humans and the gods or spirits in popular rituals. Verses used to invoke the life essence (*khwan*) or the gods were always in *rai* form. So in court literature *rai* was regarded as a "sacred" form of verse. *Rai* was always used for the invocations praising the gods, king, or royal city at the beginning of a work. And because in the Thai tradition *rai* was a sacred verse style, monks or "pundits" associated with the wat commonly used it to render sacred Pali texts into Thai.[7] The reason that *rai* was used for the whole of the *Kap mahachat,* therefore, was because it was a literary work used by monks for recitation, like *Nanthopanantha sutra khamluang* and *Phra malai khamluang*.

Prince Damrong's assumption that the *Kap mahachat* was used by monks for recitation to the faithful appears very plausible, because the style of composition in the *Kap mahachat* is exactly the same as that in the recitation versions of the *Mahachat*. The only difference is in the interspersing of Pali phrases. So the *Kap mahachat* and the recitation versions of the *Mahachat* are part of the same literary tradition and differ from that of the *Mahachat khamluang*. Of all the extant recitation versions of the *Mahachat,* therefore, the *Kap mahachat* is the oldest.

The aim of the recitation versions of the *Mahachat,* of which the *Kap mahachat* is the earliest existing example, is to translate the content of the Vessantara Jataka so that the audience can understand it—like its translation by the pundits as the *Mahachat khamluang* (or the *khamrat* versions of the *Mahachat,* for which we have no surviving example to study). In neither of the two styles of translation—by the monks or by the laity—was there a desire to omit the Pali, because listening to the religious language was a form of "making merit" demanded by the faithful. Since the *Kap mahachat* was a translation used by monks in recitations to the laity it was believed that the Pali should not be omitted, especially the Thousand Verses (*khatha phan*). But in the version that has survived, most of the Pali has been omitted except for the *chunniyabot* or short phrases that begin each section. Take, for example, this verse: "*chatiparam* Yonder to the happy, bright shore of Liberation and Deliverance from Mara / The end of the cycle of existence of birth, aging, sickness, and death / To gain the treasure of the higher world / Because of you Chali my finest son..." Where have the Pali passages disappeared to, especially the Thousand Verses? We can assume that at this recitation ceremony the monks had already recited the Pali before beginning the recitation of the Thai translation. The brief Pali references remaining

7. I have already explained in detail the use of *rai* in 'Bourgeois Culture and Early Bangkok Literature' (see chapter 1 of this book).

in the translation were to indicate to those who understood Pali what point the translation has reached in the original text. This would be convenient for checking the translated text with the original Pali text. It avoided the problem of boring the general audience who could not understand Pali, although they still had to endure listening to the Pali original first in order to gain "merit." The surviving *Kap mahachat* text is therefore the one that monks used to recite the story in Thai after having first already chanted the Pali version.

This assumption is supported by evidence from the custom in some parts of the central region of reciting the *Mahachat* over three days, namely the *Thet mahachat* festival. On the first day the monks will chant the Thousand Verses from start to finish. The recitation in Thai starts on the second day. If it is a royal event (*khong luang*), the recitation in Thai will also include sections of Pali. But if it is a village recitation sometimes the Thousand Verses are omitted and sometimes included, as in the royal recitation. On the third day there is a recitation of the Four Noble Truths (Anuman Ratchathon 1960, 442–4). In some wat in central Thailand today the monks chant the Thousand Verses from before dawn in order to finish by morning, after which they begin the recitation of the *Mahachat* in Thai, in time for the participation of the laity in the ceremony. In this kind of recitation only the monks and more pious among the laity come to listen to the Thousand Verses. In the recitation ceremonies of the *Mahachat* in the south and the northeast, the Thousand Verses are also recited separately from the recitation of the *Mahachat* in Thai. In the northeast it is believed that the recitation of the Thousand Verses conveys the greatest merit (Somsak 1975, 149–51). In some parts of the south the notion of listening to the complete recitation of the *Mahachat* within one day is understood to mean listening to the Thousand Verses in Pali. The recitation of the Thai version can take as many days as are required (according to Professor Akhom Phatiya, Songkhla province). These customs demonstrate that the Pali content, especially the Thousand Verses, is the most important thing, or more important than the recitation of the *Mahachat* in Thai. At the very least, the Pali verses must be retained at the heart of the custom of reciting the *Mahachat*. So it is possible that formerly also the monks recited the Pali and Thai separately.

If this is correct the next development in the recitation as it appears in the *Kap mahachat* was the mixing of Pali phrases with the translation. The entire Pali version was not used as in the *Mahachat khamluang*, but the Pali verses which are central to listening to the recitation of the *Mahachat* could not be omitted. This meant that the faithful could listen to the recitation without becoming bored, while they gained merit from listening to the Thousand Verses at the same time. The recitation of the *Mahachat* mentioned in *Khun chang khun phaen* is an example of this development in the *Mahachat*. It does not matter that the historical context of *Khun chang khun phaen* is the early Bangkok period. Here it seems that there was no recitation of the Thousand Verses in Pali because it is not mentioned. The beginning of the passage starts, "The sponsor of the Thotsaphon chapter / Woke up early before cockcrow..." But what the monks in the story recited was certainly similar to the recitation versions we are familiar with, namely, a text fully interspersed with Pali verses and *chunniyabot*, since it states, "and he recited the *chunniyabot*..." In addition, it was believed that the recitation had to be completed within one day, as it states: "the Thirteen Chapters of the Mahachat / at Wat Pa Lelai on the next holy day." It also states that the Chuchok chapter was recited during the day, Maharat at night-time, and Chokkasat in the "dead of night" (*Khun chang khun phaen*, 49–57). It can thus be said that the custom of reciting the *Mahachat* only in Thai and reciting the thirteen chapters within one day was by now well-established and widespread. The recitation versions of the *Mahachat* that we know today were also widely accepted.

As the popularity of translating the Vessantara Jataka into recitation versions in Thai mixed with Pali verses and *chunniyabot* grew, the Thai translations became even more detailed and elaborate with the aim of enhancing the enjoyment of the audience, and thus grew longer and longer. Different wat competed to compose versions that would appeal to the audience by mixing humorous touches, excitement, and pathos with the original text (Rit 1984). The recitation of the text also required verbal skills and a particular style of intonation such that the recitation eventually became an art form. The literary evidence for this final development of the genre of recitation versions of the Vessantara Jataka can be found in the large number of *Mahachat* recitation versions that have survived to the present day. The best-known version is that published by the Department of Education in 1910, sometimes referred to as the "thirteen chapter version of the Vessantara Jataka" (the reprint used was *Mahawetsandon chadok chabap sipsam kan* 1957; here it will be referred to as the Department of Education version).

These assumptions all suggest that formerly monks did not recite the Vessantara Jataka in Thai, since the *Kap mahachat* only appeared much later. Also the custom of reciting the Vessantara Jataka had been copied from the chanting of the *Mahachat khamluang* by laymen. Thus the monks originally would have recited the *Mahachat* in Pali. When they began to recite it in Thai they borrowed the lay custom of chanting the text. If this is correct it would mean that the popularity of the festival of reciting the *Mahachat* as it appears in *Khun chang khun phaen* must have been quite recent. In the late Ayutthaya period the Palatine Law which had been in use since the reign of King Trailokanat, made no mention of the *Mahachat* in its account of royal ceremonies, even though it did mention that the Rains Retreat was part of a royal ceremony. The literary work known as the *Thawathotsamat*, which describes the various ceremonies carried out during the year, likewise makes no reference to the recitation of the Vessantara Jataka. Even in the early Bangkok period the recitation of the *Mahachat* had still not become a regular royal ceremony. During the Third Reign, if not enough sons of the aristocracy and nobility had entered the monkhood in that year then no recitation of the *Mahachat* was held. The *Mahachat* itself was also mixed up with recitations of other texts throughout the year (Chulachomklao 1960, 71–5). According to the evidence, the royal alms-giving ceremony of the recitation of the *Mahachat* incorporating the "great baskets"[8] was first organized on a

8. These baskets were to receive the alms offerings presented by those attending the recitation. [T]

large scale only in the First Reign, in 1807. It was a particularly grand affair: "the old people said that in former times there was never an occasion such as this / a massive ceremony of worship, an amazing, stupendous sight" (Records of the First Reign, 1807, Manuscript Division, National Library).

From late Ayutthaya when recitations of the *Mahachat* were first held, through to the reign of King Rama IV in the Bangkok period, it became very popular to compose recitation versions of the *Mahachat*. Many have survived until today. It is from this time that various customs associated with the recitation of the *Mahachat* developed. such as decorating the preaching hall with banana tree fronds and sugarcane to imitate the Himavanta forest, and decorating the alms offerings for each chapter of the story with papaya into which are carved motifs based on events in the story, as described in *Khun chang khun phaen*. This only became popular in the late Ayutthaya period, because it was only possible for these decorations to be meaningful when the recitation of the story by monks could be understood and enjoyed by lay audiences. Thus the chanting of the *Mahachat* by laymen, which appears to have been an old custom among the Thai people, only became a major festival when recitations in Thai by monks began in the late Ayutthaya period. It was an important festival for local communities. Both the laity and the monks joined in portraying the ideals which the society considered important in narrative form. These were ideals which they could sense and understand by listening to this sacred story, and by seeing the reliefs and decorations of scenes from this story on the inside of the wat. These ideals lived in the imagination of people who grew up with a deeply-held belief in them.

If we compare literature from Lanna it appears likely that the recitation versions of the *Mahachat* there originated prior to those in the central region. The oldest *Mahachat* manuscript so far discovered from Lanna was inscribed in 1712, which means that such manuscripts may have been composed at a considerably earlier date. Among the versions of the Lanna *Mahachat* so far discovered, most were inscribed after 1759, which indicates that even in Lanna the custom of reciting the *Mahachat* probably became widespread not long before the central region (Prakhong 1976, 151–62).

The large number of recitation versions of the *Mahachat* is a sign of the popularity of the custom of reciting the *Mahachat* in Thai (in the central region), which had spread rapidly since the late Ayutthaya period. This was a custom that truly belonged to the people (which is why we have versions of the *Mahachat* called *khamluang*.) It was usually monks who composed these recitation versions of the *Mahachat*, because a knowledge of Pali was important in writing the story. The authors whose work was included in the Department of Education's recitation version of the *Mahachat* were either monks or people who had spent many years in the monkhood, for example Prince Paramanuchit Chinorot, the "Wat Thanon School," Phra Thepmoli, and King Rama IV. It should be pointed out that since the recitation versions of the *Mahachat* and even the recitation of the *Mahachat* itself truly belonged to the people and the monks, court poets and poets from the upper class did not have a major role in composing recitation versions of the *Mahachat* in the late Ayutthaya period. The practice of adapting folk literature to become the literature of the court was a prominent feature of the early Bangkok era, and resulted in poets of the court and upper class competing with the wat in composing recitation versions of the *Mahachat*, for example Chaophraya Phrakhlang (Hon), Prince Paramanuchit Chinorot, and King Rama IV. The versions composed by these poets later became very popular. Following their selection for inclusion in the thirteen chapter version of the *Thet mahachat* the popularity of these versions increased even further, resulting in their domination of the other recitation versions. For this reason the discovery and publication of the Phetchaburi *Mahachat* is a breath of fresh air to those interested in recitation versions of the *Mahachat*. The Phetchaburi version is written in a style that is quite different to the Department of Education version (except for the Thankan chapter, which appears to be the same as that used by the Wat Thanon school in the Department's version).

DATING THE PHETCHABURI VERSION OF THE *MAHACHAT*

If one looks carefully at the Phetchaburi *Mahachat* there are two chapters which are the same as in other versions: Wanapawet and Thankan. The Phetchaburi version of Wanapawet is virtually the same as the one believed to have been composed by Prince Paramanuchit Chinorot (Kan Wanapawet in *Mahawetsandon chadok sipsam kan* 1964, 75–92, hereafter referred to as the "Cremation Volume version"). When these two versions of Wanapawet are compared it is quite clear that the Phetchaburi *Mahachat* is older. Prince Paramanuchit Chinorot adapted it into a new version which is more refined and polished to suit the tastes of the audience in the early Bangkok period. Composing a new version of an older work appears to have been common practice for this particular poet. For example, his *Kritsana son nong khamchan* was adapted from an earlier version written by a monk by the name of "In" during the reign of King Borommakot. This is obvious if we compare sections of Wanapawet in the Phetchaburi *Mahachat* with that written by Prince Paramanuchit Chinorot.

Phetchaburi version

bhikkhave O monks, who hold tightly to the precepts.
The mighty Thao Thep Kunchon Suthamabodi [Indra] commanded Lord Vissukam to come to build an ashram
As well as provide utensils used by ascetics
To present them to the great king.
Lord Vissukam received the divine command
And magically created the ascetic's ashram
Situated in a lonely place on Crooked Mountain,
And ordered the wild animals in the Himavanta mountains to avoid the place.
They fled to a distance three *yojanas* from there.
He had the other animals sing sweet melodies in chorus near the ashram
And miraculously caused the area to bloom with flowers
And the air to be fragrant with the sweet scent of pollen.

He placed an inscription upon the entrance *antaradhayitva*
And disappeared into the heavens whence he came.
Then *bodhisatto* the great king of the lineage of enlightened victors crossed the mountains, hills, and ponds.
All the trees of the forest stood upright, a wondrous sight,
As the sun god visited the peak of Yukhandha mountain.
He arrived at the splendid ashram in the forest.
Upon seeing the inscription he realized that the Thousand Eyed One [Indra] had built it as a gift to him.

(*Mahachat mueang phet*, 86–7; written according to contemporary orthography but retaining the original tones)

Prince Paramanuchit Chinorot in the Cremation Volume version

bhikkave O monks, who hold tightly to the precepts.
Ming Amon Makut Thewarat Surarit [Indra] ordered Lord Vessukam to magically produce an ashram
As well as the utensils required by ascetics
To present to the great king.
Lord Vessukam respectfully received the divine command
And came to magically build the ascetic's ashram in a lonely place on Crooked Mountain,
And miraculously caused the wild animals in the forest to flee
Three *yojanas* away from there.
He caused the animals to sweetly sing
A song in chorus near the ashram,
And he miraculously caused the trees to be adorned with flowers fragrant with the sweet scent of pollen.
akkharam likkhitva He placed an inscription upon the entrance
antaradhayitva And disappeared into the heavenly abode of the gods.
Then the great king of the lineage of enlightened victors crossed the mountains, hills, and ponds.
All the trees of the forest stood upright, a wondrous sight,
As the Sun god visited the peak of Yukhandha mountain.
He arrived at the splendid forest ashram.
Upon seeing the inscription he realized that it was a gift created for him by the Thousand Eyed One [Indra].

(Cremation Volume version, 89–90)

In revising the older version of Wanapawet, Prince Paramanuchit Chinorot thus omitted lengthy, drawn out phrases and changed those words whose meaning was unclear. For example, the older version refers to Indra as *Thep kunchon suthamabodi*, which might have been misunderstood by the audience as referring to some other god. So he has changed the god's title to *Ming amon makut thewarat surarit* or "Lord of the Gods," which according to Buddhist belief meant Indra. Apart from this he also edited certain sections. For example, the old version stated he "miraculously caused the area to bloom with flowers." This reads as if the trees had to be created in a forest which should already be full of trees. So he changed this passage to read, "And he miraculously caused the trees to be adorned with flowers fragrant with the sweet scent of pollen," i.e., to make something that already existed produce flowers. However in every line he is careful to preserve the original rhyming scheme.

The Thankan chapter in the Phetchaburi *Mahachat* is almost identical to that in the Department of Education version. There are only minor differences which are probably due either to a lack of care on the part of the copyist of the Phetchaburi version, or to someone wanting to improve on the Department of Education version. Let us compare the introductory section in the two versions

Phetchaburi version

phussatipikhodevi Lady Phutsadi the beautiful heavenly princess
katakasasanam sutva When the Lady heard the news
That the king would banish Prince Vessantara from the palace
The Lady's breast swelled and collapsed in grief.
Her tears flowed freely.
She was full of sorrow.
cintetva She considered to herself this thought:
O my heart, what karma is this? How bitter it is
That the townsfolk have stirred up a commotion out of their anger
I must visit my two beloved children...

Department of Education version

phussatipikhodevi When Lady Phutsadi, the beautiful royal mother
katakasasanam sutva The Lady heard the news that the King
Would banish Prince Vessantara from the palace
The Lady's breast broke and collapsed in grief.
Her tears flowed freely and she was full of sorrow.
citetva She considered the thought in her mind:
O my heart, what karma is this,
How bitter it is that the townsfolk have stirred up a commotion out of their anger.
I must go to see my two beloved children...

The similarities in these two versions of the Thankan chapter shows that they must have been based on the same original. We know that the Department of Education version of Thankan is the work of the poet known by the name of the "Wat Thanon School." Nobody is certain who this poet may have been. However Sathit Semanin has stated that his real name was Thong U. He was born in the late Ayutthaya period and received his education in Ayutthaya. After the fall of Ayutthaya he traveled from wat to wat as a student until finally basing himself at Wat Thanon where he entered the monkhood. There he composed the Thankan chapter and later became famous (Sathit 1975, 94). If Sathit is right we can confidently claim that this version of Thankan was composed during the early Bangkok period, either during the reign of Taksin or that of Rama I.

Close inspection shows that the Wat Thanon School or Department of Education version of the Thankan chapter must have been based on the Phetchaburi version. The original was good and only a few passages have been changed between the two versions. One passage may be compared as an example.

Phetchaburi version

The splendid elephant,
Of such a kind that no king in ten thousand cities could find,
Was the city's auspicious palladium.
The prince was also handsome, virile, and strong
Like a Wishing Tree in the middle of a field.
One could ask from him whatever one desired.
Is it right that he should be hated? How bitter
That one should break the branches, strip their leaves, and let the fruit fall to the ground!
Your Majesty is also angry and has cut down the tree trunk.
The townsfolk gather together as an unruly mob, openly cursing him.
Your Majesty should be like a true set of golden scales.
You should carefully consider to yourself before
You decide to banish Prince Vessantara from the palace.
My lord, will he be condemned to wander from country to country?
The noble elephant, as precious to us as our own eyes, has gone;
Will our beloved son also have to leave the city?
Will this not double their anger?
Your Highness, please wait and listen.
Our precious golden white elephant,
You found in the forest and brought back to the glory of the royal city.
If former merit still abounds, then others can also be found.
But it is so hard to find a beloved son such as ours,
Like finding the jewel of the Emperor.
Your Highness, you are old now,
You should think about yourself.
Should you banish your son from the palace?
What will happen if later you should fall ill from disease?
Who then will care for us and protect us?
Or will the palace ladies
Have to sit beside you night after night caring for you?
O my lord, in happy times the ladies all walk in a dignified manner

But if there is a crisis will they not promenade straight out of the palace?
If children are plentiful, this can be avoided.
Without your son here, who will fear the King's command?
The riches in the kingdom will disappear.
ambavapatitajama Like a mango tree with sweetly fragrant fruit,
The fruit turn yellow and fall to the ground one after the other.
It is of no use to forbid people from eating them,
The townsfolk will eat them all, leaving none,
Like your treasures, without a king to protect them.
anatha appa vittho Your Majesty,
It is difficult to control the hearts of the courtiers, great and small.
In good times they will fall over themselves to serve your every wish.
They will flatter you from morn to night.
But in bad times they will persuade one another to make things worse.
hamsonikhhinnapatove Like a royal swan with a broken wing stuck in a swamp
The crows will arrive to pick out its guts…

Department of Education version

The splendid elephant
Which the kings of a thousand cities could not find
Was the auspicious palladium of the city.
The prince was also most handsome.
Banishing him from the royal city will not make the elephant return.
Your Highness is too willing to heed the words of wicked men.
The townsfolk blame him and have become angry.
Having lost a handful, will you now lose an armful, Your Highness?
My lord, don't make this decision lightly, you should consider it carefully.
When in difficult times, when there is no way out,
How can the war horses and victory elephants help our son and his wife if they perish by Your Majesty's hand?
O my lord,
Do not be sad, do not be upset.
As for the royal auspicious elephant, the palladium of the city, former merit still abounds so it could be found again.
But it is so hard to find a son such as ours.
It is like searching for Indra's discus.
Your Majesty, would you drive your son far away from you?
Who will act in your place?
Soon our city will be deserted like a crow's nest.
When Your Highness becomes old,
The royal possessions will be in chaos.
ambava patitajama Like a mango tree with sweet-smelling fruit

Which turn yellow and fall to the ground one after the other,
There is no need to tire oneself reaching up to pick the fruit,
The crowd will grab them and eat them all, leaving none,
Like the treasures of Your Majesty
Without any royal relatives to protect them. *appavittho*
Also, it is difficult to control the hearts of the courtiers, great and small.
When times are good they will be quick to serve you,
They will carry out your every wish,
Curry favor with you from morn to night.
But in difficult times they will all get together to make things worse.
hamsonikkhinapatamtova Like a royal swan with a broken wing stuck in a swamp,
The crows will arrive to pick out its guts...

Apart from these sections which show that the Phetchaburi version is the original used by the Wat Thanon School, the Pali phrases used in the beginning of each section called *chunniyabot* are in most respects the same in both versions, except that some of them have been omitted in the Wat Thanon School version.

Such similarities between the two versions can also be seen in the Matsi chapter. The version of this chapter in the Department of Education's edition was written by Chaophraya Phrakhlang (Hon), but it is not known who wrote the chapter that appears in the Phetchaburi version, or when. However some sections of the Phetchaburi version are arranged in exactly the same order as in the version by Chaophraya Phrakhlang (Hon), and in some cases they even use the same words. For example, the Phetchaburi version reads, "...if we still lived in the great royal city as before / You would not dare do this to me / For better or for worse I would have cut your body in two with my own right hand." This passage in the version by Chaophraya Phrakhlang (Hon) reads, "...if I lived in the great city like before / If you had done this / Your body would immediately have been cut in two by my own right hand..." Or, in the Phetchaburi version, "How sad, the black plum tree near the ashram..." while the Department of Education version reads, "We should be sad, the black plum tree near the ashram...."; or, in the Phetchaburi version: "...the pebbles and sand glittering in the sunlight / Like ground crystal scattered all around" while the Department of Education version reads, "when touched by sunlight the shiny pebbles and sand under the tree sparkle and glitter, bright and shining / Like someone had ground crystal and scattered it all around the area." Both versions say that Matsi heard the same sound from the forest as if her children were crying: "*nguem ngeum.*" In some passages both versions use almost exactly the same words. For example, the Phetchaburi version reads, "Would you have this dense forest be your graveyard? / Would you have the hermitage here be your cremation pyre?" which is almost the same as the Department of Education version: "Would you have this dense forest be your graveyard / And would you have this hermitage be the place of your golden cremation pyre...?" Nevertheless, the differences between the Chaophraya Phrakhlang (Hon) version and the Phetchaburi versions are greater in the Matsi chapter than in the Wanapawet and Thankan chapters.

Even though there are many differences, the fact that the content is arranged in the same order and in many cases exactly the same words are used means we can be confident that the Chaophraya Phrakhlang (Hon) and Phetchaburi versions of the *Mahachat* must be related. Both must have been adapted from the same earlier version. If we consider the similarities between the two, the Phetchaburi version of the *Mahachat* appears older than that by Chaophraya Phrakhlang (Hon), since the latter has made numerous changes to the former version to improve its literary qualities, even though the content is virtually the same.

We can approximate the date of the composition of the Phetchaburi version by comparing the two versions of this chapter. The Phetchaburi version—or at least the three chapters referred to here—must be older than those by Prince Paramanuchit Chinorot, the Wat Thanon School, and Chaophraya Phrakhlang (Hon). Chaophraya Phrakhlang (Hon) died during the First Reign, and the revised version of Thankan by the Wat Thanon School must have been completed before the end of the First Reign as well. Therefore it is possible that the Phetchaburi *Mahachat* dates from before the First Reign, that is, some time between the late Ayutthaya period and the reign of King Taksin. The fact that manuscripts of the Phetchaburi version survived and were copied in Phetchaburi makes it very likely that it was based on a version from the late Ayutthaya period, since numerous documents from the Ayutthaya period have been discovered there. Phetchaburi is close to Ayutthaya and was once an important city. Religious texts and other documents were copied from Ayutthaya and kept in Phetchaburi since the time that Ayutthaya was the kingdom's capital. Also, after the fall of Ayutthaya, people seeking refuge from the wars may have brought with them religious texts and documents that they considered important. Phetchaburi was not seriously affected by the fighting at this time. For these reasons numerous important documents have been discovered there, such as the Luang Prasoet version of the Royal Chronicles. The Phetchaburi version of a *Mahachat* recitation text was probably copied in Ayutthaya and was most likely composed from various versions which were well-regarded and hence copied by later poets. It is a good example of the early Bangkok literary practice of adapting and improving on older texts.

In terms of prosody and literary style the text also appears old enough to date from the late Ayutthaya period, and undoubtedly older than the literary style of the chapters in the Department of Education's version. The Phetchaburi version's use of old expressions and words can be seen in every chapter. For example, the Buddha is referred to as Phra Sithat (or Prince Siddhattha) (p. 6); the phrase used for being hungry is "to have a sore belly" as in "if you have a sore belly you should try to eat something" (p. 15); Mount Yukhondhara is referred to as "Sacred Mount Yukhandharesha" (p. 139); Princess Matsi calls out to her children, Kanha and Chali, "awake my jewels, don't sleep in late" (p. 141); the expression "to act condescendingly" (*du thuk*) is rendered differently as "before, none looked down upon (*du tam*) and reproached your father" (p. 148); the expression "our *kamma* has caught up to us now" (p. 158) for ever (*talot pai*) or for own's whole life (*talot chiwit*) is rendered as: "it's not possible to protect your lord against evil *at all times (rot chua)*" (p. 179).

THE VALUE OF THE PHETCHABURI VERSION OF THE *MAHACHAT* FOR THE STUDY OF EARLY BANGKOK LITERATURE

If we accept that the Phetchaburi version of the *Mahachat* is based on or at least is very similar to versions from the late Ayutthaya period, it is very useful for the study of the literary qualities of *Mahachat* literature from the central region. In terms of literary merit the Phetchaburi version cannot compare to the Department of Education version, but for the study of the literary history the Phetchaburi version is useful in helping us understand the poets who composed recitation versions of the *Mahachat* in the early Bangkok period.

Comparing two major poets of the early Bangkok period, Chaophraya Phrakhlang (Hon) and Prince Paramanuchit Chinorot, reveals quite major differences. Chaophraya Phrakhlang (Hon) was a poet with new and different ideas who attempted to break through existing literary conventions. For example, he was the first poet to render tales (*nithan*) into verse. He searched for new and different tales which had never previously been used in Thai literature, such as *Sombat amarin*, *Phetmongkut*, and *Siwichai chadok* (*Sivijaya Jataka*). He also experimented with new literary forms. Chaophraya Phrakhlang (Hon) was thus an innovator. His work is quite original, so it is not surprising that the Kuman and Matsi chapters written by him are quite different from versions of the late Ayutthaya period, even though they must have been based on a version that had survived from Ayutthaya. This is clear when we compare the Phetchaburi version with that by Chaophraya Phrakhlang (Hon) in the passage where Prince Vessantara calls to his son Chali to come out of the lotus pond so he can be like a merchant junk on which Vessantara can lead sentient beings across the Sea of Becoming.

Phetchaburi version

Like a trading ship in this world
A merchant's junk that crosses the sea
At the auspicious moment pulls up the anchor and hoists up the sail.
The junk leaves, with the book-keeper, navigator, and crew.
The breeze blows softly and the junk sails speedily and steadily.
Then it is met by the northeasterly wind and waves splash merrily.
The force of the waves makes the junk list and shake causing it to shudder;
Storm winds thrash the red sails from all directions;
The rain and the storm winds cause the rigging to break;
The mast splinters and snaps into pieces;
The rudder breaks off and floats away;
The boards of the ship's hull, unable to withstand the pressure,
Split apart and are washed away in the current;
The merchants die and become prey for fish. (p. 149)

This passage or one very similar to it was greatly improved upon by Chaophraya Phrakhlang (Hon). Even though in various places he uses many of the same phrases and expressions as in the Ayutthaya period version, Chaophraya Phrakhlang (Hon) did not follow the original particularly closely, and there are subtle shifts in emphasis.

Chaophraya Phrakhlang (Hon) version

A junk of some merchant
Has its hull constructed
Out of wooden planks nailed sturdily and tightly together,
Sheets of metal fitted together, covered with a layer of caulking rubber to make watertight.
The boards on the ship's deck are straight, there's a winch to haul up the anchor,
The mast stands tall and steady, fastened by plates, attached to a pulley; it looks strong.
The rigging on the mast is secure.
The flag with a centipede insignia flaps in the breeze.
The craftsman has carved out reliefs of animals:
The royal lion proudly pushes out its chest decorated in the *kranok* style, holding a crystal ball in its mouth.
When the monsoon winds blow the shouts go up.
The cargo is lowered into the ship's hold and the stagnant water is bailed out.
The junk is heavily loaded, up to the washboards.
At the auspicious moment for departure three cheers go up.
A gun is fired from the ship, making a sharp bang.
The workers stand around all over the place,
Different accents and languages can be heard, "helo, lae, hela."
The anchor is hauled up and the gong is struck giving out a loud clash.
Flags flutter and wave atop the sail, blown by the wind god.
The book-keeper and the navigator look around intently.
They set the compass and look through the telescope to determine the direction in which the boat should sail.
The helmsman changes the boat's direction out towards the deep ocean;
soon the coast can no longer be seen.
Then the Selatan wind begins to blow and waves break merrily here and there.
Buffeted by the waves the junk sways boisterously;
The mast shears off; the planks on the ship's deck split apart;
A giant wave crashes, smashes, and dashes the boat, ba-bam-blam;
The junk sinks in the middle of the vast ocean;
No human being is left alive,
They all become prey for the turtles and fish, since it is but a worldly ship, which does not last...

(Department of Education version, 239–40)

Even though the basic theme in each version is the same, Chaophraya Phrakhlang (Hon) greatly improves upon the literary quality of the older version. The first area of difference is his description of the boat and of the merchant junks leaving port. Chaophraya Phrakhlang (Hon) makes full use of his own direct experience, as we can see from his description of the junks which leave the port of Bangkok amidst noise and commotion. He describes in full the chaos surrounding the port, the boats themselves and their construction, the rituals associated with the boats' leaving the port such as letting off firecrackers and banging gongs. All this brings the reader into contact with reality as he himself has experienced it. Such emphasis on actual experience renders the Vessantara Jataka less a religious sermon and more a piece of literature. The narrative acquires a greater or at least an equal importance to the religious point it is designed to convey. In the section which uses a metaphor comparing man to a merchant's ship at the mercy of nature, the lengthy description based on the poet's actual experience of boats and navigation results in the blurring of the religious point of this passage as the reader becomes engrossed in the vividness of the picture painted by the poet, the excitement and force of the style, and the clarity of the description. In other words Chaophraya Phrakhlang (Hon) has added metaphors from *this* world which results in a considerable weakening of the other-worldly meaning.

Another difference that should be noted is that the version by Chaophraya Phrakhlang (Hon) brings something new to the description in this passage: the emphasis on the strength of the merchant vessel, which is absent from this passage in the Phetchaburi version. The description of the construction of the boat at the beginning of this passage—intended to express the boat's sturdiness—reflects not so much advances in ship-building techniques, since the passages in both versions were composed at approximately the same time, but rather change in the nature of thinking between two different eras. The boat which was carefully constructed to endure sea voyages uses many kinds of nails and clasps and metal plates stuck together in sheets, which ensure that the mast, which is one of the weak points of a junk, is strong and sturdy. All of this appears to reflect a confidence in the ability of humans in their struggle with the elements. Although it is true that at the end of the passage the boat sinks, the sinking is only briefly mentioned and is explained as being the result of a storm. In any case it is necessary to include the passage about the boat's sinking here as it is part of the original passage in the Vessantara Jataka. So it is interesting that this emphasis on the strength of the boat, which is a product of human effort, does not appear in the Phetchaburi version. The version by Chaophraya Phrakhlang (Hon) who is an important poet of this era thus reflects the greater confidence in human ability which is characteristic of the thinking of the upper class generally in the early Bangkok period.

Prince Paramanuchit Chinorot, on the other hand, is a poet who attempted to preserve older literary traditions. There is not a single work by this poet which does not have its roots in an older work. *Taleng phai* was modelled on the earlier *Yuan phai,* but inserts *lilit nirat* verse like that used in the poem *Lilit phra lo*; *Samutthakhot khamchan* is the completion of an older work; *Kritsana son nong* is also an adaptation of an older work from the reign of King Borommakot. Nevertheless,

Prince Paramanuchit Chinorot is a poet of the early Bangkok period, and he could not help but be influenced by the age in which he lived. A comparison between his composition of the Wanapawet chapter and the Phetchaburi version suggests that he in fact did not write a new version of Wanapawet but rather used and improved upon an older version written in the Ayutthaya era. This may have been because the version of Wanapawet dating from the Ayutthaya era was of high literary quality. But if we compare other chapters in the Phetchaburi version with those he composed himself we find interesting changes, similar to those in the work of Chaophraya Phrakhlang (Hon). See, for example, the two versions of the Chulaphon chapter.

Phetchaburi version

> Now I will describe the birds and flora of the Himavanta forest.
> Flocks of parrots perch on *ket* trees eating their fruit.
> Throngs of heron perch on the upper branches of Burma reed trees.
> Storks perch on the branches of *krasang* trees and cry out loudly.
> A night-owl stares out from the tip of a moke tree.
> The watercock sits on the *ulok* tree, turns around, and flies away.
> The weaver birds sip water noisily.
> The thrush catches horseflies sadly looking for a mate.
> The fireback pheasant perches atop a fan palm, looking as if floating.
> The pygmy goose perches in a *khoi* bush, looking pitiful.
> The bamboo bird flits back and forth to perch on the *kralamphak akkhanit.*
> Some sit in the nest, as if in contemplation, and then fly away.
> The partridge perches on the lead tree singing sweetly.
> The *sua saew* bird hovers to eat the abundant ripe fruits of the banyan tree.
> Flocks of doves sit in pairs on the *pliao* tree nestling closely in couples, looking contented.
> The red breasted parakeet dances along the branch of a *taew* tree.
> The mynah bird perches on the orange jasmine tree, chirping away.
> The pheasant perches on the *mafo* tree, crouching down.
> The crane hovers here and there crying out loudly.
> The *khla* bird sits on the *krasang* tree singing.
> The hoot of the scops owl sitting on the garlic pear tree echoes through the vast forest.
> Swans nestle up to the *hiang* tree.
> Flocks of peacocks prance and strut on a branch atop the yang tree.
> The barbets sit on the Burmese ebony tree, cooing loudly to their lovers.
> The sweet singing of the cuckoo resounds through the forest. (p. 145)

Prince Paramanuchit Chinorot version

> *nanavanana bahu dija* There are many different varied species of wonderful birds.
> All are twice-born.

Before this they were eggs; later they were born as animals.
annyamannya pakujajino The whole forest was aloud with the sweet sounds of the birds screeching,
Calling to each other noisily as birds are wont to do.
nanthika Merrily the swans and geese fly in,
Descending to play in the Mucalinda pond.
Splashes of water stick to the lotus flowers in drops.
piyajino The heron arrive in mating pairs,
Looking for food to skewer with their beaks to feed to their chicks waiting in their nest.
What a noise they make!
The watercock walks along the edge of the pond then disappears into the bushes.
Cormorants dive into the water hunting for fish.
All of these species of bird live happily by the water, where they find their food.
Their nests are in the bushes on the banks; their noisy singing fills the forest.
(Cremation Volume version, 149)

The difference between the two versions clearly lies in the fact that Prince Paramanuchit Chinorot is stricter in retaining the content of the original Pali verses. For example, he tries to explain the words *bahu* and *dija* meaning "to be twice born," which the Phetchaburi version simply omits; the entire section contains no Pali *chunniyabot*. But this difference is not particularly important, besides showing this royal poet's strict maintenance of tradition. The more important difference is the way in which the poet describes the bird life. The Phetchaburi version emphasizes the rhyming scheme. For example the *nok yang* (heron) perches on the *yot yung* (upper branches of the Burma reed tree); the *salika* (mynah bird) sits on the *ton kaew* (orange jasmine tree), and so on. These descriptions of flora and fauna became popular during the late Ayutthaya and early Bangkok periods. But once a literary tradition has been followed for a long time, its novelty fades and becomes something lacking in spirit. The rhyming pattern, which once conveyed a feeling of lightheartedness, becomes blander and less enjoyable for the reader. The forest, a thing that actually exists in the world, loses its importance because it is reduced to the demands of the rhyming scheme of a particular literary convention. Poets in the early Bangkok period began to move away from this convention of describing the forest, as can be seen in a considerable number of descriptions in the work of Sunthon Phu where the forest described is a real forest. What the poet wants to convey is the beauty that human beings can experience through their five senses. The words used are closer to the actual meaning, rather than chosen to meet the demands of a rhyming pattern that aims principally to affect the reader's feelings. Prince Paramanuchit Chinorot's version of this passage describing the bird life in the Chulaphon chapter has escaped from this older literary tradition and reflects more the actual world as it is, similar to the literature of the early Bangkok period generally which reflects a greater interest in the real world than the literature of the Ayutthaya period. This is an important difference between the two versions since it reflects a changing literary trend.

Another change to the *Mahachat* in the early Bangkok period is the clearer characterization of the people in the story. They have more distinct personalities and have been transformed into human beings who carry out actions according to their own intentions to a much greater extent. In actual fact, the Vessantara Jataka is a moral parable in Pali. The behavior of the various characters in the story enables the Bodhisatta to perform the great Perfection of Giving (*than barami*), and for this reason the characters do not always act according to their own motivations. They are like puppets that act in certain ways determined by extra-worldly forces. For example, the gods tell Amittada about Prince Vessantara and urge her to go to Chuchok to have him ask for the royal children to be her servants. This emphasis on Prince Vessantara, who is a sacred hero, and his quest to achieve the Perfection of Giving, thus renders the other characters lifeless. We might say that Chuchok helps Prince Vessantara to achieve this high level of Perfection (*barami*) no less than his two royal children enable him to lead sentient creatures across the Sea of Becoming. However, the recitation version of the *Mahachat* has changed the nature of the characters to a certain extent by adding material about them which does not appear in the original Pali. The original aim was probably simply to make the story more entertaining and lively for the listeners. Unintentionally the characters begin to appear more independent. Another important development of the *Mahachat* in the early Bangkok period was the increasingly distinct personality of the characters. The result is that these characters begin to be transformed into people who act according to their own personality and self-interest. This change releases the Vessantara Jataka from the genre of moral parable and transforms it into something more like fiction (*niyai*). A clear example demonstrating this point concerns one of the most important characters of the story, Chuchok.

Chuchok is a cruel, selfish, wicked, and heartless man. He is cunning, afraid of his wife, and a coward. This personality dictates his actions. In the passage when he accepts his friend's proposal to give him his daughter Amittada instead of the money which is owed to him, the Phetchaburi version (pp. 92–3) reads, "the old man began to think lustfully / Even though I lose another five chang I don't regret it / The old man gave a respectful *wai* to the woman's mother and said..." This passage does not seem to accord with the miserliness and selfishness of Chuchok. Surely such a miserly person would regret losing another five chang. And giving a *wai* to the woman's mother demonstrates that he knows proper manners and how to be respectful—something out of keeping with the basic personality of Chuchok, who is unlikely to have acted in this way. The Chuchok chapter of the Wat Sangkrachai version written in the early Bangkok period is much more consistent with Chuchok's personality. When Chuchok sees Amittada he is so satisfied that, "The old man cried out, Oh! Ah! Come on, sir / Hurry up! / Quickly! / *tang adaya* / Chuchok hurriedly led Amittada away / And hastily sped off to his home" (Department of Education version, 130).

When Amittada threatens Chuchok and forces him to go and ask for Kanha and Chali, the Phetchaburi version reads, "Old Chuchok whose mind was deluded by lust / Fearing that his young wife would leave him and go far away / Soothed her feelings saying, 'My beautiful young thing / Don't be angry with me, my fair-skinned, delicate maiden / I will go to ask for the two royal children to be your servants / So don't be sad and weep...'" (*Mahachat mueang phet,* 102). The passage in the Wat Sangkrachai version is more consistent with Chuchok's cunningness and boastfulness, which makes it both funny and much more in keeping with Chuchok's real personality: "The old man pretended not to be moved / By his wife's harsh words / And cried out, 'Who said I would not go? / If you want me to go I'm not afraid / How many hundreds or thousands of miles to Crooked Mountain? / Before I used to go there quite often / Even if it was a bit further than Crooked Mountain I would still go / Wherever you want me to go I am willing to go...'" (Department of Education version, 152).

Similarly when Chuchok deceives Chetabut, the hunter, the Phetchaburi version says simply that, "Chuchok laughed and quickly slid down the tree exclaiming, how tired I am" (*Mahachat mueang phet,* 107). But this passage in the Wat Sangkrachai version is much better:

> As for the old man
> He timidly climbed his way down the tree,
> Holding close to himself his shoulder bag
> From which a rattling sound was heard.
> The hunter called out, 'Sir, what is that sound?'
> The old man lied that it was an ivory box containing a letter with a royal seal.
> Chetabut happily raised the box above his head in respect.
> The old man cried out, warning him, 'Hold it carefully, the box is old and heavy, make sure you don't break it.'
> Chetabut spread out a cloth and made prostrations before it, believing what the old man had said was true.
> He did not realize that he was paying respect to a box containing chili and ginger.
> The old man thought to himself, 'Now I'll enjoy this! This wicked man
> Threatened me, cursed me, abused me, did everything except shoot me dead.
> Let him pay respect to this box over and over.'
> He had been outwitted by the cunning devious old man...
>
> (Department of Education version, 175)

This latter version enables us much better to see the scheming, vengeful character of Chuchok, without his sympathetic side. It is also very funny for the listener.

This greater characterization in the story gives the characters more independence in their actions. They are not merely the instruments of a larger narrative that determines their actions in order to suit its own requirements. The Vessantara Jataka is thus transformed into fiction (*niyai*), and its character as a moral parable decreases. This is consistent with the changing literary trend in the early Bangkok period, which saw the replacement of "other-worldly" content by "worldly" content.

Studies of the literary qualities of the *Mahachat* up to now have been rather careless. There has been no cross-checking of the various versions, which has resulted in blind praise for this genre of literature. It should be understood that the talents of the poets who composed the *Mahachat* in the early Bangkok period were limited by two things which meant that they had to sacrifice their own poetic skill to a certain extent. These limitations were the following:

1. All the versions of the *Mahachat* are translations from the Pali. No matter how popular the recitation versions were, the *Mahachat* was still a genre of religious literature. So it has a character unlike other Jatakas, upon which a large amount of Thai literature is based. In these other Jatakas the poet has the right to make changes according to his own will. It is possible that the narrator of the outer-drama, *Sangthong,* might not ever have seen the Pali version of the *Suwannasang chadok* in the *Panyatsa chadok* collection of Jatakas. But the Vessantara Jataka is a "sacred" Jataka. So the alterations that can be made to the story are much more limited than with the *Suwannasang chadok*. The tradition of "translation" was never completely discarded with the *Mahachat.*[9] So we can see that the practice of *chunniyabot* or placing Pali phrases at the beginning of a passage, continues in the recitation versions of the *Mahachat*. The original function of these Pali phrases was simply to check how far the translation had progressed. The oldest version of the *Mahachat*, the *Mahachat khamluang* (or the wat versions of the *Mahachat* for chanting by laymen, of which no version has survived which we could study today) was simply a sentence by sentence translation, in which the entire sentence in Pali would be given, followed by its Thai translation. Hence in the recitation versions, the Pali content is not omitted; the poet is allowed to insert a considerable amount of other material, but he has no right to omit the Pali content. Thus many kinds of Pali expressions find their way into the recitation version of the *Mahachat*. For example, when Vessantara is waiting for Chuchok to ask for a gift, the phrase, "His generosity sought a beggar to receive the royal gift, in the same way that a drunkard searches for a whisky merchant" sounds strange in Thai. However this phrase is not an invention by Chaophraya Phrakhlang (Hon), the author of this Kuman chapter, but comes from the Pali, which in the original *Nibat chadok* (Pali: *Nipata Jataka*) reads: "*...Pipasito viya surasoado tassagaṃanamaggam olokento nisidi*. The phrase used when Princess Matsi faints, "like a golden banana tree that has been felled by the stroke of a sword (*Mahachat mueang phet,* 187) is consistent with the Pali verse, "*...pitta suvannakaddalikhandam viya.*" However, Chaophraya Phrakhlang (Hon) changed it slightly to make it sound a little more Thai: "Like a golden *chat* tree, struck and broken by a thunderbolt, collapses and falls down..." (Department of Education version, 297). Nevertheless, the source of the metaphor is still to be found in the Pali.

If one is to praise the literary merits of a recitation version of the *Mahachat*, one needs to first check it against the original passage in the *Nibat chadok* to see what belongs to the original Pali and what is due to the skill of the poet.

2. During the late Ayutthaya period many literary styles, expressions, metaphors, and mourning verses (*bot khruan*) had become standard in the recitation versions of the *Mahachat*. That is to say, the metaphors, descriptive passages, and mourning

9. This discussion is limited to the central region. Due to this author's limited knowledge it does not include the *Mahachat* versions of the south, northeast, and Lanna.

verses had become a form of composition that was commonly accepted. Poets from different schools simply competed with each other to compose versions based on these accepted stylistic conventions. All of the content which was outside of the Pali verses conformed to fairly fixed patterns of composition. For example, in the Matsi chapter, Princess Matsi faints and Prince Vessantara believes that she is dead. His expression of grief in the Pali original is merely a lament that if she had died in the royal capital her body would be decorated according to her status, but in the loneliness of this forest what is to be done? (*Mahachat khamluang*, 373). At least since the late Ayutthaya period Thai poets have elaborated on Prince Vessantara's expression of grief. They compare the forest and nature to mourners at a royal funeral, as in the Phetchaburi version:

> How sad that Matsi is dead.
> Alas, she lies prostrate upon the ground. What a pitiful sight!
> Will you make this dense forest your graveyard?
> Will this hermitage be your golden cremation pyre?
> Will the singing of the birds, crows, and cockerels be the laments of the funeral choir?
> Will the moon's clear, pure radiance be your sparkling crystal lantern?
> Will the radiance of the stars be your shining lamp?
> Will the looming canopy of the forest be your golden funeral curtain?
> Will the incessant droning of the cicadas take the place of the playing of the palace musicians...?
>
> (*Mahachat mueang phet,* 188).

Mourning verses in this style from the late Ayutthaya period appear to have been copied from the mourning verse of Rama in the narration verse (*bot phak*) from the *Ramakian* of the Ayutthaya period, in the *Nang loi* episode:

> I shall smooth out the sand to make it
> like the royal bed.
> I shall embrace your body like a funeral urn.
> Only my own voice, hot from weeping,
> Will replace the mourning of the court ladies
> whose duty is to cry and weep.
> The sea will take the place of the city.
> Mountains will be like your cremation pyre.
> The dragon and kilin
> instead of pictures of endless forest.
> Stars and moon, instead of candles
> and lotus shaped lanterns.
> Clouds and misty stars
> instead of tassels hanging from the ceiling.
> Plants instead of the royal-tiered umbrella
> The great golden parasol.

The flowers of Himavanta forest
Instead of bouquets hanging in rows.
The edge of the Ocean
will cover your beautiful body
    Instead of a funeral shroud
    laced with gold and jewels.
    The sound of waves will replace
    the playing of drums and the gamelan orchestra.
The singing of cicadas and insects
instead of the conch shell and horn.
I shall gather flowers
and arrange them at the foot of the pyre
    And I shall raise your beloved corpse
    to place it upon the leaping flames

Chaophraya Phrakhlang (Hon) also composed a mourning verse similar to that in the Phetchaburi *Mahachat* (and as already mentioned, his version may have been based upon the Phetchaburi version, or an earlier one related to it) which itself copied the narration verse from the *Ramakian*. However his version is better than the older one. It is one of the most famous passages of the recitation version of the *Mahachat*:

Will you make this dense forest your graveyard?
Will you make this hermitage your golden funeral pyre?
Will the constant singing of the mynah bird be your funeral choir?
Will the buzzing of the cicadas and crickets take the place of the sound of
    conch shells and string orchestra?
Will the clouds and mist in the sky be like a ceiling?
Will the yang trees in the Himavanta forest be your gold and silver tiered
    umbrella?
Will the pure white moonbeams be the beautiful crystal lanterns?
(Department of Education version, 288).

Similarly, the description of the merchant ship in the Kuman chapter, the description of Chuchok's repairing of his house before leaving Amittada in the Chuchok chapter, and the description of the flora and fauna outside the original Pali text in the Wanapawet, Chulaphon, and Mahaphon chapters, were all initially composed in the Ayutthaya era, and had become a literary style. Poets from the early Bangkok period made use of these accepted conventions but competed amongst themselves to make them sharper, more beautiful, and more appealing to the audience. So in praising the abilities of the early Bangkok poets who composed these recitation versions of the *Mahachat*, one needs to compare their work with the Phetchaburi version, which dates from the late Ayutthaya period, in order to evaluate the literary talent of these later Bangkok versions. The changes made by the early Bangkok poets to these older versions are very striking, as shown in the examples given above. In some instances, through their use of short, concise expressions, the early Bangkok poets compete admirably with the poets of Ayutthaya. For example, there is a passage in the Chuchok chapter when the Brahman takes Chuchok's money for safekeeping and is then unable to return it, so proposes to give his daughter to Chuchok instead. In the Pali original it states only that he gave Chuchok his daughter, whose name was Amittada (*Amittatapanamam dhitaram tasasa adasi*). However, the Ayutthaya author of the recitation version of the *Mahachat* creates a whole scene of conversation between the Brahman father and mother of Amittada and Chuchok, so that the giving away of their daughter does not appear too heartless. The Phetchaburi version reads, "My daughter is equal to the gold you left with me / You can take her as your wife, or as a servant, as you wish." The Wat Sangkrachai School of the early Bangkok era follows the Ayutthaya version but changes the words of Amittada's father and mother to make them sharper and more precise: "You can either keep her at your side / Or let her share your pillow / Or let her sleep at your feet…" (Department of Education version, 129).

The publication of the Phetchaburi version of the Vessantara Jataka is therefore extremely useful for the study of the literature of the central region. Besides giving us a recitation version of the *Mahachat* from the Ayutthaya period, it can be used to compare the literary quality of the *Mahachat* versions which developed to a high level in the early Bangkok period. It will help us gain a true understanding of the genius of the poets who composed recitation versions of the *Mahachat* in the early Bangkok period, as opposed to the blind praise taught by schoolteachers. The Phetchaburi version helps us appreciate both the limitations and the genius of the poets who wrote the *Mahachat* in the early Bangkok period.

Given the value of the Phetchaburi version of the *Mahachat* I cannot help wondering about the many other recitation versions of the *Mahachat*, currently in the care of the National Library, which also date from the Ayutthaya period and which have never been collected and published. Even if they do not contain the full thirteen chapters, or if their literary merit is not high, they would still be of huge benefit to the study of literature. Their publication ought to be considered.

I can think of no better way of ending this article than by expressing my appreciation and respect to all those involved in the publication of the Phetchaburi version of the *Mahachat*.

4

THE WORLD OF LADY NOPHAMAT

TRANSLATORS' NOTE

During the Fifth Reign, the court was anxious for Siam to have a long and splendid history. A text about Lady Nophamat was accepted as an ancient work about a real historical figure. This "fact" has been passed through school books into popular tradition. She is credited with the invention of the float festival of Loi Krathong. The government's Public Relations Department states it this way:

> Evidence has been found in the Sukhothai Period, when Nang Nophamat, the originator of the Loy Krathong Festival, made the floating lantern from various kind of colorful flowers in the shape of a lotus to present in a royal ceremony on the full moon night of the twelfth lunar month. From that day, the *krathong* made of banana leaves with flowery decorations in the shape of a lotus became the master pattern of *krathong* floating on Loy Krathong Day in the present time.
> (www.prd.go.th/ebook/focus/july02_04.html)

A manual of flower arrangement is equally straightforward:

> It was Nang Nophamat who invented a floating lantern in the shape of lotus made with colorful flowers of various kinds, adorned by candles, incense sticks and a lantern. This floating lantern was placed on the river at the Royal Ceremony of Chong Prieng on the night of the full moon of the twelfth lunar month. The King was so delighted by the floating lanterns in the shape of a lotus that he declared a tradition of floating lanterns on the night of the full moon of the twelfth lunar month, the festival which has been passed on until the present day, now known as the Loi Krathong Festival. The floating lantern is made of banana leaves and decorated with flowers. (ML Tui Jumsai, *Flowers and People*, Thai Wattana, 1972)

The same story is repeated in countless tourist publications. The beauty contest which forms part of the Loi Krathong celebration in Sukhothai is named after Nang Nophamat.

The abbreviation *NN* refers to the 1964 edition of *Nang nophamat.*

4

THE WORLD OF LADY NOPHAMAT[1]

PLACING *NANG NOPHAMAT*

NANG nophamat or Lady Nophamat, also known as *Tamrap thao si chulalak* (The treatise of a royal consort) is a text that refers to events in the Sukhothai period (thirteenth to fifteenth centuries AD), but neither its idiom nor its contents are evidence that it dates back to the Sukhothai era. According to Prince Damrong Rajanuphab, King Chulalongkorn maintained that it must really date back to Sukhothai on grounds that its claims were respected by "earlier students of antiquity, such as King Mongkut and Prince Wongsathiratsanit."[2] He believed that an original from that era had really existed but later had been so modified and extended that few traces of the original remained. In his treatise *Phraratchaphithi sipsong deuan* (The Royal Ceremonies of the Twelve Months), Chulalongkorn used the work as a source for the origin and development of various state ceremonies. In so doing, the king seems to have been over influenced by his personal respect for his predecessors.

Nang nophamat's claims are easy to disprove, as Prince Damrong himself has shown. The work contains various passages that demonstrate it could not have been composed in the Sukhothai era; for example, it refers to Americans and to cannon. In addition, its literary style shows clearly that it was written in the Bangkok period. Indeed, some believe that King Rama III (r. 1824–1851) composed about half of it.

1. Achan Saichon Wannarat of the Faculty of Arts, Chulalongkorn University, kindly copied for me manuscripts from various texts on royal ceremonies in the Manuscript Division, National Library. These manuscripts were of great help in determining the age of the *Nang nophamat* text. After the publication of this article in the *Thammasat University Journal*, Professor Craig Reynolds of Sydney University, Australia, graciously wrote a personal letter to the author, critically discussing the article. Some parts of that letter have been selected and included in this edition of the article, specifically those which extend the scope of the problems raised, and those which point out some flaws in the article upon which the author is incapable of improving. Therefore, any merits this article may contain owe a lot to the contributions of the two persons mentioned. However, only the author is to be held responsible for any deficiencies.

2. Damrong, "Exegeses", in *Nang nophamat* 1964 (hereafter, *NN*), 212. King Chulalongkorn (Rama V) reigned 1868–1910; Prince Damrong was one of his chief advisors and principal interlocutor on political affairs. King Mongkut (Rama IV) reigned 1851–1868. Prince Wongsathiratsanit was a son of Rama II and a younger half-brother of King Mongkut.

To fix a date in the early Bangkok period for *Nang nophamat*'s composition, we need look no further than its discussion of the royal ceremony of Wisakha Bucha. There is no evidence that this rite was ever performed in the Ayutthayan period (1350–1767). It was first held in 1817, during the second Bangkok reign. The royal decree establishing the rite claimed it had been performed by kings of ancient times, but none of these rulers were named except for a King of Lanka.[3] At the same time, if we look at the description of ceremonies in *Nang nophamat*, we can see that all date from before the time of King Mongkut, as they show no tendency for Buddhist rituals to encroach upon Brahmanic ceremonial. From these facts we can date the work's composition roughly between 1817 and the end of the Third Reign in 1851. It so happens that in the National Library there is a manuscript of *Nang nophamat* among the archives of the Third Reign (No. 57, Saka year 1197). Only volumes 3 and 4 remain, but the table of contents states that the document was copied in the Saka year 1197 (1835). Thus the original must have existed before 1835. On the cover is written that it is the "Royal Treatise of Phra Si Chulalak," the title of someone holding the office of principal royal consort. Another manuscript version is No. 497 in the collection of royal ceremonies; it is in cursive writing, has been corrected in several places, and is also incomplete. The contents and language of these two copies correspond to those of the printed version. Although this documentation is limited, it leads us to suspect that the tale of *Nang nophamat* was probably composed more or less at one go, and was not subject to the insertion of material over a long period of time. Had that been the case, there should exist fragments whose contents depart from the printed version. We can thus narrow the timing for the composition down to the period between 1817 and 1835 at the latest. *Nang nophamat* is thus a product of the early Bangkok period; and, as we shall see, bears the literary hallmarks of that era.

We should also note that it was endorsed by the "earlier students of antiquity" because they did not delve deeply enough into the evidence concerning state ceremonies at the close of the Ayutthayan period. At the time King Chulalongkorn composed his *Royal Ceremonies of the Twelve Months* the only document readily available for research into the late Ayutthayan era was the version of the *Khamhaikan khun luang ha wat* (Testimony of the Monarch Who Sought a Monastery) by K. S. R. Kulap, who modified his account of the rites to make them conform to what was seen in Bangkok times. Thus antiquarians who examined the passages on the annual ceremonial cycle in *Nang nophamat* were led to believe that the cycle depicted was in some respects even older than the late Ayutthayan period. For example, ceremonies which in the late Ayutthaya period were held in the second lunar month, such as

3. Damrong 1962, 548–52. However, it should be pointed out that the text of *Phraratchaphithi thawathotsamat krung kao krung kamphocha* (Royal Ceremonies of the Twelve Months in the Old Capital and Cambodia) (document no. 496, cabinet 112, shelf 5/4, package 60 of the Manuscript Division) states that there was a "Buddhasatra" ceremony on the day of the full moon in the sixth month at which the King of Cambodia vowed adherence to the Buddhist commandments, presented food to the monks, and conducted other religious ceremonies, but it does not definitely specify this ceremony was for Wisakha Bucha.

the *triyampawai* and *tri pawai* or swinging festivals,[4] are placed by *Nang nophamat* in the first month (*Nang nophamat*, hereafter *NN*, 316); while royal ceremonies of the second month which at the close of the Ayutthayan era were moved to the first, such as *butsaya phisek* or kite flying and *chawian phrakho kinliang* or veneration of the sacred bull, are returned to the second month.[5] This ordering corresponds to that given in the *Khlong thawathotsamat* (Lay of the Twelve Months)[6] and the *Kot monthianban* (royal household law) (*Kotmai tra sam duang*, I, 129–30). *Nang nophamat* also mentions ceremonies that do not appear in the *Khamhaikan khun luang ha wat* or the royal household law, namely the *phirunasat* or rain-calling and the *khenda* or top-spinning rites. Its description of the *raek na* or first plowing also differs from that in the royal household law.

But the significance of *Nang nophamat*'s distinctiveness on the matter of state ceremonies was misconstrued by the "earlier students of antiquity." The rites it described do not in fact differ from the royal celebrations in late Ayutthaya and early Bangkok times. At least, they correspond to the manuals for traditional royal ceremonies which were compiled during the First Reign. The author of *Nang nophamat* relied on the *Khamhaikan khun luang ha wat* (royal version), or the *Khamhaikan khun luang wat pradu songtham* (Testimony of the Monarch of Wat Pradu Songtham),

4. Chulachomklao 1960, 6. However, in *Phraratchaphithi thawathotsamat krung kao lae mueang kamphocha* (*PTKLM*, Royal Ceremonies of the Twelve Months in the Old Capital and Cambodia), which is another version of the document referred to in the previous footnote (this one being document no. 495), it is definitely confirmed that the *triyampawai* and *tripawai* ceremonies (Brahman swinging ceremonies performed for Siva and Vishnu respectively) were held in the first month. This document, copied in 1812, was part of the attempt to collect various Ayutthaya texts during the early Bangkok period which resulted in the recovery of mostly late Ayutthaya versions.

5. Chulachomklao 1960, 68. However, Chulalongkorn used the evidence of the late Ayutthaya period from the oral account of Rama IV and *Khamhaikan khun luang ha wat* (Testimony of the Monarch who Sought a Monastery, *TMSW*) compiled by K. S. R. Kulap, published by Dr. Smith's printing house. A cross-checking with *Khamhaikan chao krung kao* (Testimony of the Inhabitants of the Old Capital, *TIOC* 1967, 268) reveals that the *butsaya phisek* and *thaloeng phrakho kinliang* (night-bathing and sacred cow ceremonies) were still held in the second month. The original manuscript of *TMSW* which was used by Kulap has now been found, but the part on royal ceremonies is missing. Hence there is no way of finding out whether or not Kulap had revised the manuscript to fit what he found to be the case in the early Bangkok period. A recently discovered copy of *Khamhaikan khun luang wat pradu songtham* (Testimony of the Monarch of Wat Pradu Songtham, *TWPS*) contains no account of royal ceremonies of the twelve months, therefore it is still difficult to solve this question conclusively. Nevertheless, both the primary documents in the Manuscript Division and *TIOC* certify positively that in the late Ayutthaya period the royal ceremonies of the first and second months had not yet been shuffled as in Chulalongkorn's judgment, and thus there is no trace that *NN* dates back further than the late Ayutthaya period.

6. *Thawathotsamat*, 31–2. This is a *nirat* or verse tale, in which a romance is recounted through the passing seasons and their appropriate ceremonies.

copies of which certainly existed before 1807,[7] and on his own experience since as a member of the court, he would have been familiar with the state ceremonies and celebrations of early Bangkok. He then dressed these rites up as dating from the Sukhothai period. This is why he included the top-spinning ceremony, which was only established as a state ritual at the beginning of the Bangkok period (or else the Brahmans previously performed it on their own),[8] and the rain-calling ceremony, which was not mentioned in the royal household law but was performed in the time of King Borommakot towards the end of the Ayutthaya period, was set down in a manual, and was subsequently continued as a state ceremony in Bangkok times. His description of these rites differs from their actual performance in the Bangkok period because the actual performance contained obscene elements which had to be censored or modified on paper.[9] His version of the plowing ceremony also diverges from the description in the royal household law because he describes the actual procedures in Bangkok times when the king was not absolutely required to carry out the plowing himself but could have a noble act on his behalf, and might attend.[10]

7. See Nidhi 1978, 251–4 (chapter 6 of this book), which assumes that this text is in accordance with *TIOC* as far as the ceremonies of the twelve months are concerned, even though it may contradict *TMSW* in Kulap's version.

8. Chulachomklao 1960, 452–5. On page 335 of *NN* concerning the *khenda* ceremony (literally the top ceremony) it is clearly stated: "The king does not attend the *khenda thing khang* ceremony." This seems to be an accurate account of this ceremony as it was actually performed in the early Bangkok period. Hence it was not mentioned anywhere in the late Ayutthaya testimonies or in the royal household law since it was not a royal ceremony. However, *PTKLM* (document no. 495, already cited) recorded that the "khenda thorani thing khang" ceremony was a royal ceremony in which the king himself held a string to spin the top while praying to prophesy the kingdom's fate. It is possible that this ceremony continued to be practiced in Cambodia as a royal ritual while it was abolished from the roster of royal ceremonies of the twelve months in both Ayutthaya and Bangkok.

9. Chulachomklao 1960, 540–5. In *Chotmaihet ratchakan thi 1* (Records of the First Reign), no. 2, [jo so 1148] 1706, there is a text of the *phirunsat* royal ceremony which was presented to the king by Phra Yankosonthera of Wat Saket. Phra Yankosonthera was ordained as a Buddhist monk in the Ayutthaya period, and used to chant prayers in this kind of royal ceremony during the reign of King Borommakot (r. 1733–1758), and thus was able to remember it. According to this text, this royal ceremony was more Buddhist than Brahman, and the king had no role. This accords with the account in *NN*. In the reign of Rama IV, the ceremony was modified to give the king some role, as can be seen in *Tamra phraratchaphithi phirunsat tham phithi kho hai fon tok* (Manual of the *phirunsat* rain-making ceremony) Manuscript Division, no. 428, cabinet 112, shelf 4/2, package 55.

10. Chulachomklao 1960, 409–11. According to the primary evidence found in the Manuscript Division, the *raek na* (first plowing) ceremony followed several patterns. For example, in *PTKLM* no. 495, the king himself performed the role of Phraya Raekna. But in the no. 496 version, the king was supposed to transfer the throne to Phraya Phonlathep for three days, and let him perform the first plowing, attended only by officials of the land department. The same text also says that King Borommakot had added some merit-making to the ceremony, that is, ordering the nobles to present food to Buddhist monks in eight different

One can sympathize with the error of the "earlier students of antiquity." Documentation from late Ayutthaya was not readily available for them to consult, and it was therefore easy to accept that *Nang nophamat* must be ancient and date from Sukhothai. However, we must reiterate that there is no evidence or reason to suppose this work contains any elements dating back to the Sukhothai period. We have to accept this crucial fact first of all; only then can we examine *Nang nophamat* as part of early Bangkok literature. Indeed, the book's great interest lies precisely in the fact that it is a product of this period. Attempts to place it within the literature of Sukhothai (which can be found in any number of literary histories) have for a long time obscured the really exciting elements hidden in this work.

Everyone accepts that *Nang nophamat* was composed by more than one person, and there is good reason to believe it includes a considerable input written by King Rama III.[11] This multiple authorship makes it difficult to discern the work's real intent. To discover this intent, we have to analyze the aims of each section separately. In so doing, we find that *Nang nophamat* has two distinct purposes.

1. A biography of Lady Nophamat from her birth until she made a name for herself at the court of Phra Ruang, a legendary king of Sukhothai. This is a most interesting section, and we will discuss it in detail later.

2. Instruction on good behavior for a lady of the royal household, and thus for women in general. The table of contents makes this purpose crystal clear by stating "the ancient teachings of Phra Si Chulalak will be of benefit to those ladies who follow her advice" (*NN*, 217). Such instruction was a common feature in the literature of this period. Well-known works in the same vein include Sunthon Phu's *Suphasit son ying* (Sayings for the Instruction of Ladies), and Prince Paramanuchit Chinorot's *Kritsana son nong* (Krishna Teaches a Younger Sister). It is into this part of *Nang nophamat* that King Rama III inserted much of his own writing, changing it from a general guide for upper-class women (the purpose stated in its table of contents) to advice for ladies of the royal household. In addition, anecdotes have been inserted

directions, and dedicate the merit to the gods so that they would protect the paddy shoots. The description in this text conforms with *Phraratchaphithi thawathotsamat,* Vol. 2. no. 498, cabinet 112, shelf 5/4, package 60, which also mentions the transfer of the throne to Phraya Phonlathep. This shows that up to the late Ayutthaya period, the throne was still formally transferred to Phraya Raekna, but the practise may have become looser, allowing Borommakot's injection of some Buddhist merit-making into the ceremony. It was only in the Bangkok period that the transfer of the throne, even though only formal, was completely abolished. The fact that this is in accord with the account in *NN* proves even more clearly that the *NN* text describes the royal ceremonies as practiced during the early Bangkok period, and not during the early Ayutthaya or Sukhothai periods.

11. At the end of the story, dancing is criticized as follows: "so much effort is wasted studying this subject of no substance . . . . according to Buddhist commentary. . . whatsoever binds life to the eternal cycle of suffering is sinful . . . . those who still love dancing set themselves up as teachers, and train students to go on dancing until their old age and death. This should be considered habitual sinning" (*NN*, 359–60). This seems to reflect the mind of King Rama III's court superbly.

which appear to be royal barbs aimed at the behavior of certain real-life officials of the inner palace (*NN*, 261–98).

We should also mention that King Vajiravudh, Rama VI (r. 1910–25) once issued a royal judgment declaring that this text was originally a manual for royal ceremonies during the nine months that fall outside the *phansa* period, the Buddhist Lent or Rains Retreat, and that the title was simply Nophamat, meaning Nine Months (Damrong in *NN*, 214, fn. 1). However, there is no evidence to support this opinion: Nophamat is the heroine's personal name, given because at her birth "my complexion had a yellow sheen, as if my whole body had been anointed with *saraphi* flower paste, so they gave me the name Nophamat" (*NN*, 247) which meant pure gold.

The descriptions of royal ceremonies found in the text are not those of a manual of state ritual. The text makes no effort to specify who is supposed to do what. In contrast, the royal household law is very explicit on ceremonial procedures and personnel. In addition, the inclusion of the top-spinning and rain-calling ceremonies makes it clear these are not "royal" rites because the king is shown to have no part in them. The author's concern lies in describing the public's participation in the celebrations and the general atmosphere surrounding royal ceremonies. Lady Nophamat herself remarks that "what I relate regarding the annual cycle of state ceremonies is brief and without details, because I have seen some and not others, remembered some things and not others" (*NN*, 353–4). Her main purpose in describing the ceremonies is to connect them with her own history, and as a means of enhancing her own fame. In addition, they are an essential literary device, a point I shall take up later. At this stage we need simply to be clear that *Nang nophamat* is not a manual of royal ceremonies nor is there any evidence of it ever having been used as one.

THE WORLD OF *NANG NOPHAMAT*

The work was composed and added to around the Third Reign, and although we cannot assert the authors' exact intent we do know that they were all children of their time; they lived in the "world" of their day. This environment was vastly different from that of Ayutthaya. The volume of trade, especially of export goods, had greatly increased. The long war in the east had forced the government to supply its armies with rice from the central plain. These economic changes undoubtedly explain why the government, beginning in the Second Reign, reduced by half its claims to phrai labor, cutting the statutory corvée period to three months a year. Among the diverse novelties of the Bangkok era, the most influential on Bangkok upper class thought was the influx of foreigners, foreign products, and foreign ideas. The most prominent of the alien groups, by virtue of sheer weight of numbers, was the Chinese. At the beginning of the Bangkok period the rate of Chinese immigration rose sharply (for various reasons connected to conditions both in Siam and China). Since these settlers penetrated far more extensively into Thai economic life than had their predecessors, it is not surprising that their cultural influence became very conspicuous. The acceptance of Chinese culture, especially in matters of scientific technique, was nothing new in

Siam. Yet the huge influx of Chinese at the beginning of the Bangkok era, and the speed at which Chinese culture was accepted, meant that Chinese ways could not be assimilated into Thai culture at the gradual pace characteristic of Ayutthaya times. Chinese customs and artistic tastes were adopted without acquiring much of a Thai flavor. For example, the architectural preference for the *keng* curved roof quite clearly preserves a purely Chinese style (and no Thai word has yet been invented for it). Stone figures imported from China were haphazardly set up in and around Thai buildings. The book *Sam kok* (Three Kingdoms) was translated from the Chinese without losing its Chineseness (which is not a comment on the quality of the translation), and entered into Thai culture precisely by preserving its exotic character, by being something frankly alien. Compare this to the impact of Indian culture, which took centuries to become established, and then remained over many further centuries. Its Indian-ness completely disappeared or, to put it another way, was absorbed and transformed into something very Thai. The Ramakian is not an "Indian" romance, even though it has origins in the Ramayana. Even Buddha (as the *tamnan* and popular belief would have it) stepped down and bestowed his teaching on every nook and corner of the country.

Nonetheless, the foreignness of the Chinese culture imported at the beginning of the Bangkok era did not become a serious threat to Thai culture. At least two factors made for this compatibility: first, the Thai had been exposed to Chinese cultural influence for a very long time; second and, more importantly, there was no great contrast between the bases of science and technology in Thai and Chinese civilizations. Take, for example, pharmacology. Although there was a growing preference for Chinese medicines, these were prepared in the same way as Thai remedies, that is, by boiling and oral intake. The differences lay in the ingredients used, not in the principle of preparation. Both were based on the concept of maintaining the balance in the body between the four elements or between yin and yang.

It was the culture of the west which presented the greater challenge, even though it was imported to a lesser degree, and even though there were many fewer westerners than Chinese in Siam. In the early Bangkok era, elements of western culture became increasingly visible in Siam and increasingly familiar for the Thai. Modern military science and strategy proved themselves spectacularly in the Anglo-Burmese and Opium Wars, events followed closely by Bangkok officialdom. Even before the end of the Third Reign, new types of military equipment and training had been widely adopted. Steamships demonstrated their efficiency to an enthused upper class, and were rapidly adopted. Similarly, a new kind of medicine, brought by the missionary doctors, found speedy acceptance, first by the lower and then by the upper classes. Printing, also introduced by the medical missionaries, was taken up by the government with little delay.[12] Just as with Chinese culture, there was not enough time for their foreignness

12. At this point, Professor Craig Reynolds has offered the following comment: "In the discussion on the reception of western culture, the author and others often considered changes in thought and culture as separable from political changes, or more specifically from the pressure of imperialist powers. The appeal of western science might be because it was more

to be adapted into something Thai. They retained a distinctly alien air (as shown by the addition of the word *farang* to denote various new military, medical, and technical commodities and practices). But the foreignness of these western imports challenged Thai culture far more than those of China and by the same principle: the cultural products of a west which had experienced scientific and industrial revolutions had a philosophical and technological basis which differed absolutely from Thai culture. The mere acceptance of products or methods from the west shook the foundations of Thai civilization with a vengeance. For one thing, it meant a total shift in ways of thinking. Thus to adopt the western method of calculating an eclipse, which was more accurate than that used by Thai astrologers, meant accepting a mechanical conception of the universe. Following modern astronomical understanding, the west based its calculations on the idea of the earth circulating a stationary sun, whereas Thai astrologers saw the earth as fixed and the sun circling it through the firmament. Thus the western method of calculating an eclipse entailed not simply a change in technique but also a crucial transformation of the way the Thai imagined the universe.

The acceptance of western cultural products also meant discarding things that hitherto had constituted "knowledge." For example, the use of steamships for sea transport meant abandoning lore about different kinds of waves and winds, warning skies, the use of sail, and so on. In particular, as people came to adopt the highly accurate western barometers and navigational charts, the main knowledge of Thai seafarers immediately lost any value. The steamships in turn established "knowledge" of a kind which had never been valued before and indeed might not have been considered "knowledge" at all, for example, the techniques of working with steam, uses of steam pressure, and the like. In other words, the acceptance of certain western products had a violent impact on the Thai value system. This "foreignness" of the west was something that could not be assimilated gradually, because the fundamental differences in science and technology gave no possibility for Thai civilization to absorb western cultural products and make them its own while preserving the basis of its own civilization. We can see this simply enough in the case of vaccination; vaccine affected the body for reasons which had nothing to do with the balance of the four elements, and Thai physicians were unable to turn it to effective use by mixing it in their decoctions.

Such violently "foreign" things rapidly inundated Bangkok and increasingly penetrated the way of life of people of all strata, but particularly the upper class (the

---

'suited' to explaining reality. A part of its appeal might lie in the fact that it was also extolled by the western powers themselves. The Thai ruling class certainly saw the obvious cultural, social, economic, and political differences between Siam and the west. The doubtful thing is whether science would have had such a great appeal if it had had nothing to do with power." In Professor Reynolds' opinion, the more interesting question is how the Indianization in the ancient Thai worldview and the westernization in the later one were similar or different, given the fact that during Indian cultural expansion into Southeast Asia since ancient times up to the eighteenth century, Indian knowledge was very popular but India did not have, or threaten to have, any political power over the region.

aristocracy, royalty, and some of the monkhood). As part of this process, the worldview of the literati was increasingly affected. They could see the efficacy of these "foreign" things, and the need to accept many of them. The old Thai worldview could not absorb all this and still retain its familiar contours. How could one explain the world so as to encompass the new knowledge, the new realities, and the new aesthetics? And how would such explanations affect the old familiar ideas of the good? We should not think of these problems or questions as ones which the literati confronted self-consciously as such. But it was now impossible to think about almost anything without some "foreign" elements being latently present. The changes were hidden in the byways of thought, where people did not notice them, but where they were unconsciously retained.

Nang nophamat was composed and read in the midst of these challenging transformations. The authors of the work were by no means philosophers trying systematically to present a new worldview; yet (consciously or otherwise), they did create a new "world" capable of encompassing this "foreign" way of thought, no matter in how undigested a form. It was a world which was unlike the old and yet did not differ from it completely. From this viewpoint, *Nang nophamat* merits special attention for it reflects very clearly the changing mental universe of the Thai elite, and it seems to have been the first literary work of its kind to do so.

In order to understand this "world" we need to examine the text in some detail. And to grasp its distinctiveness we must discuss first of all its characteristics as a work of literature.

NANG NOPHAMAT'S CHARACTERISTICS AS A LITERARY WORK

First of all, one is struck by the fact that the text was composed in a semi-stylized prose idiom.[13] In the Thai literary tradition, this mode of composition was typically employed only in connection with religious and state affairs. We find it used for royal chronicles, decrees, royal medical texts, and so on. It also occurs in religious documents such as translations of Jataka tales or Buddhist histories written by monks such as the *Mulasatsana* (Founding of the Religion),[14] pharmaceutical texts, histories of holy sites,

13. The term *roi kaeo* means a prose with free rhyming and specially selective wording, which seems to be called "stylized prose" in English. See for example Sriphuripricha (1956), composed by Phra Sriphuripricha, head of the Royal Scribes Department, or *Pathom somphothikatha*.

14. The *Tamnan mulasatsana* was composed before 1420 AD by two monks in the Chiang Mai region, Phra Phuttaphukan and Phra Phutthayan. It was primarily concerned with the arrival of Buddhism in Siam and it set the style for Buddhist historical composition thereafter. It was written in Thai Yuan. The first Thai translation was published in 1939. An English translation by Sommai Premchit and D. K. Swearer appeared as 'A translation of *Tamnan Mulasasana Wat Pa Daeng*: the chronicle of the founding of Buddhism of the Wat Pa Daeng tradition', *JSS*, 65, 2 (1977).

or the *Traiphum phra ruang* (Three Worlds of King Ruang),[15] which was originally a religious text. All through the Ayutthaya period and into the early Bangkok era there was almost no exception to the rule that a literary work with a "story" had to be written in verse. The very few exceptions that we do have occur at the beginning of the Bangkok era and clearly exhibit "foreignness:" for example, *Three Kingdoms* (and other Chinese historical romances) and the *Ratchathirat* (King of Kings), a chronicle of the Mon Kings of Pegu translated during the First Reign. It is striking that in every case, the text is a translation from a foreign language, including the *Nithan iran ratchatham* (Duodecagon, or Tales of the Persian Court), which was a half romance, half didactic transmission of Jataka tales. The use of stylized prose for a work of "fiction" was thus something quite new in the literary tradition in early Bangkok. If we accept *Nang nophamat* as a work of fiction, it marks the first time that prose was used for a work that was not a translation. However, *Nang nophamat* is by no means purely a work of fiction, since it also includes elements of an etiquette manual for ladies. Even so, it represents a stage in the spread of prose in Thai literature and is thus on a level of significance with the autobiography of Prince Wachirayan Warorot or the work of the first generation of Thai novelists.

Next, *Nang nophamat* tries to place itself in a real world. In fact, this was a technique favored by many writers of "fiction" at the beginning of the Bangkok period, and the reality portrayed was usually that of Bangkok. Thus in *Inao*, all four of Suriyawong's cities have a "shrine for the guardian spirit, a sacred foundation pillar venerated throughout all Krung Krai, a ceremonial swing by a Brahman temple; and traditional magical rites were carried out in a Drum Hall in the middle of the city. In spite of a fire set by conspirators, the elephant bridge still stood, constructed of bricks overlaid with heavy planks; the canal stretches as far as the eye could see" (Phutthaloetla 1955, 4–5).[16] In this respect *Nang nophamat* followed the pattern of the literature of the time. We must realize that the authors made no effort to describe any "special" flavor of Sukhothai. Rather the unusually interesting thing about their picture of Sukhothai is that they did not, like their contemporaries, use Bangkok as the story's backdrop. In fact, they made great efforts to create a feeling of "not-Bangkok." But there is no doubt they had no real idea of what Sukhothai was like in the era of King Ruang (and perhaps had no interest in acquiring one), and they had no model other than Bangkok with which to build "not-Bangkok." They were thus careful at the beginning of the text to emphasize for readers Sukhothai's "uniqueness" by, for

15. The *Traiphum phra ruang* (the three worlds refer to heaven, earth, and hell) was a cosmological treatise supposedly compiled during the Sukhothai period under the auspices of King Lithai (r. 1347–1374). It has also been claimed that it was composed by Lithai himself in 1345, before he ascended the throne. No copies exist from that time, but several recensions survive from the late Ayutthaya and early Bangkok periods. The Pali original has been translated into English by Frank and Mani Reynolds (1982). The work is also sometimes called the *Tephumikatha*, which was the name by which King Lithai referred to it.

16. *Inao* is a dance drama, drawing on the Panji stories from Java, for which a version was composed by Rama II.

example, saying that Sukhothai was surrounded by a river (which Bangkok is not). The Drum Hall of Sukhothai is called Chai Pheri Hall, and the main throne halls in the palace of King Ruang do not have names like Chakrawatphaichayon or Phaisan Thaksin but are called Inthraphisek, Udomratchasak, and Phisansaowarot. These and many other small details denote the "difference" from contemporary Bangkok (*NN*, 237–41). Aside from this, in the narrative itself the authors try to give a flavor of something "specially" Sukhothai, as they conceived it must have been. For example, in the Wisakha Bucha ceremony King Ruang goes to venerate three important Buddha images: Phra Chinnarat, Phra Chinnasi, and Phra Lokanatsattarot. The first two of these were well-known in the early Bangkok period as "Sukhothai" images, while the last has a name close to Phra Lokanat, the Ayutthaya Buddha figure which was placed in Wat Phra Chetuphon from the time of the First Reign and which was also considered an "ancient" image.

This attention to creating a "specialness" for the setting for the action of the story marks *Nang nophamat* as widely different from *Inao*. Both works use settings remote from the authors in time and place, but the author of *Inao* did not bother to differentiate between that time and his own, whereas *Nang nophamat*'s composers were fully aware of Sukhothai's distance. Nonetheless, they were not sufficiently concerned about this distance to make any effort to research the real setting. Just for this reason, all the more importance was attached to making the characters and events special. Lady Nophamat is depicted as a woman unlike all others; the events which take place in her tale are singular happenings, which will never recur because they took place under "special" circumstances. To speak in this way probably is an exaggeration, in that it makes *Nang nophamat* too much like a modern novel whereas in fact the authors' central purpose remained didactic. The teachings themselves are not unique, for the values they express were general and widely accepted, i.e., nothing "special." But the emphasis on the "special" setting distinguishes *Nang nophamat* from other literary products of its day. Even though the text follows the literary practices of its time and is unlike present-day literature, one can still read it as exemplifying the slow metamorphosis of Thai literature in the early Bangkok era. We will discuss the significance of the narrative's "special" setting below.

Another distinguishing feature of *Nang nophamat* is that the leading character is female. As with the text's other special literary features, such use was not something utterly new to the Thai tradition, but it was also not in the mainstream of literary practice. In the literature of early Bangkok (folk literature excluded), female characters were by no means merely the objects of competition between males. This may have been because in old Siam women played a comparatively important role both in the economy and in society; and hence they were not portrayed as passive characters in literature. We can see this very clearly in the depictions of the ladies Wanthong (in *Khun chang khun phaen*), Butsaba, and even Sida (in *Ramakian*), all of who are "active" characters on whose action or inaction the changing events of the tale hinged. In the same period as Nang Nophamat was born as a literary figure, we find Nang Laweng, a distinctly active character in the story of Phra Aphaimani in which she occurs, to the extent that her role is of equal importance to that of the principal male. Not long after *Nang nophamat* there was Nang Kaeo Na Ma, who is more important to the story in which she figured than the hero, because she is the only active character.

Still, we must admit that Lady Nophamat differs from Nang Laweng or Nang Tiaosian (in *Three Kingdoms*), for the authors claim that Lady Nophamat was a real individual—or rather, they try to make us believe in her existence (later we will take up the matter of this emphasis on her "reality"). Unlike Nang Laweng, she possesses no magical powers. Lady Nophamat is bold and has strong personal desires, unlike other female characters in the literature of the time. She ponders on the difficulties placed in the way of her dreams by the fact that she was born a woman: "It is extremely difficult to serve the king so well that my name would be known throughout the land. Evidently, everything in the palaces is done by those holding the posts of the two chief royal consorts." Even so, she is determined to "make mine a name that will long resound in the land" (*NN*, 281–2).

When considered from the contemporary perspective, which values custom and ritual less and less, Lady Nophamat's accomplishments seem trivial[17] as most of the ceremonies have been changed or abandoned, though some have become traditional. But in fact rites and traditions were important at the time in which the tale of *Nang nophamat* was composed, more so than we can easily comprehend today. To be the origin of a practice or prescription for any tradition was then no small role, and was not entrusted to just anyone. In many northern *tamnan* the role of originating various prescriptions and traditions is usually assigned to hermits, heavenly beings, or even gods, if not to the king himself. But *Nang nophamat* makes the purveyor of wisdom a woman, a mortal being who, though upper-class, is not of royal blood. Lady Nophamat is thus quite justified in exhibiting some pride: "I want other women in the same situation as me...in the future to know how I, little Nophamat, performed a service for King Ruang...and so made a name for myself as a woman, a sage, and a skilled craftsman, a name which will last for all time" (*NN*, 354). We should bear in mind that a female sage is not a figure one comes across often in the literature of early Bangkok. Lady Nophamat's lasting reputation is distinctive because it comes from her being a sage, unlike Nang Tiaosian in the *Three Kingdoms* who wins renown only for her womanly wiles—which is also a way of putting women down. I do not wish to argue that the authors of *Nang nophamat* were proclaiming the equality of the sexes, but undoubtedly they saw women as having much greater capabilities than did earlier writers.

17. Owing to the making of a lotus-shaped floating lamp by Lady Nophamat, a commandment was issued to continue the practice (*NN*, 308–9). A poem about this practice was composed and later became a ritual text. It says that in some years the king took his concubines out to enjoy the *chong priang* (lantern-lighting) royal ceremony (*NN*, 315). Lady Nophamat embroidered flowers into the shape of a betel tray for use in the *khachentharatsawasanan* (elephant and horse bathing) ceremony. Later a commandment was issued to make this kind of floral arrangement in various other ceremonies until it became customary (*NN*, 323). Lady Nophamat made drawings of golden flowers arranged in a bunch and in the shape of a lotus, and these became models for later practice (*NN*, 340).

In its narrative form too, *Nang nophamat* departs considerably from the literature of its day. It is scarcely a typical feature of contemporary *niyai* (tales) to have the narrative built round the life story of the leading character, with other aims treated as mere appendages. Notably, there is no attempt to create problems in Lady Nophamat's life. She has a normal birth, is not the child of a heavenly being or dragon, and is not raised by a hermit. As is stated at the outset, her lot in life is to be a consort of the king. She is born into a socially respectable Brahman family.[18] She gets a first-class education without any difficulty because her father is a prominent Brahman. Her final reception as a royal consort goes smoothly. She cherishes the ambition to make a name for herself, and she succeeds. The uneventfulness of this plot marks it off from the contemporary literature, but probably this is because *Nang nophamat* is not a real *niyai*. As we noted earlier, the way the tale is presented is more striking than the plot itself, as if the authors were trying above all to represent the "reality" of Lady Nophamat's life. The avoidance of any claims for miraculous powers for its protagonists makes *Nang nophamat*'s plot differ from those of the Jataka tales. The things which happen to her, especially her ultimate success, are "logical" and in accordance with the "real life" of the time as laid out from the beginning of the text. Thus the authors spend pages explaining in detail Lady Nophamat's education (*NN*, 248–9). From early childhood she was not taught to play games like ordinary children but day and night, "I was taught to play at making verses, drawing, and the art of clever conversation filled with poetry and proverb." At the age of seven she was made to "learn to read Siamese and Sanskrit fluently, and then I was put to study the teachings of the Buddha.... then they had me make a thorough study of the Three Vedas." From there she went on to study composition until "it was second nature for me to be a good person." She studied prosody "in order to express myself in the manner of the sages." Then she learned the Three Sciences from an astrological treatise which "taught how to calculate the movements of the nine planets, moon, and stars in order to predict good and bad events." All these were subjects for study by princes, and the best that society in the early Bangkok period could offer its young upper class males. The authors equipped Lady Nophamat with all this learning in order to make it believable that she could make a great name for herself in the future. More than any earlier Thai literary work, the plot of *Nang nophamat* is concerned with human beings. Man is the shaper of man, and man achieves greatness by being

18. The author of *NN* specified that the royal family was the most prestigious family, greater than other families in general. Among other patriarchal families, Lady Nophamat also mentioned the Brahman and the wealthy as having high status (*NN*, 227). The idea that these three categories of family were prestigious also appeared in the Northern Chronicle in which it was said that only members of these three categories of family should become a king (*Phongsawadan nuea,* 1963). In the Wat Pho Hom inscription dated 1609 in the Ayutthaya period, the person making merit by leaving this inscription prayed that, "In whatever world I shall be born, let me be born into the three honorable families of the wealthy, the great Brahman, or the great king" (Text no. 96 in *Prachum silacharuek phak thi 4*, 67). This indicates that Lady Nophamat's family qualified her to be a royal consort and to make a contribution to the kingdom which deserved to be recorded as a text.

formed by other men. It is a story which revolves entirely around human behavior (to be sure the behavior of human beings of the upper class), and no supernatural or other magical force come into play.

Nonetheless, the narrative construction of *Nang nophamat* still depends heavily on the literary conventions of its day. We can see this in the way the stage is set at the beginning, with a celebration of the capital city quite like that in *Inao* and similar works. In addition, the influence of social conditions at the beginning of the Bangkok era is reflected in *Nang nophamat* in the same way as in other texts of the time. We can see this clearly in, for example, the description of city life: trade and merchants are important features, bearing witness to the city's prosperity, as "Merchants both from this land and from abroad come to trade in the royal city of Sukhothai, bringing their goods by sloop, kampan, junk, raft, barge, oxcart, buffalo cart, on elephant-back and camel-back, by horse, by mule, and by donkey, by boats that are punted, paddled, rowed sitting, rowed standing, sailed, or sculled. They come and go in all seasons, never a month passes without them" (*NN*, 226). Such descriptions of a trade-based prosperity are perennial features of the literature of early Bangkok. In contrast, the Ayutthayan *Khlong chaloemphrakiat somdet phra narai* (Lay in Praise of King Narai) of Phra Si Mahosot devotes only one verse to trading junks (stanza 26) and does not discuss commerce at all. *Nang nophamat* also takes note of various other professions, such as that of physicians (who are divided into specialists in various illnesses), as well as goldsmiths, silversmiths, glaziers, scribes, sculptors, potters, turners, smiths, and so on (*NN*, 228–9). These trades reflect the spread of specialized skills which is a hallmark of urban civilization. The urban features of *Nang nophamat* are striking, though they are something we can find elsewhere in the literature of early Bangkok.

Another feature of the plot is its borrowing of devices from ancient literature, such as its account of the annual cycle of state ceremonies (which led to the earlier cited misapprehension that *Nang nophamat* was a manual for such rituals). We now need to consider what literary "functions" this description actually served.

First of all, the twelve-month ceremonial cycle fits well into the story plot from the beginning, for at the outset it is said of Lady Nophamat's father, the court astrologer Phra Si Mahosot, that he "was honored above other literati, having charge, for example, of ornamenting the capital for the royal ceremonial cycle of the twelve months" (*NN*, 246). And, as mentioned above, the authors were much concerned with providing credible background details for their story.

Next, a woman of that time, especially one of the upper class who had to live in the court, could find no better way to relate the activities around her than through the royal ceremonies, for these were probably the only kind of activity which connected her to the outside "world." Moreover, these rites were a link to the world of the future, because they had been performed in the past and would continue to be performed in the future. Again, if we bear in mind the importance which royal ceremonies had at the time this text was written, we can appreciate the appropriateness of Lady Nophamat's emphasizing them.

Lastly and most importantly, it had been customary in Thai literature since the Ayutthayan period to use royal ceremonies as a device to mark the passage of time. The *Thawathotsamat* is a good example of the use of royal ritual to evoke the poet's recollection of time past. In today's world we are used to dividing time into periods of years, months, days, and hours. Time goes "by the clock." But this sense of its passage is new. Earlier, people in most societies organized time by events. Time itself was empty: it could only be evoked by the events which filled it. In Thai literature from ancient times up to the early Bangkok period, time itself was rarely defined; sequencing or the passage of time could only be discerned from the contents of the story. Many local chronicles and annals still use events rather than calendrical markings as devices to fix time's passage. In this respect, *Nang nophamat* makes use of a very ancient literary device, as does *Thawathotsamat*. And of course from the viewpoint of the main character, royal ceremonies were major happenings. Finally, we should note that both *Nang nophamat* and *Thawathotsamat* show no development of their characters and are almost without development of the plot; their authors thus had a particular problem in demonstrating the passage of time. State ceremonies furnished events with which the authors could fill time's void.

Nang nophamat is part of a literary transformation that emerged from many decades of change in the thought and worldview of upper-class people. This kind of literature did not spring from nowhere; it reflected intellectual changes that had already taken place, but at the same time *Nang nophamat* did propose "new" things more sharply and clearly than before, and took these changes forward to a higher stage.

LADY NOPHAMAT'S WORLD

From the viewpoint of the history of thought, the most interesting and apparently inexplicable aspect of *Nang nophamat* is that in the first part of the story the authors devote space to describing the world using the ancient framework for this purpose, and yet the human world described is starkly different from that in the belief of the ancient Thai. The clearest change in worldview thus appears in this part of the text.

The authors begin by referring to the origins of man who was created "by the will of Brahma"' before the present era (*kalpa*) began. This account of the creation differs somewhat from the version in the *Tephumikatha* (King Lithai's compilation of the Three Worlds) in that it is openly Hindu. The reasons why the writers felt they had to avoid a Buddhist basis will be explained below. It conforms to the ancient way of describing the world to begin with the origins of man, but the authors were not really concerned with those origins. They merely wanted to claim that formerly all men spoke "Pali" as their only language, and to explain the difference in language that they knew existed. This was a world which did not have nations or nation-states and where no one paid attention to ethnicity. In the authors' view, the differences between peoples lay in their culture, or way of life, and this variety was expressed most clearly through language. The authors tried to explain the various "kinds" of man by a typology determined by language.

They began by dividing the world into three parts, stating that this division was originated by the ancient sages. These parts are: Chomphu Thawip, the "Land of the Rose-Apple Tree;" territories other than Chomphu Thawip which are collectively called Patchantaprathet; and all those islands around Lanka (in other words, territories separated from the above two by ocean) along with Lanka island itself, collectively called Singhonprathet (*NN*, 218). This division of the world also derives from the *Tephumikatha*, which states that Chomphu Thawip consists of Machimprathet (central India) and Patchantaprathet (border lands) (*Traiphum phra ruang*, 754–5). But the differences are important and noteworthy. *Nang nophamat* does not mention the other three continents referred to in the *Tephumikatha*. The world of *Nang nophamat* does not have a center, nor does it have a Mount Meru, rose-apple tree, or Bo Tree Throne as its center unlike the *Traiphum lokawinitchai* (the last royal recension of the Three Worlds, which was sponsored by Rama I and appeared in 1803) (Nidhi 1978, 229; chapter 6 of this book). The Chomphu Thawip of *Nang nophamat* is simply a territory like others; it is not a land where the Lord Buddha or a Universal Emperor will come to achieve enlightenment. This world without a central point—a world composed of territories which all have equal importance—this is the new world of the Thai.

Lady Nophamat then explains that ancient sages held that long ago there were only three languages, but that the poets and sages preferred to divide them further into: Makhot or Pali and Khaek, used in Machimprathet (meaning here the Indian subcontinent in particular); Siamese or Thai; Singhalese or the language of the Sri Lankans; Sanskrit or the tongue of the Brahman; the Taleng spoken by the Europeans (I cannot explain this attribution); the Phukam language of the Burmese; the Talum language of the Mon; the Hariphunchai speech of the "Black Lao" (meaning black bellied); and the Kamphut tongue of the Khmer (*NN*, 219). We can see that this second typology of languages differs fundamentally from the first. It is not that the first is incorrect, but the second is more true to the differences among language and more concerned to describe the real situation. It respects the individuality of each language much more. Thus the Khaek (as the Thai use the term) speak three distinct languages—Pali, Sanskrit, and Singhalese. Burmese speak Burmese and Mons speak Mon; Thai and Lao are distinct languages, peculiar to their own peoples.

Next, Lady Nophamat states that she "will divide the tongues of the various nations," and lists the names of thirty-two languages, both those previously mentioned and some new ones. The thing to note is that she does not say the sages of old were wrong; she merely claims that one must elaborate on what they related. Her explanation of language places more emphasis on the reality of the world and time which the authors knew, a world which stressed the particularity of languages. Thus she divides the Lao language into Lao, Lao Lue, Lao Ngiao, Black Lao, and White Lao. Likewise, Khmer becomes Khmer Kamphut, Forest Khmer, Khmer Lamat, and Khmer Suai. In "Burma" there is spoken Burmese, Raman (Mon, Peguan), Thawai, Krasae (Assamese), Yakhai (Arakanese), Shan, and Tongsu. A variety of Khaek languages are also presented; apart from various "Brahmanic" languages, we find Arabic, Mahon (referring to the Parsis, and thus the Persian language), Sunni (confusing a language with a religious sect),

Mangkali (Bengali), Malela (probably the Malabar Coast), Khura (unidentified), Hui-Hui (unidentified), Malay, Mu-ngit (probably Bugis), Javanese, Cham, and Prueksa (unidentified). *Farang* or western languages are divided into those of the French, Dutch, English, Portuguese, Americans, "Isbanyot" (Spanish, espanol), and "Farangkarani" (probably colonies).[19] The noteworthy aspect of this listing of languages is that the authors derived it from the world they experienced; even if they did get some things wrong, they were concerned to present the reality of this world rather than the supernatural reality one finds in the *Traiphum lokawinitchai*, written not many decades before (Reynolds 1976, 210–11). And for their descriptions of the different languages they evidently relied on enquiries among these language's speakers, for the linguistic communities mentioned were mostly those of traders who had settled in Siam in the early Bangkok era.

An accurate account of the world's linguistic communities was then knowledge worth knowing, and therefore worth setting down. The writers had no doubt about what "reality" was, but at the same time they extended the boundaries of "knowledge" to include things that were of secondary importance in the past; and this in turn raised the question of what would be "reality" in the near future.

The absence of a center to the world affects the status of countries in it. In the *Tephumikatha* the state ruled by a *chakravartin* or universal emperor served as the center for all countries in the world and was even the pivot of the universe in a certain sense since the *chakravartin* was the patron of the *thamma*, which in turn was the supreme motive force of the cosmos. He was no ordinary patron, but immensely great. The power of this universal ruler, according to the *Tephumikatha*, is such that "when they know that the Great Chakravartin is proceeding towards their lands, princes great and small gather their forces and come to do battle with him; but they find they cannot succeed" (*Traiphum phra ruang*, 588–9). By contrast, in *Nang nophamat* the universal ruler has no role, for the text describes a world which has more than one great state, and the various countries are subject to no single, superior universal force. Lady Nophamat speaks of many states in which the kings have "vast might," and powerful armies which bring smaller towns and cities under their control "and hence become great capitals, of which there are several in the independent countries of Chomphu Thawip" (*NN*, 222). The territories of these "independent countries" adjoin each other, even if they are separated by mountains and forest. Should the kings on either side "desire the wealth and lands of the other," they will take to the battlefield against each other, for many generations, resulting in

19. *NN*, 219–22. During the Third Reign, the idea that the characteristics of various *chat* (nations) were matters of knowledge was shown in the drawings and *khlong* descriptions of various *chat* in Wat Phra Chetuphon (Wat Pho). Most of the names of *chat* listed there are the same as those in this text, including the inscrutable *chat* "Khaek Hui-Hui." The *khlong* descriptions of various *chat* in Wat Phra Chetuphon further confirm that all these names were intended to refer to real peoples in the real world, unlike the peoples speaking "dozens of languages" customarily mentioned in traditional works. See *Prachum charuek wat phra chetuphon*, 771–87.

the collapse of commerce in both countries. But if both "independent" monarchs "behaved according to royal tradition" they would be friends and "peaceful progress would extend throughout their capitals.... their lands would prosper with goods of all kinds, including gold and silver; their praises would be sung in all tongues, in all lands" (*NN*, 223–4).

We can see the consequences of the lack of a center in the case of language as well: no one tongue forms the standard or is otherwise set above the others. To be sure, Lady Nophamat relates that according to the sages of yore there were only three languages; but when she comes to describe the thirty-two tongues of her day she does not connect them to the three ancient languages, and although she mentions Thai she does not see it as something special, superior to the other thirty-one. In the same way, Lady Nophamat portrays the world with many powerful states, but no one state more important than the others. Furthermore, expansionist policies may have negative effects on society. States are equal and no state is the locus of Mount Meru, the center and pivot of the states surrounding it. Hence, both geographically and socially Lady Nophamat's world diverges drastically from the world of the *Tephumikatha*; it presents a horizontal surface on which no center can be found.

We should bear in mind that though the ideology of the *chakravartin* derived from India, an Indian ruler of this grandeur existed only as a theoretical construct. In India, real kings, no matter how mighty, were still "tributaries;" that is they were independent rulers but at the same time tributaries of a (purely hypothetical) universal monarch.[20] In Siam, however, the Thai king in Ayutthaya always claimed directly or indirectly to be a universal ruler, probably as a result of Angkorian influence. We can see this claim clearly in the coronation ceremony when the act of sitting on the Throne of the Eight Directions proclaimed the monarch's centrality in the world (Wales 1931, 77–82). Other rulers could only be tributaries of the Ayutthayan king. Hence the term *prathetsarat,* tributary state, has a different meaning in Thai from that of Pali usage in India. Upper-class Ayutthayans would have had no difficulty in understanding the underlying reality of the Thai theory of universal monarchy. They experienced wars with Cambodia and Burma, alliance with Luang Prabang, and the looming power of Vietnam at the end of the Ayutthaya period. They could see that the governments of Ava and Saigon hardly corresponded with the "tributary" status in the sense of the Thai theory of universal monarchy. But even so, this theory persisted without any modification. It upheld a truth without any reference to the real world. In the early

20. This idea came from a conversation with Professor Yoneo Ishii of Kyoto University, who investigated this issue in Pali documents. In addition, see Thassanee (1976, chapter 4) which surveys the titles of emperors in Pali and Sanskrit literature, and finds that they were all imaginary figures e.g., the emperors in the Jataka tales or Yudhisthira, Phra Ram, Phra Phrot, and so on in Sanskrit literature. Hence Thassanee (1976, 194) concludes that: "The emperor was an imaginary ruler, a super-hero of the nation." It should also be mentioned that since the First Reign, the Thai kings preferred to present themselves as *thammaracha* (moral kings) rather than emperors, and "emphasized only those imperial tasks that could actually be performed by the king" (Saichon 1982).

Bangkok period, the divergence between theory and reality became even more glaring. Hue, Ava, Penang, and later Singapore and Calcutta were definitely not tributaries of a "universal monarch" in Bangkok. On the contrary, the Thai *chakravartin* often had to adjust his policies to accommodate the encroaching power of these states. In this respect, *Nang nophamat* is the first literary work to reflect the real world and ignore completely the old theory of states.

At the same time, the repeated wars and intermittent tension with neighbors which resulted from Bangkok's efforts to impose its power over its tributaries—such as the campaigns to suppress the Malay rulers and the troubles with the British East India Company in Malaya—meant that in the early Bangkok period the country was constantly either actively fighting wars, or formally in a state of war. It is very likely that such conflicts were for the most part to the disadvantage of the class of bourgeois officials.[21] There is little doubt that all the authors of *Nang nophamat* were connected with this group, and instead of viewing expansionist wars with the enthusiasm demanded by the Thai theory of universal monarchy, they explicitly condemned them and stressed the economic losses they entailed.

Hence the world portrayed by *Nang nophamat* is far removed from the ideal presented in the old texts. Instead it is based on "real life" as the authors experienced it in their day.

Another particular feature of Lady Nophamat's world is that it is inhabited only by human beings. Gods and demons, heavens and hells, evil spirits—none of these have any role. Places where ordinarily people do not live, such as Himmaphan forest, are not mentioned. The human world is not part of a great chain of being extending from the gods to the beasts of hell, in which roles change as beings pass through the cycle of births and deaths, as in the *Tephumikatha* and the *Traiphum lokawinitchai* (Reynolds 1976, 208–9). Mankind is the center of the universe; man's fate is of his own making alone and not affected by the power of any other order of beings.

Notable, too, are the authors' attempts to avoid dealing directly with the Buddhist religion. We have seen that in Lady Nophamat's account of the languages of various nations she states that she uses material from the ancient sages, meaning explicitly the "Book of the Three Vedas." She thus does not venture to improve on Buddhist canons. Although in fact her "knowledge" contradicts the *Tephumikatha* and the *Traiphum lokawinitchai*, the author never refers to the contradiction in any conspicuous way. Similarly, in order to account for a "knowledge" which does not come from Buddhism, the authors make Lady Nophamat a Brahman versed in the Three Vedas, and thus possessed of another, non-Buddhist source of authority. It is as if they were trying to preserve Buddhist learning as a sacred source by presenting the new knowledge as simply a different species of truth, not something that might replace

21. Concerning this class, see Wyatt 1979. Professor Wyatt and I are of the same opinion that members of the bureaucratic class in the early Bangkok period had increasingly bourgeoisified themselves, although they still steadfastly guarded their bureaucratic status. This class played a great role in shaping the form and content of Thai culture and politics in this period.

the old one. This is a compromise typical of the first stages in the transformation of a worldview. It may well be that the authors did not see the contradictions as sharply as we do today, and that hence the omission was unintentional. But as the pace of Thai ideological change quickened, such equivocation would become increasingly difficult, and a need would grow to recreate the source of sacred "knowledge," as we shall see below.

We have already spoken of the attempt to present reality in the literature of early Bangkok. Reality based on "experience" lies at the heart of *Nang nophamat*. The authors' literary technique is thus closely bound up with their worldview. Their Sukhothai and their King Ruang are meant to be a real country and a real individual, not fanciful ones like Sawatthi and Varanasi in the Jataka tales. We have seen that the Buddha images in their Sukhothai bore the names of real ancient images. This attention to making the story appear authentic extends to the use of the title Thao Si Chulalak for the heroine. By the early Bangkok period, this title had been abolished, but it was preserved in the Three Seals Law as the title of one of the four principal royal consorts, and our authors seem to have seized upon this "ancient" name in order to seem realistic.[22] The name King Ruang seems to be fictional rather than real because of the references to the magical power of King Ruang as ruler of Sukhothai in the *Phongsawadan nuea* (Northern Chronicle, 28–30).[23] However, the authors try to make King Ruang into a real historical individual. Indeed, instead of simply referring to the *Northern Chronicle* they suggest those who wish to know the virtues of King Ruang should turn to the "treatise about Chamathewiwong" (*NN*, 245).[24] In fact there is no mention of King Ruang in *Chamathewiwong*. There is only a ruler who may be confused with him, King Athittayarat, but the *Chamathewiwong* states clearly that "he was born and ascended the throne in Hariphunchai" (Phorangsi 1967, 83). Very likely the writers did not consult the *Chamathewiwong* at all, especially as it had then not yet been translated into Thai; but they cited it because they wanted to give a source for King Ruang that had no element of fiction, so as to make King Ruang appear as "real" a person as possible. The King Ruang of *Nang nophamat* thus differs from the Thao Phrommathat of the Jatakas and from the King Ruang of the *Northern Chronicle*.

22. This title had also been used in the Sukhothai period, but it seemed then to denote a queen rather than a consort. See *Charuek wat asokaram* (Wat Asokaram Inscription) no. 93 in *Prachum silacharuek phak thi 4*, 42. Presumably, Ayutthaya must have later retained the title of Si Chulalak for a favorite consort. Its initial use was possibly reserved exclusively for those ladies who came from the former Sukhothai royal family.

23. The *Northern Chronicle* was written in 1807 by Phra Wichian Pricha (Noi), a pundit serving the Front Palace under Rama I. It is as much legend as chronicle, and seems to have drawn on documents from the Ayutthaya period.

24. The *Chamathewiwong* or *Camadewiwamsa* is the story of the founding of the kingdom of Hariphunchai (present-day Lamphun) in the seventh century AD by Princess Chamadewi of Lopburi, who thus brought Buddhism to northern Thailand. It was composed in Pali by the monk Bhodirangsi in 1570 AD and was first published in Thai in 1920. See D. K. Swearer and Sommai Premchit, *The Legend of Queen Cama: Bodhiramsi's Camadewiwamsa, a Translation and Commentary* (New York: State University of New York Press, 1998).

We have often spoken of "reality" in discussing this work, as if earlier Thai writings were not concerned with "reality" at all. But that is not so: no literature can exist which does not respect what is "real." We must understand, however, that there are different kinds of "reality." The "realities" of *Nang nophamat* and of our own day are similar in that they consist of things which we can apprehend with our five senses (together with the wisdom and knowledge which derive ultimately from our sensory experience). It seems realistic to us when the writers, referring to various languages, list all those they have seen, heard, or been told of. For us, all this is evidence that they respect "reality." However, perhaps because of the influence of Buddhism, the literature prior to *Nang nophamat* accorded little importance to this kind of "reality" on grounds it was something impermanent, constantly in flux, and thus not worth knowing, unlike the more permanent and indeed eternal "reality" of the *thamma*. Such "reality," as embedded in the Jataka tales for example, was the "reality" worth knowing. The literature before *Nang nophamat* emphasized this reality, but as a truth-beyond-truth. Using experience as the standard to judge such reality would reduce its value. The question of whether a king like Vessantara actually gave alms on such a large scale—and whether he should have—arises only when viewing the world through the prism of experience. But the Vessantara Jataka was composed with the intention of illustrating the truth-beyond-truth that alms-giving is meritorious conduct.

For this reason we cannot consider *Nang nophamat* as more "realistic" than the Vessantara Jataka; we should rather say that its authors were more concerned for the truth revealed by experience than were previous Thai writers.

The stress on experienced reality clearly reflects a crucial change in worldview. In the first place it was bound to influence ideas of what constituted knowledge. Experience now became the means for achieving knowledge. This meant an immeasurable expansion of potential knowledge, for it was no longer restricted to what was revealed in religious texts, but extended into the unbounded realm of experience. Secondly, experience was human experience (for we cannot know the experience of animals and gods). Human experience thus had value; it was not just part of a superficial, endlessly repetitive flux with no significance in itself. On the contrary, it was the instrument by which mankind moved closer to truth of another kind; it implied that man is capable of discovering "knowledge" and "truth" for himself, without the aid of religious texts, gods, or *rishi* holy men. Not long after *Nang nophamat*'s time, the Thai literati would confront the problem of deciding whether knowledge derived from human experience was more valid than that contained in sacred books.[25]

25. At this point, Professor Craig Reynolds has offered the following comment: "I think your discussion concerning reality, knowledge, and experience needs to be included into this article. But I get a feeling that you yourself were not so sure of your own opinions. You seemed to talk a little too much which shows that you were not very certain, were you? Perhaps, I have misunderstood you. The idea that we are closer to Nang Nophamat's conceptual world than that of ancient documents, such as these written before 1800, because the world conception of Nang Nophamat was built on empirical experience is, I think, questionable. 'Experience'

Thirdly, the view that experience is the path to "knowledge" and "truth" also undermined the certainty and fixity of "knowledge" and "truth." Human experience varies, and this variety can lead to very different kinds of knowledge. New experiences are bound to discredit old knowledge, and hence what is held to be knowledge is constantly changing. This view would shake the Thai thought-world to its foundations. In old Siam, knowledge had been characterized by perfection; the highest truths were seen as eternal because they were not temporally conditioned. Knowledge of perfect truth was the end goal of all study. But when experience became the pathway to knowledge, then truth was no longer perfect. In *Nang nophamat* we cannot yet see this new perception of the world clearly; it would be a long time before the idea of relative knowledge would emerge distinctly in Thai thought. Indeed, even today the old vision of knowledge as something perfect has not really lost its hold on Thai society—something which has posed problems for western-style teaching in the country.

This change in worldview ensured that *Nang nophamat* exhibits the distinctive literary characteristics we have noted above. The use of a "special" setting makes the characters specific as well. The attention to delineating the particularity of the actors, background, and events, together with the attempt at "realism," is surely the product of a worldview that values the kind of truth that is derived from experience. We might compare it with the state of mind prevailing in the period that gave birth to the English-language novel.[26]

The changes in worldview evoked in *Nang nophamat* are limited to matters of geography, values concerning reality and knowledge, and relations between states. In regard to the relationship between mankind and the world, especially where that involves religion, there is no trace of any such change. The same is true of the treatment of social relations: broadly speaking, the political worldview seems to have undergone no alteration. Lady Nophamat calls for loyalty and the willingness to sacrifice—even one's life—for the king's sake: "I must be willing to give up flesh and blood, indeed my very life, should this be required to win favor and speed the accomplishment of His Majesty's royal purpose" (*NN*, 282). She does so because the king is the most powerful and exalted being, and because understanding the royal intent is beyond the

---

in the sense that you used here is in fact a matter of modern men's self-indulgence. Isn't it possible that 'experience' or what is held to be 'experience' changes with time? I think you can say that the flying Buddhist relics mentioned in the Sukhothai stone inscription (or even a magical *chakra* in Traiphum) were all very real for people in that time. Anyway, this is just my conjecture. I think you have to contextualize reality according to time and place too (I know that you have already put reality in quote marks, but you need to say still more). But I haven't thought about this matter carefully enough to suggest any creative advice as of now." I fully agree with Professor Reynolds' arguments. However, after trying strenuously to distinguish between the "experience," "reality," and "knowledge" of the early Bangkok period and those of the former period, I cannot think of any clearer explanation. Hence my surrender at this point despite my appreciation that this question is important and should be resolved.

26. See the analysis of the origin of the English novel in Ian Watt, *The Rise of the Novel* (Berkeley: University of California Press, 1967), 9–60, which links the expansion of empiricist philosophy with the rise of the novel in England.

power of ordinary mortals. It is as if the ruler is a god beyond the norms of mankind. Thus Lady Nophamat says: "a person who enters royal service will find it difficult to fathom why the king grants mercy or withholds it. He should not presume to think about it. Even if he is supported by a vast store of merit accumulated in previous incarnations, reward will still be a matter of the royal pleasure" (*NN*, 258–9). It would be a long time before the change in the worldview of the Thai literati would reach its logical conclusion and encompass a corresponding change in political worldview.

THE TALE OF *NANG NOPHAMAT* AS PART OF THE CHANGING WORLDVIEW IN THE EARLY BANGKOK PERIOD

As noted earlier, the particular literary characteristics of *Nang nophamat* were not completely without precedent in Thai writing. The same is true of its worldview: we can find traces of such a transformation in earlier works. Of particular interest in this connection is the *Traiphum lokawinitchai*, a work composed on royal initiative in the First Reign. The text sets out to describe the Three Worlds of the Buddhist universe, but in so doing it reveals a change in the cosmological view of the literati compared to that expressed in the *Tephumikatha* or the *Traiphum phra ruang*. It moved the center of the universe from Mount Meru to the Throne of Enlightenment, in line with new beliefs about the king which early Bangkok monarchs wished to stress (Nidhi 1978, 228–9, see chapter 6 in this book; Dhammapricha 1977). It is concerned as much to teach the fundamentals of Buddhism as to describe the Three Worlds, and it includes instruction from the most basic principles up to the level of metaphysical doctrine. The entire work is devoted to explaining natural phenomena, such as flood-tides and ebb-tides, thunder, rainfall, eclipses of the sun and moon—things which the *Traiphum phra ruang* did not deem worthy of mention. Moreover, the *Traiphum lokawinitchai* takes the origin of mankind as its starting point and stresses the importance of the world of man over other worlds.

We can see, therefore, that *Nang nophamat* is not the first Thai literary work to emphasize the importance of human kind.

Sometime after *Nang nophamat* was written, a book appeared which showed even more clearly the changing worldview of the Thai literati. The *Sadaeng kitchanukit* (On Diverse Subjects) of Chaophraya Thiphakorawong was composed in 1865 (as the writer declares at one point that "from this time we must step back a thousand eight hundred and sixty-five years" to the birth of Christ) and was published in 1867 (Thiphakorawong 1970, hereafter *SK*, 49).[27] Its author lived in the same social world as the authors of *Nang nophamat* and faced the same problems, but more acutely because he had to deal more with foreigners, especially those from the west. The impact on the worldview of the author of *Sadaeng kitchanukit* was more

27. Chaophraya Thiphakorawong (Kham Bunnag) was minister of foreign affairs to King Mongkut at the time he composed this work.

violent and made him more conscious about the confrontation between the old and new worldviews. He could not simply hedge the issue any longer. Because he himself was equipped with western scientific knowledge, he could not explain matters as mere "elaboration" of ancient teachings, as Lady Nophamat had; he needed explicitly to confront and ultimately undermine the old authorities. Of course, the class origins and upbringing of Chaophraya Thiphakorawong ensure he was no revolutionary of the kind that seeks to root out all traces of the old worldview. There were aspects of the old worldview which he took to be of enduring and precious value. The problem for him was how to recast only some parts of the old worldview so that it could accommodate the new knowledge from the west. Moreover, one purpose in composing *Sadaeng kitchanukit* was to reply to attacks on Buddhism mounted by the missionary doctors. He was concerned to explain Buddhism in a way which did not clash with the scientific knowledge that was beginning to engulf the Thai literati. This amounted to defining and delimiting Buddhism in a world which was experiencing dramatic change in worldview.

In so doing, Chaophraya Thiphakorawong did not avoid confrontation with Buddhist cosmology and did not refrain from referring to the Three Worlds; for example, in explaining why rain falls, why there is a dry season (*SK*, 12), and what causes solar and lunar eclipses (*SK*, 42). The explanations provided in Buddhist teachings surely did not accord with scientific principles based on experienced reality. Yet Chaophraya Thiphakorawong argued that such explanations did not come from the Buddha's own teachings, but were concocted by monks when the religion spread beyond India. The monks had not dared tell kings outside India that the Buddha viewed such questions about natural phenomena as "ephemeral" for fear they would lose faith and turn to the Hindu way of thinking (*SK*, 55–6). For Chaophraya Thiphakorawong, there was no real need to refrain from confronting ancient teachings of this sort. Hence when explaining why the world is round, he states that "this is what the evidence reveals; so how can one believe that the earth is flat and has Mount Meru as its pivot?" (*SK*, 59). The teachings of the missionary doctors are treated in the same vein: Chaophraya Thiphakorawong tries to prove that, as with the Three Worlds or other teachings not part of the Buddhist canon, they are superstitions, without foundation and without the truth that comes from "experience" (*SK*, 60–71).

Such thinking was not peculiar to Chaophraya Thiphakorawong. A traveler who visited Bangkok in 1856 reported that the contents of the Three Worlds of King Ruang "are frequently denied by many of the shrewder Buddhists in Siam."[28] Chaophraya Thiphakorawong himself evidently shared this view long before he wrote *Sadaeng kitchanukit*, for it was reported that in a conversation with a foreigner in 1863, he remarked that the Jatakas were nothing but fairy tales and that King Nagasena could certainly not have descended from Brahma's heaven as in the *Milintha panha* (The Questions of King Milinda[29]) (Reynolds 1976, 213).

28. Reynolds 1976, 214, quoting William Maxwell Wood, *Fankwei, or the "San Jacinto" in the Seas of India, China and Japan*, New York: Harper, 1859, 256.

29. This work was composed in Pali in north India about two thousand years ago. There is an English translation by T. W. Rhys Davies (New York: Dover Press, 1963). It recounts the

Chaophraya Thiphakorawong's effort to reconcile Buddhism and its cosmology with science also represented a new limitation on the religion, since it held that only that part which represented the Buddha's own teaching was "real" and thus in accordance with scientific principles, which were also "real." He declared that "if one takes the view that the world is flat, this is the same as asserting that there was a creator to make it so; but if one holds that the world is round it is in accordance with the Buddha's teaching that this is its natural bent" (*SK*, 58). In the matter of religious texts, he believed those in Pali to be sacred because, even if they do not represent the exact words of the Buddha, they are in the words which the Buddha employed, and therefore "true." If some Pali texts appear to contradict science, they must be re-interpreted to find their real meaning. Indeed, "if we find Pali words referring to earth, heaven, and hell strewn throughout various treatises, we will see that some are meant metaphorically, and some correspond with people's perception of the world, and that is why they are still found in the Pali text" (*SK*, 56). All non-Pali texts (including later commentaries) which are an important part of Buddhism in Thailand, are thus of lesser value and open to attack and overthrow if they contradict scientific principles.[30]

The new limitations on Buddhism and the "return to original texts" were also defining characteristics of the religious reform movement known as the Thammayut sect (and were furthermore characteristic of religious reform movements elsewhere in the world over the last century). The way in which monks wore their robes now had to conform to that described in the Pali texts, not because the monks would thereby economize on cloth or have a more pleasing appearance but in order to be "authentic" as a way of respecting a "real truth" uncorrupted by the ideas of commentators. Chaophraya Thiphakorawong, like the authors of *Nang nophamat*, was an intellectual who found himself carried along by the tides of a changing worldview.

THE PLACE OF NANG NOPHAMAT IN THE HISTORY OF THOUGHT

Work on the history of Thai thought, to which very few scholars have as yet devoted themselves, no longer attaches importance to the tale of *Nang nophamat*. The very interesting study by Craig Reynolds (1976) on the Thai worldview in the nineteenth century focuses heavily on Chaophraya Thiphakorawong's *Sadaeng kitchanukit* and makes no mention at all of the tale of *Nang nophamat*. Research on Thai political history in general has also neglected it. This is why Reynolds sees in *Sadaeng kitchanukit* a drastic intellectual change among Thai intellectuals, so violent that it cut them off

story of King Milinda, or Munandar, a Greek king who ruled in northwestern India about 200 BC and was converted to Buddhism by Nagasena, who descended to earth for the purpose.

30. The majority of the texts quoted in *Traiphum phra ruang* were non-Pali, i.e., texts composed wholly by commentators. See Eugene Denis, 'La Lokapannatti et les idées cosmologiques du Bouddhisme ancien,' thesis presented at the University of Paris, 1976, p. li.

from their past. But if we use Chaophraya Thiphakorawong's compendium as our point of departure we are likely to lose sight of the fact that the religious reforms of Prince Mongkut had already taken place in the Third Reign. And if a religious reform succeeds it is not because a single wise man took it into his head to carry it out but also and necessarily because there were many "intelligent" people who supported the endeavor, from fervent disciples to passive accepters. If historians do not take into account the social and economic base of the "great reforms" of the Fourth and Fifth Reigns, then the age of reform seems to spring from nowhere and can be explained only by emphasizing external pressures. Such explanations are self-contradictory because historians also portray the reforms as proceeding very smoothly, but no power on earth, not even the greatest, could force an old society to change peacefully unless the internal foundations for the change had already been laid.

In the history of thought, the tale of *Nang nophamat* serves as a link between *Traiphum lokawinitchai* and *Sadaeng kitchanukit.* Hence it should not be ignored. Each of these works represents in itself a change and together they form a series of tiny bridges which lead seamlessly from one situation to another without any violent break. It was not an individual genius who opened up the new era but small, gradual adjustments in the thinking of Thai literati who found their world in continuing flux. Some of them left behind for us traces of this metamorphosis in their thought. The world of Lady Nophamat is an important world linking the age of early Bangkok to that of the "great reforms" which followed, at least as far as the thought of the literati was concerned.

If we look at the course of the history of thought in this way, we may be stimulated to reconsider other aspects of the history of these two eras.

5

THE LIFE OF THE BUDDHA AND THE RELIGIOUS MOVEMENT OF THE EARLY BANGKOK PERIOD

TRANSLATOR'S NOTE

In addition to the Thai text in *Pakkai lae bai ruea*, this translation is based on an English version of the article written by Professor Nidhi for an English-speaking audience. Places where my translation may appear too free are places where I thought the language in the English version was more readable and appropriate than an "exact" translation from the Thai.

In this chapter, Buddhist terms and names are rendered in the forms based on Pali. However, Thammayut(ika) is given in the conventional spelling based on phonemic transliteration from Thai. (CJR)

5

THE LIFE OF THE BUDDHA AND THE RELIGIOUS MOVEMENT OF THE EARLY BANGKOK PERIOD[1]

INTRODUCTION

In the central Thai language at least three literary works on the life of the Buddha have been found and published widely. Written over a span of about eighty years, all three works were composed by famous authors. The author of the first, Prince Paramanuchit Chinorot, wrote it in the first half of the nineteenth century, that is, before the "opening" of the country by the Bowring Treaty (1855). This prince was the son of King Rama I (r. 1782–1809), went into the monkhood as a child, and remained there his entire life. King Nangklao in the third Bangkok reign (r. 1824–51), who was his nephew, paid him great respect as a sage and considered him the final authority on all religious matters. The entire elite probably regarded him as one of the most notable poets of that time. Although there is evidence that he was close to Prince Mongkut who started the so-called "religious reform," he kept himself aloof from the Thammayut movement both before and after Prince Mongkut ascended the throne. In the Fourth Reign (1851–68) he received the highest ecclesiastical honors and was made head of the monastic order in Siam. The second author of the life of the Buddha, Supreme Patriarch Sa, was one of the original disciples of Prince Mongkut. When Prince Mongkut became king, Sa ultimately decided to remain a monk rather than disrobe and undertake lengthy government service as some of Mongkut's other disciples had done with great success. In the Fifth Reign (1868–1910) he was promoted to Supreme Patriarch of the Sangha. The third author, Prince Wachirayan, a son of King Mongkut, went into the monkhood when he was a young man and remained there until his death in the first quarter of the twentieth century. When this prince became a monk, it had become the tradition for princes descended from Mongkut to be ordained in the Thammayutika or "reformed" order. His long-term stay in the monkhood was actually the expressed intention of his brother, King Chulalongkorn. In the Sixth Reign (1910–25) the prince-monk received a special ecclesiastical

1. Professors Likhit Likhitananda and Saeng Chandrangam of Chiang Mai University and Professor Praphot Aswawirunhakarn of Chulalongkorn University have kindly and patiently answered questions on Pali literature and Buddhism, and I would like to thank them for their generous assistance here. I would also like to thank Professor Craig J. Reynolds of Sydney University and Professor Yoneo Ishii of Kyoto University who read the original draft and kindly made valuable comments. Any shortcomings in this essay, however, are solely the responsibility of the author.

title reserved for royalty and was made Supreme Patriarch. He was responsible for "modernizing" changes in the monastic education system, and he played a part in establishing religious instruction both inside and outside the Sangha (reinforcing, at the same time, Thammayutika teachings in the content of that instruction). This prince-monk also carried out vital tasks in Chulalongkorn's policies of reorganizing the Sangha to facilitate its control by the centralized supervision of the state.

These three literary works have been republished many times, and they have formed part of the curriculum at various levels of Thai monastic education. And the three works, especially the last, have served as a model for the writing of the Buddha's biography in Thai, both in school textbooks and in books for the general public.

It might be presumed that writings on the Buddha's life in Thailand, a country with a long history of belief in Buddhism, would be numerous, but in fact this is not the case. The corpus of literature in the Central Thai language has relatively few versions of the Buddha's life (and it is likely all these works date from the early Bangkok period). The earliest reference to a biography of the Buddha in Central Thai, no longer extant, is in a document from the reign of the founder of the Chakri dynasty. The series of lives of the Buddha mentioned above came after this text that no longer survives. Not until modern times when western literature began to circulate in Thailand did various versions of the Buddha's life begin to proliferate in Thai language. The scarcity of Thai biographies of the Buddha may surprise those who look at Buddhism from a Christian point of view, because in Christianity the life of Christ and the doctrine he preached are inseparable. But Sakyamuni, the historical Buddha, is of less importance in Buddhist doctrine, and treatment of the Buddha as a historical figure is perhaps irrelevant to his own teachings. When looked at from this perspective, the interest of the Thai elite of the central plains in the Buddha's life since the late eighteenth century indicates a subtle change in its religious thinking that merits serious study.

The three biographies of the Buddha mentioned above were written by two groups of monks: non-Thammayut and Thammayut. In view of the fact that the Thammayut has usually been regarded as the only "change" in the religious thinking of the elite from the late eighteenth to the middle of the nineteenth century, we might expect significant differences if we compare the two groups of texts. But in fact the three biographies in their basic elements and frames of reference are congruous. In order to explain this remarkable congruity, it is necessary to reinvestigate the religious movements taking place among the elite during the early Bangkok period and to try to place all three biographies of the Buddha in the context of intellectual history. This essay aims to do just that.

THE BUDDHA'S BIOGRAPHY

Compared with Christianity and Islam, Buddhism, especially in the Theravada order, attributes little significance to the life of its founder. The New Testament of the Bible actually contains biographies of Jesus as told by different disciples, and as far as the biography and way of life of Mohammed is concerned, these are described in great detail in the Hadith, a scripture of oral origins whose importance is second only to that of the Qur'an. The canon of the Theravada Buddhists nowhere contains a comprehensive biography of Sakyamuni, although many parts of the Suttas and the Vinaya refer to various episodes in the Buddha's life. The main reason for this neglect is that according to Buddhism's principal teaching, the figure of the Buddha as a person is of minor importance. As Edward Conze explains,

> The existence of Gautama, or Shakyamuni, as an individual is, in any case, a matter of little importance to Buddhist faith. The Buddha is a type that has been embodied in this individual—and it is the type which interests the religious life.... In the official theory, the Buddha, "the Enlightened," is a kind of archetype which manifests itself in the world at different periods in different personalities, whose individual particularities are of no account whatsoever. (Conze 1957, 34–5)

In actual fact, it may be misleading to say that Buddhist scriptures have little interest in discussing the Buddha. There is a strain of thought about the Buddha in the Mahayana doctrine (which is probably present in the Theravada as well, though this cannot be confirmed) which is useful in understanding the interest of Buddhist scripture in the founder. The Mahayanists hold that the Buddha exists in three bodies.

1. Niramanakaya (The Created Body) refers to the body, manifest in the form of Prince Siddhattha in flesh and blood, which must change and decay like any other human body. This was the body in which the Buddha at first manifested himself to others. Nowadays when we talk about the Buddha's biography, in point of fact we are alluding to the history of the Niramanakaya, that is, to the Buddha's human body (because it is the only body subject to change and thus the only one to have a "history").

2. Dhammakaya (The Dhamma Body) refers to the principle or nature of Buddhahood not visible to the human eye. Thai inscription no. 54, discovered at Phitsanulok and dated 1448, explains "Dhammakaya as the characteristics of being a Buddha," all of which are metaphors for different kinds of dhamma. For example, the Buddha "has a head as sublime as Knowledge and Enlightenment; he has hair which is as sublime as Nibbana, the feeling experienced after the deepest meditation." (This passage corresponds to one in the Dhammakayadi, suggesting that the concept of the Dhammakaya occurs in the Theravada as well.) It is this body that is alluded to in a saying of the Buddha, "Those who see Dhamma see the Tathagata."

3. Sambhogakaya (The Glorified Body) is the body of the Buddha that generates joy and delight in those who gaze on it. The features of this body, beautiful and radiant, inspire faith. These features, which in Thai texts are identical to the signs of the Mahapurisa (the Great Man), are in fact the embodiment of the Sambhoga body of the Buddha (cf. Conze 1957, 35–8).

By distinguishing among these three bodies, one finds that "the Buddha" alluded to most frequently in the Theravada texts is the Buddha of the Dhamma and Sambhoga bodies, while very little attention is given to the Niramana body. When we refer to the

Buddha's biography we mean the story of a man who lived in India over two thousand years ago, whereas the Buddha of the Dhamma and Sambhoga bodies is incapable of having a "story." So it is not surprising that the Tipitaka pays little attention to the "biography" or "story" of the Buddha, because the Tipitaka most often aims to expound on the Buddha in his Dhamma and Sambhoga bodies. And naturally the Buddha's life narrated in this way accordingly differs from the biography of the Buddha that we are familiar with and understand today. Let us therefore call this kind of narrative of the Buddha's life a "dhammography," as opposed to the story of the Buddha in his Niramana body which nowadays we refer to as biography.

THE BUDDHA'S LIFE IN THAI TRADITION

Owing to religious influence from Ceylon, the life of the Buddha in Thai tradition is not so different in character from that which exists—and is written or told—in Ceylon. Thus it is necessary at the outset to explore briefly the Buddha's life-story in the Ceylonese tradition.

Three distinguishable yet related themes may be found in the Ceylonese tradition of the Buddha's life, a tradition that has its roots in both the canon and the commentaries.

1. Buddhahood is a spiritual state attained by a number of people, and the story of the Buddha is in fact a narrative of one of two things, either a) the story of all Buddhas, including Sakyamuni, who have or will have attained that spiritual state; or b) the story of Sakyamuni in his previous existences, beginning with his first vow to become a Buddha millions of eons ago and running through the myriad of his transmigrations during which he met, and was shown "the way" by, all previous Buddhas. The most exemplary narrative of this type of life of the Buddha is the Buddhavamsa, a late canonical work which contains among its twenty-eight chapters only one short chapter on the life of Sakyamuni in his last incarnation. This type of theme of dhammo-graphical description of the Buddha thoroughly permeates the commentaries written in Ceylon. For example the Madhuratthavilasini, Jinalamkara, Jinacarita, and the Nidanakatha are just a few among the more famous ones that can be cited. (Malalasekera 1960; Likhit 1969, 103–11; Malalasekera 1958, 105–16, 230–1).

2. A story line exists in which the Buddha figures centrally, but it is focused on his previous existences rather than on the empirical span of his lifetime. The Jatakas are important in this story of the Buddha, ten of the Jatakas being selected to show the Buddha's attainment of the Ten Perfections (*dasaparami*). A canonical work, the Cariyapitaka, is the best illustration of this story line. In short, the Jatakas' role remains vital in many Ceylonese texts on the life of the Buddha.

3. The history of the *satsana* (literally, the Teaching) is also a part of the Buddha's life. In most cases, the history of Buddhism is embodied in the story of significant relic monuments (*chedi*), and in almost every case it is inseparable from the two themes described above. Many of these Pali works from Ceylon—such as the Mahabodhivamsa, Bodhivamsa, Dathavamsa, and Thupavamsa (see Malalasekera

1960, 157, 160, 216)—were quite well known to Thai scholars. The Teaching, like the Buddha, existed in infinite time, extending back to the immemorial past as well as into the unforeseeable future. Sakyamuni's vow to be a Buddha, taken eons ago, is just as much a part of this "history" of relics as it is of the eventual disappearance of these relics two to three thousand years hence.[2]

These texts do not narrate the story of the Buddha as a human being but as a principle of Dhamma. The condition of being a Buddha is not limited to empirical time and space. The presentation of the essence of the Buddha's story in this way corresponds closely with the central core of Theravada teaching, namely, that the Dhamma "discovered" by the Buddha is timeless. It had come into existence before his enlightenment and will be in existence forever. Consequently, this Dhamma, as well as Buddhahood itself, could not be tied to a specific time or a specific individual.

The Ceylonese dhammographical story of the Buddha established a model for telling the Buddha's life story in Siam. Presumably, there were also models from Burma as well, but the present writer has had no opportunity to study Burmese commentaries and so cannot discuss this point. Popular texts from Ceylon concerning the Buddha's life have been cited since Sukhothai times. The Traibhumikatha, for example, refers to Jinalamkara, Bodhivamsa, Buddhavamsa, and, in the index, Madhurattha-puranivilasini (*Traiphumikatha*, 787–8). The last-mentioned is probably Madhu-ratthavilasini, which itself is a commentary on the Buddhavamsa. Although Jinalamkara was not well-known in Ceylon, it had gained an enduring respect in Siam up to the early Bangkok period. In the first Chakri reign high-ranking monks referred to this text and its subcommentary in order to respond to the king's inquiry about the number of tiers on the royal umbrella (*Prachum phraratchaputcha*, 134).

The Buddha's life in this dhammographical form was plentiful enough in the commentarial literature of Ceylon (and also from Burma). Thai authors had no need to search for the Buddha's life in the canonical literature which, in any case, contains no comprehensive version of the Buddha's life (as biography). What was more important, moreover, was that in any effort to use the canon as a source, passages from the various Suttas and the "Vatthu" in the Vinaya made the Buddha into someone with a human life, limited to a specific time and historical context. The narrative of the life of the Buddha according to the canon thus became biography. The notion of narrating the Buddha's life as biography had not yet emerged in Siam. The evidence used to narrate the Buddha's life came, therefore, from the commentaries or the Buddhavamsa in the Khuddakanikaya.

2. Interestingly, the "biography" of the Buddha in the textbooks for children in Ceylonese Sunday school today is still told according to these traditional themes. The story begins with Sakyamuni's vow to attain Buddhahood when he meets Dipangkara, a previous Buddha; it continues with stories of previous Buddhas in the Jatakas; and it ends with the religious history of Ceylon (Gombrich 1971, 84–97). The persistence of this tradition in Sri Lanka is of great significance for comprehending the breadth and depth of changes in religious thinking in Thailand.

In the dhammographical life of the Buddha, the inclusion of the Buddha's virtues in his previous lives many, many eons ago is of no less importance than the moment of his enlightenment as a Buddha. For this reason, the Jatakas were considered indispensable in the life of the Buddha. Thai inscription no. 90 with its fourteenth century paleography declares that the image above the inscription is that of "the ascetic Phetsandon (Vessantara)." Incised stone slabs in the *wihan* of Wat Si Chum at Sukhothai are all pictorial representations of the Jataka tales. The incorporation of Jatakas would remain an integral part of the Buddha's life in Thai tradition for a long time, especially in oral recitations as will be discussed below.

The dhammographical narration of the Buddha's life is also clearly evident in Ayutthaya. A text called Saddhammasamgaha, believed by some Pali students to have been composed in Ayutthaya, opens with the story of the Buddha (meaning, in this case, the Buddha's life), beginning with the Bodhisatta's vow to become a Buddha and ending with his enlightenment and the Buddhist councils. A shorter version of the same story is found in another text written in Ayutthaya times, Cula-saddhammasamgaha (Likhit 1969, 199–201).

In Lanna the dhammographical approach to the Buddha's life was standard for writings on the subject. Mulasasana relates the Buddha's story from his vow to achieve Buddhahood and his long cycle of rebirths up to his enlightenment as a Buddha. His pre-Sakyamuni lives cover fifty-seven pages, while his life as Sakyamuni takes only three pages (*Tamnan mulasatsana*, 1–57). The number of pages used in each section clearly indicates the attitude towards "biography," which forms only a minor part of a lengthy "dhammography" of the Buddha. Following this is the story of the Buddhist councils and the propagation of Buddhism to Lanna. The structure of the text is an imitation of ecclesiastical history (the history of the Teaching) established in Ceylon.

Another Pali text from Lanna, Jinakalamalipakaranam, is structurally identical to Mulasasana and works from Ceylon. The great attention paid to the first vow of the Bodhisatta to achieve Buddhahood is reflected at the beginning of the Buddha's story where temporal units are given for his vow-making in past lives:

> By his thought our Lord Buddha made a vow to achieve Buddhahood for seven incalculable world-periods (*asamkhya*), by word for nine incalculable world-periods, and by body and word for four incalculable world-periods. Uncountable lives before he even met a Buddha, our *bodhisatva* experienced an instant in which he intended to become a Buddha. (Ratanapañña 1958, 3)

Although time is firmly established in this passage, the chronological frame does not make dhammography into biography. The time scale used in the story is beyond the human scale, and it is even beyond the time scale of the universe (that is, it is before this age of the Buddhas when the universe had already devolved and reemerged many times). This is virtually the time scale of Dhamma itself.

This dhammographical description of the Buddha's story prevailed in Siam until the early Bangkok period. The renowned Pali scholar and historian, Phra Wannarat of Wat Phra Chetuphon, began his History of the Buddhist Councils (*Samgitiyavamsa*) with the prophecy of Buddhahood given to the Bodhisatta by Dipangkara and ended it with his imminent departure from the Dusit heaven as he looks down and considers his rebirth in the human world. His life as Siddhattha and Sakyamuni is narrated briefly with no details. Even Sariputta, the most important disciple in Theravada tradition, is not mentioned (Wannarat 1978, 5–26). *Samgitiyavamsa*, however, devotes proportionately greater space than previous works to the Buddha's life as Siddhattha and Sakyamuni, because *Samgitiyavamsa* and its author were a part of the current of changes in Thai thought and religion which began to be apparent in the early Bangkok period, as will be discussed below. Nevertheless, the dhammographical approach to the Buddha's life left its unmistakable mark on the Buddha's story in early Bangkok. Inscriptions on a pavilion in front of a reliquary included the Jatakas and began with the first story, the preeminent one about the lives of the Bodhisatta under twenty-four previous Buddhas and the nature of the prophecies he was given by each of them (*Prachum charuek wat phra chetuphon*, 118–26).

The dhammographical tradition discussed above was one maintained entirely by means of written texts. The people had a different tradition kept alive through oral transmission, the best source of which was probably the reports of foreigners who had visited Siam in various periods. At a later time, however, namely in the nineteenth century, westerners became better informed about the Buddha's life, owing to their increasing familiarity with India and the scholarly works of European orientalists. Consequently, the Buddha's life as revealed in these later sources does not really reflect Thai thinking.

In the seventeenth century Nicolas Gervaise was not very successful in narrating the life of the Buddha, despite having lived in Siam for four years. He reported that the Thai believed the Buddha after several rebirths was born a Thai prince who finally ascended the throne. When the Buddha renounced the world he observed ascetic practices: "The Buddha gave away all his belongings when asked by beggars. . . . He even donated one of his eyes." In addition, the French friar also recorded stories reminiscent of the story of the Five Disciples and the story of Devadatta. Moreover, the Buddha in this version even visited Lavo (presumably the Buddha's Footprint at Saraburi), and in returning to Ceylon the Buddha simply leapt with one step, leaving his footprint there at Lavo. After he had established Buddhism, says Gervaise, the Buddha "vanished from human view, entered Nibbana, and enjoyed its bliss with all past Buddhas ever after" (Gervaise 1928, 75–6).

A number of observations may be made about these reports of Gervaise.

1. The biographical version of the Buddha's life was not well-known in Siam. Whether the idea that the Buddha was a Thai prince was a misunderstanding of Gervaise or of the Thai people is impossible to say. But in actuality, how many Thai would have known that Kapilavatthu, the principality of the Sakya, was in India, or "Muang Thet" as it was then called? More probably, people thought that the Buddha was born in Ceylon, and Gervaise's own report of the Buddha's footprint and return to Ceylon indicates as much. Whatever the case may have been, our discussion here concerns the Buddha's life as biography. As long as the Buddha's life was treated as dhammography, whether his birthplace was in India, Ceylon, or Siam was insignificant.

2. The reference to multiple births of the Buddha and to the final stage when he joined with many previous Buddhas suggests that the Buddha's life as recited by monks and people in seventeenth century Ayutthaya placed heavy emphasis on deeds which accumulated merit in preparation for the attainment of Buddhahood in the last life. That is to say, the Jataka stories were emphasized. The reference to the Buddha's donation of worldly possessions is probably an allusion to the Vessantara Jataka, the Buddha's last human birth before being born as Gotama. In other words, the Jatakas were still an important, inseparable part of the life of the Buddha in Thai thinking. The reference to past Buddhas emphasized an older idea that merely brought the life of Gotama Buddha into the context of the dhammographical tradition. There was no biography of the Buddha in the religious tradition of the Thai masses.

3. The reference to the Five Disciples and Devadatta illuminates the fact that the First Sermon and the story of Devadatta constituted important elements in the story of the Buddha's life.[3] This is corroborated by La Loubère (1969, 149–57), who in his work provided great detail on Devadatta.

The story of the Buddha in La Loubère's work is not so different from that in Gervaise's, despite some discrepancies in detail. The basic outline of the story is the same. La Loubère began his account of the Buddha's life by relating the Buddha's donation of his wife and children, which we can see clearly is from the Vessantara Jataka and is identical to Gervaise's account. This confusion reconfirms the interpretation that the Jataka stories and the story of the Buddha were inseparable in Thai thinking. On the story of the Buddha proper, La Loubère was presumably referring to some well-known episodes such as the extreme asceticism practiced by Gotama before his enlightenment, the story of the Five Disciples, Buddha's victory over Mara, and the Great Death. La Loubère (1969, 136) himself reports that he was unable to obtain a book on the Buddha's life and was thus obliged to rely on oral sources. His alleged effort to obtain such a written account is quite credible, because when we discount the misunderstandings from his version of the Devadatta story, we can see that it corresponds in almost every detail with one of the commentaries. It is virtually identical to the commentary on the Dhammapada (see the Devadatta story in U Nissako 1963). La Loubère claimed to have obtained the Devadatta story from a translation of a Pali text, thus tending to confirm the interpretation above that the life of the Buddha as biography was not widespread in Siam. When the French ambassador was looking for just such a text of the Buddha's life no one could supply him with one, as it had to be compiled from numerous Pali texts. This is why La Loubère was forced to rely on oral sources rather than written ones for his life of the Buddha.

3. It is interesting to note that according to Thai belief, Devadatta, the villain and arch-enemy of the Buddha, had heard a prophecy from the Buddha that he himself would become a Buddha in the remote future after living out a torturous time in hell. The attention given to Devadatta among the Thai arises, I think, from the potentiality of his Buddhahood. The future Buddha, like Metteyya, always played an important part in folk religious thinking in Thailand, as attested to by numerous merit-making vows that we can find in inscriptions.

In the early Bangkok period, Crawfurd (1967, 366) narrated the story of the Buddha by using the research of a member of the Royal Society of Bengal. He reported that monks in Siam had insisted there had been four Buddhas (that is, in this epoch called Bhaddakappa, the Civilized Epoch, there had been four Buddhas). Crawfurd (1967, 367) then related the history of the expansion of Buddhism to Ceylon and Siam, thus indicating that the story of the Buddha told by the monks was still in the same dhammographical form that had been passed down from ancient times. In other words, the previous Buddhas and the history of *the* religion were one and the same history.

By the same token, Bowring related the story of the Buddha by returning to the 550 Jataka stories, but the parts dealing with Gotama were now closer to the Thai version, except for some errors owing to his own misunderstandings.

It is obvious that the story of the Buddha in popular or oral tradition was not essentially different from the story of the Buddha as written by Thai intellectuals and available in both Pali and Thai. This version we have characterized as dhammographical. It is appropriate at this point to summarize the structure of the story of the Buddha in this older Thai tradition before proceeding further.

THE STRUCTURE OF THE BUDDHA'S STORY IN THAI TRADITION

1. The story of the Buddha in his incarnation as Gotama Buddha is inseparable from his life in previous incarnations. And in order to emphasize the point that "the Buddha" is clearly a spiritual principle, a number of Gotama's significant deeds are not unique to him but are "duties" that all previous and future Buddhas perform. Metteyya, for example, who is yet to come, is to live a life almost exactly the same as that lived by Gotama Buddha: he will reside in the three pavilions; he will be enlightened under a tree; he will eat rice porridge; he will float a container; he will sit under a thatch shelter; he will speak to the craving nature of beings (*tanha*); and so forth.

2. In the Mahaparinibbana Sutta the Lord Buddha attributed earthquakes to eight causes: wind; persons with supernatural powers; the passing away of the Bodhisatta; the birth of the Bodhisatta; the Enlightenment; the preaching of the First Sermon; the Buddha's death and the Buddha's entry into Nibbana. Leaving aside the first two causes of earthquakes (wind and persons with supernatural powers), the remaining ones form the basic structure of the Buddha's life according to the Sutta literature, namely, the Bodhisatta's passing away from the Dusit heaven, his birth, his Enlightenment, the First Sermon, and his death and passing into Nibbana (Phutthathat 1954, 313). It is possible to extract from this sequence four essential events which correspond to the four sacred sites stipulated by the Buddha in the Mahaparinibbana Sutta: the site of his birth; the site where he attained Enlightenment; the site where he preached the First Sermon; and the site of his death (Phutthathat 1954, 326). In other words, the life of the Buddha must, according to this Sutta, comprise these essential events.[4]

4. In the fifth century Fa Hsien reported that each Buddha retained, as a rule, four sacred sites: the site where he attained enlightenment; the site where he "turned the Wheel

In Siam, however, the Sutta literature was not regarded as a source for the Buddha's life. Most—I would even like to say all—of the works on the Buddha's life relied on the later commentaries as sources. As late as the reign of Rama III (1824–51), an inscription referring to an event involving Kondanna referred to a commentary, the Manorathapurani (*Prachum charuek wat phra chetuphon*, 56). Nevertheless, the four (or six) essential events in the life of the Buddha according to the tradition of the Suttas remained intact in Thai works, although the commentaries gave importance to other events as well. Jinakalamalipakaranam specifies the "horoscopic" events in the Buddha's life as follows:

> It is said that, by nature, all Buddhas descend into their mother's wombs, go forth to pursue spiritual salvation, preach the First Sermon, perform magic of duality (*yamakapatihariya*) when the moon is in the Uttrasalha section of the sky; the Buddhas attain Enlightenment, are born, and die when the moon is in the Visakha section of the sky; the descent from the heaven known as Devorohana occurs when the moon is in the Assujja section of the sky. (Ratanapañña 1958, 44)

The series of important events in the Buddha's life in this version are: the descent into his mother's womb; his birth; the "going forth;" the First Sermon; Devorohana; the performance of magic of duality; and his death.

3. It should be observed that in this series of events in his life, the Buddha is the sole "dramatis persona" of the entire account. His actions after the Sangha is established are condensed into only two events, namely, the descent from the Tavatimsa (Devorohana) and the performance of magic of duality, both of which are totally unrelated to the historical circumstances in which the Buddha found himself.

Nowadays when we narrate the biography of someone, we commonly discuss the individual's relationship to others, and we relate the individual's responses to historical circumstances. For this reason the episodes in the Buddha's life concerning his chief disciples, his return to Kapilavatthu to preach a sermon to his father, the story of Ananda, the story of Devadatta, and so forth are important, but only when we see the Buddha as a human being (Niramanakaya, the Created Body), who necessarily interacts with his environment through people and circumstances. The traditional concept of the Buddha's story, on the other hand, treats him as a Buddha only (Dhammakaya and Sambhogakaya, the body of Dhamma and the Glorified Body), and most assuredly sees interactions with his environment as irrelevant. In the traditional Buddha's story it is not necessary for important episodes to have any bearing on other people, and the same is true for the life of the Buddha according to

---

of the Law" (preached the first sermon); the site where he preached the sermon on purity (Ovadapatimokkha); the site where he returned from the Tavatimsa heaven (Devorohana). The structural outline observed by each monastic order's tradition may differ somewhat, although the accounts of the Buddha's life in both orders contain the same events. See *Chotmaihet haeng phuttha-anachak*, 121–2; and Ratchabanditsapha 1932.

ancient oral tradition. As we have already pointed out, the Jinakalamali does not even mention the name of Sariputra, the most important disciple in Theravada Buddhism (for the importance of Sariputra in Theravada Buddhism see Conze 1957, 90–3).

One very good example of the disinterest in the historical context of the Buddha's life in this traditional writing can be seen in the absence of reference to Maghapuja. The events of Maghapuja day are vitally important to the Sangha, because it was on this day that the Buddha first gave the sermon called Ovadapatimokkha. Afterwards it became the Buddha's practice to give the Ovada to the assembly of monks every half lunar month. In olden times the Ovadapatimokkha was regarded in Siam as one of the "hearts" of Buddhism (see Phra ratchakamnot mai, no. 33, in *KTSD*, V, 313–8). Subsequently this custom was discontinued, and instead the Buddha permitted the assembly of monks to recite the monastic regulations every half lunar month (Wachirayan 1980, II, 5). We can see that this custom, which lies at the foundation of the Sangha, had its inception on this day. But the Sangha itself is of no great importance to the traditional life of the Buddha, so this event is ignored. Even the royal ceremony for Maghapuja was, after all, organized only in the Fourth Reign (Chulachomklao 1960, 127).

THE IMPORTANCE OF THE COMMENTARIES

It has been mentioned above that the information used in writing the Buddha's story has tended to come from the commentaries rather than from the canon. In addition to the fact that no complete story of the Buddha is available in the Tipitaka, there is an even more important reason that the canon was not a source of religious knowledge in Sukhothai and Ayutthaya.

I believe that the main reason the Tipitaka was not as dominant as the commentaries over religious thought in Siam arose from the fact that this religious tradition came from foreign lands (from both the Mon country and Ceylon), what we refer to broadly as Ceylonese Buddhism (*lankawong*). In all probability the Tipitaka (Theravada version) existed in Siam before the propagation of Ceylonese Buddhism. At the very least, Pali was already known in Sukhothai. Every instance in which Pali is used in the Sukhothai inscriptions, *khom* characters are employed rather than the Sinhalese characters that had been taught from Ceylonese texts. *Khom* characters also prevailed for writing Pali in the central plains of Siam, and they continued to prevail until the late eighteenth century. All of this suggests that the Thai were already acquainted with Pali in *khom* characters, and the Pali texts which were well-known were bound to be from the Tipitaka in *khom* before the spread of Ceylonese Buddhism to Siam. When monks from Sukhothai, Ayutthaya, and Lanna traveled to study religion in the Mon country or Ceylon, the most important texts for them were the commentaries, because the Tipitaka was already present in their own countries. Going abroad to study meant learning from the commentaries; otherwise, there was no need to go abroad. Understandably, the attention given to the Tipitaka by the monks who were "graduates" of the

Ceylonese school decreased, and educated monks held the commentaries in high esteem. Commentaries meant texts from abroad, while the Tipitaka was a "local" text, so monk-intellectuals placed great importance on the commentaries. When King Lithai cited commentaries in his Three Worlds cosmology (*Traiphum phra ruang*), at the time it was regarded as a mark of distinction. That is to say, he was able to cite "up-to-date" commentaries on a par with monks who had gone to the Mon country or to Ceylon for their ordinations. The commentaries dominated the education of monks in Siam, especially in the central plains, for a long time.

All Pali works written in Thailand are similar to the Traiphum cosmology in the sense that they favor the commentaries over the Tipitaka, with the sole exception being the Mamgalatthadipani which makes extensive use of the Tipitaka. In the time of King Borommakot when religious missions were dispatched from Ayutthaya to Ceylon, the king sent as a gift ninety-seven texts, not one of which was canonical. All were commentaries, grammatical texts, and the like, including some which had been composed originally in Ceylon such as the complete works of Buddhaghosa. Answers given by Thai monks to royal queries tended to cite commentaries more than the canon. Even the term "*phra bali*," reserved in later times for canonical texts, was once used differently to refer to the commentaries as well as the canon, for example in the First Reign (*Prachum phraratchaputcha,* 97).

In modern times Thai scholars tend to rank the canon highest in a hierarchy of validity, while the commentaries, sub-commentaries, manuals, and so forth have progressively less validity and credibility. Some scholars nowadays even rank the canon in terms of declining credibility: the Sutta, the Vinaya, and the Abhidhamma, respectively. Religious texts are arranged in a vertical order according to their validity, with the Tipitaka at the top and the manuals at the bottom, although this notion has arisen only in recent times with the critical approach taken towards religious studies. In former times it is probable that the view of the validity of religious texts meant that they were arranged in a horizontal rather than a vertical order. That is to say, the Tipitaka was at the center, and because the canon was thought to be not easily comprehended, it was surrounded by the commentaries, sub-commentaries, grammars, manuals, and other texts. These latter texts did not contradict the Tipitaka but supplemented it and made it more accessible and more accurate. The validity of the Tipitaka and the other texts was thus equal; one was no better than the other, as we believe to be the case today. The conventional Thai reckoning of Buddhist councils in Ceylon included Buddhaghosa's trip to Ceylon and his translation of the commentaries from Sinhalese into Pali as the Sixth Council (the Tipitaka was already in Pali by that time) (Wannarat 1978, 98–112). The history of Buddhist councils terms this corpus of commentaries the Atthakathapitaka (Wannarat 1978, 102). A legend of Buddhaghosa's composition of the Visuddhimagga tells that a certain deity repeatedly stole the manuscript from him, causing him to rewrite it three times. When the deity returned the three rewritten manuscripts to Buddhaghosa who showed them to the assembly of monks, it was found that all three were absolutely identical. As this legend implies, the Visuddhimagga endured as absolute truth, and for this reason, however many times it was rewritten, the texts would never differ. All this demonstrated the belief that the commentaries were as valid as the Tipitaka, rather than being subordinate to the canon as we believe nowadays.

In reality, however, there is a difference between the commentaries and the canon. The canon, especially the Sutta section, is clearly more "rationalist" than the commentaries. In the parts concerning the life of the Buddha, for example, the Sutta makes hardly any references to miracles. Prince Siddhattha's "going forth" is not neglected, but he takes his leave from his relatives. He ceases his ascetic practices by dint of his own will with no mention of Indra playing his harp and admonishing the prince. The Buddha resolves by himself to end his life without the warnings of Mara. And so forth. All these episodes make the Buddha more humanlike. The sources for the life of the Buddha that had be of the dhammographic kind thus did not use the Sutta for information, as opposed to the commentaries that narrated the Buddha's life in terms of his "Dhamma body" and the "Glorified body." And since the commentaries and the canon were regarded as equally valid, there was every reason to use the commentaries as a basis for writing the Buddha's life.

The respect paid to the commentaries began to decline in the early Bangkok period. Many of the royal queries put to the monks in the first Bangkok reign amounted to an inquiry into the contradictions in the commentarial literature. This critical approach in terms of logic was the primary cause of the erosion of the high status of the commentaries. In some cases the monks admitted that the commentaries conflicted with *atthathibai* (or what we now call *takka* or logic). For example, the high-ranking monk Phutthakhosachan in the First Reign admitted that one of his explanations was wrong because he had relied on a commentary called Paramatthadipani and "had not been careful enough in considering the logic (*atthathibai*) underlying the Pali writings" (*Prachum phraratchaputcha*, 55–7).

The decline in respect shown the commentaries became really visible, however, only in the religious movement called the Thammayutika Nikai, because the basis of this movement was the reinstatement of the canon. Reinstatement of a basic text is characteristic of religious reform movements in other countries, religions, and periods as well. Prince Mongkut, the leader of this movement, referred to the Tipitaka as "the big Pali text" and to the commentaries as "texts of countless fables and legends." He stated clearly that he would neither defer to nor be intimidated by those ancient individuals known as "master-commentators."' He proclaimed himself a believer in Buddhism: "but I believe only in its essential messages; the husks and the dirty and nasty trash that have accumulated and become mixed up with Buddhism are not part of my faith" (*Prachum phraratchaputcha*, 243–8).

FROM "PHRA PATHOMSOMPHOTHIKATHA" TO PRINCE WACHIRAYAN'S "THE LIFE OF THE BUDDHA"

PHRA PATHOMSOMPHOTHIKATHA (HEREINAFTER CALLED *PP*)

Various authors had been writing Pali works on the life of the Buddha known as Pathomsomphot and works with similar titles for a very long time. The oldest version was probably a text composed in Burma or Ceylon, though the original is no longer extant. But its title is mentioned in Gandhavamsa, a Pali compendium found in Burma and Ceylon (see Malalasekera 1960). The text known as Pathomsomphot was not popular in either Burma or Ceylon, as it is not cited in other works. In Siam the Buddha's life with this title existed in many versions since Ayutthaya times. Many Thai-language versions existed in Lanna, the evidence so far indicating that the oldest recension was copied in 1769. According to *A Bibliography of Palmleaf Manuscripts and Blackbooks from Chiang Mai District* by Sommai Premchit, six versions of Pathomsomphot in different styles have been found in Chiang Mai City district alone. *A Bibliography of Palmleaf Manuscripts from Lampang* (The Northern Palmleaf Manuscript Research Project, Institute of Social Science Research, Chiang Mai University, 1981) grants the title Pathomsomphot to versions found in a great many Lampang monasteries, even more than in Chiang Mai itself, suggesting that the Buddha's life written up as Pathomsomphot was widespread in the Lanna region.

As far as can be ascertained from an inspection of these bibliographies, all versions of the Lanna Pathomsomphot treat the Buddha's life in the dhammographical tradition. The story begins in the time before his human birth and continues into his coming as a future Buddha. That is to say, the life of the Buddha embraces all time, beyond the human condition.

There are also many versions in the central plains, but those found so far are all in Pali. We can assume that a Thai version existed before Prince Paramanuchit wrote his own Thai edition, as will be discussed below. I am not in a position to examine the version in the National Library, so I am unable to say whether or not that text treats the Buddha's life as dhammography or as biography. Nevertheless, when Prince Paramanuchit composed his life of the Buddha first in Pali and later on translated it into Thai, there already existed in Siam Pali and Thai versions of the life of the Buddha, and these versions were probably available to the court as well as to him. This fact is rather important, because unlike some of the literary activity in early Bangkok, Paramanuchit's undertaking was not an attempt to recover literary or scholarly work which had been known and then lost to the royal collection.

The Pali version of the work informs us that King Rama III, through Prince Kraisonwichit, invited Prince Paramanuchit to write a Pali "treatise" on the life of the Buddha, and in 1825 he finished the work after seven months. Prince Paramanuchit tells us about his own authorship as follows:

> Now I have finished composing a text about the Buddha with the title of Pathamabhisambodhi, which is an old text with defective passages. Additionally, I have elaborated

> the account where the original was inadequate. This undertaking is to fulfill the wishes of the exalted king.

The passage clearly shows that there already existed a text called Pathamabhisambodhi, and that the prince "elaborated the account where the original was inadequate." But examining Phrapathomsomphot, the Thai translation of this work (Paramanuchit 1962), leads us to the conclusion that Prince Paramanuchit did more than simply edit the original. He also made many interpolations in a number of places. For example, when he related the descent of the Buddha from the Dusit heaven he inserted material from the Jatakas about the Bodhisatta's accumulation of merit in previous lives before his incarnation as Prince Vessantara, and said, "Now my response to the royal request will resume with the account of the Dusit heaven in the old text. Continuing on, the authors of the texts then composed more praises of the Buddha's virtues for another two chapters, saying . . . " (*PP*, 42). These kinds of remarks are common throughout the Thai version, even though Prince Paramanuchit was not himself the original author of the entire text. What is significant is that he *chose* to proceed in this way from selecting the texts he wanted to translate to deciding what comments of his own to insert according to his own views. The important point that is apparent in this work is that the prince was responsible for *choosing* to make the text appear as it does.

Rama III also requested Prince Paramanuchit to translate this work of his into Thai, which we know today as *PP*. Rama III apparently had a special interest in Pathamasambodhi, the life of the Buddha preferred by previous kings in the Bangkok dynasty as well. In 1831 Rama III had the Pathamasambodhi story painted on the walls of the sanctuary at Wat Phra Chetuphon, and he favored the recitation of this life of the Buddha in years when the royally-sponsored recitation of the Vessantara Jataka was not held (Chulachomklao 1960, 71). As a matter of fact, the Thai version of the Pathomsomphot had already existed for some time. In sermon form, it was sixty chapters in length, and in the First Reign the king had attended the sermons from time to time (*Chotmaihet phraratchaphongsawadan*, 6, C.S. 1164, "banchi raichue"). Rama III's invitation to Prince Paramanuchit to write both Thai and Pali versions must not, therefore, have been motivated by the unavailability of the works, but for some other reason he simply wanted to have a life of the Buddha in Pali and Thai.

PP is different from other versions of the story of the Buddha written in Ceylon and Siam. This version does not emphasize the theme of the Bodhisatta's accumulation of merit, and thus it does not begin with the Bodhisatta's vow to become a Buddha. It is true that *PP* opens with a brief history of the lineage that gave rise to the first king in the world who was said to be the Bodhisatta (the Aggana Sutta does not specify that the first king, Mahasammata, was the Bodhisatta; only later do the Ceylonese texts claim that Mahasammata was the Bodhisatta). The purpose of the first chapter, on the contrary, is not to relate the past lives of the Bodhisatta but to follow the lineage of the Buddha as Prince Siddhattha, from the first king down to the Buddha's father, King Suddhodhana, including the history of the Sakya clan. When examined from this perspective, the content of chapter one of *PP* truly concerns this world, because the Buddha's ancestors were all human. Even the Bodhisatta himself was a descendant of human beings rather than from twenty-four previous Buddhas who had attained enlightenment before him.

This beginning of the story alone is enough to distinguish *PP* from other comparable works, because it treats the Buddha's life as biography rather than dhammography. The main theme of *PP* is concentrated on the life and works of Gotama Buddha, from his birth through his enlightenment and the propagation of his teachings until his extinction. Although the final section of the text ends with the division of the Buddha's relics and their ultimate disappearance, drawn from the Anagatavamsa, these parts expand the temporal framework in the life of the Buddha beyond human time (that is, into an as yet unrealized future). But when we consider the work in its entirety, this final section comprises but a small part of what is a very large text, whose core is the life of Gotama Buddha which occurred in the empirical time of this world (or at least time that can be reckoned according to the calendar).

The concern to cast the Buddha's life in this-world empirical time is clearly discernible in the first part of "the death of the chief disciples" (*PP*, 445–7), because there is an account of the time following the Buddha's first awarenesses and of certain events in his life from year to year up to the age of twenty-seven. After the enlightenment the account jumps to his forty-fifth year, the year that involves "the death of the chief disciples" and his Nibbana. The failure to provide an account for all forty-five years is because it was difficult to do so, particularly when the evidence in the commentaries or even the canon itself did not specify the dates of events in the Buddha's life, nor did it arrange events in order. Nevertheless, this account of time gave the Buddha's life biographical characteristics, because it was lived within the context of this-world empirical time as distinct from metaphysical time (such as eons, *kalpa*, *asamgkya*, *buddhantara*, or intervals of Buddhas, etc., all of which are meaningful in terms of Dhamma but not in terms of verifiable, empirical time).

The main outline of the story told in *PP* is not very different from that told in older accounts, the only exception being that *PP* omits previous incarnations and the lives of former Buddhas. But the important thing is that *PP* also contains various additional episodes. The Jinakalamalipakaranam, for example, mentions the essential events in the Buddha's life as follows: the entry into his mother's womb; his birth; the going forth; his enlightenment; the first sermon; Devorohana; the practice of the magic of duality; and his Nibbana. But *PP* inserts many other episodes between these essential ones, beginning with an account of the Sakya line and the wedding of King Suddhodhana. And it adds after the Buddha's birth the prophecy of the signs of the Great Man on his body and an account of his life before he became an ascetic; after his going forth it adds the practice of extreme asceticism and the Lady Sujata story; after his enlightenment it adds the invitation of the god Brahma to propagate his teaching; after the first sermon it adds the disciple Yasa's story, the subduing of the Uruvela ascetics, and the account of the two chief disciples, Sariputta and Moggallana, his return to Kapilavatthu and his encounter with his wife, the ordination of King Sakya, and the account of his father's death; and after Devorohana it adds the death of the chief disciples. The inclusion of all these episodes detracts from the Buddha as a "principle of Dhamma," while the essential events mentioned in Jinakalamali-pakaranam condense the Buddha's life into episodes related only to the principal of Dhamma. But the inclusion of Yasa's story, the account of Uruvelabasa, the account of the Buddha's kinsmen in the Sakya lineage, and so forth make the Buddha's life just like any other human life related to the human and cultural environment (for example, the account of the belief of the Uruvela-Kassapa or the pride of the members of the Sakya clan in their seniority to the Buddha). In other words, when we read the Buddha's life in *PP* we feel the Buddha's humanity more than when we read the dhammographical Jinakalamalipakaranam where he is nothing but a Buddha (as the Dhamma body and Glorified body).

Another interesting point is that although *PP* does not deny the various miracles in the Buddha's life, on many occasions it attempts to explain them metaphorically in terms of Dhamma. For example, the miracles that accompanied the birth of the Bodhisatta are explained as signs of eventual Buddhahood: the world shook at the moment of his enlightenment; that the mute were able to speak was a "sign" he had achieved the Four Foundations of Mindfulness; that he was able to take seven steps at his birth is explained as a "sign" of his attaining the Seven Requisites (*PP*, 60–62).

An explanation given elsewhere in *PP* about the Bodhisatta's birth adds another factor: "it has been asked whether the Buddha was walking on air or on the ground, whether he was an adult or a child, and whether he was dressed or naked." The answers are that he walked on the ground but was seen by others as walking on air; that he was actually a child but was seen by others as an adult; and that he was actually naked but was seen by others as fully clothed (*PP*, 63). These explanations render the Bodhisatta's miracles true in terms of experience, while the supernatural aspects are in the eye of the beholder.

This reinterpretation of miracles was not new but was an old tradition taken from the Sutta in which miracles were always understood rationally. The fact that the author of *PP* has chosen to follow this Sutta tradition is of great interest, because as mentioned earlier, in old Thai society the canon was not so significant as the commentaries as a source of knowledge. The interpretation of miracles in *PP* thus corresponds to trends in the religious movement discernible from the early Bangkok period which had begun to lean in the direction of greater rationalism.

As with other kinds of supernatural qualities, the quality of Buddhahood is seen in *PP* as more a matter of spirituality rather than physical strength. At one point *PP* describes the physical strength of the Buddha as equal to that of ten herds of elephants, and it even describes in great detail how much physical strength that amounts to. But then *PP* says, "Actually, if the Bodhisatta had used this great strength alone he would not have been able to be enlightened as to the nature of suffering, nor would he have been able to relieve its cause, namely craving, nor would he have been able to practice the noble eightfold path, nor would he have been able to be enlightened as to the fruit of Nibbana, nor would he have achieved victory over the three forms of Mara." All these are only possible because he possesses other forms of mental power (strength through knowledge), such as the "knowledge of the ten powers," the power of the five "higher knowledges," which enabled the Buddha to be victorious.

This emphasis on spiritual aspects corresponds with the interpretation of Buddhism in favor with a certain group of intellectuals from the beginning of the Bangkok period (see below), and it was consistent with parts of the Thammayut doctrine.

Although *PP* is different from its predecessors, it is in large part a work based on information from these older versions of the Buddha's life. Some traces of "dhammography" are, therefore, to be found in this "biography." Besides, *PP* is basically a text for Buddhist sermons, and monks did occasionally use it for reciting sermons at royal ceremonies. The dhammographical elements in the story to a considerable extent thus suited the purpose of those sermons at the time. "The account of the future Buddha," for example, was included in the life of the Buddha in order to stress the important principle of Dhamma that Buddhahood is for all time; it is timeless (*PP*, 367–85). When these features of "dhammography" are gathered together, however, they are still less distinct than the more prominent features of "biography."

PATHOMSOMPHOT OF SUPREME PATRIARCH SA PUSSADEVA

Not long after the emergence of *PP* and its success in generating interest in the biographical approach to the Buddha's life, and after the so-called religious reform of the Thammayut was well-established, another work on the life of the Buddha appeared that was even more biographical in character. It is worth pointing out that this life of the Buddha used the same approach as *PP* and did not contradict that work as we might expect coming from a Thammayut author who differed with monks of the Mahanikai. This life of the Buddha, Pathomsomphot (hereinafter called *P*), is by Supreme Patriarch Sa Pussadeva (Sa 1979).

In the same manner as *PP*, *P* attempts to separate decisively the Buddha's life from that of the previous Buddhas. The reference to previous Buddhas over the last ninety-one eons is made only in order to stress that in this immense length of time a mere seven Buddhas appeared. This reference supports the emphasis at the beginning of *P* that Buddhahood is rare in the world (implying that the Buddha's life is therefore interesting, that Buddhism is an excellent religion, and that neither is commonplace) (*P*, 8).

The Bodhisatta is introduced into the story at the moment of his birth with no reference to his departure from the Dusit heaven (*P*, 11–2). This introduction gives a particularly strong impression of the Bodhisatta as a human being. The part that describes the signs of the Great Man on his body declares that the signs were based on belief in texts written by ascetics long before the present Buddha-age (*P*, 12–3). This reference makes the signs of the Great Man less miraculous, because they were merely the signs in which people believed at that time according to the texts. It is not the case that he possessed those signs because he was to become a Buddha.

The main source of information for *P* is the canon; the commentaries are totally ignored. The exclusive reliance on the canon was consistent with Thammayut doctrine which insisted on a return to the authentic, original texts. The Bodhisatta in *P*, therefore, discontinued his practice of extreme asceticism, as described in the Sutta, without Indra and his harp. Also in accordance with the Sutta, the Buddha realized his own death without exhortations from Mara the ogre. The going forth is described almost verbatim from the Sutta: "When the Buddha's kinsmen on both sides wept, their faces covered in tears," the Buddha departed for the ascetic life (*P*, 25).

It was the author's intention to reduce the importance of the commentaries. As he stated in the preface, "so that people will maintain a firm faith in the Buddha, information without canonical support will be discussed only briefly by using the interpretations of commentators of old" (*P*, 6).

The account in *P* also tried to relate the Buddha in the story to the world surrounding him. After the Buddha's visit to Rajagrha, *P* shifts its theme to the Buddha's "works" that manifest Dhamma: the proclamation of the Vinaya for the four who had become supporters of the faith. Then the story proceeds to the Buddha's death. In fact, this section concerning the Buddha's "works" brings forth the participation in the Buddha's life of people and social context, thus making the Buddha all the more into a human figure. And the style of the Buddha's life is all the more that of a biography as well.

The interpretation of the Buddha's experiences before the going forth in terms of explanation is also very interesting. *P* explains these experiences in the Bodhisatta's life in a way that would be useful to the Buddha in his subsequent propagation of the religion. For example, the Bodhisatta's enjoyment of life when he was a householder with a family prevented him from being castigated by his foes later for taking up the mendicant life as an escape from his failures as a layman (*P*, 23–4). When we compare *P* with *PP*, we can see that both works supply explanations, but what each work chooses to explain as well as the manner of explanation are different.

The basic purpose of *P* is to serve as a text for sermons by monks, but rather than allow the dhammographical elements to infiltrate the story, the work gives detailed translations of excerpts from the Suttas. Preaching sermons in this way was congruous with Thammayut thinking which proclaimed a return to the original texts. Hence the Sutta on the Wheel of the Law, the Sutta on the Not-Self, the Fire Sutta, and various teachings taken from the Sutta, are available in full translation in *P*.

THE LIFE OF THE BUDDHA BY PRINCE-PATRIARCH WACHIRAYAN

This version of the Buddha's life turns the Buddha into a completely historical figure in the sense that it attempts to put him into historical context. Its first appendix (Wachirayan 1980, I, 96–103) gives an account of the names of places as well as principalities and their capitals in northern India at the time of the Buddha according to the author's investigation of the canon and of western scholarly works. At the beginning of the story the Prince-Patriarch also described conditions in Jambudvipa and the way people in northern India lived during the Buddha's time. In the preface to the book the author explained clearly that he intended to compose a biography of the Buddha in the manner of a chronicler (*nak tamnan*) or, as we would say nowadays, a historian.

There is no question that the Prince-Patriarch's main source of information was the Sutta, which was also the case with *P* and which was congruous with Thammayut thinking.

In an attempt to present events in the Buddha's life in a rational ways the Prince-Patriarch explained miracles that appeared in the Sutta in terms of symbolism (or, as *PP* would say, "omens"). For example, the Bodhisatta's ability to take seven steps at birth is explained as a literary strategy that the ancient commentators used to allude to the Buddha's alternate residence in seven states (I, 104–5). There is even a second appendix in which the Prince-Patriarch explained these miracles rationally, "dismissing the miraculous meanings associated with the Buddha's birth." In this vein the author believed that in listening to the story of the Buddha's life which was steeped in miracles, one had to be selective and extract the essence: "Rather like eating a mangosteen or a rambutan, it is too acidic to eat the whole fruit. One has to peel off the rind first and take only the fleshy part—this is the way to eat such a fruit." Miracles involving the Buddha which were in olden days an integral part of the life of the Buddha (in order to show his Glorified Body) had become by that time merely "the rind" that had to be peeled off and discarded. Such an attitude was not, however, one that emerged only in this *Life* but evolved gradually from the time of *PP* (or even earlier), explaining all miracles in the Buddha's life in terms of "omens" or "parables."

Though it is unfinished, this *Life* has a structure that clearly makes it into biography, because we are made to see the development of a particular man through actions and works which are related to those of other individuals. This is not the account of an individual who is disconnected from other individuals of his time and whose life is patterned after important events in the lives of Buddhas that preceded him.

OTHER ARTISTIC EXPRESSIONS OF THE BUDDHA'S LIFE

The life of the Buddha, narrated in dhammographic form in Siam for centuries, gradually changed into biography. Beginning with *PP* through to *The Life* and manifested in the Ministry of Education's textbooks of moral instruction, the Buddha as a principle of Dhamma has become progressively less meaningful in the story of his life written in biographical form; it is now the Created Body of the Buddha as a human figure that lies at the center of the story. This change also corresponds with developments in the portrayal of the Buddha's life in painting during the early Bangkok period. Paintings of the Buddha that were popular in the Ayutthaya period and at the very beginning of the Bangkok period depicted him as a Buddha image and as a principle of Dhamma (the Glorified Body). In the illustrated Book of the Three Worlds, which dates from the reign of King Taksin, the Buddha as Prince Siddhattha before his ordination is portrayed as a human being like the kings and heroes of literature. Once the Bodhisatta has attained Buddhahood, however, the artist prefers to portray him in symbolic form such as a lotus or as the dais of the Master (Samnak nayok rathamontri, 1982). Mural paintings also reflect the same concept. Although there are many pictures of the Buddha, all of them are clearly Buddha images and

The Invulerable Buddha, Phra Nirantarai

are gilded. Still, from the Fourth Reign on, the Buddha in Thai mural paintings was portrayed as an image less frequently and in many cases was no longer gilded.[5] At the same time, the Thai began to see the Buddha less as a principle of Dhamma and worshipped him more as a "human being" (to the regret of the present writer, who sees in this trend a change in the direction of the profane).

In the field of sculpture a remarkable development occurred in the making of Buddha images during the Third Reign. The king commanded Prince Paramanuchit to select images of the Buddha in various postures from episodes in the Buddha's life. Additional postures were then created, and the total, including those already in use, amounted to forty (Atchara 1980, 206). The traditional postures of the Buddha were in fact also drawn from the Buddha's life, and what we refer to as the Four Postures depict the most significant episodes: seated (the Enlightenment); standing (the First Sermon); walking (Devorohana); and lying down (Death). It is obvious from these Four Postures of the Buddha image that, while they depict the Buddha's life, this is the life in dhammographic form only. The dhammic essence is distilled from the life of the Buddha and made graphic. The increase in postures to forty in all represents the addition of details to the life story which give significance to things that happened to the Buddha as a human being. In other words, the portrayal of the Buddha in statuary has also become biographical.

In artistic terms, Thai sculpture, which was dominated on the whole by images of the Buddha, departed significantly from convention during the Fourth Reign. When he ascended the throne, Mongkut had Buddha images cast to celebrate his safe deliverance from the threats and dangers at the hands of his enemies. He named these images the Invulnerable Buddha (Phra Nirantarai). The style created by the king for this Invulnerable Buddha image was unique in Thai sculpture, because it was the first time that the Buddha had been depicted realistically. The robe hangs on his body in pleats, as a cloth would hang in reality. The topknot (*ushanisha*), a prominent feature of the Buddha image throughout Asia, was not made for these images; the head is just like any other human head. The realism of Mongkut's Buddha

5. I am grateful to Professor Kamol Chaiyawattana of Thammasat University for kindly supplying this information.

images served as an inspiration and a model for art in Thailand up to modern times, and while it is easy for art historians to see western influence behind this change, Mongkut claimed that the departure from conventional images was made in order to conform to descriptions of the Buddha's features in the canon. It is indisputable, however, that this claim is an inadequate explanation for the changes. Wrinkles in the cloth, for example, are a change totally unrelated to any canonical material. Nor does western cultural influence explain the changes adequately. Deep down in the thinking of the Thai, I would suggest, a gradual change was taking place in the perception of the Buddha. Among the members of the elite and, later, throughout the general population as a result of modern education, the Buddha came to be seen more and more as a human being. He was an exalted human being, to be sure, but basically a human being all the same. The Buddha image according to convention—non-human, sexless, impersonal, and merely an abstraction of a principle—became less and less satisfying to Buddhists in Thailand. Realistic portrayals attempted to represent the Buddha in a way that was situated firmly in the modern Thai mind.

CHANGES IN RELIGIOUS THINKING DURING THE EARLY BANGKOK PERIOD

The evolution that took place in the Thai attitude towards the life of the Buddha is reflected clearly in these three works, written one after the other. The last two were written by leaders of the Thammayut movement, while the first work was written by an author who was in no direct way connected with the religious movement known as the Thammayut reform. Nevertheless, these three works are obviously related and lie within the same course of development. A number of historians of Thailand tend to think that the Thammayut movement marks a break from the religious thinking prevalent at the time of the movement's inception. And for that reason, the movement is frequently called a "religious reform" (see Lingat 1954). The Buddha's life in the Thammayut versions is not, however, what one might expect. That is to say, it is so close to the previous versions that we might even say it follows the same trends in religious thinking. So it would be prudent to review the development of this thinking in the early Bangkok period to see if we can realistically place the Thammayut in the context of the intellectual history of nineteenth century Siam.[6]

It is generally understood that the destruction at Ayutthaya by the Burmese caused confusion and decline in Thai Buddhism, which was not easily reversed by the founding of the new kingdom. The confusion and decline are understood to have occurred with respect to two components of Thai Buddhism: the Sangha; and the religious texts (Lingat 1958). The notion of a decline in Buddhism after the fall of Ayutthaya probably comes from an uncritical acceptance of the Thammayut's

6. The extent to which my ideas derive from three MA theses by Atchara Kanchanomai, Naruemon Thirawat, and Saichon Wannarat can be seen clearly in the references to their work in this section. However, responsibility for conclusions in this study rests solely with me.

outlook on Thai Buddhism. Prince Mongkut was reported by one of his disciples to have thought that, "the monastic order vanished from Siam when Ayutthaya fell to the Burmese" (Pawaret 1962, 2).

This misconception about the development of Thai Buddhism in the eighteenth and nineteenth centuries is the basis of the theory of "restoration of the faith" by post-Ayutthaya kings. Religious activities carried out by all Bangkok kings are seen as attempts to "restore" Buddhism to the perfect form supposed to have existed in Ayutthaya. The gathering together of religious texts by Taksin as well as Rama I is understood in this theory to be part of the restoration effort. The task, though difficult in the pre-printing age, was not insurmountable and was finally achieved. The restoration of the "pure" Sangha, however, was much more difficult, and no matter what measures the kings took, the Sangha was still "impure," "bad," and "not conforming to Buddhist principles." The Christian missionaries, who began arriving in Bangkok in the 1820s, even contributed to this "crisis in religion," according to the theory, and called for urgent reform. It was Prince Mongkut during his monkhood, claims the theory, who first succeeded in restoring the Sangha's purity by establishing the rival Thammayut "order." When the history of Buddhism in the early Bangkok period is looked at in this way, one cannot help seeing the movement known as the Thammayut as a change of great magnitude in the Thai Sangha.

But the Thammayut movement is quite unique in Thai history. The Thammayut, unlike any other monastic "order" established in Siam, originated locally, whereas other orders owed their inception to monks who had been to Ceylon or the Mon country for reordination. It was not the ruling king who supported the establishment of the new order, at least not in its initial stages. This situation differed from previous cases in which the king sponsored the dispatch of monks to other countries for reordination. The Thammayut order was a movement created and nurtured independently by a group of intellectuals in a society where there were no effective intellectuals outside the control of the state. According to its accepted history, the Thammayut movement seems to have emerged abruptly without an intellectual tradition within the society to support its growth. It is thus necessary for supporters of the "restoration" theory to conclude that the source of inspiration for the creation of the Thammayut order must have come from outside the society, and they state explicitly that this external origin was the west. The Thammayut is thus simultaneously a "restoration" of the traditional standard of monastic practice and an "adaptation" of that standard according to western science and "rationalism" (Griswold 1961). The similarity of texts on the life of the Buddha by Thammayut and non-Thammayut authors suggests that if the Thammayut movement was a change in religious thinking, it neither occurred abruptly nor was it unrelated to the trends in religious thinking that prevailed among intellectuals at that time.

From the beginning of the Bangkok period, changes in many aspects of elite life, including religious thinking, are perceptible. Their personal experiences, the way resources were shared among the elite, and changing socioeconomic conditions all resulted in change in intellectual and cultural domains as well. There is no doubt that the kings of early Bangkok undertook a number of significant religious activities, but their purpose was not the restoration of Ayutthayan Buddhism. Saichon Wannarat's 1982 study shows that these activities were aimed at "changing" rather than "restoring" the religious thinking of the Ayutthaya period.

Rama I's interest in encouraging the study of religious texts was distinctive in comparison with the kings of Ayutthaya. The king established a religious school within the grounds of the Temple of the Emerald Buddha when it was first constructed, and monks and novices received instruction in Pali texts from officials in the Department of Buddhist Learning (*Krom ratchabandit*). Princes and nobles followed the king's lead and invited learned teachers to give religious instruction to monks and novices (Saichon 1982, 95). In the realm of ideas Rama I's thinking was in many ways "rationalist" when it came to his belief (Saichon 1982, 102–3). He attempted to make religious practice more comprehensible and less ritualistic. He admonished people to "understand the Thai meaning in each precept" when they vowed to keep the precepts (Saichon 1982, 104). The king also had many Pali works such as the Questions of Milinda, Jinakalamalipakaranam and others translated into Thai, and he commissioned the compilation of religious texts such as a Thai version of the Three Worlds cosmology (*Traiphum lokawinitchai*). These royal initiatives had no precedent when Rama I is compared to the kings at Ayutthaya. It is probable that parts of the canon and the more famous commentaries were translated into Thai by his order to commemorate the cremation of his brother, the Front Palace prince (Thiphakorawong n.d., 254). The trend towards the vernacularization of religious teaching had begun long before Prince Mongkut gave sermons in simple Thai and before the Thammayut undertook the translation of parts of the canon from Pali into Thai. Rama I's interest in the canon, as opposed to the commentaries, is also worth noting. In the twentieth year of his reign a list was compiled of sermons given to him by Buddhist monks which shows that of 237 texts recited to him as sermons, 202 were from the Sutta (Saichon 1982, 119). Considering the traditional pre-dominance of the commentaries in Siam, we can see that this interest in canonical literature represented a significant event of religious change. The author of *Traiphum lokawinitchai* pointed out that listening to the Vessantara Jataka—the preeminent Jataka which yielded much merit for those who heard it—actually yielded less merit than listening to the Vinaya, the Sutta, and the Paramattha (the canon) (Saichon 1982, 113). At the same time, he emphasized spiritual gain over the material benefits of merit-making. He said that each and every time one realized the impermanence of all things (*anicatta*) one gained more spiritual benefit than one did from constructing a pavilion and dedicating it to a Buddha image; more than from keeping the precepts and more than from practicing the Dhamma of compassion and indiscrimination (*brahmavihara*) (Saichon 1982, 114). In an action unprecedented in the history of the Thai legal system, the king promulgated royal decrees for the Sangha, the first time the state attempted to exert direct control over the Sangha rather than work through the monastic institution itself (see the Kotphrasong in *KTSD*, IV, 164–228). It then became a custom for all subsequent kings to issue laws of this kind, though these of course are not contained in the Three Seals Law.

Rama I's policies with respect to religion may be summarized as follows:

1. As far as the Sangha is concerned, his policy was aimed at making monastic discipline more rigorous and at promoting knowledge of the Pali texts.

2. In terms of religious belief, the king encouraged understanding of religious texts, and thus he regarded the translation and composition of texts in Thai as essential. At the same time, he sought to make religious belief more rational; at the very least, all that was taught should be logical. Many of his queries addressed to ecclesiastical dignitaries concerned contradictory statements in the commentaries.

3. He placed great importance on religious practice, especially because the interpretation of religion among the elite was increasingly spiritual rather than ritualistic.

4. Probably because of factors mentioned earlier, there was greater interest in the canon, not only in the compilation of its various parts but also in the convening of the Buddhist Council during the First Reign. There is no doubt that Rama I's Buddhist Council was highly charged with political purpose, but the idea of organizing a Buddhist Council to enhance political prestige had not even occurred to any Ayutthaya king. The political benefit to be derived from organizing the Council was realized only as a result of the esteem for the canon itself among those who held political sway.

These policies were not entertained and supported by Rama I alone but had their foundations in the religious outlook shared by large numbers of the elite (Saichon 1982). And for that reason, we can observe the continuation of these policies in subsequent reigns. The fact that these policies continued to be pursued without substantial protest indicates that these attitudes toward religion on the part of the elite were becoming even more widespread.

According to the royal chronicles, both Rama II and Rama III took an interest in enforcement of strict monastic practice. On some occasions, such as in 1842, serious disciplinary violations resulted in the disrobing of large numbers of monks (Thiphakorawong 1961, II, 61). As far as the encouragement of religious instruction is concerned, Rama III issued an authoritative plea for more extensive teaching in the monasteries. The senior ecclesiastical hierarchy was asked to provide more Pali study. Monk-teachers who had many degree holders among their students would have their stipends increased; those with few degree holders would have their stipends reduced (Atchara 1980, 99–100). Rama III promoted spiritual practice as well as religious studies. In all the monasteries he built or renovated he had meditation quarters (*khana kuti*) constructed for monks who wanted to practice meditation. Members of the aristocracy who built monasteries in this reign followed the king's example. Prince Rakronnaret ordered Krompalat Kham to build Wat Phleng as a meditation center, and he gathered there meditation masters who usually roamed the kingdom (Atchara 1980, 175–6). The importance of the canon itself was still recognized. Rama III had many copies made, one of which he presented as a gift to Cambodia. He also commissioned translations of the canon into Thai, most of which, it would appear, were from the Sutta (Atchara 1980, 93–4; Naruemon 1982, 125).

It is obvious that the major trends of this religious movement had started in the elite class at least from the very beginning of the Bangkok period. Saichon (1982, ch. 1) even argues that this kind of religious interpretation had already taken shape by the end of the Ayutthaya period. These trends, when analyzed, are not incongruous with the orientation and principles of the Thammayut. On the contrary, they were one and the same movement.

THE RELIGIOUS MOVEMENT KNOWN AS THE THAMMAYUT

Previous studies of the emergence of the Thammayut have been carried to two mutually exclusive extremes. Earlier studies tend to view the founding of the Thammayut as a purely religious movement with no political implications whatsoever, the best example of this view being the work of Prince Damrong (1954, 21–49). The other extreme position views the founding of the Thammayut order in political terms only, completely unconnected to any religious movement at all (e.g., Ki 1975). The truth, in my opinion, probably lies somewhere in between these two extremes.

As for the political aspects, the excellent work by Naruemon Thirawat (1982, 45–141) renders any further discussion of the matter here unnecessary. However, any political movement will be effective only when its ideas are rooted in society. Utterly new ideas will not be understood by one's followers, let alone induce the faith that would transform them into a political force. Before Prince Mongkut disrobed and ascended the throne, he had at least 130 monastic disciples (Atchara 1980, 158; Naruemon 1982, 105); Thammayut teachings were spreading to the provinces, to the tributary states, and to another country (Ceylon). Prince Mongkut's political ingenuity is beyond doubt, but this ingenuity in itself is not sufficient to explain the enthusiasm of monks and novices who supported him and who believed in the Thammayut unless they were completely taken in as political pawns by Prince Mongkut. In instances where political movements take the form of "peasant revolts" led by mystics (*phi bun*), we look for explanations behind the followers' devotion towards their leaders, rather than credit the blind adherence that we find described in official sources. For the Thammayut, then, it is equally reasonable to look for explanations behind the devotion of a particular group towards Prince Mongkut. To do so requires us to investigate the origins of the Thammayut as a religious movement. In summary, it should be said that the political and religious movements respectively are not necessarily in conflict to the point that they are mutually exclusive. Actually, some of the success of Prince Mongkut's political movement must be attributed to the fact that it was congruous with a religious movement that had existed in Thai society for a long time. The potentiality of being a Thammayut follower existed before the Thammayut's inception and for this reason I think it is worthwhile to examine the Thammayut in the context of the wider religious movement, which is what I intend to do in the rest of this paper.

In studies of the Thammayut's origins as a religious movement there has been a tendency to treat the Thammayut separately from the religious movement that was already underway in Thai society. Thammayut teachings are thus presented as a novelty, even though Prince Mongkut's inspiration is attributed explicitly to a foreign origin, namely to Mon monks (see Pawaret 1962; Wachirayan 1957; Chulachomklao 1956; Narathip n.d.). Consequently, it is not possible to explain the basis of Mongkut's thought without referring to the inflow of ideas from outside, as in the work of Griswold who gives credit to the American missionaries (Griswold 1961). But the fundamentals of Thammayut thinking cannot have come from the west. As Naruemon has shown, the first missionaries arrived in Bangkok in 1828, three years after Mongkut had established his group for practicing Dhamma. Bishop Pallegoix arrived in 1830 and is likely to have had even less to do with the founding of the Thammayut (Naruemon 1982, 83).

One of the most prominent features of the Thammayut movement is its emphasis on strict adherence to the Vinaya code of monastic discipline in such matters as the style of wearing the robe, the handling of money, the way a man was ordained, the way Pali was pronounced, and so forth. Whether or not Thammayut monastic practice actually adhered to the Vinaya is another question altogether, but it is certainly the case that Thammayut leaders claimed to observe the Vinaya more strictly than other monks. The attempt to emphasize strict observance of the Vinaya—or the attempt to make others believe that this was the case—is closely connected to the concept of preserving the purity of the Buddhist order.

Of all the different ways that Buddhism could be endangered, the most significant was the disappearance of Buddhist ascetics, because the withering away of the Enlightenment, religious study, religious practice, the Sangha, and the relics all stemmed from or were dependent on the disappearance of Buddhist ascetics. In other words, belief in the Five Disappearances led to the idea that keeping the monastic order pure was an important condition for ensuring the continuation of the Buddhist religion. The existence of a pure Sangha was vital because only with a pure Sangha could authentic ordinations without blemish be performed, and thus would the order procreate itself. Whenever a society of Buddhists thought that there were not enough pure monks left to perform ordinations, it could expect that Buddhism would eventually die out in that land. It was necessary, therefore, to send monks for ordinations whenever such a situation arose. Thus kingdoms in Southeast Asia and Ceylon exchanged missions back and forth many times through the centuries.

The efforts of Thai kings from Taksin onwards to disrobe "shameless" (*alajji*) monks and to "clean up" the Sangha stemmed from their determination to keep the Sangha pure. This was a duty expected of a Dhammaraja ruler in Thai society. When Prince Mongkut insisted that the Sangha at that time had decayed to the point that pure monks would eventually disappear from the Siamese kingdom, it became necessary to "reinstitute" a pure order. This course of action was well understood in those days, because it was along the same lines as the action taken by Buddhist leaders, in fact, by all the early Bangkok kings. However, the establishment of a pure group of monks went too far in the sense that Prince Mongkut had no political power to "clean up" the Sangha. This creation of a new monastic order, guaranteed to be pure and ordained without the slightest blemish, was considered to be a highly significant contribution to religion in the eyes of Buddhists. And whether he intended to or not, Prince Mongkut was demonstrating his "royal might" by this action, an action which in the past had been the prerogative only of Great Dhammaraja rulers of Buddhist kingdoms to pursue.

The Thammayut order tried to make its teachings comprehensible to the lay community at large. Prince Mongkut established a printing house in his monastery to print religious pamphlets for distribution, and the Thammayut gave sermons twice on the Buddhist "sabbath" (*wan phra*), in the morning and afternoon. In giving these sermons, Thammayut monks preferred to use vernacular speech, rather than Pali phrases, to facilitate comprehension, and they also trained their Thammayut disciples to give sermons in the same way (Atchara 1980, 149). These initiatives seem to be innovations, and it is easy to compare them to the methods of propagation used by the missionaries. In fact, however, these initiatives are one and the same with Rama I's promotion of Thai translation of Pali texts, his commissioning of the composition of religious texts in Thai, and Rama III's commissioning of inscriptions at Wat Phra Chetuphon to give religious instruction in Thai language. The idea that religion must be based on understanding rather than on ritualistic practice was neither an innovation of Mongkut nor was it a western borrowing. It was already a prominent feature of the religious movement underway among members of the elite in Thai society at least from the first Bangkok reign.

Prince Mongkut proclaimed that return to the original teachings of the Buddha was the heart of Thammayut practice (Naruemon 1982, 75–8). In his "In praise of the Dhamma" he wrote,

> The Buddha's words were uttered from the mouth of one who was completely free of defilements. They are words which have value for attaining salvation. As for the statements of the learned commentators, they are impregnated with the defilements of people steeped in defilements (*buthuchon*) (quoted in Naruemon 1982, 82).

Prince Mongkut also "encouraged the study of religious texts and was not content with studying the Vinaya as were the Mon monks. He urged study of the Sutta as well" (Chulachomklao 1956, 46).

The return to the original texts—i.e., to the canon—actually formed an important part of the religious movement which began at least as early as the first Bangkok reign when the commentaries began to be questioned and on some occasions even opposed. The return to the canon on Mongkut's part was thus congruous with an existing trend in the religious movement, and it can be said that Mongkut's position was also congruous with Rama III's order to Mongkut and the Thammayut to translate the Sutta into Thai. The claim to have returned to the canon was seen as correct and proper because the canon was rising in status to become the foremost repository of Truth, surpassing the commentaries. This change in the canon's status did not occur abruptly, but required the passage of time and the actions of others for a long while before Prince Mongkut could establish the Thammayut order.

The attention given to the canon, especially the Sutta, deeply affected the thinking of the elite in the early Bangkok period and led in the direction of what we may loosely describe as "rationalism."[7] The nature of this rationalism is clearly visible in the

Suttas which themselves were probably more responsible for the spread of "rational" thinking among Thai intellectuals than western ideas which had not yet found their way to Siam in the early Bangkok period.

This rationalism was yet another notable feature of the Thammayut movement. Prince Mongkut was averse to all explanations based on tradition. He declared that when he first began to practice meditation, he was dissatisfied with his teachers who, when asked for reasons for particular practices, could give no answer except by calling on the authority of tradition. Mongkut attacked the Sayamvamsa monks (now called the Mahanikai) for their disrespect towards the canon and for their failure to act according to the Pali texts. Instead, they adhered to traditional practice which they accepted without question as correct (Atchara 1980, 148). Mongkut insisted that even strict observance of the Vinaya should rest on an understanding of the reasons behind the disciplinary code: "One had to be clear about the original intention behind each regulation—how changes had taken place and what particular practices were originally supposed to achieve" (Chulachomklao 1956, 29).

As mentioned earlier, however, this "rationalism" did not appear only when Prince Mongkut founded the Thammayut movement. It had always been a prominent feature of the religious movement among the elite at least from the first Bangkok reign. Rama I himself on several occasions put queries of a "rationalist" nature to high-ranking monks. For example, he expressed his objection to a sermon given to him about a fish swimming around listening to Dhamma teachings and becoming enlightened as a result. Such a sermon would lead to the misunderstanding that listening to Dhamma teachings alone could bring enlightenment (Saichon 1982, 108). Phraya Thammapricha, a religious author in the court of Rama I, explained that the great merit to be derived from listening to the complete Vessantara Jataka in one day along with one thousand articles donated as alms was only a metaphor. One acquired merit from listening to other sermons as well. And even the poor could obtain the same amount of merit if they listened to the Vessantara Jataka along with the rich who were providing the alms donations (Saichon 1982, 113). This kind of "rationalism" was widespread in the religious writings produced or sponsored by the elite.

The Thammayut placed importance on the spirituality of religious practice. Prince Mongkut, for example, in one of his sermons said,

> What is this thing called 'merit?' Where can one find 'merit?' In fact, 'merit' is in one's mind. And what is the mind that is meritorious? It is the mind purified of greed, of anger, and of ignorance. *This* is what merit really is.

Mongkut also taught that alms-giving should be undertaken in order to purify one's

7. I would say that "rationalism" in this limited sense is not very prominent in the Abhidhamma in which a very systematic logic is used to analyze the human psyche. The emergence of this "rationalism," I would argue, is connected to the expansion and intensification of the export economy which began to dominate the economic activities of the early Bangkok elite. Details of this thesis and its application in a study of early Bangkok literature are discussed in chapter one of this book, "Bourgeois culture and early Bangkok literature."

mind. Setting one's mind on heaven through alms-giving caused the accumulation of greed. His interpretation of the Buddha's teachings was directed at spiritual practice in this life, at obtaining merit in a spiritual sense in this life (Chomklao n.d.).

Teachings that emphasized spiritual values were also a legacy of earlier trends at least from the first Bangkok reign. Rama I disagreed strongly with ecclesiastical dignitaries who forced Laotian monks to undergo reordination on the grounds that they pronounced Pali incorrectly. Rama I reasoned that the mind was far more important than the pronunciation of Pali.

> Having vowed to take the Three Gems as his refuge and to observe the ten precepts, does a man become a novice? What should be taken as the criterion in this case? Pronunciation or belief and dedication? A person who maintains a firm and genuine belief and who vows to take refuge in the Triple Gems and to keep and practice the ten precepts rigorously and steadfastly is better than a person who vows to take refuge in the Triple Gems with perfect pronunciation but who has insufficient faith to keep the precepts. (Cited in Saichon 1982, 107).

Rama III's support for meditation practice in the monasteries is a measure of the importance he gave to the spiritual aspects of Buddhism. The decline of ritualistic Buddhism in the thinking of the elite was thus not a new development but was a trend visible long before the founding of the Thammayut.

The entire discussion above leads to the conclusion that the Thammayut was but one part of a broader religious movement that dominated the elite from the early Bangkok period. It was not the product of ideas from outside the country, and it was not something alien and incomprehensible to people at the time. And it was for these reasons that the Thammayut became such an effective political instrument for the leader of the movement.

The congruity of the Thammayut and the broader religious movement at the beginning of the Bangkok period helps to explain the similarities of *PP* and subsequent texts down to *The Life. All these texts on the life of the Buddha were products of a unitary religious movement. So it is not surprising that they affirm the same currents of thinking. The differences among these texts mark a gradual evolution in religious thinking rather than a sharp break from an older tradition.*

6

THE HISTORY OF BANGKOK IN THE CHRONICLES OF AYUTTHAYA

TRANSLATORS' NOTE

A correct translation of the title would specify the *Royal* Chronicles of Ayutthaya. The adjective has been omitted because it makes the title read better. For simplicity, the documents are referred to as "chronicles" throughout since no category of chronicles other than the royal ones are mentioned.

Some of the early passages may be daunting for those not familiar with the Thai chronicles. For those daunted, the section on 'Chronicles from the Ayutthaya period' can be skipped or skimmed. It argues from internal evidence that sections of three chronicles must have been written during the late Ayutthaya period, and not disturbed by later recensions. These sections are: the original Luang Prasoet chronicle or a parallel unabridged version upto 1662/3; the Chakraphatdiphong version from late Narai to the close of the Thaisa reign; and the Phan Chanthanumat version for the reigns of Phetracha and Suea. These sections then form a baseline for Nidhi to

Chronicle	*Material on what era*	*Composed in what era*
Luang Prasoet (or unabridged parallel)	A. Upto 1662/3	In Ayutthaya period (? Narai)
Chakraphatdiphong	A. End Narai to Thaisa B. Remainder	During Ban Phlu Luang (1688–1767) Same as Phonnarat version
Phan Chanthanumat	A. Chakkaphat to Naresuan B. Phetracha–Suea C. Thonburi upto 1778/9 D. Remainder	Probably Rama I During Ban Phlu Luang (1688–1767) During Thonburi (1767–82) 1795/6
Phonnarat/Br. Museum		between 1795 and 1807
Bradley	Thonburi	Possibly early Rama II
Royal Autograph		Rama IV

analyze the changes introduced by the versions written in the Thonburi and early Bangkok periods. This table summarizes Nidhi's judgements on when the various parts of various chronicles were composed.

Wherever possible, Nidhi's references to the Thai chronicles have been matched with references to Richard Cushman's English translation, *The Royal Chronicles of Ayutthaya* (2000). These citations are in the form (*RCA*, 32/24–6) which means lines 24–6 on page 32. Wherever possible also, Cushman's translations are used for Nidhi's extracts, with some spelling of names adjusted to conform to the conventions used in this book.

Abbreviations used for citations of chronicles and other sources are given on p. 347.

The dating of the major reigns in the late Ayutthaya and early Bangkok periods are given on p. 343.

6

THE HISTORY OF BANGKOK IN THE CHRONICLES OF AYUTTHAYA

THE genre of chronicle literature from various countries of Southeast Asia has not been accorded much historical value by western historians since the mid twentieth century, especially in the classic histories, on grounds that these chronicles are not primary sources. Some of these works, such as the Burmese Glass Palace Chronicle, recorded events which had happened a thousand years earlier.

Chronicles have thus tended to be viewed as secondary sources and not such good ones at that, because of the legend-like quality of some passages. The muddling of events further reinforces the view that even as secondary sources, chronicles are difficult to trust. The dating, especially in the Thai and Cambodian chronicles, has consistently been proven wrong by other contemporary sources.

Even so, for the era after the time for which there are many inscriptions available, chronicles are the most important local sources in the region. Although there are other western sources for the history of this era, the interests of western travelers, traders, and missionaries were limited, and these sources do not help us understand the Southeast Asian region from the viewpoint of its own people. Studying from external sources gives us an understanding of the region's history no better than the westerner's view "from the deck of the ship, the ramparts of the fortress, the high gallery of the trading house" (Van Leur 1955, 261).

With growing awareness of the importance of local sources, the study of Southeast Asian history has subsequently accorded them greater importance. The key starting point of this approach is to have respect for a way of thinking which is not the same as ours today. The attitude towards the past and towards history differs among people of each era and civilization. Respecting this difference is the starting point for a creative approach to historical study. Only through efforts to understand the ideas and cultural environment of people in the era when the chronicles were written will historians be able to understand what those people wanted to write, and why, and with what meanings.

Even though there has been pioneer work in this direction and this has achieved some exciting results, there are still many local sources, both printed and manuscript, which await the abilities of a new generation of historians to apply the knowledge of anthropology and other social sciences in their analysis, as a first step towards their effective use.

In Thai history, the importance of the chronicles in the form of either *tamnan* or royal chronicles is already evident (Wyatt 1976, 107–22). The discovery of a new chronicle by Michael Vickery (1977, 1–80) has further increased their importance.[1] Internal analysis of this text gives reason to believe that this chronicle, or the part which has survived, was written before the reign of King Trailokanat (1448–88?), or at least before the administrative reforms of that era (Vickery 1977, 54). This chronicle is an unabridged (*phitsadan*) version, showing that the Thai tradition of writing such chronicles is very old. Although there may be errors in later chronicles, we know for sure that this "tradition" was copied and passed down without a break until the Fourth Reign of the Bangkok era when western-style history began to influence Thai scholars.

The fact that this tradition of writing about the past has been the foundation of Thai history, and goes back so far, should further increase historians' respect for the chronicles. Such respect should not be merely a (public) display of credence, but should involve attempts to analyze the chronicles and explain their contents in a careful and thorough way.[2] This essay is a small attempt by one small student of history to do just that.

This long tradition of writing "history" has rested on the continual practice of what is known as "recension of the chronicles." From sources about recension in more recent times, we know it was always an activity carried out on royal commission or under royal patronage.

Prince Damrong (1962, 18–9) makes a distinction between "recension" and "composition" but in fact recension of the chronicles involved everything from correcting the style and spelling, to extending the coverage, inserting new material, and altering old material (as will be seen below). Hence recension of the chronicles was not simply a matter of adding material to bring an old version uptodate, but also involved a complete revision of the view of the past to accord with ideas prevalent at the time of the recension. Contemporary political interests, aspirations, fears, and needs of the government which presided over the recension are thus deliberately inserted into the image of the past which is totally, though quite unconsciously, redrawn.

The periodic recensions of the chronicles thus record changes from one era to another. Changes in the aesthetic standards of language from one era to another result in a different style of language in the new recension. Changes in the government's ideas about political institutions, individuals, and historical events form the background against which a new recension is written. When we know for sure that certain things in the recension have been misrepresented, revised, embellished, or added, it may

1. Apart from the reasons relating to royal rank cited by Vickery, the age of this work is clearly proven by the style of language used. For example the word "tha" meaning "wait" as in "tha fang khong samkhan" (wait to hear the sound of the main *gong*); or the phrase "Khun Nagar Jaiy and all the dao bana retreated. The enemy was encouraged and came on strongly;" also calling the Mon as "Meng" (Vickery 1977, 6) and using the town name of Sa Luang (Vickery 1977, 24).

2. A chronicle was printed for the first time in 1864. Over the period of more than a century since then, various chronicles have been printed or reprinted around ten times, but there is still no printed edition with analysis and full explanatory references of any single chronicle except the Royal Autograph edition for which Prince Damrong wrote an unfinished introduction. Does this neglect of the chronicles among Thai historians indicate the level of their interest in them?

mean the chronicles have no historical value as secondary sources. Yet by the same token it means they have enormous value as primary sources if we try to understand why such stories had to be altered, misrepresented, elaborated, and embellished with great artistic skill.

In sum, the chronicles which contain traces of successive recensions confirm the view of E. H. Carr (1961, 30) that history is "an unending dialogue between the present and the past."

In the Thonburi and Bangkok eras there were several recensions of the chronicles. The interest in their past among the ruling class of the time (which had its own character not comparable with today's interest in the past) seems to have been rather active judging from the collection and copying of old chronicles, the recension or composition of chronicles in the Thonburi era, and the several recensions and composition of Thai history in Pali and Thai in the First and Second Reigns of the Bangkok era (Wyatt 1973, 26–7).

This should not be surprising. The ruling class in that era had just passed through a major shock from the destruction of Ayutthaya, the "unconquerable city." It was thus an era when the ruling classes turned to the past in order to understand themselves. There was self-criticism of a sort which is not often found in Thai literature, for example in the poem (*klon phleng yao*) by the Front Palace prince in the First Reign analyzing the reasons for the fall of Ayutthaya,[3] and in *Nirat narin* with its dreams of resurrecting the ideology of the past, and so on. The recensions of the chronicles in this era are thus full of the dreams, hate, detestation, love, pride, shame, and prejudice of the upper class of the time. The chronicles of the Ayutthaya era are thus good primary sources for the history of the Bangkok era, as they record matters lodged in the thoughts and beliefs of the ruling class of the time—matters that do not surface in the usual historical sources such as government appointments, orders, and records.

At the same time, this approach provides us with a way to analyze the Ayutthaya chronicles as secondary sources. If we can isolate the influences which affected the recensions in the Thonburi-Bangkok eras, or define broad principles for isolating such influences, we will be able to use these chronicles more efficiently as sources for the history of Ayutthaya.

To achieve this aim, we must first be certain which of the Ayutthaya chronicles were affected by recension in the Thonburi-Bangkok era, and which were not, so that we can then make comparisons. Apart from this, we need to identify other non-chronicle sources which can be used to examine the "revisions" made in the course of the recensions.

As my judgements about the Ayutthaya chronicles are somewhat different from those of others, it is necessary first to explain the inventory of chronicles in some detail.

3. Whether this analysis is right or wrong, fair or unfair to the Ban Phlu Luang dynasty, people have continued to find it credible for a very long time. Down to the present day, we can hear analysis of the reasons for the destruction of 1767 not very different from that in the royal *phleng yao* poem. This historical theory has been amazingly resilient.

CHRONICLES FROM THE AYUTTHAYA PERIOD

The following are the chronicles which have been discovered or which have left some traces.

1. 2/K.125 chronicle

Here this will be called the Michael Vickery Chronicle (in the same way that the Luang Prasoet and Dr Bradley versions are named). This is the oldest unabridged chronicle found to date.

Michael Vickery, who published and analyzed this text, believes that this chronicle, like the Luang Prasoet version, was based on government documents (Vickery 1977, 53).[4] It is clearly not in the tradition of *tamnan*, but that of chronicles.

2. Luang Prasoet Chronicle

The preface states clearly that this chronicle was written in the reign of King Narai. The preface also refers to "events in the chronicles," suggesting other chronicles existed before this version was compiled—something confirmed by the evidence of the Michael Vickery Chronicle. This may be the first abridged chronicle. The preface states that King Narai ordered that stories be collected from chronicles and other sources, and be "copied into a single place," as if such an abridged version had not existed before.

It is difficult to determine what was the final year of the narrative in the original Luang Prasoet chronicle (the narrative in the extant version ends in 1604). Prince Damrong (1962, 19) surmised that at most it would have run to the end of King Prasat Thong's reign (1656). But this judgement conflicts with the statement in the Luang Prasoet chronicle's own preface about "counting all the years together up to now" which places the year of composition as 1680/1. However, the chronicles composed later than this era have material about the Narai reign which is full of errors, and material about the part of this reign after Phraya Kosathibodi (Lek) returned to Ayutthaya from the war against Burma which is clearly a later addition.[5] Hence historians tend not to accept the date in the preface of the Luang Prasoet chronicle.[6]

4. The writer is not so confident of this judgment. This style of writing, interleaved with discussion, seems to be common also in government documents. An example may be seen in the daily despatches of the Thonburi army. But among its sources, the Luang Prasoet chronicle makes great use of astrological records which are another kind of documents from the royal archives, and these give the chronicles a distinctive style.

5. Most famously, the account of Kosa Lek's embassy to France has him demonstrating his invulnerability to French gunfire, and returning to report that the French king's body changed from green to red to white during the course of the day (*RCA*, 293–5). [T]

6. On grounds that, if the Luang Prasoet or a parallel unabridged chronicle had existed with material upto 1680/1, then the later chronicles would have kept the basic narrative from these works, as they did for the period before Narai. [T]

However, analysis of later recensions reveals that the material which must have originated in the Ayutthaya period itself comes to an end around 1662/3.[7] Hence it is highly likely that a copyist of the Luang Prasoet chronicle miswrote the date in the preface with digits transposed (i.e., CS 1042, 1680/1 in place of CS 1024, 1662/3). This mistake in the original from Phetchaburi then affected the royal version copied in the Thonburi era. If that is the case, the Luang Prasoet chronicle must have been one of the sources used for the recensions done later in the Ayutthaya period. There may have been an unabridged chronicle written in parallel with the Luang Prasoet version and retaining the original facts up to 1662/3. How far the Luang Prasoet version was used as a major source for recensions later in the Ayutthaya period is another issue, as all later recensions are of the unabridged type.

7. The Chakraphatdiphong chronicle has coverage up to CS 1025, 1663/4, and then skips to 1683/4 (*CC-8*, 170–1). For the year 1663/4, the chronicle has a story about corralling elephants, which cannot be verified, and two other events which were unlikely to have been written down in Narai's reign, and are probably wrong. The first story is about a contest in horse and elephant riding between Nai Chai Khan, son of a wet-nurse, and King Phetracha (*RCA*, 268–9). Whether or not such events did indeed take place in 1663/4, they would only have been deemed worth writing down later after Phetracha had ascended the throne. At the time of writing, the composer of the Luang Prasoet chronicle had no way of knowing that Phetracha would become king. Hence it must be concluded that this story was written after Phetracha ascended the throne.

The other story is about the revolt of Prince Ram and Prince Thong (Goldie in *RCA*), Narai's younger brothers (*RCA*, 269). This event was probably confused with the revolt of Phra Traiphuwanathit which happened earlier, and is confirmed by the testimony of Amdaeng Kaen as witness (for example *PR*, 379–80, see details in *PC*, 236–44; *RCA*, 234–5, where Phra Traiphuwanathit is translated as the Holy One of the Solar Lineage of the Three Worlds). In this Phra Traiphuwanathit revolt, the plan was to kill the king when he came out for the Ceremony of Yampawai, and the same plan reappears in the revolt of Prince Thong and Prince Ram. Also, in the Phra Traiphuwanathit revolt, the name of Prince Thong appears as Phra-ong Thong who was executed on that occasion. The revolt of Phra Traiphuwanathit was reported by the missionaries in Ayutthaya, as noted in Turpin (1908, 33) where the account is consistent with the chronicles. Thus it is likely that the revolt of Prince Ram and Prince Thong recorded for 1663/4 is actually the same event as the revolt of Phra Traiphuwanathit around 1657–9.

This story also must have been written after the Narai reign. Thus, ignoring these two stories dated to 1663/4, the latest material in the Chakraphatdiphong chronicle before the later insertions must be dated to 1662/3.

In the Phan Chanthanumat edition, there is a note inserted (at some unknown date) that two volumes had been lost since 1668/9 (*PC*, 260–1). In fact, as noted above the contents stop around 1662/3.

In the British Museum edition, which was the model for the Phonnarat version (or they may be called the same edition for the passages about Ayutthaya), the narrative comes down to around 1660 to 1662, and then goes back to tell the account of Phaulcon in 1657/8 which is evidently a later insertion (*BM*, 408).

3. The Chakraphatdiphong Chronicle

Most of the contents of this chronicle are the same as the Phonnarat version which is known to be a Bangkok era recension. The exception is material from the end of Narai's reign up to the close of King Thaisa's reign.

Some historians believe that the contents of this chronicle are so erroneous—for example the statement that Tham Thian was a former crown servant (*khaluang doem*) of Prince Khwan (*RCA*, 322/6)—that it cannot credibly have been written in the Ayutthaya period. But analyzing the contents in detail, especially the segments that are different from other versions, shows that these passages must have originated in the Ayutthaya period and been written under the patronage of the Ban Phlu Luang dynasty (1688–1767).

The Chakraphatdiphong Chronicle is the only one that relates events at the end of Narai's reign with some accuracy. Other versions diverge from other primary sources. For example the Chakraphatdiphong Chronicle does not state that Prince Aphaithat is a son of King Narai as other versions do. It has the correct year for King Narai's death, while other versions differ by up to six years (*CP*, 171). It has the dates of all reigns except King Suea correct in line with other primary sources, while other chronicle versions are inconsistent in varying degrees.[8] Besides this, the Chakraphatdiphong version is the only chronicle which accepts that the despatch of the Thai army to establish Siam's authority in Cambodia during Suea's reign was a total failure—"they attacked the Vietnamese of Lawaek, were routed, and came back" (*RCA* 397/14). This agrees with missionary reports (Turpin 1908, 113), while other chronicles (for reasons to do with later politics which will be explained below) added that the Khmer faction which sided with the Vietnamese still agreed to send tribute to Siam.

Most of the contents of the Chakraphatdiphong version are likely to have been written in the Ban Phlu Luang period. The kings of this dynasty are attacked by the other chronicles but in this version they completely escape any condemnation. King Phetracha accepts a challenge to ride the chase elephant and bait horse (*CP*, 170–1; *RCA*, 268–9; this is a sort of gladiatorial contest)—a story which implicitly glorifies Phetracha's abilities, and which is omitted by all other chronicles. Phetracha refuses to become king immediately on Narai's death, and merely claims he will "preserve royal affairs in the interim until a person with merit appears" (*RCA*, 331/34) which is the correct behavior the chronicles always ascribe to those contesting for the

8. This edition states that King Suea died in CS 1077 (1715/6), but is obviously a copyist's mistake which probably should be 1071 (1709/10) as the length of the reign is clearly specified as seven years and the year of ascending the throne as CS 1065. However Prince Damrong investigated this and decided that King Suea died in CS 1070 but he counted the length of the reign as six years which would be 1071 (see *PC-S*, 177). As for the year in which King Thaisa's reign ended, the Chakraphatdiphong edition is not explicit, but the last date mentioned is CS 1094 (1732/3) which must be another copyist's mistake because it precedes events in CS 1089 (1727/8). All other editions of the chronicles give the last year of King Thaisa's reign as CS 1094 (1732/3).

throne. This material is also omitted by other versions. In addition, Phetracha does not have himself crowned immediately, as in other versions, but waits another 7–8 months before holding the Anointment of Attainment (*CP,* 174; *RCA* 332/11; a rite of enthronement after conquest).

Another passage which does not appear in other versions occurs when King Phetracha returns to Ayutthaya from Lopburi after "overcoming the era of hardship." A bone relic of the Buddha performs a miracle by passing in front of the royal barge (*RCA* 331/41). This passage attests to the accumulated merit of Phetracha in his status as king, as it is believed that only those with sufficient accumulated merit will discover relics. Along the same lines, King Ramesuan dug up a relic, and King Ramkhamhaeng had a relic disinterred for worship.

In the Chakraphatdiphong version, King Phetracha belongs to one of the inner lineages of the Narai court and enters government service without using the supernatural means found in other versions. King Suea shows bravery and resolution in suppressing the Tham Thian revolt. He patronizes Buddhism. He has the power to suppress a revolt in Nakhon Si Thammarat which does not appear in other versions[9] but for which there are supporting primary sources in the missionary reports (*CC-37,* 185). King Thaisa, who is attacked in other versions for not abiding by the Buddhist precepts and killing animals, appears here as a perfectly normal monarch who is not evil in any way. His error in assigning the succession to his son rather than his brother who held the office of Front Palace prince is "excused" on grounds it was manipulated by dishonest officials.

The Chakraphatdiphong chronicle is sometimes said to be wrong about the relations between Tham Thian and Prince Khwan. But if these passages are studied in detail, it can be seen there is no mistake. Prince Aphaithat is invited from Ayutthaya, and when he reaches Lopburi, goes to meet King Phetracha abiding by the rules of audience. The chronicle states: "Lord Phra Khwan ascended and arrived riding on His holy palanquin. Phraya Surasak commanded he be taken out to the Monastery of the Carrion.... and thereupon directed lord functionaries to do away with him" (*CP,* 122; *RCA*, 311/11–4).

The name, Prince Khwan, is used again in this chronicle during the reign of King Suea who, after ascending the throne, got rid of all his brothers right at the start of the reign following a revolt by "Prince Khaek Dam" (it's not known whether this is two persons or one) (*CP,* 176). The Phonnarat chronicle states that the prince named Dam was a half-brother of King Suea by another mother (*PR*, 557). When he is executed on the order of King Suea, the Chakraphatdiphong chronicle states: "Another two days later Lord Holy Khwan was seized and ordered to be taken and executed at the Monastery of the Knoll of the Phraya." It can be seen that the term "Prince Khwan" is not an individual name but a term used to refer to first-ranked (*chaofa*) royal princes such as Prince Aphaithat. Hence the "Prince Khwan" who appears in King Suea's reign

9. Among other editions of the chronicles, the Phan Chanthanumat version compiled in the Bangkok period does not mention the Nakhon revolt at all, while the Phonnarat version places it in the reign of Phetracha (*PR*, 512–24; *RCA*, 348–55).

is likely to have been a prince of the first rank. The Chakraphatdiphong chronicle says that King Phetracha had only two first-ranked sons called "Phra Ratcha Somphan" (likely to be a nickname), a son with Narai's daughter, and Narai Thibet, a son with Narai's niece (*RCA*, 332/40–6). The "Prince Khwan" who was executed in the Suea reign must have been one of these two, not someone else named "Prince Khwan" as the later recensions report.[10]

Hence the fact the Chakraphatdiphong version reports that Tham Thian was a "former crown servant" of Prince Khwan is not illogical, as "Prince Khwan" here means Prince Aphaithat. This also explains why Tham Thian disguises himself as Prince Aphaithat; he was a former servant of this prince and hence knew the prince's everyday activity and princely manner well enough to disguise himself.

However, because this version is linked to the recensions made in the Thonburi-Bangkok period,[11] it can be expected that some modifications were made under the same influences which affected these recensions. For example, the treatment of the succession on the death of Narai seems to stress the lack of legitimacy of the Ban Phlu Luang dynasty—a point stressed also by the other recensions of this period. But for the most part, the account of the transition from Narai in the Chakraphatdiphong chronicle seems rather free of the influence of the recension work of the Thonburi-Bangkok period.

4. The Phan Chanthanumat Chronicle

In the preface to this chronicle, it clearly states the recension was made in CS 1157 or 1795/6. However, this chronicle also has an insertion or new preface in the passage on King Suea's reign which states: "This much—the accounts of Holy Phetracha and of Holy Lord Suea—were composed earlier. At this time the Supreme Holy Buddhist Lord Omnipotent has issued a command for Chaophraya Phiphit Phichai to compose accounts of Holy Reigning Lord Narai, of Holy Phetracha, of Holy Lord Suea, of

10. There is a letter from a French missionary written in the first year that King Suea ascended the throne stating that King Suea had a younger brother aged only 14–15 years and "in fact the throne should belong to the younger brother because this prince was born of a queen who came from the old dynastic line." Suea declared that he would not kill this younger brother and would pass the throne to him when he had attained an appropriate age (*CC-37*, 182). The execution of Prince Khwan according to other editions of the chronicles was done in the last year of Phetracha's reign. But it can be seen from this primary source that "Prince Khwan" was still alive until at least the first year of King Suea's reign, and thus the king's intention to execute him must have been revoked, as reported in the Chakraphatdiphong edition.

11. In *Collected Chronicles,* Part 8, which printed only those sections of this chronicle which differed from other editions, some of the important phrases analyzed here are different from printed editions such as that by Khlang Witthaya Press, 1963. For example the Khlang Witthaya edition changes the wording "Prince Khwan," when used to refer to Prince Aphaithat, into "Prince Aphaithat" (*CP,* 2506, 935). The writer is not in a position to examine the original manuscript in the National Library, and decided to follow the *Collected Chronicles,* Part 8, because this edition was thoroughly checked in great detail at the time of the first printing when Prince Damrong was editor.

Holy Borommakot and of the Holy Lord of the Eternal Sun Indra Holy Throne and to arrange [the years of] the Royal Era in [their proper] sequence." (*PC*, 217; *RCA*, 309/29–33).

On the dating of this preface, some historians believe that "composed earlier" here means in the Thonburi period (Busakorn 1968, 90) and that Chaophraya Phiphit Phichai was the person commissioned by King Rama I in the early Bangkok era to update the chronicle to the end of Ayutthaya, or the end of the Thonburi period. If this judgement is correct, then the account in this chronicle up to the Suea reign is a Thonburi period recension.

The Thonburi period was another era when the ruling class had a great interest in writing history. A number of complete and partial versions of the chronicles were collected, including the Luang Prasoet version. The CS 1136 version is a copy made in the Thonburi period. But this reign had too many other concerns to proceed far with this kind of work. The only chronicle truly written in this period was the Thonburi Chronicle of Phan Chanthanumat. Recension work on the Ayutthaya chronicles, as the preface cited above shows, was confined to the Suea reign. Any correction and updating must have been limited to certain passages, and in some places the old Ayutthaya chronicles must have been copied completely. There are traces that the material in the Phan Chanthanumat version about the Phetracha and Suea reigns, which was recompiled in the Thonburi period, tends to be very respectful towards the early Ban Phlu Luang dynasty, as will be analyzed below.

Although the recension of the Ayutthaya chronicles in the Thonburi period did not add much material, it did initiate an important process that had great influence on later recensions: it revised the dating. The vestiges of the Ayutthaya period recensions which can be found in the Chakraphatdiphong and CS 1136 versions tell us that, up to the end of the Ayutthaya period, the dating was not yet confused and wrong. It tends to agree with the dating in the Luang Prasoet version which is probably correct up to 1662/3. The revision and confusion of the dating began during the Thonburi era in the Phan Chanthanumat chronicle, which became the model for the recensions made in the Bangkok First Reign.

There is no good evidence or rationale to explain why the dating had to be revised to the new sequence. However, dates that are wrong, and wrong in the same way as in the chronicles, are found in many places in the astrology almanacs. If the astrology almanacs and records were to be printed in full, it might reveal the reasons why the later recensions of the chronicles have incorrect dating (*CC-8*, 86–115).

There is an important piece of evidence which shows that the contents of the Phan Chanthanumat version prior to Chaophraya Phiphit Phichai's recension were greatly influenced by writing from the Ayutthaya period. These are the passages which are very amicable towards the Ban Phlu Luang dynasty. The troubles in Lopburi are not mentioned. More importantly, Phetracha's ascent of the throne is both peaceful and correct "according to the *thamma*" because when Narai fell gravely ill, "He issued a rescript, being pleased to say that Phra Phetracha was an important person and then to relinquish the royal affairs of the realm to Phra Phetracha for him to oversee all the nobles and all of the servants in royal service" (*PC*, 261; *RCA*, 309/24–6). This does not appear in any other chronicle. But there are missionary records which confirm that, before the end of Narai's reign, Phetracha was appointed as regent (Turpin 1908, 70–1). This fact was something known among people in early Bangkok, as shown by the 'Abridged Chronicle of Prince Paramanuchit Chinorot' (Wyatt 1973, 47).

In the Phan Chanthanumat version, Phetracha has a blood connection to Narai, and uses neither trickery nor magic. The central government is portrayed as strong during his reign; revolts may happen but they can be suppressed. The chronicle tries to build continuity between the Prasat Thong and Ban Phlu Luang dynasties by giving "legitimate rights" to Phetracha, along with a beautiful and eloquent account of the funeral which Phetracha organizes for King Narai (*PC*, 262–3; *RCA*, 319–20). By contrast, the passages recomposed by Phraya Phiphit Phichai revert to portraying the disorder in the central government. The people who join together to seize Narai's throne are killed. The suppression of the revolt in Nakhon Ratchasima is not very successful, and results in people from the capital region having to flee and scatter (*PC*, 278–9).

The version prior to Chaophraya Phiphit Phichai's recension portrays the Suea reign in a good light. King Suea promotes Buddhism, even performing a sword dance as an offering to Buddha at the Holy Footprint (Phraphutthabat), and having no royal siblings killed during his reign. Visiting the Holy Footprint does not result in King Suea becoming angry with his son, as related in later chronicle versions. The passages on King Suea's cruelty towards the end of his reign are understood to be insertions made in the Thonburi era recension.[12] The treatment of the Suea reign in Chaophraya Phiphit Phichai's recension is evidently very different—indeed diametrically opposed—to the earlier material. Thus the Phan Chanthanumat chronicle, at least these earlier passages, must be dated to Ayutthaya, because they were greatly influenced by the recensions made in the Ban Phlu Luang era. These passages will be referred to here as the Phan Chanthanumat-Ayutthaya version, to distinguish them from the recension by Chaophraya Phiphit Phichai during the First Reign.

5 and 6: CS 1136 and CS 1145 chronicles

The CS 1136 (1774/5) version is believed to be a recension from the Borommakot reign (Damrong 1962a, 12, 20). The CS 1145 (1783/4) version is similar to the Phan Chanthanumat chronicle, differing only in a few words. As these two chronicles have little new to study, they are not used in this analysis.

In sum, at the end of the Ayutthaya period, there must have been unabridged versions of the chronicles up to the end of the Thaisa reign, as proven by the Chakraphatdiphong and Phan Chanthanumat-Ayutthaya chronicles. This was the very least. Possibly there were other recensions in the Ekathat reign, and later chronicles reused their material about the Borommakot reign, but this cannot be clearly proven.

12. The narrative about the land procession (*PC*, 268–9) is very detailed, and believed also to have been inserted during the Thonburi period recension because there are sources stating it was composed as a manual.

There are other documents which are closely related to the chronicles and which are useful for validating the chronicles' information. These documents provide further light on the process of recension in the Thonburi-Bangkok era. Those documents are as follows.

1. *The Short History of the Kings of Siam* (or in the title of the original, Chronicle of the Ayutthaya Dynasty); *Testimony of the Inhabitants of the Old Capital*; and the *Northern Chronicle*.

The first document was written in 1640 by Van Vliet using oral sources to a large extent. At that time, there were histories in written form in both the chronicle and *tamnan* style. Wyatt has pointed out that Van Vliet probably also used written sources. Wyatt also noted the similarity between certain passages in the *Short History* and in the chronicles of Nakhon Si Thammarat (Wyatt in the introduction to Van Vliet 1975, 7).

However, the sources used by Van Vliet, whether oral or written, mostly belong to the category of *tamnan*. Comparison to the Michael Vickery Chronicle indicates that Van Vliet probably never saw that document. For this reason the *Short History* belongs together with the *Testimony of the Inhabitants of the Old Capital* (*Khamhaikan chao krung kao*) and the *Northern Chronicle* (*Phongsawadan nuea*), both of which are documents written after the Ayutthaya period. Although the contents of both these documents were preserved in memory and passed on from generation to generation by oral transmission, and although from the time of Van Vliet to the period after Ayutthaya's fall is more than a century, we can still find similarities between several passages. Beyond the fall of Ayutthaya, the tradition of oral history, which is similar to folk tales and closely linked to the *tamnan* form of history, clearly still had vitality. This tradition existed in parallel with the development of the chronicles.[13]

Comparing these three documents reveals many similarities between the stories. In all three, the foundation of Ayutthaya by U Thong is associated with a rishi or hermit

13. In early Bangkok down to the Fifth Reign, oral history attracted increasing interest from the court. Prior to this, oral history seems to have been the province of the wat, as can be seen from the historical works produced in Lanna in the fifteenth to sixteenth centuries, and the *Sangkhitiyawong* written by Somdet Phra Phonnarat in 1789 in celebration of King Rama I for holding the grand council to revise the Tipitaka (Wyatt 1976, 1156). In 1807, while still holding the title of Front Palace prince, the future Rama II presented to the king a history of this type about events before the foundation of Ayutthaya, as a single-volume in *samut thai* form. Phra Phonnarat included this material at the start of the chronicles which King Rama I commissioned in 1795. In the same year that he presented this pre-Ayutthaya chronicle to the king, the Front Palace prince also ordered Phraya Wichiankhiri to collect historical legends and write them up as the *Northern Chronicle.*

During the Fourth and Fifth Reigns there was a considerable effort to collect histories of localities and tributary states to keep as the property of officialdom (*luk khun na sala*). Interest in this sort of history at this time probably had a political purpose, especially the history of tributary states (see for example, Osborne and Wyatt, 1968). However, these histories of localities and tributary states preserved a great deal of oral history and history of the *tamnan* type.

(Van Vliet 1975, 57–8; *TIOC*, 54–5; *NC*, 64). The man called Khun Worawongsathirat in Van Vliet's account has the duty to "read old stories and foreign histories in the king's language." The equivalent character, named Nai Bunsi or Khun Chinnarat in the *Testimony*, recites poetry for Somdet Paramesuan in Chaiyaracha's court (Van Vliet 1975, 71–2; *TIOC*, 71). In the chronicles, he is usually called Phan Butsithep and described as an official in charge of the office of registration (*RCA*, 22/24). In both the *Testimony* and Van Vliet, the Burmese army's first attack on Ayutthaya ends in a similar way, namely, the Burmese king kills the Thai king or causes his death, and as a result the Burmese king loses heart and withdraws his army (*TIOC*, 80; Van Vliet 1975, 73–4).

In addition, the *Testimony* tells us there were some facts which were known to those responsible for the recension of the chronicles in early Bangkok but which the chroniclers chose to omit, and there were some things known to people in late Ayutthaya which they were not happy to talk about but which the chroniclers chose to include in their work.

2. Astrological records

For this work I have only been able to use those records that have been printed in the *Collected Chronicles* part 8.

RECENSIONS IN THE THONBURI-BANGKOK ERA

If the insertion in the Phan Chanthanumat chronicle about Chaophraya Phiphit Phichai was truly written in the First Reign, then during the Thonburi era the Ayutthaya chronicles underwent recension up to the Suea reign, and the Phan Chanthanumat version is the oldest recension after the fall of Ayutthaya, and the model for later recensions.

In 1795, King Rama I ordered another recension, meaning the Phan Chanthanumat version completed up to the end of the Thonburi period. This recension made almost no corrections to the Thonburi version, except for the following.

a. Material was added on late Ayutthaya from the end of the Narai reign to the fall of the city in order to bridge the gap to the Thonburi chronicle composed in the Thonburi period (see below on the Thonburi chronicle). Also the Thonburi chronicle was extended from around 1779 to the end of the reign.

b. Although there is no clear evidence, it is highly likely that the accounts of wars with Burma from around the Maha Chakkaphat reign to the end of Naresuan were expanded at this time. The style is obviously different from that used in the Ayutthaya period, and similar to that used in early Bangkok (compare the style of the CS 1136 version with that in Phan Chanthanumat). During the Thonburi period, there was probably not enough time or interest to elaborate the elegant unabridged style; for the Suea reign, a lot of the material was simply copied from the Borommakot reign, adding only the part at the end in order to defame King Suea (as analyzed above); and there was no interest in completing the missing events from 1662/3 to the end of the Narai reign.

The recensions of this time were probably not greatly to the royal liking. For this reason, Somdet Phra Phonnarat made a new recension, though in what year is unknown. The preface of the written manuscript states that a recension had been made in 1795 (meaning the Phan Chanthanumat version) and "then Somdet Phra Phonnarat of Wat Phra Chetuphon...made a new recension from beginning to end, appending material to extend the coverage" (preface of *PR*, 5). This recension must have been made after 1795 and completed in some year before 1807, since in that year, when the Front Palace prince (future Rama II) presented a pre-Ayutthaya chronicle to the king, Phonnarat's recension was finished at least up to the end of Ayutthaya, as can be seen from the British Museum version.

Hence in the Phonnarat chronicle, the sections on Ayutthaya were completed between 1795 and 1807, and those on Thonburi were probably copied from the 1795 recension of Phan Chanthanumat (see below about the Thonburi chronicle "Phonnarat version" printed together in two volumes).

In sum, the past which the government of Rama I's time most wanted to construct for their "present" involved only stories about wars with Burma in the time of Naresuan, and the events of the Ban Phlu Luang dynasty. Even the image of Ban Phlu Luang presented by that dynasty's enemy (that is, King Taksin) in the Phan Chanthanumat version was not satisfactory. The material in the British Museum version about the Ban Phlu Luang period is thus very different from the Phan Chanthanumat version.

The Phonnarat and British Museum versions are the same. Small differences of wording are mostly attributable to the copyists, such as "siri" in place of "si," and many differences in numbers. But this similarity between the two ceases at the end of the Ayutthaya period. The contents of the Thonburi chronicles printed for the first time by Dr Bradley in 1864 are very different.

In 1850 King Rama III asked Prince Paramanuchit Chinorot, a former student of Phonnarat, to compile an abridged chronicle. This chronicle was greatly influenced by the Phonnarat version. The legends about the pre-Ayutthaya period in this abridged chronicle differ from those in the British Museum version, but are similar to the *Chulayutthakanwong* (Wyatt 1973, 25–7). The interesting aspect of this abridged chronicle is that in some places it has a dating unlike any other version (Wyatt 1976, 121). In addition, it has some material which the Rama I recensions do not mention at all.

Apart from the chronicles, there are other related sources which are useful for analyzing the process of "recension" in the Thonburi-Bangkok era. Most important are other written works by the major chronicler, Phra Phonnarat of Wat Phra Chetuphon, who wrote a Thai history in Pali called *Chulayutthakanwong*. This work, for which at present there is no complete version, must have been the model for the *Chulayutthakanwong khwam riang* and *Thetsana chulayutthakanwong*. Comparing accounts of the same event across these three volumes—such as the King of Chiang Rai's migration to escape war—demonstrates that the other two are translations or summaries from *Chulayutthakanwong*.[14]

14. For example, in the *Chulayutthakanwong* (p. 5), "the king of Chiang Rai led all those

There are no sources which show for certain the age of these documents, but the *Thetsana chulayutthakanwong* is known to have been written in the Second Reign (*CC-66*, 92), and Phonnarat passed away at the beginning of that reign. These texts were probably written around that time. The interesting part is that the author mentioned certain events that he himself omitted from the recension of the chronicles.

RECENSION OF THE AYUTTHAYA CHRONICLES AND ITS OBJECTIVES IN THE THONBURI AND BANGKOK ERAS

Comparing the recensions made in the two periods reveals a great number of changes in the form of revisions, deletions, and additions in the later period, apart from changes in the literary style.

In many places, revisions were made because of new data, especially about Burma, Cambodia, and Laos. But in some places, facts about events which are known to have taken place are omitted or not stated clearly and completely. Such revision cannot be called wholesale misrepresentation, because misrepresentation is only one element. There are many cases where we cannot decide between the conflicting accounts in the Ayutthaya and Thonburi-Bangkok recensions, because there are no external sources for verification.

But the main concern in this study is not whether or not some event really took place in Ayutthaya. Historians choose to include one event and exclude another because they believe the former has "meaning" for them. Such meanings do not exist in isolation but are always based on some set of values. In other words, the decision to "select" the facts in history is always related to some values (political, moral, aesthetic, philosophical, etc.) on the part of the historian. Hence the problem whether the Thonburi-Bangkok recensions are correct or incorrect is not as important for this study as the question why the recension "chose" to pick up this fact and throw away that one, and why as a result certain facts have since been expanded upon in detail in history and literature.

---

people to Siam to the forest near Kamphaengphet. The power of the merit of the king of Chiang Rai inspired Thao Sakka Thewarat to transform himself into a hermit ascetic." The *Chulayutthakanwong khwam riang* states: "The king of Chiang Rai brought all his followers to Siam to the forest temple around the forest at the mouth of the Kamphaengphet river on the western side. He related all of the events to the ruler and officials, and asked to come under the protection and be subjects within the boundary (*kha khanthasema*) and remain staying there. At that time Somdet Amarintharathirat understood the reason why that Phraya had such great merit and would be the origin of a line of kings.... so he came down from the world of the gods in the form of an ascetic" (*CC-66*, 345). The account in the "*khwam riang*" edition is obviously a translation and precis of the Pali *Chulayutthakanwong*. So too is the *Thetsana chulayutthakanwong* whose account of the same incident runs: "at that time the king of Chiang Rai...led the peoples of Chiang Rai to flee to Siam to the forest around Kamphaengphet. Seeing the power of his merit, Pra-ong Somdet Amarintharathirat (magically) changed his body into a hermit" (*CC-66*, 67).

The relationship between a historian and his data is also a relationship between the society of the historian's time and the data from the past. E. H. Carr (1961, 35) warned us: "The historian, then, is an individual human being. Like other individuals, he is also a social phenomenon, both the product and the conscious or unconscious spokesman of the society to which he belongs; it is in this capacity that he approaches the facts of the historical past."

Hopefully, looking at things from this angle will help reveal the "values" of early Bangkok society, especially of the elite for whom the chronicles were both a product, and one factor in the production of their own class.

What emerges most clearly from the comparison of the recensions in the two periods is the hostility towards the Ban Phlu Luang dynasty during the Thonburi-Bangkok period. In the recensions made in the years following the most terrible disaster in the history of the state, namely the fall of Ayutthaya, this disaster had to be explained. At the same time, that explanation had to be "useful" for the present day. The chroniclers chose to explain this disaster by fixing the blame on the Ban Phlu Luang dynasty.

In the view of the Thonburi-Bangkok period recensions, the members of the Ban Phlu Luang dynasty were not fit to be rulers, not fit to be warriors, not fit to be the centre of "royal authority," and not fit to be patrons of Buddhism. Presenting the Ban Phlu Luang dynasty in this way helped confirm the legitimacy of both the new dynasties. It also taught readers, who needed to learn from the past, a "lesson" about the value of unity and orderliness under a strong government. In addition, it strengthened a new ideology about the monarchy which the kings of this period, and particularly the Chakri dynasty, wanted to give special emphasis (see below).[15]

There are some points about the chronicles' view of the Ban Phlu Luang dynasty which deserve special mention.

a. This dynasty's rise to power was not only illegitimate but also ruthless in nature. To seize power from one of the best and greatest kings of Ayutthaya amounted to a massive show of ingratitude.

King Narai was already revered in the recensions made in the Ayutthaya period, even in the Chakraphatdiphong recension made in the Borommakot reign. This was because the Ban Phlu Luang dynasty claimed its legitimacy as rulers through marriage with senior ladies of the Narai dynasty. This legitimacy by descent was reinforced by the "political legends" about secret connections between King Suea and King Narai. Hence there was no reason to view the Ban Phlu Luang dynasty as a discontinuity in the dynasty and hence condemn Narai in their chronicles.

This respect and admiration for Narai was widespread in the official nobility until the end of the Ayutthaya period, as can be seen from the *Testimony of the Inhabitants of the Old Capital* which is highly reverential towards Narai (*TIOC*, 105–27). The

15. The success of the chroniclers in the Thonburi-Bangkok period is rather amazing. Because their interpretation of the reasons for the collapse of Ayutthaya was accepted by Prince Damrong, this interpretation is still generally upheld down to the present day. This must be one of the most enduring interpretations of a historical incident in the world, without contest or challenge from new generations of students.

British Museum (or Phonnarat) chronicle compiled in the Thonburi-Bangkok era is even more reverential. The gap in the narrative from 1662/3 to the end of Narai's reign gave the chroniclers an opportunity to add material which mostly is very far-fetched, namely the passages about Constantine Phaulcon, and about the Thai envoys' travel to France (*RCA*, 269–77, 303–7). These were written to reinforce the greatness of Narai as a king who was known and honored by the king of France. At the same time, the Thonburi-Bangkok recensions make Phaulcon into a clever and honest official who is elevated to the high rank of Chaophraya, and holds the ministerial post of *samuha nayok*, even though in real life he was no more than Okya in rank and held the title of *chakri* for a short time only.

The narrative of the seizure of power in Lopburi is written to stir the emotions (*RCA*, 311–8). Phra Phetracha and Okluang Sorasak execute the rightful heir, Prince Aphaithat, along with Phaulcon, in a daring fashion. Mom Pi is executed before Narai's own eyes. To help the courtiers who are still loyal, Narai even gives up a palace to become a wat so the courtiers may escape into the monkhood. And importantly, Narai refers to those establishing the new dynasty in his own words as "these two wretches, father and child, are making plans for rebellion" (*PR*, 482; *RCA* 316/5).

Such a tragic portrayal like scenes from a drama cannot be found in the Chakraphatdiphong version or even the Phan Chanthanumat recension commissioned by Rama I in 1795. The *Testimony of the Inhabitants of the Old Capital* relates that Narai died normally, and the nobles agreed to invite the "secret" son to ascend the throne, but this son maneuvered to have his (step)-father become king before himself.

The Thonburi-Bangkok recensions undermine the sacredness of the Ban Phlu Luang dynasty's claims to legitimacy through marriage by having King Suea execute the son born to Phetracha with the senior royal lady in Narai's lineage. This execution of "Prince Khwan" may have happened in reality as both the Chakraphatdiphong version and the *Testimony of the Inhabitants of the Old Capital* report the same thing (*TIOC*, 129–30).[16] But the British Museum and Phonnarat chronicles turn this passage into more of a "drama" by having this Prince Khwan executed during Phetracha's reign in a most pitiful fashion; they portray Prince Khwan as a child[17] playfully eating a watermelon and have the deed committed in a cruel fashion which greatly distresses his mother (*RCA*, 367/31–2). Even though Suea's act makes Phetracha fly into a rage, Phetracha is not in a position to respond in any way. The situation thus resembles the events at the end of Narai's reign (*PR*, 545–7, 537–9). Both the Chakraphat-diphong version and the *Testimony of the Inhabitants of the Old Capital* state similarly that the execution of Prince Khwan took place in the Suea reign. The narrative of this tragic

16. The *Testimony* explains that Prince Khwan is executed because of a secret gathering to plot a revolt. There may be some evidence pointing to this. The Chakraphatdiphong version seems to connect the execution with the revolt fomented by Prince Khaek Dam at the start of Suea's reign.

17. From the dating in the Chakraphatdiphong edition, this "Prince Khwan" must have been older than 14 years at the time of his execution.

event, which happened to Phetracha as to Narai, is a way of reiterating the Buddhist teaching that "you reap what you sow."

Another prince of the Narai lineage who appears in the Chakraphatdiphong version is not mentioned again either in the Chakraphatdiphong or Phan Chanthanumat-Ayutthaya versions or in the *Testimony*, but the Phan Chanthanumat recension of 1795 states that he was executed by the Front Palace prince and Phra Banthun Noi in the Suea reign (*PC*, 282; *RCA*, 374). This execution of Trat Noi ("Little Highness") has probably been confused with the execution of Prince Khwan because the details are very similar. The later recensions "removed" this prince of the Narai lineage by having him enter the monkhood which is equivalent to ending his political life, and strengthens the legitimacy of the Ban Phlu Luang dynasty. Whatever the truth of these events, the accounts of the deaths of the two princes of the Narai lineage achieved two purposes: first, they totally removed the males of the Narai lineage from the Ban Phlu Luang dynasty; second, they associated the unseemly death of Trat Noi with the king of the Ban Phlu Luang dynasty whose reign was remembered as "the good old days," that is King Borommakot who, as Prince Phon, took part in the execution.

The Thonburi-Bangkok recensions also exploit the ambiguity about the origins of the Ban Phlu Luang dynasty by adding that the family came from ordinary commoner origins and was not part of the ruling class at all.

In the British Museum and Phonnarat versions, after Phetracha ascends the throne, his relatives from Suphanburi pay a visit to the court in Ayutthaya. This visit provides the chroniclers with an opportunity to write a comic scene into the history, as the relatives are country bumpkins who do not know court customs and conduct themselves towards Phetracha just as relatives would in the countryside (*RCA*, 336–7).

We have sources which show clearly that the ancestral line of Phetracha were not country bumpkins. La Loubère (1969, 89) states that, "His family has continued a long time in the highest offices; is frequently allied to the Crown." Turpin even states that Phetracha might have been a first cousin of Narai, and that, in agreement with what is stated in Thai sources, his mother was a wet-nurse in the palace, and his sister was presented to Narai as a concubine (Turpin 1908, 66). In old Thai society, social status did not alter so rapidly that someone could become king while his close relatives were still peasants. Making up such stories about the origins of the Ban Phlu Luang dynasty was in line with the Chakri dynasty's policy to "lay bare" rights to dynastic descent on grounds of blood, which were something the kings of the Chakri dynasty never tried to claim, at least not until the Fourth Reign.

b. The Thonburi-Bangkok recensions portray each of the Ban Phlu Luang kings as either ruthless, irrational, or weak. In each case, the criteria for the "evil" which the chronicles use to denigrate this dynasty seems to be the moral values of Buddhism.

In one passage, the Phonnarat chronicle refers to King Suea as follows:

> In those days His Majesty, the Supreme Holy Lord of the Realm, failed to remain within the Holy Metropolis for long ... Then His Majesty would proceed with a holy throne barge ... And the King angled for all the diverse and multifarious piscine forms and only accumulated sinful demerit by breaking holy royal traditions stemming from the examples

> of the past. Now His Holiness killed off those groups of the various piscine forms with hooks and nets, felling them dead in great numbers. (*PR*, 559–60; *RCA*, 384/30–8)

In truth, hunting was nothing new for Siamese kings. Foreign records show that Narai liked to hunt (Turpin 1908, 88). Also, hunting is a sport of the kings who appear as lead characters in some Thai literary works, for example Phra Phanwasa in *Khun chang khun phaen*.

Another passage about King Suea from the same chronicle runs:

> At that time the Supreme Holy Lord of the Realm possessed a holy royal heart rough, coarse, cruel and savage, without trustworthy goodness. The King in His behavior broke the holy royal traditions and failed to possess shame or fear of sin. And His holy heart was thick with lewd evilness, and there was anxiety in the sources of anger and the sources of folly compounded within His mental disposition without fail. Now His Holiness drank clear alcoholic beverages regularly and then liked to take pleasure in the practice of copulating with young ladies who had not yet menstruated. Now, if any lady was able to persevere and endure it, the King accordingly made holy royal gifts of rewards of silver, gold and cloth of variously colored silk to that lady in great amounts. If any lady was unable to bear it, however, the King accordingly manifested His holy wrath and beat her down on her central region to make her reach the point of death. Then He had a coffin brought in and the corpse of that lady placed in it. [Such coffins] went out by way of the gate of the Holy Royal Palace Enclosure to the rear of [the residences of] the consorts continually and that gate was accordingly called the Gate of the Ghosts' Exit. (*PR*, 571–2; *RCA*, 391/28–42)

There is no doubt at all that this sort of passage does not appear in the Chakraphatdiphong version or the *Testimony*. This wild imagining seems to have begun during the recensions of the Thonburi era. There are some irrelevant insertions in the Phan Chanthanumat-Ayutthaya version, but they are in the style of folk tales, unlike the revisions in the Bangkok recensions which state, for example, the king liked to "indulge in sexual intercourse with young girls and female children eleven to twelve years old. If any girl shoved, struggled and rolled around, the King manifested His holy wrath by inflicting on her the holy royal punishment of striking her on the upper part of her chest with His elbows and killing her right there. If any girl did not struggle, shove or roll around but remained still and satisfied His holy inclinations, the King gave her holy royal gifts of bounties and rewards" (*PC*, 270; *RCA*, 373/13–8). It is also worth noting that in early Bangkok the death of commoners in the royal palace was considered a bad omen, and in the event of such a death a relative of the deceased had to perform a ritual of sacrifice to the spirits of the palace gate. Thus the character which the chronicles create for King Suea not only denigrated Suea himself but also portrayed the declining auspiciousness of the cosmic centre of the Ayutthaya state, namely the Ayutthaya royal palace.

There was one further event which the post-1795 recensions added to the Suea reign about an elephant round-up which resulted in an accident and severe punishment for the Front Palace prince and his brother (*PR*, 562–70; *RCA*, 386–9). The 1795 recension passes over this event (*PC*, 282–3) but mentions the punishment of the Front Palace prince and his brother as resulting from the killing of Trat Noi. The treatment in the post-1795 recensions seems designed to show the irrational and quick-tempered nature of King Suea, and the lack of capability of the Front Palace prince and his brother who later become King Thaisa and King Borommakot respectively. It also demonstrates the difficulties experienced by nobles and people who live under a royalty that lacks capability and morality. Similarly, an account of building stockades in the Phonnarat version states: "The various people who were building the stockades waded through water to do their work and hurried each other on to erect the corral stockades both by day and by night.... Starved for food and grown emaciated, many accordingly fell dead" (*PR*, 563; *RCA*, 386/42–6).[18]

King Thaisa is also not shown reverence in the Thonburi-Bangkok recensions which state that he "practiced behavior in constant sinfulness. Now His Majesty went around on tour to angle just like His Supreme Holy Royal Father." Furthermore, he issued a decree forbidding the eating of carp, his personal favorite, and imposing a fine of five tamlueng (*PR*, 583; *RCA*, 399/10–12) which was a rather high sum for a society where a cash economy was not yet established, and even high for the Bangkok era when laws imposed a fine of only thirteen tamlueng for a case involving the death of an able-bodied male aged 21 to 25 (*KTSD*, I, 200). Thaisa's punishment for eating carp seems unrealistic and was probably inserted during the post-1795 recension.

The next king was Borommakot. He is probably the king of the Ban Phlu Luang dynasty who created the most difficulty for the chroniclers of the Thonburi-Bangkok recensions because he was highly popular among the Thai people (as can be seen from the reports of Ayutthaya war prisoners in the *Testimony of the Inhabitants of the Old Capital*). The style of outright condemnation used for King Suea and King Thaisa was not possible. However, the chroniclers managed to undermine Borommakot's reputation with methods much cleverer than open condemnation.

18. Cross-checking among the different versions suggests that this event may not have taken place. The execution of Trat Noi which appears in the Phan Chanthanumat edition may not have taken place as it is not mentioned in either the Chakraphatdiphong or British Museum editions. In addition, it seems to have been a fixed pattern for the recensions compiled in the Bangkok period to make the *upparat* or Front Palace prince, prior to ascending the throne, do something wrong or not to the liking of the reigning king. For example King Suea executes Prince Khwan which makes his father so angry that he entrusts the throne to his son rather than the Front Palace prince. Similarly, King Borommakot criticizes the future King Suriyamarin as "lacking perseverance," and does not allow him to reign. Possibly all these stories were invented along the lines of a fixed pattern. If that is the case, the story of Chao Mae Wat Dusit is likely to be another event which may not have taken place (and if it did, who was she?). (Chao Mae Wat Dusit, mentioned as a wet nurse of King Narai in this part of the chronicles, is claimed as the earliest identifiable progenitor of the Chakri dynasty. See *RCA*: 305/25–6. [T])

The episode for which Borommakot is most famous is the despatch of monks to Sri Lanka to sustain Buddhism. This event was something which the chroniclers and people in early Bangkok could probably still recall, as it features in the *Testimony of the Inhabitants of the Old Capital* (*TIOC*, 144–8). The mission of monks to Sri Lanka is also mentioned in *Thetsana chulayutthakanwong* which may have been written by Phonnarat, author of the chronicle (*CC-66*, 86). Phonnarat's pupil, Prince Paramanuchit, also included this event in the abridged chronicle (Wyatt 1973, 49). However, this episode which earns the highest glory for the Ban Phlu Luang dynasty (at least in the Bangkok view) is excluded from the early Bangkok recensions including Phan Chanthanumat, British Museum, and Phonnarat.

The image of Borommakot created by the chronicles at some times lacks rationality and is "packed with odds and ends which don't add up to anything" (in the view of King Chulalongkorn 1916, 71). The story about the Mon leader named Saming Tho, who set himself up as king of the Mon in Pegu before the end of the Toungoo dynasty, is similar to the account in the *Hmannan Yazawin Dawgyi* (1954, V, 198–200). Saming Tho flees to the shelter of the Siamese king when his father-in-law, Phaya Thala, seizes the Mon throne. Borommakot throws him into jail because he has disliked him ever since Saming Tho asked for Borommakot's daughter and Borommakot noted, "This miserable Saming Tho is of vile race and lowly line" (*PR*, 613, 620; *RCA*, 439/7–8). The Phonnarat chronicle gives the impression that, because of his self-regard on this matter, Borommakot decided to receive an envoy from Ava and even send a return mission (which the *Hmannan Yazawin Dawgyi* confirms). Ultimately, instead of sending Saming Tho to Phraya Thala to strengthen the power of the Mon, Borommakot banishes him from the kingdom.

The Phonnarat chronicle presents these actions on the part of Borommakot as exhibiting self-importance and lack of foresight (since ultimately Burma attacked Ayutthaya) (*PR*, 621–2; *RCA*, 475–6). Yet there was a more logical explanation which people in early Bangkok could probably still recall as it appears in the *Testimony of the Inhabitants of the Old Capital.* When Saming Tho came to Ayutthaya, he raised a revolt: "he commanded many groups of followers, and attacked the small towns along the border of the royal territory" (*TIOC*, 143–4). These many groups of followers must have been Mon migrants.

The control of manpower and the loyalty of large numbers of Mon immigrants were not problems for the Ayutthaya government alone, but also for the early Bangkok government. However neither the Phan Chanthanumat recension of 1795 nor the British Museum or Phonnarat versions make reference to the internal political imperative which forced King Borommakot to overlook the long-term consequences and be more arrogant than he needed to be.

Another event in the early Bangkok recensions again places Borommakot in a derisory situation for the Thai of the period after Ayutthaya fell.

The chronicles report that an Ava envoy arrived at the Ayutthaya court and informed King Borommakot, perhaps untruthfully, about the court customs of Ava on the proper receipt of a royal missive. The king thus issued a royal proclamation that, when a page came to read the royal missive, even the seniormost ministers must place their hands together in salutation while listening, and then prostrate themselves in the direction of the royal palace, and only when the reading was finished would the page formally return the respectful salutation to the ministers (*PR*, 615; *RCA*, 440–1).

Both King Taksin and King Rama I were leaders of the official nobility. Their governments were rule by the class of official nobility and differed from rule by the royal court (see below). This regulation by King Borommakot must have created disgruntlement among the nobles. The more Borommakot followed the customs of Burma, the more his reputation declined.

The reputations of the last two kings of the Ban Phlu Luang dynasty were easily denigrated and destroyed. One of them (Uthumphon) was interested only in saving his own soul, and entered the monkhood even when political affairs were in crisis. The other (Ekathat) is portrayed by the chronicles as weak, stupid, and full of prejudice in his dealings with the nobility. His father says openly to the nobles that his son lacks perseverance, and were he to occupy the throne it would bring disaster to the country. Hence even though this son is the elder prince, he is commanded to enter the monkhood to make way for his younger brother to ascend the throne smoothly. The stupidity of King Ekathat is not detailed by the chronicles themselves but comes from the mouth of King Borommakot, his father as, "That Department of the Fourth Rank Anurak Montri is endowed with a disposition lacking perseverance" (*PC*, 301; *RCA*, 458/34–5). But the Phonnarat version is not satisfied with this alone, and quite straightforwardly uses the word "foolishly" in the narrative of events after Ekathat has ascended the throne; King Alaungpaya leads his army via Mergui but Ayutthaya gets the confused information that he is coming via three routes; Ekathat, "because He lacked the transcendental knowledge of holy reflection and holy fast thinking, foolishly accepted [the idea of an invasion by] all three routes" and thus despatches armies on all three (*PR*, 636, compare with *PC*, 304; *RCA*, 476/30–2). No other chronicle condemns a king to this extent.

The *Hmannan* account of the Siam-Burma war at the time of King Alaungpaya is different from that in the Thai chronicles. Even though the narrative is generally similar, the resistance by Ayutthaya is not as weak and muddled as portrayed in the chronicles. Even the defence of the city is carried out with courage. In Harvey's account of the war, Alaungpaya's risk-taking at Ayutthaya almost ends in a disastrous failure for the Burmese side (Harvey 1967, 241–3). But the Thai chronicles attribute Ayutthaya's survival on this occasion to the illness of Alaungpaya which forces the Burmese to withdraw (*PR*, 640; *RCA*, 483).

c. The Thonburi-Bangkok recensions try to show that the Ban Phlu Luang dynasty lacks the "royal authority" to rule

The royal authority of the Ayutthaya king is manifested in royal rituals which place the royal palace at the "centre of the universe" and demonstrate the accumulated merit of the king in his status as the supreme protector and patron of Buddhism—as the king of the white elephant and other royal regalia. The chronicles withhold all of these attributes from the Ban Phlu Luang dynasty as kings of Siam. But importantly the chronicles seem to emphasize the Ban Phlu Luang kings' lack of royal authority on grounds they fail to be proper patrons and protectors of religion. The kingdom cannot survive because there is nobody to uphold the *thamma.* One example is the rulers' failure to abide by Buddhist morality, as mentioned above.

In the view of early Bangkok governments (as will be shown below), the state exists only to serve as a ladder for people to accumulate merit so they may achieve nirvana on some day in the future, either quickly or slowly according to each individual's accumulation of merit. The *thammasat* or laws of the country do not exist only to regulate relations between people in this world. The state must also take care of the spiritual welfare of its people. When the state lacks a ruler who nurtures the Buddhist *thamma,* either that state has no reason to exist, or else the ruler who has not fulfilled his duty has forfeited his right to rule. In other words, such a ruler has completely lost his "royal authority" as a Buddhist monarch in the view of the governments of the Bangkok period.

The Phonnarat chronicle summarizes this idea well in relating an event which for many reasons is believed not to have taken place in reality. This occurs when King Alaungpaya is leading his army towards Ayutthaya through the region of Kui and Pran. Three Siamese are arrested by the Burmese when they sneak out to observe the Burmese army. Under interrogation these men address Alaungpaya with words worth reproducing in full:

> "May Your holy royal punishment be upon my head for not fearing Your holy and powerful power! As for there being someone making use of us to come and spy on Your army—it certainly is not the Supreme Holy Buddhist Lord Omnipotent. The entire reason why we have been courageous, have failed to be afraid of death and have come is because our ancestors have decreed that, during 1122 of the Royal Era, a year of the dragon, second of the decade, there would be a Holy Grand Ruler of Kings and Lord who, endowed with the constant condition of a holy accumulation of merit, would receive the Anointment of Attainment under the white tiered umbrella to become the paramount ruler, grand and unique, within the Capital of the Country of the Phukam to the west, and [that] His Majesty would come this way in holy royal procession with an army of the four divisions to subdue an enemy sovereign and royal opponent of the Age of Kali, and to foster and nourish the Holy Buddhist Religion and the populace without favoritism. The Servants of the Holy Lord, never having seen [such a sovereign] since being born, thereupon audaciously persuaded each other to come to hide and wait to admire the Lord of the Accumulation of Merit of the Paramount Fig. Thus the saying our elders have handed down for generation after generation has been realized. May it be as the King is disposed!" (*PR*, 637–9; *BM*, 622–3; *RCA*, 478/45–479/13)

This passage is not found in any Ayutthaya chronicle other than the Phonnarat version. It was probably written between 1795 and 1807 at the time when Siam's hatred of Burma was at its height. But the praise for the Burmese king here has nothing to do with the hatred and resentment which existed towards Burma. It is a device for portraying the early Bangkok period's ideas about king and state. A king who does not uphold the Buddhist *thamma* gives rise to *kaliyuga*, an age of calamity. The right to be a king does not come from dynastic descent; rather, a "world emperor" who comes to overcome that *kaliyuga* is "crowned" as king because he "nurtures Buddhism."

This passage also shows the influence of writing "universal" history, in which there is no single centre of affairs in one single country and no single royal dynasty in one place. Rather, such history describes the dynasty and country which, in each era, is the most prominent patron and protector of Buddhism (Wyatt 1976, 109–11). There may be some influence of the *tamnan* type of history in this passage, but it seems of less importance than the political thinking of the time in which it was written. Accounts of the wrongs which the Burmese committed against Buddhism are available elsewhere in large quantities, and even attacks on Burma as an enemy of Buddhism exist in contemporary documents of the same era.

The chronicles undermine the accumulated merit of the Ban Phlu Luang dynasty in other ways that show its merit had lost its significance.

In Borommakot's reign, gold was discovered in Bang Taphan. The *Testimony of the Inhabitants of the Old Capital* links the "appearance" of this gold mine with the meritorious deeds of Borommakot such as building wat, and forbidding the killing of animals in Ayutthaya (*TIOC*, 149–50).[19] The discovery of this gold mine is also reported in the Phonnarat version but is not linked with the "merit" making of Borommakot at all (*PR*, 618; *RCA*, 446–7). In the same fashion, the rites to overcome drought, which in the *Testimony* are performed by the elders of the monkhood on the orders of Borommakot and which are able to bring rain (*TIOC*, 153), are not mentioned at all in the chronicles. These events were still in the memories of people in early Bangkok as they reappear in the Royal Autograph edition (*RA*, II, 230; *RCA*, 454). The Phonnarat chronicle reports that one of the several special elephants of Borommakot fell ill so badly that he could not be retained and had to be released into the forest (*PR*, 627; *RCA*, 459). The possession of special elephants was a symbol of possessing high "royal authority," and thus the loss of a special elephant for any reason was also a symbol of the decline in "royal authority."

At the end of Borommakot's reign, the Phonnarat chronicle inserts an additional passage, not found in the Phan Chanthanumat version, to emphasize this is the end of an era—not just the end of King Borommakot's reign, but of the Ban Phlu Luang dynasty as a whole. That insertion states:

19. The account of this event in the *Testimony of the Inhabitants of the Old Capital* is intended to elevate King Borommakot as a world emperor according to Buddhist theory, or *thammaracha*, which is the name which this book uses for King Borommakot. The world emperor has a crystal treasurer who is capable of seeing "the decorative gems, silver and gold on the land, under the land, as deep as sixteen *yojana* under the land, or even in the depths of the ocean" (*Traiphum phra ruang*, 616; Reynolds and Reynolds 1982, 168). And because King Borommakot "while he reigns, acts righteously and does righteous things.... because of the accumulation of merit of the one who is Lord above all ... [r]ice and water, plus fish and other food, the ten thousand measures of gems and ornaments, the nine kinds of gems, silver, gold, clothing and garments of silk will all be available in abundance" (*Traiphum phra ruang*, 597; Reynolds and Reynolds 1982, 153).

> When death came to His Holiness, a variety of unnatural and ominous events thereupon [occurred] because His Holiness was the major sovereign in the Thai Country ... in the middle of the night, the kite winds blew heavily and the Holy Grand Reliquary, which was the foundation of the Monastery of the Fig [Wat Pho], collapsed and fell down. Even the atmosphere displayed evil abnormalities. Lotus meteors fell and hit the Grand Bow in luminous streaks of light. In addition, the orb of a star accordingly eclipsed the sphere of the Holy Moon, while comets [appeared in] the Canal of the Albino Elephants. The populace accordingly was cold and clammy [with fear] throughout the Metropolis, because the Divine Lords were influencing them into perceiving [what was about to happen]... (*PR*, 628; *RCA*, 460/25–40)

This passage resembles another about the end of Taksin's reign in the Phan Chanthanumat chronicle (which was written in the Bangkok period for certain), that "in the atmosphere there were many unexpected things, such as a meteor and a falling fire-vehicle (*pratuk-kat*)" (*CC-65*, 126). Both accounts refer to comets which are believed to appear at an evil time. Hence readers of the chronicles in the Bangkok period would understand immediately that the Ban Phlu Luang dynasty's rights to kingship had definitively ended at the close of Borommakot's reign. The fate of the Ban Phlu Luang dynasty was sealed.

The international politics of the Bangkok era imposed some limitations on this destruction of the Ban Phlu Luang dynasty's reputation. The chroniclers sometimes altered or misrepresented events for the sake of Siam's external interest. Mostly these instances concerned Siam's rights over territories which in early Bangkok were held to be tributary states according to ancient traditions. Sometimes these passages happen to augment the reputation of the Ban Phlu Luang dynasty. One clear example is the case of Cambodia.

An important instance of Siam's intervention in Cambodia during the Ban Phlu Luang period was the despatch of an army to assist the faction of Khmer royalty which sided with Siam to expel Vietnamese influence from Cambodia in Thaisa's reign. The Ayutthaya recensions such as the Chakraphatdiphong version do not conceal the failure of the Siamese side in this venture. They report straightforwardly that the Siamese army was "attacked by the Yuan, routed and fled" (*CC-8*, 178; *RCA*, 402/29–31, recast). This accords with external sources (Turpin 1908, 133).

Such an account was possible because late Ayutthaya had lost interest in Cambodia. Even Siam's victorious war against Cambodia in Naresuan's reign is not mentioned at all by the inhabitants of the old capital taken away as war captives by the Burmese (*TIOC*, 89–98). The places which Naresuan attacked and took, as listed in the *Testimony of the Inhabitants of the Old Capital*, do not include Cambodia (*TIOC*, 96). But in the Thonburi and Bangkok periods, Cambodia had great significance in the foreign policy of both King Taksin and the Chakri kings. The defeat by Cambodia in Thaisa's reign was effectively a disruption of Siam's claims over Cambodia. The recensions from 1795 onwards spread the story that the Cambodian side was defeated by the Ayutthaya army and subsequently consented to offer tribute of silver and gold flowers (*PC*, 284; *RCA* 403/42–3). The British Museum version elaborates on this to make it abundantly clear that the Siamese achieved a definite victory (*BM*, 574–77; *RCA* 402–4).

The insertion of a passage about the cruel execution of a Cambodian king in Naresuan's reign (*RCA*, 153) is also understood to have been the work of the chroniclers in the Thonburi and Bangkok periods. The Luang Prasoet chronicle states only that "the King advanced with his army in procession to seize the city of Lawaek.... In the campaign on that occasion King Si Suphan was captured" but has no mention of a ritual execution (*RCA*, 142/30–4). We know from contemporary sources that the Cambodian king was able to flee, and went to reside in Vientiane until his son returned to rule in Lawaek again (Hall 1968, 255–9). The ritual execution invented by the chroniclers seems to have been a lesson for Cambodian royalty who came to "take education" at the Bangkok court in the early Bangkok period.

The whole narrative of King Naresuan's first major war with Burma is highly likely to have been written afresh in the Thonburi-Bangkok period, perhaps making use of old chronicles from the Ayutthaya era, as the literary style is clearly that of the Bangkok period, and as there are additions like the Cambodian example above. King Naresuan may already have been a hero for the people of Ayutthaya, but the chronicles make him an even greater hero for the Bangkok period. He was the ideal king—clever, a brave warrior, and a patron of Buddhism. He was constantly mindful of his duty to be the supreme patron and protector of Buddhism. Even in the throes of battle, he proclaimed to the gods, "You had Us born into the lineage of the great white umbrella and would have Us support the Holy Buddhist Religion, so why don't you help to clear the air so We can see the enemy?" (*PR*, 197; *RCA*, 130/36–9). Even when angry about the mistakes of his generals, he listens to one Phra Phonnarat (it is interesting why this character happened to be called Phonnarat) expound about "His Holiness the Supreme Crown of the World" [i.e. Buddha] and as a result "contemplated the Holy Merit beyond all bounds and felt joy and exultation fill the lotus of his heart. Raising his hands above his head in reverent obeisance..." (*PR*, 202; *RCA*, 133/9–12).

The chronicles' account of the great war with Burma on this occasion is a rousing work, well written of its kind. How much or little value this passage of the chronicles has for history still needs to be ascertained by a great deal of verification with external sources. But its value as literature is such it would be difficult to find anything comparable from the same period. It is written in elegant stylized prose (*roi kaeo*). For the reader it is both beautiful and inspirational. There are pieces of dialogue aptly inserted into the story. This part of the chronicles must have made a great impression on the Thai of early Bangkok who had just experienced a national disaster and still faced a constant threat from Burma. The story begins with the weakness of Ayutthaya and its defeat at the hands of King Bayinnaung (Burengnong), but continues on to Siam's revival under King Naresuan, and ends with the disaster that befell the Bayinnaung dynasty. The story is impactful not simply because victory eventually falls to the Thai, but because the story confirms the Buddhist belief that virtue is its own reward.

The values on prominent display in the recensions of this time are military courage and patriotism. The chronicles paint an image of Naresuan as a brave warrior. When he leads the army out to battle, the chronicles have Naresuan say, "We shall have to advance forth first to have fun playing war with the Mons" (*PR*, 184; *RCA*, 140/10–11).

This story was developed to its peak in another literary work written by Prince Paramanuchit Chinorot, *Taleng phai* (Defeat of the Mon), which uses the chronicle narrative to such an extent it is little more than a translation of stylized prose into poetic verse. This usage of the chronicles followed the trend of literature in the early Bangkok era. A Mon chronicle was adapted on royal command into the story *Ratchathirat* (King of Kings) with the objective of showing the Thai that the Burmese were not always victorious but had been defeated by (even) the Mon. The *Sam kok* (Three Kingdoms) story was also translated in the First Reign because it was thought it would have military value, and would inspire military valour.

Another important change in the recensions of the Ayutthaya chronicles made in the Thonburi-Bangkok era was to portray the government in Ayutthaya as unstable and discontinuous.

The Luang Prasoet chronicle written in the Narai reign refers to the contests over the throne in successive reigns in a vague fashion. In 1370, King Boromracha came from Suphanburi, "ascended the royal throne of the Capital City of Ayutthaya, and then sent King Ramesuan to ascend the royal throne of Lopburi." In 1534 when King Chairacha seized the throne and executed either his own son or the minor king (according to different versions), the Luang Prasoet chronicle says only "his young son had an accident and so the royal throne went to Prince Chairacha." Similarly in 1548, "King Yot Fa met with an accident and Khun Chinnarat obtained the throne." After that "Khun Chinnarat and Queen Si Sudacan met with an accident. So Prince Thianracha ascended the royal throne" (*CC-1*, 115, 124, 126; *RCA*, 11/39–42, 20/14–7, 23/11–6). In the absence of explanations from other chronicles, we would have no way of knowing what happened to these unfortunate kings.

The Luang Prasoet chronicle tends to present a picture of stability. The succession disputes and power struggles are played down through the device of vagueness. This may be because this version of the chronicle had to use the astrologers' records and almanacs as its major source. The compilers of the astrological almanacs seem to have tried to avoid using violent or coarse words in relating events that took place in the court.

The Michael Vickery Chronicle, even though only a fragment remains, seems to confirm that the Ayutthayan chroniclers did not like to describe violence in disputes over the throne or over power. This chronicle in the unabridged style concludes the suppression of a revolt in the time of King Rachathirat III as follows: "Because the king observed the ten principles of royal conduct excellently he killed people who were traitors. Those whom he did not also consider traitors, he did not have them killed" (Vickery 1977, 22–3). In reality, the many power struggles in Ayutthaya probably had no severe impact which undermined the stability of the government, especially when those who acquired the throne got a firm grip on power. Turpin, whose work was written from contemporary French missionary records, spoke of the "coup" of King Phetracha that, "The revolution was managed so adroitly, that there were no perceptible changes in public affairs.... as soon as there appeared nothing more to fear from their actions, he promoted all those of whom he had previously cause to complain" (Turpin 1908, 89).

Many changes of regime must have been of this nature; changing the dynasty did not mean an attempt to change anything fundamental, and any bloodbath was simply a somewhat excessive elimination of enemies.

This elision of the openly violent seizures of power seems to have been continued through to the recensions made in late Ayutthaya.

The Chakraphatdiphong chronicle has little to say about the coup at the end of Narai's reign. Furthermore, it stresses the continuity between the new dynasty and the old one by stating that Phetracha was appointed to the highest post in charge of the nobility. The Phan Chanthanumat-Ayutthaya chronicle does not mention the coup at all and stresses that Phetracha had marriage relations with senior royal ladies of the Narai lineage. The attempt to construct an image of continuity for the Ayutthayan monarchy is even more explicit in the *Testimony of the Inhabitants of the Old Capital.* King Prasat Thong, who Van Vliet (1954) says was the most cunning of all those who contested for the throne, in the portrayal by the inhabitants of Ayutthaya ascends the throne peacefully as the son of the previous king. The succession disputes decided by civil war (on a large or small scale) at the end of the reigns of Ekathotsarot, Songtham, and Prasat Thong are not mentioned at all. King Suea becomes a secret son of King Narai.

While the Ayutthaya recensions wanted to tone down these violent and bloody struggles for power, the Thonburi-Bangkok recensions wanted to play them up.

King Rama I did not seek legitimacy by concluding a marriage alliance with the inner part of the previous dynasty, or by claiming a legitimate but secret blood connection (such as being the hidden son of a previous king). King Taksin took some members of the Ban Phlu Luang lineage into the palace but King Rama I took nobody from the Thonburi lineage as a consort. It seems he accepted quite straightforwardly that he was someone who had seized power, and he established his legitimacy to rule with a different type of ideology which will be explained below.

This change is readily understandable. In the time before the fall of Ayutthaya, both Taksin and Rama I were only mid-level or rather junior nobles. Taksin had been appointed as Phraya Wachira Prakan and had not yet gone to take up his post in Kamphaengphet.[20] Furthermore, Kamphaengphet was not a major city in late Ayutthaya. As for Rama I, he was ranked only as *luang yokkrabat* of Ratchaburi. His mother, according to the explanation which King Mongkut gave to Bowring, came from a Chinese trading family in Ayutthaya (Bowring 1969, I, 65–6). Furthermore, Rama I was probably related to the Chinese community of Amphawa.[21] Hence, if Ayutthaya had not fallen apart, he would probably have spent his life in Ratchaburi

20. In some accounts, Taksin is supposed to have been appointed governor of Kamphaengphet with the title of Phraya Wachira Prakan shortly before the Burmese attack. In his later study of Taksin, Nidhi (1986, 116–21) reckons this is one of many later myths about Taksin's career. [T]

21. Skinner (1957, 19, and 80) states that, since at least the early fourteenth century, Chinese settlement had spread up various rivers including the Maeklong as far as Kanchanaburi, making it likely that Amphawa was one of the early Chinese settlements.

and sought his fortune in some way other than government, for example as a trader or capitalist (moneylender) in agricultural products.

There was no occasion at all in Ayutthaya history when a low-ranked noble on the level of Taksin or Rama I was able to ascend the throne. For this reason, neither monarch was interested in preserving the "sacredness" of the Ayutthaya monarchy. In the chronicle recensions made under their rule, legitimacy by blood descent is exposed as only a myth because many of the Ayutthayan kings (in the chronicles, not in true history) were commoners.

THE CHRONICLES OF THONBURI AND THE RECENSIONS IN EARLY BANGKOK

Kachorn Sukhabanij found definite proof that part of the Phan Chanthanumat chronicle of Thonburi was written in the Thonburi period itself. The chronicle has a reference to someone who had been "Phraya Thibet Borirak" in the Ayutthaya period and "is [now] Chaophraya Si Thammathirat," meaning in the Thonburi period (Kachorn 1977, 92–5). Kachorn stated it was certain that Chaophraya Si Thammathirat was promoted further in 1774, hence the Thonburi chronicle must have been written by that year. The source Kachorn used was the copy of a government order printed in the *Collected Chronicles* volume 66, but this order does not inform us when this person became Chaophraya Si Thammathirat (*CC-66*, 147). Furthermore, a reference to Chaophraya Si Thammathirat has been found in the daily military register from 1771 (*CC-66*, 237).

In 1782, King Rama I appointed someone new to the title of Chaophraya Si Thammathirat, namely Phraya Takto, the Thonburi astrologer (Thiphakorawong 1960, 10). It thus can be concluded that the section of the Phan Chanthanumat chronicle about Thonburi must have been written in some year between whenever Phraya Thibet Borirak was appointed as Chaophraya Si Thammathirat and, at the latest, the end of Taksin's reign. The exact year this part of the chronicle was written is still uncertain.

As there are no external sources to settle this matter, the contents of the document itself have to be submitted to internal analysis.

This chronicle has very detailed and careful description of events in each year. But around 1779–80 the narrative starts to contract noticeably. For example, only two events are reported in 1779, only one in 1780, and in 1781 only a story of the king ordering the army to Cambodia before the chronicle goes into the disorder at the end of the reign. Thus it can be seen from the process of composition that the chronicle commissioned by King Taksin probably extends up to roughly 1778–9, and the remainder was added after the end of the reign.

The contents of this chronicle glorify King Taksin throughout. Conspicuously, there is nothing about the Chakri family, and nothing special to glorify the Chakri family in any way. This is different from the versions revised later. Yet in 1807, when the recension commissioned by Rama I and compiled by Phra Phonnarat was completed, the material on Thonburi was still the same as the Phan Chanthanumat version, word for word. This means that, up to almost the last year of the First Reign, there was no new chronicle written about the Thonburi era except for material appended about the end of the reign (compare the coverage of the Thonburi era in the British Museum version).

The tolerance exhibited by King Rama I about the chronicles written under the authority of Taksin is not easy to explain. From the perspective of political rivalry, the Ban Phlu Luang dynasty was not a problem for the Chakri dynasty, and yet the Rama I recensions of the Ayutthaya chronicles about the Ban Phlu Luang period have a great deal of addition and elaboration. Conversely, King Taksin, who had to be openly declared a true political enemy, is allowed to "speak" quite openly. This paradox is best explained by the fact that Taksin and Rama I shared a similar attitude to kingship. The chronicles of King Taksin, while glorifying Taksin himself, were tolerable because they upheld principles about the role of the king and the king's duty to the state which were identical with the principles of Rama I.

There is another version of the chronicles of the Thonburi era which Dr Bradley printed together with the Phonnarat version, known as the two-volume edition. The contents differ greatly from the Phan Chanthanumat or British Museum version,[22] even though that volume was the basis for drafting this recension. Most of the variation lies in additional material, and changes of style, rather than omission. Who made this recension and when is not known for certain. It is highly likely it was done after the First Reign, since this volume did not exist in 1807. Possibly, Somdet Phra Phonnarat made the recension before his death early in the Second Reign. Anyway, here this version of the Thonburi chronicle will be called the Phonnarat version.

This Phonnarat version was the basis for drafting the recension currently known as the Royal Autograph edition which was compiled in the Fourth Reign and revised subsequently to become the final recension of the chronicles.

As the complete recension of the Thonburi chronicle was compiled rather long after King Taksin's reign, the need to denigrate the king had waned, other than over the events surrounding the king's derangement at the end of the reign. If a recension of the Thonburi chronicle had been made early in the First Reign, probably it would have been designed to bring down the reputation of King Taksin. Hostility towards the previous king was much stronger at the start of the First Reign, as evident from an order appointing Chaophraya Nakhon Si Thammarat in 1784 as follows: "Phraya Taksin governed the realm at that time. He was full of anger and greed. He did not behave properly according to ancient customs" (Krom Silapakon 1962, 188). The recension of the Thonburi chronicle in the early Bangkok period had the narrow objective of enhancing the reputation of the Chakri dynasty, rather than lowering the reputation of King Taksin. The revisions may be summarized as follow.

22. The Phan Chanthanumat chronicle of Thonburi is missing the middle part about the war with Asewunki (Atthi-wongyi), but as the other contents are identical with the more complete British Museum edition, these can be used where the Phan Chanthanumat edition is defective.

1. Narrative was added about the life histories of people in the Chakri family, especially Rama I and the Front Palace prince. For example, a passage was added on the *luang yokkrabat* of Ratchaburi (i.e., the future Rama I) being presented at court and entering government service, with Phra Mahamontri, his younger brother, as sponsor (*PR*, 37). This passage does not appear in the Phan Chanthanumat version, but was simply inserted without explaining when the *luang yokkrabat* was appointed, and what was the new post of Phra Ratchaworin who had held the post earlier and had figured in the battle at Chanthaburi.

Besides details on the histories of members of the Chakri family, material was also added about some prominent nobles of the Thonburi era. For example, the Phonnarat volume added material from the Ayutthaya period about the presentation at court and entry into government service of Luang Nai Sak who was later promoted to Chaophraya Chakri (*PR*, 21, 49), and known as Phraya Chakri (Khaek). He was a military officer who fought at Nakhon Si Thammarat and had a son whose name is mentioned in the chronicles as Laksamana which suggests he was a Muslim and explains why he was named "Khaek" (*CC-65*, 40). This individual was rather important as he is understood to have been an enemy of Phraya Aphai Ronnarit, as will be mentioned below.

2. The narrative was revised where it might be damaging to the reputation of the Chakri dynasty, especially on two points. The Phan Chanthanumat and British Museum editions have similar passages about the despatch of an army to attack Nakhon Si Thammarat in 1769. Phraya Yommarat (younger brother of the future King Rama I, who both editions say was promoted from the title of Phraya Anuchitracha in 1768) (*CC-65*, 39; *BM*, 671) and Phraya Aphai Ronnarit (future King Rama I) both merged their armies with that of Phraya Chakri (Khaek) (*CC-65*, 39; *BM*, 672), and yet the attack failed. Military officers laid charges against Phraya Chakri (Khaek) to King Taksin "who gave his learned judgement that there had been a falling out and argument, and it had been his misfortune to have only unsuccessful officers" (*CC-65*, 40). This passage was clearly not at all favorable to the reputation of King Rama I and his younger brother. The Phonnarat version of the Thonburi chronicles thus revises the whole passage. When the king orders the army to Nakhon in 1769, Phraya Anuchitracha and Phraya Aphai Ronnarit are detailed to take their armies to attack Siam Reap. On arrival they receive news that King Taksin has died, and thus withdraw their armies and return. In military law, this would be counted as a mutiny because the armies were withdrawn without receiving any order. But as they declare their loyalty and show no wish to become subjects of anyone else, King Taksin's anger abates and he praises both of them. In sum, the attack on Siam Reap is not successful but this is not due to the pair's lack of military ability but because of accidental circumstances (*PR*, 48–9, 59–61).

What was the truth in this matter cannot be ascertained. Yet the two or three contemporary sources that are available do not agree with the revisions in the Phonnarat chronicle and suggest that no attack was made on Siam Reap in 1769. A letter from the French missionaries in Thonburi at that time refers to the army attack on Nakhon in 1769 but not an expedition to attack Siam Reap, even though these missionaries were highly interested in Cambodia as some had just escaped from there to Thonburi, and their previous letter had been wholly about Cambodia (*CC-39*, 446). Conversely in 1772, when the king led an army against Cambodia and towns in southern Vietnam, the missionaries reported this expedition (*CC-39*, 461). The records of Prince Narintharathewi include the military expedition to Nakhon but do not have the names of Phraya Aphai Ronnarit or Phraya Anuchitracha among the officers. The officers' names appearing in these records are admittedly rather confused, but what is important is that there is no mention of an attack on Siam Reap in 1769 (Chulachomklao 1916, 5).

Although the Phonnarat chronicle revised the account of the two Phrayas' involvement in the attack on Nakhon, the revision was not made very carefully. The chronicle simply lifted a passage from another edition compiled in the Thonburi period which states that Siam Reap had been seized by these two Phraya in 1768 when the king led an expedition to suppress the ruler of Phimai (*PR*, 42). This tallies with the account in the Phan Chanthanumat and British Museum versions (*CC-69*, 37). A careful revision would have cut this out because there would not have been two military expeditions to attack Siam Reap within such a short space of time.[23]

Another passage which underwent revision was about the defence of Phitsanulok during the war with Asewunki (Atthi-wongyi). The Phan Chanthanumat and British Museum editions seem to imply that the Burmese poured in forces to take the city and the Thai were unable to hold onto it. Also, Phitsanulok seems finally to have fallen without an engagement, as these chronicles state: "Chaophraya Chakri and Chaophraya Surasi realized the forces were too much and so led their troops to break through the Burmese lines and escape from Phitsanulok. The whole army was scattered in utter confusion. The Burmese army had the field and pursued them..." (*CC-65*, 104). These two chronicles do not report the story about Asewunki wanting to meet Chaophraya Chakri as, from the standpoint of the laws of both Siam and Burma, such a meeting would amount to mutiny. The Phonnarat chronicle has a great deal of additional material on this war. Some additions (for example, about the negotiations to see Phraya Chakri) seem to show some influence from the *Three Kingdoms*. The retreat from Phitsanulok is described as happening in an orderly fashion. Chaophraya Chakri has the camp outside the town abandoned in order to fight inside the town. Then he sends a Thai orchestra to play on the walls as a diversion (another influence from the *Three Kingdoms*). When the opportunity arises, he leads the army to break through the encirclement in an orderly fashion, "the units left at the rear waited to intercept the forces mid-way with great capability." The loss of Phitsanulok thus still presents an opportunity for the Phonnarat chronicle to "cast a spell" so that Bangkok may remain safe from the Burmese for ever: after entering Phitsanulok, the Burmese

23. King Chulalongkorn declared that the attack on Siam Reap in 1769 was a fact, but the attack on Siam Reap in 1768 did not take place, citing the Khmer chronicles as his source (Chulachomklao 1916, 43). But the Khmer chronicles about this event were compiled at a much later date and followed the material in the Thai chronicles. Also the business about making war in two places at the same time at the start of the reign is unlikely to have taken place.

general Asewunki declares: "Burma can come to fight Siam again in the future as long as the army commander shows cleverness and skill equal to ours; but if their skill is less than that, it would be better not to come to fight the Thai at all because victory will be impossible" (*PR*, 154–6). At the same time, this chronicle has additional history about Asewunki's ability based on stories obtained from Burma which show he was even able to engage and defeat the Chinese (*PR*, 76–8). These do not appear in the British Museum or Phan Chanthanumat editions.

The truth about the fall of Phitsanulok cannot be ascertained as there are no reliable external sources on the subject, but it is likely that the city was not breached even though the subsequent retreat from the city was not so orderly, and full of feints and ruses, as in the Phonnarat version. More likely, King Taksin himself ordered a break-out from the siege, and as a result Chaophraya Chakri was promoted in rank to Phrachao Mahakasatsuk in 1777 after the war. If he had lost to the Burmese and been the cause of the breach, he would have faced punishment rather than promotion.

Other than revisions to protect or enhance the reputation of the Chakri dynasty, there were some other revisions which may have had a more profound objective, including reducing the passages which glorify King Taksin but have no utility as reinforcement for the view of kingship held in early Bangkok. For example, in the Phan Chanthanumat chronicle, when King Taksin received news of the battle against the Burmese at Bang Kung, "as soon as he knew, he felt pleased, as if he had received the ultimate good fortune. With a heart full of royal courage, on that night itself, he led the forces by sea so swiftly as if he were Phraya Chawan Ratchahong, leader of all the golden swans (*suwannahong*)" (*CC-65*, 31). The Phonnarat chronicle omitted this passage, and stated that the king appointed Phra Mahamontri as leader of the vanguard and ordered this vanguard alone to attack and defeat the Burmese (*PR*, 38). In the Phan Chanthanumat edition, the king himself leads the vanguard.

Conversely, passages which glorify King Taksin very highly yet agree with the ideal of kingship in early Bangkok are retained in their existing form. For example, one passage which made Prince Damrong decide that the Thonburi chronicles were probably not written in the First Reign, runs "at the time when the capital had not yet fallen, the king who had the supernatural power of an embryonic Buddha stated that Ayutthaya was in danger because the officers and people of the city did not follow the *thamma*" (*PR*, 1; Damrong 1962, 24–5). Even if it were true that this passage was written in the Thonburi era, the Bangkok recension did not change even a single letter (until the Royal Autograph edition), because these words were not over-glorification: the person who is king has the status of being a future Buddha. One title for royal princes in the Ayutthaya period was *No phutthankun*, "embryonic Buddha." King Rama I himself was glorified as an embryonic Buddha by the writer of *Thetsana chulayutthakanwong* as follows: "both princes who were of the lineage of the Buddha observed Buddhist practices with a wish to attain nirvana and become a Buddha" (*CC-65*, 91). Every king was accorded the right to be an embryonic Buddha. There was no reason for Rama I to deny this right to someone else while he enjoyed the right himself. In addition, this passage reiterated an idea about kingship which will be covered below.

There was one further interesting revision on the subject of moving the capital.

The Phan Chanthanumat chronicle states that when Ayutthaya was recaptured from the Burmese, King Taksin, seeing the corpses and other calamities, declared "he was distressed and weary of the throne and wanted to go to Chanthaburi." But the "monks, ministers and people" implored him to ascend the throne and "he saw the benefit of being consecrated for attaining enlightenment, so accepted the invitation, and halted at the residence (*tamnak*) in Thonburi" (*CC-65*, 29). This should be read as a decision to use Thonburi as a temporary capital. The Phonnarat chronicle adds a passage in which Taksin decides to move the capital from Ayutthaya permanently: while staying in the old palace, Taksin has a prophetic dream in which he is chased out of the palace by a member of old Ayutthaya royalty, and as a result he decides to abandon Ayutthaya permanently (*PR*, 4).

It appears there was no definite policy about the location of the capital during the Thonburi period. Throughout Taksin's reign, no royal palace was built, and no large-scale building was constructed of durable material in Thonburi. Even though the king tried to preserve several symbols of Ayutthaya culture such as the dramas, chronicles, Tipitaka, and various manuals of royal ceremonial, these were all things that could be easily transported.

The policy to abandon Ayutthaya was made by King Rama I who established a new capital immediately on ascending the throne. In the first year of the reign, he ordered the building of the Amarintaraphisek palace and Wat Phra Si Ratthana Sasadaram as the court temple, instead of using Wat Photharam in the way that Taksin had used Wat Chaeng (later named Wat Arun). In early Bangkok, people probably retained a considerable attachment to Ayutthaya. In the hopes of the Front Palace prince, if the Burmese could be captured as war prisoners, "the Burmese will become slaves of the Thai and can be used to build Ayutthaya." The policy to build Bangkok like the old capital was intended to lessen the nostalgia for the old "sacred center" of the Thai state. In the Phonnarat chronicle, the narrative was revised so that the decision was taken and remained unchanged from the previous reign.

The Phonnarat edition's wish to ring down the curtain on Ayutthaya also resulted in another additional passage summarizing that Ayutthaya had thirty-four kings and lasted as a capital for 417 years (*PR*, 23). The British Museum and Phan Chanthanumat editions do not count the number of kings or the capital's age (*BM*, 663–4; *CC-65*, 29–30). The Phonnarat edition was the first chronicle to do so.

The Phonnarat edition has rather detailed additional passages about the disorder after the fall of Ayutthaya (*PR*, 22–31, some of which repeats *CC-65*, 34–7). But apart from preserving details for future scrutiny, the most meaningful aspect of these additions was probably the Phonnarat chronicle's summary that "there arose killings and disorder throughout every part of the realm of Siam because no king could be found. It was like the era (*kalpa*) of animals and the era of famine" (*PR*, 24). Similarly, in the Phonnarat edition, Prince Thep Phiphit[24] was not executed at Phimai, as stated in the Phan Chanthanumat version, but brought to Thonburi on the king's orders

24. A maverick prince of the Ban Phlu Luang family who represented a restorationist alternative to Taksin's new polity. [T]

and executed there (*CC-65*, 37). This agrees with contemporary records that state he was executed in Thonburi (*CC-39*, 443–4). Phonnarat adds passages about the investigation of Prince Thep Phiphit who refuses to pay homage on grounds that he considers himself a descendant of old royalty. It has King Taksin rule that "you no longer have your old fortune and status.... you must die now once and for all, so that there will no further disorder in the realm in the future" (*PR*, 43). This revision is closely bound up with a profound change which arose in early Bangkok (possibly originating earlier in the Thonburi period) which will be explained below.[25]

Not all the revisions in the early Bangkok recensions were made in order to change the meaning. Some resulted from new and better knowledge about events. The execution of Prince Thep Phiphit is one example. Most such additions tend to concern events in neighboring countries, especially Burma, about which more information was available in early Bangkok. This can be found in the Phonnarat chronicle on Thonburi. Examples include the story of a Chinese army attacking Ava; events in Burma after the end of the reign of Hsinbyushin (1763–76; in Thai history known as King Mangra) (*PR*, 168); and the Tayson revolt in Vietnam (*PR*, 169–72). Such additions relating to the Ayutthaya period were not extensive until the last recension in the Royal Autograph edition.

THE THINKING BEHIND THE THONBURI-BANGKOK RECENSIONS

As can be seen from the many examples presented above, the revisions in the Thonburi-Bangkok recensions were not simply what Wyatt called "heeding the king's sensibilities" (Wyatt 1976, 120). There were deeper intentions. The condemnation of the Ban Phlu Luang dynasty was not done simply to eliminate political rivals. It is true that Ban Phlu Luang descendants challenged the power of King Taksin, namely Prince Thep Phiphit and Chao Si Sang who fled to Ha Tien (Phutthaimat) and Cambodia (see about Chao Si Sang in *CC*, 39). But both these Ban Phlu Luang descendants were eradicated early in Taksin's reign. There was no reason to revise the chronicle to condemn this dynasty any further.

25. There were other revisions for which the facts cannot be checked and the reasons for the revision cannot be explained. For example, the Phan Chanthanumat edition reports that Suki, the head of the Burmese garrison left at Ayutthaya, submitted to King Taksin and was commissioned to continue looking after the old capital. The Phonnarat version revises this so that the garrison head dies in the fighting. It seems that hatred of the Burmese had deepened in the early Bangkok period to the point they were seen as being irreligious and enemies of Buddhism (see the law on conscription 1810 in Sathian 1935–53, IV, 2). The tales of evil deeds and destruction of religious places by the Burmese at Ayutthaya all come from documents written in the Bangkok era. Thus possibly it was now unthinkable to have a Mon on the Burmese side looking after the old capital. However, I am not certain on this point because I cannot find sources for the ruling class view of the Burmese in the Thonburi period to use for comparison.

The attempts to revise the past, no matter who did it and in what period, arose from the complex relationship between the past and the present. Possibly they simply made no attempt to understand changes in the conditions of different eras. Possibly they just hoped to make the past "be of use" for the present. In part, there may have been complexity arising from the conditions of the time. But in part, events known from the past must have been concealed or misrepresented because the image of the past from the sources available at that time was considered unsatisfactory, and because there was a desire to construct a new image of the past that was satisfactory for the present. This newly constructed image did not need to be beautiful and glorious in all respects, but had to embed the moral judgment or ideals of the present so that it "had meaning."

What was it about late Ayutthaya that the ruling class of Thonburi-Bangkok was unhappy with and wanted to change?

As observed already, the revisions of the chronicles about the Ban Phlu Luang dynasty were made to destroy the reputation of the dynasty through reference to moral and political principles in Buddhist teaching. The fact that certain values are used to judge the past indicates that these values have great significance in the present. In part, Buddhism was used as a value in order to explain why the country experienced a disaster under the Ban Phlu Luang dynasty. But more importantly, the revision announced the values of the new government which had just been established. And as the "royal" chronicles were a matter of the king and state, the values which both new dynasties announced in these works were about the king and the state.

Thus we should first examine theories about king and state in Buddhist teaching.

The oldest text in Buddhism about the origins of the state and government appears to be the Aggana (Akanya) Sutta (Rhys Davids 1965, 77–94). In the Thikanikai (Dighanikaya), this text offered a Buddhist explanation about the origins of the world and universe. Humans were formerly gods of the Brahma level who descended as beings into the world that had just been newly created. The behavior of these beings degenerated by stages, and at each stage of degeneration their lives became more difficult because nature changed and no longer provided them with such a comfortable existence. For example, they had to start finding their own food; male and female genders developed; and lust arose. From that point, humans never ceased to do evil. Robbery and conflict appeared. In the end, someone among them had the idea of leading them to search for a person "who was the handsomest, the best favored, the most attractive, the most capable" (Rhys Davids 1965, 88). It was decided to make this person their commander, judge, and ruler in exchange for food and other necessities of life which the people provided as recompense. This individual was thus named the first Great Elect (*mahasommuti*) or first king of the world.

The important points about this theory are as follows.

1. Personal property, state, and society originate from the degeneration of mankind, meaning that if mankind was still mentally pure as at the time of the first descent into the world, these things would not be necessary.

2. The institution of kingship is based on an agreement or social contract between government and people, defining their different duties to one another. Such thinking

does not necessarily support democratic ideas. It might just limit the king's duties to maintaining orderliness in society, and oblige the people to work to provide the king's upkeep without having any rights at all.

3. Under this agreement between king and people, the king performs his duties by imposing punishments on those who do wrong (Goshal 1966, 64–5).

For a long time, Buddhist writers have drawn on this passage in the Aggana Sutta for theory. It appears in later religious texts such as certain Jataka stories (Goshal 1966, 68), Vasupanthu's *Apithammakot*, and Buddhaghosa's *Wisutthimak* (Goshal 1966, 377–8).

From this theory, Buddhist states in Southeast Asia developed further ideas about state and king as follows.

1. The state is modeled in the form of a large universe according to Buddhist-Hindu geography.

2. The person who is king is believed to have accumulated the most merit. This is indicated by his superior status in life, above all others in the same incarnation. He possesses the royal insignia, the palace, and a lifestyle of conspicuous wealth. The fact that he has the most accumulated merit is proven by his ascent of the throne. This action intrinsically indicates that this person has the most merit. If there were someone else with greater merit than the ruling king, then there would be consequences such as that person successfully seizing the throne (Heine-Geldern 1965).

3. By analogy to Indra, the god who supports religion, the duties of the king, apart from building the palace and apportioning the provincial cities, is to be the chief patron of Buddhism within his own little universe. He acquits this duty by constructing places of worship, and protecting and promoting the Sangha.

4. In Buddhism, the ultimate goal in life is nirvana. The current existence is only one stage in the passage to this destination. In each life, a human being should accumulate more merit in order to achieve nirvana in the future. In his role as the patron of Buddhism, the king has a duty to keep people moral so that they do not fall into the bad ways which lead to hell, but accumulate merit according to their fortune. From this angle, the state is a tool to achieve nirvana and the king is like a Bodhisatta who leads people to that goal. As noted above, Buddhist political theory views the state as a product of man's own degeneration, but the state in Southeast Asia has the additional role of enabling man to recover his goodness.

This whole line of thinking has been present in Siam for a long time. The first documentary source, the *Traiphum phra ruang* or Three Worlds of King Ruang, dates back to the time of King Lithai of Sukhothai. It centers on the principle of the king as the possessor of the highest accumulated merit, and makes the Great Elect into a Bodhisatta (*Traiphum phra ruang*, 773–4; Reynolds and Reynolds 1982, 324–5). This idea of the king as a Bodhisatta continued down to the Bangkok period, as can be seen from the *Trailokawinitchai* (Treatise on the Three Worlds)[26] which was written in this period and which states the king is a Bodhisatta. Just this single statement conveys the full theory about the king being the possessor of the highest merit.

26. This book was later called the *Traiphum lokawinitchai*. This may be a misunderstanding

The Ayutthayan kings, including the Ban Phlu Luang dynasty, were also inheritors of this tradition. But although these ideas were important in the Ayutthaya period, they were not emphasized as much as in early Bangkok. The Ayutthayan king had a sacredness that was intrinsic. This sacredness did not arise merely from some duty under a "social contract" which had been agreed since the time of the Great Elect, but as a result of being a king. The idea of *devaraja*, god-king, was still of some significance.[27] A royal decree issued in the reign of King Borommakot well illustrates the thinking behind the authority of the king:

> ...moreover, the kingdom is supreme but the king because he is an Elect, a god, can bring down the great and raise up the small. If the king orders any mission, it is like a heavenly axe falling on trees and mountains that may not be able to withstand this and must be broken and destroyed. If the king forbids anything, then those rights are void. (Bradley 1873, 383)

It can be seen that in this decree, royal authority does not depend at all on the duties of the king. It is based on the king's approximation to a *devaraja*. Conversely, laws issued in the early Bangkok period tended constantly to mention that the foundation of royal authority lay in the *duties* of the king. For example, a royal decree from 1795 states that:

> ...the king today supports all the world's beings to live according to morality, promotes the flourishing of Buddhism, looks after the restoration of some wat by his own hand, and orders his officials both great and small to restore many Buddha images, stupa, chedi, and wat and clad them with lacquer and gold so they can flourish as places of worship for all the good people to inculcate good behavior and enable monks, individuals, and saints (*arahat*) to escape from the cycle of rebirth and the four evils (*chaturabai*). (Bradley 1873, 432)

Here it is necessary to stress that this Buddhist theory about state and king also had quite some influence in Ayutthaya. This is evident from the recording of the

---

on the part of the staff of the National Library, as the two original manuscripts possessed by the Manuscript Division show clearly that the writer gave the name *Trailokawinitchai* which is more correct on linguistic principles.

27. The word *devaraja* or god-king always tends to create confusion. But however much this word is disliked, there is no better way to explain the idea than by using this vague term, whose meaning is so broad it is virtually meaningless. It should also be understood that the *devaraja* theory had its own internal development like other ideas or institutions created by mankind. The nature of *devaraja* changes according to time and place. The *devaraja* of the Khmer in the time of Angkor Thom and in the time of Lawaek were not necessarily the same. In Thailand it is usually believed that Ayutthaya copied the *devaraja* model from the Khmer. Thus it is disappointing that there has been no attempt to study seriously what was the nature of *devaraja* in Ayutthaya and how it could be the ideology of the government for administering the country.

Ayutthayan kings' religious activities in the Luang Prasoet chronicle which treats these activities as an important element of the realm. Yet this idea was not as prominent as it became in the early Bangkok period. The Ayutthaya kings used other ideas to "rationalize" their rule and their institution. The Chakri rise to power (or possibly from the Thonburi period, though the records are not reliable enough) made this the most prominent aspect of Buddhist theory, and the major foundation of Chakri rule.

As a result, the institution of kingship changed. New opportunities opened up for kings to undertake various "royal activities" which were not considered as such in the past. At the same time, the monarchy could innovate more easily because the philosophical basis of rule had begun to change, although this change was not so marked as to constitute a revolution or even reform. Many of the innovations were done in the name of "reviving" old practices or copying ancient forms. Because the past became a standard for dealing with the problems of the present, recension of the chronicles, or in brief the recreation of the past to be "of use" for the present, was an imperative for the leaders of early Bangkok.

It is time to pay closer attention to Buddhist theory about state and kingship and how it became more prominent in early Bangkok.

It seems a little surprising that one of the things it was felt necessary to do urgently in the first year of the First Reign (1782) was to convene a meeting of the Sangha to study religious texts for rewriting the *Tephumikatha* (*Trailokawinitchai*, handwritten manuscript in the Manuscript Division of the National Library, bundle 1, cupboard 107, referred in the sources here as *Traiphumikatha*). In truth, in 1782, the *Traiphum phra ruang* (Three Worlds of King Ruang) was already in the royal library, because the extant version had just been inscribed in 1778. But why this version did not meet royal approval, with the result that the monkhood had to be ordered to prepare a new version, is not known because unfortunately at present the original version cannot be found and compared against the *Traiphumikatha* written in the First Reign. However, even if the document no longer exists, it probably was not greatly different in content from the *Trailokawinitchai* since the royal scholars used the *Traiphumikatha* as the basis for writing the *Trailokawinitchai*.

The preface of the *Trailokawinitchai* states that the king commissioned the composition by the assembly of royal scholars in 1783, after the Sangha had completed the *Traiphumikatha*.[28] Also he ordered a search for more copies of the Tipitaka "and had it rewritten correctly according to the Pali." The royal scholars also mention that the king took part in the compilation. For example, passages where the king's words were used to expound the Pali text are indicated in the form "at this point the king wishes it be written that…"

This text of the *Trailokawinitchai* describes the cycle of the universe, the origins of the world and of man, and importantly the origins of man and government. In the

28. In the Manuscript Division there is another version of the *Trailokawinitchai* written in 1784 but it is merely another copy of the royal version; so the royal version can be used as the model.

Traiphum phra ruang, this material appears at the very end, but in the *Trailokawinitchai* it is right at the very front. In addition, it is highly possible that the *Trailokawinitchai* used material from the Aggana Sutta, which the *Traiphum phra ruang* did not. The *Trailokawinitchai* contains certain phrases which appear only in the Aggana Sutta and not in any other scriptural text. For example, in the passage about the first man who thought of gathering food, both the Aggana Sutta and the *Trailokawinitchai* attribute this to "indolence" while the *Traiphum phra ruang* attributes it to greed arising from the establishment of the family. Although the Aggana Sutta was used in the composition, the *Trailokawinitchai* was not written "correctly according to the Pali" because it maintains that the Great Elect was a Bodhisatta, even though this idea does not appear in the Aggana Sutta or any other scriptural text.

The most important addition to the Pali in the *Trailokawinitchai* comes in the passage about the time when the waters begin to recede prior to the origin of the world. The first territory to emerge out of the water, if considered from the angle of Buddhist cosmological principles, should be Mount Meru, but the *Trailokawinitchai* instead has the Bo Tree Throne, on which the Buddha will sit and attain enlightenment, appear above the water first. It also explains, "as for the head of the land, the site of the Bo Tree Throne where Buddha will reach enlightenment under the white umbrella, when the world is destroyed, this will be the last part to be destroyed.... when the world is created, this part is created first.... thus it is called the head of the land meaning that it presides over the surface of Chomphu Thawip (Jambudvipa)." Changing the pillar of the world from Mount Meru to the Bo Tree Throne has profound implications for thinking about the state and kingship because it amounts to changing the centre of the world or universe. The king is not a "god" of the world who resides atop Mount Meru, but the king is a "Buddha" of the world who will lead all beings to find release in both body and soul. For the king to go fishing is immediately wrong because it is a betrayal of his duty to lead the people to find release according to each person's fortune and merit.

The new duties which the early Bangkok kings of the Chakri dynasty created for themselves were reflected in the issuance of a great many laws. One part of these were the Sangha Laws which had no precedent from Ayutthaya (and which have been covered by many people so it is not necessary to cover them again here). But another part was the issuance of decrees to protect the souls of the king's subjects, the ordinary people. Many decrees issued from the First to Third Reigns are evidently very different compared to old laws from Ayutthaya. They forbid various things which are not directly related to affairs of state, or else they have reasons which are not related to affairs of state but instead are based on religion. For example, a law of 1790 forbids cock-fighting "because gambling on cock-fighting is a sin" (Bradley 1873, 66). Similarly, the declaration forbidding opium smoking by King Rama III refers to consequences in the next world, namely, a fall into hell. The same tendency is found in the decree issued in 1800 to repeat the ban on cock-fighting and fighting fish. It is worth presenting at length:

> Nowadays it is the royal wish to strengthen Buddhism so that the people may live in peace and happiness...so that people may live by the four principles of *thamma*, setting the mind

> to follow the four principles, obeying morality, and giving alms. They will gain the planes of happy rebirths, blessings as humans, blessings of the heavens, and blessings of nirvana. As for officials and people who at present do not see danger in the future, who get together and persuade one another to go cock-fighting and quail-fighting, who use tricks, lies, and corruption to get wealth for self-interest, without wisdom, without considering the virtue of previous merit, indulging in money and wealth, committing bad deeds, being dishonest, quarrelsome, sinful, obscene... once dead, with five aggregates destroyed, they will fall into hell for a long time. After hell they will become suffering ghosts (*prêt*), carrying flaming iron bars, beating one another, inflicting dire actions. Because done habitually, these weighty deeds lead them to the realms of misfortune without fail. (Bradley 1873, 506)

From this perspective, the duty of the king is to lead people along the path towards nirvana, not just to take decisions on court cases and assign punishments to wrongdoers. His role is comparable to a Bodhisatta who has compassion towards mankind and leads all beings to happiness in both wordly and spiritual matters. This idea is recorded in another decree which is also worth presenting, even though it is rather long, because it reflects this thinking very clearly.

> All Buddhas when practicing the perfections within the cycle of rebirth surely have great kindness and compassion for the entire world of beings, and would like them to attain happiness in this world and in the supramundane sphere. This is the basis of their accumulated merit. Even when [these Bodhisattas] are born as paramount rulers, at times when there is no Buddhism to be found, all beings in the world rely on the paramount ruler who is accumulating perfections. The king should surely have the kindness to persuade ascetics, Brahmans, and all citizens to adhere to good deeds and honesty, and habitually practice good deeds, so when their time comes and they die, their minds will reflect upon the good deeds which they have practiced habitually. This will function as a great focus with the power to block their bad deeds completely, enabling them to ascend to enjoy heavenly blessings or human blessings, because the Lord Bodhisatta is a great king (thao phraya) with the kindness to lead worldly beings thus, as has always been the tradition. (Bradley 1873, 447–8)

The concern of the "Bodhisatta" towards the people thus extends to many details which are not connected with matters of state, such as whether or not they have knowledge of the five, eight, or ten precepts. Hence the decree presented above was a royal order enjoining all government officials to understand fully the meaning of all the precepts. It described the content of these precepts in detail, and enjoined any official attending court on any day first to abide by those precepts.

These instructions were not issued because certain kings had a special veneration for religion and turned to such matters when politics were fine and normal and they were free from "royal duties." In 1782, the first year of the First Reign, there was a decree for all officials to behave according to the Ten Wholesome Actions (*thotsakuson kammabot)* which the king compared to the disciplinary code of the Sangha in this way: "The Phra Patimok is the code of discipline of the monkhood.... the Ten Wholesome Actions is the code of discipline of the laity." This amounted to incorporating religious teaching as part of the law of the realm. The decree ordered all people to behave according to "the royal instructions concerning religion which determine this law." It explained the content of the Ten Wholesome Actions in detail, and stated that offenders "will be subject to punishment, either light or severe according to the offence" (Bradley 1873, 471–3). This order was one part of the "royal activities" which the king had to perform in his status as a Bodhisatta. Under this theory, the state would have meaning for the people when the king acted in this way.

There was also a decree in which the king was concerned that people would worship guardian spirits and the "male *linga*" to the point of forsaking the Refuge of the Three Jewels: "the king wishes for the sages and royal scholars to search in the Tipitaka that there is nothing" about making people worship the "male *linga*." The decree referred to the Buddhist teaching that "the Refuge of the Three Jewels is the crowning glory of the whole *thamma*.... the Refuge of the Three Jewels will be secure because of respect for the merit of Buddha, the merit of the scriptures, and merit of the Sangha. These are the true merit. The mind should not change to adhere to other merit and think of that as more uplifting than the Refuge of the Three Jewels." The king ordered all *linga* to be collected and burnt. As there were some references to guardian spirits in Pali texts, they were allowed to remain, but with a severe ban on revering them more than the Three Jewels (Bradley 1873, 474–7).

Prioritizing Buddhist ideas over all other ideas about state and kingship in this way often brought the kings of early Bangkok into conflict with royal customs passed down from Ayutthaya. Such conflict appeared in the writing of history and other matters, but surfaced especially clearly in at least one decree which King Rama I issued on changing the royal ceremony of drinking the water of allegiance. In the Ayutthaya period, the king ordered the nobles first to worship the Phrachetthabidon image of King Ramathibodi[29] and then the Three Jewels. Rama I ruled that

> this custom is wrong because under former kings, all the royal family members arrogantly thought of [Ramathibodi] as the most elevated king born in the past, and thus created royal customs which made officials and all royal family members pay respects to this image before the Three Jewels, which have merit beyond this world, more than the Three Worlds. This arrogance has the intention of giving prestige to the king. They did not have the critical wisdom to consider this wrong, because all officials big and small, when they follow that custom, will forsake the Refuge of the Three Jewels. It is arrogance that is disrespectful to the Refuge of the Three Jewels. (Bradley 1873, 503)

We tend to understand that early Bangkok was an age of "revival" of the arts and culture of late Ayutthaya but we should note that this "revival" had a limited scope. That is, it was a revival of form more than of content. Further, the forms revived were those that were not in conflict with the new mentality of the early Bangkok era. The ruling class could accept the "revival" of Ayutthaya forms, but when those

29. U Thong, the first king in the chronicles' account of Ayutthaya (1351–69). [T]

forms were dangerous to the new mentality of the age, the early Bangkok kings were equally prepared to challenge and destroy them. This readiness to sacrifice old models is reflected in administration, relations between the core kingdom and tributary states, legislation, literature, economic activities, and so on. It paved the way for the large-scale changes which followed in the Chakri age of reform.

For the next king (Rama II), who still used the form of the Ayutthayan-style "Great Elect," the monastic writer of *Thetsana chulayutthakanwong* gave a sermon summarizing the lessons of history suffused with royalty in this way: "The core matter which is held to belong to the self is not real, and even great kings, all of whom possess great power and great merit, cannot escape the power of Phraya Machurat, the lord of death. Some kings die of old age; this is a matter of the normal world. Some have their life destroyed in an untimely death due to the efforts of other people, or because of the royal wealth, even though nobody is really its owner. There is no substance at all" (*CC-66*, 92–3).

When the royal wealth is public property, that is, has no owner, one way the person who is king can prove his legitimacy is by displaying he has the highest accumulation of merit, and another is by showing that he is a person with the ability to undertake fully the duties of kingship according to Buddhist theory.

For such displays of accumulated merit, early Bangkok totally adopted the forms used in Ayutthaya, for example: being the owner of white elephants, a fact worth making known to all on the flag of the royal fleet; being the sole owner of a towered hall or *prasat*; being in possession of the royal regalia; being the sole owner of a female drama troupe; and so on. At the same time, the king's nature as a Bodhisatta was emphasized much more clearly than before. The eulogy of the ruler in the *Trailokawinitchai*, which follows the Aggana Sutta, runs: "his bodily form which is beautiful, when seen, should exude and portray his great intrinsic power, and his most incisive and excellent wisdom beyond that of any other being, so that he may ride roughshod over those who commit wrong, and praise and promote those who do right."

The early Chakri kings, especially King Rama I, conducted royal affairs and ceremonies according to these principles in every respect.

In truth, a "bodily form which is beautiful" was something expected of those who held the position of king since the Ayutthaya era. The royal robes and regalia, crown, throne, water-borne vehicles, and land vehicles were all crafted and decorated to make the "bodily form which is beautiful" of the king. These devices were all things which King Rama I unearthed or created as a complete package during his reign. When he came out to receive foreign guests, as described in foreign records, he was presenting the king as the "bodily form which is beautiful" to the eyes of the world.

The things which made up this "bodily form which is beautiful" were reserved for one person alone. Other people were not allowed to imitate the various devices, articles, and regalia. In the first reign, the *lakhon* dramas copied the original royal robes and regalia, which made the boundaries of the "bodily form which is beautiful" begin to blur. There could be people other than the king who began to have some share in it. Thus a law forbade dramas from copying royal costumes and regalia, and regulated exactly how drama costumes and regalia should be (Damrong 1965, 27–8). Being born beautiful was in itself a kind of accumulated merit, but the bodily beauty which the king jealously wished to reserve for himself alone was not an ordinary beauty like that of Khun Phaen but a kind which "when seen, should exude and portray his great intrinsic power" as well.

The Thai kings displayed their "most incisive and excellent wisdom" by making the court a gathering place for philosophers and scholars with the king as patron. The meetings of philosophers and scholars in early Bangkok were more active than in any earlier era of Thai history, especially in the spheres of religion and literature. Early Bangkok produced more literary works than any period of Ayutthaya (even though there were several "golden ages" of literature in Ayutthaya they seem to have had more gold than literary works).

The early Bangkok kings were not mere patrons in name only but participated fully in the work of the philosophers and scholars. They took decisions about both religious and literary issues. The *Trailokawinitchai* text describes how King Rama I posed questions to the meeting of knowledgeable persons from the senior Sangha. He asked questions "with the insight born of his abundant wisdom and merit accumulated from the past, and with great composure." The monks could "answer sometimes, not in others." This epitomized his "most incisive and excellent wisdom" because the king could debate among the "scholars" and perceive problems in the *thamma* so profound that the "scholars" did not always have the answers. In addition, the king intervened to explicate issues and interpret the Pali texts in the *Trailokawinitchai* in several ways, demonstrating his "most excellent wisdom" very clearly.

In relation to the king's ability to punish those who did wrong and praise those who did good, King Rama I arranged for laws to be collected for making a new code. This directly demonstrated his undertaking the royal duties of a Buddhist monarch, especially considering that such a code may not have existed previously in the Ayutthaya era. It shows even more clearly how fully he undertook his "duties" according to Buddhism.

From this perspective, we can better understand the revisions made in the recension of the Ayutthaya chronicles. The narrative was totally changed to construct Naresuan as the ideal king who gave protection against the "five enemies" troubling Buddhism. The preface to a government order issued in the Second Reign runs as follows:

> For Buddhism to prevail, develop, and flourish further, it must depend on the royal power to act as protector, and prevent the "five enemies" trampling over it. The custom of the great kings of old was to promote and maintain Buddhism so that it would develop, progress, and endure. This is the reason for nurturing courageous soldiers who have the capacity to campaign in war, and all the manpower and arms of all kinds, which together with the great and expansive royal power are able to suppress the five enemies and stop them from trampling over the supreme Buddhism, following the ancient royal traditions which have been passed down. In Bangkok nowadays it has been the vulgar Burmese enemy who was a deviant, hurtful, and exploitative demon

> (*mara*) that often and incessantly brought troops to fight against rural communities in the dependent states and outer regions in order to destroy Buddhism and create chaos. (Sathian 1935–53, IV, 2)

At the same time, the Naresuan story aroused the elite of society to be enthused about war, and to join with the king in the "pious act" of repelling the five enemies which come to trouble Buddhism. The Naresuan story also demonstrated that the Thai had right and justice on their side as they had not attacked the Burmese first, while the Burmese were in the wrong because they had invaded Siam first, and had in the end to suffer the consequences of their evil actions.

Conversely, the kings of the Ban Phlu Luang dynasty were examples of monarchs who lacked the right qualities according to Buddhist theory. They had not accumulated enough merit; the origins of the dynasty were unmannered peasants; when they occupied the throne they acted in impious ways and did not add to their stock of accumulated merit. Thus their royal auspiciousness (*monkhon*) was steadily reduced; their good elephants fell sick and had to be released; people kept dying in the sacred space of the palace; the dynasty suffered such internal decay that a son made love to his father's wife; the king and his successors stabbed one another in the back or had reasons to dispute over the succession; when enemy armies attacked, the people saw them as coming to overthrow an age of hardship; and finally the country was lost and Buddhism was crushed to pieces.

Even though the Thonburi-Bangkok recensions of the chronicles mention birth as a demonstration of the merit accumulated from past lives, they deny any birthright in the ruling class itself, that is among the royalty and nobles. The chronicles certainly do not endorse conflict over the throne, but they do not claim that legitimacy derives solely from blood descent. Someone who can prove his ability to undertake the duties of kingship, both worldly and religious, according to Buddhism is accorded high legitimacy to control the throne. Opposing such a person's ascent to the throne is useless, and hence royalty and nobility accepted Songtham, Prasat Thong, Narai, Phetracha, Taksin, and Rama I as kings. Offering violent opposition against someone who has sufficient accumulated merit would only create an unnecessary bloodbath. With this education, royalty and nobility would in the future allow Prince Chetsadabodin and Prince Mongkut to ascend the throne without such unnecessary bloodletting.

THE CHRONICLE TRADITION AND THE ROLE OF CHRONICLES FOR THE ELITE

Ideas about king and state in early Bangkok, as analyzed above, had great influence on the recension of the chronicles in this period. They were the main values used for revising the past.

The real question is why such trouble and effort was taken with the chronicles. They were not literature (in truth, literature was affected by these ideas in the same way) and they were not plans for the construction of the capital.

To answer this question, we must examine the tradition of using the chronicles in the past and in the early Bangkok period, or in other words, the role of the chronicles for the state and the institution of kingship.

In early Ayutthaya, chronicles were important enough to have been written from the earliest period. This importance had nothing to do with literature. When we come to the early Bangkok period, the chronicles evidently had very little or no relation with literature. The only literary work which may have some connection with the chronicles is the *Lilit yuan phai* (Defeat of Lanna). The chronicles were not books to be read for pleasure, but had some role in government. The importance of the chronicles must have increased for some reason so that in the Narai reign an abridged version was commissioned, namely the Luang Prasoet version, which was more convenient to use and refer to.

If we surmise what the ruling class in Ayutthaya down to the Narai reign looked for in the chronicles, then the only answer can be "model customs and traditions" which former kings had practiced. In traditional society, traditions or their "models" were devices for finding solutions to problems which arose. Had such problems occurred before? If so, how were they solved? The answers to these questions dictated how these problems should be met when they recurred. Thus a traditional society changes slowly because most challenges are met with an old kind of response. Any new response has risks and must be essayed with caution. Thus the chronicles were a sort of "manual" like the manuals on Royal Offerings (*kalapana boromratchuthit*) and other subjects. But the Ayutthaya chronicles focus on one subject not covered by any other manuals, namely relations between states. For this reason, the chronicles have a great deal about war, because war is a kind of relations between states under the model of the universe understood by states in Southeast Asia (according to Ayutthaya theory, trade was not a relation between states but between merchants who took refuge under states). The chronicles also describe the hierarchical relationships between states, under which certain countries present tribute in the form of royal daughters and white elephants, and request to find shelter under the protection of the ruler.

Before the end of Ayutthaya, the chronicles became an inseparable part of the state, as the testimony of Ayutthaya people shows (*TIOC*, 73). The collection and recension of the chronicles figured among the many things that King Taksin did to strengthen the state in social and cultural ways. King Rama I also made recensions of the chronicles as one part of his royal activities to build up the Siamese state. The political significance of the chronicles is thus clearly evident, and is reflected in the refinement of style in the later recensions.

Even though the chronicles underwent considerable development in early Bangkok, both in the extent of revision and in their value as literature, the chronicles were still a cultural property of the upper class alone, or even of the court alone. There was no noble, official, or monk who wrote or updated a chronicle independently on his own. The fact that the contents of the chronicles were never transferred to popular literature either as *sepha* ballads, dramas, or murals is clear evidence that the chronicles were the property of a minority. In a society where most people could not read, the channels through which upper class culture was passed down to the lower classes were monks' sermons and dramas. But sermons on royal history or the chronicles were only ever offered to the court.

The Jataka stories and folk tales were extensively adapted into literature and drama, but never anything from the chronicles. The only literary work which adapted material directly from the chronicles in this era was *Taleng phai* (Defeat of the Mon) which was very much a work of the upper class. It could be read or listened to only by people who had adequate knowledge of language. It was written in the *lilit* verse form which could not be used for drama. Comparison with *Lilit phra lo* is revealing, because this story was adapted for performance, beginning with *Phra lo noralak* written by Prince Mahasakdi Ponlasep of the Front Palace. Yet *Taleng phai* was not adapted into any other literary form.

The chronicles were not used in other ways because they were the property of royalty. Adapting them for drama might have been inappropriate and might have created problems for the players. In this respect the chronicles had an intrinsic "sacredness." It required almost another century before historians of Prince Damrong's generation could make the chronicles into a property of the "nation." Then the contents of the chronicles were sufficiently interesting to be adapted into mass art such as stage drama and cinema.

Although the chronicles were not communicated to the majority of the people, there are sources which lead us to believe that they were disseminated widely within the upper class or ruling class in the early Bangkok period. Members of the upper class were expected to know the stories in the chronicles. The chronicles became part of the education of the ruling class.

In the early Bangkok period, the chronicles were developed as a repository of a great many things to do with the "world" of the ruling class: relations with neighboring countries and some excerpts of their history; the role of nobles loyal to the kingdom such as Phanthai Norasing;[30] war tactics; the ideal king; proper royal language; the conventions of the court; and most importantly, the philosophy of government and state according to the theory founded by King Rama I. The chronicles thus helped to construct a worldview for the ruling class. They painted a picture of the outside world, and the role of the ruling class in relation to this outside world. For these reasons, there was no place more fitting than the chronicles for presenting a new theory of king and state, as the chronicles enshrined the power of dominating the past, and the hope of controlling the present and the future.

THE FINAL DIALOGUE IN CHRONICLE FORM: THE ROYAL AUTOGRAPH EDITION

The changes that took shape in the reign of King Mongkut were very extensive. This chapter will not enter into complex matters beyond the knowledge of the writer,

30. A helmsman who insisted so repeatedly that King Suea should execute him for having caused damage to a royal barge that his wish was finally granted (*RCA*, 392–3). [T]

but will just draw attention to a certain change in this period that has not been mentioned by historians, according to the writer's knowledge, and that influenced the last recension of the Ayutthaya chronicles.

In Mongkut's reign, there was a more obvious distinction between the institution of kingship and the king himself. Mongkut was the first king who separated his own finances from the wealth of the realm. For instance, he stated that "while I am lord of the realm, I must act as the protector of the realm, and not treat the treasury finances, old or new, inner or outer, as my own wealth" (*Prachum prakat ratchakan thi 4*, 230). The king as an institution, and the dynasty as members of that institution, acquired much greater importance. There were many royal proclamations designed legally to separate this institution from others, and many other detailed laws and customs governing relations with the royal institution and similar matters. These can be analyzed under several headings as follows.

1. Many royal proclamations laid down detailed and precise laws about the use of language to address the throne. For example the 11th proclamation forbade use of the phrases "taken by the flesh, captivated at heart" and "liking the flesh, the heart blooms" on grounds they were "coarse language." The 36th proclamation allowed use of the word "body" (*tua*) in certain contexts but forbade it where it was used as a pun or had a lewd meaning. The 43rd proclamation laid down forms of address for women in the writing of petitions. Several other proclamations of the same sort show that the complex and detailed *ratchasap* language known today effectively originated in this reign. Records from earlier generations show that *ratchasap* was much less systematic and complex before this time.

2. Personally King Mongkut was on close terms with officials and monks, and not strict about observing old conventions. At the Phetchaburi palace, for example, he invited ministers to sit on chairs. But as the apex of the institution of kingship, he was very conscious of the "sacredness" of the institution. For the first time, regnal years became important in day-to-day affairs, as Mongkut ordered the use of regnal years when specifying dates (62nd proclamation). For literate Thai, the royal institution became part of the thinking about time, in addition to the Buddhist era ("when the Buddhist age has passed...") and the former *tamnan* form (the Chula era which King Sakdam established). Mongkut also forbade those addressing the monarch at court from referring to his appearance in either critical or eulogistic terms by using such words as thin, short, dark, or light on grounds "this is too much" (215th proclamation).

3. More emphasis was placed on the special and exclusive character of the royal institution which distinguished royalty from other people. In truth, the Thai royal institution had had such distinguishing customs and laws since ancient times. But in the early Bangkok period, the emphasis on the duties of the king according to Buddhist theory, and marriage links between the royal family and the nobility, caused the status of royalty to decline. While the policies of the early Bangkok period continued into the Fourth Reign, there were new attempts to make members of the royal institution become conscious of being very different and distinctive from other classes. The 205th proclamation laid down forms of address in detailed hierarchical order, beginning from the highest levels of royalty and descending to those of the common people

(*nai, amdaeng, ai-i*). Mongkut also reiterated the blood difference between royalty as a class and commoners in another proclamation which ran: "thus women from the countryside who were born to retainers of the king, retainers of others, slaves, or nobles may not be taken as consorts of the king lest there may be children which damage his reputation" (322nd proclamation). He was concerned that confusion between ranks of the monkhood and of senior royalty might result in royalty being addressed wrongly and thus ordered that royal titles always be prefixed with the word "krom" (9th and 71st proclamations). He drew a line defining membership of the royal institution to include Mom Chao as the lowest level, and proclaimed that Mom Ratchawong and Mom Luang should not be called royal—"do not dream or speak such crazy things" (255th proclamation).

The development of such ideas about the royal institution in the Fourth Reign resulted in royalty having a greater consciousness of their own class. In truth the trend in this direction began before this reign, and might be traced back to Rama II's instruction for royalty to enter government service (in Ayutthaya times, senior royalty had been kept distant from political power) (Damrong 1962, 432–6). The duties according to Buddhist theory imposed on the king and other members of the dynasty gave rise to a consciousness that those duties were something held in common. The proclamations and instructions of King Mongkut further emphasized this consciousness, paving the way for his son to establish a feeling of "noblesse oblige" among his brothers and sons in the Fifth Reign.

The Ayutthaya chronicles underwent a recension in the Fourth Reign against the background of this new consciousness of royalty as a class, and of the "sacredness" of the institution of kingship. This affected the recension in several ways.

1. More material was added about neighboring countries which had close relations with Siam. For example, there is more detailed treatment of the rising power of the Konbaung dynasty in Burma than in other versions (*RA*, 223–5; *RCA*, 472–5). Sources about these neighboring countries had become better known, for example from the testimonies of war prisoners. Additions of this sort made the chronicles into much better "social science" texts for the ruling class.

2. The condemnation of the Ban Phlu Luang dynasty was scaled back in the Royal Autograph edition, mainly by omitting material which tended to impair the "sacredness" of the Thai institution of kingship.

Where in the Phonnarat version King Borommakot criticizes Prince Anurak Montri as only "lacking perseverance," the Royal Autograph chronicle expands this to "he is dull and stupid. Intelligence and perseverance cannot be found in Him" (*RA*, 234; *RCA* 458/44–5). Yet the Royal Autograph version then omits the material appearing in other versions about King Ekathat being stupid and lacking judgment in sending an army against Alaungpaya. When Prince Anurak Montri is only a royal son, he may indeed be criticized as stupid, but when he ascends the throne as king of the realm, to be criticized as stupid would affect the sacredness of the institution as a whole.

The Royal Autograph chronicle is the first source to report that King Alaungpaya was injured by the explosion of a great gun which he was directing to fire at a *prasat*.

As a result, the Burmese army had to retreat (*RA*, 253; *RCA* 483/17–34). Burmese chronicles are rather unclear about the cause of Alaungpaya's death (Harvey 1967, 242). Other Thai chronicles report only that he fell ill. The interesting point is not so much the cause of Alaungpaya's death, but the fact that the Royal Autograph version reports that the great gun was aimed to fire on a *prasat*, a form of building with a distinctive roof which was one of the prerogatives of the Thai king. Other royalty, however high in rank, could not reside in such a building. There is a special implication in having this gun explode when it was aimed to damage this symbol of the Thai institution of kingship.

In the Phonnarat version, Alaungpaya vows to overcome an era of hardship in Siam and to nurture ascetics, Brahmans, and other people no matter who they are. Unsurprisingly, these passages were omited from the Royal Autograph version because they directly undermined the Thai king in his status as an institution.

The Royal Autograph edition also includes certain points which are not found in other versions and which add to the prestige of the Thai institution of kingship. The most important of these is about the despatch of a Buddhist mission to sustain Buddhism in Sri Lanka during Borommakot's reign (*RA*, 228–9; *RCA*, 452). The sick elephant which, in other chronicle versions, had to be released into the forest during Borommakot's reign, here walks back into Lopburi by itself only two to three days later (*RA*, 235; *RCA*, 460/10–4). The Royal Autograph edition greatly glorifies Borommakot, and after his death there are no bad omens for Ayutthaya such as a clammy fog, which was the way that other versions brought down the curtain on the Ban Phlu Luang dynasty.

DIALOGUE WITHOUT END

After the Royal Autograph edition, the influence of western-style thinking and methods of historical study began to expand into Siam. The first wave of western influence resulted in Thai historians making more efficient use of source materials. But as with the assimilation of outside cultures since the remote past, western influence was limited within a small circle that lacked a philosophical foundation for absorbing such influence. Assimilation is the main theme of cultural history. In the chronicles, the past was used to serve the present. In the period of western influence, the past could still be used in the same way. As the central government tried to establish a "nation-state" within Siam's traditional polity, the past was still extensively used for guidance in the present. Much more study is needed to understand the role of history in the building of the nation and the new institution of kingship in the reign of King Chulalongkorn. With mass education and printing, the contents of the chronicles became the property of larger numbers of people.

For many different reasons, the people who created the history of the nation were "students" of the chronicles. If the "father of Thai history" had been a monk instead of Prince Damrong, the history of the "nation" might have been influenced by the traditions of *tamnan* and "universal history," and might have followed Buddhist lines more than it did. The chronicles had a large role in creating the Thais' image of their own past. They shaped part of the Thai worldview, namely the past as seen from the present, and certainly have had a deep influence on the behavior of people down to the present day. One amazing thing worth recording is that even after the change of government in 1932, the chronicles remained "textbooks" for history in secondary schools for many years.

However strong the influence of the chronicles, Siam changed too much for them to construct an adequate image of the past. Most importantly, the chronicles were written to paint a picture of the past for an upper class presided over by a king, but this past was now disseminated to other classes as well. The chronicles had to give an image of the past for something which was newly created, namely the nation-state of Siam, something to which the chronicles had paid no attention (because it was unknown to those compiling the recensions). The most powerful western influence in Thai historical study is the shift of focus from the king and upper class to the "nation."[31]

At present, some historians are conscious of the problem of confusing the present with the past. But how many "customers" do such historians have in a society which has been accustomed to "using" the past for the present over many centuries? A past which has no color or beauty, which fits nobody's ideology, and which does not support any special institution, may be closer to the truth. But in such a society, will it have any value to command people's attention?

However much effort they invest, the work of historians who present such a dry reality will always fail in part. We cannot remove ourselves completely from the "present," and thus we are forced to conduct a dialogue with the past, even without knowing it. As we are human, this limitation is something we have to accept. The utmost of which tiny humans such as we are capable is to strive constantly to break out of this limitation, even though we must always fail. It is just this failure on the part of historians which ensures that the dialogue with the past will be never-ending, and that in all secondary sources there exist primary sources, or as Marc Bloch calls them, unintentional sources.

APPENDIX

There is another set of documents worth mentioning as they illuminate the process of recension of the early Bangkok chronicles. These are the documents which the committee for printing documents of the Historical Recension Commission call the *Khamhaikan luang wat pradu songtham* (Testimony of the Monarch of Wat Pradu Songtham), here called *TWPS*.

31. In truth, the writing of history was still suffused with stories about kings and the upper class for a long time to come, but there was a noticeable change: the deeds of the king and upper class were now explained primarily by examining their effect on the "nation." See for example Prince Damrong's explanation of the construction of the Garden of the Right in the chronicles of the Second Reign of the Bangkok era.

In truth, *TWPS* is a mixture of at least three documents.

The first part is another version of the "map of the city of Ayutthaya" which Phraya Boranratchathanin has already elucidated. This "testimony" must undoubtedly have been written after the fall of Ayutthaya. If Ayutthaya still existed, there would have been no imperative to compile such a map in early Bangkok (or even Thonburi). The government made efforts to collect whatever traditional maps they could find, both in written form and as people's memories. The "map of the city of Ayutthaya" was probably written or taken down as testimony as part of this effort.

The second part of *TWPS* is a manual of various royal ceremonies.

The third part is a chronicle from the reign of King Suea to the fall of the city. The contents and wording match those in the printed volume known as the *Testimony of the Monarch Who Sought a Wat* (royal version), but *TWPS* is superior as it includes several passages which are missing from the *Testimony of the Monarch Who Sought a Wat.*

The third part is specially worth attention because, without such a complete version as that found in *TWPS*, we would not be able to appraise the *Testimony of the Monarch Who Sought a Wat.* The original *Testimony of the Monarch Who Sought a Wat* is known as "the chronicle translated from Mon" and is believed to be testimony which was taken down in Burmese from the Thai who were taken to Burma, then translated from Burmese into Mon, and from Mon into Thai (alternatively, the testimony may have been first taken down in the Mon language and then translated to Burmese). Comparing the *Testimony of the Inhabitants of the Old Capital*, which was translated from the Burmese, with the *Testimony of the Monarch Who Sought a Wat*, this assumption used to be believable. But with the later discovery of this more complete version in *TWPS*, it can be seen that this assumption may need some modification concerning the final part.

From around the time of King Borommakot until the fall of the capital, *TWPS* has detailed treatment which diverges from the *Testimony of the Inhabitants of the Old Capital* so much that it is not believable that they were translations of one another (through however many stages of translation). Apart from this, *TWPS* is a more detailed and reliable source with a very different narrative style from the *tamnan* type used in the earlier passages. For example, in the account of the power struggle between Prince Aphai, Prince Poramet, and King Borommakot, *TWPS* does not mention the release of an elephant with a secret letter as related in the *Testimony of the Inhabitants of the Old Capital*, but instead states that officials of the royal palace, who were thinking of abandoning and betraying the two princes, escaped with a letter to the Front Palace. Apart from this, *TWPS* and the *Testimony of the Monarch Who Sought a Wat* record several royal ceremonies in full and correct detail beyond what would be necessary in testimony for the Burmese. This makes it likely that this "chronicle translated from Mon" was specially researched and compiled as a "manual" for royal ceremonies and is another version of the royal chronicles, at least in those passages from King Borommakot onwards. The Thai prisoners of war who gave such detailed and correct testimony must have had written documents.

It is usually understood that these various *Testimonies* were translated into Thai in the Fourth Reign because the original of *Testimony of the Monarch Who Sought a Wat* (royal version) is in handwriting of this reign. But in truth, the translated version and the additions must have originated at least before 1807, the year when the Phonnarat and British Museum versions of the chronicles were completed. This is because there are many passages in these chronicles which are copied from *TWPS* word for word, or phrase by phrase. The contents of *TWPS* must have been in existence and used as sources by the chroniclers of early Bangkok. They were not just memories.

Whoever translated and embellished *TWPS* had a different, indeed totally opposite view of the Ban Phlu Luang dynasty from that of the compilers of the early Bangkok chronicle recensions. King Ekathat is criticized in the chronicles as "stupid, without judgment or cleverness" but *TWPS* states that, "The king adhered to *thamma* and honesty. He went to worship Phra Si Sanphet on every occasion without fail. He walked in meditation constantly. He upheld the ten virtues, and governed the city and borders to the appreciation of the monks and Brahmans. Happily without suffering and danger, he had compassion and merit. The rains were plentiful. There was much happiness and no drought. Rice, fish, other food, and fruit had excellent taste. All of the people and the inhabitants of the rural settlements were comfortable and contented" (*TWPS*, 36). There are many other passages with views diametrically opposite to those of the chronicles. In summary, the chroniclers had an opportunity to "choose" how to present the image of the Ban Phlu Luang dynasty. The image which appears in the chronicles was shaped by that "choice," not by the availability of sources.

The interesting question is the dating of this "chronicle translated from Mon." We know for sure it was not later than 1807 as mentioned above. There is another passage which invites us to think it must be after the Thonburi period. The final passage about Phraya Taksin and Phraya Phetchaburi going out to fight during the war with Burma says "thus Phraya Taksin was made commander of the army" (*TMSW*, 1967, 436). If this passage had been written in the time of Ayutthaya or by Ayutthaya prisoners, the name would have appeared as Phraya Tak or Phraya Wachira Prakan, in the form which other nobles were called at that time. If the passage had been written in the Thonburi era, he would have been called the king (compare the Phan Chanthanumat chronicle of Thonburi which refers to him in that way). Only after the Taksin reign was the name Taksin or Phraya Taksin used for the King of Thonburi.

Hence in the First Reign when the recension of the Ayutthaya chronicles was made, there were people who had a different view of the Ban Phlu Luang dynasty from the "official" thinking as it appeared in the chronicles. They were able to put their views into the "royal edition" of a book. Such views were not completely smothered by the official version. In fact they became the basis for further recension of the chronicles in the Fourth Reign. Hence although the government in early Bangkok established its own view about the past through the chronicles, it did not completely crush unofficial opinions. With "gentle" circumspection it relied on time for the views in the chronicles bit by bit to exert growing influence among the elite. Such "brainwashing" is cleverer than violent methods, or burning the books of the "opposition party." However, the opinion of the government was inscribed in the "sacred" books of the state (Chandler 1975, 343–8 demonstrates that the Cambodian chronicles were also likely to have been "sacred").

One other interesting point concerns Somdet Phra Phonnarat as a historian. Considering the period and social environment, this monk was a historian of considerable interest. *TWPS* reveals some of the sources he used in his work. In addition, Phonnarat had access to sources which in some form or other had been used by Van Vliet. The Van Vliet chronicle and the *Sangkhitiyawong* used sources which were the same or from the same tradition (Vickery 1976). As a historian, Phonnarat was very interested in source materials. The questions worth studying are how he used his sources, what did he want to achieve in his work, and, as someone "making a recension of history" for government, how much freedom did he have to work (Reynolds 1979).

REIGNS

The major reigns of the late Ayutthaya and early Bangkok periods are conventionally dated as follows.

	Maha Thammaracha	1569–1590
	Naresuan	1590–1605
	Ekathotsarot	1605–1610
	Si Saowaphak	1610–1611
	Songtham	1611–1628
	Prasat Thong	1629–1656
	Narai	1656–1688
Ban Phlu Luang	Phetracha	1688–1703
	Suea	1703–1709
	Thaisa	1709–1733
	Borommakot	1733–1758
	Uthumphon	1758
	Ekathat	1758–1767
Thonburi	Taksin	1767–1782
Chakri (Bangkok)	Yotfa (Rama I)	1782–1809
	Loetla (Rama II)	1809–1824
	Nangklao (Rama III)	1824–1851
	Mongkut (Rama IV)	1851–1868
	Chulalongkorn (Rama V)	1868–1910

GLOSSARY

avatar	an incarnation of a god
Ban Phlu Luang	name given to the dynasty of late Ayutthaya (1688–1767)
barami	accumulated merit, innate power, especially of a king
Bodhisatta	Buddha-to-be; future Buddha
bot	a verse, or form of verse
chadok	Jataka
chakravartin	universal emperor in Buddhist political theory
Chakri	name given to the ruling dynasty of the Bangkok era
chan	a metrical form, probably derived from India
chao sua/je sua	merchant prince, especially Chinese (Thai adaptation of a Chinese phrase)
chek	pejorative term for Chinese in Thailand
chotmaihet	a record; a genre of poetic works recording events
chunniyabot	Pali phrases used to punctuate the *Mahachat*
farang	westerner, European
Front Palace	residence of the *upparat* or heir designate
Isan	the northeast region
Jataka	collection of tales of the former lives of the Buddha; often used for preaching, or as the subjects of temple murals
kalahom	the ministry overseeing provinces and tributaries to the south
kalpana	offerings of land, people, or other materials for the upkeep of wat
kamsuan	an old poetic genre of love lament
kap	recitation; a verse form for recitation
keng	a building (especially roof) style adopted from China
khaek	a foreigner, usually of Malay or Indian origin
khamluang	a royal version of a literary work
khanom chin	a type of noodles
khlong	a metrical form
khom	old Khmer, e.g., of script
khun nang	the nobility; a collective term for senior officialdom
klon	a metrical form
krapung	a basket; a measure of volume

krathong	a decorative float used in festivals
lakhon	drama
lakhon nai	inner drama, meaning performed in the court
lakhon nok	outer drama, meaning performed outside the court
linga	lingam, symbolic representation of male sex organ
mahathai	the ministry overseeing provinces and tributaries to the north
mo lam	practitioners of a form of singing from the northeast
munnai	an overseer (of phrai).
nak leng	a tough; in early Bangkok usage, a playboy
nirat	a poetic form combining travel, remembrance of loved one(s), and observation of nature
nithan khamklon	a folk tale in verse form
nithan	a folk tale or fable
niyai	a story, fiction
phaya	a lord
phleng yao	a poetic genre, originally in the form of a love letter, used for poems of love, travel, prophecy, etc. (lit: long song)
phleng	a generic term for folk forms, mostly involving group singing
phrabat	a footprint of the Buddha
phrai	a commoner; someone subject to corvée labour
phrakhlang	the ministry overseeing trade and the treasury
phraratchaniphon	a composition by, or on commission from, the king
phu di	"good people", gentlefolk; the aristocracy
pranamphot	eulogy or invocation at the start of a literary work
rai	a metrical form, used especially for religious themes
Ramakian	the Thai version of the Ramayana story
rishi	holy man
sakdina	"power over fields"; traditional system of numerical ranks; sometimes used as referent for Thai equivalent of feudalism
sepha	a poetic form for recitation with meter and intonation, sometimes translated as ballad
tamnan	legend, old form of historical writing
thamma	dharma, Buddhist teaching
Thammayut(ika)	name of the Buddhist order founded by Prince Mongkut
thao	an old word for a chief or king; a lord
that	slave
thotsabarami	the Ten Perfections achieved by the Bodhisatta or Buddha-to-be
Traiphum	the Three Worlds, a Buddhist cosmogony
upparat	appointed heir apparent

wai	gesture of greeting or respect with hands joined in front of the body or above the head
wat	Buddhist temple, monastery
yokkrabat	a central official with judicial functions appointed to provincial towns

Weight, length, and currency

hap	60 kilograms
kwian	25 *hap* or 1500 kilograms
chang	600 grams
phara	400 *chang* or 240 kilograms
krabung	14–16 *chang* or around 9 kilograms
sen	40 meters
yojana	400 *sen* or 16 kilometers
fueang	8 satang
salueng	25 satang
baht	100 satang
tamlueng	4 baht
chang	80 baht

ABBREVIATIONS

BM	*Phraratchaphongsawadan krung sayam chak ton chabap khong britit miosiam* (The Royal Chronicles from the British Museum original).
CC	*Chut prachum phongsawadan* (Collected Chronicles) The number following refers to the part. All references cite the Kaona Press editions, except parts 64, 65 and 66 which are cited in the bibliography.
CP	*Phraratchaphongsawadan krung si ayutthaya chabap chakraphatdiphong* (Royal Chronicles, Chakraphatdiphong edition).
CS	Chula Sakkarat.
JSS	*Journal of the Siam Society.*
KTSD	*Kotmai tra sam duang* (Three Seals Law).
NC	*Phongsawadan nuea* (Northern Chronicle).
NN	Nang nophamat.
PC	*Phraratchaphongsawadan chabap phan chanthanumat* (Royal Chronicles, Phan Chanthanumat edition); the part about Thonburi is cited as *CC-65.*
P	Sa Pusadeva, Somdetphra Sangkharat. 1979. *Pathomsomphothi* (Life of the Buddha). Bangkok: Mahamongkut University.
PP	Paramanuchit Chinorot, Somdet Kromphra. 1962. *Phra pathomsomphothikatha* (Life of the Buddha). Bangkok.
PR	*Phraratchaphongsawadan krung si ayutthaya chabap somdet phra phonnarat* (Royal Chronicles, Phonnarat edition); for Thonburi section, the version used is that printed by the Department of Textbooks.
RA	*Phraratchaphongsawadan chabap phraratchahathalekha* (Royal Chronicles, Royal Autograph edition).
RCA	Cushman, Richard, tr. 2000. *The Royal Chronicles of Ayutthaya.* Bangkok: Siam Society.
SK	Thiphakorawong Mahakosathibodi, Chaophraya. 1970. *Sadaeng kitchanukit* (On Diverse Matters). Chiang Mai.
TIOC	*Khamhaikan chao krung kao* (Testimony of the Inhabitants of the Old Capital).
TMSW	*Khamhaikan khun luang ha wat* (Testimony of the Monarch Who Sought a Wat).

TWPS 'Khamhaikan khun luang wat pradu songtham' (Testimony of the Monarch of Wat Pradu Songtham).

BIBLIOGRAPHY

Anchalee Susayanha. 1981. 'Khwam plian plaeng khong rabop phrai lae phon krathop to sangkhom thai nai ratchasamai phrabatsomdet phrachulachomklao chaoyuhua' (Change in the phrai System and its Impact on Thai Society in the Reign of King Chulalongkorn). MA thesis, Chulalongkorn University.

Anuman Ratchathon, Phraya. 1960. 'Prapheni mi ngan thet mahachat' (Traditions of Mahachat Recitation). In *Watthanatham lae prapheni tang tang khong thai* (Thailand's diverse culture and traditions). Bangkok: Kaona.

Arunnipha Khunakon, Phra-ongchao. 1938. 'Thetsana phraratchathan prawat ratchakan thi 3' (Sermon on the Biography of King Rama III). In *Thetsana phraratchaprawat lae phongsawadan krungthep* (Sermons on Biographies and Chronicles of Bangkok). Bangkok.

Atchara Kanchanomai. 1980. 'Kan fuenfu phraphutthasatsana nai samai rattanakosin ton ton (BE 2325–2394)' (The Revival of Buddhism in Early Bangkok, 1782–1851). MA thesis, Chulalongkorn University.

Athibai phaenthi phranakhon si ayutthaya kap kham winitchai khong phraya boranratchathanin (Introducing the Map of Ayutthaya and Analysis of Phraya Boran Ratchathanin). 1963. 2nd edition, Bangkok.

Benchawan Suntharangkun. 1975. *Wiwatthanakan khong baep rian thai* (Development of Thai textbooks). Bangkok.

Bendix, Reinhard. 1962. *Max Weber. An Intellectual Portrait.* N.Y.: Doubleday and Co. Inc.

Bock, Carl. 1884. *Temples and Elephants: The Narrative of a Journey of Exploration through Siam and Laos.* London: Sampson Low, Marston, Searle and Rivington.

Bot lakhon khrang krung kao rueang nang manora lae sangthong (Ayutthaya Era Dramas of Manora and Sangthong). 1965. Bangkok: Khlangwitthaya.

Bot lakhon ramakian phraratchaniphon somdet phrachao krung thonburi (King Taksin's Version of Ramakian). 1963. Bangkok: Khurusapha.

Bowring, Sir John. 1969. *The Kingdom and People of Siam.* 2 vols., Kuala Lumpur: Oxford University Press.

Bradley, D. B., ed. 1873. *Kotmai mueang thai* (Thai Law). Bangkok: Rim pom pak khlong bangkok yai.

Bruguière, M. 1844. 'Notices of the religion, manners and customs of the Siamese.' (Translated from *Annales de la foi*). *Chinese Repository*. XIII, 4 (April, 1844), 169–217.

Bunnowat khamchan. 1959. Bangkok.

Burney, Henry. 1910. *The Burney Papers.* Vol. I. Bangkok: The Vajirayana National Library.

Burney, Henry. 1911. *The Burney Papers.* Vol. II. Bangkok: The Vajirayana National Library.

Busakorn Lailert. 1968. 'Phraratchaphongsawadan krung si ayutthaya.' *Silapakon*, 12, 2 (July).

Busakorn Lailert. 1972. 'The Thai monarchy in the Ban Phlu Luang period, 1688–1767.' PhD thesis. University of London.

Carr, E. H. 1961. *What is History?* London: Macmillan.

Chai Ruangsin. 1974. *Prawattisat thai samai BE 2325–2453 (ton thi nueng dan sangkhom)* (Thai History, 1782–1910, part 1, social). Bangkok.

Chai-anan Samudavanija. 1979. *Chiwit lae ngan khong thianwan lae ko so ro kulap* (Life and Works of Thianwan and K. S. R. Kulap). Bangkok.

Chandler, David P. 1975. 'The duties of the corps of royal scribes.' *JSS* 63, 2, 343–8

Chaophraya Phrakhlang (Hon). 1960. *Sombat amarin kham klon.* Bangkok.

Chaophraya Phrakhlang (Hon). 1964. *Lilit phayuhayatra phetphuang, lilit sriwichaichadok, klon charuek rueang sang phukhao wat ratchakhrue.* Bangkok.

Chaophraya Phrakhlang (Hon). 1972. *Wannakhadi chaophraya phrakhlang (hon)* (The Literary Works of Chaophraya Prakhlang (Hon)). Bangkok: Phrae Phitthaya.

Chatthip Nartsupha and Suthy Prasartset. n.d. *The Political Economy of Siam, 1851–1910.* Bangkok: The Social Science Association of Thailand.

Chindamani. 1961. Bangkok: Sinlapabannakhan.

Chinese Repository.

Chit Phumisak. 1975. *Bot wikhro wannakam yuk sakdina* (Critique of Sakdina Era Literature). Bangkok.

Chomklao Chaoyuhua, Phrabatsomdet (King Rama IV). 1968. *Prachum prakat ratchakan thi 4* (Collected Proclamations of the Fourth Reign). Bangkok: printed on the cremation of Phra Mahaphothiwongsachan.

Chomklao Chaoyuhua, Phrabatsomdetphra (King Rama IV). n.d. *Nangsue phrommachan somdet phrachomklao phu pen chao khong tham* (A Book on Leading a Pure Life by King Mongkut). Mss in William Gedney library, University of Michigan.

Chotmaihet haeng phuttha-anachak khong phikasu fa-hian (Records of the Buddhist Kingdoms by Fa Hsien). 1967. Translated by Phraya Surinluechai. Bangkok: cremation volume for the translator.

'Chotmaihet hon' (Astrological records). In *Prachum phongsawadan phak thi 8* (Collected Chronicles, part 8), Bangkok: Kaona.

Chotmaihet raiwan thap samai krung thonburi (Daily Military Records of the Thonburi era). 1969. In *Prachum phongsawadan phak thi 65* (Collected Chronicles, part 65), Bangkok: Khurusapha.

Chuan Phetkaeo et al. 1981. 'Khrongrang ngan wichai rueang kan sueksa wikhro withichiwit khong chaoban nakhon si thammarat thi prakot nai wannakam lailak-akson' (Study of the Way of Life of Nakhon Si Thammarat Villagers as Revealed in Literature). Papers of a seminar on local art and culture.

Chuea Satawethin. 1973. *Sunthon phu.* Bangkok.

Chulachomklao Chaoyuhua, Phrabatsomdetphra (King Rama V). 1916. *Phraratchawichan* (Royal Commentaries). Bangkok: printed on the cremation of Prince Nakhon Chaisi Suradet.

Chulachomklao Chaoyuhua, Phrabatsomdetphra (King Rama V). 1956. *Rueang wat samorai an mi nam wa rachathiwat* (On Wat Samorai, Renamed as Rachathiwat). Bangkok: cremation volume of the royal grandfather.

Chulachomklao Chaoyuhua, Phrabatsomdetphra (King Rama V). 1960. *Phraratchaphithi sipsong duean* (Royal Ceremonies of the Twelve Months). Bangkok: Sinlapabannakhan.

Chulayutthakanwong khwamriang. In *Prachum phongsawadan phak thi 66* (Collected Chronicles, part 66), Bangkok: Khurusapha.

Conze, Edward. 1971. *Phuttasatsana: sara lae phattanakan* (Buddhism: Teaching and Development). Translated by Nidhi Eoseewong. Bangkok.

Crawfurd, John. 1820. *History of the Indian Archipelago.* Vol. II. Edinburgh.

Crawfurd, John. 1915. *The Crawfurd Papers.* Bangkok: The Vajiranana National Library.

Crawfurd, John. 1967. *Journal of an Embassy to the Courts of Siam and Cochin China.* Kuala Lumpur: Oxford University Press.

Cushman, Richard, tr. 2000. *The Royal Chronicles of Ayutthaya.* Edited by David K. Wyatt. Bangkok: Siam Society.

Damrong Rachanuphap, Prince and Dhanit Yupho. 1956. 'Prawat sunthon phu' (Biography of Sunthon Phu). In *Phra Aphaimani*, Bangkok.

Damrong Rachanuphap, Prince, ed. 1920. *Phra bowon ratchaniphon.* Bangkok.

Damrong Rachanuphap, Prince. 1934. 'Tamnan nangsue sam kok' (History of the Three Kingdoms). In *Sam kok* (Three Kingdoms), Bangkok: Udom.

Damrong Rachanuphap, Prince. 1950. 'Tamnan sepha' (History of the sepha). In *Khun chang khun phaen,* Bangkok: Khurusapha.

Damrong Rachanuphap, Prince. 1954. *Khwam song cham* (Memoirs). Bangkok: Ministry of Interior.

Damrong Rachanuphap, Prince. 1962. *Phraratchaphongsawadan krung rattanakosin ratchakan thi 2* (Royal Chronicles of the Bangkok Second Reign). Bangkok: Khlangwitthaya.

Damrong Rachanuphap, Prince 1962a. 'Kham athibai phraratchaphongsawadan chabap phraratchahatalekha' (Preface to the Royal Autograph Edition of the Royal Chronicles). In *Phraratchaphongsawadan chabap phraratchahathalekha* (Royal Autograph Edition of the Royal Chronicles), Bangkok: Khlangwitthaya.

Damrong Rachanuphap, Prince. 1964. *Tamnan wang na* (History of the Front Palace). Bangkok: Kaona.

Damrong Rachanuphap, Prince. 1965. *Tamnan lakhon inao* (History of the Inao Drama). Bangkok: Khlangwittaya.

Damrong Rachanuphap, Prince. 1971. 'Kham athibai' (Foreword). In *Nirat sunthon phu* (The Nirat of Sunthon Phu), Bangkok: Khurusapha.

Dhammapricha, Phraya. 1977. *Traiphum lokawinitchaikatha* (Treatise on the Three Worlds). Bangkok: Department of Fine Arts.

Dhani Nivat, Prince. 'Siamese literature.' SEATO Lectures. Bangkok: SEATO, 1960.

Dhani Nivat, Prince. 'Thai theatre and music.' In *Aspects and Facets of Thailand.* Bangkok: Public Relations Department, 1961.

Dhanit Yupho. 1960. 'Thi ma khong anirut khamchan lae bot lakhon rueang unarut' (Background of the Anirut Poem and Unarut Drama). In Si Prat, *Anirut khamchan*, Bangkok: Krom Sinlapakon.

Dhanit Yupho. 1963. 'Lao rueang nangsue ramakian' (About the Ramakian). In *Bot lakhon ramakian phraratchaniphon somdet phrachao krung thonburi* (King Taksin's Version of the Ramakian Drama). Bangkok: Khurusapha.

Dhanit Yupho. 1965. *Khon* (The Mask-play). Bangkok: Khurusapha.

Em-on Chittasophon. 1970. 'Phra niphon praphet chan khong somdet phra mahasamana chao kromphra paramanuchit chinorot' (Chan Compositions of Prince Paramanuchit Chinorot). MA thesis, Chulalongkorn University.

Frankfurter, O. 1914. 'The unofficial mission of John Morgan, merchant to Siam in 1821.' *JSS*, 11, 1, 1–8.

Gervaise, Nicolas. 1929. *The Natural and Political History of the Kingdom of Siam*. Bangkok.

Griswold, A. B. 1961. *King Mongkut of Siam*. New York: Asia Society.

Gutzlaff, Charles. 1832. 'Journal of a residence in Siam, and of a voyage along the coast of China to Mantchou Tartary.' *Chinese Repository*. I, 1 & 2.

Hall, D. G. E. 1968. *A History of South-East Asia*. London: Macmillan.

Harvey, G. E. 1967. *History of Burma*. New York: Octagon Books.

Heine-Geldern, Robert. 1956. *Conceptions of State and Kingship in Southeast Asia*. Ithaca: Cornell University.

'Hmannan Yazawin Dawgyi.' 1954. *Selected Articles from the Siam Society Journal*, V, 1 and 2; VI, 1 and 2. Bangkok: Siam Society.

Hong, Lysa. 1981. 'The evolution of the Thai economy in the early Bangkok period and its historiography.' PhD thesis, University of Sydney.

Hudak, Thomas J. 1993. *The Tale of Prince Samuttakote: A Buddhist Epic from Thailand*. Ohio University Monographs in International Studies, Southeast Asia Series 90.

Ingram, James C. 1955. *Economic Change in Thailand since 1850*. Stanford: Stanford University Press.

Kachorn Sukhabanij. 1977. 'Khrai khuea phu taeng phraratchaphongsawadan krung si ayutthaya' (Who Wrote the Royal Chronicles of Ayutthaya?). In *Komun prawatisat* (Historical data), Bangkok: printed for the cremation of Mani Krachangsat.

Kamsuan si prat. 1958. Bangkok: Chulalongkorn University.

Kap mahachat. 1964. Bangkok: Khlangwittaya.

Khamhaikan chao krung kao (Testimony of the Inhabitants of the Old Capital). 1963. Bangkok: Khlangwitthaya.

Khamhaikan khun luang ha wat (Testimony of the Monarch who Sought a Wat). 1967. Bangkok.

'Khamhaikan khun luang wat pradu songtham' (Testimony of the Monarch of Wat Pradu Songtham). 1969. *Talaengkan prawatisat ekkasan borankhadi* (Reports on Historical and Archaeological Records), 3.

Khattiyaratpatiphat (Royal Romance). 1978. In *Phongsawadan krasip*, edited by Banchoet Inthuchanyong. Bangkok: Praphansan.

Khun chang khun phaen. 1950. Bangkok: Khurusapha.

Ki Thanitson. 1975. *Prawat khana song thai kap thammayut prahan* (History of the Thai Sangha and a Criticism of the Thammayut). Bangkok: Manikonwitthaya.

Kiattisak Wongmukda. 1980. 'Saphap kan kha khong thai rawang pho so 2325–2398' (The state of Thai trade, 1882–1955). MA thesis. Srinakharintharawirot University.

Kong wichakan krasuang thammakan. 1932. *Phraratchaphongawadan krung thonburi* (Royal Chronicles of Thonburi). Bangkok.

Kotmai tra sam duang (Three Seals Law). 1962–3. Bangkok: Khurusapha.

Kritsana son nong khamchan (see Paramanuchit 1970).

Krom Silapakon (Fine Arts Department). 1962. *Ruam rueang mueang nakhon sithammarat* (Collection on Nakhon Si Thammarat). Bangkok: printed on cremation of General Chaophraya Bodintharadechanuchit.

Kukrit Pramoj. 1980. 'Soi suan phlu.' *Siam Rath*, 7 April.

Kusuma Raksamani. 1978–9. *Nithan panchatantra chabap phasa thai* (Thai Version of Panchatantra). Bangkok: Sinlapakon University.

La Loubère, Simon de. 1969. *The Kingdom of Siam.* Kuala Lumpur: Oxford University Press.

Likhit Likhitananda. 1969. 'The Pali literature of Thailand.' PhD dissertation, Magadha University.

Lilit phra lo. 1969. Bangkok.

Lingat, R. 1954. 'La vie réligieuse du roi Mongkut.' Siam Society, fifitieth anniversary commemorative publication. Bangkok: Siam Society.

Lingat, R. 1958. 'La double crise de l'église bouddhique au Siam (1767–1851).' *Cahiers d'Histoire Mondiale*, IV, 2.

Mahachat khamluang (The Royal Mahachat). 1955. Bangkok: Mahamongkhut Ratchawittayalai.

Mahachat mueang phet (The Phetchaburi Mahachat). 1980. Transcribed into Thai by Saman Sohem. Bangkok: Board of National Culture.

Mahanuphap, Phraya. n.d. 'Nirat kwangtung.' In Sang Phatthanothai, *Thiao mueang taechio* (Visiting the Taechiu Country). Bangkok: Sunkanpim.

Mahawetsandon chadok chabap sipsam kan (Vessantara Jataka in Thirteen Chapters). 1957. Bangkok: Khurusapha.

Mahawetsandon chadok sipsam kan (Vessantara Jataka in Thirteen Chapters). Cremation volume for Mrs Song Suphap. 1964. Bangkok.

Malalasekera, C. P. 1958. *The Pali Literature of Ceylon.* Colombo: M. D. Gunasena.

Malalasekera, C. P. 1960. *Dictionary of Pali Proper Names.* London: Pali Text Society.

Malleret, Louis. 1968. *Un manuscrit inédit de Pierre Poivre: Les mémoires d'un voyageur.* Paris: EFEO publication LXI.

Montri Umavijani. 1990. *Sunthorn Phu: An Anthology*. Bangkok: Office of the National Culture Commission.

Moore, R. A. 1914–5. 'An early British merchant in Bangkok.' *JSS*, 11, 21–39.

Nang nophamat (The Lady Nophamat). 1964. Bangkok: Khlang Wittaya.

Narathip Praphanphong, Kromphra. n.d. 'Praditsathan phra song khana thammayutikanikai' (The Establishment of the Thammayut Order). In *Rueang chao lai.* Bangkok.

Narisaranuwattiwong, Somdet Kromphraya. 1958. *Wichan rueang tamnan sepha* (Critique of sepha). Bangkok.

Naruemon Thirawat. 1982. 'Phraratchadamri thang kan mueang khong phrabatsomdet phrachomklao chaoyuhua' (Political Thinking of King Rama IV). MA thesis, Chulalongkorn University.

Nattawut Suttisongkram. 1979. *Wannakam phaktai* (Southern Literature). Bangkok: Rueangsin.

Nidhi Aeusrivongse. 1994. 'The early Bangkok period: literary change and its social causes.' *Asian Studies Review*, 18, 1.

Nidhi Eoseewong. 1978. 'Prawatisat rattanakosin nai phraratchaphongsawadan ayutthaya' (History of Bangkok in the Chronicles of Ayutthaya). In *Ruam pathakatha chak samakom sangkhomsat haeng prathet thai* (Collected Lectures from the Social Science Association of Thailand), Bangkok: Social Science Association of Thailand.

Nidhi Eoseewong. 1979. 'Lok khong nang nophamat' (The World of Lady Nophamat). *Thammasat Journal*, 9, 1, July-September.

Nidhi Eoseewong. 1980. *Kanmuang thai samai phrachao narai* (Politics in the Era of King Narai). Bangkok: Sathaban thai khadi sueksa.

Nidhi Eoseewong. 1980. *Prawatisat rattanakosin nai phraratchaphongsawadan ayutthaya* (The History of Bangkok in the Chronicles of Ayutthaya). Bangkok: Bannakit.

Nidhi Eoseewong. 1986. *Kanmuang thai samai phrachao krung thonburi* (Politics in the Era of the King of Thonburi). Bangkok: Silpa Wattanatham.

Nithan iran ratchatham chabap ho samut haeng chat (Persian Tales, National Library Version). 1961. Bangkok: Khlangwitthaya.

Nittaya Kanchanawan. 1972. *Wannakam ayutthaya* (Ayutthayan Literature). Bangkok: Ramkhamhaeng University.

Osborne, Milton and David K. Wyatt. 1968. 'The abridged Cambodia chronicle, A Thai version of Cambodian history.' *France-Asie*, 193, 2, 189–96.

Paitoon Sayswang.1978. 'An economic history of the Chao Phya delta 1850–1890.' Bangkok: Faculty of Economics, Research Report Series, Thammasat University.

Pallegoix, Monsignor Jean-Baptiste. 2000. *Description of the Thai Kingdom or Siam*. Translated by Walter E. J. Tips. Bangkok: White Lotus.

Pallegoix. 1963. *Lao rueang mueang thai* (Description of Siam). Translated by San Tho Komonlabut. Bangkok: Kaona.

Panya Rungrueang. 1974. *Prawat kan dontri thai* (History of Thai Music). Bangkok: Thaiwatthanaphanit.

Paramanuchit Chinorot, Somdet Kromphra. 1960. *Taleng phai* (Defeat of the Mon). Bangkok: Khurusapha.

Paramanuchit Chinorot, Somdet Kromphra. 1962. *Phra pathomsomphothikatha* (Life of the Buddha). Bangkok.

Paramanuchit Chinorot, Somdet Kromphra. 1963. *Prathom ko ka, prathom ko ka hat an, prathom mala* (Primers for reading). Bangkok.

Paramanuchit Chinorot, Somdet Kromphra. 1970. *Kritsana son nong khamchan* (Kritsana's Instruction of her Younger Sister). Bangkok.

Pawaret Wariyalongkorn, Somdet Kromphraya. 1962. *Phraratchaprawat phrabatsomdetphra chomklao chaoyuhua* (Biography of King Rama IV). Printed for the cremation of Prince Praditthasari.

Phitthayalap Phruethiyakon, Krommuen. 1974a. 'Rueang phraram' (About King Ram). In *Chumnum phraniphon* (Collected writings), 3.

Phitthayalap Phruethiyakon, Krommuen. 1974b. 'Wichan rueang nithan panyi rue inao' (Critique of Panji or Inao). In *Chumnum phraniphon* (Collected writings), 1.

Phitthayalap Phruethiyakon, Krommuen. 1974c. 'The shadow play as a possible origin of the masked play.' In *Chumnum phraniphon* (Collected writings).

Pho Na Pramuanmak. 1970. *Prachum nirat kham khlong* (Collected nirat in khlong Form). Bangkok: Phraephitthaya.

Pho Na Pramuanmak. 1971. 'Chao sam lo kap nang upim' (Prince Samlo and Lady U-Pim). *Chalongbandit*, Chiang Mai University.

Pho Na Pramuanmak. 1972. *Kamsuan siprat nirat narin.* Bangkok: Phraephitthaya.

Phongsawadan nua (Northern chronicle). 1963. In *Prachum phongsawadan lem 1* (Collected Chronicles, Vol. 1), Bangkok: Kaona.

Phothirangsi, Phra. 1967. *Chamthevivongse* (Legend of Chamadewi). Published on the occasion of the 72nd birthday of Mrs Kimho Nimmanhaeminda.

Phraratchaphongsawadan chabap khong britit miosiam (Royal Chronicles, British Museum Version). 1964. Bangkok: Kaona.

Phraratchaphongsawadan chabap phan chanthanumat (Royal Chronicles, Phan Chanthanumat Version). 1960. Bangkok.

Phraratchaphongsawadan chabap phraratchahathalekha (Royal Chronicles, Royal Autograph Edition). 1962. Bangkok: Odeon Store.

Phraratchaphongsawadan krung kao chabap chakraphatdiphong (Royal Chronicles, Chakraphatdiphong Version). Bangkok: Khlangwitthaya.

Phraratchaphongsawadan krung si ayutthaya chabap phan chanthanumat (Royal Chronicles of Ayutthaya, Phan Chanthanumat Version). 1970. In *Prachum phongsawadan phak thi 64* (Collected Chronicles, part 64), Bangkok: printed on the cremation of Nai Mae Chawalit.

Phraratchaphongsawadan krung thonburi (chabap phan chanthanumat) (Royal Chronicles of Thonburi, Phan Chanthanumat Version). 1969. In *Prachum phongsawadan phak thi 65* (Collected Chronicles, part 65), Bangkok: Khurusapha.

Phutthathat Phikkhu. 1954. *Phutthaprawat chak phra-ot* (The Buddha's Biography as Told by Himself). Bangkok.

Phutthayotfa Chulalok, Phrabatsomdetphra (King Rama I). 1956. *Dalang.* Bangkok.

Phutthayotfa Chulalok, Phrabatsomdetphra (King Rama I). 1965. *Bot lakhon rueang unarut* (Unarut Drama). Bangkok.

Phutthayotfa Chulalok, Phrabatsomdetphra (King Rama I). 1972. *Unarut.* Bangkok: Phraephitthaya.

Phutthaloetla Naphalai, Phrabatsomdetphra (King Rama II). 1955. *Inao.* Bangkok: Khurusapha.

Phutthaloetla Naphalai, Phrabatsomdetphra (King Rama II). 1958. *Bot lakhon nok ruam 6 rueang* (Six Outer Dramas). Bangkok: Sinlapbannakan.

Plueang Na Nakhon. 1963. *Prawat wannakhadi thai samrap nak sueksa* (History of Thai Literature for Students). Bangkok: Thai Watthanaphanit.

Prachum charuek wat phra chetuphon (Collected Inscriptions of Wat Phra Chetuphon). 1967. Bangkok: Phanfawitthaya.

Prachum kap he ruea (Collected Boat Songs). 1961. Bangkok: Khurusapha.

Prachum khamphak ramakian (phak 7, 8 lae 9) (Collected Ramakian Scripts, Parts 7, 8, and 9). 1969. Bangkok.

Prachum phraratchaputcha (Collection of Royal Queries). 1973. Bangkok.

Prachum prakat ratchakan thi 4 (Collected Proclamations of the Fourth Reign). 1968. Bangkok.

Prachum silacharuek phak thi nueng (Collected Inscriptions, Part 1). 1978. Bangkok.

Prachum silacharuek phak thi sam (Collected Inscriptions, Part 3). 1965. Bangkok.

Prachum silacharuek phak thi si (Collected Inscriptions, Part 4). 1970. Bangkok.

Prakhong Nimmanhaeminda. 1976 'Mahachat lanna: kan sueksa nai thana thi pen wannakhadi thongthin' (Lanna Mahachat Studied as Local Literature). Seminar paper.

Praphakonbowonwisutthiwong, Momchao. 1938. 'Thetsana phraratchaprawat ratchakan thi 2' (Sermon on Biography of King Rama II). In *Thetsana phraratchaprawat lae phongsawadan krungthep* (Sermons on Bangkok Biographies and Chronicles). Bangkok.

Prathom ko ka, prathom ko ka hat an, prathommala (Primers for Reading). 1963. Bangkok.

Prathueang Wongruen. 1981. 'Phon ngan wichai bueang ton rueang wannakam chak tambon rongchang amphoe pa mok changwat angthong' (Result of primary research on literature from Pa Mok, Ang Thong). Seminar paper.

Preecha Changkwanyuen. 1972. 'Kan chai phasa roi kaeo nai phasa thai samai ayutthaya' (Use of prose in Thai in the Ayutthaya period). MA thesis, Chulalongkorn University.

Prem Chaya. 1955. *The Story of Khun Chang Khun Phaen*. Bangkok: Chatra Books.

Rachaphilap khamchan (nirat sida). n.d. Leaflet, Thai Language Department, Chiang Mai University.

Rachathirat. 1959. Bangkok.

Raffles, Sir Thomas Stamford, ed. 1826. *The Mission to Siam and Hue the Capital of Cochin-China in the Year 1821–1822.* London: John Murray.

Ramakian. 1963. 4 vols. Bangkok: Khlang Witthaya.

Ratanapanna Thera. 1958. *Jinakalamalipakaranam* (The Sheaf of Garlands of the Epochs of the Conqueror). Translated by Saeng Manavidura. Bangkok: Krom Sinlapakon.

Ratchabanditsapha (Royal Academy). 1932. *Phutthaprawat fai mahayan nai thibet riang tam chabap khong dabboenyo rokhin* (Mahayanist History of the Buddha from Tibet According to W. Rockhill). Bangkok printed for the cremation of Kromluang Samon Rattanasirichet.

Reynolds, Craig J. 1976. 'Buddhist cosmography in Thai history with special reference to nineteenth-century culture change.' *Journal of Asian Studies*, 35, 2.

Reynolds, Craig J. 1979. 'Religious historical writing and the legitimation of the first Bangkok reign.' In A. J. Reid and D. G. Marr, eds., *Perceptions of the Past in Southeast Asia.* Singapore: Heinemann for ASAA.

Reynolds, Frank E. and Mani B. Reynolds. 1982. *Three Worlds According to King Ruang: A Thai Buddhist Cosmogony.* Berkeley: Berkeley Buddhist Studies Series.

Rhys Davids, C. A. F. and T. W. 1965. *Dialogues of the Buddha, Part III* (Sacred Books of the Buddhists, vol. IV). London: Pali Text Society.

Rit Ruangrit. 1984. *Khrueang len mahachat.* 2 vols, Phranakhon: Wathanaphanit.

Ruschenberger, W. S. W. 1838. *Voyage Round the World Including a Narrative of an Embassy to the Sultan of Muscat and the King of Siam.* Philadelphia: Carey, Led and Blanchard.

Sa Pusadeva, Somdetphra Sangkharat. 1979. *Pathomsomphothi* (Life of the Buddha). Bangkok: Mahamongkut University.

Sahai, Sachchidanand. 1976. *Ramayana in Laos. A Study in the Gvay Dvorahbi.* Delhi: B. R. Publishing Corporation.

Saichon Wannarat. 1982. 'Phutthasatsana kap naew khwamkhit thang kanmueang nai ratchasamai phrabatsomdetphra phuttayotfachulalok (BE 2325–2352)' (Buddhism and political thought in the reign of King Rama I, 1782–1809). MA thesis, Chulalongkorn University.

Samnak nayok ratthamontri (Office of the Prime Minister). 1982. *Samuphap traiphum* (Illustrated Book of the Three Worlds). Bangkok.

Samphanwibak (Abbot's Hardship). 1957. Translated by Nakhaprathip. Bangkok: So Thammaphakdi.

Samutthakhot khamchan. 1959. Bangkok: Khurusapha.

Sanit Bunsong. 1981. 'Wikhro bot suat lam phetchaburi' (Analysis of Phetchaburi prayer chants). Paper presented at a seminar on local culture.

Saowalak Anantasan. 1977. *Wannakam ratchakan thi 2* (Literature of the Second Reign). Bangkok: Ramkhamhaeng University.

Sarasin Viraphol. 1977. *Tribute and Profit: Sino-Siamese Trade, 1652–1853.* Cambridge, Council on East Asian Studies, Harvard University.

Sathian Wilailak. 1935–53. *Prachum kotmai pracham sok* (Collected Laws in Chronological Order). Bangkok.

Sathit Semanin. 1975. 'Phasa sawan' (Language of heaven). In *Wannasin parithat* (Literary Review), edited by Chaloemsak Silaphon, Bangkok: Bannakit.

Si Mahosot, Phra. 1959. *Bot kawi niphon khong phra simahosot* (Poetic Works of Phra Si Mahosot). Bangkok: Sinlapakorn.

Si Prat. 1960. *Anirut khamchan.* Bangkok: Sinlapakorn.

Skinner, William G. 1957. *Chinese Society in Thailand: An Analytical History.* Ithaca: Cornell University Press.

Sombat Chantonwong. 1980. 'Lokkathat thang kanmueang khong sunthon phu' (Political outlook of Sunthon Phu). In Sombat Chantonwong and Chai-anan Samudavanija, *Khwam khit thang kan mueang lae sangkhom thai* (Thai Political and Social Thought). Bangkok.

Somphan Lekhaphan. 1975. *Wannakam samai rattanakosin ton ton* (Early Bangkok Literature). Bangkok: Ramkhamhaeng University.

Somsak Chanphosri. 1975. *Pramuan prapheni mongkhon isan* (Isan Traditions). Bangkok: Thammabannakhan.

Sriphuripricha, Phra. 1956. *Chotmaihet rueang patisangkhon wat phrasrirattana satsadaram khrang ratchakan thi sam* (Records of the Restoration of Wat Phrasrirattana Satsadaram in the Third Reign). Bangkok: cremation volume for Colonel Phraya Ratanaphimphaphiban.

St. John, Spenser. 1879. *The Life of Sir James Brooke, Rajah of Sarawak.* London: William Blackwood and Sons.

Sunthon Phu. 1956. *Phra aphaimani.* Bangkok: Khurusapha.

Sunthon Phu. 1960. *Prachum nirat sunthon phu lae khong but kap khong sit* (Collected nirat of Sunthon Phu and his Disciples), edited by Nai Chan Khamwilai, Bangkok. (References to 'Kap phra chaisuriya,' 'Phleng yao thawai owat,' 'Aphainurat,' and to Samian Mi's 'Klong phleng yao sansoen phrakiat phrabat somdet phra nangklao,' 'Nirat phra thaen dongrang,' and 'Nirat suphan' are all from this collection.).

Sunthorn Phu. 2001. *Nirat mueang klaeng* (To Klaeng). Translated by Prem Chaya (H.H. Prince Prem Purachatra). Edited by Montri Umavijani. Bangkok: Suksaphanphanit.

Suraphon Wirunrak. 1979. 'Nang yai wat sawang arom' (Puppets of Wat Sawang Arom). *Siam Rath Sapda Wichan*, 18 March.

Tamnan mulasatsana (A History of Buddhism). 1975. Bangkok: cremation volume for ML Det Sanitwong.

'Tamra len nang nai ngan mahorasop' (Manual of Puppetry) 1972. In *Latthi thamniam tang tang (phak 6)* (Various customs, part 6), Bangkok: Khlangwitthaya.

Thammathibet, Chaofa. 1962. *Chaofa thammathibet phrom duai phra prawat lae phra niphon bot roi krong* (Prince Thammathibet and the History and Composition of bot roi krong). Bangkok.

Thassanee Sinsakul. 1976. 'Chakkraphathirat nai khadi india' (The Indian concept of the emperor). MA dissertation, Faculty of Arts, Chulalongkorn University

Thawathotsamat. n.d. Bangkok: Khao Phanit.

Thetsana chulayutthakanwong. In *Prachum phongsawadan phak thi 66* (Collected Chronicles, part 66), Bangkok: Khurusapha.

Thiphakorawong Mahakosathibodi, Chaophraya. 1970. *Sadaeng kitchanukit* (On Diverse Matters). Published by Sukit Nimmanhaeminda for distribution at a united kathin offering at Wat Ketkaram, Chiang Mai.

Thiphakorawong, Chaophraya. 1960. *Phraratchaphongsawadan krung rattanakosin ratchakan thi 1* (Royal Chronicles of the Bangkok First Reign). Bangkok: Khurusapha.

Thiphakorawong, Chaophraya. 1961a. *Phraratchaphongsawadan krung rattanakosin ratchakan thi 2* (Royal Chronicles of the Bangkok Second Reign). Bangkok: Khurusapha.

Thiphakorawong, Chaophraya. 1961b. *Phraratchaphongsawadan krung rattanakosin ratchakan thi 3* (Royal Chronicles of the Bangkok Third Reign). Bangkok: Khurusapha.

Thiphakorawong, Chaophraya. n.d. *Chotmaihet phraratchaphongsawadan phaendin phrabatsomdet phraphutthayotfa* (Records for the Chronicle of King Rama I). Unpublished mss in possession of Professor Yoneo Ishii, Kyoto University, Center for Southeast Asian Studies.

Thornely, P. W. 1923. *The History of a Transition.* Bangkok: Siam Observer Press.

Traiphum lokawinitchai (Treatise on the Three Worlds). 1977. Bangkok: Krom Sinlapakon.

Traiphum lokawinitchai. Manuscript division, religious records, cupboard 107, no. 1.

Traiphum phra ruang (Three Worlds of King Ruang). 1955. Bangkok: Sinlapabannakan.

Turpin, F. H. 1908. *History of the Kingdom of Siam and of the Revolutions that have Caused the Overthrow of the Empire upto A.D. 1770.* Bangkok: Committee of the Vajiranana National Library.

U Nissako, tr. 1963. *Phra thammapathatthakatha (8 phak)* (Commentary on the Dhammapada, 8 parts). Bangkok: Mahamongkhut University.

Van der Heide, J. Homan. 1906. 'The economical development of Siam during the last half century.' *JSS*, 3, 2; reprinted in Chatthip Nartsupha and Suthy Prasartset, eds., *The Political Economy of Siam, 1851–1910,* Bangkok: Social Science Association of Thailand, 1981.

Van Leur, J. C. 1955. *Indonesian Trade and Society.* The Hague.

Van Vliet, Jeremias. 1954. 'Historical Account of Siam in the XVIIth Century.' *Selected Articles from the Siam Society Journal,* VII: 31–90. Bangkok: Siam Society.

Van Vliet, Jeremias. 1975. *The Short History of the Kings of Siam.* Bangkok: Siam Society.

Vella, Walter F. 1957. *Siam Under Rama III.* N.Y.: Association of Asian Studies.

Vella, Walter F. tr. 1986. 'Lamentations. Sunthon Phu.' In *Anuson Walter Vella,* ed. Ronald D. Renard, Chiang Mai: Payap University and University of Hawaii at Manoa.

Vickery, Michael. 1976. 'The Short History of the Kings of Siam: A review article.' *JSS*, 64, 2, 207–36.

Vickery, Michael. 1977. 'The 2/k. 125 fragment, a lost chronicle of Ayutthaya.' *JSS*, 65, 1, 1–80.

Wachirayan Warorot, Somdet Kromphaya. 1957. *Thetsana phraratchaprawat phrabatsomdet phraporamenthara mahamongkut phrachomklao chaoyuhua* (A Sermon on the Biography of King Mongkut). Bangkok, merit-making volume for King Mongkut and Prince Thiwakorawongprawat.

Wachirayan Warorot, Somdet Kromphaya. 1980. *Phutthaprawat* (Life of the Buddha). 2 vols. Bangkok: Mahamongkut ratchawittayalai.

Wales, H. G. Quaritch. 1931. *Siamese State Ceremonies*. London: Bernard Quaritch.

Wannarat, Somdetphra. 1920. *Chulayutthakanwong phak 2.* Bangkok: printed on cremation of Phraya Phahonyothin Ramintharaphakdi.

Wannarat, Somdetphra. 1978. *Samgitiyavamsa/Sangkitiyawong* (History of Buddhist Councils). Bangkok: cremation volume for Phra Ubalikhunupamachan.

Waraphon Thinanon. 1979. 'Kan kha samphao khong thai samai rattanakosin ton ton' (Siam's junk trade in the early Bangkok period). MA thesis, Chulalongkorn University.

Weber, Max. 1958. *The Protestant Ethic and the Spirit of Capitalism.* New York: Charles Scribner.

Wertheim, W. 1984. 'The trading minorities in Southeast Asia.' In *East-West Parallels.* The Hague: van Hoeve.

Wichianpricha, Phra. 1931. *Phongsawadan neua* (Northern Chronicle). Bangkok: printed on the cremation of Phraya Thanarattanabodi.

Wyatt, David K. 1973. 'The abridged Royal Chronicle of Ayudhya of Prince Paramanuchit Chinorot.' *JSS*, 61, 1, 25–30.

Wyatt, David K. 1976. 'Chronicle traditions in Thai historiography.' In C. D. Cowan and O. W. Wolters, eds., *Southeast Asian History and Historiography.* Ithaca: Cornell University Press.

Wyatt, David K. 1979. 'The subtle revolution of King Rama I of Siam.' Unpublished article, subsequently published in Wyatt and A. Woodside, eds., *Moral Order and the Question of Change*, New Haven: Yale University Southeast Asian Studies, 1982; and in Wyatt, *Studies in Thai History*, Chiang Mai: Silkworm Books, 1994.

Wyatt, David K. 1980. 'Family politics in seventeenth and eighteenth century Siam.' A paper presented at the 8th conference of the IAHA, Kuala Lumpur, August. Reprinted in Wyatt, *Studies in Thai History*, Chiang Mai: Silkworm Books, 1994.

Yada Praphaphan. 1981. *Rabop chaophasi nai akon samai krungthep yuk ton* (The Tax Farming System in Early Bangkok). Bangkok: Sangsan.

Yuan phai rue yo phrakiat phrachao changphueak krungkao (chabap phrachao borommawongthoe kromphra sommata amornphan) (Defeat of Lanna or Celebration of the Deeds of the King of the White Elephant). 1959. Bangkok: Faculty of Arts, Chulalongkorn University.

Nidhi in 1981 by Arun

AFTERWORD[1]

THE essays in this collection helped to establish Nidhi Eoseewong as the most innovative and admired Thai historian of his generation. Nidhi had already written *Politics in the Era of King Narai* (1980) and would subsequently publish the massive *Politics in the Era of the King of Thonburi* (1986) and several other historical articles. But the essays presented here, especially 'Bourgeois culture and early Bangkok literature,' 'Sunthon Phu: bourgeois poet laureate,' and 'The history of Bangkok in the chronicles of Ayutthaya,' founded his reputation. Some of those who attended the first presentation of 'Bourgeois culture' in 1982 can still recall the details of who said what, and the general excitement of the event ("I could sense something very significant was coming"), over two decades on. This afterword tries to show why this was so, and how the essays were received.

BEFORE *PEN AND SAIL*

Nidhi Eoseewong was born in Bangkok in 1940 into a Teochiu trading family. He went to Assumption College in Siracha, Chonburi, and then studied for his BA and MA at the Faculty of Arts, Chulalongkorn University. He studied both literature and history, and was active in literary societies. In 1966, he became a lecturer in history at the newly founded Chiang Mai University where he remained until retirement in 2000.

In 1964, while a master's student, he published a short story, a favourite genre of this era. Although set in France during the Second World War, 'To humanity' was written at the time Thailand was being drawn deeper into the US war in Indochina. A US soldier in Normandy accidentally comes under bombing by Allied planes. After watching his friend succumb to panic and be killed by his own sergeant, he contrasts "one person who is a human, a little animal which loves life and the peace of the natural world, and another person who is a soldier, a machine which works according to rules and discipine." He concludes, "humans are fragile animals, unsuited to life

1. This piece began as a handful of pages and grew because many people made suggestions, found sources, and corrected mistakes. Thanks to Attachak Sattayanurak, Ben Anderson, Chalong Soontravanich, Chatthip Nartsupha, Chetana Nagavajara, Hong Lysa, James Ockey, Patrick Jory, Pasuk Phongpaichit, Porphant Ouyyanont, Saichon Sattayanurak, Thanet Aphornsuwan, Thongchai Winichakul, and Ukrist Pathamanand.

in this violent world, until such time as they can truly control its course." He is then himself hit by bomb shrapnel and lies paralysed and dying, his thoughts drifting across everything of value in his life—maternal love, friendship, and natural beauty. In a note appended to the story, Nidhi thanked "love, friendship, understanding, empathy, mutuality, and peace—everything which inspires confidence, hope, love, and warmth in humanity," and "everyone who reads this story with the feeling of being beyond the assumptions in the word 'nation'."

In the late 1960s, Nidhi contributed to the stirring of critical debate which led eventually to the successful 1973 student revolt against military rule and US neocolonial domination. He wrote several articles for *Sangkhomsat parithat* (Social Science Review), the journal edited by Sulak Sivaraksa which was the leading mouthpiece for dissent (Anderson 1985, 27, fn. 27). Nidhi's two main themes were the duty of intellectuals to take a public role by "asking the questions and questioning the answers" (on which more below), and the need to overthrow the traditional approach to Thai history. On the latter theme, he contributed an article on 'Prince Damrong and Arnold Toynbee' in 1969 (Nidhi 1969).

The text part of the article is a review of the western historians which Damrong[2] himself read (on the evidence of his library) including Ranke, Mommsen, and especially Toynbee. Nidhi highlighted two points. First, these historians believed history was a branch of natural science, and the key task of the historian was to collect more sources to subject to scientific analysis. As a result they tended to select topics for which sources were available rather than topics that were significant. Second, under the dominating influence of nationalism in their era, these historians wrote national histories in which modern states were read back into the past.

The footnotes, which are in total fifty percent longer than the text and only loosely connected to it, are a string of criticisms of the "Prince Damrong school of history." Nidhi argued that the historians of this school still dominated the profession in Thailand. They made a fetish of historical "accuracy," and believed that amassing detail would result in a history that was "right." They convinced themselves they were applying scientific method, and could not recognize their own biases. Damrong in particular had elevated the role of the king in the past. They focused on events not trends. They portrayed these events as the outcome of the actions of great figures. They paid no attention to society, economy, or culture. They concentrated on the Sukhothai era because sources were available even though Sukhothai's legacy for the present was sketchy, and neglected the Ayutthaya era because sources were lacking even though the legacy was dense. They focused narrowly on the history of the "Thai" and their interaction with the west, and neglected Siam's debts to India and China

2. Prince Damrong Rachanuphap was a half-brother of King Chulalongkorn and a leading official during the Fifth Reign, credited especially with shaping the powerful Interior Ministry and the provincial bureaucracy. From 1915 onwards, he devoted his attention to history and literature, writing and editing several chronicles, and authoring over fifty works of history, biography, and literary analysis.

and its role in Asian trade. They failed to study other countries to give any sense of perspective. They saw no value in history for itself but only as a tool for inducing nationalism: "I can remember that in my first year at university a history lecturer began his course by stating that among the several objectives of studying history the first was to increase love of one's country" (Nidhi 1969, 31). These historians used nationalism, which was a recent idea, to explain the motivation of people in the past. The other two "gods" they celebrated were monarchy and "democracy," meaning the paternalistic "Thai" version of democracy supposedly exemplified by the Sukhothai era. Indeed, Sukhothai had been so celebrated that "King Ruang has entered our current politics in many ways" and "seems set to become the person who founded the Democrat Party rather than Khuang Aphaiwong" (34). On monarchy, Nidhi wrote:

> The histories written at present are virtually eulogies of past kings. They constantly attempt to analyze the successes of kings in the past, but never their failures. Qualities which are valued at present are ascribed to kings in the past. As a result, King Ramkhamhaeng becomes one of the world's pioneer democrats because he made a declaration of the people's rights and freedoms just like his English colleagues.... We study history full of a bias that kings do only what is good and beneficial for the country, and that anything seemingly otherwise arises only because the people of the time could not keep up with the king. (33)

In such an atmosphere, Nidhi observed, it was not surprising if the keepers of the archives were destroying or hiding records. He rounded off this display of fireworks by announcing that "the study and writing of our history has not yet begun" (34).

The essay caused a stir.[3] Kachorn Sukhabanij, whom Nidhi identified as a leading living exponent of the "Prince Damrong school," sent a pained letter suggesting "when Khun Nidhi tries [writing history] for himself, he will find out how difficult it is" (Kachorn 1969, 130). Others upbraided him for showing disrespect for such an eminent figure as Damrong, the "father of Thai history." Nidhi commented later: "Nobody denies the greatness of Prince Damrong but having to bow down is too much" (quoted in Jiraporn 1996, 46).

When the student revolt took place in October 1973, Nidhi was in the US, where he studied from 1971 to 1975 for a PhD at the University of Michigan. He had already become interested in studying the early Bangkok period (Jiraporn 1996, 11), yet he said later he could not see the point of studying Thai history with non-Thai teachers, and so focused on Indonesia. He learnt Dutch and Bahasa Indonesia, and wrote his thesis on 'The intellectual elite and modern literature in Indonesia,' broaching themes about the interplay between authors and audiences within their economic, social, and political context which prefigured the approaches in the essays of *Pen and*

3. This article was exceptionally daring for its time. The monarchy's social role and political meaning had expanded rapidly in the 1960s. Prince Damrong had been baptized as the "father of Thai history." He was also the favourite half-brother of King Chulalongkorn who had been canonized as the architect of Thailand's modernity.

Sail. Because he was unable to get financial support for fieldwork in Indonesia,[4] he felt the thesis was imperfect, though other scholars hold it in high esteem. He never published anything based on his doctoral research, but before returning to Thailand wrote an article on 'The *Devaraja* cult and Khmer kingship at Angkor' (Nidhi 1976), one of only two academic works he published in English.[5]

On his return to Thailand, the left-right polarization which would lead eventually to the massacre at Thammasat University on 6 October 1976 was well under way. While Nidhi was a fierce critic of Thailand's old order, he was not attracted to organized communism as a replacement. In a 'Letter from Chiang Mai' sent to *Sangkhomsat parithat* in 1968, he had shown his hope for a middle path. He described two recent incidents in Chiang Mai: a scrap between students and local gangsters, and a fire in the market believed to have been started as terrorist provocation. Both incidents reflected badly on the authorities. One of the gangsters was revealed to be a close relative of a senior policeman, and soldiers sent to the burning market engaged in looting. Beijing radio had tried to exploit these incidents, which Nidhi took to be part of a Maoist "people's war" strategy of polarization. Nidhi (1968, 116) stated his belief that "students for the most part have no interest in the temptations of Beijing" but he could see how such incidents might reduce people's trust in government and ultimately drive them to seek the protection of the communists. Nidhi also noted that the government's tendency to demonize all opponents as communist hastened such polarization. He concluded:

> Mao Zedong's 'people's war' is a brilliant product of an Asian strategist. It helped the world escape from the era of nineteenth-century colonialism completely or almost so. But if we follow the dialectical theory of the communists themselves, Mao's strategy is only the thesis, and there must be an anti-thesis too. Countries which may be in danger from the people's war such as Thailand, Malaysia, and Indonesia will have to think up the anti-thesis to the people's war.... Don't be afraid of communists like kids afraid of ghosts who scream and shut their eyes... We need to understand them and, though not supporting them, should not oppose or contest with them by either legal or social means. (119–20)

If the authorities simply treated people properly, "victory will go to the government side for sure" (120).

On return to Thailand in 1975, Nidhi was dismayed by the atmosphere of conflict. Chiang Mai was especially tense because of the protests by the Peasant Federation of Thailand over land rents and rural debt. Nidhi tried to remain independent of both camps at a time when polarization had virtually obliterated any middle ground. He was accused of being unsympathetic to the student movement and the left (Jiraporn 1996, 11) but privately helped leftist colleagues during the denouement in late 1976.

4. He was financed by the Ford Foundation which at the time did not have any provision to support a scholar from one Asian country to do research in another.

5. He later published an English summary of 'Bourgeois culture and early Bangkok literature,' see Nidhi (1994).

He later claimed that he had devoted little attention to Marxism which was the language of critical debate in this period:

> I hardly read what Marx wrote, but rather Pho Intharapalit [a popular writer of bandit romances]…. the bandit community is a free society which has escaped from state power… they have escaped the terrible oppression by the state's bad people. This is a refuge of freedom in a certain sense. (Nidhi 1998, quoted in Saichon n.d., 7)

In fact his earlier contributions to *Sangkhomsat parithat* had shown considerable appreciation of Marxist theory and practice.

In the late 1970s, he wrote further on Thai historiography advocating a more critical approach. He also spearheaded a collaborative project analyzing state, economy, and society in early Ayutthaya, published later in a book entitled *Sriramthepnakhon* (1984). More importantly, with intellectual life deadened after the violent right-wing reaction of 1976, Nidhi buried himself in research. Two years later, the results began to appear in rapid succession: 'The history of Bangkok in the chronicles of Ayutthaya' in 1978, the essay on Nang Nophamat in 1979, the study of the King Narai era in 1980, the essays on Sunthon Phu and the Phetchaburi Mahachat in 1981, and the essays on 'Bourgeois culture' and 'The life of the Buddha' in 1982.

HISTORY AFTER 1976

The first appearance of these essays was immediately recognized as a landmark of significance not only for academic history but for intellectual life in general and its role in Thai society.

From the late 1960s, students and intellectuals had risen in revolt both against the political regime and against the orthodoxies dominating intellectual life. Studies of literature and history had been at the forefront of this movement: "history became one of the arenas of struggle between old thinking and new thinking" (Patcharaphon and Chukiat 1981, 59). The writings of Chit Phumisak, who had studied at the same Chulalongkorn Faculty of Arts as Nidhi from the late 1950s[6] and been shot dead as a communist guerrilla in 1966, were rediscovered from the early 1970s and widely celebrated (Reynolds 1987). Chit had linked literature and history, analyzed literary works through a lens of class, and dramatically reinterpreted key documents of mainstream Thai history—all practices which Nidhi would continue.[7]

6. Nidhi became a freshman a year after Chit had left.

7. Nidhi rarely refers to Chit. In a review of Craig Reynolds' translation of Chit's *The Real Face of Thai Feudalism Today*, Nidhi (1987a, 127, 129) remarked "*Real Face* has no value as theory. Marxists in general view the Marxist theory that Chit applied in this work as too superficial…. In his academic work, Chit pushed aside the old meanings of old signs, sought what he believed was the real essence, and built new meanings for old signs (such as 'sakdina')." For the remainder of the review he concentrated on Reynolds' contextualization and interpretation of Chit.

But in October 1976, the army, with the tacit support of a nervous urban middle class and establishment, had bloodily smashed the student movement and retaken power by coup. The intellectuals were scattered—some in jail, some to the jungle camps of the communists, and some into self-imposed exile. The new regime abolished parliament, imposed tight controls on intellectual activity, banned books, and initially proposed a 12-year interlude before the return of democracy. While this extreme approach was moderated after one year, the military remained firmly in command, and state authorities still hoped to control political and intellectual life for the immediate future. The army laid plans to manage the political system from the parliament down to the grassroots. Senior bureaucrats drew up a new "national ideology" built around the unifying symbol of the king. This was not broadcast for public consumption like Indonesia's Pancasila, but guided government activities such as the revision of school textbooks, training of village heads, and campaigns for national unity orchestrated by the National Culture Commission (Connors 2003).

In this stifling atmosphere, history became an area where intellectuals defiantly demanded more freedom of thought, and revived the trends of critical and politically engaged scholarship which had flourished over 1973–6. Nidhi was neither the sole figure in this revival nor its pioneer. From 1978, a handful of other historians (mainly economic historians associated with Chatthip Nartsupha) published works which reestablished the critical study of history from a political economy angle (Somsak 1982; Reynolds and Hong 1983). In November 1979, Sujit Wongthet founded the magazine *Sinlapa watthanatham* (Art and Culture) to serve as a platform for challenging the state's control of history and culture (Hong 2000). Yet amid several such initiatives, Nidhi stood out. In a special 1981 issue of *Warasan thammasat* (Thammasat Journal) on historiography, Nidhi was identified as the spearhead of a new generation of historians who "try to find new answers to old questions" (Patcharaphon and Chukiat 1981, 62). In an article which appeared in June 1982, Somsak Jeamteerasakul[8] reviewed several recent historical works and pronounced Nidhi "the most important academic historian at the present time." He explained:

> Nidhi Eoseewong is a major historian, the most capable of the present era. Although his output is not large—around ten pieces (about half of which are on historiography)—yet almost every one of his works has won rapid and widespread acceptance...and it is perhaps not too much to say that each one of Nidhi's works from 'The history of Bangkok in the chronicles of Ayutthaya' and 'Politics in the era of King Narai' to 'Sunthon Phu: bourgeois poet laureate' has resulted in a change in the historical interpretation of its subject. This single point makes Nidhi's work stand out from that of other historians in this era. (Somsak 1982, 140, 143)

8. Somsak had been arrested in October 1976 and jailed until an amnesty in 1978, when he returned to Thammasat University to complete his BA. He was one of relatively few intellectuals who would remain a Marxist over years to come. He made a name for excoriating other historians on grounds of both wrong interpretations and poor scholarship (see especially the footnotes of his doctoral thesis, Somsak 1993).

Moreover, Somsak went on, 'Bourgeois culture and early Bangkok literature,' which had just appeared, made these four earlier works appear to be "just the overture" in advance of this "climax." Somsak announced: "not since Chit Phumisak has there been someone who analyzes the social roots of literature in such a systematic and exciting way" (Somsak 1983, 147).

ATTACKING TRADITIONAL HISTORIOGRAPHY

Nidhi's keynote speech at the annual conference of the recently formed Historical Association in 1979 was an attack on the state's use of history, and a manifesto to transform the practice of history for a new era (Thongchai 1995, 102). In the first part of the speech, Nidhi expanded on his earlier criticism of the "Prince Damrong school" which had dominated the writing of Thailand's history since the early twentieth century, and whose interpretations suffused school textbooks. As Nidhi noted, this school's cultural heritage was the writing of chronicles which focused solely on kings and their activities—rituals, wars, and family politics. The Damrong school had introduced modern critical methods, but only to a limited extent. They had taken up the western approach to political history but tended to ignore society, economy, and culture. The result was a new history which superficially appeared modern and international but which still focused on kings as heroes. These kings were now part of a "state," but this state had no origin, dynamic, or development until the nineteenth century "reforms" when the kings themselves became the progenitors of the modern nation-state. Nidhi argued it was time to "cut loose" from such history:

> Writing history to serve the state and monarchy, which are new and constantly changing, makes the analysis faulty or shallow.... The Thai state is now strong enough that there is no need to create history in its support. History should have more lasting value than serving something impermanent. (Nidhi 1980a, 12)

After reviewing the many alternative approaches in the historian's repertoire, including social science techniques and quantitative methods, Nidhi asked his colleagues "the key question of our occupation: what are we teaching history for?"

> At one time, the discipline of Thai history was inserted into the curriculum to create a unified past for the Thai people. Now, we no longer see any virtue or necessity for history to serve the 'nation.' Thai history viewed from the perspective of 'the nation' was highly distorted. (17)

He pointed out that everybody uses information about the past to make decisions in their everyday lives. The value of history as a discipline lay in its ability to teach critical thinking, and "the facts of history have less importance than understanding why these particular facts have historical importance." He ended by giving this proposition a pointed political significance:

> At a time when the state in all its forms tries to control information, the heart of the history discipline, namely its attention to critical evaluation of facts, is even more necessary.... History should teach people how to cope with the information which they receive from various sources in a well-rounded and creative way, in the hope that they will be able to deal intelligently with hearsay, and that there will never again be a time when a small group of people will be able to fool the majority and create political chaos through radio. (17)

This last sentence referred to the army's use of radio from late 1974 onwards to whip up opposition to students as enemies of the nation, climaxing on 6 October 1976 when army radio incited the right-wing forces to attack and kill the students inside Thammasat University. Nidhi and other defiant intellectuals of this era were openly resisting a fiercely ideological conservative revival which aimed to control politics, the social order, and intellectual activity. They attacked the "Prince Damrong school" and other scholarship of an earlier era because these were sources which the conservatives invoked as orthodoxy to stifle new thinking and to legitimate their attempts to stem change.

As with his earlier essay about Damrong and Toynbee, this piece provoked strong reactions. After Nidhi's lecture, Prince Subhadradis Diskul, art historian and Damrong's son, argued that Damrong's only failing was that he could not bring himself to write anything which reflected badly on his family, especially his half-brother and mentor, King Chulalongkorn. Sulak Sivaraksa also spoke and later committed his reaction to print (Sulak 1980). Among a lot of rant (new historians made mistakes in *ratchasap* and court titles; Sulak could write better articles than all of them), Sulak made two points: the concept of a "Damrong school" was illusory as there was no lineage of students or followers; and Luang Wichit Wathakan rather than Damrong should be held responsible for the poor state of Thai history.[9] Sulak also cautioned Nidhi and others for disrespect, and strongly restated the traditionalist role for history: if Nidhi and others could "view Prince Damrong in a Thai way without influence of *farang* methodology... it would help them understand the New Siam and its legacy of thinking, identity, and culture as well" (Sulak 1980, 49).[10]

Nidhi replied to Sulak that a school was a group that "used the same direction for analyzing history," with no need for there to be any other relationship between them. He also offered a more precise definition of the characteristics of the "Prince Damrong school:"

9. Nidhi responded to this point in a later essay by arguing that Damrong was the real thing while Luang Wichit was only a pale copy (Nidhi 1986a).

10. Sulak focused most of the article on Kobkua Suwannathat-Pian, who had written an article on the Prince Damrong school in 1976. He said he would criticize Nidhi only in general terms because of their personal relationship. He did however note that he preferred to read Ben Anderson since Anderson wrote English better than Nidhi wrote Thai. In his reply, Nidhi returned the compliment by insisting he "respected Khun Sulak too highly" to engage in an unseemly public argument, but then in the next sentence adding that "Sulak's criticisms have no content to reply to" (Nidhi 1981a, 49).

> 1. A belief that the study of history provides lessons for the present, and a tendency also to believe that those lessons will be useful in practice; 2. as a result of the above belief, coupled with the political situation of that time, a special focus on political history to the neglect of local history and other types of history, rendering the state as something fixed and static with no development, and believing the past can be understood through politics alone; 3. a view that any change in the state stems solely from the monarchy, embracing the 'great man' theory of history (perhaps unintentionally). (Nidhi 1981a, 51–2)

To scotch any idea that this "school" was only a mental construct, Nidhi described three people: one of his history lecturers at Chulalongkorn University who "used one volume of Prince Damrong's works per hour, point by point;" another historian who had followed Damrong closely in his work on a committee on early Bangkok history; and a third whose printed lecture notes "copied Prince Damrong word for word, page after page." All three were of royal lineage (Nidhi 1981a, 52).

BEYOND TRADITIONAL HISTORIOGRAPHY IN PRACTICE

'The history of Bangkok in the chronicles of Ayutthaya,' which had appeared in a preliminary form a few months before Nidhi's speech at the Historical Association, exemplified what Nidhi meant by concentrating not on the facts but "why these particular facts have historical importance." The proposition that the chronicles were very specifically a tale about kings was nothing new. Indeed, in 1907 King Chulalongkorn had warned people not to "carelessly misconceive them as a history of Siam" (Baker 2001, 96). But as Nidhi noted in mock-amazement in the footnotes to this essay, the chronicles were still taught as "history" in schools for decades after the end of the absolute monarchy in 1932, and some of the historical interpretations in the chronicles survived intact down to the present. Nidhi showed how the chronicles about the Ayutthaya era, especially those composed between the early and mid nineteenth century, were much more interesting sources for analyzing the era in which they were written rather than the era they were written about. In a 1981 essay on historical method, he seemed to describe how he arrived at this approach:

> [A historian] must start with a set of easy questions. Trying to answer these using strict historical methods will throw up another set of questions. Repeating this process several times will make the historian arrive at another question or set of questions which are the ultimate questions on that issue or period, overshadowing all the prior questions, and giving hope that the answer will throw light on the period or issue better than earlier accounts. (Nidhi 1981)

By showing that the chronicles were political documents written with a very clear agenda, Nidhi challenged both the authenticity and the magic of the major source of traditional Thai historiography.

'Bourgeois culture and early Bangkok literature' attacked the old approach to Thai history from another angle. In the mainstream view of the time, Siam in the early nineteenth century was a traditional rural society, totally dominated by a king and court who had overcome the shock of 1767 by reviving the form and substance of the Ayutthayan polity. In this view, change came from outside at mid century with capitalism, the western colonial threat, and western ideas of progress; and the court elite managed these external forces splendidly.

The first two words of Nidhi's essay title—bourgeois culture—were a challenge to this view, in several ways. They disrupted the social model of a traditional peasantry and dominant monarchy by placing a dynamic new urban society in the historical foreground. The essay portrayed the court, not in traditional garb as warriors and rulers, but as merchants. It offered a view of history driven by social conflict which was very different from the version all about "unity" which the bureaucrat ideologues were simultaneously writing into the school textbooks.

Another aspect of these pieces and of Nidhi's historical writings in general is a deliberate attempt to undermine the "sacredness" of history in the Thai intellectual tradition. The royal chronicles had been part of the royal regalia. Besides being manuals of statecraft and claims to monopoly ownership of the past, they were also sacred objects in their own right. Prince Damrong and other royalist historians had maintained a great deal of this sacred aura in their adaptation of the chronicles into the forms of modern history. In 'The history of Bangkok in the chronicles of Ayutthaya,' Nidhi brought the chronicles down to earth—something which provoked some fierce reactions.[11] Similarly, Nidhi's study of King Narai was titled *Politics in the Era of King Narai*, just like one might write of *Politics in the Era of General Prem*. The portrayal of factional politics in Narai's court was written with the same vocabulary and tone used for contemporary political analysis so that "the ruler Thais today call 'King Narai the Great' is depicted as just a political animal like everybody else" (Thongchai 1995, 104). In 'Bourgeois culture,' Nidhi wrote about the past with the vocabulary of modern analysis such as the "market economy" and "export-led growth." He repeatedly emphasized the continuities between the bourgeoisie of the early Bangkok era (meaning, mainly the court) and the bourgeoisie of the present day. Nidhi's study of the Thonburi era presented King Taksin as a former cart-trader who probably started his political career by bribing his way to a minor official post. In 'The history of Bangkok,' Nidhi suggested that a certain minor official in Ratchaburi might have become an agricultural trader, not King Rama I, if historical circumstances had been different.

11. Wimon Phongphiphat (1982) defended the reliability of the chronicles by taking the example of King Taksin's overthrow and comparing the chronicles to other accounts, especially those of resident missionaries. Wimon did not refer to Nidhi by name, and made no response to Nidhi's major argument that the chronicles had to be read as political documents. Rather, he asked rhetorically where Thai history would be without the chronicles. Nidhi demolished Wimon's arguments about the overthrow of Taksin in his 1986 book on the Thonburi era.

BEYOND THE MODE OF PRODUCTION

While challenging traditional historiography, Nidhi also offered an alternative to the Marxist histories which had flourished during 1973–6 as the rival to traditional approaches.

Before and during the 1973–6 era, Marxist social science in Thailand had focused on the analysis of the mode of production as a guide to revolutionary strategy. Since the late 1940s, the Communist Party of Thailand (CPT) had borrowed Mao's description of China as a "semi-feudal, semi-colonial" society, along with its strategic implication that the revolution must be led from the villages ("countryside surrounding town"). Chit Phumisak had emphasized that sakdina could be equated with feudalism, and had argued that Thai society remained predominantly feudal down to the present (Reynolds 1987). The debates of 1973–6 had largely confirmed the picture of Thailand as still an overwhelmingly rural and traditional society.

After 1976, this analysis lost its intellectual grip. The students who fled Bangkok after the Thammasat massacre were glad for refuge in the CPT's jungle camps, but could not agree with the party's strategy. The events of 1975–6 had shown the power of the Thai state and army, and their ability to mobilize urban forces for a right-wing reaction. By comparison, Thailand's peasants were not convincing as a revolutionary base. In addition, growing information about the Khmer Rouge's regime of primitive agrarian communism in neighboring Cambodia further lessened enthusiasm for rural-based revolution. The historical debates from 1978 onwards took place as students and intellectuals straggled back from the jungle camps with a message of disillusion.

In different ways, the contributors to these debates were searching for ways to move beyond earlier concerns and conclusions. The works by Chatthip Nartsupha and colleagues which appeared from 1978 onwards were exciting because they were based on much deeper archival research on the last 150 years of Thailand's economic history than the contributions to the debates of 1973–6, and because they moved away from the Maoist approach by drawing on Marx's idea of an Asiatic mode of production. They focused on the question of what factors had impeded Thailand from developing its own capitalism. Chatthip would soon shift to arguing that peasant society should be preserved, rather than be superseded by capitalism or revolution (Chatthip 1984).

Nidhi's approach was exciting in a different way. It signaled a shift away from this rural-focused history to something which recognized the historical role of Thailand's urban society. His use of the term "bourgeois" for an era much earlier than it had hitherto been applied in Siam flirted with the idea that Siam had an intrinsic, indigenous route to capitalism which did not depend on imports from the west, and which in fact was aborted by the Siamese elite's acceptance of a semicolonial role in the "reform" era. More strikingly, Nidhi departed from the whole obsession with the mode of production. Having positioned himself clearly as an enemy of the conservative mainstream and its "gods" of nationalism, monarchism, and state-building, he presented a major work of historical analysis which took no interest in modes of production, placed the peasantry in the background, and found the vectors of historical change in the interplay between the trading economy and the mentality of the urban elite.

Nidhi not only challenged conservative historiography in the teeth of a conservative shift in national politics, but also showed a way beyond the Marxist-Maoist orthodoxy at a time the Thai communist movement was collapsing. In his review essay, Somsak (1982, 152) marveled at the way Nidhi's novel and iconoclastic use of the term "bourgeois" won almost instant acceptance.

THE CHINESE IN THAI HISTORY

The essay on 'Bourgeois culture' was also a landmark in writing the Chinese into the national history. In the official version, the people of Siam/Thailand were all "Thai" and the role of all others, especially the Chinese, was to "become Thai" and accept this linear heritage. From time to time in campaigns for national unity, the establishment had demonized the Chinese as a divisive force. By shifting the focus of history from village to city, Nidhi also brought the Chinese from the periphery to the centre of historical interpretation.

Again, Nidhi was not the pioneer. In his thesis, published in 1975, Charnvit Kasetsiri had deftly argued that the Chinese role in Thai history went back at least to the start of the Ayutthaya period. But Charnvit's book was in English and published abroad. Nidhi's 'Bourgeois culture' was written in Thai and presented in Bangkok at an institute of "Thai studies." It made the Chinese the dynamic element in early Bangkok economy and society—as one subheading put it, the "main factor of change." The Chinese did not fade into Thai society, but transformed it. They did not imbibe Thai culture in a one-way process, but also imported Chinese architecture, stories, medical skills, accounting and much else which was valued and eagerly adopted by the old elite.

In his 1986 study of the Thonburi era, Nidhi took this argument further. He portrayed King Taksin as a Chinese adventurer who put the Siamese state back together after the monarchy and old court elite had allowed it to fall apart—a total inversion of the conservative denigration of the Chinese as a divisive force in Thai society. To ensure no reader missed the point of the book, he inserted in the preface a definition of *chek* which turned this normally derogatory term for the Chinese in Thailand into something positive:

> Being *chek* means receiving through birth and culture certain customs related to the customs and culture of people in China. This is not total imitation because local Thai culture along with social and economic imperatives demands some modification. What the *chek* mean by *chek* culture is not exactly like Chinese, but is clearly different from Thai. It is their own culture.... A powerful society is one which allows variety in culture. The distinctive ways of life, tastes, and preferences of the *chek* are one of the social assets of Thai society similar to the distinctiveness we find among the hill peoples, the Mon, the Vietnamese, and so on in Thailand. (Nidhi 1986, 13–4)

NEW MENTALITIES

The unifying theme of the *Pen and Sail* essays as a whole, was not the economic history but the intellectual history of the early Bangkok period. In yet another essay published in 1982, Nidhi explained that he tackled intellectual history as a counterweight and supplement to political history, but also because it provided a different perspective on Siam's development over the nineteenth century (Nidhi 1982).[12]

In this essay and in the opening paragraphs of 'Bourgeois culture,' Nidhi noted that mainstream history portrayed "Old Siam" as inert tradition, with the only moving parts being the westerners who brought change and the kings who dealt with it creatively. By contrast, Nidhi set out to show that Siam's history had an internal dynamic, and that social forces other than the kings—especially the new bourgeoisie—had a major historical role. By studying the chronicles, literature, and key religious texts, he presented a change in the elite's mentality which began in late Ayutthaya and flourished in the first half of the nineteenth century. This change was predicated on the dislocation of the old order by the Burmese attack, the development of an urban market economy in which the new Chinese were a significant factor, and greater social mixing and interchange made possible by the disruption of old rules and hierarchies. The new outlook encompassed a greater sense of individualism, new views of time and space, correspondingly different interpretations of history and geopolitics, a more rational interpretation of Buddhism, revised codes of elite social conduct, and a new conception of kingship.

In this version of Siam's nineteenth century history, the critical phase was not the vaunted "Age of Reform" but the decades which preceded it, marked by a surge of intellectual activity. By contrast, Nidhi presented the "reform" era as a massive cultural failure when this indigenous creativity was buried by slavish imitation of the west and by a retreat to formal classicism. More than any other aspect of Nidhi's work, this overriding theme of the whole *Pen and Sail* project was a direct challenge to the mainstream view which elevated the Fourth and especially the Fifth Reigns as the formative era of modern Thailand.

Nidhi's history is "inward" in several complementary ways. He hardly ever cited theoretical works or even other historians or histories as models. He repeatedly claimed that he adopted no particular theoretical approach, and that his ideas arose out of the study of historical sources. In all his historical works he has been intent on finding an internal dynamic driven by indigenous forces, and has argued strongly against relying on external factors to explain change. In the essays collected in this book,

12. This trend was wider than Nidhi alone. Hong Lysa (2000, 29) notes that the appreciation of Chit's work changed over the course of the 1970s. During 1973–6, the focus was on his "economistic" work, especially *Chomna sakdina thai* (The real face of Thai feudalism today). In the late 1970s the focus shifted to his "linguistic-oriented" works, especially *Khwam pen ma khong kham sayam, thai, lao lae khom* (The origin of the words Siam, Thai, Lao, and Khmer).

he describes the development of a new rationalism within the indigenous culture prior to any influence from the west. He deliberately conducted his academic career within Thailand, not writing anything for publication in English since returning from Michigan in 1975 (except one short summary article), and routinely refusing most invitations to overseas conferences and appointments. Yet this "inwardness" is clearly deliberate as Nidhi cannot be accused of any naïve parochialism: he chose to study Indonesia, wrote about Cambodia, commented on Toynbee, translated Bertrand Russell (and Edward Conze's study of Buddhism), and wrote a university textbook on early Islam. This "inwardness" is perhaps best interpreted as a declaration of independence.

THEMES AND CRITICISM

Contemporary written reactions to these essays are sparse. As far as I know, there has been no academic review of *Pen and Sail* since it appeared in book form, and there has been no general attempt to review Nidhi's historical work as a whole. The retrospectives which appeared around Nidhi's retirement in 2000 tended to present these works as a prelude to his later and longer career as one of Thailand's most prominent "public intellectuals." However, a handful of written reactions and reviews give some flavour of the themes which excited and irritated the audience when these essays appeared.

LITERATURE AND HISTORY

Nidhi's use of literature in 'Bourgeois culture' challenged the conservative project of building a unifying "national ideology." Literature, like history, was taught as an instrument of state-building and national unity. During the 1973–6 interlude, Chit Phumisak's Marxist rejection of this approach had become one of the key texts of the students and intellectuals, sparking new schools of literary criticism. But with the intellectuals scattered to the winds in 1976, the conservatives regained their monopoly. Nidhi, like Chit, had studied both history and literature in the Chulalongkorn Faculty of Arts, and followed Chit in analyzing literature within a framework of class division. As in his approach to history, he was bent on undermining the "sacredness" of the great authors and great works in the Thai literary canon. In particular, he celebrated Sunthon Phu precisely for being "shallow" and "entertaining," and ridiculed those who subjected Sunthon Phu's works to ponderous literary criticism. The impact can be gauged from one of the few critical reactions to Nidhi's work to appear in written form.

Sumali Wirawong's 'Reflections on Nidhi Eoseewong's "Bourgeois culture and early Bangkok literature"' appeared in Silpakorn University Arts Journal in 1982. Sumali argued that Nidhi had been intent on proving his proposition that "there may be more continuity between the reform era of the late nineteenth century and the early Bangkok era, than between early Bangkok and Ayutthaya." To this end, "he has used material selectively to support his argument without studying literary works in a sufficiently thorough and balanced way, and without appreciating the state of research on Thai literary history. As a result, his material in many places is regrettably outdated, erroneous, illogical, unsupported, and not credible" (Sumali 1982, 113).

Sumali's criticism of Nidhi had two main points. First, Nidhi's idea of "two cultures" based on class division was an inappropriate way to analyze Thai society and literature. Nidhi had taken the approach from western theory which did not fit Thai society.[13] It certainly could not be applied to early Ayutthayan society which, like Sukhothai, must have been a rural society with little social division. Even though late Ayutthaya was more layered, the social gradient was still gentle and upward mobility was possible. Thus instead of portraying Thai society in terms of class and class conflict, it was more appropriate to stress that "each group is just one part of a single, united culture, and all changes take place in parallel driven by the same reasons and forces of time and place.... Relations of family, occupation, religious belief, and ritual enabled the two groups of *phrai* and *munnai* to be constantly intertwined, to exchange thinking, and to copy one another's literary forms" (Sumali 1982, 114).

Sumali thus argued that the differences which Nidhi found between upper-class culture and popular culture were largely illusory. Both cultures drew on the same pool of folk tales, especially the Jataka. All people participated in the same festivals and ceremonies. Verse forms could not be divided into complex upper-class forms (*chan*, *rai*) and simpler popular ones (*klon*), as there was a unified literary tradition which gradually progressed from simple to complex forms over time. The outer and inner dramas were not so different; court drama was performed by women because there were many women in the court, while the popular drama was played by men because they had a lot of leisure time during their non-corvée months. Nidhi's biggest error was to portray the upper-class tradition as bound up with ritual, and the popular tradition with entertainment; old puppet dramas were not ritualistic, and upper-class works were also written to entertain.

Sumali's second argument was that the changes Nidhi detected in late Ayutthaya and early Bangkok were over-done. In her view, Thai literature developed seamlessly over time on the basis of tradition. She denied any shift from ritualism to realism in the invocations of poems. Upper class literature did not adopt folk sayings and metaphor from the popular tradition for constructing the "wondrous scenes;" instead these were a shared tradition which again changed over time in a gradual trend from free treatment of sex to more sophisticated and symbolic approaches as the society became more complex and restrictive. Literature for reading did not appear in the Bangkok era but existed earlier. There was no simplification of literary forms; the changes in meter which Nidhi detected were actually traditional. Old works like *Kamsuan* and *Nirat hariphunchai* were very entertaining and showed the same features which Nidhi supposed emerged only with the new form of *nirat* in the Bangkok era.[14]

13. Elsewhere Nidhi (1982, 46) notes that he was influenced by Robert Redfield's idea of Great and Little Traditions.

14. In a thesis that first appeared in 1991, Duangmon Chitchamnong (1997, 204) repeated some of Sumali's specific criticisms, namely that Nidhi drew too stark a division between elite and popular culture in terms of ritualism vs. entertainment, oral vs. written, and different

Sumali concluded, "Nidhi did not use literary evidence to compose his argument, but his personal feelings and present-day standards.... Literature must be studied in a balanced way, without bias or pre-formed theory, otherwise the conclusions will be mistaken and give rise to major misunderstandings" (Sumali 1982, 135).

Sumali's critique restated the conservative proposition that Thai literature, like Thai history, is a sacred object which expresses the unity of the Thai people in space and over time.

In reply, Nidhi noted that the difference between himself and Sumali was not a matter of facts but of framework and approach. He preferred the model of class conflict because the division of power, status, and economic benefits in Thai society was so clearly unequal. Although his approach accorded with western "materialist" theory, he arrived at this view not by beginning from theory but by developing his own view of Thai history. The model of one unified culture and one unbroken tradition simply buried popular culture as unimportant and subordinate, but he believed it deserved study in its own right. Overall he argued that his approach had "more explanatory power," but he also welcomed debate, and gently ribbed Sumali for portraying a difference of approach as a matter of good or bad scholarship.[15]

THE MARKET AND CAPITALISM

'Bourgeois culture' also prompted a less heated debate among economic historians. As Somsak's 1982 review article showed, Nidhi's essays appeared after a batch of publications by Chatthip Nartsupha and his disciples arguing that Thai rural society prior to the Bowring treaty of 1855 was still largely oriented to subsistence. Two years later, Chatthip published *The Thai Village Economy in the Past*, portraying a dual economy in which the subsistence rural economy and the urban export economy existed side-by-side with only very limited linkages. Nidhi was the only contemporary historian mentioned in the text of this book. Referring to the account of growing trade and individualism in 'Bourgeois culture,' Chatthip noted "While Nidhi may be correct in identifying change of this nature, the growth in trading towns during the sakdina period was limited to the towns indicated [by Nidhi]" (Chatthip 1999, 37).

In 1989, Chatthip's colleague, Somphop Manarangsan, wrote a review essay on 'The expansion of the Thai economy in the early nineteenth century' which developed this point further. The essay also covered Sarasin Viraphol's *Tribute and Profit* and Hong Lysa's *Thailand in the Nineteenth Century* but was directed mainly at Nidhi's 'Bourgeois

---

traditions of prosody. But Duangmon accepted that there was a big difference of emphasis between the two traditions, and she accepted Nidhi's proposition that early Bangkok was a novel and highly creative period in Thai literature, though her analysis took a more conventional literary approach and ignored Nidhi's work for the most part.

15. Although Sumali's review is isolated, the contention that Nidhi misused literary evidence is often repeated in the tradition of oral criticism down to the present day. Indeed, some literature experts refused to assist this translation project on precisely those grounds.

culture.' Somphop's main intention was to question the extent and scope of the market economy in the early nineteenth century by introducing some measurement into the qualitative data used by Nidhi and others.

Nidhi had argued that the growth of a market economy, driven by exports and demand from a growing non-subsistence population, had made it possible for government to switch to tax collection in cash from the Third Reign. Somphop suggested the size of this market economy was really very small. Although the proportion of government revenue collected in cash was not clearly known, Somphop suggested it might be as low as 10 percent.[16] He also reckoned that the value of total exports and imports in 1850 was equivalent to only 40 per cent of the government's total income, while domestic demand was also small. He estimated that the total volume of rice needed for both exports and urban supply was only 17 percent of the production capacity of the central region and required only 1.7 percent of the total labor force.

Somphop also argued that the shift to tax-farming probably stimulated the growth of a market economy rather than being proof that such an economy already existed. He then went on to question the dynamism of the economy in the Third Reign. Siam's chief market in China was dull. Although Rama III liberalized trading at the Siamese end, the Chinese state was still restrictive. The junks were inefficient for bulky cargoes such as rice so that the selling price in China was high; hence imports were significant only in years of shortage and Siam enjoyed no steady demand which could stimulate an increase in production. From 1820 onwards, China's trade balance was negative because of the imports of opium. In 1840, Britain attacked China and imposed the Nanking treaty of 1842, opening up Chinese ports to western shipping—first efficient clippers, then steamships—which drove the junks out of business.

Finally Somphop argued that the lack of communications in Siam severely limited the geographic spread of any economic change. The new canal building was all around the capital, and land travel remained very slow. He summed up: "Although the economy may have had more dynamism, yet its scale was still rather limited and did not expand the market economy as it might have" (Somphop 1989, 107).

Nidhi replied by welcoming such serious criticism as a contribution to the process of learning. He felt the difference of opinion between himself and Somphop was not great. His major concern had been to study the intellectual development in the early nineteenth century. Prior to his essay, intellectual history of this era had been analyzed in terms of a revival of Ayutthayan ideas and practices. But Nidhi believed worldviews and mentalities had changed as a result of shifts in society and economy. Existing academic works did not analyze these shifts (Hong Lysa's book on Siam's economic history was not published until two years later), hence in writing 'Bourgeois culture,' Nidhi felt he needed to analyze the economic history of Siam in detail. He might have been too eager to make his case, and might have overstated some things and created misunderstanding. He agreed wholeheartedly with Somphop that the

16. Yet Somphop also pointed out that half of total revenues came from the "vice taxes" on opium, liquor, and gambling, and these would certainly have been collected in cash.

extent of the market economy was still limited, particularly in geographical extent. Yet, however small it was, the market economy still affected the worldview of the elite, which itself was a very small social segment.

Besides, Nidhi went on, his major argument was not about the scale of exports but their nature. Siam had exported for a long time; the shift in early Bangkok was in the nature of the goods—from things collected from the forests, to things grown and made by farmers and artisans. From the early nineteenth century, there was growing tension between an old economy of subsistence production and tax-in-kind, and a new economy of production for the market. The old social structure and political system were built around the old economy and its flows of conscripted labor and goods collected as tax-in-kind. As the market economy became a rival for resources, the tension between these two economies grew, and conflict arose within the elite—over goods and later over control of manpower.

Nidhi did not want to devalue the importance of the arrival of capitalism and western ideas, but pointed out that the impact of these outside factors was different in different countries precisely because the local conditions varied. The Siamese elite's response to the inroads of capitalism and western ideas was shaped by the bourgeois culture which had already developed with the market economy. The Bowring treaty obliged a much more decisive shift towards a market economy, which the Siamese elite managed relatively well because of the changes in outlook that had already taken place. Indeed, in Nidhi's view, the underlying story of the "Age of Reform" was the success of the elite in translating the kind of benefit they enjoyed in the traditional economy and polity into an equally impressive level of benefit in the age of capitalism.

CHANGE AND EVOLUTION

Nidhi's dismissal of the Bowring treaty as a key turning point in Thai history was also questioned in a 1985 essay by Ukrist Pathamanand who raised wider issues about Nidhi's approach to historical change.

Ukrist (1985, 16) noted that "in every work, Nidhi thanks his colleagues, students, and even typists but never his teachers." Yet Nidhi had clearly been influenced by the Annales school, especially Marc Bloch's idea of "total history" and Lucien Fevre's focus on historical periods rather than historical events. Ukrist pointed out that, "In all of Nidhi Eoseewong's works, even though they address social change, yet change is always evolutionary in nature, underpinned by prior foundations—economic, political, and social" (18). This was true of Nidhi's analyses of early Ayutthaya, early Bangkok, and even the 1932 revolution. Ukrist argued this bias to evolution was built into Nidhi's annalist-like approach. There was no analysis of the reasons behind the internal, evolutionary changes in society; no ability to judge when small changes accumulated into something big; and hence all change "ultimately becomes no change at all" (19).

Ukrist accepted Nidhi's argument that the economic changes of late Ayutthaya and early Bangkok paved the way for what came later, "yet when Siam made the Bowring treaty there was undeniably a change that was new and qualitative" (27). Old systems no longer functioned. Government was obliged to shift from exploiting trade to exploiting production. The money economy spread. A market in land appeared. The elite shifted into investments in land, tin, rice milling, and banks. Although Ukrist did not make the point directly, it was clear from his own citations that he preferred an idea of historical dialectic moving society on from one stage to another.

In 1988, Nidhi presented a conference paper in English in London entitled 'The social foundations of the Thai elite and non-elite cultures.' It is his most systematic presentation of his view of nineteenth-century social change, and it offered a response to Chatthip, Somphop, and Ukrist.[17]

Nidhi argued that the twin supports of the traditional Thai state were the profits of international trade and the control of manpower. The two were interconnected, but trade was the most important, with two results. First, the state had little reason to dominate the village and so developed no standing army, no lines of communication into its hinterland, and no systems for commanding the economic production of the village. Taxes were low and corvée obligations modest compared to other states. The village was thus "autonomous in every aspect of life, creating and nourishing its own culture, making its own decision on economic matters, and distributing power among its members" (Nidhi 1988, 4). "Production in the village was primarily subsistent" (5), which nurtured an "anti-individualist" (6) culture of mutual cooperation.

Second, changes in trade drove changes in the state and its relations to the village. The expansion and changing nature of trade from late Ayutthaya "largely affected only the town and the town culture" (11) in a direct sense. The state responded to these changes in trade by relaxing corvée requirements and developing tax farming, but these adjustments did not change the subsistence orientation of the village except in a few limited areas. The coming of "free trade" (Nidhi skirted mentioning the Bowring treaty directly) forced another shift but "although this adjustment was more encompassing than that undertaken formerly, it was still along the same lines as adjustments which the Thai elite had made since the Ayutthaya period in response to changes in international trade" (14–5). The elite developed a centralized revenue bureaucracy to replace tribute and manpower dues, and began also to profit from land rents. Still "only a small fraction of the rural people was really affected," namely those who migrated to the rice frontier, but otherwise "the Thai peasants still clung to their subsistent way of life. Although production for the market might have grown larger, it never dominated the farm" (17).

In short, Nidhi conceded Somphop's argument that the changes of the early Bangkok era were limited in extent. He also gave a description of the village's subsistence economy, community ethic, and distance from the state which substantially agreed with that of Chatthip. But Nidhi's explanation of why things were this way was very different. Chatthip emphasized the strength of village culture, while Nidhi pointed to the weakness of the state. Chatthip used a modified version of the Asiatic

17. The paper has no citations, and ends rather abruptly. Nidhi withheld it from the book which resulted from this conference. As far as I know, there is no Thai-language equivalent of this paper.

mode of production, while Nidhi rejected this approach totally, and emphasized the political dynamic—the state's orientation to trade and resulting failure to develop the mechanisms for dominating the village.

Similarly, Nidhi conceded Ukrist's point that the shift to "free trade" in the second half of the century was a qualitative change, but insisted this was merely the reiteration of an old pattern, not something momentous. He reasserted the specialness and internal dynamic of Thai socioeconomic history.[18]

RATIONALISM

Another written criticism of the *Pen and Sail* essays challenged Nidhi's theme of new elite mentalities in the early Bangkok era, especially a new "rationalist" view of man, the world, and religion. The Buddhist scholar, Sathianphong Wannapok, made comments at Nidhi's initial presentation of the essay on 'The life of the Buddha,' and then committed his comments to print. He objected to Nidhi's argument that early nineteenth century biographies of the Buddha "exhibited a rationalism which became even more evident in the Thammayut movement" (Sathianphong 1981, 79).

First, Sathianphong suggested this rationalism was nothing new. Nidhi had assumed that Prince Paramanuchit Chinorot's life of the Buddha innovated a rational and realistic approach to portraying the Buddha's biography. Yet Paramanuchit had stated in his preface that he compiled his life from earlier Pali versions, and Sathianphong argued that Paramanuchit copied the rationalism from these. Second, Sathianphong ridiculed the proposition that the Thammayut was rationalistic by arguing Thammayut was narrowly obsessed with petty rules (especially on monastic dress and chanting) and showed little interest in philosophy.

Sathianphong contended that this theme of a new rationalism was "a presumption by Nidhi" which also underlay the essays on Nang Nophamat and Sunthon Phu. But Sathianphong did not expand into a general critique of this theme. Rather he used his response to Nidhi as a hook for an attack on the Thammayut order and Mongkut's reasons for founding it. He argued that Mongkut had been expecting to ascend the throne in 1824 when he was shouldered aside by King Rama III, and that all Mongkut's subsequent actions were devoted to building his political standing. Hence he "founded the Thammayutika for political reasons" (76). Mongkut's historical researches, discovery of the Sukhothai Manangkasila "throne" and the stele of Inscription I were similarly "all efforts to build up his political position" (76). He invented the concept of a purer Mon monastic practice in order to attack Wat Mahathat and the traditional order. He had himself reordained six times to claim superior purity "which was a political stratagem used earlier by King Songtham in the

18. In the latter part of the paper, however, Nidhi's mode of argument changed. The bureaucratic power and rentierism developed in the "reform" era enabled a small royal elite to monopolize power and profit, creating an unbalanced and divided society. New urban classes which emerged in the economy of "free trade" reacted to this "clumsiness" by overthrowing the absolute monarchy in 1932. There is a dialectical mechanism in this passage.

Ayutthaya era" (77). Sathianphong described the Thammayut order as pettifogging troublemaking which eventually King Chulalongkorn found to be too narrow and a danger to Buddhism (78). Sathianphong challenged Nidhi to show "what actually is the Thammayut philosophy" and how it was different or more rational than the mainstream.

AFTER *PEN AND SAIL*

In 1986, Nidhi completed his study of the transition from Ayutthaya to Bangkok with publication of *Politics in the Era of the King of Thonburi*, by far his longest historical work. Just as the 'History of Bangkok in the chronicles of Ayutthaya' had revealed how late Ayutthaya history had been composed to "make the past useful" for the early Bangkok period, so this book showed how the history of the Thonburi era had been constructed in the late nineteenth century to explain the origins of the Chakri dynasty. Where the mainstream version argued that Burma smashed a glorious Ayutthaya in 1767, Nidhi argued the Ayutthaya polity had already fallen apart from internal tensions. Where the mainstream version made Taksin a Chinese who was well acculturated into the traditional elite, Nidhi made him a *chek* adventurer whose noble connections had been invented later. Where the mainstream version showed that Taksin became mad, making it necessary for the Chakri to step forward, Nidhi makes 1782 into a coup—in fact, "one of the bloodiest coups in Thai history" (Nidhi 1986, 576)—just like 1947, 1957, or 1976, plotted by the old elite to reinvent a traditional polity in which they enjoyed power and status, and justified only later by stories about insanity.

Beyond this unraveling of mythification, the striking message of the book lay in its portrayal of the society and polity of the Taksin era, marked by more local autonomy, social mixing, mobility, and experiment than the periods both before and after. Although Taksin's state proved fragile, Nidhi concluded, "he created a startling and exciting success story in Thai history" (Nidhi 1986, 586). The parallel between the Chakri reimposition of centralization, hierarchy, and social order with the coup of 1782, and the resurgence of military and monarchy after the coup of 1976, is unmistakable.

By this time, Nidhi had begun another project. In his 1979 speech at the Historical Association, he had advocated the study of local history as one strategy to counter the state's attempt to monopolize historical interpretation. He now put this advice into practice. In a series of studies on the *mueang* along the southern peninsula, he showed the very distinctive character of these local societies, and traced their negotiations with Ayutthaya and other would-be overlords from positions of relative autonomy (Nidhi 1983; 1985; 1987).

But his attention was turning from the past to the present. From his earliest writings in the late 1960s, he had urged academics to take a more active role in society. In 1969, he wrote a criticism of Thai academics for remaining too confined within the ivory tower while Thailand suffered from corruption, lack of economic justice, a growing gap between rich and poor, government spending diverted to help only the urban elite, materialism spreading through mass media, migration of villagers to work in awful factory conditions, and lack of art and culture. Nidhi attributed these problems chiefly to industrialization and made no mention of American influence. Military rule was not cited as a cause, but condemned because of its failure to make any improvement. This dire situation had arisen, Nidhi argued, because intellectuals did not "ask the questions and question the answers." The ideal state would perhaps be the "dictatorship of intellectuals" proposed by Herbert Marcuse but that had never arisen anywhere in the world. Confucius' idea of intellectuals acting as the moral monitors of government seemed more practical, yet in reality intellectuals always got shouldered aside. Until recently in Thailand, most of the educated were employed by the state and lacked the independence necessary for criticism. Nidhi was conscious of being part of a new and broader intelligentsia created mainly by the expansion of universities. But most of his colleagues, he found, were easily compromised by grants of money, status, and other benefits from those in power. The state was a "monster" (*yak*) which gobbled up potential dissenters. "When this is the case, Thai society totally lacks any awareness of its own true problems" (Nidhi 1969a, 109). In order not to become easy victims of the monster, intellectuals had to live moral lives and not be bought off by offers of "stuff, sex, and status" (110). Ultimately the only way for intellectuals to control the monster state was by the same methods that the Buddha had used against his own demons, namely morality, clarity of thought, and wisdom. Nidhi ended by urging those who "happen to agree with some of this country teacher's ideas" to "raise an army to seize all of Thailand's universities" (102).

A year later, Nidhi published a Thai translation of Bertrand Russell's *Authority and the Individual* which argued that intellectuals had a social duty to criticize and oppose government (Jiraporn 1996, 19–20). In his articles on historiography written around the same time, Nidhi argued that the value of studying history was that it taught people how to think critically and thus be in a better position to empower themselves. In the dedication of his doctoral thesis, he expressed "my deep gratitude to the peasants of Thailand, the source of my salary." In a 1986 essay on 'Two hundred years of Thai history and the way ahead,' he praised the new trend of community history "because it allows the ordinary people of the country to own the history of the nation" (Nidhi 1986a, 39).[19] He also argued

19. The bulk of this article was a further episode in Nidhi's critique of the "Prince Damrong school." He argued that the Thai elite only became interested in history when its "identity" (*ekkalak*) was threatened. This had happened three times: in early Bangkok because of the Burmese aggression; in the Fourth and Fifth Reigns because of colonial pressure; and over 1957–75 because of American influence. In each of these eras, historians sought new sources and new methods in order to explain the past (the examples from the three eras are: Paramanuchit Chinorot; Prince Damrong; Prasert na Nagara and Kachorn Sukhabanij). At other times, the elite ignored the past, or reworked old research (e.g., Luang Wichit Wathakan). The professionalization of history in the universities had altered the situation, making it important for historians to escape the ivory tower.

> there are many kinds of new media which give easy access to the general population such as television dramas, cinema films, video, novels, and magazines like *Sinlapa watthanatham* (Art and Culture). Thai historians should not ignore these media but experiment with them and develop new ways to use them so they can communicate with the broader society. (Nidhi 1986a, 40)

From 1985 he wrote regularly in the monthly magazine, *Sinlapa watthanatham*. While many of the first pieces were historical, often summarizing his longer works, increasingly Nidhi applied the techniques of the historian to analyze issues of the present day in a series of long reflective essays.[20] In addition, he wrote an advice column in a magazine for teenagers, and columns of current comment on society and culture in several daily and weekly newspapers. At a time of rapid change, when so much of the content of education remained under tight state control, Nidhi and several other teachers believed that education had to spread beyond the formal institutions and exploit new opportunities in the relatively free space of public media. Intellectuals had a duty to "teach" *society*. Nidhi's writings from 1985 onwards aimed to demystify the past and provide insight into the present so that ordinary people would be better equipped to deal with the impersonal forces of state, capitalism, and globalization.

CONCLUSION

Nidhi's famed historical writings, from 'The history of Bangkok in the chronicles of Ayutthaya' to the study of Taksin, appeared over just eight years from 1978 to 1986.

The enthusiastic reception for the essays collected in this book, as well as the critical reactions from literary conservatives and political economists, can probably be explained by four factors. First, at a time of suffocating conservatism, these essays challenged the old conservative historiography with its sacred aura and its focus on the heroic role of kings. Second, against a background of rapid urbanization sparked by the American era, they gave a central historical role to urban Siam and especially to the immigrant Chinese whose descendants were rapidly becoming the dominant element in urban society, culture, and politics. Third, at a time when Thailand's communist movement was collapsing, they offered an approach to history which was innovative and radical yet significantly different from the Marxist focus on modes of production. Fourth, as Thailand was becoming increasingly globalized, they argued for an indigenous dynamic in Thai history.

In addition, the essays are full of insights which cut across mainstream history and attitudes, including the disarmingly simple analysis of Chinese migrants in 'Bourgeois culture,' the exposition of a new Buddhist-based theory of kingship in 'History of Bangkok,' the shifting cosmology revealed in *Nang Nophamat*, the changing conception of the Buddha over time, and the explicaiton of Suthon Phu's

20. One of these is translated as Nidhi (2001).

cheerfully shallow appeal. For many also, Nidhi is simply a good read—because of the energy of his prose, and the regular appearance of something new, exciting, and perhaps outrageous.

The evolutionary, organic, and indigenous pattern of change in *Pen and Sail* reflected the loss of trust in either of the international camps of the Cold War, and anticipated the coming era of democratic process, civil society, and "people politics." Nidhi's celebration of early Bangkok, when old state structures were discredited making space for new ideas, more social interchange, and a resulting cultural upsurge, and his downgrading of the "reform" era, when state power increased, hierarchies ossified, and creativity gave way to imitation, reflected the close of an era marked by competing conceptions of a strong state's ability to transform society, and the emergence of new concerns to roll back state power in order to make more space for community and individual. Nidhi, in his historical work and political life, has been a prophet and proponent of this major historical transition.

Chris Baker

REFERENCES

Anderson, Benedict R. O. G. 1985. 'Introduction' in Anderson and Ruchira Mendiones, *In the Mirror: Literature and Politics in Siam in the American Era.* Bangkok: DK Books.

Baker, Chris tr. 2001. 'The Antiquarian Society of Siam speech of King Chulalongkorn.' *JSS,* 89, 1 & 2.

Chalong Soontravanich. 2002. '"Dae manutsayachat" lae nithi iaosiwong' ('To humanity' and Nidhi Eoseewong). *Warasan kong thun siburapha* (Siburapha Fund Magazine), 5 May.

Charnvit Kasetsiri. 1976. *The Rise of Ayudhya.* Oxford University Press.

Chatthip Nartsupha. 1999. *The Thai Village Economy in the Past,* translated by Chris Baker and Pasuk Phongpaichit. Chiang Mai: Silkworm Books.

Connors, M. K. 2003. *Democracy and National Identity in Thailand.* New York and London: Routledge Curzon.

Duangmon Chitchamnong. 1997. *Khun kha lae laksana den khong wannakhadi thai samai rattanakosin ton ton* (Value and distinctiveness of early Bangkok literature). Bangkok: Thammasat University Press.

Hong Lysa. 2000. 'Twenty years of *Sinlapa watthanatham*: Cultural politics in Thailand in the 1980s and 1990s.' *Journal of Southeast Asian Studies,* 31, 1, March.

Jiraporn Witayasakpan. 1996. 'Mueang thai nai khwam khit lae khwam fai fan khong satsatrachan doktoe nithi iaosiwong' (Thailand in the thought and dreams of Professor Dr Nidhi Eoseewong). Bangkok: Thailand Research Fund.

Kachorn Sukhabanij. 1969. 'Chotmai thueng bannathikan' (Letters to the editor). *Sangkhomsat parithat* (Social Science Review), 7, 2, Sep–Nov.

Nidhi Aeusrivongse. 1976. 'The *Devaraja* cult and Khmer kingship at Angkor.' In Kenneth R. Hall and John K Whitmore, eds., *Explorations in Early Southeast Asian History: The Origins of Southeast Asian Statecraft,* Ann Arbor: Michigan Papers on South and Southeast Asia 11, University of Michigan.

————. 1988. 'The social foundations of the Thai elite and non-elite cultures.' Unpublished paper presented at the conference on 'Thai constructions of knowledge,' SOAS.

————. 1994. 'The early Bangkok period: literary change and its social causes.' *Asian Studies Review,* 18, 1, July.

Nidhi Eoseewong. 1964. 'Dae manutsayachat' (To humanity). *Mahawitthayalai* (University), 23 October 1964; reprinted in *Phayiya* (Bouquet), Bangkok: Chulalongkorn Student Association, 1966.

————. 1968. 'Chotmai chak chiang mai' (Letter from Chiang Mai). *Sangkhomsat parithat* (Social Science Review), 5, 4, March.

————. 1969. 'Somdet kromphraya damrong ratchanuphap kap arnot toibi' (Prince Damrong and Arnold Toynbee). *Sangkhomsat parithat* (Social Science Review), 7, 1, Jun–Aug.

————. 1969a. 'Patikiriya: pannyachon thai?' (Response: Thai intellectuals?). *Sangkhomsat parithat* (Social Science Review), 7, 2, Sep–Nov.

————. 1980. *Prawatisat rattanakosin nai phraratchaphongsawadan ayutthaya* (The History of Bangkok in the Chronicles of Ayutthaya). Bangkok: Bannakit.

————. 1980a. 'Kan sueksa prawatisat thai adit lae anakhot' (The study of Thai history, past and future). *Ruam botkhwam prawatisat* (Collected historical articles), 1.

————. 1981. 'Prawatisat lae kan vichai thang prawatisat' (History and historical research). Papers from National Research Council seminar on research in the humanities, 22–4 July, reprinted in Charnvit Kasetsiri and Suchat Sawatsi, eds., *Pratya prawatisat* (Philosophy of history), Bangkok: Thai Wattanaphanit, 1984.

————. 1981a. 'Patikiriya: sakun damrong rachanuphap ik thi' (Comment: the Prince Damrong school revisited). *Sinlapa watthanatham,* 3, 1.

————. 1982. 'Kan sueksa prawat khwam khit khong Thai' (The study of Thai intellectual history). *Warasan thammasat* (Thammasat Journal), 11, 4, December.

————. 1983. 'Khati thi kiao kap rat khong prachachon thai chak wannakam pak tai' (People's beliefs about the state from southern Thai literature). *Warasan Thammasat* (Thammasat Journal), 12, 3.

————. 1985. 'Chak rat chai khop thueng monthon thesaphiban: khwam sueam salai khong klum amnat doem nai ko phuket' (From peripheral state to province: the decline of the old power group in Phuket). In *Sinlapa watthanatham,* 6, 5 (March).

————. 1986. *Kanmueang thai samai phrachao krung thonburi* (Politics in the era of the King of Thonburi). Bangkok: Sinlapa Watthanatham.

————. 1986a. '200 phi khong kan sueksa prawatisat thai lae thang khang na' (Two hundred years of Thai history and the way ahead). *Sinlapa watthanatham,* 7, 4, reprinted in Nidhi, *Krung taek, phrachao tak lae prawatisat thai* (The fall of Ayutthaya, King Taksin, and Thai history), Bangkok: Matichon, 1995.

————. 1987. 'Nakhon sithammarat nai ratcha-anachak ayutthaya' (Nakhon Si Thammarat in the Ayutthaya kingdom). In *Yu mueang thai* (In Thailand), essays presented to Professer Saneh Chamarik on his 60th birthday, Bangkok: Thammasat University Press.

————. 1987a. 'Review of Craig J. Reynolds, Thai Radical Discourse: The Real Face of Thai Feudalism Today.' *Warasan manutsayasat* (Humanities Journal, Chiang Mai), 14, 1–2.

————. 2003. 'The Thai cultural constitution.' Translated by Chris Baker. *Kyoto Review of Southeast Asia, 3* (<kyotoreview.cseas.kyoto-u.ac.jp>).

Patcharaphon Changkaeo and Chukiat Sakunchokchai. 1981. 'Nithi iaosiwong kap prawatisat thai' (Nidhi Eoseewong and Thai history). *Warasan thammasat* (Thammasat Journal), 10, 2.

Reynolds, Craig J. 1987. *Thai Radical Discourse: The Real Face of Thai Feudalism Today.* Ithaca: Southeast Asia Program, Cornell University.

Reynolds, Craig J. and Hong Lysa. 1983. 'Marxism in Thai historical studies.' *Journal of Asian Studies,* 43, 1, November.

Saichon Satyanurak. n.d. 'Bot wichan ngan wichai rueang "Mueang thai nai khwam khit lae khwam fai fan khong satsatrachan doktoe nithi iaosiwong"', (Review of "Thailand in the thought and dreams of Professor Dr Nidhi Eoseewong").

Sathianphong Wannapok. 1982. 'Wichan bot khwam khong doktoe nithi iaosiwong pathomphothikata: thamprawat rue chiwaprawat' (A critique of Dr Nidhi Eoseewong's essay on the life of the Buddha: dhammography or biography). *Sinlapa watthanatham,* 3, 7, May.

Somphop Manarangsan. 1989. 'Kan khayai tua thang sethakit khong thai nai chuang ton sattawat thi 19' (Expansion of the Thai economy in the early nineteenth century). *Asia parithat* (Asia Review), 10, 1, Jan–Apr.

Somsak Jeamteerasakul. 1982. 'Sangkhom thai: chak sakdina su thun niyom' (Thai society: from feudalism to capitalism). *Warasan thammasat* (Thammasat Journal), 11, 2, June.

Somsak Jeamteerasakul. 1993. 'The communist movement in Thailand.' PhD thesis, Monash University.

Sulak Sivaraksa. 1980. 'Somdet kromphraya damrong kap sakun prawatisat damrong rachanuphap' (Prince Damrong and the the Damrong Rachanuphap school of history). *Ruam botkhwam prawatisat* (Collected historical articles), 1.

Sumali Wirawong. 1982. 'Kho khit nueang chak bot khwam rueang "Watthanatham kadumphi kap wannakam ton rattanakosin" khong nithi iaosiwong' (Reflections on Nidhi Eoseewong's "Bourgeois culture and early Bangkok literature"). *Aksonsat mahawitthayalai sinlapakon* (Silpakorn University Arts Journal), 5, 2.

Thongchai Winichakul. 1995. 'The changing landscape of the past: new histories in Thailand since 1973.' *Journal of Southeast Asian Studies*, 26, 1, March.

Ukrist Pathamanand. 1985. 'Khwam plian plaeng khong sangkhom thai nai thatsana khong doktoe nithi iaosiwong' (Social change in the view of Dr Nidhi Eoseewong). Social science papers no. 2, Arts Faculty, Krirk University.

Wimon Phongphiphat. 1982. 'Phraratcha phongsawadan—chuea dai rue mai?' (Are the royal chronicles reliable?). *Warasan aksonsat (Arts Journal, Chulalongkorn University), 14, 2, July.*

INDEX

CPSIA information can be obtained
at www.ICGtesting.com
Printed in the USA
BVHW081019200322
631818BV00001B/47

9 789749 575925